ISBN: 9781313854955

Published by:
HardPress Publishing
8345 NW 66TH ST #2561
MIAMI FL 33166-2626

Email: info@hardpress.net
Web: http://www.hardpress.net

DISEASES OF THE SKIN

DISEASES OF THE SKIN

BY

JAMES H. SEQUEIRA

M.D.Lond., F.R.C.P.Lond., F.R.C.S.Eng.

*Physician to the Skin Department and Lecturer on Dermatology at the London
Hospital ; in charge of Queen Alexandra's Department for Light Treat-
ment ; Honorary Consultant for Diseases of the Skin to Military
Hospitals in London ; Consulting Dermatologist to the Radium
Institute ; Secretary of the British Section of the International
Association of Dermatology and Syphilology ; Fellow
(late Secretary of Dermatological Section) of the
Royal Society of Medicine ; formerly Physician
to the North Eastern (now Queen's)
Hospital for Children*

THIRD EDITION

With 52 Plates in Colour and 257 Text-Figures

London

J. & A. CHURCHILL

7 Great Marlborough Street

1919

Printed in Great Britain.

PREFACE TO THE THIRD EDITION.

THE Second Edition of this work was exhausted soon after publication. The delay in presenting this edition has been due to pressure of work caused by the war.

The employment of so large a proportion of the profession under abnormal conditions has limited research, but much of value has been learnt, especially in relation to skin affections of parasitic origin. The attention directed to venereal diseases and the unique opportunities of observing the effect of the modern methods of treating syphilis have been utilised to great advantage.

In this edition I have endeavoured to bring the work up to date, and I have again to acknowledge the useful criticisms of numerous reviewers. A number of the sections have been rewritten and a general revision of the whole work has been made. New plates and figures in the text have been added. The book, however, by rearrangement and the use of fresh types, has not been increased in size.

Dr. Malcolm Simpson has been good enough to read the proof sheets and I am greatly indebted to him for this and for many useful suggestions.

J. H. S.

PREFACE TO THE FIRST EDITION.

THIS book began with notes for a course of lectures delivered in the Skin Clinic of the London Hospital in 1902, and has gradually grown with the experience of nine years' teaching. The work being primarily designed for the student and in the hope that it may also be of use to the practitioner. I have devoted special attention to diagnosis and treatment, omitting historical references and discussions of debated points. The general arrangement of the chapters is on etiological lines. a system which modern developments have rendered possible, though still incomplete. Where such a classification has been impracticable, the diseases are grouped according to their morphological characters. If any apology is needed for such an arrangement, I can only say that I have found it exceedingly useful in teaching.

Great care has been taken in the selection of the illustrations, which, with a few exceptions, are from my own cases. I cannot express adequately my gratitude to Dr. Arnold Moritz for the time and trouble he has expended over the photographs, taken direct from patients, in three colours. From these the plates have been made. Only those who have had experience in this kind of work can appreciate the enormous difficulties involved. The black and white illustrations are from photographs taken by Mr. E. E. Wilson. late clinical photographer at the London Hospital. For the photographs of the animal parasites I am indebted to my former clinical assistant, Dr. T. J. Williams, and to Dr. C. W. Daniels for the illustrations of tropical affections.

For the convenience of students and others desiring to study more in detail particular subjects, I have appended to each section a few references to recent articles, and especially to those in which the literature of the subject is to be found. In a work of this scope, no attempt has been made to give complete bibliographies, and I trust that authors whose names are omitted will pardon the absence of direct references to their work.

In conclusion. I have to acknowledge my indebtedness to the writers in *La Pratique Dermatologique*, and in Mracek's *Handbuch*, to the text-books of Radcliffe-Crocker. Malcolm Morris and others, to Unna's "Histopathology." and to the many friends who have kindly sent me monographs and reprints. In the tiresome work of reading the proof sheets and for many suggestions I have to acknowledge the great assistance afforded me by my brother. Staff-Surgeon W. S. H. Sequeira. R.N.. M.B. It is also a pleasing duty to thank my publishers for their courtesy and generosity, especially in the matter of illustrations.

JAMES H. SEQUEIRA.

MANCHESTER SQUARE. W.

TABLE OF CONTENTS.

LIST OF PLATES.

DISEASES OF THE SKIN.

CHAPTER I.

HISTOLOGY OF THE NORMAL SKIN.

THE integument is composed of three layers, the epidermis or cuticle, the dermis or corium, and the subcutaneous tissue or hypoderm.

The **epidermis** (Fig. 1) is a non-vascular protective covering composed of stratified pavement epithelial cells. It has four layers— (1) the stratum corneum, (2) the stratum lucidum, (3) the stratum granulosum, and (4) the stratum mucosum.

(1) The *stratum corneum.* The superficial part of the horny layer consists of cells which are constantly shed. They do not stain well with osmic acid, and owing to their loose attachment are sometimes called the stratum disjunctum. The main part of the stratum corneum varies in thickness in different parts of the body. It reaches its highest degree of development on the palms and soles and is enormously thickened in regions exposed to pressure. The cells are flattened and lie in lamellæ. They have no nuclei and are composed of keratine, and in the horny plaques of the workman's hand there is a little eleidine. There is also an epidermic fatty material which gives suppleness to the corneous layer.

(2) The *stratum lucidum* lies immediately under the stratum corneum and may be looked upon as intermediate in its structure between the horny and granular layers. It has a homogeneous appearance, its cells are non-nucleated and devoid of fatty matter. Eleidine is present in the form of granules.

(3) The *stratum granulosum* consists of one to three or four layers of cells, lozenge shaped in section, and containing granules of eleidine, staining easily with carmine. The intercellular fibrils of the mucous layer have disappeared.

(4) The *stratum mucosum* consists of several parts. The basal layer, or stratum germinativum, stands on the basement or hyaline

membrane. It consists of cylindrical cells in one or two layers, with large nuclei showing karyokinetic figures. In this part of the epidermis the pigment is chiefly developed. Above it lies the prickle cell-layer consisting of several rows of irregular polygonal nucleated cells, united by filamentous processes. As the stratum granulosum is approached the cells become flatter and fusiform, and finally stratiform.

Pigment. Melanin is a lipo-chrome produced by the nucleus. Its formation is a normal function of epidermal cell-metabolism.

The **corium**, or **cutis vera**, is composed of dense fibrous tissue with strands of yellow elastic tissue. It contains the vessels, lymphatics, nerves, and touch corpuscles, the glandular elements and

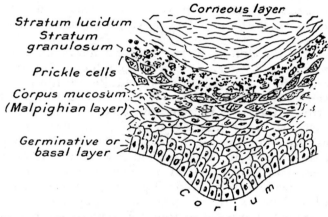

FIG. 1.—Vertical section of epidermis (diagrammatic).

the hair follicles (Fig. 2). There are two main divisions—(1) the papillary layer or pars papillaris, and (2) the pars reticularis.

(1) The *papillary layer* consists of finger-like processes, which fit into the irregularities of the mucous layer of the epidermis. The papillæ are supplied with blood-vessels, lymphatics, and fine nerve twigs and touch corpuscles.

(2) The *reticular layer* is formed of bundles of connective tissue. It is continuous with the papillary layer, and there is no essential difference in the structure. Elastic tissue fibres are met with in varying quantity in this layer. It is traversed by the vessels, nerves, and glandular structures, and by the hair follicles.

It is now believed that the true skin does not normally produce pigment.

The **subcutaneous tissue** or hypoderm consists of loose connective tissue bundles containing masses of fat-cells in their meshes. The sweat glands and the deep hair follicles reach the hypoderm.

The vessels of the skin. There are two plexuses, the superficial, forming loops in the papillary layer, and the deep, lying in the subcutaneous tissue. Branches of supply pass from the latter to the sweat glands and to the hair follicles and sebaceous glands. Renaud has demonstrated that the distribution of the blood-vessels in the skin is mapped out into areas which are supplied by a central deep artery and drained at the periphery by a plexus of veins. Arterial congestion produces erythema or redness of the central area, while venous congestion causes a purplish reticular mottling due to distension of the peripheral venous plexus.

The lymphatics form two plexuses following the distribution of the blood-vessels. Spaces filled with lymph are found in the corium, and by the apices of the papillæ the lymph reaches the deeper layers of the epidermis.

The **nerves of the skin** are (1) medullated nerve fibres terminating in touch corpuscles at the apices of the papillæ, and in the Paccinian bodies in the hypoderm; (2) non-medullated fibres, which pass through the corium and apparently end in the stratum mucosum. There are three kinds of corpuscle connected with the nerve terminals —(1) the corpuscles of Krause, occurring in the conjunctivæ and other sensitive mucous membranes; (2) the Paccinian bodies, chiefly in the hypoderm, and particularly numerous on the fingers and toes, consisting of a central nerve fibre surrounded by a core, and with a capsule of concentric layers; (3) touch corpuscles, also rounded or oval bodies at the apices of the papillæ.

Muscle. Striated muscle is found in the platysma of the face and neck. The arrectores pilorum are of smooth muscle; they run obliquely downwards to the root of the hair, and have the power of erecting the hair and of expressing sebum from the sebaceous glands connected with it. The skin of the scrotum also contains smooth muscle.

The **sweat or coil glands** are long narrow tubes extending from the sweat pore to the subcutaneous tissue. In the epidermis they are coiled spirally, while in the corium they run nearly straight and end in a coil which is copiously supplied with blood-vessels.

The **sebaceous glands** are usually in relation with the hair follicles, but on the edge of the lip and on the penis they are independent of the hairs. They consist of acini opening into a duct which communicates with the hair follicle. In some parts of the skin they are of large size and the hair follicle in connection is comparatively

1—2

small and unimportant. Such large sebaceous glands are seen on the nose and in the naso-labial furrows, etc. On the other hand, on the hairy parts of the body, the scalp and face, the hair follicles are large, while the small sebaceous glands are sacculated diverticula opening into the upper part of the common pilo-sebaceous duct.

The **hair** is a modified epidermal structure. It consists of a

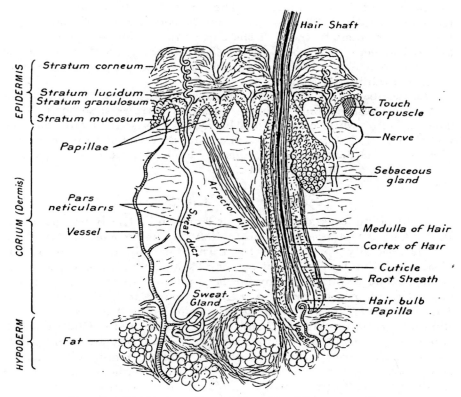

FIG. 2.—Vertical section of the skin (diagrammatic).

shaft above the level of the surface of the skin, a root in the skin, and a bulb at its lower end. The bulb is concave on its under surface and stands on the papilla containing the vessels for the nourishment of the hair. Each hair is contained in an invagination of the skin called the follicle. The follicle is a narrow cylindrical tube formed partly of the dermis and partly of the epidermis.

The wall of the hair-follicle consists of (1) a dermic coat, composed of an external longitudinal layer of fibrous tissue, a middle layer of transverse fibres, and an internal, glassy, homogeneous layer ; (2) an epidermic coat consisting of a layer continuous with the prickle layer of the epidermis, a root-sheath of two layers and the cuticle.

The hair itself is covered by a fine cuticle, within which lies the cortex, comprising the bulk of the hair substance. The cortex surrounds the medullary cavity containing the medulla.

The **nail** is an epidermic plate lying on the nail-bed. At the proximal end is the matrix. The ungual plate is composed of flattened keratinised cells. The matrix consists of cells similar in their arrangement to those of the corpus mucosum elsewhere ; deep cylindrical cells, then polygonal cells, flattening as they approach the surface. The stratum granulosum is replaced by a fine granular layer, containing no eleidine.

The nail-bed is covered by a mucous layer ; there are no papillæ in the dermis, but longitudinal ridges and furrows take their place. The lunula or white crescent at the root is less translucent than the rest of the body of the nail. The thin skin which forms over the surface at the base is the remains of the epidermic covering which envelops the whole nail in the fœtus.

Functions of the Skin.

It will be unnecessary to enter at length into the functions of the skin. The integument is a protection to the subjacent structures and is specially constructed to resist a certain degree of injury. Heat regulation is carried out by the vascular network and the sweat glands. The respiratory function is of minor importance, but small quantities of oxygen are absorbed and carbonic acid is given off. The excretory function is of greater moment. The sweat glands eliminate waste products and water, and it is estimated that in health two pounds weight of sweat leave the adult body in twenty-four hours. The sensory function of the skin is highly elaborated ; tactile sensation, the sensations of pain, pressure, heat, and cold are all observed through specially developed nervous apparatus.

REFERENCES.—A valuable paper on the pigment of the skin by DR. W. DYSON appeared in the *British Journal of Dermatology*, XXIII., p. 217. "The Functions of the Skin." M. PEMBREY. *British Journal of Dermatology*, May, 1910, p. 156. On the sensory functions the papers of DR. H. HEAD (with DRS. CAMPBELL, RIVERS, and THOMPSON, and MR. SHERREN). "Brain." 1900, 1905, 1906, 1908.

CHAPTER II.

MORPHOLOGY.

THE student beginning the study of dermatology is frequently bewildered and may actually be deterred from its pursuit by the complexity of its nomenclature. The terminology is, however, the least important part of the subject, and I cannot too strongly advise the novice to get rid of the common idea that a knowledge of skin diseases consists in the application of polysyllabic appellations and in attaching to each of them one or more appropriate prescriptions. The study of cutaneous affections is much more interesting and affords an admirable training in observation. In no other branch of medicine can so much be learned from the objective phenomena. The lesions lie spread out before the eye, and with the assistance of a lens and a microscope their most important characters can be studied. Exactitude of description is to be aimed at, and to attain this it is a useful practice to sit down in front of patients and to write out in simple language what is to be seen. Diagrams should also be made of the distribution of the lesions, and if the observer can use his pencil he will derive great help from sketches. Systematic observation of cases in the out-patient clinic and in the wards will soon make the student familiar with the essential features of the commoner skin diseases, and the nomenclature will come gradually and easily.

The objective phenomena are also valuable aids in determining appropriate treatment. Certain diseases of the skin are the result of local irritation, others are caused by animal or vegetable parasites, while some depend upon toxic conditions of the blood. In these we are often able to effect a cure by the removal or destruction of the cause. Thus, an eruption of scales may be due to a vegetable fungus, as in tinea versicolor, and the organism can be destroyed by the application of parasiticide remedies. Another scaly affection is caused by the spirochæta pallida. Salvarsan given internally causes the disappearance of the lesions by its action on the parasite in the blood.

But we are still ignorant of the causation of some of the commonest skin diseases. Treatment under such conditions, unless absolutely empirical, must be symptomatic, and to be successful the symptomatic treatment of cutaneous affections depends upon the accurate observation of the elementary lesions. Suppose we have before us an eruption of scaly patches whose cause is unknown. We may treat the condition empirically or rationally. Rational treatment will direct the application of remedies which are known to influence the keratin formation of the epidermis. Such remedies may be applied locally or administered internally. Our success will depend upon the exact interpretation of the objective phenomena, and not upon the name or label which we attach to the disease.

To facilitate accurate description it is necessary to know the meaning of certain terms which are applied to the elementary lesions of skin disease, and a little time spent in mastering the short vocabulary which follows will be of great assistance to the student in the reading of the subsequent chapters.

Elementary cutaneous lesions are *primary* and *secondary*, and in examining an eruption it is important to determine which is the primary element. In many cases this is fairly easy ; in others the history and the observation of an intelligent patient will be helpful ; but where there are extensive secondary changes it may be exceedingly difficult to be certain what has been the primary manifestation. With the growth of experience these difficulties diminish, and there is one thing which should never be omitted, and that is the examination of the *whole* of the affected area, for it is highly probable that at some part, often the periphery, the primary lesion unaltered by retrograde or evolutionary change will be found.

Primary Lesions.

Macules are circumscribed, non-elevated alterations in the colour of the skin, of any size or shape. Examples : the eruption of measles, the macular syphilide, the cutaneous nævus (port-wine mark).

Papules are solid, or apparently solid, elevations of the skin not larger than a pea. Examples : the shotty papules of variola, flat papules of lichen planus, flat warts.

Nodules are inflammatory swellings larger than a pea, but not exceeding a hazel-nut in size. They commonly involve the true skin. Examples : nodular syphilide, nodular leprosy.

Nodules are often called "tubercles," but for descriptive purposes this term is better avoided, to prevent confusion with lesions caused by Koch's bacillus.

Nodes are flat subcutaneous inflammatory swellings, *e.g.*, syphilitic nodes. The adjective " nodosum " is applied to a special form of erythema.

Tumours are (1) new growths of the skin, such as fibromata, or epitheliomata, and (2) large inflammatory swellings, granulomata occurring occasionally in tuberculosis, and in a number of tropical affections of the skin.

Wheals or pomphi are circumscribed swellings caused by hyperæmia and œdema, and characterised by a white centre and red margin. Examples : the nettle sting, urticaria.

Vesicles are circumscribed swellings of the skin smaller than a pea, containing serum or (rarely) lymph. Examples : the eruption of chicken-pox and herpes zoster.

Bullæ, blisters or blebs, are elevations of the epidermis larger than a pea, containing serum or blood. Examples : blisters caused by a scald, pemphigus.

Pustules are swellings of the skin containing pus. Examples : common acne, impetigo.

Secondary Lesions.

The primary lesions mentioned above may pass by evolution or devolution into other forms, or they may be modified by super-added conditions. Thus a vesicle may dry up to form a crust or scab, or it may pass into a pustule. The secondary lesions are important because they are often the most prominent feature when a case comes under observation.

Scales or squamæ are dry exfoliations of the epidermis. Example : the lesion of psoriasis is covered with a silvery scale.

Crusts or scabs are dried masses of exudation and other products of inflammatory action. Example : the crust of common impetigo.

Excoriations are superficial lesions characterised by removal of the epidermis. Examples : abrasions caused by injury or scratching.

Fissures or rhagades are linear ulcers extending usually to the papillary layer. They occur in the normal fissures of the skin and rarely leave scars. Examples : the cracks on the hands associated with " chapping " and chronic eczema.

Ulcers are circumscribed lesions characterised by loss of sub-stance of the true skin. Examples : varicose ulcer, gummatous ulcer.

Scars or cicatrices are new formations of connective tissue to replace loss of substance of the true skin. It is important to remember that scars only occur when the true skin is involved. Examples : cicatrices of burns, and of syphilitic ulcers.

Stains are local discolorations of the skin from (1) extravasation of blood, (2) diapedesis in inflammation, and (3) the local application of pigments and certain drugs. Examples : the stains left by a bruise, by a syphilitic eruption, and by picric acid.

General Morphology.

Assuming that the vocabulary of terms is mastered, it will now be useful for the student to consider the general morphology or forms of eruption and other morbid conditions of the skin. In this section I shall indicate the essential features of each group, and with a view to helping those unfamiliar with the subject, I have appended to the brief description of the form of eruption under consideration a list of the important conditions in which it occurs, with references to the chapters in which the details are discussed. I believe that such an arrangement will be of use also to those who have lost touch with the skin clinic, and that a summary of the important affections characterised by erythema or papules, to take examples, will refresh the memory and assist in diagnosis.

Erythema is the name given to redness of the skin of a congestive character. The colour disappears under pressure, but returns when the pressure is removed. This feature distinguishes erythema from hæmorrhage into the skin, which is unaffected by compression. Cutaneous nævi are excluded from the erythemata because they are not congestive, and the history of their congenital origin is usually obtainable.

Erythemata are described as macular, scarlatiniform, morbiliform, diffuse, polymorphous, etc., according to their distribution and characters. The names are sufficiently distinctive and require no further definition.

Causes of erythema.—Erythema may be active or passive. In the active form the colour is bright red and the surface feels hot to the touch. The redness is due to active dilatation of the capillaries. In the passive variety the colour is livid or purplish and the surface is cold. The cause is stasis in the small blood-vessels. In some conditions passive congestion takes a reticular form from the arrangement of the venous plexuses (*vide* Livedo, p. 66).

Active erythema occurs as a result of local irritation, friction, pressure, heat, cold, light, X-rays, radium, and some chemicals, including drugs locally applied (Chapter IV.).

It is also a prominent feature in the exanthemata, the eruption of syphilis (p. 286), leprosy (p. 263), and in septic and toxic diseases. The importance of toxæmia in the causation is discussed in Chapter XIV. Erythema may also follow the internal administration of a number of drugs (p. 338).

Passive erythema occurs on the extremities in some apparently healthy children and adolescents, and in cachectic conditions, particularly in tuberculosis. The term " acro-asphyxia " is given to the more marked forms. Passive erythema is intensified by cold weather.

Erythemato-squamous eruptions. In a considerable number of skin affections the lesions are characterised by congestion and by scaling. Psoriasis is perhaps the commonest of these. The lesions are congested areas covered with masses of silvery scales (p. 451). In the squamous form of seborrhoic dermatitis the scales are greasy (p. 211). In pityriasis rosea (p. 449) the patches are rose coloured and covered with fine scales. Some forms of tinea and erythrasma form scaly patches on a congested base (p. 141). The squamous syphilide has scaly and congestive characters (p. 290). Some rare chronic conditions of this type simulating psoriasis are called " parapsoriasis " (p. 459).

Erythrodermia is the name given to *generalised,* persistent inflammatory conditions of the skin, attended with scaling, which is often profuse, a regular exfoliation. The erythrodermias may be primary or secondary. The primary forms are classed as exfoliative dermatitis and pityriasis rubra (p. 401). Generalised redness with scaling may also occur in the premycosic stage of mycosis fungoides (p. 574), and in leukæmia (p. 404). The secondary conditions follow eczema, psoriasis, and pemphigus foliaceus (p. 404).

Urticaria is a condition of localised hyperæmia with œdema. It is characterised by the formation of wheals or pomphi.

It occurs as the result of local irritation, *e.g.,* the nettle sting, and the bite of the bug, and of trauma, such as the blow of a whip or cane. When generalised it is usually an evidence of toxæmia. It frequently follows the ingestion of decomposing or unsuitable food, but may be due to auto-intoxication from the alimentary canal (p. 371). Some drugs, *e.g.,* copaiba, antitoxins, etc., may also cause it (p. 340). It is a rare complication of nervous disease and is a feature of the premycosic stage of mycosis fungoides (p. 573).

Cutaneous hæmorrhages are characterised by red macules which do not disappear on pressure. At first they are bright red, then purplish, and finally brown or greenish in tint. They occur as the result of injury, including the bites of insects, or from venous congestion, as in varicose veins ; but an eruption composed of hæmorrhages into the skin is usually caused by circulating microbes or toxines, as in the hæmorrhagic fevers, cerebro-spinal meningitis, septicæmia, and toxæmia. Cutaneous hæmorrhages are also seen in certain " blood diseases," pernicious anæmia, leukæmia, scurvy, hæmophilia, and in grave visceral disease, especially of the liver and kidneys. The name " purpura " is applied to many of these eruptions, and if the cause is known, they are classed as symptomatic purpura, while those of unknown origin are grouped as idiopathic purpura (p. 376).

Papular eruptions. Papules may be inflammatory or non-inflammatory. Those which are confined to the appendages of the skin are dealt with later (see Follicular Affections, p. 14).

Papules may be of the normal colour of the skin or red or brown in tint. They are described as flat, conical, acuminate, pointed, hemispherical, etc., according to their form.

Non-inflammatory papules occur as congenital anomalies—certain nævi and moles ; as evidence of senile degeneration—senile warts ; and from contagion—the common wart.

Inflammatory papules appear in variola, varicella, and vaccinia, and some other fevers, e.g., measles, typhus, typhoid, and in syphilis (p. 287), tuberculosis (p. 251), and leprosy (p. 260). In some forms of ringworm the lesions consist of a ring of papules (p. 140).

Papules are characteristic of lichen planus (p. 462), of the itching eruptions classed as prurigo (p. 429), and of strophulus or gum rash of infants (p. 428). They also occur in certain varieties of eczema (p. 101) and erythema (p. 361), and from local irritation. Both the local application and internal administration of certain drugs may be attended by a papular eruption (p. 341).

Diffuse papular conditions occur as a sequel to chronic irritation, chronic eczema, prurigo, and many itching diseases. To these secondary developments the term " lichenisation " is often given (p. 101).

Vesicular eruptions are produced by an effusion of serum in the epidermis. In extremely rare cases the fluid is lymph (Lymphangioma and Lymph varix, p. 417).

Vesicles are essential features of the eruption of variola, vaccinia, and varicella. They occur in dermatitis due to many forms of chemical irritation (p. 83), and in the reaction of the skin to heat, cold and actinic light (p. 71). Vesicles are characteristic of eczema and eczematised conditions (p. 101). They also occur in some forms of ringworm (p. 141), and in scabies (p. 115).

Grouped vesicles on an erythematous base are seen in herpes zoster (p. 441) and the labial and genital varieties of herpes (p. 434), and in association with bullæ in dermatitis herpetiformis (p. 487). In rare cases the eruption of strophulus is vesicular as well as papular (p. 428). Sudamina are dealt with among the affections of the sweat glands (p. 582).

Bullous eruptions. Blisters or bullæ are caused by the elevation of the epidermis by serum or blood. They may be the result of trauma, or of irritation by heat, cold, and light (p. 70), and, in the congenital anomaly called epidermolysis bullosa, develop in response to slight degrees of pressure or friction (p. 53). Coccal infection causes bullous impetigo, including the so-called pemphigus neonatorum (p. 181), while the spirochæta is responsible for the bullous congenital syphilide (p. 305).

The most important group of bullous eruptions are the varieties of pemphigus (p. 490), dermatitis herpetiformis (p. 486), and hydroa (p. 490). With the exception of the acute malignant form of pemphigus, which is believed to be microbic, the etiology of these affections is unknown.

Circulating toxines produce bullæ as an epiphenomenon in some forms of erythema (p. 361) and urticaria (p. 372), and closely allied to these are the bullous drug eruptions (p. 344). In Morvan's disease and in nerve-leprosy bullous lesions also occur (p. 263). A bulla also is situated at the orifice of exit of the Guinea worm (p. 129).

Pustular eruptions. Pustular affections of the skin are primary or secondary. The lesions may form in the superficial layers of the epidermis, or in the deeper structures and in the follicles (see p. 14). Pustules may be of any size, rounded or oval in shape, tense or flaccid, and they are often surrounded by a red areola. In many cases when the lesions first come under observation there is already a transformation into crusts or scabs.

The eruptions of variola and vaccinia (and occasionally varicella) become pustular, and pustules may occur in tuberculosis (p. 252) and syphilis (p. 239). The commonest causes, however, are streptococcal and staphylococcal infection. Impetigo (p. 189) and ecthyma (p. 182) are instances of primary coccogenic conditions, but many forms of irritant dermatitis, eczema, and itching eruptions become " impetiginised," i.e., secondarily infected with pus-cocci (p. 103). Some varieties of ringworm (p. 141) and many fungous diseases, blastomycosis, sporotrichosis, actinomycosis, etc. (p. 166), are characterised by the formation of pustules.

Ulceration. Ulcers vary very much in their characters. They may be rounded, oval, polycyclic, reniform, etc. The edge may be well or ill defined, steep, shelving, punched out, undermined, or everted. There may be infiltration, while the base may be irregular, covered with granulations or with slough, and the discharge may be clear, purulent, sanious, or bloody. Ulcers run an acute or chronic course. They occur as a result of physical irritation— from injury, heat, cold, X-rays, and chemicals (Chapter IV.) ; from microbic infection, as in soft sores (p. 270), syphilis (p. 299), tuber- culosis (p. 239), leprosy (p. 264), ecthyma (p. 182), farcy (p. 203) ; in certain mycotic infections, sporotrichosis (p. 172), blastomycosis (p. 169), mycetoma (p. 168), and actinomycosis (p. 165). Impaired circulation is the cause of the varicose ulcer, and perforating ulcer is due to nervous disease (p. 447). In many tumours characteristic ulceration occurs—*e.g.*, rodent ulcer (p. 541), epithelioma (p. 536), carcinoma (p. 536), and mycosis fungoides (p. 571).

Gangrene is local death of the skin and may result from traumatism, from compression, as in the bed-sores of myelitis and the like. It may also be caused by heat, cold, X-rays, and high- frequency currents, and the local action of chemicals, the caustic acids, alkalies, corrosive sublimate, chloride of zinc, and arsenic and in ergotism (Chapter XVII.). Gangrene of the extremities occurs in obliteration of the vessels, in Morvan's disease and nerve leprosy, and in Raynaud's disease and diabetes. Necrosis of the skin is occasionally produced by direct bacterial infection, as in dermatitis gangrenosa infantum (p. 186).

Cutaneous atrophy may be idiopathic or cicatricial. It may be localised or diffuse. The commonest forms are, naturally, cicatricial. Cicatricial atrophy occurs after burns, scalds, chronic X-ray and radium dermatitis, and chemical irritation. It may follow any form of deep-seated pustulation, *e.g.*, acne vulgaris, syphilis, follicular tuberculides. It is the common sequel of ulcera- tion of any kind, *e.g.*, syphylitic, lupoid, leprous ulcers, In lupus erythematosus and the dry forms of lupus vulgaris it is the result of interstitial inflammation. It occurs rarely in certain nervous diseases, and idiopathically. Stretching of the skin and probably certain toxic conditions are the cause of striæ atrophicæ. (Chapter XXIV.).

Sclerosis of the skin is characterised by thickening and toughening of the integument, which may feel like a piece of hide. It may be generalised, as in sclerema neonatorum (p. 50), or localised, as in sclerodermia or morphœa (p. 514), and in the tropical disease called ainhum (p. 517).

Facial hemiatrophy is an interesting form probably of nervous origin. Pachydermatous conditions occur in chronic congestive conditions, *e.g.*, in varicose veins.

Hypertrophy of the skin occurs in elephantiasis (p. 443), pseudo-elephantiasis (p. 414), pachydermia (p. 413), in the rare condition known as trophœdema (p. 420), in rhinoscleroma (p. 267), and rhinophyma (p. 385).

Dyschromias are discolorations of the skin. They may be local, as in the pigmented mole, a congenital anomaly (p. 29), and often follow exposure to light (freckles), heat (ephelis ab igne), and the X-rays (p. 78). The stains left by inflammatory and ulcerative conditions may also be classed as local dyschromias. Chloasma uterinum is associated with pregnancy, and uterine or ovarian disease may also cause pigmentation (p. 502). In some cases there is no explanation of the local increase of pigment (Melanodermia, p. 499). Arsenic and silver given over prolonged periods may cause pigmentary changes (p. 341).

General dyschromias occur in Addison's disease, syphilis, leprosy, and some nervous diseases, in Raynaud's disease, myxœdema and exophthalmic goitre. The bronzing of diabetes is now recognised as a form of hæmochromatosis. Blue discoloration is seen in hæmochromatosis and in argyria. Jaundice produces a yellow discoloration.

Absence of pigment occurs as a congenital anomaly in local and general albinism (p. 28), and in leucodermia, often associated with melanodermia, which may be idiopathic (p. 499) or the result of syphilis (p. 292).

Follicular lesions. A cutaneous affection may start in and be limited to the follicles. Many forms of staphylococcal infection attack the hair follicles, *e.g.*, impetigo of Bockhart, boils, carbuncle, sycosis, folliculitis, dermatitis capillitii (Chapter VIII.).

Fungi often invade the hair follicles and also the hairs themselves, *e.g.*, tinea favus (p. 153).

The sebaceous glands may be over-active, as in oily seborrhœa (p. 587), or they may become infected, *e.g.*, acne (p. 215), tuberculous folliculitis (p. 251) and syphilitic folliculitis (p. 288).

Folliculitis of the acne type may be caused by chlorine, tar, and oil of cade applied locally, and may follow the internal administration of bromides and iodides (p. 344).

Horny plugs are seen at the mouths of the hair follicles in pityriasis rubra pilaris (p. 475), keratosis follicularis (p. 479), lichen pilaris (p. 473), and psorospermosis follicularis vegetans (p. 479).

Affections of the hair, nails, and sweat glands are dealt with in Chapter XXVI.

Diseases of the hypoderm. A number of affections of the subcutaneous tissue come under the observation of the dermatologist. They commonly begin about the blood-vessels, and are doubtless often of embolic origin. Such conditions occur in connection with varicose veins, phlebitis, and periphlebitis. Syphilitic phlebitis produces a chronic form of hypodermic swelling, one form of syphilitic node (p. 299). Tuberculosis is the cause of the erythema induratum of Bazin (p. 255) and various toxaemias cause erythema nodosum (p. 363). Subcutaneous fatty and other tumours are also often brought to the notice of those practising in skin diseases.

CHAPTER III.

CONGENITAL AFFECTIONS OF THE SKIN.

ANOMALIES of the development of the skin are common. They are usually noticed at or soon after birth, but a few conditions, doubtless also of congenital origin, do not attract attention until some months or possibly years later. To many circumscribed lesions of the skin of congenital origin the term " nævus " is applied. It is no longer limited to vascular anomalies. It is difficult to classify these affections rationally, and they will be considered here as far as possible on an anatomical basis.

Development of the skin. The integument is derived from the epiblast and the mesoblast. The epidermis, nails, hair, and glands are of epiblastic origin, while the corium and the subcutaneous tissue and their vessels are formed from the mesoblast.

The Epiblast. At the second month of intra-uterine life the primitive single layer of epiblast has developed into two strata, representing the stratum corneum and the stratum mucosum respectively. At the fifth month the corneous layer is double, but the superficial epitrichial layer is shed at the seventh month. The corpus mucosum develops between the fifth and the eighth month, but the stratum granulosum does not appear until the ninth month.

Cellular downgrowths from the epidermis form the hairs and the sebaceous and sweat glands. The hair is first noticeable on the forehead in the third month, and on the trunk in the fifth. The sebaceous and sweat glands begin to develop in the fifth month. The nails form within the epidermis and the superjacent layer is shed shortly before maturity. From the sixth month onwards the surface is covered with the vernix caseosa derived from epidermal cells and not from the secretion of the sebaceous glands. Pigment appears in the course of the first year after birth in the white races, but the negro infant shows evidence of colour in the first week.

The Mesoblast. The dermis is developed from the primitive skin plate of the mesoblast, and at the end of the second month is composed of spindle cells of a fibromyxomatous character. It is differentiated from the hypoderm in the third month, and the papillary bodies begin to appear a month later. In the fifth month the myxomatous character of the corium undergoes a change, the layer taking on a collagenous appearance, but the elastic tissue does not appear until the seventh month. The vessels are present as early as the twelfth week.

The Vernix Caseosa, the waxy covering of the fœtus, has been classed by some as " Seborrhœa." It may persist for some days to two or three weeks after birth. In uterine life the cells of the corneous layer accumulate on the surface to form the vernix. The cells differ from those formed later in life, chiefly because they are constantly soaked in the liquor amnii. They contain little free fat, and washing with ether does not appreciably diminish their weight, nor do they take the osmic stain. The persistence of the waxy covering after birth may be taken as evidence that the epidermis has not yet adapted itself to its new conditions, but it may also be due to a time-honoured custom of leaving the layer on the scalp, where it is most commonly found, untouched in the ablutions of the infant. Occasionally the groins and other flexures remain covered with the vernix.

CONGENITAL AFFECTIONS OF THE EPIDERMIS.

The horny layer of the epidermis may undergo excessive growth, hyperkeratosis. This condition occurs congenitally in xerodermia, ichthyosis, ichthyosis hystrix, and in tylosis.

Abnormal vulnerability of the epidermis occurs in the condition known as epidermolysis bullosa.

Ichthyosis and Xerodermia.

Ichthyosis is a congenital hyperkeratosis or hypertrophy of the horny layers of the skin. Xerodermia is a mild degree of the same process.

Etiology. Ichthyosis frequently occurs in several members of the same family, and heredity is often traceable. It is said to be endemic in certain tribes. The cause is unknown.

Pathology. The disease is a hypertrophy of the horny layers of the epidermis. The cells of the rete mucosum develop directly into horny cells, the prickle-cell layer being imperfectly formed. The sebaceous glands are absent or atrophic, but the sweat glands are usually normal, and the subcutaneous fat is atrophied.

Clinical features. The ichthyotic skin is dry and scaly and looks dirty. The parents often state that the child's skin has been rough and dry from birth, but careful enquiry will usually

elicit the history that nothing abnormal was noticed until some weeks
or months later.

A general dryness of the skin with a tendency to the formation
of small scales is called xerodermia (dry skin). The furrows are
more distinct than in the normal epidermis, and there may be some

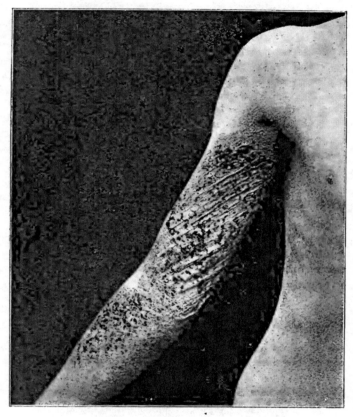

FIG. 3.——Ichthyosis.

roughness, resembling goose-flesh, from keratosis or prominence of
the hair follicles, particularly on the limbs (keratosis follicularis).
In more marked cases there are branny scales of a dirty brown
colour, most developed on the extensor surfaces of the limbs. The
face is dry and rough, and radiating cracks are often seen about the
orifices. Although this form may affect the whole of the epidermis,
we often find that the skin of the flexures, axillæ, front of the elbows,

popliteal spaces, and groins is smooth and supple. The scalp is usually covered with a fine branny scurf.

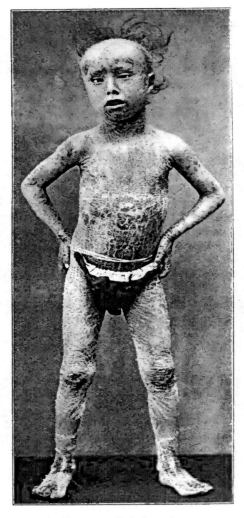

FIG. 4.—Ichthyosis.

In the severe forms of ichthyosis there are scales of various sizes, diamond-shaped or polygonal, resembling fish scales. The squamæ may be thin or thick, and in the worst cases the condition is greatly disfiguring. The hair in such instances is thin and scanty. In

2—2

neglected cases the scales may be dark brown or nearly black. The palms and soles are rarely scaly, but the epidermis is obviously thickened and the normal fissures are exaggerated.

After scarlatinal desquamation the skin may become normal temporarily, but the hyperkeratosis soon recurs.

Except in the flexures, the skin is always dry, and perspiration is imperceptible. In the hot weather there is an amelioration of the condition, doubtless because there is some sweating. Itching is sometimes a troublesome feature.

A form of xerodermia characterised by redness and scaling of the whole surface, including the flexures, is sometimes met. It is believed to be related to the erythrodermias (*vide* p. 400).

Ichthyosis and xerodermia appear in the first year and increase in severity, as a rule, from the fifth to the fifteenth year, and then remain stationary, persisting throughout life. The ichthyotic skin is peculiarly vulnerable, and " chapping " takes place easily. Slight exposure to chill or easterly winds frequently produces eczema (Pl. I.). The roughness of the skin causes the adhesion of particles of dust and dirt, especially on the lower limbs of young children, and the mother often complains that it is impossible to keep the parts clean. Ichthyosis is a troublesome complication of renal disease, as the measures adopted to induce diaphoresis are of little effect.

Diagnosis. A slight degree of scaly eczema might be mistaken for ichthyosis, but the absence of inflammation and the universality of the disease, with the history of its appearance and persistence from soon after birth, should make the differential diagnosis easy. Ichthyosis hystrix is a localised condition, the rough skin being in lines or streaks (*vide* p. 21). On removing the scales of true ichthyosis the subjacent skin is found to be normal, while hystrix affects the whole thickness.

Prognosis. The disease persists through life. It is worse in the second decade and tends to become stationary, and even less severe, in adult life. Treatment affords great relief, but the condition is incurable.

Treatment is purely palliative. Thyroid extract administered internally will sometimes improve the condition, but the effect is transitory and not to be recommended. No other drugs have any influence. Constant local treatment is important. Frequent bathing is useful to remove the scales. The ordinary warm bath or alkaline baths with one drachm of sodium bicarbonate to the gallon may be given. In the mild cases rubbing the whole surface once daily with equal parts of glycerine and water is all that is

Plate I.

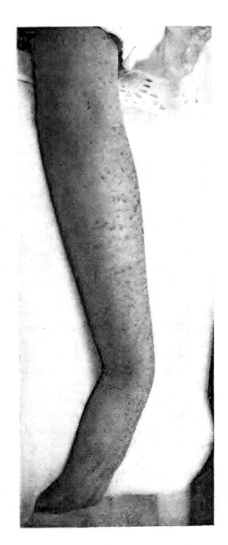

ECZEMA ON A XERODERMATOUS SKIN.

The exaggeration of the normal tissues and general dryness are best seen about the wrist. The patient had had several attacks of eczema.

necessary to keep down the scaliness and impart smoothness and suppleness to the skin. In the more severe forms oily preparations are to be preferred. Equal parts of olive oil and lanoline rubbed in after a daily bath cleared off all the scales in the case represented in Fig. 4. Eucerin, a glycerine of wool fat, in combination with vaseline is also a valuable remedy. It is rubbed in once a day. Constant attention is required, or relapses will occur. To prevent chapping washing with warm water and, above all, careful drying are required. The eczematous lesions are treated by applying zinc paste or the ointment of zinc oxide and salicylic acid. In bad cases care must be taken against exposure to easterly winds and cold.

REFERENCES —Histology : UNNA. "Histopathology," translated by DR. NORMAN WALKER, pp. 332 and 1154. Heredity : STAINER. "The Hereditary Transmission of Defects in Man." Oxford, 1910, p. 16, etc.

Ichthyosis Fœtalis : Harlequin Fœtus.

Harlequin fœtus is usually described as a form of ichthyosis, but on very unsatisfactory grounds. It is a rare condition occurring in the infant. The skin is tough and like parchment, with large deep cracks or furrows forming plates. The lips and eyelids are stiff and the child is unable to suck. Death occurs a few days after birth. In some instances the infant is stillborn. There is a milder degree of this affection in which the scales are thin and ultimately peel off, leaving a normal smooth surface. By some the latter form is believed to be the persistence of the epitrichial layer which should be shed by the fœtus at the seventh month.

REFERENCE.—BALLANTYNE. "Manual of Ante-Natal Pathology," Edinburgh, 1902, Vol. I., p. 306.

Keratolysis is a very rare condition in which the whole epidermis is shed at intervals, sometimes yearly, very much in the way the snake sheds its skin.

Ichthyosis Hystrix or Linear Nævus (Nævus unius lateris).

Linear nævus is the name given to congenital lines or streaks composed of warty elevations covered with scales. The localisation of the lesions and their usually limited character demand that these anomalies should be classed as nævi.

Etiology. The cause is unknown.

Pathology. The unilateral arrangement of the bands and streaks, which, however, is not essential, as there is a group of cases in which the lesions are bilateral, although not symmetrical, suggests that the affection is of nervous origin, but in many cases the lesions do not

FIG. 5.—Ichthyosis hystrix.   There was an epithelioma on the face and lipoma of the shoulder.

follow the lines or areas of nerves.   Some suggest that Voigt's lines are the determining factor, but the streaks are often quite irregular. The individual lesions consist of thickening of the prickle layer and hyperkeratosis, with hypertrophy of the papillary layer.   The elastic tissue is atrophic and there is often evidence of inflammation in the true skin.   Dilatation of the sweat ducts may occur.

Clinical features.   The condition may be noticed at birth, but often does not attract attention until the child is a few years old. The lesions may be insignificant streaks an inch or so long, or bands

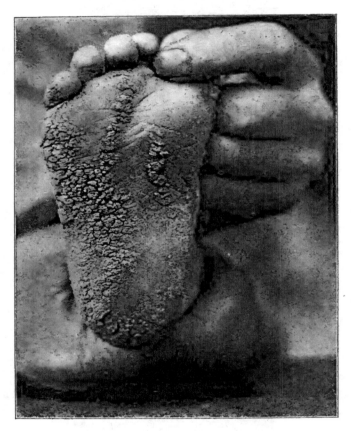

FIG. 6.—Ichthyosis hystrix.

of irregular width extending the whole length of a limb or round the trunk.   As a rule, the streaks or bands are unilateral ; hence the name Nævus unius lateris.   Each streak is composed of closely-set small waity swellings covered with scales.   It may be almost the colour of the surrounding skin or brownish or blackish in tint. Occasionally squamous-celled carcinoma may develop in later life upon such nævi. I have seen one case in which the nævoid condition involved the soft palate, as well as the skin of the face.

In the rare condition known as Ichthyosis hystrix gravior (Porcupine skin disease) there is an extraordinary development of warty

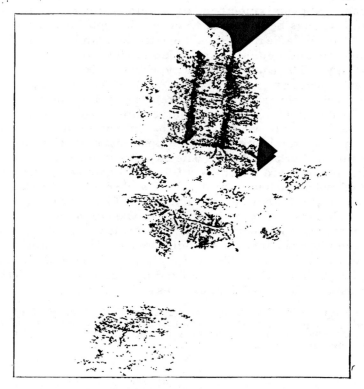

Fig. 7.—Tylosis. The left palm was similarly affected. The affection was known to have occurred in four generations.

masses involving a large part, but never the whole, of the integument. In one family this affected the males for four generations.

Treatment. Unless giving trouble by their position, the linear nævi may be left alone. Caustics will thin them down, but, if radical treatment is desired, they should be excised, or destroyed by the Paquelin or electric cautery or by radium or solid carbonic acid.

References.—" Histology of Linear Nævus." H. G. Adamson. *British Journal of Dermatology*, 1906, XVIII., p. 235. " Manual of Antenatal Pathology." Ballantyne, Vol. I., p. 306.

Tylosis (Keratodermia palmaris et plantaris).

Tylosis is an hereditary and family hyperkeratosis of the palms and soles.

Etiology. Several members of a family may be affected, and the condition has been known to occur through four or five generations. The "Maladie de Méleda " occurring in an island off Dalmatia is an endemic and hereditary affection of this type.

Pathology. The condition is a hyperkeratosis.

Clinical features. The palms and soles are symmetrically affected, being covered with thick horny yellowish plates with a well-defined margin. The normal fissures are exaggerated. In some cases the skin is darker, often brown or nearly black, the fissures producing a mosaic-like appearance or a rough surface resembling the bark of a tree. The movement of the parts is impeded and the fissures are often painful. I have seen the condition associated with ichthyosis hystrix. The disease is generally noticed when the subject is about four or five years of age and persists through life. Amelioration is sometimes seen in the summer.

Treatment is palliative only. The thickened epidermis may be softened by plasters of salicylic acid or by the application of lotions of the same drug. Temporary improvement follows exposures to the X-rays, but if these be persisted in, cicatricial contraction with cutaneous atrophy and telangiectases may occur.

REFERENCES.—H. RADCLIFFE CROCKER. *British Journal of Dermatology*, Vol. III., p. 169, plates. BESNIER. International Atlas, 1889, 5. A. M. GOSSAGE. *Quarterly Journal of Medicine.* Oxford, I., p. 331. Pedigrees and references.

Epidermolysis bullosa.

This condition, which was formerly called congenital traumatic pemphigus, is a developmental anomaly in which slight traumatism causes the formation of bullæ.

Etiology. The disease sometimes runs in families for generations, and several members of the same family may be affected. In other cases heredity cannot be traced.

Pathology. Nothing definite is known as to the cause. It is supposed by some to be a congenital hyper-excitability of the vaso-motor system. Elliot and others have found in the apparently normal skin of subjects of epidermolysis degeneration changes in the basal epithelial cells. The bullæ are formed by the exudation of serum, and by some authors an embryonic condition in the vessels is believed to be the essential feature.

Clinical features.   The disease appears in infancy and may persist to adult life.   The parents notice that slight friction and pressure, which normally would have no effect on the skin, produce

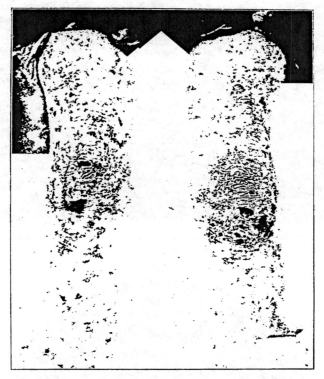

Fig. 8.—Epidermolysis bullosa.   Blebs and atrophic skin about the knees.

blisters.   The parts most exposed to pressure, viz., the knees, ankles, feet, elbows, wrists, and knuckles, are consequently affected.   The blebs appear with great rapidity and vary in size from a pea to half a walnut, or larger.   Most of them contain serous fluid, but blisters containing blood are not uncommon.   The bullæ on rupture dry up quickly, and there may be some atrophy of the skin.   In one type of the disease white pinhead-sized shining spots form on the sites of old lesions, and these on microscopical examination are found to be epidermal cysts.   Such cysts, formerly miscalled " milia," occur after

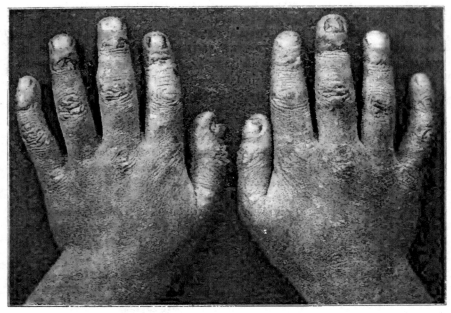

FIG. 9.—Epidermolysis bullosa. Atrophic nails and epidermal cysts in sites of old bullæ.

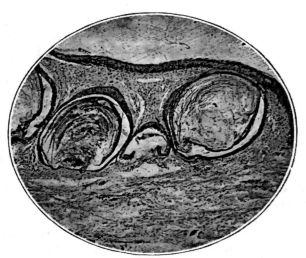

FIG. 10.—Epidermic cysts from case of epidermolysis bullosa. Micro-photograph of section.

other bullous eruptions, but in this form of epidermolysis bullosa they are more numerous than in any other condition.

The finger and toe nails are atrophic and in some instances consist merely of small horny pegs. In others the nails are yellowish or dirty brown and opaque and do not reach the ends of the digits.

In none of my cases has there been any eosinophilia or other noteworthy blood change.

A few cases in which the disease has started in adult life are on record. A noteworthy instance was described by Wise and Lautman, who give references to the previously reported cases.

The **prognosis** is usually bad. I have seen a tendency to improvement at the approach of adolescence, but in many cases the patient is crippled for life, every kind of work being impossible on account of the formation of blisters on slight provocation.

Treatment is purely palliative. Drugs have no influence on the disease, and all that can be done is to protect the parts and apply soothing ointments to the blisters on rupture. Ergot has been tried, it is said, with temporary benefit.

REFERENCES.—WALLACE BEATTY. *British Journal of Dermatology,* August, 1897. A. M. GOSSAGE. *Quarterly Journal of Medicine,* 1908; I., iii., gives family tree of Bonajuti's cases, in which thirty-one out of sixty-three persons in five generations were affected. L. B. CANE. *British Medical Journal,* May 8, 1909. References and family tree showing disease in four generations. COLUMBINI. *Monatsheft. f. Prakt. Derm.,* May, 1900. Twenty-four out of forty-seven members of a family in three generations. WISE and LAUTMAN. "Acquired Epidermolysis Bullosa." *Journal Cutaneous Dis.,* 1915, p. 441.

CONGENITAL PIGMENTARY ANOMALIES.

The pigment of the skin may be congenitally absent, as in albinism, or in excess, as in pigmented moles.

Albinism.

A congenital absence of the pigment of the skin, hair, and choroid. The cause is unknown. Albinism is more common in the tropics than in temperate zones. It sometimes occurs in several members of a family, and may be associated with mental defect.

Albinism is usually complete. Local absence of pigment is exceedingly rare. The skin of the albino is white or pale pink, the hair is very fine and of a white or pale yellow colour. The iris is commonly pink and the pupil shows the red reflection from the non-pigmented choroid.   Photophobia and nystagmus are constant symptoms.   No treatment is of any avail.

REFERENCES.—" Heredity."   SYM.   *Lancet*, 1901, July 11.   " Partial in a Hindoo."   HUTCHINSON.   Smaller Atlas, Plates I. and II.   " A Negro Albino."   BLASCHKO.   *Berlin. Klin. Wochenschrift*, 1912, XLIX., p. 2128. " Albinism in Man."   K. PEARSON, E. NETTLESHIP and USHER.   Biometric Series, VI., many plates and pedigrees.

Mongolian Blue Spots.

A congenital condition characterised by dark bluish spots on the lower sacral region and elsewhere.

This anomaly, of which the cause is unknown, occurs in 80 to 90 per cent. of the Chinese and Japanese and in about 1 in 300 white persons.

The spots are rounded or oblong from one-fifth of an inch to five inches in diameter.   They are well defined or shade into the colour of the surrounding skin.   The surface is normal and the colour does not disappear on pressure.   There may be one macule or several.   The sacral region and buttocks are most commonly affected, but the spots may occur elsewhere.   The spots are present at birth and usually disappear by the fourth year.   Histologically there are fusiform cells containing melanotic granules in the corium.

No treatment is necessary.

REFERENCE.—CASTOR.   *Journal of Tropical Medicine*, 1912.

Nævus pigmentosus (Pigmented Mole).

The **etiology** of pigmented moles is unknown.   Maternal impressions are often invoked as causes.

Pathology.   Sections show masses or rows of cuboidal cells of epidermal origin in the corium.   The corium being a mesoblastic structure, it would appear that the epiblastic cells are abnormally included in it in the process of development.   In addition to the cuboidal cells there is excess of pigment, and hypertrophy of the hair follicles is common.

Clinical features.   Pigmented moles may be present at birth and occur on any part of the body.   They may be single or multiple, and of all sizes, from a pin's head to large tracts covering one half of the head or extensive areas of the trunk and limbs.   The mole is a circumscribed spot or patch of brownish or brownish-black skin, usually covered with hair.   The hairs may be fine and downy

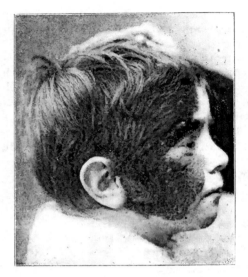

FIG. 11.——Pigmented hairy mole.

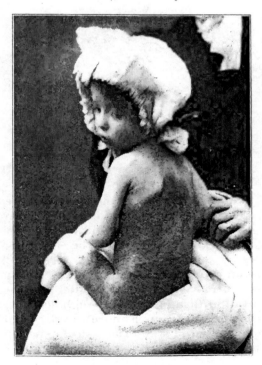

FIG. 12.——Pigmented mole.

or strong and stiff. The surface of the mole may be smooth or irregular and warty, especially if there be also hypertrophy of other elements of the skin.

Prognosis. Except for the disfigurement the pigmented moles are of little significance until middle life is reached. In patients over forty years of age there is a risk of their developing into malignant growths of melanotic type. These neoplasms are carcinomata, and rapid metastases may occur.

Treatment. Removal may be demanded on account of the disfigurement. Small pigmented nævi may be destroyed by elec-

FIG. 13.—Nævus verrucosus.

trolysis or by radium. The larger areas may be excised and skin grafts put on. The hairs can be removed by electrolysis, and after their removal there is often some diminution of the pigment. I have recently had remarkable success in the treatment of extensive pigmented moles by solid carbon dioxide. The stick of the dioxide is pressed firmly on the area for forty seconds. A moderately severe reaction with the formation of bullæ results, and the hair comes out and the pigmentation disappears. Though several sittings may be necessary, the treatment is much more rapid than that by radium, and I think the method will stand the test of experience. For details of treatment, *vide* p. 37.

In the adult any pigmented mole which is increasing in size should be removed without delay.

Nævus verrucosus is the name given to a pigmented mole with hyperkeratosis (Fig. 13).

Nævus lipomatodes is a pigmented mole with hypertrophy of the connective tissue and fat (Fig. 14).

FIG. 14.—Nævo-lipoma.

The treatment of these nævi, if limited, is on the same lines as for the common pigmented mole.

REFERENCES.—UNNA. " Histopathology," translated by NORMAN WALKER, p. 1125. A. WHITFIELD " Histology." *British Journal of Dermatology*, 1900, XII., p. 267. WILFRID FOX. *British Journal of Dermatology*, 1906, XVIII., pp. 15, 47.

Milium congenitale.

A very rare condition, of which Dr. Radcliffe Crocker described two cases.

The lesion is a pale reddish-yellow plaque on the head or face. The surface is finely granular and composed of closely aggregated pale yellow papules the size of a pin's point. Comedones are present at the borders and scales on the surface. Patches on the scalp are hairless. The lesions are present at birth and do not alter. They are apparently nævoid structures and consist of nucleated epithelial cells in the corium enclosed in a kind of capsule. They thus resemble the non-pigmented mole and are probably due to abnormal inclusion of epiblast.

REFERENCE.—H. RADCLIFFE CROCKER. "Diseases of the Skin," 1903, p. 699.

CONGENITAL ANOMALIES OF THE CUTANEOUS VESSELS.

Nævus anæmicus. This name is given to a condition in which there are one or more scattered patches of skin which are paler than the normal integument. These are caused by an abnormally small development of the cutaneous vessels. They are sometimes associated with small vascular nævi.

REFERENCE.—STEIN. *Archiv. für Dermatol.*, 1910, p. 411.

Nævus vascularis.

The vessels of the skin and the subcutaneous tissue may be congenitally hypertrophied, forming the local or diffuse vascular overgrowths called nævi vasculares. They are the commonest congenital affections of the skin, and it has been estimated that one person in ten has a vascular nævus of some sort. When the term "nævus" is used without a descriptive adjective, this form of congenital anomaly is usually implied.

Vascular nævi are classified, according to the parts involved, as cutaneous, subcutaneous, and mixed. They are further subdivided into (1) simple angioma, port wine mark; (2) angioma cavernosum, the common nævus, often called popularly "strawberry mark"; and (3) nævus araneus, spider or stellate nævus.

Etiology. The simple angioma and angioma cavernosum are congenital anomalies, though they may escape notice until some time after birth. There is no adequate explanation of their origin, but as the head and neck are the parts most frequently affected, it has been suggested that injury at birth may be the cause. The spider or stellate nævus does not usually appear until some years after birth, and sometimes follows an injury. It should perhaps be considered as a form of telangiectasis, but for convenience is dealt with here. Vascular nævi occur twice as frequently in females as in males.

Pathology. The *simple angioma* or port wine mark is a capillary hyperplasia. The vessels are dilated, but there are no lateral communications between them. The *cavernous nævus* is a hyper-

s.   3

trophy and dilatation of the capillaries of the corium or of the subcutaneous tissue, or of both, with communications between the dilated vessels forming cavernous spaces.   The subcutaneous nævus may be enclosed in a fibrous envelope, or it may be diffuse.   Combinations of subcutaneous tissue and fat overgrowth with the vascular hyperplasia occur.   Congenital vascular nævi are often associated with other congenital affections, such as adenoma sebaceum, pigmented moles, fibromata, etc.   The *nævus araneus* consists of a

Fig. 15.—Angioma simplex.

central cavernous dilatation with radiating large capillaries extending from it.

Clinical Features :—

Angioma Simplex (port wine mark).   The lesions are macules of a bright red or purple or violet colour.   They are usually of considerable size and may affect large tracts of skin.   They are often unilateral, involving perhaps one half of the face and neck, or forming extensive bands along a limb or on the trunk.   Occasionally lesions of small size occur in the neighbourhood of an extensive patch.   The macules are of varying shape, and the surface may be perfectly smooth, or there may be small erectile tumours on a generally flat area.   The colour varies from time to time, effort, crying, coughing, and exposure to cold tending to deepen the tint.

Plate 2.

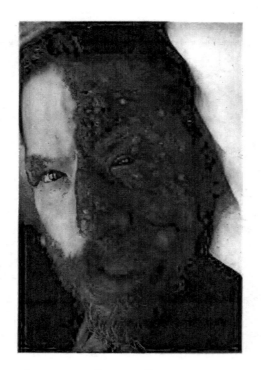

AN EXTENSIVE VASCULAR NÆVUS WITH MANY
ERECTILE TUMOURS.

The mucous membrane of the lips and tongue were
also involved.

Pressure causes a temporary disappearance or diminution of the colour. In some cases the vascular dilatation occurs in the mucous membranes as well as on the skin. The face and neck are the parts most affected, and the condition causes great disfigurement. A slight nævoid condition of the median part of the forehead and nape is common.

Cutaneous nævus. The common strawberry mark is generally smaller than the port wine stain. It varies from a pin's head to an inch or so in diameter. It is elevated above the surface of the surrounding skin and is of a bright red colour. Compression causes partial or complete disappearance of the colour and swelling. Effort, crying, coughing, and the like tend to cause erection or turgescence of the tumours. They may occur anywhere on the skin and occasionally on the mucous membranes.

Subcutaneous nævus. The skin over the swelling is of normal colour, but compression causes the nævus to diminish in size, though it rarely completely disappears. Sometimes it has the erectile character of the common cutaneous variety.

Mixed nævi are more common than the purely subcutaneous. The swelling is in part red, but the affection of the vessels of the skin is rarely so extensive as that of the subcutaneous tissue. Large mixed nævi are sometimes met with at the muco-cutaneous junctions of the mouth and external genitals.

Fibro-angioma. In rare instances a vascular nævus of large size may be associated with a hyperplasia of fibrous tissue.

Course. Vascular nævi may (1) disappear spontaneously, (2) remain stationary or simply increase with the growth of the child, or (3) grow rapidly. Authors often lay stress upon the frequency of spontaneous disappearance, but, with the exception of the pale pink areas on the forehead and nape of the neck already referred to, I do not think that spontaneous cure is common.

Injury or friction may cause ulceration of the nævus, especially if it is situated on the genitals, in the groins, or on mucous surfaces. The ulceration may involve the whole or part of the angioma and, as a rule, cures it by the formation of a scar.

Hutchinson's "Infective Angioma." Angioma Serpiginosum. A peculiar form of vascular nævus characterised by red patches, some of which have a purplish tint, round which are clusters of minute red spots—the cayenne pepper grains of Hutchinson. In a girl of twenty under my care the history was that a few scattered red spots were noticed when the patient was two years old. The nævus had gradually spread by the formation of minute red spots until it reached from the right shoulder and part of the neck and chest, down the arm and forearm as far as the dorsal surface of the forefinger and thumb. This form of angioma differs from those previously described in its slow extension.

Nævus araneus. Stellate nævus, Spider nævus.

This common variety demands special notice. The lesions consist of small bright red spots varying in size from a pin's head to a millet seed, and from this as a centre thread-like dilated capillaries radiate. Occasionally the central spot is erectile. Although it may be visible at or soon after birth, the stellate nævus sometimes does not appear until the second decade of life, or even later. It is possible that all are derived from small congenital lesions, but there is often a history of injury or the sting of an insect or the like. In any case, most of these nævi do not attract attention till the child is in its teens. They are commonly multiple and usually on the face.

Diagnosis. Only an ulcerated nævus is likely to give rise to difficulty in diagnosis. The history that there has been some abnormality noticed at birth or soon after, and that recently this has taken on an ulcerative character, will be a guide. Moreover, the ulceration is often incomplete, and some portion of the lesion will show the true nævoid character.

Prognosis. Nævi may disappear spontaneously, particularly the superficial variety which affect the forehead and nape of the neck. Others remain stationary and some increase rapidly.

Treatment. Nævi require treatment when they are increasing in size, when they cause disfigurement, and when they are ulcerated. Remembering that they may disappear spontaneously, many advise waiting in all cases where the nævus is not obviously growing, to allow time for this spontaneous involution. While waiting it is a good plan to paint the nævus daily with non-flexile collodion, which exerts a steady pressure on the vessels and occasionally appears to effect a cure.

Unless rapidly increasing, there is rarely any necessity for treating a nævus on covered parts of the body. On exposed parts, and especially on the face and neck, it is of the utmost importance to effect the removal with the least possible disfigurement.

Treatment of simple angioma and cutaneous nævi. The most satisfactory results are obtained in superficial angiomata by the local application of extreme cold. This may be carried out by liquid air or by solid carbon dioxide.

The *liquid air* is obtained in globular receptacles containing a litre. (A litre costs about fifteen shillings.) Pledgets of cotton wool held in a pair of sponge-holders are dipped into the liquid and instantly applied to the surface to be treated and pressed firmly for a few seconds. The immediate effect is a contraction of the vessels, the surface becoming white as if an escharotic had been applied. The skin soon resumes its normal colour, and increase of vascularity follows. This is usually succeeded in a few hours by vesication. The vesicles or bullæ are dressed with lint spread with boric acid ointment, and the lesion is treated as a burn. Healing takes place in from ten to fourteen days with some desquamation. It may be necessary to treat the same area more than once. I have seen admirable results in superficial cases, the only scarring noticed being where the parts have been irritated by the child. Care must therefore be taken to keep the parts covered, and, if necessary, to restrain the hands. The little operation is not very painful, although the liquid air has a temperature of $-182°$ Centigrade. The thawing which occurs a few minutes afterwards is attended with considerable pain, but this soon passes off. It is not necessary to give an anæsthetic, except when treating in the neighbourhood of the eyes, which must be most carefully protected.

Liquid air may also be used in the treatment of the common nævus ; its only drawback is the expense, for the liquid rapidly evaporates. If possible, several cases should therefore be treated at one time.

The treatment by *solid carbon dioxide* is not so simple, but is very much cheaper and equally successful, especially for small areas. The following method I have found most efficient. A wash-leather bag, about the size of a sponge bag, is held against the nozzle of a carbon dioxide cylinder, and the tap is slowly turned so that the escaping gas rushes out into the leather receptacle. The rapid exit of the gas causes a large portion to become solid, forming white snow-like flakes. With a little experience it is easy to determine when a sufficiency of the " snow " has been obtained. The tap of the cylinder is then closed and the bag removed and inverted so that the snow is turned out on to a slab. By means of a metal scoop the snow is introduced into a brass or vulcanite cylinder and rammed tight by a suitable plunger or rammer which closely fits the tube. In this way a solid stick of the snow is formed, which is easily pushed out of the cylinder and is then ready for use. It can be held in folds of lint and can be cut with a pen-knife into any required shape. It is then applied to the area to be treated for ten, fifteen. thirty, or forty seconds, according to the effect required. At the same time pressure can be exerted if necessary. On the removal of the stick from the nævus a white cavity with indurated edge and

base is seen.   In about five minutes the cavity fills up and resumes
its normal colour.   The actual application of the carbon dioxide
may be attended with very little pain, but the thawing process is
sometimes very painful.   In six hours or less there is a strong
inflammatory reaction with the formation of blisters.   These are
allowed to heal under simple boric acid dressings.   If too prolonged
an application be made, especially if considerable pressure be used,
sloughing may occur.   The results in most cases are highly satisfactory, but it is important to cover exactly the area under treatment ;
overlapping of the normal skin by the pencil of the snow produces
an undesirable scar.   An area about one inch in diameter, or square,
can be treated at one time.   The temperature is — 79° C.   The cost
of the application is only a few pence.

For irregular areas Sibley suggested that the carbon dioxide
snow may be dissolved in acetone and applied to the affected area
by a camel-hair brush.   I have found this method convenient.

Fulguration or sparking with the high frequency electrode introduced by Dr. Reginald Morton has given satisfactory results in the
treatment of some port wine marks, but as it requires an anæsthetic
and sometimes causes keloid, it is not to be preferred.

The application of *radium* also gives satisfactory results ;   it
does not require an anæsthetic and can be carried out while the
patient is sleeping.   The radium is applied on a flat surface and
allowed to remain in position for half an hour to an hour at the time.
When dealing with large surfaces it is best to have a square applicator,
as it is much easier to fit in the areas treated.   Unfortunately the
radium treatment is very tedious, and in the treatment of nævi
does not give better results than those obtained by the application
of intense cold.   Sometimes the scar is covered with telangiectases.
Wickham's suggestion of a combination of treatment by radium and
the mercury-vapour lamp appears from my recent experience to be
of service in port wine marks.

The *X-rays* should not be used ;   unless pushed to the production of inflammation they are useless, and whenever inflammation
is caused by the rays there is a liability of telangiectases in the
scar, which are even more unsightly than the nævus.

The *Finsen light* is much too tedious for ordinary cases.   After
prolonged treatment simple angiomata certainly become paler, but
many months and perhaps years may have to be devoted to the cure
of a large area.

On many port wine stains small erectile spots of the cavernous
type occur.   These require touching with the electric cautery or
electrolysis needle as described in the next section.

Small cutaneous and subcutaneous nævi can be removed by *excision*. Most of the lesions are encapsuled and removal is easy. In the diffuse variety also, provided the incisions are made well outside the nævus, the hæmorrhage is usually trifling. In deep nævi it may be necessary to compress with a clamp, or to pass hare-lip pins under the growth and by winding rubber tubing round them prevent excessive bleeding.

Puncture with the *galvanic cautery* is also a satisfactory method. The point should be fine and heated to dull redness. The punctures are made vertically at a distance of one-sixth of an inch apart. The scar is usually slight.

Electrolysis is more tedious than cauterisation, but if carefully done leaves little or no scar. There are two methods. Very small lesions may be treated by the unipolar method. The negative needle is introduced into the nævus and the circuit completed by the positive pole being placed on some indifferent part. The negative needle may be of steel, but irido-platinum is better. Lewis Jones advocated the use of a zinc needle. The current employed is from five to ten milliampères. Bubbles of gas coming from the puncture indicate when sufficient current has been passed. The needle may be introduced at several points.

In larger nævi the bipolar method is better. Both poles are connected with irido-platinum needles, and these are inserted into the nævus. The current is passed until bubbles of gas are evolved. The needles may be moved from time to time until the whole nævus is treated. After the application the tumour feels solid and doughy. A steel needle should never be used at the positive pole, as a deposition of iron takes place and causes a permanent pigmentation, in fact a tattooing.

It is best to give a general anæsthetic for electrolysis, especially if the nævus is situated near the eye, as a slight movement on the part of the patient may lead to irreparable damage.

Strict antiseptic precautions must, of course, be employed in this as in all operations. After treatment the patch is covered with fine gauze and collodion.

Repeated treatments may be required in deep nævi, but many cases are cured at one sitting. It is always better to do too little than too much at one time, because sloughing may occur, and this causes scarring. Lewis Jones's multipolar apparatus is often used in the treatment of nævi of large size.

In the rare cases of widespread cavernous angioma a combination of *excision with galvanic cauterisation* may be employed. and if the cautery is used after incision to puncture the nævoid tissue and the parts are closed by fine sutures, extensive nævi, for instance of the lips, may be removed with remarkably little scarring. Where the orbit is involved careful dissection has given good results in the hands of some surgeons.

The *stellate nævus* is best treated by puncture of the central swelling by a fine-pointed galvano-cautery, or by the electrolysis needle, using the negative pole. The scar left by the cautery is small and that by electrolysis imperceptible.

REFERENCE.—H. LEWIS JONES. *Trans. Royal Soc. Medicine* (Electro-therapeutical Section), 1909, p. 107. A valuable paper with statistics of 1,600 cases. "Angioma Serpiginosum." J. H. SEQUEIRA. *Brit. Journ. Dermatology,* 1912, p. 355, coloured plate.

CONGENITAL AFFECTIONS OF THE LYMPHATIC VESSELS.

Lymphangioma circumscriptum is a rare condition of over-growth of lymphatic vessels and spaces in the skin. It may co-exist with a common vascular nævus. The lesions are multiple, closely-set transparent vesicles with thick walls. The tumours appear in infancy or early childhood, and the chest and upper limbs are the parts most commonly affected. There are no symptoms and there is no tendency to spontaneous involution as in some of the congenital angiomata.

A rare form of diffuse lymphangioma causing elephantiasis is described at p. 416.

Treatment. If causing trouble from their position, lymph-angiomata may be removed by excision or destroyed by electrolysis.

REFERENCE.—"LYMPHANGIOMA Circumscriptum." SIR MALCOLM MORRIS. International Atlas of Rare Skin Diseases, Fasc. 1.

CONGENITAL AFFECTIONS OF THE APPENDAGES OF THE SKIN.

Congenital Affections of the Hair.

In the albino the hair is fine and devoid of pigment (*vide* p. 28).

Congenital alopecia may be universal or partial. Complete absence of the hair is very rare. I have had four cases, two in one family. The scalp and eyebrows are completely bald, and the eyelashes few in number and non-pigmented. The baldness may persist, but in some instances there is merely delayed growth, and after several years the hair begins to appear as fine down, and later it becomes normal or nearly normal. Congenital alopecia may be associated with dystrophy of the nails (Fig. 16).

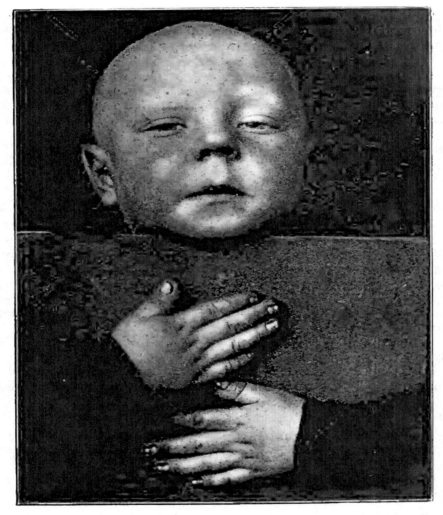

FIG. 16.—Congenital alopecia with congenital dystrophy of nails.
Boy æt. 4.

Partial congenital alopecia is less rare. Tracts of the scalp of varying size and shape are devoid of hair and may remain so. They may be classed as a variety of nævus.

In certain families the development of hair is deficient throughout life.

No treatment, either external or internal, appears to have any influence upon congenital alopecia.

Congenital hirsuties. Excessive growth of hair in infancy is very rare. I recently saw a female child born in Canada of English parents with a thick growth of downy hair on the face, particularly on the upper lip, chin, and nose. Large tufts of long silky hair were present on both auricles. According to the history the child was covered with fine hair at birth, but that on the trunk had been

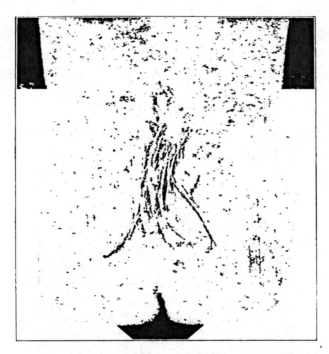

Fig. 17.—Hairy tuft (congenital). There was no evidence of spina bifida.

gradually shed, while the hair on the face and ears had increased in length. In other respects the child appeared to be well developed. No treatment has been suggested for such conditions. I did not feel justified in trying the X-rays, as there is a great risk of producing telangiectases, while the fact that the hair on the trunk and the extremities had fallen led me to hope that ultimately the downy growth on the face might also disappear.

Local excessive growth of hair is seen in the pigmented hairy mole (p. 29). and also in the form of hairy patches without pigmentation. Such patches occur sometimes just above the gluteal cleft, where they may be associated with spina bifida. The condition is illustrated in Fig. 17, where the tuft of hair forms a veritable tail.

Where treatment appears advisable from the position of the hair electrolysis gives the best results (*vide* p. 600).

Ichthyosis thysanotrichia.   This name has been given to comedo-like black spots in which numerous tuft-like hairs grow from the same follicle. Each hair is spread out like a spray at its free end. The cheeks, forehead, and upper part of the trunk are the usual sites.

REFERENCE.—S. WEIDENFELD.   *Wien. Med. Wochenschrift*, April 5, 1913.

CONGENITAL TUMOURS OF THE GLANDS.

Adenoma sebaceum.

Adenoma sebaceum is a congenital overgrowth of the sebaceous glands. In some cases the hair follicles and the sweat glands are involved in the hyperplasia.

There are three types—(1) where the lesions are pale (Balzer);

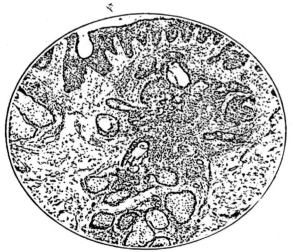

FIG. 18.—Adenoma sebaceum (Pringle type).
Microphotograph of section.

(2) where the tumours are pink (Pringle); and (3) where the surface is warty (Hallopeau and Leredde).

Etiology.   The cause of sebaceous adenoma is unknown.   The tumours are present at birth, but tend to enlarge and increase in number.   The children are usually mentally deficient, and other cutaneous anomalies, such as vascular nævi, moles, and fibromata, are often present.   Stopford Taylor has described three cases of the Pringle type in one family, and Adamson showed a mother and

FIG. 19.—Adenoma sebaceum (Pringle type).

son who were affected, and I demonstrated cases in mother and daughter.

Pathology.   The tumours are circumscribed overgrowths of the sebaceous glands (*vide* Fig. 18), with involvement sometimes of the hair follicles and sweat glands.   In the second type (Pringle) there is also vascular hypertrophy, and in the third (Hallopeau) there is hyperkeratosis.

Clinical features.   The tumours are small yellowish or red nodules, rarely warty, affecting the middle third of the face, and especially the naso-labial furrows (Fig. 19).   They increase slowly until puberty is reached, when they become stationary. Small cutaneous horns may develop on the surface. In addition to the vascular nævi and pigmented moles and fibromata which often accompany them, there is sometimes a curious form of flat fibroma above the iliac crests on each side. The mental defect is due to tuberose sclerosis.

Treatment. Sebaceous adenomata may be removed by the knife or destroyed by electrolysis.

REFERENCES.—J. J. PRINGLE. *British Journal of Dermatology*, Jan., 1890, p. 1, with literature. DICKSON and FOWLER. *Quarterly Journal of Medicine*, Oxford, 1910-11, IV., p. 43.

Spiradenoma.

Spiradenoma is a congenital adenoma of the sweat glands. It is very rare. As a rule the tumour is single and larger than the sebaceous adenoma. As already mentioned, the sweat glands may be involved in sebaceous adenoma. Hypertrophy of these glands may also occur in ichthyosis hystrix and in moles. See also p. 526 on tumours of the appendages of the skin.

Epithelioma adenoides cysticum (Brooke). Tricho-epithelioma. This is a very rare congenital affection. The face, scalp, and back are the parts affected. The tumours vary in size from a pin's head to a pea. They are white, bluish yellow or pearly, and quite painless. They are usually two to a dozen or more small tumours, discrete and scattered. Females are most often affected, and heredity has been traced in several cases. The tumours are embryonic solid coil-like masses derived from the rete mucosum and from the hair follicles.

Treatment. The growths may be removed by the knife or curette, or destroyed by electrolysis.

REFERENCES.—H. G. BROOKE. *British Journal of Dermatology*, 1892, IV., p. 269. FORDYCE. *American Journal of Cutaneous and General Urinary Diseases*, Vol. X. SIR E. C. PERRY. International Atlas of Rare Skin Diseases, Plate IX., Part III. J. E. R. MCDONAGH. *British Journal of Dermatology*, 1912.

TUMOURS OF CONGENITAL ORIGIN.

Neuro-fibromotosis. von Recklinghausen's Disease, Molluscum fibrosum.

This rare condition is characterised by the formation of multiple fibrous tumours in the skin, tumours on the nerve-trunks and pigmentation.

FIG. 20.——Multiple fibromata.

Etiology. The cause is unknown. The condition is often associated with pigmented and other nævi. Occasionally several members of a family are affected.

Pathology. The tumours consist of fibrous tissue of an embryonic type or more or less developed. In some there are gelatinous masses and mast cells. Primitive nerve fibres are also found in them.

Clinical features. The disease may be first noticed in infancy, but attention is usually called to it by the development of the tumours about puberty. The whole surface of the body is studded with soft, roundish tumours, embedded in the skin, or sessile or pedunculated. They may be the colour of the surrounding skin, or bluish or brown, and in later stages often become irregular and warty. They may be of all sizes, and in later life sometimes attain enormous proportions. Tumours weighing as much as thirty-five pounds have been met with. It is often easy to herniate the tumours under the surrounding skin when they are of small dimensions. The pigment is in the form of freckles or large yellow patches. The patients are often, but not always, of low mental development.

The tumours gradually enlarge, but are of no danger to life. They often entail serious discomfort from their position and dimensions.

Treatment. Where their presence causes trouble from friction or pressure, or where the mass of the tumour is an impediment to movement, excision may be practised. In the patient figured (Fig. 20) the small tumours on the eyelids obstructed vision, and many were removed at different times. It is said that the injection of thiosinamine causes the growths to shrink.

REFERENCES.—v. RECKLINGHAUSEN. Monograph, Berlin, 1882. TAYLOR. *Journal of Cutaneous Diseases*, February and May, 1887. MORRIS and WILFRID. Fox, *British Journal of Dermatology*, 1907, XIX., p. 109. Familial cases. J. D. ROBERTS and N. S. MACNAUGHTEN. *Review Neurolog. and Psych.*, 1912, X., p. 1.

Xanthoma congenitale.   Nævo-xantho-endothelioma.

Xanthoma congenitale is a rare condition, characterised by the appearance of numerous yellowish tumours.

The **cause** is unknown.

Pathology. The tumours consist of fatty cells which are looked upon as the result of an inflammatory process, or as embryonic cells undergoing a special change. Mr. McDonagh believes they are derived from the endothelium of the capillaries. The cellular growth may disappear spontaneously. There are no mast cells as in urticaria pigmentosa.

Clinical features. The lesions are scattered yellow nodules, varying in size from a pin's head to a pea, and occasionally larger. A red tinge is sometimes noticed in very early lesions, but this changes to the characteristic yellow. They are hard and indolent, and there are no subjective symptoms. The parts most commonly affected are the face, especially the eyelids, the hands, feet, knees, elbows, and buttocks, but the lesions may occur anywhere, even on the mucous membranes. The condition may be noticed at birth or in early life, and may entirely disappear in a few years leaving little or no scarring. It has been observed in several members of a family and is sometimes hereditary.

Diagnosis. Xanthoma occurs in the subjects of glycosuria and jaundice (p. 559), but in the congenital form there is no evidence of visceral disease. The nodular form of urticaria pigmentosa resembles congenital xanthoma, but in this affection there is itching, and wheal-like tumours form from time to time. Mast cells are present in the lesions of urticaria pigmentosa, and in cases of doubt a biopsy may be necessary to make the diagnosis.

Treatment. Xanthoma congenitale may be excised or cauterised. The tumours disappear under treatment by the X-rays.

REFERENCE.—J. E. R. McDonagh. *British Journal of Dermatology,* 1912, XXIV., p. 85: plates and references.

Xerodermia pigmentosa.

Xerodermia pigmentosa is a rare affection characterised by permanent freckling, telangiectases, atrophy of the skin, and the formation of warty tumours which frequently become malignant.

Etiology. The disease may affect several members of a family. In one family seven children suffered from it. It does not appear to be hereditary, the fact that the patients rarely survive puberty probably explaining this. The irritation of the actinic rays of light is believed to be the exciting cause. The condition closely resembles the chronic dermatitis which occurs in X-ray workers (*vide* p. 79).

Xerodermia pigmentosa may be considered as a precocious senility of the skin, all the lesions characteristic of the disease being found in the skin of the aged, in which also there is great liability for pigmented warts to become malignant.

Pathology. Kaposi, who first described xerodermia pigmentosa, believed that the first part to be affected is the papillary body and the epidermis. Atrophy of the papillary layer is always present, and the rete is thinned in the white patches of the skin. In the

Plate 3.

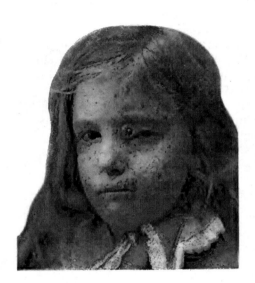

XERODERMIA PIGMENTOSA.

Girl, aged ten, affected from early infancy. Multiple
freckles, pigmented warts, telangiectases, atrophic
spots and an epithelioma at the left inner canthus.
The scar at the left angle of the mouth was the site
of another epithelioma. Many similar neoplasms
have been removed. The backs of the hands were
also affected.

pigmented spots granules of pigment are found in the epidermal cells and also in the corium. The warty nodules consist of stratified masses of epidermis which send down processes into the true skin. The malignant growths are usually described as epitheliomata, and in sections of one of my cases numerous cell-nests of the usual type were found in the many tumours removed. Melanotic carcinomata have been observed, and Kreibich described cancers of the medullary type.

Clinical features. The child usually in the first summer after birth becomes freckled on the face, neck and shoulders, and on the forearms and hands and occasionally on the legs, that is, on the parts which are more or less exposed to sunlight. The freckles are yellowish brown in colour, but, unlike the common ephelides, do not disappear with the approach of winter. As time goes on they increase in number, and then minute permanently dilated capillaries —telangiectases—are noticed. The next feature is the formation of a number of small dry warty papules and nodules. The nodules usually fall off after a time, leaving small atrophic patches, which ultimately become white. The scarring about the lids leads to ectropion and its attendant troubles. From time to time, however, the warty nodules, instead of dropping off, begin to grow rapidly, producing in a few days or weeks large tumours, which are true carcinomata. The little girl figured (Plate III.) had been under my care for seven years, and during that time about twenty growths of this type had been removed. I saw the child once a month, and was able to remove the tumours before the glands were involved. She was, however, removed from my observation for some months, and when I saw her last was obviously near death from extensive malignant disease. Occasionally, as in the case just mentioned, there is a xerodermatous condition of the scalp and covered parts. The activity of the process varies from time to time, and is always increased in the summer months.

I have seen one case in which the disease, apparently of the same type, developed in a young man constantly exposed to wind, weather, and excessive sun in the fields. Similar cases have been recorded.

Prognosis. Nearly all the patients die early. In some cases the malignant neoplasms produce metastases in the internal organs.

Treatment is purely palliative. The skin may be protected from the actinic rays of the sun by thick red veils, or by the application of pigmented powders and salves. Early removal of the cancerous tumours is important. Treatment of the warts and

4

tumours by X-rays and radium has been recommended, but they often fail.

REFERENCES.—KAPOSI. Hand Atlas, 367 to 376. H. RADCLIFFE CROCKER. *Med. Chir. Trans.*, 1884. KREIBICH. *Archiv. f. Derm. u. Syph.*, 1901, Vol. LVII., p. 123. " Epitheliomatosis of Solar Origin." W. DUBREUILII. *Annales de Derm. et de Syph.*, June, 1907, p. 387.

Sclerema neonatorum. Hidebound Skin.

This rare congenital anomaly is characterised by rigidity of the skin and subcutaneous tissue, with subnormal temperature and other evidence of low vitality.

The **cause** is unknown. It is believed to be malnutrition, and may occur after severe diarrhœa, but whether this is a cause or an associated symptom is not clear. Paterson suggests from the association of bronchitis, broncho-pneumonia, hæmorrhages into the serous cavities, and polyarthritis found *post-mortem* that the disease is septicæmic in origin.

Pathology. The prickle layer of the epidermis is shrunken and the fat of the hypoderm is atrophied, and red and brown in colour. There is an apparent or real hyperplasia of the connective tissue.

Clinical features. The skin may be hard at birth or begin to indurate soon after. The lower limbs are first affected, and the disease spreads upwards and gradually becomes universal. The surface is of a dirty yellow colour and quite smooth. On palpation the skin feels as hard as a board, and cannot be moved over the subjacent structures and does not pit on pressure. The child becomes rigid and sucking is impossible. The temperature is always subnormal ; it may fall as low as 90° and even to 80° F. The infant is drowsy and apathetic, and there may be diarrhœa. Death is the rule. Occasionally the sclerema is partial, and the patches are then well defined and feel like pieces of hide let into the skin. In these cases recovery is possible. A male infant, aged fifteen months, suffering from congenital sclerodermia and sclerodactylia was shown at the Royal Society of Medicine by Dr. Cockayne. The extremities showed the usual contraction. The skin of the face, abdomen and chest was also affected. The child suffered from hydrocephalus.

Diagnosis. Sclerema neonatorum has to be distinguished from œdema neonatorum. In the latter the skin at first pits on pressure and is blue and mottled.

Treatment. The infant should be placed in an incubator or wrapped up in cotton wool and surrounded with hot bottles, and fed through a tube if unable to suck.

Œdema neonatorum.

Œdema neonatorum is rather rarer than sclerema. The infant is debilitated, apathetic, and somnolent. The pulse and respiration are feeble, and there is a very low temperature. The disease begins on the lower extremities and spreads to the body. The skin feels doughy and pits on pressure at first, but finally gets so tense that pitting is not produced. The swelling may be so great that the palms and soles are convex. The skin is dull red or bluish and mottled. Recovery is extremely rare.

Puerperal infection has been suggested as a cause. The infants are often premature, and cardiac, renal, and pulmonary affections have been found. The disease is a true œdema, serum escaping from the sections of the tissue. The fat is not solid, red, and brown like that of sclerema.

The **diagnosis** from sclerema has been mentioned above.

Treatment is on the same lines as that of sclerema neonatorum.

REFERENCES.—" Sclerema Neonatorum." CARPENTER and NEAVE. *Lancet,* July 21, 1906. " Remarks on Sclerema and Œdema Neonatorum." BALLANTYNE. *Brit. Med. Journal,* 1890, I., p. 403. PATERSON. *Quart. Journ. Med.,* 1915, July, p. 317. E. A. COCKAYNE. "Congenital Sclerodermia and Sclerodactylia." *Brit. Journ. Dermatology,* XXVII., p. 288.

CHAPTER IV.

ERUPTIONS DUE TO LOCAL IRRITATION.

THE normal skin is specially constructed to withstand a moderate amount of irritation, but in certain conditions, some congenital and some acquired, the resisting power is defective. The most remarkable example of an inherited low resistance is seen in the condition called epidermolysis bullosa, already discussed (p. **25**). Here the least pressure or friction causes an outbreak of blisters. But short of this there are numerous slight anomalies which render the skin peculiarly vulnerable. Some of these will be mentioned incidentally in this chapter, but we are here specially concerned with the eruptions which physical and chemical irritation may excite in a normal or apparently normal skin.

Most of these affections are of an inflammatory type, and are described as various forms of " dermatitis," *e.g.*, X-ray dermatitis, sugar dermatitis, etc. It is important to remember that on an eruption primarily caused by local irritation bacterial infection often supervenes and masks the essential features of the original inflammation.

The following groups will be studied :—

Eruptions due to (1) mechanical irritation,
                (2) heat,
                (3) cold,
                (4) light,
                (5) X-rays,
                (6) radium,
                (7) chemical irritants.

The Effects of Mechanical Irritation on the Skin.

Blows, contusions, pinches, friction, and scratching may cause several kinds of lesion.

Erythema, or acute congestion, is produced by a slight injury. There is local redness, with perhaps slight swelling, heat, tenderness, and itching. The colour disappears on pressure. Lesions of this type rapidly disappear. Prolonged pressure over bony prominences is the cause of erythema paratrimma, the first stage of the bed-sore.

Wheals come next to erythema in severity. The lesion is a raised flat swelling, at first red, but later the centre becomes pale. There is a sensation of burning and itching or tingling. The skin is in a condition of hyperæmia and œdema. A smart blow, as with a whip or cane, produces a wheal. It must be remembered that excessive wheal formation upon slight irritation is characteristic of urticaria (*vide* p. 370).

Ecchymoses and petechiæ are effusions of blood into the skin ; the common bruise is the familiar type. Blows and pinches are the usual cause of these hæmorrhages. The colour does not disappear on pressure, and the stain may persist for some time, going through a series of changes in tint. Pinches of the end of the finger may lead to subungual hæmorrhage and cause the loss of the nail.

Blisters or bullæ may also form from injury, but friction is the most common cause, as in the blisters on the hands from the use of unfamiliar tools, rowing, etc. The epidermis is raised by an effusion of serum, but sometimes the bleb contains blood. Excessive blister formation from slight traumatism is a characteristic of epidermolysis bullosa.

Abrasions and excoriations are superficial breaches of the surface, due to friction and to scratching. It is necessary to bear in mind that there is often some itching affection, *e.g.*, scabies, which may be the cause of the patient scratching, and also that abrasions may be produced intentionally by hysterical patients or malingerers.

Treatment. Simple soothing applications are all that are required in all these conditions, which in normal subjects tend to spontaneous cure.

Intertrigo.

Intertrigo, or chafing, is the name given to lesions produced by the friction of two opposed surfaces of skin.

It is commonest in babies and may be due to excessive fatness. The worst cases, however, occur in neglected infants.

The regions affected are the groins, the sides of the scrotum, and the flexures of the thighs. Here the irritation of the urine and fæces and improper cleansing of the parts are important factors. Intertrigo in the folds of the neck caused by the irritation of fluid food is also seen in young infants.

Intertrigo also occurs in the obese adult, the parts affected being the groins, the gluteal cleft, and, in fat women, the submammary folds. Colliers, labourers and others engaged in dirty work and soldiers on active service who are unable to attend to personal hygiene are frequent sufferers.

The friction first produces an erythema, and the moisture due to retained perspiration or irritating urine and fæces causes the sodden epidermis to be removed, with the result that a raw oozing surface is formed.

Infection by micro-organisms may lead to ulceration and to a spread of the inflammation beyond the areas first involved.

Lesions suggesting intertrigo in the groin and between the toes

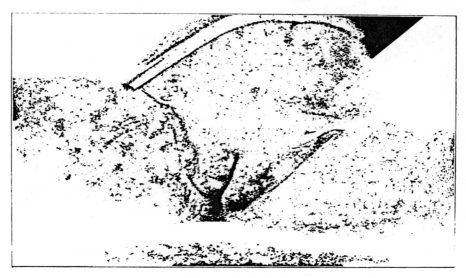

FIG. 21.—Intertrigo.

are often due to infection by a fungus (*vide* p. 141), and a so-called intertrigo in the sulcus between the ear and the scalp is caused by pus-cocci (*vide* p. 180).

Treatment. The parts must be properly cleansed, and irritant soaps must be avoided. The napkins must be changed frequently and well washed and thoroughly dried before again being used. Among the careless it is not uncommon to find that the napkin, after being wet, is simply dried and used again.

Dusting powders are applied after washing. A useful one is made of equal parts of oxide of zinc and powdered starch or talc. Emol keleet is another soothing preparation. If the parts are ulcerated a little calomel, 1 in 10, may be added to the powder, or boric acid ointment or a mild mercurial ointment (Hydrarg. Ammon. grs. 5 to Ung. Zinci ʒi) may be applied.

Napkin Erythema.

In babies, eruptions due to local irritation, but differing from intertrigo in affecting the convex surfaces, are common. They have received special attention from Jacquet, who classifies them as " dermites infantiles simples." The eruption is of a dark red colour,

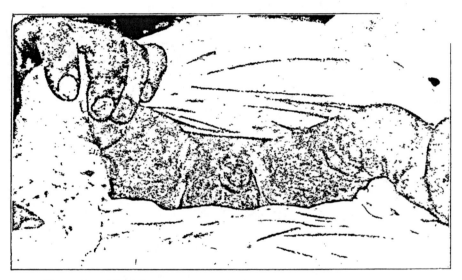

FIG. 22.—Napkin erythema (the actual flexures are unaffected)

and the surface is smooth and shining. It is confined to the convex surfaces of the buttocks, the lower part of the back, the backs of the thighs, the calves and heels, and the perineum and scrotum. The flexures are free from the eruption.

Jacquet describes several stages of the affection : (1) erythema. (2) erythema and vesication, (3) papules, and (4) ulcers. Brocq believes the eruption is caused by streptococci. The more severe lesions are doubtless due to secondary microbic infection.

These conditions are common in neglected infants seen in hospital and dispensary practice, but they are occasionally met with in well-tended babies.

It will be seen that the eruption is confined to the parts which are in contact with the napkin, and neglect in changing is the common cause. In some infants, however, the excreta appear to be extremely irritating, and the cause of this is usually gastro-intestinal trouble.

Diagnosis. These eruptions are of considerable importance from the point of view of diagnosis, because they are frequently erroneously called congenital syphilis. They have also to be distinguished from intertrigo, from seborrhoic eczema, and from impetigo.

Differential diagnosis of the eruptions in the " napkin region " :—

The *napkin dermatitis* is dark red and shining and diffuse. It affects the convex surfaces, buttocks, back, back of the thighs and calves, and the perineum and scrotum. These are parts actually in contact with the napkin.

Congenital syphilis. The eruption is of small coppery red lesions not specially confined to the napkin area. The palms and soles are often affected, and there may be lesions on the face. There are snuffles, and a peculiarly wizened expression of the face. The specific eruption comes out from three to five weeks after birth, and the napkin erythema often starts later.

Intertrigo is distinguished by the lesions beginning in the flexures of the groins, thighs, and elsewhere. The eruption may, however, spread on to the convex surfaces, but the flexures themselves are always affected.

" *Seborrhoic* " *dermatitis* may affect the napkin region. The areas involved are well defined and moist, and are usually covered with a greasy scale of a yellowish colour. The lesions may also be found in other flexures, particularly in the axillæ, and it is common to find that the child's mother has pityriasis capitis.

Impetigo may complicate the napkin erythema or intertrigo. The lesions are phlyctenules, which in a part subject to irritation are ruptured early and produce raw oozing surfaces. There is frequently evidence of impetigo of the common type elsewhere, or there may be other cases of pus-coccal infection in the family.

Treatment of napkin erythema. The treatment is on the same lines as that of intertrigo. The parts must be kept clean, and no irritant soap must be used. Protection of the affected areas is best obtained by the application of powders, or by Lassar's paste (zinc oxide 24 parts, powdered starch 24 parts, salicylic acid 2 parts, and vaseline 50 parts). If there is ulceration, the boric acid ointment, or Ung. Hydrarg. Ammoniat. 5 grs. to the ounce, may be used with advantage.

• REFERENCES.—JACQUET. " Dermites Infantiles Simples." *La Pratique Dermatologique*, Vol. I., p. 881. H. G. ADAMSON. " On Eruptions of the Napkin Region of Infants." *British Journal of Children's Diseases*, January, 1908, V., 131.

Scratched Skin.

Scratching of the skin produces excoriations or denudations of the epidermis as deep as the stratum mucosum. These are common epiphenomena of the itching diseases, such as scabies, pediculosis, eczema, strophulus, and the prurigos. They are also met with in the rare diseases mycosis fungoides and leukæmia cutis. The excoriations are usually linear, but where the primary eruption is papular, the tops of the papules are scratched off and small blood crusts form at the apices. In some rare conditions the scratching is deep, the patient endeavouring to tear out the irritating spots. The worst lesions of this kind I have seen were in a case of leukæmia cutis. Infection of the abrasions by pyogenic cocci causing impetigo, boils, etc., is common. Prolonged scratching causes **pigmentation** and **thickening** of the integument, and sometimes "**lichenisation.**" The last term is applied to a chronic papular condition, the closely set minute elevations of the skin producing a quadrillated surface which resembles shagreen leather (*vide* p. 432).

The **treatment** of the scratched skin is the treatment of the cause. The irritation should be allayed by destroying the itch parasite or the pediculi, by appropriate treatment in eczema, etc. If the cause can be removed the itching ceases, and simple soothing remedies rapidly heal the excoriations. For the more chronic conditions emollient ointments and keratolytic preparations to destroy the thickened horny layers are necessary (*vide* Formulæ). Applications of the X-rays and of the Kromayer lamp are sometimes of great service.

Callositas.

A callosity is a localised hyperkeratosis or thickening of the horny layers of the hands and feet due to friction.

Etiology. Frequently *recurring* friction and pressure cause callosities. The horny patches on the hands are produced by the use of tools, those on the feet by badly-fitting boots. Slighter degrees of hyperkeratosis are seen on the fingers of players on stringed instruments, *e.g.*, harpists, violinists.

Pathology. The lesion is a hypertrophy of the corneous layer of the epidermis—a reaction to frequently repeated irritation.

Clinical features. The callosity is a horny, raised, flat plaque of a yellow or greyish yellow colour. As a rule there is no inflammation, but occasionally suppuration occurs. The hand lesions are painless, but those on the soles may be tender and cause great discomfort in walking.

Treatment is rarely required, except when they occur on the sole. If removal be called for, the parts are soaked in hot water and pared down with a sharp knife. The salicylic plaster (Leslies) or salicylic collodion regularly applied will remove the horny layers. A full pastille dose of X-rays will often cure the condition.

Clavus or Corn.

A corn is a painful overgrowth of the horny layer of the epidermis of the toes and soles.

Etiology. Friction and pressure from tight or badly-fitting boots are the cause.

Pathology. The corneous layer is hypertrophied as in the callosity, but in addition there is a conical mass of epidermal cells whose apex is on the papillary layer. The pressure of this cone causes the pain.

Clinical features. Corns are round, flat elevations of the skin on the toes and soles. They are often multiple. Except when they exist between the toes, corns are hard and horny, but in the inter-digital spaces they are soft and whitish in colour, from the maceration of the epidermis by warmth and moisture. Whether hard or soft, they are painful and tender, and in many instances variations in the temperature, especially cold and damp, cause spontaneous pain.

Treatment. After softening in hot water, the hard corn may be pared down with a sharp knife and the conical plug removed with the point. A corn-plaster, a ring of thick plaster worn over the area to relieve the parts from pressure, will often effect a cure. Salicylic acid collodion (1 in 5) painted on for several nights, followed by fomentation in hot water, often removes the hard corn.

Soft corns may be pared down or treated with the salicylic collodion, the toes being afterwards kept apart by a pledget of cotton wool. After removal it is imperative that properly fitting boots be worn, or the corns will recur.

Dermatitis repens (Crocker).

An inflammation starting usually from an injury and spreading by the formation of vesicles which erode the epidermis. The injury may be quite insignificant, but vesicles form at its site, and rupture. The epidermis is thrown off, leaving a raw red surface which oozes. From the margin the lesion spreads slowly by the formation of fresh vesicles under the epidermis. Sometimes the vesicular lesions are of large size. As a rule, the hand is affected, but the disease has been known to spread up the limb to the trunk and down the opposite arm. Dermatitis repens is of slow development and may last for several weeks or many months. Radcliffe Crocker considered the condition as a neuritis primarily, with secondary coccal infection.

Treatment. The undermined epidermis is cut away, and a 10 per cent. lotion of potass. permanganate is applied. Lactate of lead lotion or ointments of iodoform or aristol are also used.

REFERENCES.—H. RADCLIFFE CROCKER. " Diseases of the Skin," 1903, p. 196. J. H. STOWERS. *British Journal of Dermatology*, 1898, VIII., p. 1.

Feigned Eruptions. Dermatitis artefacta.

Dermatitis artefacta is the name applied to an eruption produced by the patient to excite sympathy or to evade work. In civil practice the subjects are usually hysterical girls and women, paupers and others desiring admission to hospitals and infirmaries, and workpeople anxious to obtain compensation under the Workmen's Compensation Act. In the Services the eruption is produced by men who want to obtain their discharge. A large number of cases have been seen in men desiring to evade military service. Ormsby is of opinion that in some of the so-called hysterical cases the acts are unconscious.

The lesions are produced in a variety of ways; sometimes by friction, scratching with the nails, etc., and in other instances by the deliberate application of irritants, such as alkalies, acids, cantharides, phenol, croton oil, tobacco-juice and mustard. It is often very difficult to determine the means employed, and the patient naturally uses every artifice to escape detection.

Clinical features. All varieties of dermatitis may occur, the type depending upon the irritant employed. Friction, scratching with the nails and with sharp instruments, such as scissors, cause abrasions and even superficial ulcers. Deeper lesions are generally produced by caustics and acids. Sometimes the destruction is so great that virulent bacterial infection is suspected. The lesions are erythematous, bullous, ulcerating, and even gangrenous.

They generally present features which strike an experienced eye at once, but occasionally it is extremely difficult to make a diagnosis. The points upon which stress should be laid are :—

(1) The lesions do not conform to the known types of skin disease.

(2) They are in parts which can be reached by the patient's hands.

The left side is more commonly affected than the right, owing to most people being right-handed.

(3) The lesions are remarkably circumscribed, the surrounding skin being normal. Their outline is often rectangular, while pathogenic lesions are rounded or ovoid.

(4) In the hysterical there are often changes in the field of vision, and anæsthesia of the palate and of the stocking and glove areas, and occasionally hemianæsthesia.

The photograph (Fig. 23) illustrates an exceptional case. It shows the leg of a young girl in whom the lesions were remarkable for their arrangement in sets of three, all of the same length, and equidistant. They consisted of rather deep longitudinal abrasions covered with dried blood and small crusts formed by dry exudation. Recent lesions and the stains of older abrasions are well shown in the photograph. The patient had complete anæsthesia of the palate and right hemianæsthesia, affecting the face, limbs and trunk, with the exception of a spot the size of a shilling over the right eyebrow, where sensation was normal. It was suggested that the excoriations were produced by a three-pronged fork, but scratching by the finger nails might have caused them.

Another recent case of mine had ulcerative lesions on the right arm, probably produced by caustics. One ulcer the size of a half-crown was well defined and covered with dried blood. Some of the smaller spots resembled very closely vaccination lesions. Below these were areas of simple erythema. There was complete anæsthesia of the palate. The patient was twenty-six years of age. She was an inmate of an inebriates' home for the cure of the chlorodyne habit.

One of the most interesting cases I have met was a maternity nurse who produced blisters with liquor epispasticus on the right hand and fingers. She had stocking and glove anæsthesia and was for a long time supposed to be suffering from syringomyelia. She gave the history that she had submitted to the removal of the nails on eighteen occasions for whitlow. By covering the affected areas with an occlusive dressing and gradually increasing its size, the blisters appeared higher and higher up the limb until the neck was reached. By a ruse a small bottle labelled adrenalin and cocain was found in the patient's possession. She insisted that she used this for hay asthma, but an examination of its contents proved it to be blistering fluid. She indignantly denied an association between the lesions and the cantharides.

Plate IV. shows the breast of a young maidservant with characteristic lesions and numerous scars. She presented the phenomena

Plate 4.

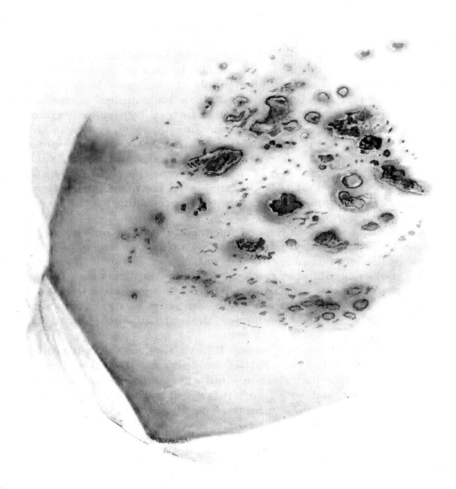

FEIGNED ERUPTION (DERMATITIS ARTEFACTA).

Right breast of a young girl with artificially produced lesions. She had symptoms of hysteria, anæsthesia, etc., and had had abdominal section performed for supposed gastric ulcer. No ulceration was found at the operation.

of hysteria.   The nature of the agent used was not discovered.   It is interesting to note that she had had a laparotomy performed for supposed gastric ulcer.

Napoli has shown that a bullous dermatitis was produced by Italian soldiers by the local application of the leaves of *Ranunculus acer* to the skin.   The root of *Daphne gnidium* and juice of cactus leaves were also used (Caraccio) to simulate skin disease.

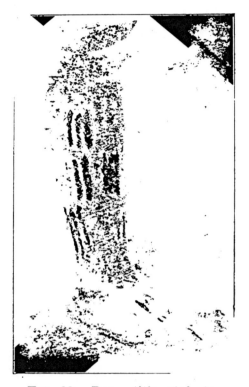

FIG. 23.—Dermatitis artefacta.

Dr. Whitfield has called attention to the value of testing the surface of the lesions by litmus paper, which may reveal the use of an acid.

These cases are not uncommon and may give rise to great difficulty It is impossible to get the patients to confess by what means the dermatitis is produced, and they have been known to submit to extensive operation rather than acknowledge that the lesions were self-inflicted.   Moreover, it is often surprisingly difficult to get the

patient's friends to believe that the physician is taking a correct view
of the case. One mother insinuated that I was in collusion with the
dermatologists at two other general hospitals because I at once
suggested the cause of her daughter's trouble. She believed that
her unfortunate child was the object of persecution on the part of the
hospital doctors.

The most satisfactory method of dealing with the condition is to
catch the delinquent in the act, but this is rarely effected. I have
several times pointed out the diagnostic value of other signs of
hysteria. particularly anæsthesiæ. Another feature is forcibly
brought out in the histories of several cases, viz., that some slight
traumatism, a small burn or wound, often appears to suggest auto-
infliction of injuries to the patient. The worst type of malingerers
seen in civil practice are those who have some dermatitis produced
by their employment and continue to keep up the irritation. The
payment of five pounds to a servant employed in a large institution
as compensation for dermatitis alleged to be caused by irritant soap
and alkalies led to an epidemic of similar cases which came under my
notice.

Treatment. The remarks made above show how difficult it
is to treat this type of patient. The part may be put up in a fixed
dressing, and over that a plaster of Paris case of some thickness
and weight may be applied. The patient has impressed upon her
that this will have to be done at the slightest suspicion of the return
of the eruption. The hands may also be confined in cotton wool.
Simple protection of the lesions leads to their rapid healing, but the
patient, finding that she is the object of suspicion by one doctor,
passes on to another. In all cases removal from the anxious care
of credulous friends and relatives is important, and the discipline
and routine of hospital often prove of great value.

REFERENCE.—ORMSBY. *Journ. American Med. Assocn.*, 1915, II., p. 1622.

AFFECTIONS DUE TO COLD.

The local changes met with as a result of exposure of the body or
part of the body to intense cold are—(1) freezing of the soft parts,
(2) changes in the vascular supply.

Frost-Bite.

Frost-bite is caused by freezing of the superficial tissues. The skin
of an area, *e.g.*, an ear, a finger or a toe, may be frozen hard and no
ill effects may follow thawing. More commonly, after thawing the

skin becomes red and swollen and covered with blebs containing
clear serum ; later, parts of the skin and deeper tissues may die and
come away as a dry gangrenous mass. The extent of the damage
depends on the duration of the cold and its intensity. During the
process of thawing the patient complains of intense pain, and when
the pain dies away tingling and itching follow. Healing is attended
by an inflammatory reaction. The result of such lesions is great
deformity if the nose or ears are affected. Histologically it is
found that the affected cells are swollen and the superficial nerves
are believed to degenerate. The immediate treatment of frost-bite
is the rubbing of the parts with snow. Ulcerating lesions are treated
on ordinary lines with antiseptic dressings. Surgical interference
may be required.

Trench-Foot.

Trench-foot is due to changes in the vascular supply. After
exposure to a less degree of cold over comparatively long periods,
especially in damp weather, or if the part has been in contact with
cold water, ice or snow, the smaller arteries are first contracted
and later the larger, deeper vessels are affected. The skin becomes
pale and the fingers and toes become " dead." A more intense
and prolonged cold leads to intense pain and the movements of
the digits are impaired. Later, this stage of vascular constriction
is followed by dilatation, and the parts become erythematous and
cyanotic, while the subjective phenomena increase.

During the winter of 1914—1915 a large number of soldiers were
invalided from the trenches on the Western Front on account of
so-called " frost-bite." These men were never exposed to the degree
of cold which is necessary to cause true frost-bite, and the condition
is now commonly designated " trench-foot." It has occurred in
less degree in the last two winters, but it is not peculiar to the
European war. It was described by Larrey in Napoleon's troops
in 1812, and was observed in the Balkan and Japanese wars.

The factors which appear to determine the condition are deep mud,
cold, want of exercise, the long-continued dependent position of the
feet, and the inability to remove boots and puttees for several days
and even weeks. Local infection has also been suggested.

The objective symptoms vary from gangrene with death of part
of the foot to simple erythema and swelling of a great toe. Most
of the cases presented a marbling (livedo) or a leaden grey tint of the
skin, œdema of the dorsum of the anterior half of the foot, and blisters
of various sizes (Plate V.). In some instances there were petechiæ

and blood blisters. The great toe, heel and ball of the little toe were most often the site of the blebs. Hæmorrhage into the nail-bed may lead to loss of the nail. Desquamation of large pieces of skin and also in small flakes were usual. Gangrene, when it occurred, was more often bilateral, but unequally so. The usual line of demarcation formed and healing by granulation followed. Other objective symptoms were hyperidrosis, tenderness of nerve trunks, and tension of tendons with restriction of movement.

The subjective phenomena were feelings of coldness, numbness, tingling, itching and burning with cramps, shooting and gnawing pains. The men who had the most marked objective phenomena— gangrene, œdema, blisters, etc.—complained very little. In others the subjective phenomena were more severe, and they frequently showed signs of mental strain. Hyperæsthesia and anæsthesia were common. The feet heal completely if gangrene does not occur, but the neuroses persist in many cases for a long time.

Treatment. Prophylactic measures have diminished the number and severity of the cases. The essential points are keeping the feet raised whenever possible, especially after long standing, cleanliness, and the maintenance of general fitness by good feeding, exercise, and sufficient rest.

In a declared case the patient is removed to hospital; cleansing of the feet and toe nails is of the greatest importance. The feet are elevated and either dusted with iodoform, boric acid or salicylic acid boric powders. Painting with a 1 per cent. solution of picric acid in spirit daily is also recommended. Others use a 2 per cent. iodine solution. The feet, after being dusted with powder or painted with the solution, are covered with sterile gauze and exposed to the air. Major Philip Turner recommends Bier's treatment in sub-acute or chronic inflammatory conditions. This is carried out by applying an elastic bandage above the knee, sufficiently tight to constrict the veins but not to impede the arterial circulation. The bandage is applied from eighteen to twenty-two hours in the twenty-four. It is removed at once if there be pain. Pain, swelling and anæsthesia usually clear up rapidly, and then the patient is encouraged to move the limb and to walk as early as possible. Where there has been extensive blistering or gangrenous spots the feet are so tender that walking is impossible for several weeks. All severe cases are removed from France to England, and gangrene is treated by surgical means.

REFERENCES.—E. G. FEARNSIDES. *British Journal of Dermatology,* XXVII., 1915, p. 33. RAYMOND and PARISET. *Lancet,* 1916, I., p. 1187. MAJOR P. TURNER. *Lancet,* 1917, VII., p. 638.

Plate 5.

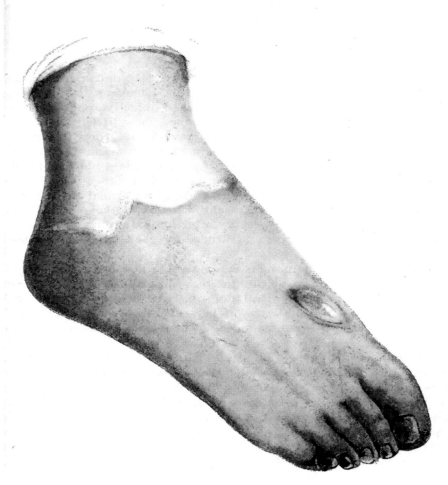

TRENCH-FOOT. (By permission of Colonel Caird.)

Chilblain.   Erythema pernio.

A chilblain is a circumscribed erythema with exudation affecting the extremities of certain predisposed people, particularly children, in damp cold weather.

The subjects of chilblain have a bad peripheral circulation, and their blood, as Wright has shown, takes twice or thrice the normal time to coagulate. The affected areas are dusky red in colour, slightly raised, itching and tender. The fingers and hands, toes and heels, are most commonly, and the ears and nose are occasionally, affected. The lesions from friction or neglect are liable to vesication and ulceration—" broken chilblains."

The only conditions which may be mistaken for chilblains are lupus erythematosus and some of the tuberculides. In the former disease similar raised red patches appear on the fingers and hands, but they are commonly chronic and do not specially occur in cold weather, though they are usually worse in the winter. There are generally lesions on the face, ears, and scalp which will aid in making the diagnosis. In the tuberculides there is the chilblain circulation (acro-asphyxia) with papular or papulo-pustular necrotic lesions on the legs and sometimes on the forearms and ears (*vide* p. 252).

Treatment. Regular exercise, good food, particularly food containing fat, cod-liver oil, iron and other tonics are indicated. The wearing of thick boots and gloves is important, and hot water must be used for washing.

Arsenic in small doses is used as a prophylactic. I have found calcium salts as recommended by Wright of value. Calcium chloride in doses of ten to fifteen grains or the lactate in fifteen-grain doses is given thrice daily for two days, and repeated in the same doses and for the same time after a few days' interval. Radcliffe Crocker recommended nitro-glycerine, but it must be used with care.

Locally, tincture of iodine may be painted on daily, or vasogen iodine, which does not stain the skin, may be rubbed in, or the linimentum camphoræ compositum may be applied. To relieve the itching menthol one drachm to an ounce of olive oil or simple ointment is a useful application. In bad cases I have seen benefit from the electric hand and foot bath, the constant current being applied for ten minutes two or three times a week. Massage of the extremities is also useful.

If the chilblain is broken the parts must be kept at rest and dressed with boric acid ointment. Fomentations of boric lint are useful if there is ulceration and sloughing.

Livedo reticularis, Livedo annularis.

These names are given to a reticular or annular purplish móttling of the skin occurring in certain subjects from exposure to cold. In tuberculosis, syphilis, rheumatism, alcoholism and hypothyroidism the condition may become persistent. The eruption begins with erythema, the result of venous stasis, the pattern depending upon the anatomical distribution of the vessels in the skin (*vide* p. 3). In some cases a syphilitic or tuberculous eruption may take on a reticular pattern owing to antecedent livedo.

REFERENCE.—H. G. ADAMSON. *British Journal of Dermatology*, 1916, p. 282.

Intense cold may be used **in treatment.** In the treatment of nævi and port wine stains, warts, and other lesions by liquid air and by solid carbon dioxide, the application of the cold is followed by an immediate shrinking of the parts with the formation of a white pellicle. In five minutes or so the parts resume their natural size and appearance, and at the end of from two to six hours vesication and the formation of bullæ occur. If the application of the cold has been prolonged, and especially if pressure has been applied at the time, as with the solid stick of carbon dioxide, there may be superficial sloughing or ulceration which may take several days to some weeks to heal. If the application be not prolonged above thirty or forty seconds the resulting cicatrix is scarcely noticeable.

Dermatitis hiemalis (Duhring).

In the Great Lake region of North America, Duhring and Corlett have called attention to a form of recurrent winter eruption, associated with high winds and cold weather, which is rarely, if ever, observed in this country. The lesions are round or horseshoe-shaped raised patches with well-defined margins and of a dusky red colour. At first the red raised patches are covered with small vesicles and closely simulate herpes. The vesicles rupture, leaving small denuded areas which weep. Later the lesions fade and are then covered with fine scales. In the late stage they somewhat resemble patches of lupus erythematosus, but have no tendency to peripheral extension. The backs of the hands and occasionally the feet are affected.

Histologically there are vascular dilatation and œdema and the formation of epidermal vesicles. Crusting may occur.

Treatment. Leather gloves are advised, and the hands should be kept dry. Diachylon ointment with three to ten grains of salicylic acid to the ounce is a suitable application.

Acrodermatitis pustulosa hiemalis (Crocker) appears to be a variety of follicular tuberculide. It affects the backs of the hands and knuckles and the sides of the fingers, and occurs in the winter and early spring in the subjects of bad peripheral circulation (*vide* p. 252).

REFERENCES.—DUHRING. *Philadelphia Medical Times*, 1874, June 10. W. F. CORLETT. *American Journal of Cutaneous Diseases*, 1891, Vol. IX., p. 41. *American Journal of the Med. Sciences*, June, 1912, Vol. CXLIII., p. 808. H. RADCLIFFE CROCKER. "On Winter and Summer Eruptions." *British Journal of Dermatology*, 1900, XII., p. 39,

RADIATION AND THE SKIN.

Heat rays, light rays, X-rays, and the emanation and rays given off by radium may all produce cutaneous changes. They are all subject to certain common laws. (1) The intensity of the irradiation is inversely as the square of the distance of the source of rays from the surface irradiated. (2) Where the rays fall obliquely upon a surface the intensity is proportional to the cosine of the angle which the rays make with the normal to the irradiated surface. To these Freund has added the following :—(3) The duration of the period of latency is in inverse proportion to the wave-lengths of the active rays, and the effect lasts longer in proportion as the wave-length is shorter, and (4) the greater the intensity of the irradiation, the earlier the reaction and the longer it lasts. For instance, the long heat waves produce an almost immediate effect on the skin, while the reaction to the ultra-violet rays which are shorter does not appear for several hours after the exposure. After exposure to the X-rays in moderate dose there is no obvious effect for fourteen to twenty-one days, while if the dose be excessive a reaction may appear in a week or ten days.

DERMATITIS DUE TO HEAT.

Heat, if sufficiently intense, produces inflammation of the skin, The various degrees of burn do not require long consideration in this work, as they are fully dealt with in the text-books of surgery. The simplest is an erythema, which may speedily pass off, with or without desquamation. The next degree is the elevation of the epidermis by serum to form bullæ or blisters. The most extensive lesions of the second degree are seen in scalds. In the third degree there is ulceration, and lastly necrosis or sloughing of the skin.

The results of burns and scalds are temporary pigmentation in the superficial cases, and permanent scars when the corium or the deeper structures are destroyed.

It will be remembered that in the treatment of rheumatism dry heat of great intensity may be employed without producing a dermatitis. The same degree of heat in a moist atmosphere causes acute inflammation.

Erythema ab igne. Pigmentation due to Heat. Ephelis ab igne.

In addition to the pigmentation left by a burn we frequently see a macular pigmented eruption due to exposure to heat. This

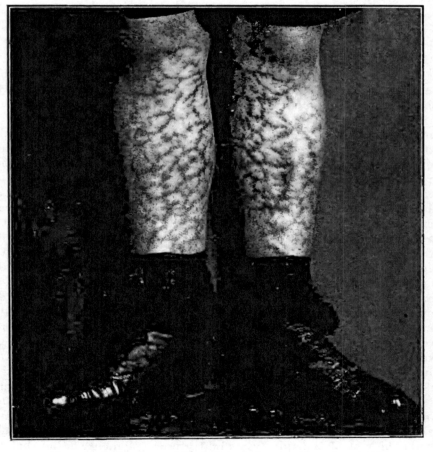

FIG. 24.—Erythema (Ephelis) ab igne. Female æt. 22.

is commonly on the front and inner aspects of the legs from the habit of toasting the limbs in front of the fire. The eruption begins as an erythema, which leaves pigmented macules. The brown macules scattered over the surface produce a characteristic mottled appearance. In Fig. 24 are shown the legs of a young woman with a marked degree of ephelis ab igne. Cooks and stokers suffer similarly. The continued application of a hot water bottle may also cause the eruption.

Microscopically, there are changes of inflammatory type in the papillary and sub-papillary layers, especially around the vessels. Pigment deposits are found in the basal cells of the mucous layer of the epidermis.

REFERENCE.—M. B. HARTZELL. *Journ. Cut. Diseases*, XXX., p. 464.

THE EFFECTS OF LIGHT ON THE SKIN.

The actinic rays of light are irritant to the skin. Two conditions occur—an acute erythema which may pass on to vesication and even ulceration, and pigmentation.

Finsen showed the effects of light on the integument in some simple but conclusive experiments. On the skin of his forearm, which being constantly covered was non-pigmented, he fastened several pieces of white and coloured glass and a small plate of rock crystal, and also painted his initials N. F. in Indian ink. He then exposed the limb to the intense light of a powerful arc lamp for an hour. At the end of the *séance* the pieces of glass and crystal were removed and the Indian ink was washed off. Three hours later the area exposed became red, and next day there was an intense erythema with swelling and tenderness, except on the parts covered with the glass and the area painted with Indian ink. An acute light dermatitis had been caused, which gradually subsided and was followed by desquamation. The area covered by the rock crystal was as acutely inflamed as the uncovered parts. The inflammation was evidently produced by rays which could pass through the crystal but which were stopped by ordinary glass and by Indian ink. The only rays which have this property are the actinic or ultra-violet rays. After the desquamation the area exposed to light was deeply pigmented, but there were white spots where the pieces of glass had been, and the initials N. F. stood out white on the bronzed skin. The same area was again exposed to the light for an hour, and the only parts which became inflamed were the white spots and the white initials, while the rest of the skin was slightly more pigmented than before. These experiments proved (1) that the actinic rays cause the so-called light "burn," and (2) that pigmentation is Nature's method of protecting the skin from the irritant effects of light.

In the treatment of disease by light, the sun's rays, the electric arc with carbon poles, mercury vapour, tungsten and some compounds of tungsten are used. The radiations have been examined spectroscopically by Russ, Schunck and others. I have shown by experiment that the penetrative power of the highly actinic rays from the tungsten arc is negligible, and Finsen's work showed the necessity of blanching the skin to allow the rays of the violet end of the spectrum to pass through the skin. By the injection locally of erythrosin and other fluorescent substances the action of the actinic rays is intensified. For instance, I have produced ulceration instead of vesication by injecting erythrosin into an area of the skin before applying Finsen light. It has been suggested from analogy with affections artificially produced in animals that certain bodies, e.g., hæmato-porphyrin in the circulation, render the skin unduly sensitive to the actinic rays. Further observations on this interesting aspect are necessary.

Finsen's red light treatment for smallpox consists in the exclusion of the actinic rays of light from the patient at the earliest possible moment. He advocated placing the patient in a room with red blinds and lighted by red lamps. By carefully excluding the actinic rays, as a photographer does from his sensitive plates, Finsen claimed to cut short the eruption of variola if seen early enough and to prevent the pustular stage and scarring. The secondary fever due to suppuration is also diminished. Observers in this country, however, have not obtained the same results which have been recorded in the Danish clinics.

Finsen's light treatment for lupus is dealt with elsewhere (p. 246). It is in exact opposition to the red light treatment, and consists in the application of concentrated actinic light to the lupus lesions to cause a dermatitis which destroys the nodules and the infecting bacilli.

REFERENCES.—FINSEN's "Phototherapy," translated by J. H. SEQUEIRA. S. RUSS. *British Medical Journal*, 1916, I., p. 124. C. A. SCHUNCK. *Lancet*, 1917, I., p. 996. J. H. SEQUEIRA. *Lancet*, 1916, I., p. 405. Also reference on "Sensitization" by DR. ADAMSON. *British Journal of Dermatology*, Vol. XXVIII., p. 275.

Solar Erythema. Sunburn.

Solar erythema is a common affection, and usually the forehead, malar eminences, and nose are its sites. In oarsmen wearing rowing costume the neck and upper part of the chest and the arms may also be acutely inflamed.

The eruption occurs usually in the early summer, before the skin has become bronzed by exposure to strong sunlight. The area affected is bright red, hot and swollen, and there are often considerable tenderness and smarting. The eruption fades in a few hours to a few days and is followed usually by desquamation, and later by pigmentation. Fair people suffer more than brunettes, and albinos most of all. Freund describes an interesting case of a man who suffered from leucodermia on the face, but who was otherwise dark. After a long exposure to strong sunlight he developed an acute erythema solare on the white patches on his face, while the normally dark pigmented parts were unaffected.

As an illustration that "sunburn" is not caused by heat rays it may be mentioned that climbers on the glaciers suffer from sunburn on the lower part of the face (chiefly on the chin and on the under surface of the nose) from light reflected from masses of ice and snow.

A similar dermatitis occurs in workers in electric furnaces, but the affection may be more severe, passing on to the stage of blistering from subcorneous effusion of serum.

The **treatment** of solar erythema consists in the application of soothing lotions and creams, such as the lotio calaminæ or the linimentum calaminæ. Susceptible persons can avoid the acute effects by protecting the face by veils (red or brown) or by applying pigments in the form of powders or salves.

Pigmentation from the Actinic Rays of Light. Lentigo, Ephelis, Freckle.

Lentigines are yellowish brown ro black pigment spots occurring on the face and elsewhere as the result of exposure to the actinic rays of light.

Pathology. Freckles are circumscribed patches of pigment in the basal layers of the epidermis.

Clinical features. Freckles are rounded or irregular yellowish brown to blackish spots, varying in size from a pin's head to a lentil seed, rarely larger, occurring on the face, neck, and the backs of the hands and wrists. They may occasionally occur on the trunk and are usually multiple. They are commonest in children and adolescents, blondes and especially red-haired subjects suffering most. Ephelides appear during the summer and fade sometimes completely in the winter.

Prognosis. They may disappear under treatment, but tend to recur.

Treatment. Freckles may be removed by causing exfoliation of the epidermis. Perchloride of mercury, three or four grains to the ounce, in glycerine or spirit applied two or three times a day will remove them if continued until the parts become red, when a little zinc ointment or cream should be applied. It is wise to begin

FIG. 25.—Permanent freckles. The hands were also affected.

with a weak solution. Red or brown veils may be worn as a protective by those specially liable to freckles. I have seen cases in which they have been very useful.

Occasionally **freckles** are **permanent.** In the patient depicted here (Fig. 25) they were in enormous numbers on the face, neck, and on the back of the hands, and caused great disfigurement. They were darker in the summer than in the winter, but fresh spots occurred during the sunny months every year, and I was assured that none had ever disappeared. The patient, otherwise in perfect health, had been affected for several years. There was no atrophy of the skin, and no telangiectases or warts appeared, so that xerodermia pigmentosa was excluded. I have seen similar less severe cases.

Pigmentary and Atrophic Conditions due to Light. Solar Epitheliomatosis.

Xerodermia pigmentosa, characterised by permanent freckling from exposure to light, with atrophy of the skin, telangiectases, pigmented warts, and malignant tumours, has been considered elsewhere (p. 48).

I have under my care a man, now 35 years of age, who works in the fields, and who every summer since puberty has suffered from freckling with atrophy of the skin, warty growths and epitheliomata. He has been in my ward several summers in succession for the removal of tumours which were characteristic epitheliomata. The condition is identical with xerodermia pigmentosa, but began later in life.

Tropical skin. Persons who have lived long in the tropics present a condition of the skin of the backs of the hands, and occasionally of other exposed parts, characterised by atrophy and pigmentation with a degree of hyperkeratosis, and the development of warty excrescences resembling those of xerodermia pigmentosa.

The **seaman's skin** described by Unna is possibly in part due to the influence of the actinic rays. It is characterised by the formation of warty growths which become epitheliomatous.

The **senile skin** is atrophic and often pigmented, and keratomata are common. In some cases the warty growths become malignant. It is possible that this condition also may ultimately depend upon irritation by light.

It is instructive to compare those conditions with chronic X-ray dermatitis.

The treatment is discussed under Cutaneous Cancer (p. 550).

REFERENCE.—" Epitheliomatosis of Solar Origin." W. DUBREUILH. *Annales de Derm. et de Syph.*, June, 1907, p. 387.

Chloasma bronzinum, Tropical mask (Cantlie), occurs in Europeans and also in natives in many tropical countries. Part of the face or neck and chest is peculiarly pigmented. The pigmented areas slowly increase, and on the ace produce an appearance like a bronze mask. It is incurable while the patient remains in the tropics. Sunlight appears to be the cause. The mucous membranes are unaffected.

REFERENCE.—CANTLIE. *Journal of Tropical Medicine*, 1908.

Summer Eruptions.

There is a group of rather uncommon conditions which demand attention in this place as being in all probability due to the irritant effects of light. To this group the term " summer eruptions " is best applied, for there are several degrees which have been described by different observers under several names.

The least severe form is Hutchinson's Summer Prurigo, while the more acute forms have been called " Recurrent summer eruption " by Hutchinson, Hydroa æstivale, Hydroa vacciniforme (Bazin), and Hydroa puerorum (Unna).

Hutchinson's summer prurigo is a papulo-vesicular eruption occurring in infancy and childhood and persisting to adult life. It is rare for it to commence after puberty.

The eruption appears in summer, and the patient may be free, or nearly so, during the winter. But there are some almost identical cases which depend on exposure to cold and wind.

Both sexes are affected, the earliest lesions appearing in infancy, and recurrences occur summer by summer up to adult life.

The face, neck, and upper extremities are affected, but occasionally the whole surface may be involved with the exception of the flexures and the palms and soles.

The lesions consist of rounded papules of a pale red colour, sometimes as much as an eighth of an inch across. Each papule may be capped by a tiny vesicle. In rare cases pustulation occurs. The lesions itch at night and the tops may be scratched off by the patient, causing small blood crusts to form. In some cases urticarial wheals occur. The lesions are always discrete.

Summer prurigo has to be diagnosed from other itching papular eruptions and from the more severe conditions to be immediately described. The history of the first appearance in early childhood and the periodical recurrences in the summer are usually sufficient to make a diagnosis from other pruriginous eruptions.

Treatment. Hutchinson recommended arsenic in gradually increasing doses, many of his patients having had as much as six or seven minims of Fowler's solution thrice daily. Ichthyol internally has also been advocated. Any deviation from the general health, dyspepsia, etc., should be attended to, and the lesions should be

Plate 6.

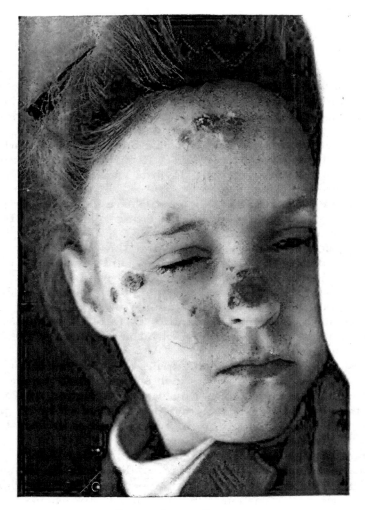

BULLOUS SUMMER ERUPTION.

Girl, aged six. The vesicles and bullæ recur year by year in the summer months. The lesions leave scars, many of which are seen in the illustration.

dressed with a soothing lotion such as Lotio plumbi et picis. Some recommend an ointment of lead and mercury (Ung. metallorum).

REFERENCES.—HUTCHINSON. "Rare Diseases of the Skin," p. 126. H. RADCLIFFE CROCKER. "Winter and Summer Eruptions." *British Journal of Dermatology*, 1900, XII., p. 39. H. G. ADAMSON. *British Journal of Dermatology*, 1906, XVIII., p. 125.

Hydroa æstivale. Recurrent summer eruption (Hutchinson), Hydroa vacciniforme (Bazin), Hydroa puerorum (Unna).

A recurrent summer eruption of children characterised by vesication which leaves scars.

Etiology. Sex has no influence, although most of the early cases described occurred in boys, hence the name Hydroa puerorum. The disease, as a rule, begins in childhood, and in most cases is worse in the summer, though a similar condition appears to occur from exposure to cold.

Clinical features. During the first two or three years of life, rarely later, an eruption appears on exposed parts in the summer. It is often preceded by a sensation of heat and pain and some general malaise. Itching is uncommon. The elementary lesions are red spots, on which develop one or more vesicles the size of a millet seed. The vesicles usually coalesce to form small flat blebs, which dry up in three or four days into scabs or crusts. In other cases umbilicated vacciniform lesions develop, which gradually dry up with the formation of scabs. To this type Bazin gave the name of Hydroa vacciniforme. In all cases the separation of the scab leaves a depressed red spot, which ultimately forms a white depressed scar (Plate VI). An attack lasts for two or three weeks, the vesicles coming out in crops.

The cheeks, nose, ears, neck, and the backs of the hands are the parts most commonly affected, but in some rare cases the eruption may be more widely spread. The attacks recur yearly, in the summer or early autumn, but as puberty is approached they become less acute. and cease when adult life is reached.

Eosinophilia has been observed in some of the examinations of th blood, and this feature is held by certain authors to show that hydro æstivale is a form of dermatitis herpetiformis (p. 486).

Diagnosis. Hydroa æstivale has to be distinguished from oth scar-leaving eruptions, particularly the tuberculides, lupus erythematosus, and syphilis. The symmetry of the eruption, its distribution on parts exposed to light, and above all the history of its recurrence every summer from early infancy, should render the diagnosis free from difficulty.

Prognosis. The outlook is bad until puberty is reached. With care in preventing exposure some mitigation of the effects may be promised.

Treatment. The patient should be protected as far as possible from the effects of sunlight. Arsenic internally has been given with benefit, but it has to be pushed. Quinine and belladonna have also been advocated. When vesicles appear they should be carefully evacuated with a sterilised needle and mild antiseptic ointments applied. Ichthyol and resorcin pastes and ointments have a beneficial effect.

REFERENCES.—HUTCHINSON. *Clinical Society Transactions*, 1889, XXII., p. 80. " Cases of Hydroa Æstivale of Mild Type : Their Relationship to Summer Prurigo of Hutchinson and Hydroa Vacciniforme of Bazin." H. G. ADAMSON. *British Journal of Dermatology*, April, 1906, p. 125.

The Effects of the Röntgen or X-rays on the Skin.

The discovery by Röntgen of Würzburg of the special properties of the rays given off by a Crookes tube led to their being widely used for diagnostic purposes. It was early noticed that the radiations caused a falling of the hair, and Freund and Schiff were led to apply them for the treatment of an extensive hairy mole. The changes which they found were produced in the skin led to a still further advance, and the rays began to be used for therapeutic purposes, and they now play an important part in the treatment of cutaneous disease. At first the application of the rays was purely empirical, frequent sittings of short duration being given until some obvious change was noticed in the integument. Thanks, however, to the researches of Holtzknecht and Kienbock in Vienna, and Sabouraud and Noiré in Paris, and numerous other workers, we are now able to estimate with some degree of accuracy the quantity of rays given off by the X-ray tube and can therefore gauge the effects which we wish to produce. The rays coming from the anode of the vacuum tube are of varying quality, and it is probable that a whole spectrum of radiations of different therapeutic value is produced. Some of these we are able to eliminate by passing the cone of rays through appropriate filters, and this procedure is of great value in the treatment of the deeper lesions.

The X-rays produce profound modifications in the structure of the skin, but the effects are most marked upon the cells of diseased tissue ; for instance the cells of a rodent ulcer and some granulomata undergo profound alteration before the normal cells of the epidermis are affected. But if pushed beyond a certain point the rays will

cause the destruction of the normal elements of the skin and even
of the subcutaneous tissue.   The quality and especially the penetrating power of the rays vary considerably with the character of the
vacuum in the tube.   This is estimated by the alternative spark
gap and also by a special instrument of Benoist, in which the rays
are passed through various thicknesses of aluminium, and the degree
of penetration is determined according to a fixed scale.

A short exposure to the X-rays produces no obvious effect upon
the skin, but with larger doses a series of phenomena is produced,
which is roughly illustrated by the annexed diagram.

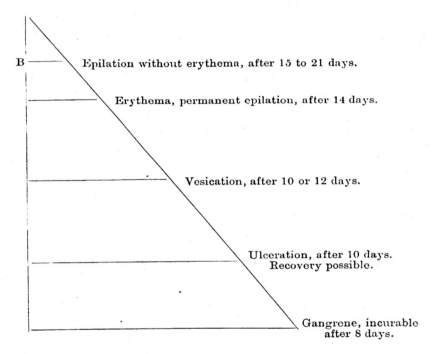

Five stages may be recognised, and in all there is a period of
latency which varies, according to Freund's second law, inversely
as the intensity of the dose, while the duration of the reaction varies
directly as the dose.

The dose is estimated most conveniently by the pastille of
Sabouraud and Noiré, and in my department at the London Hospital
no exposure is made unless the dose is thus measured.   The average
exposures to the rays in this department are 20,000 a year, and they
are given without risk of dermatitis.   The Sabouraud pastille is a

small disc covered with an emulsion of platino-cyanide of barium
in collodion and acetate of starch.   When a dose of X-rays sufficient
to turn the pastille from a pale green to an orange colour (tint B)
has been administered, the hair follicles are affected, and at the end
of a fortnight to three weeks the hair falls out.   At the end of six
weeks to two months the bald area begins to be covered with a fine
down, which a few weeks later takes on its normal character.   The
pastille is placed midway between the anode of the tube and the
area irradiated.   The distance between the anode and the area
treated should be exactly fifteen centimetres.

If the dose has been measured in this way, there is no erythema.[1]
If, however, it has been exceeded, the skin becomes red at the end
of a fortnight, perhaps a little earlier, epilation occurs, and there is a
possibility that the hair may not grow again.

When progressively larger doses are administered the area affected
may vesicate, or ulcerate superficially, the reaction appearing as
early as the tenth or twelfth day.   The **Röntgen ulcer** is indolent
and covered with a yellowish adherent slough, very like a diphtheritic
membrane.   It may take many weeks to heal.   When very large
doses have been given deep necrosis occurs, and the ulcer produced
may never heal.

It is obvious from the observations already made that frequent
repeated doses produce a cumulative effect, and repeated exposure
without measurement caused some of the troublesome early results.
When large doses are administered an interval of at least three
weeks should elapse between one applicaion and the next.

An important late result of X-ray dermatitis is the formation of
telangiectases in the scar.   These may not appear for several weeks
to some months after the exposure to the rays, and long after all signs
of dermatitis have disappeared.   They may occur after an erythema,
but are most common after superficial ulceration.   In addition to
the telangiectases, the X-ray scar is pigmented and atrophic.
Plate VII. illustrates the pigmentation, atrophy and telangiectases
left after X-ray dermatitis induced by many exposures for the
reduction of tuberculous glands.   Similar telangiectases occur after
prolonged application of radium without proper filtration, and I
have occasionally seen them after treatment with the mercury vapour
lamp of Kromayer.

X-ray dermatitis may recur after a long interval.   Darier recently
described a case in which twenty exposures were made twelve years
before for a supposed mammary cancer.   The superficial dermatitis

---

[1] A transitory erythema may occur if tungsten anodes are used.

Plate 7.

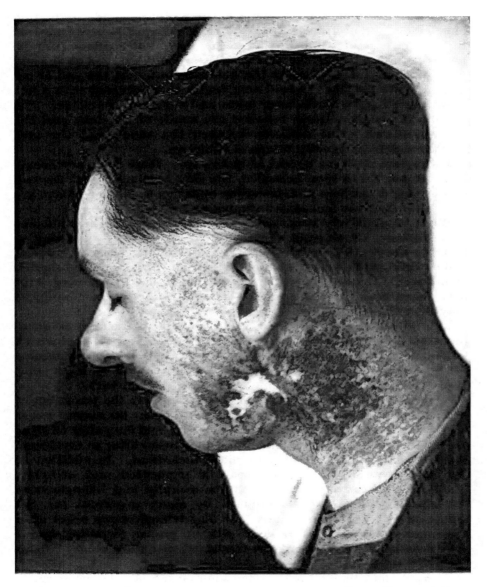

SCARRING AND PIGMENTATION CAUSED BY PROLONGED X-RAY TREATMENT.

The skin is atrophic and pigmented, and there are numerous telangiectases. The last extend far beyond the pigmented area. The rays were applied for tuberculous glands. There was a small patch of lupus erythematosus on the nose.

which followed healed. Eleven years and a half later the patient had an extremely obstinate ulcerative dermatitis. Sections showed excessive cornification, degeneration of the epidermis and papillae, and fibrosis of the capillary layer, with marked dilatations of the vessels in the corium. A somewhat similar case was shown by Beddoes. I have seen **epithelioma** develop as the result of an acute X-ray burn as well as after chronic Röntgen dermatitis.

When it is necessary to apply the X-rays for a long time, as in the treatment of deep-seated tumours, enlarged glands, or hypertrophy of the spleen, the epidermis is protected from the burning rays by thin sheets of aluminium, from 0·2 to 2 millimetres thick. Silver is also used.

Treatment of acute X-ray burns. In the erythematous stage nothing more is required than a soothing application such as Ung. Zinc. Oxid., hazeline ointment, or liniment of calamine. Where there is ulceration it is usually best to foment to get rid of the adherent slough, and, provided the ulcer be not too deep, cicatrisation usually occurs, though perhaps only after several months' treatment. Such an ulcer is prone to break down, even after complete healing, and there are often subjective symptoms in it for months and even years after, the patient complaining of itching, tingling, and other forms of irritation. Sometimes there is intense pain at first, with neuralgic twinges, which may radiate from the ulcer. Where there is deep sloughing and the locality of the ulcer permits, excision with grafting may be practised with advantage.

Frequent repetition of small doses of the X-rays produces a condition which may pass on to epithelioma ; such a disastrous result has followed the prolonged treatment of some forms of lupus by the rays. In one case brought to my notice the patient had had 1,000 sittings under the rays for lupus vulgaris. Here an epithelioma developed upon the cicatrix produced by the treatment. In another case the patient had had 300 applications of the rays, and here again cancer developed. Norman Walker and others have reported similar cases. I have seen a patient who had been under X-rays for rodent ulcer several times a week for *twelve* years ; an incurable Röntgen ulcer formed, and epithelioma developed.

X-ray dermatitis of the operator.—The early workers with the X-rays were ignorant of the dangers which attend their use. It was a common practice to hold the hand in front of the vacuum tube to determine by a fluorescent screen the penetrative power of the rays emitted. In screen examinations too the backs of the fingers of the operator were usually exposed to the rays. The result of these repeated exposures for short periods was an intractable

X-ray dermatitis.   Its clinical features are exceedingly tender and painful chronic ulceration, followed by atrophic scarring and telangiectases.   The ulcers are usually irregular tracts along the backs of the fingers, the base being covered with a yellowish-white adherent slough.   The margins of the ulcer are slightly tumid and bright red, and there may be swelling and redness of the whole finger, or even the back of the hand.   The nails always suffer ;   in the slighter degrees an excessive brittleness is first noticed ;   later painful onychia occurs, with destruction and separation of the nail.   In some cases the phalanges have undergone partial absorption, and the atrophy

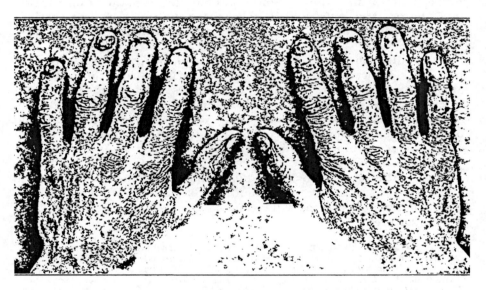

Fig. 26.—X-ray dermatitis of the operator.   The hands of a pioneer worker.

of the skin and subcutaneous tissue leads to grave deformity.   Unfortunately, this chronic and painful affection is not the only or the most serious part of the trouble, for warty nodules appear on the affected skin, and in several instances they have passed on to epithelioma, necessitating amputation of fingers or parts of the limbs.   In a few instances the face has been affected, but this has usually been in the makers of X-ray tubes, who have to test their condition in the process of manufacture.

With the use of protective shields and the recognition of the dangers, the risks have been eliminated, and no X-ray worker should now be liable to this terrible affection.

I have called attention to the appearance of *pigmented spots* appearing on the hands, forearms, and elsewhere in X-ray workers. A spot of black pigment the size of a threepenny piece developed with remarkable rapidity on the palm of one of my assistants. For fear of malignancy it was immediately excised.

The lesions of chronic X-ray dermatitis are always worse in the cold weather, and even when quite soundly healed they tend to break down into ulcers in the winter.

Treatment. The sufferer should, of course, be removed from work in which he is exposed to the rays, and the affected limb should be kept at rest in a sling. Some patients find constant fomentation give the greatest relief, but in other cases the touch of warm lotions causes intense agony. All forms of soothing application have been tried.

If possible, surgical interference should be avoided as long as possible. I have seen several cases in which the removal of an affected nail appeared to start an acute destructive process. Even the removal of a slough appears to be harmful. With rest and time many of the worst cases tend to heal with atrophy, and that is the best that can be hoped for. The keratomata are best treated by radium, but should epithelioma develop, recourse should be had to the knife without delay.

Some authors rely upon the high frequency effluve and electric baths in the treatment of chronic X-ray dermatitis, but in a not inconsiderable experience I have failed to see any real benefit from these measures.

REFERENCES.—FREUND. " Radiotherapy," translated by G. H. LANCASHIRE (REBMAN). J. M. H. MACLEOD. Collected Literature. *British Journal of Dermatology*, 1903, XV., p. 365. BÉLOT. " Radiotherapie," translated by DEANE BUTCHER. J. HALL EDWARDS. *Trans. Roy. Soc. Medicine* (Electrotherapeutic Section), 1908, p. 11. PORTER and WHITE. " X-Ray Carcinoma." (Collected cases.) *Annals of Surgery*, November, 1907.

The Effects produced by Radium on the Skin.

Radium is a therapeutic agent of great value, and it is important that the practitioner should be familiar with its effects.

Radium is obtained as bromide, sulphate, or carbonate from pitch blende and certain similar uranium compounds. It gives off three varieties of rays which are classed as α, β, and γ.

The alpha rays are canal rays which have a low penetrative power estimated as unity. The beta rays are identical with the rays given off at the kathode of the X-ray tube. They have a penetrative power as compared with the alpha rays of 100. The gamma rays are similar to the X-rays and have a penetrative power which is estimated in the same terms as 10,000.

The alpha rays will not penetrate a thin sheet of aluminium. The beta rays will pass through aluminium, but most of them are cut off by interposing a thin sheet of lead. The gamma rays will pass through lead and will influence a gold leaf electroscope even through an inch of the metal. We are thus able by interposing layers of aluminium or of lead to filter off either the alpha or the alpha and beta rays.

The alpha rays cause a superficial dermatitis, and their use is confined to the treatment of certain superficial skin affections. The interposition of a thin layer of aluminium prevents this superficial reaction and allows us to use the more penetrating beta and gamma rays without producing a severe skin reaction. When we desire to influence deep structures only we employ screens of lead, but when using them longer exposures are required. For instance, it is not an uncommon thing to expose a tumour through a lead filter to the radium for twelve, twenty-four, or thirty-six hours or longer. The filter itself, however, becomes radioactive and gives off secondary rays which are of very low penetrative power, and we can eliminate the reaction caused by them by interposing layers of paper between the lead filter and the skin.

Prolonged exposures to radium cause a series of destructive effects very similar to those caused by the X-rays ; we may get superficial or deep ulceration, and the ulcers take a very long time to heal.

The strength of radium used therapeutically is compared with the radioactivity of uranium, which is taken as unity. Pure radium is estimated as having a radioactivity of 2,000,000. As a general rule, the radium salt is mixed with three times its weight of barium salt, and we thus get a preparation with radioactivity of 500,000. This is spread evenly upon a plate, circular or square in shape, and it is kept in position by a special varnish. The varnish can be cleansed with the usual antiseptics, but must not be sterilised by heat or long solution in spirit. An applicator one square centimetre in area with ten milligrammes of radium of 500,000 activity is a useful apparatus for the treatment of small lesions. Weaker preparations are also used, e.g., in the treatment of nævi. For deep-seated growths the radium is placed in a fine glass tube encased in lead o silver tubes of varying thickness.

Workers with radium suffer from a dystrophy of the nails closely resembling that produced by the X-rays. I have also seen small warty intractable excrescences on the fingers. The use of comparatively large quantities of radium induces a curious lethargy.

REFERENCES.—" Radiumthérapie." WICKHAM and DEGRAIS (English translation by S. E. DORE). " Histological Changes produced by Radium." H. DOMINICI and RUBENS-DUVAL. Société Médicale des Hôpitaux de Paris, July 23, 1909, and *Le Journal Méd. Français*, August 15, 1909, p. 454.

Meso-thorium, which has been extensively used in some clinics for the treatment of cutaneous conditions, may produce a superficial necrosis.

REFERENCES.—FRIEDLANDER. *Archiv. f. Dermatologie ü. Syph.*, 1912, CXIII., p. 359. BUMM. *Zentralblat. f. Gynaekol.*, August 16, 1913, p. 1235.

Professional and Trade Dermatitis.

Numerous substances used in various employments cause irritation and inflammation of the skin. As a rule, the parts affected are the hands, particularly their dorsal surface, and from them the eruption often extends to the forearms. The commonest type of dermatitis is erythema, which frequently passes on to vesication. The vesicles may or may not rupture, but their rupture is followed by oozing, and we then get an eczematous condition, which may spread far beyond the area irritated. The inflammation in most subjects tends to subside on the removal of the source of irritation, the weeping areas dry up, some scaling appears, and ultimately the tissues are restored to their normal condition. In other conditions the epidermis becomes thickened and horny as a result of the chronic irritation and the thickened horny layer cracks, producing fissures which are exceedingly painful. In many cases the raw surfaces produced by the irritant dermatitis become infected with pyogenic organisms and the area becomes impetiginised (*vide* p. 103). The nails often suffer in trade dermatitis. They are often very brittle, or separate from the matrix, and sometimes show fissures and pits. The face and neck are sometimes affected secondarily, and occasionally primarily, from contact with substances carried on the shoulders. Where the patient works with gases or fine powders, or with irritant fluids, the covered parts may be attacked, and the eruption is then most marked in the flexures, particularly the groins and axillæ and the genital region.

The chapter on Eczema should be read in connection with this section, and it will only be necessary to describe in detail here the conditions which differ from the eczematous type.

The *treatment* of irritant dermatitis is discussed on pp. 107—112.

Acids, especially when undiluted, cause circumscribed burns of the skin. Nitric acid stains the skin yellow, sulphuric acid a dirty brown or red colour, and carbolic acid a greyish-white. Hydrofluoric acid causes severe ulceration. Weak solutions of the corrosive acids produce an eczematous eruption.

Alkalies. Strong solutions of caustic potash and caustic soda stain the skin a reddish or brown colour, and the burns which result from them are often severe. The nails become dull and cracked and jagged and separate from the nail-bed.

Antiseptics. Surgeons and nurses are frequently sufferers from eczematous dermatitis caused by carbolic acid, lysol, and other antiseptics. The frequent washing and scrubbing of the hands tend to increase the irritant effect of the chemicals. In rare cases the eruption resembles pompholyx, the vesicles forming along the side of the fingers .The irritant action of the antiseptics may be alleviated by the use of astringent hand lotions such as equal parts of red lotion and glycerine applied after washing at the end of an operation. In some cases the patient has to wear gloves always when operating, etc.

Arsenic causes an eczematous eruption and ulceration. Tanners and the makers of arsenical pigments are the most frequent sufferers. In some form sof arsenical pigment and weed-killer the substance is in the form of a fine powder which attacks not only the exposed parts but also those which are covered. In many cases in addition to the cutaneous affection there is perforation of the cartilaginous septum of the nose. Keratosis on the fingers leading to cancer is met with in the workers in arsenic mines.

Asphalte workers suffer from eruptions similar to those produced by tar (*vide infra*).

Barbers suffer from eczematous dermatitis from the constant wetting of the hands and also from the use of shampoo lotions containing spirit, ammonia and other chemicals, and from dyes.

Barmaids and **servants** employed in **restaurants,** whose hands are constantly wet from washing glass, china, etc., are often sufferers from dermatitis. The trouble is more common i n winter and depends largely upon insufficient drying of the hands.

Bleachers and **cleaners** using *chloride of lime* and " vitriol " suffer from a dermatitis of the hands more marked upon the palmar surfaces. Relapses are common.

Butchers and others who handle the dead carcases of animals are sometimes infected with tubercle (*vide* p. 227). An acute form of malignant pemphigus occurs rarely (p. 485).

Carbide of calcium acts as an irritant and may cause dermatitis.

Chemists are also liable to irritant dermatitis. In some cases there is remarkable susceptibility to certain substances. Knowles reported eruptions produced by *phenylhydrazin hydrochloride*.

Chimney-sweeps suffer in the first instance from an eczematous dermatitis which is followed by thickening of the skin and the production of warty tumours which may become malignant. The scrotum is the part most commonly affected.

Chlorine workers suffer from a follicular eruption which resembles acne.

Coopers are affected by the caustic soda used to clean barrels. The eruption is of the common irritant type.

Copra itch, which is caused by an animal parasite, is discussed at p. 132.

Dyes and substances used in their manufacture are common causes of dermatitis. The *aniline* dyes usually betray the cause of the eruption by the staining of the nails. *Aurantia*, hexanitro-diphenyl-amine, a dye used in the staining of the cheaper kinds of brown boots and shoes, causes a vesicular eruption (*vide* p. 86).

Di-nitro-chlor-benzole produces an erythemato-papular itching dermatitis with a distinct yellow tinge on any parts touched by the crystals. It is used in the manufacture of certain dyes.

Explosives. The manufacture of high explosives on the enormous scale demanded by modern warfare has introduced a number of cutaneous affections, which in some instances are associated with grave constitutional symptoms. Benzine and its homologues have a toxic action on the human subject, and the nitro bodies used as high explosives are the more toxic in proportion to the number of nitro groups they contain. Toluene comes first, then Mono-nitro-toluene, and lastly Tri-nitrotoluene. The poisons used as explosives or in their manufacture that are a real danger are :—

(1) Tri-nitrotoluene.
(2) Tetryl.
(3) Picric Acid.
(4) Fulminate of Mercury.
(5) Barium Salts.
(6) Di-nitro-phenol.
(7) Hexa-nitro-diphenylamine.
(8) Mixed Acids.

(1) *Tri-nitro-toluene* (T.N.T.), Amatol and Ammonal, combinations which owe their toxic effects to T.N.T. The skin and hair are stained yellow. The eruptions produced are erythema and vesication, and rarely small ulcers, "powder-holes." In some cases the vesicles on the hands and fingers resemble cheiro-pompholyx. The

sensory symptoms are itching and burning. Secondary infection leads to septic conditions of the affected skin, sometimes with thrombosis and phlebitis. Exfoliation of the affected areas is common. Moist, greasy conditions of the skin favour the development of the dermatitis; hence more cases occur in the warmer seasons of the year. The eruption may persist for several weeks after the patient has been withdrawn from the work, and septic cases may last months. Purpura is a rare phenomenon, but of great clinical import, as it signifies that there are grave blood changes—aplastic anæmia, which may be rapidly fatal. Gastro-intestinal symptoms and jaundice occur, and certain individuals show a special susceptibility in this respect.

(2) *Tetryl* (Tetra-nitro-methylaniline, or, more correctly, Trinitro-phenyl-methyl-nitramine). The skin and hair are stained yellow. The eruption is usually a diffuse erythema, often associated with gross œdema. Papulation and pustulation also occur. The eruption is commonly worst on the face and neck, the conjunctivæ being often involved. The hands and arms are not frequently affected. A transient asthmatic seizure and epistaxis may occur. Nausea and vomiting accompanied by epigastric pain are reported. Idiosyncrasy is common. I have seen an acute attack in a susceptible subject from travelling in a railway carriage with a worker.

(3) *Picric acid* (melinite or lyddite) is tri-nitro-phenol. The skin and hair are stained yellow. Occasionally a simple erythema develops on the hands and forearms.

(4) *Fulminate of mercury*, used to fill detonators, does not cause mercurialisation. Dermatitis of the hands, forearms and face, especially about the eyes, may occur. This is probably due to the mechanical irritation of fine particles.

(5) *Barium salts* are used in the manufacture of flares (Véry lights). The hair of operators may be bleached, and loss of the hair and the eyebrows has been noticed.

(6) *Di-nitro-phenol* has been used in France. It is believed to be more poisonous than T.N.T. So far no dermatitis has been reported, but covered areas of the skin may excrete the substance and show a patchy yellow discoloration.

(7) *Hexa-nitro-diphenylamine* (aurantia) was combined with T.N.T. in bombs dropped in London and elsewhere during certain raids by aeroplanes. I saw sixty cases in persons who touched the powder from broken, unexploded bombs. The skin was stained an orange tint. The eruption was an acute vesicular dermatitis with closely set lesions involving the palmar surface of the hands and fingers chiefly, and occasionally the feet. The eruption developed, as a rule, nine days after contact, and in some instances led to

extensive exfoliation and protracted inflammation due to secondary sepsis.

(8) *Mixed acids.* In the process of nitrating, operators are very liable to lesions from splashing of the mixed acids used. I have seen cases in which cheloidal scars were produced.

The *precautions* necessary to prevent the toxic effects of these bodies are :—

1. Clean working. Among unskilled workers the eruptions and general toxic symptoms are commoner when new factories are opened.

2. Ample facilities for washing are imperative. No food should be taken unless the hands and face are washed.

3. The operators must wear protective overalls and caps. Veils are sometimes employed. Clothes impregnated with the powder may convey irritation to members of a family not working.

4. Gloves must not be worn, as they tend to maceration of the skin and are easily contaminated inside. Skin varnishes and powders are sometimes used.

5. All specially susceptible individuals must be excluded.

Treatment. The patient should be removed from work. Affected areas of the skin should be cleansed with a weak alkaline solution (℥i sodii bicarb. to 2 pints of water) or with sterile olive oil. The application of a liniment of calamine (calamine 35 grains, olive oil and lime water of each half an ounce) is of great service. Septic infection is treated on the usual lines by boric acid fomentations and a mild mercurial ointment (Hydrarg. Ammon. grains 10, Ung. Paraffini. ℥1). Alternation of work should be advised.

"*Mustard*" *gas dermatitis.* During the present year a Di-chlor-ethyl-sulphide gas has been used by the Germans, and a large number of men have come under treatment. The gas has a mustard odour and acts as an intense irritant, producing an acute dermatitis which begins from four to six hours after exposure. Several weeks may elapse before the eruption clears up.

Flax, jute and **wool** may produce irritant dermatitis, which is also seen in the **silk** workers in France and elsewhere.

French polishers and others who use bichromate of potassium and similar salts frequently suffer from dermatitis, and here the staining of the nails is a guide to the nature of the affection.

Grain itch is considered at p. 130.

Grooms and **coachmen** and others having charge of horses and cattle are sometimes infected by *ringworm* (p. 141).

Hides and **skins.** Workers who handle the skins and hides of animals are liable to *anthrax* (p. 201).

Masons, plasterers and others engaged in the building trade suffer from chronic dermatitis of the hands, often with considerable thickening of the epidermis and painful fissures.

Naphtha workers suffer from a dermatitis similar to that produced by tar (*vide infra*).

Painters and workers in encaustic are also liable to dermatitis from irritants used in their employment, particularly *turpentine* and similar substances.

Paraffin is an irritant like tar (*vide infra*).

Pathologists and **post-mortem attendants** are liable to infection of the hands by the *tubercle* bacillus (p. 227).

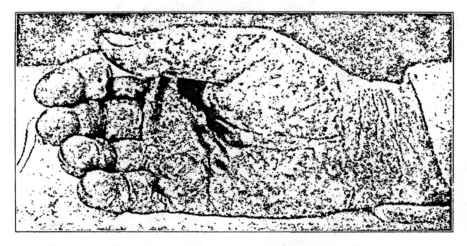

Fig. 27.—Eczematous dermatitis. Hand of a washerwoman.

Photographers are liable to an eczematous eruption produced by *metol*, and those engaged in autotype production suffer from *bichromate* dermatitis.

Printers and **electrotypers** handling lye to wash off the carbon from the formes are subject to an eczematous dermatitis.

Rubber workers who use *carbon disulphide* are liable to an irritant dermatitis.

Shellac workers are also affected, probably by *turpentine* and *arsenic*.

Silicate, used for packing round cold storage apparatus and about boilers, causes dermatitis, probably from the mechanical irritation of the material. Frequent inspection of the workmen is necessary.

Silver- and **electro- plating** cause a papular and papulo-vesicular eruption on the backs of the hands. *Mercury* and also *cyanide of potassium* are used in the processes.

Soap and **soda.** Washerwomen, scrubbers and domestic servants suffer frequently from the constant use of strong soaps and soda. The repeated maceration of the epidermis in water renders the skin more susceptible (Fig. 27). In out-patient practice it is common to see eczematous conditions of the face in young children who are

FIG. 28.—Tar acne. The back and chest were
also affected.

washed with soap intended for house-cleaning and quite unsuited to the tender skin of an infant.

Sugar. Grocers, confectioners and others who handle sugar suffer from an acute form of dermatitis which often becomes pustular. The eruption is usually irritable, and was at one time known as "sugar baker's itch." It was very commonly seen at the London Hospital when there were several sugar bakeries in the neighbourhood. I see a number of cases every year in girls who are engaged in packing sweets.

Tar workers suffer from a series of cutaneous affections. In the earliest stage there is an eczematous dermatitis. Later there are thickening of the skin and the production of warty growths, which develop into papillomatous tumours (tar mollusca) (Fig. 29), many of which fall off.   In other subjects there is a tendency for these tumours to develop into epithelial cancer.   Bayon has shown that the injection of gas-works tar into the ear of a rabbit causes epithelial proliferation. Blast furnace tar is harmless.   A severe form of acne also occurs in tar workers (Fig. 28).

Vanilla used in confectionery causes erythema, papules and vesicles.

Wet-winders working in cotton-mills may suffer from acro-asphyxia,

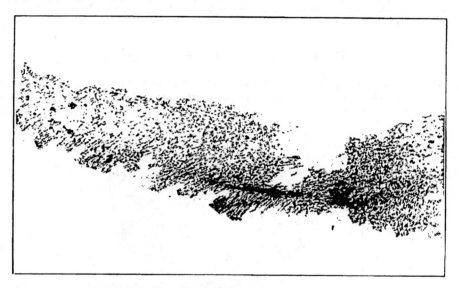

FIG. 29.—Tar molluscum.

venous stasis with marked terminal anæsthesia of the ends of the fingers, leading occasionally to superficial necrosis.   This is due to constant contact with cold water containing potash alum.

Woods.   Certain woods, notably teak (*Tectona grandis*), rosewood (*Dalbergia latifolia*), ebony (*Diospyrus ebenum*), East Indian satinwood (*Chloroxylon swietenia*), produce an irritant dermatitis.   Satinwood causes papulo-vesicular eruption with brawny swelling.   The face may be involved and the upper air passages are acutely inflamed. The irritant in this case is a crystalline alkaloid (Cash).   In other woods an essential oil is believed to be the noxious agent.   Coccus wood used in making flutes also causes an eczematous eruption. Cane cutters in Provence and other parts are liable to an irritable erysipelatoid eruption with the development of blebs. It is not certain whether this is due to an irritant in the reeds (*Arundo donax*), or to some vegetable or animal parasite.

REFERENCES:—R. PROSSER WHITE. "Occupational Diseases of the Skin," 1915, with copious references to original papers. "Dermatitis from Local Irritants." J. C. WHITE. *American Journal of Cutaneous Diseases*, October, 1903. KNOWLES. *Journal of Cutaneous Diseases*, January, 1913, XXXI., p. 11. "Bleachers." PURDON. *British Journal of Dermatology*, 1891, p. 82. "Di-nitrochlor benzole." J. M. BERNSTEIN. *Lancet*, 1912, I., p. 1534. "Flax." LELOIR. *Annales de Dermat. et de Syph.*, 1885, p. 129. "Metol." BEERS. *Medical Journal*, New York, 1908, XII., p. 596. "Silver and Electroplaters." HALL. *British Journal of Dermatology*, XI., p. 112. "Tar." H. L. BARNARD. *Polyclinic Journal*, April, 1904. H. BAYON. *Lancet*, December 7, 1912, p. 1579. "Satin Wood." J. T. CASH. *British Medical Journal*, 1911, October 17, p. 784.

Dermatitis caused by Plants.

The commonest form of plant irritation met with in this country is the nettle sting, which causes transient wheals. More severe inflammations occur from contact with the *Primula obconica* and

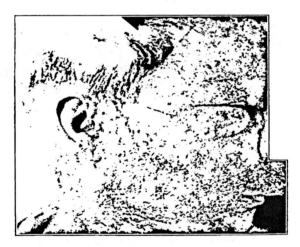

FIG. 30.—Dermatitis from *Primula obconica*.

P. sinensis. The eruption is vesicular and erythematous, and may be attended with general symptoms. The poison ivy (*Rhus toxico-dendron*), dogwood (*Rhus venenata*), and the poison oak (*Rhus divertiloba*) may also cause an acute erythemato-vesicular eruption. In the tropics lacquer (a brown balsam obtained from *Rhus verni-cifera*) by simple contact may cause fever, œdema and tension of the skin of the face, limbs and genitalia, and nasal and conjunctival catarrh. " Lily dermatitis " is the name given to an eruption occurring in the gatherers of daffodils in the Scilly Isles.

The plants which are known to have caused dermatitis are :—

Anacardium occidentale and *orientale.*
Angelica (cow-parsley).
Asparagus officialis.
Balm of Gilead (*Balsamum opobalsamum*).
Bitter orange.
Burdock (*Arctum lappa*).
Buttercup (*Ranunculus*).
Chrysanthemum.
Colchicum.
Cotoneaster microphylla.
Cowhage (*Mucuna pruriens*).
Cow-parsnip (*Heracleum giganteum*).
Cucumber.
Daffodil (juice of stem).
Daphne mezereum.
Dogwood (*Rhus venenata*).
Eucalyptus hemiphloia).
Fig (*Ficus*) (the sap).
Foxglove.
Hops (*Cannabinaceæ*).
Humea elegans.
Indian Bean (*Catalpa bignonoides*).
Indian Turnip (*Psoralia esculenta*).
Ivy (*Hedera helix*).
Lady's Slipper (*Cypridediumi calceolus*).
Larkspur (*Delphinium*).
Laurel.
Leopard's Bane (*Doronicum pardalianches*).
Lilac (*Syringa vulgaris*).
Nettle (*Urtica urens*).
Oleander (*Nerium oleander*).
Parsnip (*Pastinaca sativa*).
Poison Ivy [1] (*Rhus toxicodendron; Ampelopsis Hoggii*).
Primula obconica and *P. sinensis.*
Rhus vernicifera.
Rue (*Ruta graveolens*).

---

[1] The *Ampelopsis Hoggii* has three-lobed leaves ; the commoner *Ampelopsis Veitchii* is five-lobed.

Skunk cabbage (*Simplocarpus fetidus*).
Smart-weed or Water-pepper (*Polygonum punctatum*).
Spurge (several species of *Euphorbia*).
Squill (*Scilla*).
Thrapsia.
Tomato leaves (*Lycopersicum esculentum*).
Vanilla (*Vanilla plantifolia*).

Individual idiosyncrasy is an important factor in plant dermatitis, and in some cases the plants are more irritant at certain seasons.

In a characteristic case of plant poisoning the hands, face, and genitals are covered with closely-placed minute vesicle and bullæ on an erythematous base. There is often considerable tumefaction, particularly on the face and hands. The eruption may last from a few days to three or four weeks in susceptible subjects (Fig. 30).

The eruption is often mistaken for erysipelas, but its appearance in gardeners, amateurs or professional, should lead to careful enquiry as to the possibility of plant poisoning.

A number of remedies have been used for plant dermatitis. As a rule treatment should be on the lines of that for acute vesicular eczema. The parts should be protected by soothing lotions and creams (p. 615), and hyposulphite of soda lotion, a drachm to the ounce, is recommended.

REFERENCES.—"Poisonous Plants of all Countries." BERNHARD SMITH. "Lily Dermatitis." D. WALSH. *British Medical Journal,* September 24, 1910, p. 854. "Lacquer Poison." CASTELLANI and CHALMERS. *Tropical Medicine and Hygiene,* p. 168. PROSSER WHITE, "Occupational Affections of the Skin," gives references to original observations, pp. 110—122.

Dermatitis due to Local Application of Drugs.

Certain remedies applied to the skin for therapeutic purposes cause eruptions. The commonest met with in practice are shortly described in the following paragraphs.

Arnica, a household remedy applied in the form of a tincture to bruises, etc., may cause a papular erythema, which may spread widely from the part treated. In many cases the eruption resembles an acute rapidly extending eczema.

Atropine and **belladonna,** when used in ocular practice, occasionally cause an acute erythematous eruption and œdema, and a belladonna plaster may also excite a dermatitis.

Cade oil is often used for psoriasis and seborrhoic eruptions. It may cause erythema, but has a special affinity for the hair follicles, ·producing a suppurative folliculitis. I have once seen a condition resembling exfoliative dermatitis from its use.

Cantharides, often applied for alopecia and for the relief of pain, produces an erythema if in dilute solution, and vesication if strong. Cheloid may follow.

Capsicum. An acute erythema may be produced by the application of this substance. It is frequently used on wool as a counter-irritant.

Carbolic acid sometimes causes an eczematous dermatitis. If strong it acts as an escharotic.

Chrysarobin, used for psoriasis and for tinea, produces an acute erythema of the skin which may spread far beyond the parts to which it is applied. The characteristics of the eruption are a peculiar tint, resembling prune juice, and subsequent brownish staining. The affected skin is hot and often very irritable. Where the drug has been used near the face the acute erythema with œdema produces an appearance strongly suggesting erysipelas. In rare cases there may be general malaise and pyrexia. Very rarely a general exfoliative dermatitis has been caused by chrysarobin. I have seen one such case in which the erythrodermia lasted for several months.

Cocain. Pea-sized spots of blue atrophy of the skin in the sites of cocain-injections have been reported by Gottheil and by Réné Horand. According to these authors the lesions are peculiar to cocain.

Croton oil is sometimes used as a counter-irritant, and for the treatment of obstinate cases of scalp ringworm. Its application causes a pustular folliculitis.

Iodine, besides staining the skin, sets up an erythema which is followed by desquamation. This property of desquamation is used in the treatment of ringworm of the glabrous skin.

Iodoform occasionally sets up an acute erythema of the scarlatiniform type. Rarely a general exfoliative dermatitis may occur. In some cases there have been grave general symptoms with bullous and hæmorrhagic eruptions.

Mercury applied to the skin in the inunction treatment of syphilis occasionally causes an erythematous eruption. It should never be used in hairy regions, as a pustular folliculitis may be set up.

Mustard causes an erythema. Prolonged application of mustard plasters may cause a vesicular eruption.

Paraphenylendiamine used for dyeing the hair may cause a severe dermatitis which may spread on to the face.

Peroxide of hydrogen and the **peroxides** if strong may cause erythema and vesication.

Pyrogallic acid, used therapeutically and also in hair dyes, may cause acute inflammation with œdema.

Sulphur, used so frequently in scabies and other itching eruptions, is a common cause of dermatitis. The eruption is of the eczematous type and is attended with itching which may be attributed to the

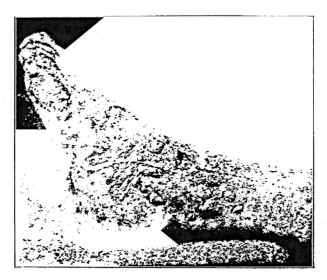

FIG. 31.—Turpentine dermatitis, from the application of a liniment.

scabies. Non-recognition of this fact sometimes leads to persistence in the use of the sulphur and the production of a severe dermatitis.

Tar acts as an irritant in many subjects. It has a special affinity for the glandular elements of the skin and produces an acne-like eruption (*vide* Fig. 28).

Turpentine and **terebene** are used as counter-irritants. In most persons they cause an erythema, but if their use is prolonged, a vesico-bullous eruption may develop (Fig. 31).

REFERENCES.—" Cocain." GOTTHEIL. *Journal of Cutaneous Diseases,* January, 1912, XXX., p. 1. " Paraphenylendiamine." BEDDOES. *British Medical Journal,* September 25, 1909.

CHAPTER V.

ECZEMA.

Definition. Eczema is a non-microbic inflammation of the skin occurring in certain susceptible subjects from external irritation or some internal cause of a toxic or nervous nature.

It is characterised by redness, vesication, exudation (weeping), and the formation of crusts and scales. The lesions, as a rule, itch intensely; they are ill-defined, and tend to spread peripherally and are specially prone to recur.

Etiology. Predisposition is a cardinal feature in the definition just given, and the exact cause being unknown, it would perhaps have been more logical to place eczema among the diseases of unknown origin. But there is a certain sense of fitness in discussing eczema in this place, because there is nothing specific in its pathology, nothing which differentiates it from the eczematous conditions which are the result of local irritation. Redness, vesication, exudation, and the formation of scales and crusts are common phenomena in irritant dermatitis without special predisposition, and there is no sound reason why such reactions to irritation should not be called " eczema." For convenience they are usually classed as forms of " dermatitis." No hard and sharp line can be drawn. Let us for a moment consider the effect of arnica or turpentine on the skin. In most persons the application causes an erythema, which is limited to the area treated, and this rapidly subsides on the removal of the irritant. In other subjects the eruption passes beyond the stage of erythema, vesicles form, and when they rupture a clear gummy fluid exudes. The process is still limited to the area to which the irritant has been applied, and the inflammation subsides spontaneously on its removal. But there are certain predisposed persons in whom the process once started is not limited to the irritated area. It spreads widely beyond it, and may appear in distant parts, and even become general. It is difficult to quell the inflammation, and when apparently cured it may recur on the slightest irritation, or even without ostensible cause, and such recurrences may occur throughout life. No one would hesitate to call the last condition " eczema," but there is no difference in the microscopical appearances in the limited dermatitis and the widely-spread eczematous lesions.

There is no doubt that in many cases which are classed as eczema the irritant is a slight one and easily overlooked, but there are others in which there does not appear to be any local cause sufficient to account for the inflammation. There must be predisposing conditions. These may be local or general.

Local predisposing causes :—

(1) Excessive dryness of the skin. This is best seen in xerodermia and ichthyosis. These congenital conditions, especially in their milder forms, are not at all uncommon. They render the skin exceedingly sensitive to° cold and damp and to easterly winds. Xerodermatous patients usually come for treatment in the late autumn and winter months, and often year after year. The dry atrophic skin of the aged is also specially prone to eczema.

(2) Excessive sweating of the hands and feet and in the flexures is a common cause of eczema. Some authorities include in the eczema group the vesicular affection of the hands and feet called dysidrosis, or pompholyx. This affection is recurrent and occurs chiefly in the summer months (p. 583).

(3) Chronic congestion, as seen in the legs of patients suffering from varicose veins, is a common condition predisposing to eczema.

(4) The local irritation of the genitals by urine containing sugar is another predisposing local cause.

General predisposing conditions :—

(1) Age is an important factor. Eczema is common in the infant and in the aged.

(2) Heredity is held by some to be a factor, but it is difficult to estimate its importance.

(3) Auto-intoxication is probably an important cause. Overfeeding and injudicious feeding are frequently found in infants suffering from eczema. High living and excess both as regards food and alcohol are doubtless predisposing causes in the adult. Constipation and other alimentary canal troubles tending to the formation and absorption of toxic bodies in the bowel often co-exist with eczema. Gout, I take it, acts not by excess of uric acid, but by intoxication from the alimentary canal. Eczema occurs also in the glycosuric and in sufferers from chronic renal disease. Rickets and teething are believed to be common causes of infantile eczema, but the associated alimentary canal troubles are more likely to be causative than the rickets, or nervous irritation from dentition.

(4) Debilitating illnesses must also be looked upon as tending to eczema. Many eczematous children are weakly, and a special form of the disease has been classed as " strumous." It must not,

s.   7

however, for one moment be taken that the tubercle bacillus has any special *rôle* in the production of eczema.

(5) Nervous conditions are often accused of causing eczema. We certainly find that worry, overwork, and anxiety appear to determine an attack. Instances of this are so common that a causal relationship appears certain.

Microbic conditions complicate eczema, but elaborate research has shown that the primary lesion is amicrobic. In the present state of our knowledge we may say that the finding of specific microbes in an eczematous lesion is evidence that the disease is either not eczema or that it is eczema which has been secondarily infected. The moist, oozing surface characteristic of the disease is particularly prone to infection, especially by pyogenic cocci, and in many instances we find abundant evidence of such infection quite early. This is most common in the eczema of children, where the itching lesions induce scratching, in the flexures, where warmth and moisture favour the growth of microbes, and on the extremities, where the opportunities for coccal invasion are frequent.

But there are primary pyogenic infections which simulate eczema very closely, and indeed some authors class them as "microbic eczema." For instance, we meet with an eruption exceedingly like eczema about the nose and ears of patients suffering from chronic discharges from these cavities. There is often an associated impetigo of the common type. The eczema-like eruption is due to pyogenic organisms. Again there are circumscribed disc-like lesions occurring about the mouth and cheeks and neck of children. They are covered with adherent scales, and are usually the colour of the normal skin, or perhaps a light pink. The trouble is contagious, and epidemics are common in schools. The affection is a trivial one, but in cold weather and with easterly winds vesication may occur. Sabouraud considers this to be a dry inflammation caused by streptococci, and it, therefore, is excluded by our definition from eczema. An erythema at the labial commissures which often goes on to maceration of the epidermis and the formation of fissures, occurring also in children, is often called eczema. It is frequently contracted at school and is due to streptococci, and is therefore a variety of impetigo, and common phlyctenular impetigo often co-exists (*vide* Fig. 77).

The intertrigo of infants and obese adults beginning in the folds as areas of erythema due to the friction of opposed surfaces often becomes vesicular, and owing to warmth and moisture of the parts the vesicles rupture early and a raw red oozing surface forms. Such a surface is very prone to pyogenic infection, and the inflammation may spread beyond the actual flexures and become widely disseminated. It is often called " eczema," but the spread of the infection is due to pus cocci.

The Eczema marginatum of Hebra, affecting the groins and axillæ, has been shown to be due to certain forms of ringworm fungus (*vide* p. 141), and an eczematoid eruption between the toes produced by the same fungi is of common occurrence. Circumscribed eczematoid lesions due to fungi are not infrequent on the hands (*vide* p. 144).

Lastly, we have to exclude the conditions known as " seborrhoic eczema." The name is an unfortunate one, for recent research has

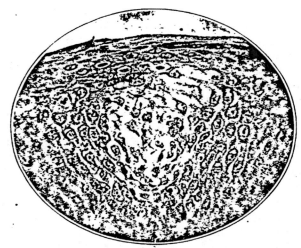

FIG. 32.—Early stage of eczema. Negative of section kindly lent by Dr. Whitfield.

shown that the process is not related to excess of sebum, nor is it eczema in the proper sense. The disease is microbic, and in the dry scaly lesions are found Unna's bottle bacilli or spores of Malassez, while in the scaly greasy lesions the staphylococcus epidermidis albus, forming grey cultures, abounds. Moreover, the anatomy of the primary lesions is different (see p. 210), and treatment by antiparasitic remedies, especially sulphur, is remarkably efficient.

Pathological anatomy. The essential part of the process is a spongy condition of the corpus mucosum due to intracellular œdema (Fig. 32). As soon as the tension of the serous exudate is sufficient to rupture the intercellular filaments, vesicles form, containing sero-fibrinous fluid and a few migratory cells. The vesicles appear first in the deep part of the epidermis, and the constant growth from below gradually pushes them up to the corneous layer, where by confluence they form the visible vesicles characteristic of one stage of the disease. The after-history of the vesicle varies. Where the stratum corneum is thick the vesicle dries up and a minute crust or scale forms, which ultimately falls off, and the epidermis is soon restored. But in many instances the vesicles rupture or are ruptured, and from the well-like cavities produced the exudation continues to pour out. This constitutes the condition known as " weeping."

Fig. 33.—Eczema in the knee-flexures.

Owing to some defect in the process of keratinisation there is no tendency to rapid healing.

In true eczema the vesicles are amicrobic at the start, but they speedily become infected with micrococci, which find the serous exudate a suitable culture ground. When pyogenic infection occurs leucocytic infiltration rapidly follows. The secretion then becomes turbid and purulent, and the crusts which form by its desiccation are yellowish and comparatively thick.

The eczema is then " impetiginised."

Defective keratinisation of the epidermis is another feature of eczema. It has already been mentioned as preventing the healing

Plate 8.

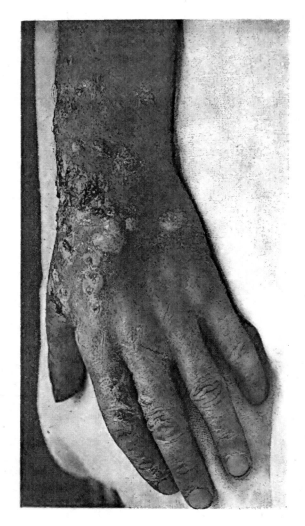

ACUTE VESICULAR ECZEMA.

The vesicles are numerous, and in parts confluent. The crusts
are due to dried exudation.

of weeping surfaces. But the special change called parakeratosis, in which the cells of the corneous layer preserve their nuclei, is the cause of the desquamation in scaly eczema. In chronic cases a still further change occurs, viz., a hyperplasia of the prickle-cell layer with increase of the interpapillary processes. This change is manifested clinically by the "lichenisation" of chronic eczema lesions. In acute facial eczema and eczema rubrum of the legs the epidermal changes are accompanied by œdema and engorgement of the papillary body and perivascular infiltration.

Clinical features. It has long been the practice to classify the types of eruption in eczema as erythematous, papular, vesicular, and pustular. It is impossible to make this distinction arbitrary, as the various stages may co-exist, or the process may undergo modifications from time to time. The terms are, however, useful as expressing the chief characters.

In **Erythematous eczema** the patients are usually adults. Its commonest site is the face, the upper limbs, and the external genitalia. The lesions are ill-defined, bright or dull red spots or patches which unite to form diffuse areas. There is usually some infiltration, and where the connective tissue is lax, as about the eyelids, or the scrotum and penis, there is often much œdema and swelling. The patient complains of heat and itching, but there is no marked pyrexia or disturbance of the general health as in erysipelas. The eruption gradually fades and is followed by a slight, usually branny, desquamation. Erythematous eczema is very prone to recur and is often mistaken for erysipelas. It generally runs an acute course, but may pass into the vesicular or scaly form. Occasionally it becomes pustular.

Papular eczema. The seats of election are the arms, legs, and trunk. The lesions are round, often acuminate, papules of a bright red colour about the size of a pin's head. In some cases the papule is capped by a tiny vesicle, visible only under a lens. The papules may be discrete, or arranged in groups, forming patches of various sizes. When the lesions are closely set, plaques may be formed which, in chronic cases, undergo lichenisation. This variety of eczema is attended with intense itching, and the clinical features are often masked by the excoriations caused by scratching. It frequently runs a chronic course and is rebellious to treatment. Recurrences are common.

Vesicular eczema. Subjective symptoms of heat and tingling often precede the eruption, which usually begins acutely. The skin becomes red and swollen, and on the red area a number of minute vesicles not larger than a pin's head appear. The closely-set vesicles soon coalesce to form larger lesions, which rupture, and a viscid serous fluid, which stiffens linen, escapes from a number of depressions which are the ruptured vesicles. The exudate dries up to form yellowish scabs or crusts, and under these the exudation continues. The itching and burning diminish when vesication occurs. The patches are ill-defined.

Vesicular eczema may occur on any part of the body. In infants the areas affected are mask-like, the cheeks, forehead, and chin being

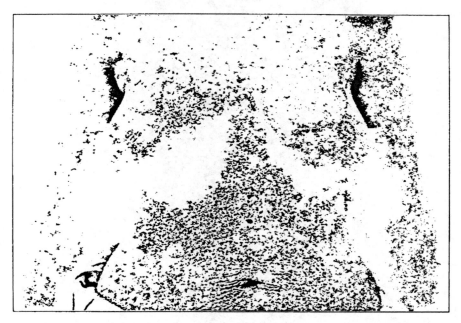

FIG. 34.—Eczema, beginning on the mamma and spreading to chest and abdomen. In this type coccal infection is the cause of the spread of the eruption.

specially involved. The hands and feet and the flexures are common sites in the adult. The itching and burning sensations lead to excoriation from scratching, and in young children it is not uncommon to find extensive bleeding areas which have been denuded by the nails.

An acute attack of vesicular eczema may last for a week or two. Relapses are exceedingly common. The diminution of the serous exudation and erythema indicates the beginning of recovery. The scabs finally fall off, leaving a red, smooth, delicate epidermis, which may be easily again excited into active inflammation. On the legs

Plate 9.

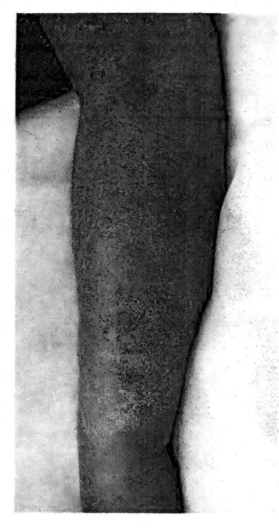

ERYTHEMATOUS AND SQUAMOUS ECZEMA.

There had been a short vesicular stage.

chronic vesicular eczema passes into eczema rubrum, and infection with pyogenic cocci commonly leads to the pustular variety.

Pustular eczema, Impetiginised eczema. Occasionally the eruption may be pustular from the onset, but this form of eczema is usually developed from one of the preceding varieties, especially the vesicular. The most frequent sufferers are children. particularly those seen in the out-patient clinics in large towns. The pustules

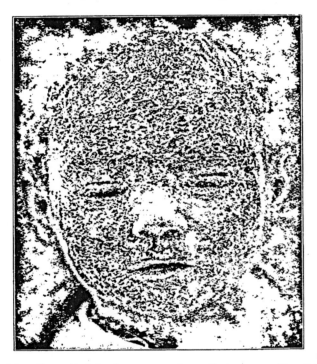

FIG. 35.—Impetiginised eczema, in a "strumous" subject, with secondary gland infection.

on rupture form dirty yellow, brown, or greenish-brown crusts. The hairy regions of the body are the most frequent sites. The glands are involved early.

Eczema rubrum is a sequel of vesicular or pustular eczema. It usually occurs on the legs of adults. The affected area is of a bright red colour, the skin is infiltrated. and the whole limb is often swollen. The corneous layer of the epidermis is absent, and the exudation may be either diffuse and hardly perceptible, or clear yellow drops of serum oozing out at various points. Scabs and crusts of yellow colour are formed by the drying exudate. Sometimes blood is mixed with the serum. The patients complain of severe burning and itching.

Eczema madidans is the name given to constantly oozing eczema.

Scaly eczema. This name is given to the scaly condition which occurs in an erythematous or vesicular eczema which is fading, and in which the active process is succeeded by the formation of scales. It is also applied to a chronic form in which erythema with scaling is the chief feature. The scales are thin flakes of a white or grey colour. They differ from the scales of psoriasis in being easily detached, and, moreover, they are scanty and never silvery.

The most advanced degree of scaly eczema is seen on the palms, and especially the soles. Here the increase of the horny layer is so great that the mobility of the parts is impeded. The surface is dry and rough, and movement causes the formation of deep painful fissures in the sites of the normal furrows of the skin. Warty and papillomatous excrescences are occasionally seen in cases of chronic eczema, especially on the extremities. They are an exaggeration of the lichenisation mentioned above. In some cases the appearance of the skin resembles shagreen, in others there is thick leathery infiltration.

Diagnosis. It would be difficult to discuss in detail all the conditions which may be mistaken for eczema in all its forms. The diagnosis will depend on the following features. The eruption is red, papular, vesicular, pustular, or scaly. The exudate is of a gummy character. The lesions are usually ill-defined. The patient complains of itching and burning.

The first point in the diagnosis is to determine whether the eruption is due to some *irritant*. The long list of irritants considered in Chapter IV. indicates the necessity for careful examination and enquiry. As a rule, dermatitis due to local irritation subsides rapidly on the removal of the cause and the application of simple soothing remedies.

Next, *scabies* should be eliminated. The linear burrows of the acarus should be sought for between the fingers and around the wrists. The eruption of scabies is, as a rule, widely disseminated, affecting the extremities, the anterior axillary folds, and the external genitals. The itching is worse at night. There may be a history of other members of the family being affected.

In *eczematoid ringworm* the lesions are, as a rule, sharply defined, but the simulation is very close. Chronic recurrent eruptions of this

Plate 10.

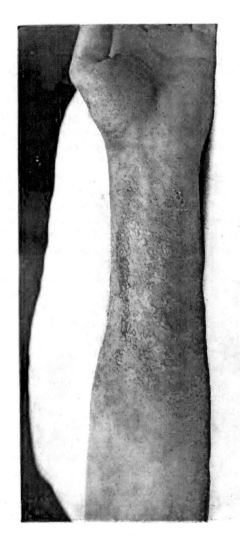

ECZEMA : Weeping Stage.

type occur in the groin and axilla and between the toes. Search should be made for fungus in all doubtful cases (*vide* p. 141).

"*Seborrhoic*" *dermatitis* is often difficult to differentiate. The presence of a scaly condition of the scalp, the predilection of the eruption for the middle line of the trunk, and the flexures and the greasy character of the scales are often characteristic. Mild sulphur preparations applied locally tend to the rapid disappearance of the seborrhoic condition.

Impetigo is differentiated by the evidence of auto-inoculation, by the scabs appearing to be stuck on, and by discrete scattered phlyctenules, but there are several eczematoid conditions which are of coccal origin, notably about the nose, ears, and mouth.

Sycosis may be mistaken for eczema of the beard region. Sycosis is a pus-coccal infection of the hair follicles and is limited to them. Eczema is not confined to the follicles, the skin between them being affected.

Erysipelas. Eczema of the erythematous type may be mistaken for erysipelas. The absence of fever and of general symptoms are sufficient to make the diagnosis.

Psoriasis may be confused with scaly eczema, especially of the knees and elbows. The scales of psoriasis are bright and silvery and on removal reveal a vascular base. In eczema the scales are yellowish and grey in tint. They are usually due to dried exudation, of which there may be a history. The lesions of psoriasis are well defined ; those of eczema shade off into surrounding skin.

Lichen planus can only be mistaken for chronic papular eczema. The papules of lichen are of a shining smooth character, they are quadrilateral or rectangular, and there is a central depression, and Wickham's silvery striæ are present. The mucous membrane of the mouth is commonly affected.

Palmar eruptions. In view of the difficulty often presented in the *differential diagnosis of palmar eruptions* it may be useful to indicate the commoner types and their special features.

Congenital palmar keratodermia or *tylosis* is symmetrical, and the soles are also affected. The horny layer is enormously thickened ; the surface may be smooth and of a yellow-brown tint, or rough and irregular and of a brown or black colour resembling the bark of a tree. It is often a family affection (p. 25).

Ichthyosis and *xerodermia.* The palms are dry and the normal fissures are exaggerated. The skin generally is dry and scaly (p. 17).

Dermatitis due to irritants. In acute cases the epidermis is covered with vesicles which may rupture and weep. The fingers are also affected. In chronic cases the epidermis is thickened and fissured, the fissures being painful and sometimes bleeding (Fig. 27). The skin may be stained by the irritant, *e.g.*, in high explosive dermatitis, dyes, etc.

Arsenical keratosis is bilateral. It may be associated with pigmentation of the trunk.

Eczema of the palms may be papulo-vesicular or scaly. It is an intensely itching eruption and often recurs. It is sometimes associated with a similar affection of the flexures and often occurs in neurotic subjects. In women beyond the menopause the eruption is often dry, thick and horny, and with painful fissures. It may be associated with hypothyroidism.

Scabies rarely affects the palms except in infants (p. 118).

Eczematoid ringworm. The eruption is usually vesicular at the onset. At a late stage there is scaling, the edge of the lesion being well defined. There is intense irritation. Fungus may be demonstrated in the epidermis at the margin.

Seborrhoic dermatitis. Palmar seborrhoides are dry and scaly and usually associated with pityriasis capitis and seborrhoides of the sternal and interscapular regions. They closely resemble certain palmar syphilides.

Psoriasis rarely affects the palms alone. The eruption is dry and scaly, and on the scales being removed the surface is florid and shows hæmorrhagic points. The elbows and knees usually show the characteristic lesions.

Syphilis. In the congenital affection there may be bullæ on the palms and soles at or soon after birth, and in the later eruptions papules and red scaly lesions are common.

In the acquired disease the early macular lesions of the stage of generalisation may appear on the palms as elsewhere. They have a dusky colour and are bilateral. Bilateral papular and lenticular lesions of a dark hammy tint, sometimes with slight scaling, also occur in the secondary stage. They are associated with a generalised eruption, buccal and tonsillar lesions, and general adenitis.

Later the lesions are exceedingly chronic, and have a red, beefy, colour with circinate or gyrate outline and dry, scaly surface. They are nearly always unilateral, and commonly on the right side. They do not itch. A chronic, scaly, non-itching eruption of the palm should always suggest syphilis.

Pompholyx affects both hands. The eruption is vesicular, the small deep vesicles extending along the sides of the fingers. In some cases the vesicles coalesce to form large bullæ, and these may be infected with pus-cocci. The affection recurs in the warm weather.

Some cases of this type are due to local irritation, others are varieties of eczematoid ringworm.

Prognosis. As a rule, eczema may be looked upon as curable, but it is often exceedingly tedious and tries the patience of the sufferer and the medical attendant. Where the underlying cause can be attacked and removed the outlook is favourable, but in all cases there is a great tendency to recurrence.

Treatment of eczema and dermatitis due to irritants. *Prophylaxis.* Certain local conditions are known to predispose to eczema. Attention to these may prevent an outbreak. For instance, the xerodermatous skin can be kept supple and in a less vulnerable condition by the daily application of glycerine and water. The more severe forms of ichthyosis usually require an oily preparation, and I have used with advantage equal parts of olive oil and lanolin. Persons who are susceptible to "chapping" should be very careful to thoroughly dry the hands and especially the wrists after washing, and the commonly used glycerine is distinctly prophylactic. Where constant washing is necessary from the avocation of the patient, equal parts of glycerine and Lotio Rubra make a suitable application.

In certain subjects soap should be sparingly used, and the superfatted basic soaps will be found of great service. In some individuals soap has to be forbidden, at least for a time, and fine oatmeal is a valuable substitute. Hard water is also to be avoided by those who are prone to eczema.

Varicose veins must receive attention. The limb should be supported by a properly fitting bandage.

In a declared case the affected part should if possible be placed at rest. In a case of widely-spread eczema the only means of properly treating the disease is confinement to bed. This not only allows of satisfactory dressing of the lesions, but ensures rest. Every source of irritation must, of course, be removed. The affected parts should be washed as little as possible, and no soap should be applied to them. In some cases sterilised olive oil may be used as a means of cleansing.

Diet. The diet in eczema should be simple. In acute cases, for instance when the face or trunk is affected, it is better to put the patient on a diet consisting chiefly of milk. Bulkeley advises limiting the diet for three to five days to rice boiled in water and eaten with butter and salt, bread and butter, and water. Some authorities exclude fresh fruit. In the more chronic and localised cases more latitude is allowable. The meat should be limited; preference being given to mutton, lamb, chicken, and game, which is not high. All twice-cooked meat, entrées, and made dishes should be avoided, and condiments, spices, and curries should be stopped entirely. Salted meats and fish should not be taken, but fresh fish may be allowed. Vegetables and cooked fruits appear to do no harm ; pastry and sweets are best avoided, but milk puddings may be taken. Alcohol should be excluded in all acute cases, and even the chronic conditions are likely to do better if wines, spirits and beer are omitted from the dietary. In some persons coffee appears to act as a direct irritant, but in cutting down the usual drinks taken it must be remembered that a sufficiency of fluid is necessary, and some water like Contrexéville, lithia, or other mineral water must be substituted. If there be glycosuria, Bright's disease, or gout, the diet appropriate to these conditions must be rigorously enforced.

Internal treatment. There is no medicine which has a curative effect on eczema. It is usually good practice to start treatment in an acute case with a saline aperient, and the action of the bowels must be carefully regulated throughout. In children rhubarb and magnesia is often useful. In very acute cases in the plethoric adult I have often seen relief from small doses of antimony wine, seven to ten minims thrice daily. It lowers the blood pressure and relieves irritation and congestion. It may conveniently be combined with alkalies. In the gouty the appropriate remedies should be given in addition. Crocker recommended turpentine in small doses, but I have not been so favourably impressed with its value. Quinine is sometimes of service in the acute erythematous type. Arsenic must never be given in acute cases of eczema, but may be beneficial in the chronic scaly forms.

One of the great difficulties is the pruritus, and for this we may give full doses of bromide at night, or antipyrin or phenacetin. Quinine in two-grain doses in a sugar-coated tablet or small doses of syrup of chloral or bromide of potassium may be given to children, but it must be remembered that some children are peculiarly susceptible to bromides.

Spas. In chronic cases in the well-to-do one is often asked as to the advisability of visiting some spa. The most important part of the spa treatment is the regular living and the general routine. These are doubtless of more importance than the actual taking of certain waters. In the overfed and constipated the regular aperients taken in the waters are of great value, and many persons find benefit from the sulphur waters of Harrogate, Strathpeffer, and Llandrindod. In other cases the alkaline waters of Royat and Vichy are of more benefit. As a rule cases of eczema do not do well at the seaside, but where the underlying cause is overwork and want of rest the tonic effects of the sea air are beneficial.

Local treatment. The local treatment of eczema and of dermatitis due to irritants is on the same lines. It is, of course, essential that the irritant, if known, should be removed. Where the patient's work is the exciting cause, he must be removed from it, if possible.

The local treatment consists (1) in the removal of crusts ; (2) the disinfection of the affected area if there be pyogenic infection ; (3) protection from irritation ; (4) the application of powders, lotions, ointment, creams, pastes, mulls, etc.

(1) The removal of crusts. This is effected by means of the boric starch poultice. One teaspoonful of boric acid and half an ounce of starch are mixed into a paste with a small quantity of cold water. Upon this is poured 15 ozs. of boiling water and the whole is well stirred. The application is spread upon butter muslin and applied cold to the affected part. It is best to keep the muslin in position by a thin bandage. The poultice softens the crusts and permits of their easy removal. Where there is pus infection I usually have the parts fomented with boric lint wrung out in hot water.

(2) Disinfection. The boric starch poultice and the boric fomentations sufficiently cleanse the parts, but where there is much impetiginisation a mild mercurial may be applied, such as the Ung. Metallorum (Plumbi acetat, 10 grs. Calomel, 10 grs. Zinc oxid., 20 grs. Ung. Hydrarg. Nitrat. Dil. to the ounce), or a solution of Nitrate of Silver, 5 to 10 grs. to the ounce may be painted on.

(3) Above all things it is important to prevent the patient from irritating the part. This can only be effected in a young child by putting thin cardboard or thick brown paper splints on the arms. These splints are tubular and extend from the armpit to the wrist. They are lined and bound with lint at each end to prevent chafing. They are long enough to prevent flexion of the elbow, and. if necessary, they may be tied together across the back. In very restless infants we may have a sleeveless nightgown made, fastened down to the bed by a row of safety pins. In adults we rarely have to resort to such measures, but there are cases in which the nurse has to exercise constant care to prevent scratching.

(4) The applications required vary with the character of the eruption. In the erythematous eczema which attacks the face, and which closely simulates erysipelas, the application of a lotion of calamine on a lint mask is very satisfactory. The lotion is made up as follows : R. Calaminæ, two drachms ; Zinc oxid., half a drachm ; Glycerine, two drachms ; Aq. Calcis, four ounces. The glycerine

may be omitted if it be found to irritate.   Lint is wrung out in the
lotion and the application is kept on constantly.

For weeping eczema it will be found more satisfactory to apply
a lotion at first, rather than an ointment or paste.   The calamine
lotion mentioned above may be used, or the following lotion of lead :
R. Glycerini plumbi subacetatis, one ounce ; Glycerine, one ounce ;
Aq. vel. aq. calcis to one pint.   The lotion is applied on lint, and it is
best to cover the part affected and to wet the lint constantly from
the outside.   This prevents undue disturbance of the eczematous area.

I have also seen great relief in the weeping stage from the application of pure coal tar.   The tar is well washed with distilled water
to remove alkali, and is painted on in a thin layer and allowed
to dry.   The application causes a sensation of burning for ten to
fifteen minutes, but this is followed by relief of the pruritus.   The
application may be repeated in three days.   The crude coal tar may
be combined with zinc as in the following ointment :—

R. Crude coal tar, forty grains ;
    Zinc oxide, forty grains ;
    Pulv. Amyli.
    Vaselin, aa to one ounce.

With such applications the exudation usually dries up rapidly,
and then an ointment or paste may be used.   These preparations
are best applied on butter muslin and kept in position by a muslin
or other thin bandage.   The ointment should be changed not more
often than twice a day, and great care must be exercised over its
removal.   If the muslin adheres and is forcibly removed the newly-
formed epidermis is torn, and actual hæmorrhage may result.   If
the dressing has stuck it is better to soften it from the outside by oil
before trying to remove it.

The following ointments and pastes are valuable in the treatment
of eczema :—

R. Zinci oxidi, one drachm ;
    Acid salicylic, ten grains ;
    Lanolin, two drachms ;
    Soft paraffin to one ounce.
R. Glycerini plumbi subacetat., half a drachm ;
    Vaselin, one ounce.

R. Emplastrum plumbi and Ol. olivæ, equal parts melted together,
a substitute for the Ung. Diachyli.

R. Zinci oxidi, one drachm ;
    Lenigallol, thirty grains ;
    Lanolin, one drachm ;
    Vaselin, one ounce.

Pastes.—Lassar's.—Zinci oxidi, twenty-four parts ;
      Starch, twenty-four parts ;
      Salicylic acid, two parts ;
      Vaselin, fifty parts.

Unna's.—Soak three drachms of gelatin in twenty drachms of water for twelve hours. Heat and add two drachms of oxide of zinc which has been rubbed up with five drachms of glycerin. Before using, melt the mixture and apply with a soft brush, and then dab cotton wool on to the surface to form a protective felt. This dressing may be left on three or four days.

Solutions of cellulose are sometimes used as vehicles for similar preparations.

In some situations creams are useful. They are excellent protective applications, but there is sometimes a difficulty in removing them. Oil is the best medium for doing this.

The calamine liniment may be used instead of the lotion.

  R. Calaminæ, thirty-five grains ;
    Olei Olivæ and Aq. Calcis, of each half an ounce.

Or the following zinc cream :—

  R. Zinci oxidi, three drachms ;
    Lanolin, one drachm ;
    Aq. Calcis and Ol. Amygdalæ dulc., of each half an ounce.

For chronic eczema, often impetiginised, and with painful fissures, daily painting with a solution of silver nitrate, ten to twenty grains in seven drachms of Spiritus Aetheris Nitrosi and one drachm of water is often valuable. The edges of the painful fissures of the finger tips are frequently thickened and horny. As a preliminary to treatment the horny edges should be rubbed down with pumice or with a pumice-soap, or cut away, before the application of an ointment or paint. Should the patient be obliged to work, the finger-tips should be protected by strips of Mead's strapping applied to form a cap.

In some cases patches of eczema of the chronic type cannot be influenced by the soothing remedies above mentioned. There may be some underlying general or more probably some local condition which has been overlooked. Varicose veins, especially of the finer variety, where there are numerous small varices, require attention. But if nothing can be found, we are often best served by treating the chronic patch vigorously to make it acutely inflamed, and for this purpose tar in the form of Ung. Picis, or, what is cleaner, an ointment of one of the allied bodies, such as Anthrasol, Ol. Cadini, or Ol. Rusci, a drachm to the ounce. Lenigallol, a derivative of pyrogallol, is also useful. If the tar preparations are used, it is well to cover the affected part with lint spread with the ointment, and to firmly bandage it on and leave it in position for twenty-four hours. I have tried small doses of the X-rays with advantage in some of these very chronic conditions. and have found it specially useful in chronic palmar eczema. Short applications of radium are also useful for limited areas. Kromayer speaks favourably of the treatment of some chronic eczemas with his mercury vapour lamp, and I have had several cases in which it has been of service in otherwise intractable conditions.

REFERENCES.—It is impossible to give adequate references in such a wide subject, but the histology may be specially studied in UNNA'S " Histopathology," translated by NORMAN WALKER, p.190 ; in SABOURAUD'S " Maladies du cuir chevelu," Vol. II., p. 331. The different views held were set forth at the International Congress, Paris, 1900. An elaborate investigation of the etiology of infantile eczema by DR. ARTHUR HALL appeared in the British Journal of Dermatology, 1905, XVII., p. 161, etc. KROMAYER discussed the modern treatment of eczema, Canadian Journal of Medicine and Surgery, September, 1904. A. WHITFIELD, Lectures. Practitioner, February, March, 1904, and Lancet, 1908, II., p. 237.

CHAPTER VI.

AFFECTIONS CAUSED BY ANIMAL PARASITES

ANIMAL parasites attack the skin (*a*) in search of food, *i.e.*, to suck the blood, (*b*) to deposit their ova, (*c*) on their way to the surface from deeper organs, and (*d*) accidentally.

Parasites which attack the skin in search of food :—

(1) Pediculi, lice ; (2) Ixodes, ticks ; (3) Leptus autumnalis, harvest bug ; (4) Pulex irritans, flea ; (5) Cimex lectuarius, bed-bug ; (6) Culex, gnat or mosquito ; (7) Pediculoides in grain itch ; (8) Tryoglyphus longior in copra itch, and various tropical parasites.

Parasites attacking the skin to deposit ova :—

(*a*) Ova are deposited in the skin by (1) the Sarcoptes scabiei, the itch insect ; (2) Animal sarcoptes ; (3) the Œstrus, gadfly ; (4) Pulex penetrans, jigger or sandfly.

(*b*) Ova are deposited on the hair by (1) Pediculus capitis, the head louse ; (2) Pediculus pubis, the crab louse ; and (3) Pediculus corporis, body louse. The last more commonly lays its eggs on the body linen.

Parasites attacking the skin on the way to the surface from the deeper organs :—

(1) Cysticercus hydatid, and (2) Dracunculus, the Guinea worm.

The skin is attacked accidentally by contact with certain larvæ, the hymenoptera, bees, wasps, hornets, etc.

Scabies. The Itch.

Scabies is a parasitic, contagious disease caused by the Sarcoptes scabiei. The characteristic lesions are the burrows produced by the female. There is intense itching and a polymorphous eruption mainly due to scratching.

The **Sarcoptes scabiei** (Fig. 36) is commonly called an insect, but it belongs to the Arachnidæ and the sub-order Acari and not to the Insecta. The parasite is frequently called the Acarus scabiei. The female, of pearly grey colour, 400 μ by 300 μ, is just visible to the naked eye. The male is somewhat smaller, 200 μ by 150 μ.

The sarcoptes have eight short legs, the four anterior provided with suckers, the four posterior with bristles. The larvæ have only six legs. The eggs are oval and of comparatively large size, 150 μ by 100 μ. The impregnated female burrows her way into the epidermis, where she lives for about two months and there lays her eggs, one or two a day. The little tunnel thus produced causes a linear elevation of the skin from one-eighth to half an inch in length. This is the " cuniculus " or " burrow." The ridge is greyish or even black in colour, and in close proximity to it there is a small vesicle. On dissecting out a burrow and examining it under a low power, the female sarcoptes is found at the distal extremity, and behind her at intervals lie the ova, from a dozen to fifty in number, the ovum nearest

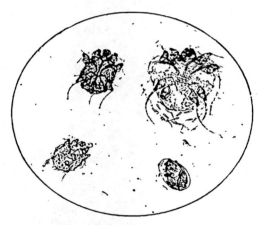

Fig. 36.—Sarcoptes.   Male, female, embryo, ovum.   x 75.

the orifice of the burrow being the first laid. There are also tiny black spots of the excrement of the acarus. The ova hatch in from three to six days and the young embryos make their way on to the surface. They reach the adult stage in a month. The females having developed and being impregnated make their way into the skin and form fresh burrows. Scratching may naturally convey the parasites from one part of the body to another. The male acarus is rarely found, as it lives on the surface.

Close contact is apparently necessary for contracting the disease. Sleeping in infected beds or with scabietic persons is the usual cause, but wearing infected clothing is also a source of infection. Scabies is one of the commonest diseases in hospital practice, but no class is exempt. In the cleanly it is frequently not thought of, and may

PLATE II.

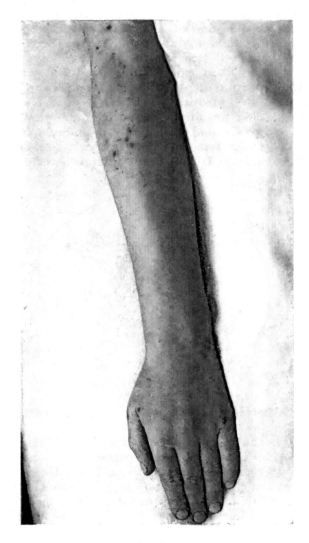

SCABIES.

An early case showing the lesions in the interdigital clefts, on the
ulnar aspect of the wrist, and on the forearm.

persist because appropriate treatment is not applied.   In war scabies is so common as to gravely interfere with military efficiency.

Symptoms.   The burrows are characteristic, and in well-marked cases there are, in addition, features which are so striking that a diagnosis can often be made on inspection.   The eruption is polymorphous, consisting of papules, vesicles, excoriations, and pustules.   The distribution of the lesions is a great help in diagnosis. The following areas should be inspected in order :—The interdigital clefts, the ulnar aspect of the wrists, the outer surfaces of the forearms, and the arms, the anterior axillary folds, the trunk, buttocks, the penis, and, in infants, the toes.   The lesions of scabies do not

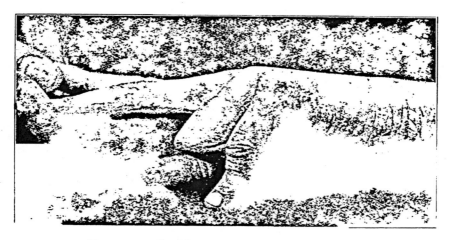

FIG. 37.— Scabies.   Burrows on the fingers.

appear on the face, except in babies at the breast, the disease being contracted there from contact with an infected mother.   The itching is intense and is always worse at night.   The intensity of the eruption varies greatly with the amount of scratching.   Impetigo of the phlyctenular and bullous types and weeping eczematous surfaces caused by scratching are common.

Scabies as seen in soldiers on active service differs in some respects from that usually met with in civil practice.   Interdigital burrows are rare.   MacCormac found them in only 13 per cent. of his cases. Vesication is more common, and the hands are often quite free from lesions of any kind.   Penile lesions are found in the majority of the patients, and may lead to a suspicion of venereal disease.   Secondary impetigo is usually severe, especially on the buttocks, elbows and knees. Furuncles are common. There is lymphadenitis in many instances.

In severe cases there is eosinophilia, and albuminuria may occur.

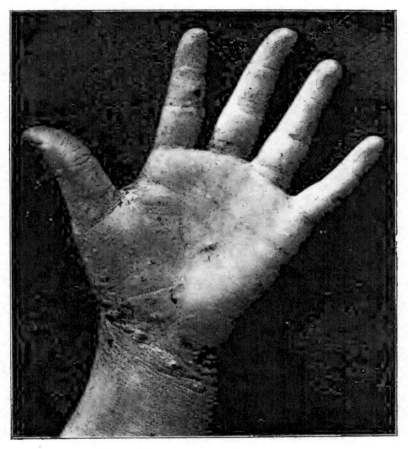

FIG. 38.—Scabies. Burrows on the palm (rare).

If unrecognised or improperly treated the disease may last for months.

In the variety known as Norwegian Itch the secondary lesions are so severe that the whole body and limbs may be enveloped in crusts and scales, in which large numbers of the parasite are present (Fig. 40).

Diagnosis of Scabies. This is usually easy, if the disease be

borne in mind.   In general practice, however, the disease is often
overlooked because it is not thought of.   The burrows are characteristic, and from them the female parasite or the ova may be removed
and recognised under the microscope.   Scabies may be mistaken for
impetigo or for eczema, and both these conditions may complicate

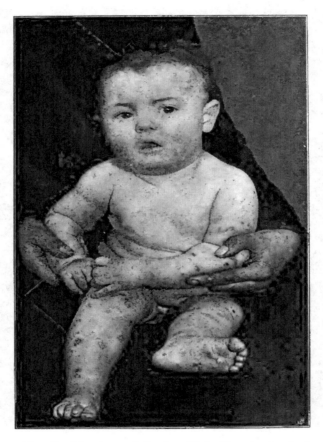

FIG. 39.—Scabies in an infant.   Note the plantar lesions.

itch.   In the male the presence of small scabbed lesions on the penis
is a valuable diagnostic feature.   As MacCormac has shown, penile
lesions are much commoner in soldiers than the interdigital lesions.
A crusted sore on the penis may lead to a suspicion of syphilis, but
there is no induration and there are itching lesions elsewhere.   Crusts
on the lower part of the buttocks are a common feature in scabies.

In babies an eruption on the hands and feet is either scabies or syphilis. In itch the lesions are often pustular and burrows may be seen. The mother may also be suffering from the disease and should be examined.

Strophulus in infants is often mistaken for itch. The lesions of strophulus are primarily small wheals with a central papule. The lesions are most developed on the extensor aspects of the limbs, and there are no burrows. The intense pruritus of *pediculosis corporis* may suggest scabies, but the distribution is different. Scabies spreads from the extremities to the trunk, while the body louse affects the trunk and especially the shoulders. An examination of the underclothing will often demonstrate the presence of the pediculus.

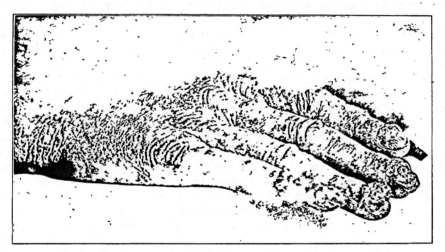

Fig. 40.—Norwegian or crusted scabies.   (Reproduced by kind permission of Dr. Wallace Beatty.)

Wallace Beatty and de Amicis remarked that their cases of the Norwegian type suggested neglected psoriasis from the heaping up of the scales. The nails may be affected.

Prognosis. Cure is rapid if the treatment is thorough.

Treatment. The patient is given a hot bath of twenty to thirty minutes' duration. The surface is well washed with soft soap and, unless the skin is delicate, scrubbed so that the burrows may be opened up. After the bath the whole of the trunk and limbs are rubbed with Unguentum Sulphuris of the British Pharmacopœia.

The patient then puts on an old sleeping suit, socks and gloves, and remains in them for twenty-four hours, when the bath and rubbing with ointment are repeated. Again the same sleeping suit, socks and gloves are worn for another twenty-four hours, when the bath and rubbing are once more carried out. On no account should more than three rubbings with ointment be given. If irritation persists after this it is almost certainly due to the sulphur, and for this a weak tar lotion—Liq. Carbonis. Deterg. 31, Aq. to ℥xx—should be applied.

In the Army there has been a revival of the old method of treating scabies by sulphur vapour. The apparatus consists of a wooden cabinet lined with brown paper. The roof of the cabinet has an opening for the head of the patient. The junction of the roof with the walls of the cabinet is lined with felt. The patient is given a hot bath and is well scrubbed with soft soap. He is then transferred to the cabinet in which he sits for fifty minutes with the head protruding through the aperture in the roof, a wet towel being applied round the neck. A sulphur candle (Jeyes) is placed in a corner of the cabinet, lighted, and the door is closed. An orderly watches the patient, who is removed immediately if there is any sign of faintness or dyspnœa. At the end of the fifty minutes the patient leaves the cabinet and puts on clean warm clothing. Itching is immediately relieved. Slight desquamation follows the application. The great merit of the method is that a soldier has only to lose one day for the treatment. The importance of this in time of war is obvious, both as regards the maintenance of the fighting strength and in the saving of hospital accommodation. To ensure satisfactory results every detail must be carefully observed. Excellent results have been reported by Major Bruce, and the measure deserves extended trial.

Chlorine gas (1 to 2 per 1,000 of air) has been used in a similar manner, the patient wearing the service gas helmet while under treatment. (Clark and Raper, *British Medical Journal*, 1917, XI., p. 113.)

Styrax, one ounce, and lard, two ounces, melted together, make a good ointment for children, as it is less irritant than sulphur.

Kaposi's naphthol ointment—Beta-naphthol, 15 parts ; Creta præp., 10 parts ; soft-soap, 50 parts ; lard, 100 parts—is a more pleasant application than Ung. sulphuris and may be used in private practice.

A rapid cure may be effected by the use of Balsam of Peru, three parts, glycerine, one part, applied all over the body after bathing at night. The patient should be kept in bed and the balsam should be allowed to remain on for a week, when a hot bath is taken, but sometimes albuminuria occurs.

In all cases the clothing and bedding should be disinfected by heat or by formalin.

Sarcoptes of animals. " Sarcoptic mange " is common in dogs and cats, and occasionally the disease is conveyed to the human

subject by pet animals. In one of my cases the face was affected.
Treatment by beta-naphthol ointment rapidly cured the condition.
By some it is believed that the Norwegian itch mentioned above is
caused by a sarcoptes derived from the wolf. Darier has also met
with cases of equine itch.

REFERENCES.—Case of Norwegian or crusted scabies : WALLACE
BEATTY. *British Journal of Dermatology*, 1913, XXV., p. 56. Plates.
Sarcoptes of Animals : NEUMANN. English translation, "Parasites and
Parasitic Diseases of Domesticated Animals," London, 1905. Sarcoptes
of Laboratory Animals : CRANSTON LOW. *Journal of Pathology and
Bacteriology*, 1911, Vol. XV. BRUCE and HODGSON. *British Medical
Journal*, 1916, II., p. 177.

The **Demodex folliculorum** is a minute acarian parasite about
350 μ long by 40 μ broad, living in the large sebaceous follicles.
It is not found in young children, but is always present in the adult.
It is believed to be non-pathogenic.

Pediculosis.

Three varieties of pediculus are met with : (1) Pediculus capitis ;
(2) Pediculus corporis vel vestimentorum ; (3) Pediculus pubis.

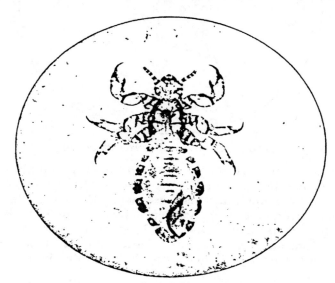

FIG. 41.—Pediculus capitis: x 25.

(1) **Pediculosis capitis.** The disease is caused by the pediculus
capitis, or head louse (Fig. 41).   The parasite is of a greyish

colour in Europeans, black in negroes, and yellow in the Chinese. It is about one-twelfth of an inch long and about half as broad. The females are larger than the males and more numerous. One female may lay 140 eggs, about four a day. They are white, somewhat conical, bodies attached to the hairs by a collagenous collar, which renders their removal difficult. If a hair on which ova are present be removed, it will be found that the nits can be pushed along the hair from the root to the free end, but not in the reverse direction. From one to a dozen or more nits may be found on one hair (Figs. 42 and 43). The ova hatch in from three days to a week, and are mature in eighteen days.

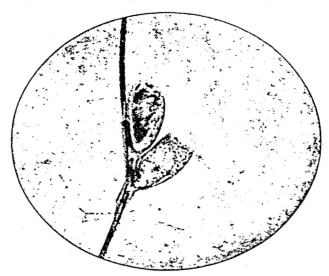

Fig. 42.—Hair with nits attached.

Pediculosis capitis is much more common in children than in adults, and in girls than in boys, owing to the length of the hair. It is one of the commonest diseases met with in hospital patients, but is not infrequent in private practice. Should it be seen in children of a household where the hygiene is good, the nurse or other attendant may be the source of infection. In boarding schools even of the better type it occurs probably from the general use of hair brushes, etc.

Symptoms. The pediculus itself does not produce any obvious lesions, but its presence on the scalp causes irritation and consequently scratching. The scratching produces excoriations which frequently become infected with pus-cocci. Crusts and scabs form which mat the hair together. The occipital region is the commonest site, but the whole scalp may be affected. Pustular lesions on the occiput, and, indeed, on any part of the face and neck, should always suggest pediculosis, and a careful examination for the parasite and nits should be made. The irritation and suppurative lesions cause enlargement and tenderness and even suppuration of the lymphatic glands of the occipital and cervical regions.

In neglected cases there may be a distinctive unpleasant odour. In the worst type, called " Plica polonica," the hair becomes matted

Fig. 43.—Pediculosis capitis in an adult male. Showing nits on the scalp-hairs.

together into a thick mass under which crowds of pediculi swarm and propagate.

Treatment. It is comparatively easy to destroy the adult parasites, but the nits are got rid of with difficulty. Even when the ova are killed the collar which attaches them to the hairs prevents their removal. In young children the most effective method of treatment is the removal of the hair by shaving and the application of the white precipitate ointment to the scalp. In cases where it is inexpedient to remove the hair, as in older girls and women, the following measures are best. The hair is soaked for twenty-four hours in paraffin or equal parts of paraffin and olive oil, the whole being covered by a linen cap. After this soaking, the scalp is washed

with warm water and soap.   The pediculi and the nits are killed,
but the latter remain attached to the hairs.   Assiduous combing
with a fine tooth-comb will remove them, and the application of
acetic acid during the combing facilitates the process.   Perchloride
of mercury, 1 in 1,000, applied to the 'hair will destroy the parasites,
and the combing and removal of nits can be carried out as after the
use of paraffin.   White precipitate ointment is used to get rid of any
impetiginous lesions which remain after the treatment.

(2) **Pediculosis corporis.**   The pediculus corporis vel vestimentorum is the largest of the human lice (Fig. 44).   The male is 3 mm.

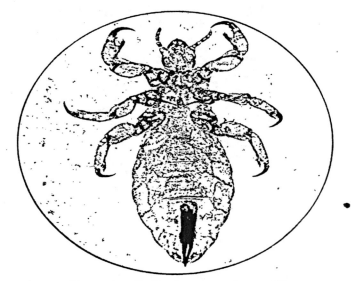

FIG. 44.—Pediculus corporis.   x 25.

long by 1 mm. broad, the female 3·3 mm. by 1·4 mm.   It varies in
colour in different races, being dirty grey in Europeans, black, smoky
orange, and yellow-brown in the darker peoples.   The parasite lives
in the underclothing and the ova are laid on it, and sometimes also
òn the lanugo hairs of the trunk, particularly about the nucha and
shoulders.   The ova, which are produced in enormous numbers,
are hatched in a week.   They develop from the larva to imago in
eleven days.   The adult life of the male is three weeks, and of the
female four weeks.   If they can get no food they die in thirty-six
hours.   The pediculus in searching for food crawls about the skin
and sucks blood.   Its presence induces itching and consequently
scratching.   Linear scratch marks, especially about the scapular

regions, chest, waist, and hips, should lead to the suspicion of pediculosis and examination of the body linen for the parasite. Hæmorrhagic points present on the skin are caused by the bites of the louse.

The disease is commoner in the adult than in the child, and especially in the elderly. It is worthy of note that it may occur in the elderly of all classes, and failing sight may sometimes account for its being overlooked.

Pediculosis corporis is of the highest importance in time of war. It is one of the greatest troubles in an army on active service, and

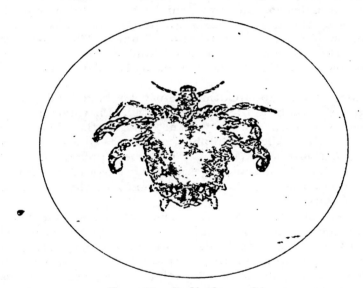

Fig. 45.—Pediculus pubis.

special attention must be directed to the disinfection of the men's underclothing. It is well known that typhus is conveyed by body lice, and the fact that the British Army has been free from this dire disease during the present war is largely due to recognition of the necessity of drastic measures directed to the extermination of body lice. Recently it has been demonstrated that trench fever is also conveyed from one individual to another by the excreta of lice inoculated by scratching. The spirochæte of relapsing fever (*S. recurrentis*) is also conveyed by the pediculus corporis.

In the tramp and vagrant seen in the poor law institutions and charitable shelters the conditions are much aggravated. The whole of the surface of the body may be deeply pigmented, the epidermis thickened and covered with scabs and crusts from secondary infection. These changes are mainly caused by constant scratching and dirt. To this aggravated condition the name phtheiriasis is given. It is popularly called " vagabond's disease." In one such case seen in my out-patient department the seams along the upper part of the man's trousers were marked by rows of ova of the pediculus. They were present in hundreds. As the man was going about without a shirt, the ova were laid on the garment next the skin, the trousers.

Diagnosis. Pediculosis corporis must be distinguished from scabies, from urticaria, and from senile prurigo. The characteristic distribution of the scratch marks about the shoulders, etc., in an old person should suggest the affection at once. The distribution of scabies on the extremities is a guide, and an examination should reveal the parasite. Urticaria should not be mistaken, as there are wheals.

Treatment. The underclothing must be baked or boiled, and the Unguent. Staphisagriæ of the British Pharmacopœia should be rubbed in all over the body after a hot bath. This should be repeated for three days. Sulphur ointment is also satisfactory. Lotions of carbolic acid (1 in 60) may be applied to relieve the irritation. Allan Jamieson suggested that a bag of sulphur should be worn round the neck as a prophylactic in elderly patients of uncleanly habits.

Prophylaxis on active service. The clothing should be turned inside out, and the seams examined. A hot iron passed along the seams will kill the parasites. Petrol or paraffin may also be rubbed into them. Where the conditions are suitable the garments may be disinfected by being placed in a Thresh disinfector for three-quarters of an hour, or boiling water for five minutes. Soaking in a 7 per cent. solution of chloride of lime for twenty-four hours, or in cresol $1\frac{1}{2}$ per cent. for an hour, is also successful.

To prevent infection the N.C.I. powder (Naphthaline 96, Iodoform 2, Creosote 2) is dusted on the underclothing. Vermijelli is also rubbed into the seams.

REFERENCES.—A. E. SHIPLEY. " Minor Horrors of War." R. F. CUMMINGS. " The Louse and its Relation to Disease." Brit. Mus. Nat, Hist., Economic Section, No. 2. A. D. PENROSE. *British Medical Journal*, May 17, 1916, pp. 745—784.

(3) **Pediculosis pubis.** The pediculus pubis (Fig. 45) attacks the pubic hairs, and occasionally the axillæ, the sternal hair, and the eyelashes and eyebrows are affected. In a very neglected child in my clinic the parasite had spread from the eyebrows on to the hair

of the anterior part of the scalp. The nits, being of different colour to those of the pediculus capitis, were quite easy to distinguish.

The crab louse is shorter than the other pediculi. It is about one and a half millimetres long. Infection usually takes place in sexual intercourse. Pediculosis pubis is occasionally seen in private practice, usually in men, and may be classed as a venereal disease. The chief symptoms are intense itching of the pubic region with excoriations from scratching. The nits are of similar shape and attached to the hairs in exactly the same way as those of the head louse. They are, however, brownish in colour, while the scalp nits are white.

On the eyelashes they form rows of tiny projections which on removal and examination under the microscope are seen to be fastened by a collar to the hair.

Treatment is simple. In bad cases it may be necessary to have the pubic area or axillæ shaved, or to remove the infected eyelashes. If this is not done the Ung. Hydrarg. Ammoniat. should be applied. The nits may be subsequently removed by the methods adopted for pediculi capitis. It is important to remember that if a too strong preparation, such as Ung. Hydrarg., be used a mercurial dermatitis may be set up, and this is aggravated by the continual application of the remedy. The patient should therefore be warned against too vigorous treatment.

Pulex irritans (Common Flea).

The common human parasite is the *Pulex irritans*. It occurs rarely in dogs and cats. The cat-flea (*Ctenocephalus felis*) and the dog-flea (*Ctenocephalus canis*) occasionally attack man. The rat-flea (*Xenopsylla cheopis* and *Ceratophyllus fasciatus*) transmits bubonic plague.

The flea lays its eggs in cracks between boards, wainscoting, animals' kennels, birds' nests, etc.

The bite of a flea causes a minute hæmorrhage into the skin, with a red areola. In some cases wheals form. Flea-bites may be mistaken for the eruptions of the exanthemata. The application of ammonia, thymol, or carbolic relieves the irritation. As a prophylactic, pyrethrum is recommended. In infected houses the floors should be washed and " crude oil " emulsion, naphthaline, or paraffin applied.

Cimex lectularius (Bed Bug).

The *Cimex lectularius* is the parasite met with in England. In warm climates another variety, *C. rotundatus*, occurs. The bed-bug is 5 mm. long, 3 mm. broad. It has a reddish-brown, wingless body. The eggs are white and 1 mm. long. The parasite peculiarly attaches itself to human habitations and may migrate with luggage. Its disagreeable odour is caused by an oily secretion. The bug hatches in eight days, and it may live for a year without food. It is known to convey the spirochæte of relapsing fever and the bacillus of plague, and recently suggestions have been made that the *Bacillus lepræ* may be carried by it. The lesions produced by the bug are more inflammatory than those of the flea. There is a central hæmorrhage where the blood has been sucked and around it a wheal or papule. The treatment is the same as that described for the irritation produced by the flea. Menthol is also useful.

To free a room from the parasite fumigation with hydrocyanic acid, burning sulphur for four hours or longer, are advised. Benzene, kerosene, oil of turpentine, and perchloride of mercury solution are applied locally.

Culex (Gnat or Mosquito).

Mosquito bites and gnat bites are attended with the formation of erythematous spots or wheals. In certain subjects the number and extent of the lesions may lead to considerable swelling. The local application of ammonia solution or of carbolic lotion will relieve the irritation.

Ixodes (Ticks).

The wood-tick (*Ixodes ricinus*) is a minute parasite of the Acarus family. Its habitat is usually pine trees. It alights on the surface of the body and inserts its proboscis to suck blood. If not disturbed it may remain for several days, and when gorged with blood it drops off. Turpentine or paraffin applied to the head of the parasite kills it, and it releases its hold. If forcibly removed the proboscis may be left in the skin and set up inflammation. The lesion caused by the tick is a small wheal.

African tick-fever is caused by *Spirochæta duttoni*, conveyed by the *Ornithodorus moubata*.

Leptus autumnalis (Harvest Bug).

The leptus is the larva of *Trombidium holosericum*, and perhaps of other species. It is of bright red colour and 3 to 4 mm. long. It attacks the human skin usually in July and August. The lower part of the legs and ankles are the areas commonly affected, but other parts are not exempt. The lesions are due to the burying of the head of the parasite in the epidermis. Probably some irritant is introduced, for violent irritation follows and red papules and wheals form. The scratching may lead to secondary lesions. The best application is carbolic acid in olive oil, or sulphur ointment.

Dermanyssus gallinæ, an acarine parasite on birds, occasionally produces a papular eczematous eruption on the backs of the hands of poultrymen.

RARER AND EXOTIC AFFECTIONS CAUSED BY ANIMAL PARASITES.

Cysticercus of the Skin. The cysticerci of *Tænia solium* and other tapeworms may reach the subcutaneous tissue and produce multiple (rarely single) tumours. The lumps are at first rounded and elastic and vary in size from a pea to a walnut. They usually occur on the trunk and extremities. The old cysts dry up, contract, and may calcify. There are no symptoms unless the size of the tumour tends to its irritation from friction, etc.

The importance of this condition lies in differential diagnosis. The tumours have to be distinguished from lipomata, sebaceous cysts, gummata, and new growths. A case in the London Hospital under Dr. Wilfred Hadley suggested multiple fibromata. The history of the tumour, its elastic character, and the finding of hooklets in the fluid evacuated by puncture are the points upon which a diagnosis is made. The tumours should be removed.

REFERENCE.—PYE-SMITH. *British Journal of Dermatology,* November, 1892.

Dracunculosis (Guinea Worm). The female dracunculus (a variety of thread worm) is the cause of the disease. It is from twenty-five to thirty inches long. Like other parasites of its class, it has two hosts. It enters the human body in a minute crustacean which lives in water. In its human host a fresh cycle of development takes place. The worm becomes sexually mature, and the female, when impregnated, starts to find her way to the surface of the body. The male disappears. Should the female escape from the body with the embryos, or should the latter emerge and get into water, the asexual cycle may start afresh, and *via* the body of the crustacean the parasite may again reach its human habitat. The life of the Guinea worm in the human body is from nine months to a year. The disease is only met with in the tropics. India, Central Asia

Egypt, Guinea, and other parts of the African continent furnish the patients seen in this country.

The lesion is characteristic. A flat swelling forms on the surface

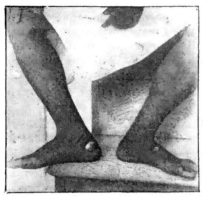

Fig. 46.—Bulla of Dracunculosis. (From Dr. Daniel's "Tropical Medicine.")

of the body, and in it the worm may be felt rolled up "like a coil of soft string." Sometimes the parasite migrates from one part to another. The foot is the part most commonly affected. When

Fig. 47.—Female Guinea Worm under skin of forearm. Photograph kindly lent by Dr. Bahr.

the worm comes to the surface a local inflammation with the formation of a bulla occurs, and occasionally severe inflammation develops. The diagnosis can only be made if the characteristic tumour is observed. There is marked eosinophilia.

Treatment consists in the injection of the area occupied by the parasite with a solution of perchloride of mercury, 1 in 1,000. This kills the worm, which may be subsequently removed. If the dracunculus is in the act of emerging when first seen, the injection may be made to kill it, and the worm may then be wound out. Douching the lesion with water for a fortnight will cause expulsion of the embryos.

Anchylostomiasis.   Hook - worm   Disease.   Tunnel - worker's Anæmia. A toxæmia with progressive anæmia caused by Nematode worms, the *Anchylostoma (Agchylostoma) duodenale* and the *Necator americanus*. It occurs in the tropics and in mines and tunnels where there is a high temperature. Infection takes place by the mouth or through the skin. The cutaneous eruption caused by the embryos entering the skin is characterised by itching wheals, papules or vesicles which may develop into pustules and ulcers. In Cornwall the lesions are called " bunches." The eruption appears on the soles of the feet and lasts ten to twelve days. Later there are leucocytosis and eosinophilia with anæmia, dropsy and fever. The ova are found in the fæces.

Other Nematodes causing cutaneous eruptions are the *Filaria Bancrofti*, producing lymphangitis with attacks of erysipelatous eruption (*vide* Elephantiasis, p. 417), the Loa loa, *Onchocerca volvulus, Rhabditis niellyi*, and *Strongylus stercoralis*.

The Loa and other species of filaria produce smooth, shiny, raised tumours about five centimetres in diameter on the face, head, arms and ankles. The lesions, which are known as Calabar swellings, are painless and last only two or three days, but they may recur after the patient has left the tropics.

The Onchocerca volvulus occurs in West Africa. It produces lymphangitis, and small tumours on the scalp, chest and limbs. The Rhabditis niellyi causes an itching papular eruption.

Craw-Craw is the name given to many itching affections in the tropics, but a special affection occurs on the West Coast of Africa resembling prurigo or scabies. The fingers and forearms are the parts most affected. The lesions are hard itching papules. Scratching causes excoriations and crusts. There are no burrows. Filariæ have been found in the lesions, but the actual cause is still uncertain. Coolie-itch is a similar refractory affection with intense pruritus and a papular, vesicular and pustular eruption. It occurs in coolies working in low-lying tropical regions. A nematode worm has been described as occurring in the lesions.

Grain   Itch.   Acaro-dermatitis   urticaroides (Schamberg). A dermatitis caused by the *Pediculoides ventricosus*. The parasite feeds on the wheat-straw worm and the joint worm (varieties of Isosoma) and on the grain moth (Silotropha).   It attaches itself to the skin by its sucking discs and claws, and apparently introduces some irritant.   Most cases have been seen in persons using new straw-mattresses, but others have occurred in men unloading grain.

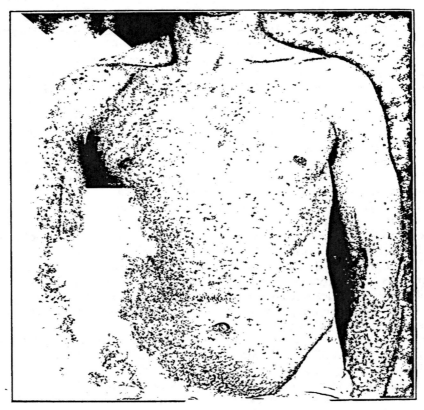

FIG. 48.—Grain itch.   Patient was one of a large number of dock porters affected, while unloading a cargo of cotton seed.

Fig. 48 shows the chest of a man under my care who was attacked with many others while unloading a cargo of cotton seed in one of the London Docks.   The eruption consisted of urticarial wheals, papules and minute vesicles on the chest, arms, face, neck and back. The incubation period is from twelve to sixteen hours.   Pustulation may occur, and in severe cases fever, sickness and albuminuria have been reported. Removal from the cause and the application of soothing and anti-pruritic lotions are required.

Copra Itch is a dermatitis attended by intense itching caused by the *Tryoglyphus longior*. It occurs in persons handling copra, the dried kernel of the cocoa-nut. The hands, arms, legs and sometimes the whole body are studded with numerous intensely itching papules often covered with blood crusts due to scratching. Papulo-pustules may occur. The affection has been carefully studied by Castellani. The incubation period is twenty-four to forty-eight hours. A 10 to 15 per cent. beta-naphthol ointment applied daily gives the most relief.

Myiasis is the name given to the invasion of the skin by the larvæ of the Œstridæ (gadflies or botflies). The lesions are suppurative and resemble boils. The actual parasite differs in various parts of the world. In tropical America the maggot is the larva of the *Dermatophilus cyaniventris*, in Africa the *Cordylobia anthropophaga* or Tumbu-fly, in Asia the *Sarcophara ruficornis*, and in Europe the *Gastrophilus nasalis*. The larvæ develop in the skin of some warm-blooded animal or in man. The stigmata of the embryo are seen at the orifice of the boil. Removal of the parasite by forceps and local antiseptic are recommended.

Black Fly Dermatitis. The black fly (*Simulium venustum*) produces a hæmorrhage by its bite, but for several days to some weeks a papulo-vesicular lesion persists. The surface weeps and heals with a thin scar. There is intense itching, heat and burning. Grouped bites form confluent lesions with much œdema. The glands are enlarged.

Brown Tail Moth Dermatitis. The brown-tail moth (*Euproctis crysorrhœa*) has attracted attention in the United States and Canada as destructive to fruit trees and in its larval state (May—June) as a cause of dermatitis. The first symptom is itching, occurring in half an hour after exposure. This is followed by an eruption of erythematous or urticarial type. The lesions are the size of a pea, raised and firm. They may occur in groups or coalesce into patches. The arms and upper part of the trunk are involved, and the eruption may last for a few days to several weeks. Mild toxic symptoms may develop.

The nettling hairs of the larva are the source of the irritant. A lotion of perchloride of mercury, 1 in 2000, followed by painting the part with collodion, is recommended.

Handling plants or vegetables in which the hairs have been embedded is the cause.

Myiasis linearis or **Larva migrans.** A linear eruption produced by the larvæ of the Gastrophilus and other parasites.   The clinical features are the development of a narrow, raised red line, $\frac{1}{6}$ to 1 inch broad and several inches long and generally sinuous.   The line extends at one end while the opposite extremity slowly fades.   The affection may last for several months to two or three years.   There is intense itching.   Hutchens advised the injection of cocaine followed by a drop or two of chloroform.

A *circinate creeping disease* characterised by rings with an elevated angry red border occurs in gardeners in tropical regions.   It lasts for two or three weeks, and is probably caused by an allied parasite. Castellani and Chalmers also describe a *dermatitis macrogyrata* of the palms, the lesions being scaly and crusted and forming large rings. Lead lotion appears to be the best application.

Pulex Penetrans (Jigger or Sandfly).   The Jigger (chigoe) is a tropical parasite, the *Pulex penetrans* or *Dermatophilus penetrans*, resembling a flea.   The impregnated female enters the skin head first to lay its eggs.   An œdematous swelling develops which is followed by the formation of pustules and rarely of ulcers and gangrene.

REFERENCES.—P. S. ABRAHAM.   *Transactions of the Dermatological Society of Great Britain and Ireland*, III., p. 62.   W. DUBREUILH.   "Les Diptères cuticoles chez l'homme."   *Archiv. de Médicine Expérimentale*, March, 1894.   SIR P. MANSON.   "Tropical Diseases."   CASTELLANI and CHALMERS.   "Tropical Medicine."   CASTELLANI.   "Copra Itch." *British Journal of Dermatology*, 1913, p. 19.   SCHAMBERG.   "Grain Itch." *Journal of Cutaneous Diseases*, 1910, XXVIII., p. 67.   KENNETH WILLS. "Barley Itch."   *British Journal of Dermatology*, XXI., 1909, p. 249. "Brown Tail Moth Dermatitis."   TYZZER.   *Trans. International Derm. Congress*, 1908, Vol. I., p. 169.   J. C. WHITE.   *Boston Med. and Surg. Journal*, 1901, Vol. CXLIV., p. 399.   "Black Fly."   STOKES.   *Journ. Cutaneous Diseases*.   XXXIII., pp. 186, 280.

CHAPTER VII.

AFFECTIONS CAUSED BY VEGETABLE PARASITES.

The Ringworm and Favus fungi.

THE labours of Sabouraud in Paris, and of Colcott Fox and Adamson in this country, have extended our knowledge of the

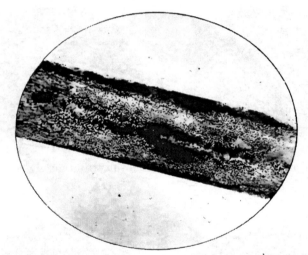

FIG. 49.—Microsporon Audouinii. Microphotograph of infected hair.
$\frac{1}{6}$ obj.

fungi which attack the human skin and hair to a remarkable degree. Four groups with many individual species are distinguished. They are (1) the Microsporons, (2) the Endothrix Trichophytons, (3) the Ectothrix Trichophytons, and (4) the Achorions.

(1) **The microsporons.** The commonest in this country is the *Microsporon Audouinii* (Fig. 49). It is peculiar to the human race, and is very rare after puberty. It causes both scalp and body ringworm. When attacking a hair it forms a mass of closely-packed small spores, resembling a mosaic around the shaft. The mycelium

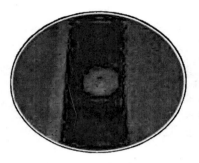

Microsporon Audouinii.

Trichophyton endothrix.

Trichophyton gypseum.

Trichophyton neo-endothrix plicatile.

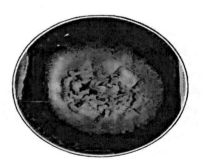

Achorion Schonleinii.

Achorion Quinckeanum.

FIG. 50.—Photographs of Ringworm and Favus cultures made by
Dr. H. M. Scott in Author's clinic.

is scanty and in the form of short rods. Grown on Sabouraud's maltose proof medium (water, 1,000 ; crude maltose (Chanut), 40 ; granulated peptone (Chassaing), 10 ; gelose 18), the cultures are snow-white downy discs, with a central tuft or knob (Fig. 50).

Microsporons of similar type have been found in the cat, dog, horse, and guinea pig. Eleven different forms have been differentiated by Sabouraud from cultures. The most important of those attacking the human subject are M. felineum, M. lanosum (vel. canis), M. equinum. Both the hair and the glabrous skin may be affected.

(2) **The endothrix trichophytons** (Fig. 51) (Trichophyton

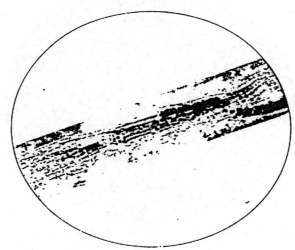

Fig. 51.—Endothrix tricophyton. Microphotograph. Note that parts of the fungus are unstained. ⅙ obj.

Endothrix). These fungi are believed to be peculiar to man. They cause ringworm of the scalp, body, and beard, and occasionally of the nails. The spores are slightly larger than those of the microsporons, but the special point of distinction is their arrangement in chains. They are found inside the hair (endothrix). The mycelium is rod-like. Sabouraud describes thirteen varieties of true endothrix and two neo-endothrix. Colcott Fox differentiated four common varieties in London : (a) a cream-coloured or white crateriform culture, T. crateriforme ; (b) a primrose crateriform culture, T. sulphureum ; (c) a greyish yellow culture with acuminate centre, T. acuminatum ; and (d) a violet culture, T. violaceum. The yellow crateriform cultures are found in ringworms of the scalp, beard, and body and nails. The acuminate form attacks the scalp only, and the violet variety the scalp and beard. Some varieties are curiously local in their incidence, *e.g.*, T. neo-endothrix plicatile is common in Denmark, but extremely rare in England and France.

(3) **The ectothrix trichophytons** (Fig. 52) (Trichophyton Megalosporon Endo-ectothrix). These fungi are derived from animals (horses, cattle, pigs, deer, cats and dogs) and birds. They are communicable to man, and from one human subject to another either directly or indirectly. They cause ringworm of the body, beard

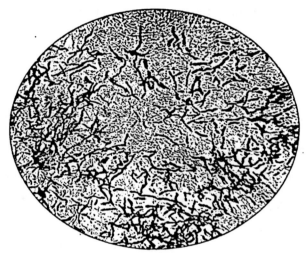

FIG. 52.—Ectothrix trichophyton. Microphotograph of scraping stained. ⅙ obj.

and nails, and occasionally of the scalp. The spores are arranged in chains, and the mycelium is made up of jointed rods.

Sabouraud describes eight varieties with small spores, and seven with large spores. Of the last, the rose variety appears to be more common in Newcastle-on-Tyne than in London (Bolam).

The common forms are :—(i.) A horse ringworm producing scaly rings in man (*T. equinum*). The cultures are yellow discs with rays at the margin. (ii.) A horse and cattle ringworm producing inflammatory, suppurative lesions in man (*T. gypseum*). The cultures are white and remarkably luxuriant. (iii.) A cat ringworm, producing vesicles in rings in the human subject (*T. felineum*). The cultures are white discs with marginal rays. (iv.) A bird ringworm, with cultures of a rose pink colour (*T. roseum*).

. Sabouraud's *Epidermophyton inguinale* (Fig. 53), as yet found only in man, is the cause of tinea cruris, the affection formerly called eczema marginatum of the groin and axilla. Castellani, Pernet, Nieuwenhuis and others have described other forms of tropical epidermophyton.

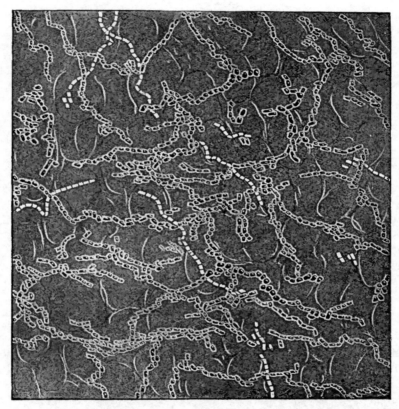

Fig. 53.—Epidermophyton inguinale in scrapings.   Kindly lent by Dr. Sabouraud.

The Achorions (Fig. 54). The favus fungi are now known to be multiple. The commonest is the *Achorion Schonleinii*. It attacks the scalp, glabrous skin, and the nails, and (rarely) the mucous membranes. The characteristic lesions are sulphur yellow cups. The mycelium is in the form of short jointed branching rods. The spores are comparatively large and abundant. Cultures on maltose agar are dirty yellowish brown with an irregular ridged surface (Fig. 50). Other forms are a mouse favus (*Achorion Quinckeanum*) with white cultures (Fig. 50), similar to those of the microsporon,

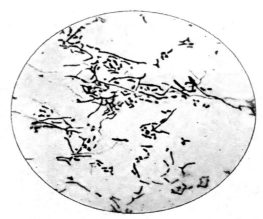

FIG. 54.—Achorion Schonleinii. Microphotograph. $\frac{1}{6}$ obj.

and a brown culture derived from the horse. Both these varieties may attack the human subject, producing clinically indistinguishable lesions.

Endodermophyton. Castellani and Perry have described three varieties of fungus causing Tinea imbricata and they are grouped under this term. A *Cladosporium* has also been described in Tinea nigra and *Malassezia* in Tinea flava of the tropics, and an *Aceladium* in an ulcerative dermato-mycosis.

Ringworm of the Glabrous Skin.

Ringworm of the glabrous skin may be due to the Microsporons, to the Endothrix and Ectothrix trichophytons, and the Epidermo-

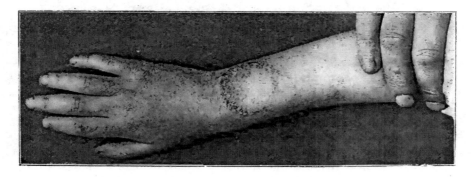

FIG. 55.—Tinea circinata. Ectothrix fungus from cat.

phytons. There may be co-existent ringworm of the scalp and of the hairy parts. The lesions are rings, sometimes concentric, and plaques. The fungus can be demonstrated by scraping the patches or rings and examining the scrapings under the microscope in a little liquor potassæ. The organism is found in the epidermal scales and in the lanugo hairs.

Microsporon cases. The lesions produced by the *Microsporon Audouinii*, the commonest scalp fungus in children, are commonly

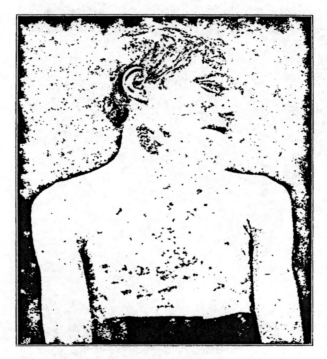

Fig. 56.—Tinea. Widely spread ectothrix infection from calf.

small red circular or oval scaly patches. They are generally confined to the neck, shoulders, and face. Occasionally the lesions are in the form of scaly rings. The microsporons of animal origin, *e.g.*, *M. Lanosum*, produce ringed lesions, and they are usually more extensive than those of the human parasite. These are also commoner in children. My youngest patient was only seven months old ; the lesion was on the wrist.

Endothrix cases. The lesions are ringed and often associated with scalp lesions. The fungus is found chiefly in the form of

Plate 12.

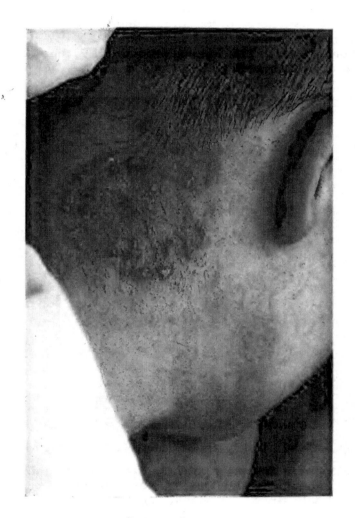

ECTOTHRIX RINGWORM.

The lesions are vesico-pustules arranged in concentric rings. The
patient was a groom.

mycelium. The differentiation of the forms of fungus can only be made by cultures. Three remarkable cases, due to the *tricho-phyton plicatile*, under my care, a boy and his two sisters, had extensive areas of the body and limbs affected. In the boy there was an extensive scaly eruption with rings, and in addition raised scaly plaques and ulceration of the umbilicus. The nails were also affected. Although cultures of the common crateriform type were obtained, the disease was probably a foreign ringworm, though I was unable to trace its source.

Ectothrix cases. In some of these it is easy to trace the infection to some animal or bird. The lesions are often of a more inflammatory type than those met with in the two preceding groups. Infection from the horse may cause scaly rings or suppurative ringed lesions which may lead to a suspicion of coccal infection (Plate XII.). Grooms, carmen, and others who come in contact with horses often suffer, but exactly similar lesions are met with in infection from cattle (Fig. 56). In some cases the beard is affected. A boy whose duty it was to lather the customers in a barber's shop attended my out-patient department some time ago with characteristic ringed scaly lesions on the right hand. Examination proved the presence of an ectothrix fungus. In ringworm derived from the cat and dog suffering from a variety of " mange " the lesions are commonly vesicular. Infection from birds affected with " white crest " may also cause tinea circinata, sometimes of a bullous type (Whitfield). The cultures, as already mentioned, are pink.

Eczematoid Ringworms of the Groins and Extremities.

Tinea cruris (Fig. 57), is a form of tinea affecting the inner side of the thigh, groin, and gluteal cleft. The disease may spread on to the genitals and down the thighs, and sometimes attacks the axillæ. It is due to the epidermophyta : *E. inguinale E. perneti, E. rubrum (Trichophyton purpureum)*. The lesions are brownish, well-defined scaly patches, which were at one time called " Eczema marginatum." From the warmth and moisture of the affected parts the scaly lesions may become eczematous. In the tropics the condition is commonly known as " dhobie itch." This form of tinea appears to be highly infectious, the infection being probably conveyed through the seats of water-closets, and is eradicated with difficulty when it appears in institutions.

Eczematoid ringworm of the extremities. Whitfield and

Sabouraud have drawn attention to the common occurrence of eczema-like lesions *between the toes*, especially the fourth interdigital space, and extending on to the plantar surface of the foot for a short distance, in patients who suffer or have suffered from Tinea cruris, and also independently (Fig. 59). This type of ringworm, which may persist for years and recur in warm seasons, is far from uncommon and is often overlooked. The following types may be recognised :—

(1) *Acute vesicular and bullous.* This comes on suddenly and has

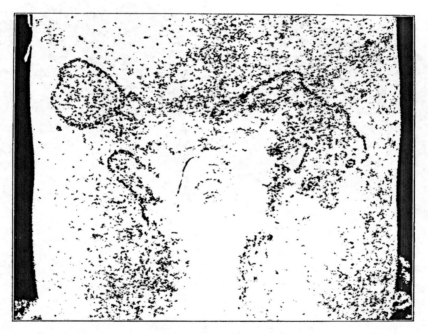

FIG. 57.—Tinea cruris. Epidermophyton inguinale in scrapings of lesions.

the character of a vesicular eczema or of pompholyx (dysidrosis). The vesicles are deep and look like boiled sago-grains. The contents are clear, and there is little or no surrounding erythema. The vesicles dry up in a few days and a brown stain is left. In other instances the vesicles rupture, showing a red glazed surface with a border of scales (Plate XIII.). The vesicles may remain discrete and the scaling may attract little attention, or a distinct hyperkeratosis may persist. Where the vesicles are in groups they often become confluent and large blebs may form. The bleb may dry up leaving an area of

Plate 13.

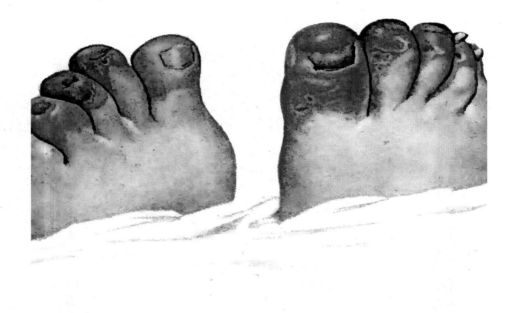

Eczematoid Ringworm of Toes of ten years' duration, contracted in the tropics.

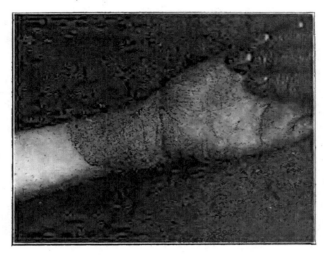

FIG. 58.—Eczematoid ringworm. Female, æt. 12.

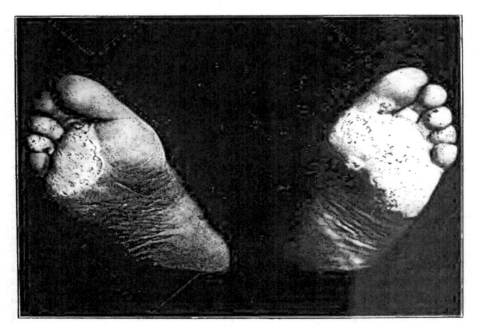

FIG. 59.—Eczematoid ringworm of interdigital clefts and soles. Female
æt 62. Disease believed to be contracted at a Turkish bath.

scale, or while central healing takes place fresh vesicles form at the margin and the whole process slowly spreads. Pyogenic infection is common.

The fingers and palms, toes and sole are the common sites.

(2) *Intertrigo type.* This occurs between the toes and is secondary to (1). White sodden masses of epidermis form in the interdigital clefts and spread on to the neighbouring plantar surface.

(3) *Hyperkeratosis.* This occurs chiefly on the heel, and is due to repeated vesication in a thick horny epidermis where there is no maceration. The horny layer may be greatly thickened.

Diagnosis of ringworm of the glabrous skin. The diagnosis is usually easy on account of the ringed character of the lesions. It will have been noticed, however, that some of the microsporon lesions are in the form of flat scaly discs, and these are usually associated with tinea capitis. The term " circinata " must not mislead the student. Psoriasis and certain syphilitic eruptions sometimes occur in rings, but those of psoriasis are covered with silvery scales, and there are usually characteristic patches on the elbows and knees. The syphilitic eruptions are polymorphous and their colour is distinctive, and there are usually other general symptoms to aid the diagnosis. The flat scaly form of tinea has to be distinguished from the scaly seborrhoide, which is usually associated with dandriff of the scalp. The ultimate diagnosis of a doubtful case rests with the finding of the fungus by the microscope.

Chronic eczematoid lesions with a well-defined edge should always be suspected and scrapings examined for fungus.

Tinea cruris has to be distinguished from erythrasma, which affects the same parts Erythrasma is more chronic, less scaly, and is caused by a different parasite (*vide* p. 149).

Eczematoid ringworm of the toes may cause difficulty. The fungus is not easily demonstrated, but there is often a history of groin ringworm which will help the diagnosis.

The **prognosis** in tinea of the glabrous skin, excepting that occurring between the toes, is usually good.

Treatment. As a rule, this does not offer much difficulty. The greasy scales are removed by washing with soft soap and warm water, and a parasiticide ointment such as Unguent. Hydrarg. Ammoniat. is rubbed in. Painting with tincture of iodine to produce exfoliation of the infected epidermis is also very useful. Whitfield's ointment, containing Ac. Benzoic grs. xxx., Ac. Salicylic grs. xxiv., Ol. Lini and Adeps Lanæ, of each half an ounce, is very useful, especially in the groin ringworms. Resorcin, 1 drachm in Tr. Benzoin Co. 1 ounce, may also be recommended. In the rare cases which resist treatment by these simple measures, chrysarobin, 5 to 40 grains, in an ointment or plaster may be necessary.

Trichophytic granulomata. In exceptional cases the ringworm and favus fungi may cause a deep inflammatory reaction, a true granuloma with epithelioid and giant cells. Most of the cases described have been in the Italian clinics. The writer had a severe case in a lad in whom there was a large ulcer about the umbilicus ; the margins of the ulcer were thick and infiltrated. In addition there were numerous flat, button-like granulomata on the trunk and extremities and on the left ear. The granulomata contained mycelium of a fungus identified by Dr. Sabouraud as the *Trichophyton plicatile.* The patient had a characteristic scaly eruption on the trunk and limbs and tinea of the nails. The granulomata left deep scars, and part of the left ear was destroyed. The patient's two sisters suffered from ringworm of the body, and one had a few similar granulomatous lesions. Other varieties of fungus have caused similar reactions, viz., *Trichophyton violaceum, gypseum,* and *regulare.* Injections of the growths with carbolic acid appeared to be the most useful treatment in my case.

Tinea unguium (Ringworm of the Nails).

Ringworm of the nails is more common than is supposed. It may be associated with tinea of other parts or may occur independently. It is much commoner in the female than in the male. Of 22 cases under my care in private practice, 16 were females and 6 were males. Of the males 4 had lived for years in the tropics and the disease had been contracted abroad. My youngest patient was fifteen, the majority being between twenty-nine and forty (11 cases). In my experience tinea unguium is commoner in private practice, and in some instances I feel convinced that the disease is contracted from manicure instruments, and there is no doubt it is spread from nail to nail by the process of manicure performed by the patient or otherwise. The fungi most commonly found are trichophyta of the endothrix type, especially *T. crateriforme* and *T. rosaceum.* Cranston Low in 19 cases found trichophyta in 16 cases, favus in 2, and in 1 an unknown fungus. Of the trichophytic cases 14 were females and 2 males. In one instance both husband and wife were affected, and there were two sisters. I had three members of one family whose nails (and other parts) were affected by the *T. plicatile.* Tinea unguium is exceedingly chronic, and may last for many years.　One or more of the finger nails may be attacked (Fig. 60).　The toe nails, from the protection afforded by the boots and socks, are rarely affected.　The nails become discoloured, opaque, and brittle, and under the free margin a scaly mass forms.　Very rarely the root of the nail is the part first involved. It may be difficult to determine whether the disease of the nails is due to a coccal infection or to ringworm, but careful microscopical examination of scrapings of the nails after soaking in liquor potassæ will clear up a doubtful diagnosis.　It must be remembered that

Fig. 60.—Tinea unguium.　Endothrix fungus grown.

psoriasis and eczema also affect the nails.　In such cases there will usually be evidence of these diseases in other parts.

Treatment.　The treatment of tinea unguium is very tedious. The nails may be removed and the matrix dressed with salicylic acid ointment (B.P.), or, after scraping, the ends of the fingers may be wrapped up in solutions of iodine, as recommended by Sabouraud. Norman Walker advises soaking the nail under lint and a finger-stall with Fehling's solution for a day or two, removing the softened nail, and then dressing with copper sulphate solution, 10 grains to the ounce.

Favus of the Glabrous Skin.

Favus rarely attacks the non-hairy parts of the body, but I have seen several instances in the Skin Department at the London Hospital. The lesions have been circular yellow cups about the size of a sixpenny

Plate 14.

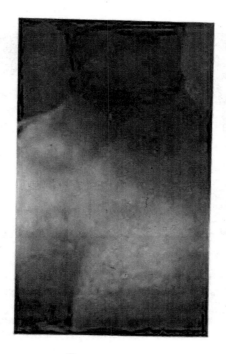

TINEA VERSICOLOR.

The lesions are scaly patches of *café au lait*
tint.   Female, aged 26.

piece. There has been some little inflammatory thickening around in some instances. On removal of the cup a superficial ulcer was found. The cups examined in liquor potassæ under the microscope showed characteristic branching fungus with spores. In four cases the scalp was quite free from disease. In very rare instances the infection of the trunk and limbs is extensive. A good example

FIG. 61.—Favus (Achorion Quinckeanum) of glabrous skin. The scalp was unaffected.

is figured in Schamberg's " Diseases of the Skin," p. 181. Here also the scalp was free. Adamson has demonstrated that some of these cases of favus of the glabrous skin are not due to the Achorion Schonleinii, but to the mouse achorion, A. Quinckeanum. Fig. 61 depicts a case of this kind.

Provided the condition is borne in mind, there is no difficulty in recognising the affection. The yellow character of the cup suggests, and microscopical examination confirms, the diagnosis. Treatment by local antiseptics is efficient.

Tinea versicolor (Pityriasis versicolor).

This disease is caused by the *Microsporon furfur* (Fig. 62). The fungus is found in the horny layer of the epidermis. It consists of an abundant mycelium of interlacing jointed threads. The spores are arranged in masses or clumps. In scrapings of the skin examined under the microscope in liquor potassæ the parasite is easily demonstrated. Cultures can be grown on epidermin agar and other media.

The lesions are fawn-coloured, well-defined patches. At the onset they are no larger than a pin's head, but they spread peripherally, and by coalescence large areas may be covered. The fine branny scales can be removed by scraping, showing the disease to be on the surface. The chest and back are the parts usually affected, but the upper extremities may be involved. It is exceedingly rare on the face. There is often some itching. McEwen has described a case in which there were papular lesions.

The patients usually perspire freely and are averse from the free use of soap and water. Enquiry will often elicit the fact that the patient sleeps in the vest worn by day. Infrequent change of underclothing is also common. Warm weather favours the development of the disease. Consumptives who sweat a great deal are frequently affected.

The disease is easily cured, but relapses are common.

The **diagnosis** is made by the microscope.

The affection has to be distinguished from pigmentary anomalies.

Leucodermia is characterised by white patches of skin with areas of excess of pigmentation surrounding them. There is no scaling, and the patches cannot be removed by scraping. Arsenical pigmentation of the trunk is of a dappled character, and here again scaling is absent. Syphilitic pigmentation is usually seen on the neck. In Addison's disease the pigmentation is of a bronze colour and is most marked where pigment is normally well developed. The mucous membranes are also affected.

Treatment. Frequent changes of the underclothing should be enjoined, and especially the removal of the day garments on going to bed. The affected areas should be washed with soft soap and warm water, and the following lotion freely applied :—

       R. Acidi sulphurosi (B.P.), one ounce ;
         Aq., three ounces.

Some apply sulphur ointment and lotions of the hyposulphites, or perchloride of mercury, 1 in 1,000.

Recurrences may be obviated by the use of a sulphur soap.

REFERENCE,—McEwEN. Papular type. *Journ. Cut. Dis.*, January, 1911.

Tinea flava (tropical pityriasis versicolor) is very common in

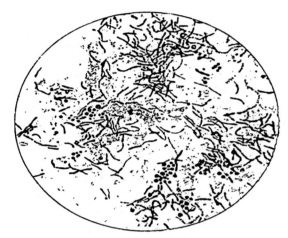

FIG. 62.—Microsporon furfur. Microphotograph. $\frac{1}{6}$ obj.

the tropics. The fungus is the *Malassezia tropica*. The eruption closely resembles pityriasis versicolor, but is very persistent, and may attack the face. In Europeans the eruption is pinkish.

Tinea nigra is another tropical affection. The patches are dull black.

REFERENCE.— CASTELLANI. "Tropical Form of Pityriasis Versicolor." *Journ. Cut. Dis.*, 1908, p. 393.

Erythrasma.

A parasitic disease producing reddish-brown patches in the genito-crural and axillary flexures and the gluteal cleft.

Etiology. The affection is a trivial one, and is often overlooked. It is, therefore, difficult to estimate its frequency. Men are more commonly affected than women. The disease does not appear to be contagious in a marked degree, for I have known instances of its persistence for years without being conveyed from husband to wife. Warmth and moisture are necessary for its development.

Pathology. The lesions are caused by the *Microsporon minu-*

tissimum (*Nocardia minutissima*), a fungus consisting of extremely fine, interlacing, jointed threads without branches. A few spores may be present. The fungus lies in the epidermal scales. Cultures are obtained with difficulty.

Clinical features. The eruption consists of well-defined brownish or brownish-red patches with a small amount of branny scale. It

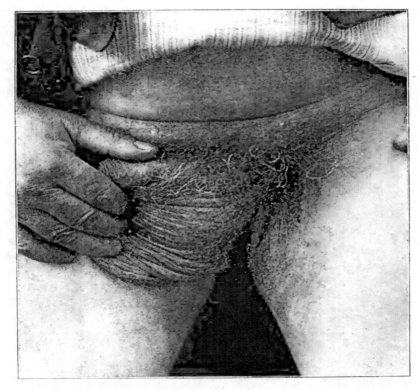

Fig. 63.——Erythrasma.

is confined to areas which are warm and moist, *e.g.*, the genito-crural flexures, groins, gluteal cleft and axillæ. In rare cases the patches extend on to the limbs. The disease is exceedingly chronic, but spreads very slowly. Relapses after apparent cure are common.

Diagnosis. Tinea versicolor is distinguished from erythrasma by the presence of lesions on the trunk. Tinea cruris is more inflammatory and its evolution is more rapid. The microscope would settle any difficulty in diagnosis.

Treatment. The treatment is the same as that of tinea versicolor.

REFERENCE.—PAYNE. "Observations on some Rare Diseases of the Skin." 1889.

Tropical Ringworms.

Tinea alba is a chronic, diffuse, powdery, squamous eruption on the limbs and trunk caused by a tropical fungus, the *Epidermophyton rubrum* (*Trichophyton purpureum*).

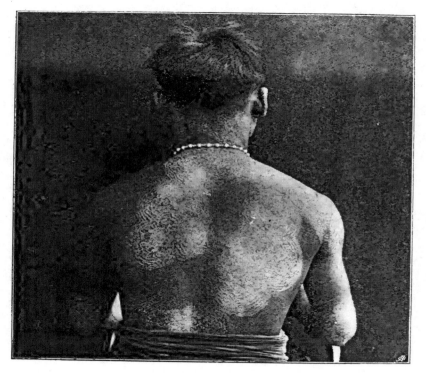

FIG. 64.—Tinea imbricata.   Photograph lent by Dr. C. W. Daniels.

Tinea albigena occurs in the Far East. It affects the palms and soles chiefly. The eruption may become bullous. Ultimately hyperkeratosis occurs. It may last for years, and is caused by a trichophyton.

Tinea tropicalis was first described by Sabouraud as occurring in patients returning to Europe from the Far East. The legs are affected first. The eruption is erythemato-squamous in small spots, which become ringed or polycyclic. There is much itching. The fungus is the Trichophyton Blanchardi.·

Tinea imbricata (Tokelau Ringworm).—Tinea imbricata is a variety of ringworm met with in the tropics. The fungus *Endodermophyton concentricum*, or *E. indicum*, is found in abundance in the epidermic scales, but the hair follicles usually escape. The mycelial threads are long, and the spores are irregular in shape.

Both sexes are equally liable, but children are more affected than adults. The disease is highly contagious.

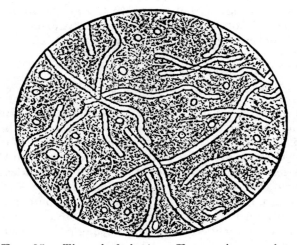

Fig. 65.—Tinea imbricata. Fungus in scrapings.

The disease may attack any part of the trunk and limbs, but avoids the scalp and other hairy parts.

The lesions consist of patches or concentric scaly rings. They spread peripherally, and produce an appearance like watered silk (Fig. 64). The scales are thin flakes, like tissue paper, which are firmly attached towards the margin of the ring and free towards the centre. The concentric rings and systems of rings are well shown in the photograph, for which I am indebted to my colleague, Dr. C. W. Daniels. The separation of the scales leaves concentric rings of fawn colour. There is no interference with the general health, and the only symptom is itching.

Manson advises destruction of the clothes, sulphur baths, and the application of strong iodine solutions. In a case recently under my care I found the application of Resorcin ʒij in Tr. benzoin Co. ʒj, as advised by Castellani, rapidly removed the eruption.   Chrysarobin ointment is also recommended.

Tinea intersecta occurs in Ceylon and Southern India.   It is caused by the *Endodermophyton Castellani.*   The eruption consists of dark brown elevated patches, which shrivel and crack.

Ulcerative dermato-mycosis.   Castellani has recently published an account of a new ulcerative dermato-mycosis occurring in Ceylon, Malaysia and the Balkans, characterised by multiple, rounded or oval, sharply defined ulcers with a red granulating base.   The ulcers are crusted or discharging pus, and are frequently mistaken for syphilis.   They run a tedious course.   A fungus of hypho-mycetic type, classified by Pinot as belonging to the genus *Aceladium,* is the cause.   Iodide of potassium (grs. xx. t.d.) internally and a weak perchloride of mercury locally are recommended.

Ringworm of the Hairy Skin.

Ringworm of the scalp (Tinea tonsurans).   Ringworm of the scalp may be caused by the microsporons, by the endothrix trichophytons, and by the ecto-endothrix trichophytons.   The proportions vary considerably in different countries and in different classes of patient   In 700 consecutive cases in children attending the elementary schools seen in the London Hospital clinic, Munro Scott found 628 patients (336 males and 262 females) affected with the microsporon and 72 (39 males and 33 females) suffering from endothrix ringworm, respectively 89 and 11 per cent.   Ecto-endothrix cases are very rare in London.   In the ringworm schools of the Metropolitan Asylums Board, Colcott Fox found the endothrix fungus in as many as 14 per cent.   He believed that the aggregation of a number of children in institutions predisposes to a higher proportion of this variety of organism.   In Paris, Sabouraud states that only one-third of his cases are due to the microsporon and two-thirds to the large-spored fungi.   Further south in Europe the proportion of the small-spored cases is even smaller.

The clinical features of scalp ringworm vary with the parasite.

Microsporon cases.   This disease is especially one of childhood.   Most of the cases occur in children between five and fifteen years.   It is exceedingly rare after puberty, but Dr. Oliver has reported cases from my clinic of two mothers infected from their children.   On the other hand, I have seen several instances in infants at the breast.   The disease is contracted by direct contact, by infected caps, hair brushes, and the like.   Though commonest in the children attending the elementary schools, no class is exempt.   Outbreaks in large boarding schools are far from uncommon.

In its earliest stage ringworm of the scalp appears as a small scaly spot, perhaps not larger than a threepenny piece, with a few broken hairs present on the patch.   It is, of course, often overlooked owing to the hair.   In the more advanced cases the areas infected may be numerous and of varying size.   Older patches are covered with ashen grey scales (Fig. 66), but the special character is the number of broken hairs scattered over the patchlike stubble   Sometimes there are many small collections of scales around the hair follicles only.

Fɪɢ. 66.—Tinea tonsurans.   Microsporon Audouinii.

In the cases of long duration the whole scalp may be covered with scales, and a diagnosis of dandriff or scurf is often made   Again, notice must be taken of the broken hairs scattered all over the patch. .These hairs are about one-tenth to one-eighth of an inch in length. They are easily removed by the forceps, and on inspection are found to be without lustre and surrounded by a white sheath.   This sheath, on examination under the microscope in a little liquor potassæ, is found to consist of a mass of small round spores closely set to form a kind of mosaic.   The fractured ends of the hairs are irregular   In the scalp lesions of young children, and also in others in whom the hair is short, a ringed arrangement of the scaly lesions is sometimes

observed. The changes in the hair are identical. In the microsporon ringworms of animal origin ringed lesions are the rule (Fig. 67).

On the neighbouring parts of the glabrous skin flat or ringed
patches often co-exist with microsporon tinea of the scalp. The
ringed character is more marked in the microsporons of animal
origin. (*Vide* Ringworm of the Glabrous Skin, p. 141.)

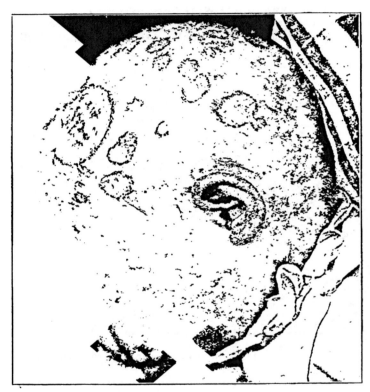

FIG. 67.—Microsporon Lanosum. Note the ringed arrangement of
the scalp lesions.

If left alone or inefficiently treated the disease may last indefinitely,
certainly for two or more years. It has no effect on the general
health, and there are usually no subjective symptoms, though itching
is sometimes complained of. Its great importance is its interference
with the education of the patient, as quarantine must be enforced
until the disease is eradicated.

Kerion. Occasionally the lesion produced by the *microsporon*

Audouinii is inflammatory, a condition known as Kerion. One or more patches become red, swollen, and boggy. The swelling does not contain pus, and on incision only a serous fluid exudes. Broken hairs may project from the swelling, and these are found to contain fungus.

Jadassohn, of Berne, and Rasch, of Copenhagen, have shown that an eruption of pale-red follicular papules may occur on the body in cases of kerion. The condition is described as a secondary lichenoid trichophytide.

Endothrix cases. This variety also occurs in childhood, but it may persist beyond puberty. As already mentioned, a greater proportion of this type is found in large aggregations of children in the barrack schools of the unions than in the children attending the elementary day schools.

The lesions differ from those of the microsporon. They are not scaly, but the hairs are brittle, and sometimes break off flush with the scalp, producing an appearance which has been described as " black-dot " ringworm (Fig. 68). In other instances the hairs may be half an inch long, or even longer. Sometimes the areas are bald, so-called " bald ringworm," and the broken hairs are only found at the margins. The disease is exceedingly chronic and even more persistent than that due to the small-spored fungus. It appears, however, to die out spontaneously after the lapse of years, but may continue to adult life.

The hairs have a normal cuticle, but the interior of the shaft contains spores in chains and rod-like mycelium (Fig. 51).

Ecto-endothrix cases. The parasite in these cases is derived from some animal, either directly or indirectly. The lesions are apt to be more inflammatory than those of the preceding classes. The areas are round and scaly, or of the *Kerion* type, inflamed boggy red swellings, which on incision do not show pus, but only a little serous oozing. I have seen cases of this type from infection by cattle and horses. The course of this form of scalp ringworm is much shorter than that of the other varieties.

Diagnosis. The diagnosis of scalp ringworm may be attended with little difficulty, but it is often missed, especially in the endothrix cases. The following rules should be borne in mind. Scaliness of the scalp in a child is more likely to be due to ringworm than anything else, and the microscope should be at once used to examine any broken hairs. This will prevent mistaking the microsporon. The endothrix cases are more difficult. If the patch is bald, alopecia areata may be suspected. The examination of hairs from the margin should be made in any doubtful case. Black spots on a bald area should at once raise the suspicion of endothrix tinea, and the coiled-up hair should be expressed like the comedo, and then examined under the microscope. Finally, hairs broken off short should always be examined for tinea. Kerion might be mistaken for forms of pustular infection, if the condition is not thought of.

Prognosis depends on the thoroughness of the treatment.

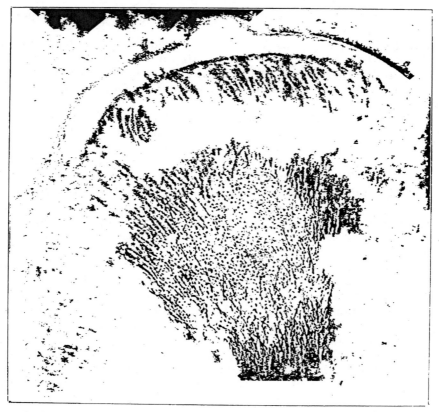

Fig. 68.—" Black-dot " ringworm of the scalp. Endothrix fungus.

Treatment. Vaccine treatment has been tried in several clinics, but the results so far have not been such as to warrant the abandonment of local measures. The local application of antiseptics in the form of ointments and lotions, even when introduced under pressure, rarely effects a cure of tinea tonsurans. Antiseptic remedies which set up a local inflammation give better results. These are oleate of copper and oleate of mercury and other mercurial ointments applied to the shaven scalp after washing with soft soap and warm water. Aldersmith's combination, Phenol 1, Ung. Sulphuris 2, and Ung. Hydrarg. Nitrat. 2, is a useful formula. Formalin, phenol, croton oil, have all been used, but great care must be employed, as scarring may be left. Adamson speaks highly of an ointment made of equal parts of sodium chloride and vaselin applied every morning, and fomentations of hot water at night. The salt ointment sets up .an acute folliculitis of the infected areas and does not affect those which are free from disease. I have tried it occasionally and have seen good results. The great trouble is the pain which the application causes in some cases.

X-ray treatment. By far the most efficient method of treatment is the application of the X-rays. It must be understood that they have no parasiticide action. They are simply used to remove the hair. The best method of procedure is Adamson's modification of Kienbock's system. The X-ray tube is enclosed in a lead glass shield with a wide circular opening opposite the anode. To the margins of this opening three pegs sloping towards the centre are fixed. These pegs rest against the scalp of the patient. They are of such a length that the area of the scalp under treatment is exactly fifteen centimetres from the anode of the tube. At one side of the aperture in the lead glass screen is placed the pastille of Sabouraud and Noiré. As a rule it is necessary to treat the whole of the scalp, and to effect this the hair is cut short all over. Five points are then taken and carefully marked with blue pencil. The first point is marked an inch and a half to two inches behind the centre of the margin of the hairy scalp in front. The second point is taken immediately above the lower edge of the scalp in the middle of the occipital region. The third point is in the middle line of the scalp, exactly midway between the two points already marked. The remaining two marks are symmetrically placed on each side, just above and a little in front of the top of the ear. Each point should be exactly five inches from its neighbours. The patient is now placed so that one of the points marked is exactly in the middle · of the three pegs attached to the tube holder, and the rays are allowed to play upon the area exposed to the anode until the Sabouraud pastille changes to the proper tint. Corbett's apparatus for exactly measuring the tint is of great value in estimating the colour of the pastille. I now use it for all cases of Tinea. I work to four-fifths of the pastille dose. The process is repeated for each of the five points. Radiation administered in this way covers a greater area than is actually required, and the parts below the scalp margin on each side of the head and the frontal and occipital regions are covered

with rubber impregnated with lead. The exact adjustment of the
application to the spots named ensures that the whole of the scalp
shall be equally exposed to the rays. The central parts of each area
get the full dose of rays, while the margins are overlapped and

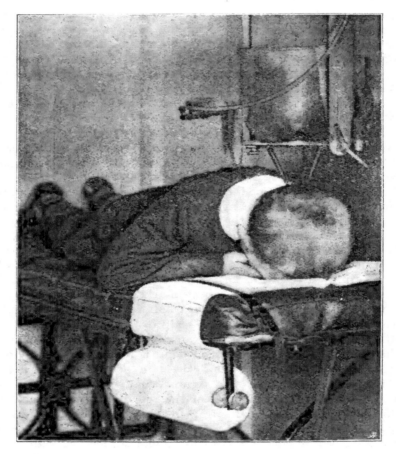

FIG. 69.—X-ray treatment of ringworm of the scalp.

receive a dose from two successive exposures. The principles upon
which this is carried out are discussed in the chapter on Radiation
and the Skin (p. 77).

If the proper dose has been given the hair begins to fall out on the
fifteenth day, and epilation is usually complete in about a week,
though the hair may continue to fall for five weeks if a rather less

dose has been given.   The new hair begins to grow in from a month
to six weeks, and it is curious to note that it is sometimes curly.
If the ringworm is limited to a small area the procedure is modified
and the rays are simply applied to the affected part after the hair
has been clipped short.

The five exposure method of treatment materially shortens the
time required for complete epilation, and with a tube in good working
order each exposure should not last longer than ten minutes, but the

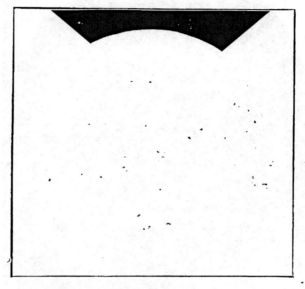

FIG. 70.—Complete epilation produced by
X-rays.   Case of ringworm.

time is of little importance, the essential point being that the pastille
should be turned to the proper tint and no more.

As soon as the hair has fallen out the child is free from infection,
but during the defluvium the falling hairs are laden with spores
and the patient may infect himself or others.   During the defluvium
the scalp is frequently washed, and a mild antiseptic ointment, such
as Ung. Hydrarg. Nitrat. Dil., is applied daily.   Occasionally a
pityriasic eruption occurs two or three weeks after X-ray treatment.
It is believed to be a " seborrhoic " dermatitis set up in a susceptible
subject by the reaction.

The treatment is most effectual, and when carefully carried out
is free from risk.   For some years past we have treated over 800 cases

Plate 15.

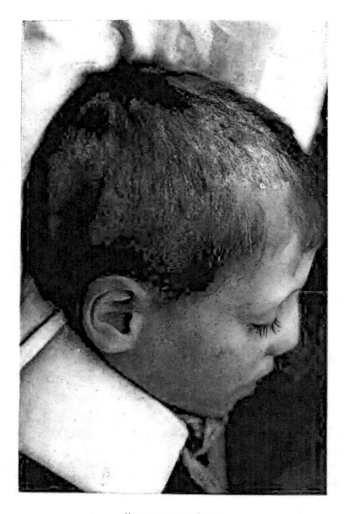

FAVUS OF THE SCALP.

The minute yellow cups on the scalp are characteristic. The patient
was a Polish immigrant.

per annum in my clinic at the London Hospital with most satisfactory results. There is no foundation for the suggestion that the brain is likely to be injured. This has been proved experimentally and also by a now lengthened experience. I do not, however, advise the use of the rays in children under four years of age, and I make a point of the parents or guardians of the child thoroughly understanding exactly what is going to be done. I insist on having the written consent of the parent, which will save trouble should one unfortunately come across a case in which there is idiosyncrasy, but with the use of the pastille such accidents as permanent baldness after the use of the X-rays are scarcely ever met with. An insufficient dose, followed by incomplete epilation, is annoying on account of the delay, for a second application of the rays should not be made until at least a month has elapsed from the first treatment.

The treatment of favus of the scalp and of ringworm of the beard region is carried out on the same lines as that of tinea capitis.

Favus of the Scalp.

Favus is a common disease in Eastern Europe and in Asia, but is rare in this country except in children of Polish and Russian immigrants. The Achorions attack the scalp, the glabrous skin (*vide* p. 140), and the nails, and exceptionally the mucous membranes. I had under my care for some time a boy whose tongue was involved.

The fungus invades the hair and the true skin, and produces inflammatory changes in the latter leading to cicatricial atrophy.

The characteristic lesions of scalp favus are small sulphur-yellow cups, about a tenth to an eighth of an inch in diameter (Plate XV.). They consist of masses of fungus, epidermal cells, dried sebum and débris. The cups are rather difficult to remove, and in chronic cases their removal discloses small bleeding cavities, showing that the true skin is involved. The involvement of the derma leads to a characteristic patchy cicatricial atrophy. The scalp affected with favus has a peculiar mousey odour. The disease is exceedingly chronic, and may persist to adult life. Darier and Hallé report a case of favus in which a granulomatous nodule developed in the corium.

Epilation with the X-rays is required, and this must be followed by vigorous treatment with antiseptics. Owing to the depth to which the fungus penetrates, favus is much more difficult to eradicate than the ringworms.

Tinea barbæ. Tinea sycosis. Ringworm of the Beard.

Tinea barbæ is a folliculitis of the hairy regions of the face caused by endothrix and ectothrix trichophytons.

Etiology. This form of ringworm is generally contracted at the barber's, the fungus being introduced by the shaving-brush and (possibly) by the razor. An interesting case has already been mentioned in which the barber's assistant, who lathered the customers, attended my clinic with ectothrix tinea on the hand. The infection may also be derived from contact with other subjects (human or animal) suffering from tinea.

Pathology. The lesions may closely resemble a coccogenic sycosis, the follicles being converted into small abscess cavities. In my clinic W. J. Oliver found the *Trichophyton violaceum* the commonest fungus in beard ringworm. The *Trichophyton rosaceum* came next in frequency. *T. fusiforme* and *T. plicatile* were found, and also *Microsporon felineum*. An avian fungus with pink cultures and an equine variety have been described.

Clinical features. The primary lesion is a round red itching spot, which may be covered with scales. In some forms a scaly ring develops ; in others, the margin of the ring is papular, or papulo-pustular, and sometimes vesicular. There are often scattered pustules about the hairs at some distance from the primary patch or ring. In a few cases the lesions are red, raised, boggy swellings like kerion of the scalp. The hairs are easily removed, and the fungus is demonstrated without difficulty. The disease may last an indefinite time, sometimes for years, and tends to relapse. Cicatrices may be left. Tinea may be present upon the glabrous skin in other parts, and such lesions may be primary or secondary. Ringworm of the moustache is very rare.

Diagnosis. The diagnosis is made by examining the hair under the microscope in a little liquor potassæ. This should be done in every case of folliculitis of the beard region.

Treatment. The most satisfactory measure is epilation by means of the X-rays, followed by the inunction of an ointment of oleate of copper (half a drachm to the ounce), or of Ung. Hydrarg. Ammoniat., or an ointment of phenol, as advised under Tinea capitis.

Tinea ciliorum. Tinea of the eyelashes is exceedingly rare. I have not met with a case.

Tinea of the pubic hair is very rare also.

REFERENCES.—R. SABOURAUD. " Les Teignes." · Many figures and plates. T. COLCOTT FOX and BLOXALL. *British Journal of Dermatology*, 1896, Vol. VIII. T. COLCOTT FOX. "Endothrix Trichophytic Flora in London." *Trans. Roy. Soc. Med.* (Dermatological Section), 1908, p. 49. H. G. ADAMSON. "Observations on the Parasites of Ringworm." *British Journal of Dermatology*, July and August, 1895, and cases with cultures in recent years. SIR MALCOLM MORRIS. "Ringworm in the Light of Recent Research." 1898. C. RASCH. "Secondary Lichenoid Trichophytides." *British Journal of Dermatology*, XXVIII., p. 9. Plates. "Eczematoid Ringworm of the Groin and Extremities." WHITFIELD, SABOURAUD, etc. *British Journal of Dermatology*, XXIII., p. 375. CRANSTON LOW. "Tinea of Nails." *Edinburgh Medical Journal*, February, 1911. H. M. SCOTT. Series of 700 cases. *British Journal of Dermatology*, XXIII., p. 330. J. H. SEQUEIRA. "Trichophytic Granulomata." *British Journal of Dermatology*, 1912, XXIV., p. 207. Plates and references. DARIER and HALLE. "Granuloma in a Case of Favus." *Annales de Derm. et de Syph.*, March, 1910, p. 129. CASTELLANI. "Tinea Imbricata." *British Journal of Dermatology*, 1913, XXV., p. 377. CASTELLANI. "A New Ulcerative Dermato-mycosis." *Brit. Med. Journ.*, 1916, II., p. 486. Plates.

Piedra. Trichosporosis.

A parasitic affection of the beard and scalp characterised by irregularly-placed white nodules on the hairs.

Etiology. The disease occurs in the Balkans and rarely in other parts of Europe. It is, however, most common in the natives of Cauca in Colombia.

Pathology. Both in the exotic and in the rare European cases fungi have been found, the swellings on the hairs consisting of masses of rather large spores, *Trichosporum giganteum*, under the epidermal layer.

Clinical features. The nodules are remarkably hard, of a black or dark brownish colour, rounded or fusiform in shape, but sometimes placed on one side of the hair only. They are removed with great difficulty, and do not tend to fracture of the hairs.

Treatment. Shaving or cutting the hair close to the root is the best remedy, but antiseptics such as 1-2,000 perchloride of mercury in an ethereal solution have been recommended.

REFERENCE.—Abstract of paper by BEHREND. *Annales de Derm. et de Syph.*, 1890, Vol. I., p. 829.

Trichomycosis axillaris flava, rubra et nigra.

A nodular affection of the axillary hair caused by a *Nocardia* with or without chromogenic cocci.

The disease is confined to hot, damp tropical districts and occurs in both Europeans and natives. It was first described by Castellani in 1911.

The fungus is a fine bacillary organism, *Nocardia tenuis*. This occurs alone in the yellow variety and in symbiosis with *Micrococcus nigrescens,* which produces a black pigment in the black type, and with a coccus producing a red pigment in the red variety.

Clinical features. The affected hairs present yellow, black or red nodular excrescences. They are easily removed by scraping. The hairs are not brittle. The affection is chronic, but usually disappears when the patient returns to a cold climate.

Treatment. The application of formalin ten grains to an ounce of spirit and a weak sulphur ointment are sufficient to remove the disease.

REFERENCE.—CASTELLANI. *British Journal of Dermatology,* 1911, p. 341.

Myringomycosis.

A scaly, dirty grey or brownish, usually moist coating lining the external auditory meatus. The surface is often dotted with round yellowish, green or blackish spots, and there is frequently serous exudation. The eruption may extend to the membrana tympani.

On removing the scale a moist bleeding surface is found. Itching is complained of.

There is no tendency to spontaneous cure. It is believed to be caused by the *Aspergillus niger* and *glaucus.*

Treatment. An alkaline lotion to remove scale, followed by an alcoholic lotion, is recommended.

REFERENCE.—BURNETT. "System of Diseases of Ear, Nose and Throat," Vol. I., p. 190.

Rarer Vegetable Parasites.

We have now to consider diseases of the skin caused by—
(1) Varieties of aspergillus—pinta and mycetoma.
(2) The ray-fungus and its allies—actinomycosis and mycetoma.
(3) Yeast-like fungi—blastomycosis.
(4) Mucedines—sporotrichosis and mycetoma.

Pinta. Caraate.

Mal del Pinto, Tina (Mexico). Cute (Venezuela). Querica (Panama).

This disease occurs in Mexico and Central and South America. The eruption consists of scaly spots of varying colour, grey, black, bluish red, dull white. The red spots are seen in white people, but in negroes the lesions are commonly dull bluish black. White spots are seen in the stage of involution. There are several forms, each probably being due to a separate organism. The disease is chronic, lasting for months or years. The face, neck, and the hands and feet are first attacked, but no part of the body is exempt. The lesions closely resemble in their character those of tinea versicolor. The general health is unaffected.

The disease is due to several forms of aspergillus, the organisms affecting the epidermis, and possibly the corium in some cases. The mycelium is composed of fine branching filaments with fructification at the termination of slender branches. *Penicillium* is found in one variety, and *Monilia* and *Montoyella* in others.

The local application of mercurial antiseptics appears to be the most successful treatment. Iodine and chrysarobin are also recommended.

REFERENCES.—SIR P. MANSON. "Tropical Diseases," 1898, p. 585. SABOURAUD. *Annales de Derm. et de Syph.*, 1898, IX., p. 673. CASTELLANI and CHALMERS. "Tropical Medicine," p. 1512. SANDWITH. *Brit. Med. Journ.*, 1905, II., pp. 479 and 1270 (bibliography).

Actinomycosis.

Actinomycosis of the skin is rare. It is characterised by the formation of chronic indurated and suppurative lesions containing the ray fungus. It may be primary or secondary to infection of the mucous membranes.

Etiology. The actinomyces (*Nocardia bovis* and *N. israeli*) is a saprophyte which grows easily in the human body. It is often directly introduced through the buccal mucous membrane or the gums. The habit of chewing grass while walking in the fields is probably a common method of infection, and many of the patients have to deal with cattle and horses, and the fungus may be introduced with hay or corn. Lord has demonstrated the organism in the contents of carious teeth and successfully inoculated guinea-pigs. In cattle it is the cause of " wooden tongue." The disease occurs in all countries, but apparently is more common on the Continent than in the British Isles.

Pathology. The organism is found in the pus or in the tissues in the form of yellowish grains about 1-250 to 1-25 inch in diameter visible to the naked eye in the pus. It is composed of a mycelium forming a small mulberry-like mass from which extend thick refracting radiating processes. Cultures are not easy to

obtain, unless the pus cocci are removed by making anærobic cultivations. The filaments segment into spores when grown on appropriate media. The inoculation of animals is difficult, but has been
successful in bovines. The parasite causes a leucocytic reaction and
proliferation of the fixed cells to form nodules. Giant cells, plasma
cells, and epithelioid cells are found in the nodules, and around them

FIG. 71.—Actinomycosis. Case seen with the late Mr. H. L. Barnard.

there is a zone of leucocytes and connective tissue cells. The vessels
are often involved.

Clinical features. Cutaneous actinomycosis is rarely primary :
in most cases the skin becomes infected when the parasite is being
extruded from lesions of the deeper structures. On account of the
frequency of infection of the buccal cavity, the seats of election are
the face and neck, which are attacked in more than two-thirds of
the cases. A decayed tooth was the site of infection in the case
figured (Fig. 71) and in two others under the author's care. The

thorax, the abdominal wall, and the anus may also be affected, but the disease is exceedingly rare on the limbs.

The primary cutaneous lesion is a nodule in the hypoderm and deep part of the cutis. The surface of the tumour is at first pinkish, and palpation reveals that it has deep attachments. Later the centre of the swelling softens and fluctuates, the skin becomes purplish and then perforates, allowing the escape of a serous, purulent, or bloody fluid, containing yellowish grains in which the fungus is found. While this process of enlargement and breaking down is proceeding, other nodules develop in the neighbourhood and fuse together, and then pass through the same stages, swelling, softening, and the extrusion of the parasite in the discharge. Ultimately an indurated nodular mass is formed with an ulcerated surface from which a number of fistulous tracks pass into the indurated base.

Progress and course. The new formation tends to invade the deeper tissues, the muscles and bones, and it may also attack the blood-vessels.

The **diagnosis** of actinomycosis is suggested by the nodosity of the tumours, their agglomeration and chronicity, and their deep attachments. The colour of the mass, the foci of suppuration, and the situation are also indications, but the diagnosis is made by the demonstration of the ray fungus. It is remarkable that the glands are not enlarged.

Actinomycosis of the skin has to be distinguished from dental abscess, which is much more acute and attended with pain. Lupus vulgaris is excluded by the absence of the apple-jelly nodules, and scrofulodermia by the character of the pus and the presence of the fungus. Syphilitic gummata are more acute and tend to break down early, and the ulcer has a punched-out character. In epithelioma the glands are involved early, but a biopsy will set any doubt at rest. Sporotrichosis can only be differentiated by an examination of the pus, for actinomycosis gives the Widal reaction.

Prognosis. Actinomycosis is exceedingly chronic and progressive, but treatment has a marked influence if applied sufficiently early and before secondary infection with coccal organisms has occurred. If the disease is allowed to run its course it ultimately proves fatal.

Treatment. Iodide of potassium should be administered in actinomycosis, but it must be given in large doses and steadily increased up to 240 grains a day. Vaccines, preferably autogenous, in doses of half a million gradually increased to fifty million elements have been given with success. The injections are made every three to seven days.

Incision and scraping of the sinuses with injection of 1 per cent. solutions of sodium or potassium iodide often hasten healing, and I have found applications of the X-rays of service.

Nodular tumours in the subcutaneous tissue caused by other varieties of Nocardia have been described. In one form the nodules are juxta-articular (Jeanselme).

REFERENCES.—SIR M. MORRIS. *Lancet,* June 6, 1896. Plate and references. J. J. PRINGLE. *Med. Chir. Trans.,* LXXVIII. The New Sydenham Society's "Microparasites in Disease" contains abstract of J. ISRAEL's "Aktinomykoses des Menschen," 1885. References. LORD. *Boston Med. and Surg. Journal,* July 21, 1910. MERIAN. *Dermatolog. Wochenschr.* References to primary actinomycosis of skin.

Mycetoma or Madura Foot.

This disease is endemic in India and East Africa, and is seen occasionally in North and South America. It appears to be caused

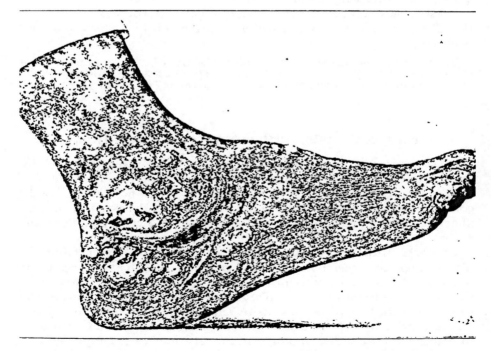

FIG. 72.—Madura foot. From a water-colour drawing by Dr. A. D. P. Hodges, of Uganda.

by several vegetable organisms. In some instances a streptothrix, closely related to the ray fungus, has been found ; in other cases a form of mucedo and numerous other fungi and an aspergillus have been demonstrated.

The disease starts in the sole in natives who go barefooted, rarely in the hand and knee, by the formation of nodosities which soften and allow a sanious fluid containing the parasites to escape. Bullæ appear on the lesions, and the breaking down of the nodules leads to the formation of fistulous tracks from which granular masses resembling fish roe are extruded. These masses contain the organisms. White, red, and black lesions have been observed. Their structure closely resembles that of a syphilitic gumma, and the infiltration may slowly spread until the whole of the foot is involved. The swollen foot is gravely deformed and in a condition of pseudo-elephantiasis (Fig. 72), while the rest of the leg undergoes atrophy, and this increases the disproportion between the enormously swollen extremity and the remainder of the limb. The disease is essentially chronic, often lasting for many years.

Treatment. Iodides have some influence in the early stages of the disease, but in most instances surgical interference becomes necessary.

REFERENCES. — MANSON. "Tropical Diseases." CASTELLANI and CHALMERS. "Tropical Medicine," p. 1527. VANDYKE CARTER. "On Mycetoma or Fungus Foot of India." London, 1874.

Blastomycosis.   Blastomycetic Dermatitis.

Blastomycosis was described by Gilchrist in America and by Busse and Buschke in Germany in 1894. It is a chronic infectious disease characterised by the formation of nodules and warty growths containing multiple minute abscesses. As a rule, the skin is primarily affected, but the disease may become disseminated throughout the body.

Etiology. Blastomycosis is caused by a pathogenic yeast fungus. Yeast fungi are occasionally found in connection with other organisms in some ulcerative skin lesions. In the condition now under consideration the lesions are due solely to the blastomyces. Most of the cases on record have been seen in Chicago and its neighbourhood and in other parts of the United States, but the disease has been seen in Europe and in India, Japan, and South America. I reported one case which appears to be of the same nature. The patient had always lived in the country and had a local reputation as a " pig doctor."

The allied affection, Coccidiosis, occurring in the Joaquin Valley in California, is due to the *Coccidiodes immitis.*

The disease commonly occurs in adults, between the ages of thirty and fifty. It is more frequent in men than in women, and the majority of the sufferers have lived in bad hygienic surroundings.

Pathology. The organism is a rounded or ovoid yeast-like body, often showing bud formation. The capsule has a double contour. The blastomyces can be grown on glucose agar and other media, and forms white cotton wool-like cultures. In the older cultivations there is a mycelium which shows some evidence of sporulation. Guinea-pigs and some other animals can be inoculated and the organism can be recovered from them.

The microscopical anatomy of the lesions is peculiar. There is an enormous increase in the rete mucosum, which sends down irregular processes containing minute abscesses full of polynuclear cells, a few giant cells, and the organism. In systemic blastomycosis the lungs are always affected, and abscesses varying in size from minute miliary collections of pus to cavities containing a pint or more are found. The abscesses are also found in other organs, including the brain, the spinal cord, and the serous cavities, and the joints and bones, including the vertebræ. There may also be large purulent collections in the retropharyngeal region, in the psoas and other muscles, and in the fascial planes.

Clinical features. The earliest manifestation is a small dry papule covered with a crust. It gradually enlarges to form a plaque the size of a coin or larger. The edge of the plaque is shelving and of a dark red or purplish colour, and in it are minute abscesses visible often only with a lens. The lesions are soft and boggy, and the surface is covered with warty or small fungating excrescences. On puncturing one of the abscesses a peculiar glairy muco-pus can be withdrawn, and in this the blastomycetes are found. The disease progresses slowly, and large areas may be involved. Ultimately cicatrisation may occur.

There is no part of the skin which is exempt, but the face, hands, including the nails, and arms are most commonly affected. Systemic blastomycosis has been described by Hyde, Montgomery, Ormsby, and others. The general symptoms are those of a chronic pyæmia, with the formation of multiple abscesses in various parts of the body. There are irregular fever, wasting and exhaustion, with symptoms due to the local infection of the different organs, particularly the lungs, kidneys, etc. The general infection may be secondary to the cutaneous disease, or the primary trouble may be in the lungs and bronchi, with secondary involvement of the skin and subcutaneous tissue.

A curious variety of blastomycosis confined to the buttocks occurs in Egypt and the East. It runs a very chronic course.

Diagnosis. Blastomycetic dermatitis has to be distinguished from the warty forms of tuberculosis and from syphilitic gummata. The miliary abscesses at the margin of the lesions may raise a suspicion, but microscopic examination is the only safe guide to the diagnosis. The systemic form simulates pyæmia, tuberculosis, rheumatism, and other general infections. The organism may be demonstrated in the sputum and in the pus drawn from the abscesses. The absence of tubercle bacilli and of the reaction to tuberculin are of some, but little, importance.

The disease called coccidiodal granuloma occurring in California is not a form of blastomycosis. Montgomery and Morrow contend that the clinical differences are so diverse that they must be distinct diseases.

Prognosis. The prognosis is favourable if the disease is limited to the skin.

Treatment. Large doses of iodide of potassium have a pronounced influence, and in combination with radiotherapy have often been sufficient to effect a cure of the cutaneous affection. Small lesions may be excised.

REFERENCES.—T. C. GILCHRIST. *Johns Hopkins Hospital Reports*, 1896, I., p. 269. *British Medical Journal*, October 25, 1902, p. 1321. F. H. MONTGOMERY and O. S. ORMSBY. " Systemic Blastomycosis." *Archives of Internal Medicine*, August, 1908. J. H. SEQUEIRA. *British Journal of Dermatology*, 1903, XV., p. 121. D. W. MONTGOMERY, RYFTSOGEL, and MORROW. *Journ. Cut. Dis.*, 1903, p. 5. *Ibid.*, 1904, p. 308. STODDARD and CUTLER. " Torula Infections." *Monographs of the Rockefeller Institute*, No. 6, 1916.

Other saccharomycetic dermatoses. A very rare form of dermatitis due to yeast infection may occur in the scroto-crural and axillary regions. The lesions are well-defined red non-elevated patches. Whitfield has reported a case in this country and Castellani has seen it in Ceylon. The yeast is easily grown on sugar media. Antiseptics such as resorcin and permanganate of potash are effective remedies.

In a case of extensive gangrenous dermatitis of the belly wall following a colotomy under my care, Western found a yeast in addition to streptococci and bacillus pyocyaneus, and B. coli communis.

A generalised ulcerative gummatous condition caused by a saccharomyces (the *Parendomyces Balzeri*) has been described by Balzer, Gougerot and Burnier (*Annales de Dermatologie*, 1912, III., p. 282).

Sporotrichoses.

Attention has lately been directed to a group of granulomatous conditions caused by sporotrichia. The earliest cases were described

in 1899 by Schenck. De Beurmann and Gougerot's researches have added considerably to our knowledge of this important group of cutaneous affections.

Etiology. The sporotrichia are lowly vegetable organisms of the mucedo group. The mycelium consists of regular septate or continuous filaments with short spore-bearing branches. The spores vary in size from three to six μ and occur singly or in pairs on the filaments or conidia. The *Sporotrichum Beurmanni* is the best known. Cultures can be grown on gelose glucose at the normal temperature ; they take about six days to develop, and by the end of the second week are luxuriant. The cultures have a characteristic appearance ; at first they are white and somewhat pointed, but later gradually become brown and flatten to form areas with convoluted borders and with radiating filaments. De Beurmann has been able to obtain positive results from inoculation of animals.

It is not yet known how the organism attacks the skin, but it is believed to be derived from animals and to be introduced through small breaches of the surface. Infection by the buccal mucosa appears also to be probable.

FIG. 73.— Culture of Sporothrix. Kindly lent by Dr. Adamson.

Pathology. The lesions are inflammatory nodules with central suppuration. Gougerot described three zones, the outer consisting of perivascular cellular infiltration resembling that seen in the syphilides. The middle zone is more like a tuberculous infiltration, and giant cells are present. In the centre there is a suppurative area with polynuclear infiltration. Sometimes portions of the mycelium are met with in sections and in the pus.

Clinical features. The lesions produced by the sporotrichia are of various forms, but it may be stated generally that they fall into two groups, one resembling the manifestations of syphilis and the other those of tuberculosis. The primary lesion is followed after a short interval by a subcutaneous nodule which enlarges to the size of a small nut. This ultimately softens and discharges. A succession of several such formations develops along a lymphatic trunk which can be felt as a cord. Some of the lesions do not break down. They may increase to the size of a small orange, and after some months a gradual involution occurs. The lesions may be grouped or widely spread, and the subcutaneous tissue, the bones and joints, and the mucous membranes and viscera, e.g., lungs, kidneys, etc., and special sense organs may be attacked.

The common clinical types are (a) a sporotrichic " chancre " with associated lymphangitis, (b) disseminated gummatous lesions,

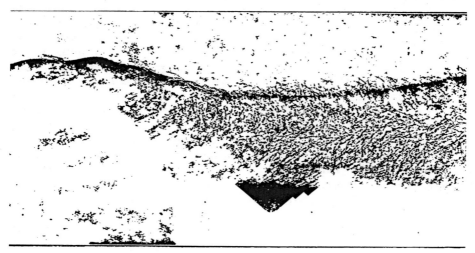

FIG. 74.—Sporotrichosis. Plate kindly lent by Dr. Adamson.

(c) disseminated ulcers. Other varieties resemble the warty form of tuberculosis, the ulceration of Bazin's disease, ulcerating tertiary syphilides, ecthyma, and boils. All these conditions leave scars which closely resemble the cicatrices of syphilis. In many cases the general health is very little affected.

Diagnosis. The importance of recognising the sporotrichoses is evident from the clinical features briefly indicated above. The diagnosis depends upon the multiplicity of the lesions and the variety of their forms, and the viscous character of the pus which exudes from the broken-down tissue. The patient's health is usually unimpaired. The actual diagnosis is made by culture, which takes from one to two weeks, and by Widal's agglutination reaction. The serum of patients suffering from sporotrichosis agglutinates an emulsion of the sporotrichia spores. The serum of sufferers from actinomycosis also agglutinates this emulsion, but in a different proportion.

Prognosis. If untreated the lesions multiply and extend. They readily yield to iodides.

Treatment. In most cases a course of iodides of a fortnight's to a couple of months' duration causes the disappearance of the lesions. Large doses should be given. Suppurative nodules are punctured and injected with 1 per cent. iodine solution. Dressings of lotions of similar character are used. Relapses are common if the treatment has not been carried out strenuously.

REFERENCES.—" Les Sporotrichoses," by DE BEURMANN and GOUGEROT, with many illustrations and full bibliography. Cases by NORMAN WALKER and RITCHIE. *British Medical Journal*, July 1, 1911, p. 1, coloured plates and references. H. G. ADAMSON. *British Journal of Dermatology*, XXV., pp. 33, 60, illustrated. " Sporotrichosis," by H. G. ADAMSON. *British Journal of Dermatology*, XX., No. 9, p. 296.

CHAPTER VIII.

MICROBIC AFFECTIONS OF THE SKIN.

A LARGE number of cutaneous eruptions are caused by micro-organisms. In some of them the infection takes place from within, *via* the blood stream, but in the majority the attack is made from without.

By means of cultures many varieties of micro-organism have been shown to make the epidermis their habitat, but the majority of these are not pathogenic. The non-pathogenic bacteria occur chiefly in the flexures, such as the axillæ and between the toes, where warmth and moisture favour their growth. According to Sabouraud, pathogenic organisms are met only as individual units upon the *normal* skin, but if the epidermis has been damaged in any way, as by friction or injury or some other condition which lowers the natural resisting power of the corneous layer, the bacteria develop colonies and produce an inflammatory reaction. The demonstration of *colonies* of an organism in, or upon the surface of, any cutaneous lesion is taken as evidence that the pathological process, at any rate in part, is due to the microbe found. It appears also to be probable that at least one organism constantly found on the skin, viz., the *Staphylococcus epidermidis albus,* may under certain conditions become pathogenic. The reasons why this organism is sometimes capable of exciting cutaneous reaction are unknown. It will be remembered that the bacillus coli, a normal denizen of the bowel under certain circumstances imperfectly known, undergoes a similar change and produces an acute inflammatory reaction.

The common microbes causing cutaneous lesions are :—

(1) The streptococci in erysipelas, several forms of impetigo, and whitlow ;

(2) the pyogenic staphylococci, producing follicular impetigo, boils, carbuncle, sycosis, cutaneous abscesses ;

(3) the *Staphylococcus epidermidis albus* in many conditions, and of particular interest in the " seborrhoides " ;

(4) the micro-bacillus of acne in comedones and pustules of acne vulgaris ;

(5) the strepto-bacillus in the soft chancre ;

(6) the tubercle bacillus in lupus vulgaris, scrofulodermia, and other varieties of cutaneous tuberculosis ;
   (7) the bacillus of Hansen in leprosy ;
   (8) the bacillus anthracis in malignant pustule ;
   (9) the bacillus mallei in glanders (farcy) ;
   (10) the Klebs-Loeffler bacillus in diphtheria of the skin ;
   (11) the bacillus of Frisch in rhinoscleroma ;
   (12) the spirochæta pallida in syphilis ;
   (13) the spirochæta pallidula in yaws.
   The bacillus pyocyaneus and the bacillus coli communis are usually met with in association with streptococci in some forms of gangrenous dermatitis.
   The " bottle bacillus " of Unna or spores of Malassez are organisms more closely related to the fungi than to the bacteria ; they are found in the scales of dandriff, in the comedones of infants, and in " seborrhoides."

STREPTOCOCCAL INFECTIONS OF THE SKIN.

Streptococci are cocci arranged in chains of greater or less length, but sometimes in pairs only (diplococci). They prefer anærobic media and grow best at the body temperature. They do not liquefy gelatine. Sabouraud separates the streptococci from the other coccal organisms by growing them in a capillary pipette on fluid media.
   The streptococci differ very much in their virulence, but those met with in skin practice probably all belong to one variety, the *Streptococcus pyogenes* or streptococcus of Fehleisen. Streptococci are commonly found in the cavity of the mouth, but they are less common on the normal skin than the staphylococci.

Erysipelas.

Erysipelas is an acute inflammation of the skin and subcutaneous tissue caused by the *Streptococcus pyogenes* of Fehleisen.
   Etiology. The organism gains entrance by a breach of the surface of the skin or an adjacent mucous membrane, *e.g.*, that of the nasal cavity. The breach of surface may be obvious, as in the erysipelas of wounds, burns, scalds, and the like, or it may be microscopic and impossible to locate. The patients are generally young adults, between twenty and forty, but no age is exempt.
   The predisposing causes are chronic alcoholism, Bright's disease, and other weakening conditions. The lesions of vaccinia and variola are sometimes the points of entrance of the streptococcus.

Epidemics in surgical wards were common before the introduction of antiseptics, and it must be remembered that wounds like those caused by the introduction of trocars into dropsical legs, or into the abdomen for the relief of ascites, are prone to be infected unless scrupulous care is taken.

Symptoms. General. A rigor usually marks the onset of the disease. The temperature rises rapidly to 102° to 105° F., and there are the usual symptoms of fever—malaise, headache, coated tongue, and thirst. The temperature chart shows remissions in the morning and rises in the evening ; and an extension of the eruption is often indicated by a further rise of the temperature. As the disease progresses the furred tongue becomes dry and brown, there are sordes on the lips, and the patient may pass into a " typhoid " condition. In severe cases vomiting and delirium occur. The urine contains albumen and casts.

Local. The eruption may start from a wound, but in many cases the point of entry of the organisms is so minute as to escape careful search. The initial lesion is a small raised shining red area with a well-defined margin, tender and hot to the touch. Where the subcutaneous tissue is lax, as in the eyelids, there is great swelling, and the swollen lids may completely close the palpebral fissure. If the affected area lies over a flat surface of bone there is very little swelling, but the tenderness and pain are more pronounced. In the centre of the patches small vesicles and bullæ containing clear serum are common. The clear fluid may become purulent and dry into crusts. Heat, pain, and itching are complained of. In four or five days the eruption at any one part fades and desquamation follows. A characteristic of the disease is the peripheral extension of the area, but in the form called **erysipelas migrans** the eruption appears in one part of the body, and, rapidly subsiding there, reappears in another region, and such attacks may go on for some weeks.

Erysipelas may attack any region, but the face, the part most exposed to infection, is the most frequently affected. From the face it may spread to the scalp and on to the neck. If the scalp is affected the hair usually falls, but grows again.

With the decline of the eruption the temperature drops to the normal by lysis, the subjective symptoms gradually disappear, the tongue cleans, but the patient is often left enfeebled, and convalescence may be tedious. In young healthy adults, however, the improvement may be rapid.

Duration. In a mild case the disease clears up in a week to ten days, but a duration of three weeks or more is not uncommon.

Recurrences are frequent, especially where the disease attacks

s.   12

the alæ of the nose and the cheeks, and repeated outbreaks lead to great thickening of the parts, a form of elephantiasis (*vide* p. 185).

Diagnosis. The well-defined margin is sometimes absent, and this may lead to difficulty, but the tense shining red areas with minute vesicles upon them, together with the constitutional symptoms, fever, etc., are generally sufficient to make a diagnosis.

Erythematous eczema of the face is often.diagnosed as erysipelas ; in both there are redness and swelling of the eyelids, but in eczema there is little or no rise of temperature and the general symptoms of erysipelas are absent.

The **prognosis** is good except in the debilitated or in those addicted to intemperance or suffering from Bright's disease. In the very old and in young infants the prognosis is grave.

Treatment. General. The patient should be confined to bed, and a light and nutritious diet should be enjoined. The administration of alcohol depends upon the condition of the heart. Other cardiac stimulants such as strychnine and digitalis may be necessary.

Medicinal. The tincture of the perchloride of iron in 10 to 30 minim doses is the remedy usually prescribed.

Local. The parts should be covered with ichthyol 20 to 40 per cent. in lanolin, applied in the form of a paint. Hot lead lotions are comforting. In the recurrent form starting from the nose, the nasal cavity should be treated, and if there are abrasions with suppuration the Pigmentum hydrarg. nitratis is a useful application.

Impetigo contagiosa.

Impetigo contagiosa or phlyctenular impetigo is an acute inflammation of the skin characterised by the formation of flat vesicles or bullæ which become pustular. It is caused by the streptococcus pyogenes.

Etiology. Children are more often affected than adults, and in out-patient clinics impetigo contagiosa is one of the commonest diseases. Auto-inoculation is frequent, and the disease rapidly spreads from one individual to another where there is close contact. In men the infection often takes place in the barber's shop. Irritant discharges from septic wounds is a common cause of impetigo in the military hospitals.

Diseases like scabies, pediculosis, strophulus, and prurigo, in which there is severe itching, are commonly complicated with impetigo, and eczema and other forms of dermatitis in which there are moist surfaces afford a suitable ground for streptococcal infection.

To describe this secondary infection the word " impetiginisation " is often used.   Sabouraud has shown that the streptococcus can be obtained from the lesions in pure culture by growing them on fluid media in a capillary pipette, if the exudation is taken from the vesicles early.   Inoculation experiments give positive results.   In most cases the staphylococcus invades the lesions, and cultures made on solid media show abundant growth of these organisms.   It appears certain,

FIG. 75.—Impetigo contagiosa.   Phlyctenular impetigo.   ×2.
Diagrammatic (after Darier).

however, from the researches of Dohi that staphylococci may also cause lesions resembling common impetigo.

Pathology.   The lesions of impetigo contagiosa are superficial. The epidermis is elevated by an effusion of serum which rapidly becomes opaque and purulent.   There is a moderate amount of leucocytic infiltration in the corium.   Secondary infection with pyogenic staphylococci is common, and when this occurs the follicular type of lesion (*vide* p. 189) follows.   In ecthyma the epidermis

FIG. 75A.—Ecthyma.   ⅔.
Diagrammatic (after Darier).

is destroyed and there is ulceration of the true skin leading   to scarring.   The ulcer has a shelving edge (Fig. 75A).

Clinical Forms of Impetigo :—

Common type.   The eruption begins as flat vesicles containing clear fluid, which becomes purulent and rapidly dries, forming yellow crusts   As a rule, when the patient first comes under observation the lesions are already yellow or yellowish brown or greenish crusts varying in size from a pea. to a sixpence or larger.   They appear to be " stuck on," as Tilbury Fox pointed out.   Leslie Roberts has called attention to a common arrangement of the spots like a budding yeast organism.   A larger spot has in close apposition a smaller spot, and this again a still smaller one, and so on.   This feature can be demonstrated frequently.   On removing the crust

12—2

from a recent lesion a red oozing surface is exposed, but when the spots are dying away the subjacent area is dry.

Minute papules and vesicles are occasionally seen in association with the typical phlyctenules.

The eruption itches, and auto-inoculation is exceedingly common. By scratching and simple contact fresh spots form with great rapidity, and large areas may be involved. Lesions may appear on distant parts, e.g., the fingers, where phlyctenular whitlow is not uncommon. Impetigo often spreads from one member of a family to another.

No parts of the body are exempt, but on account of exposure, those most commonly affected are the face, particularly about the mouth and nose, and the scalp and nape of the neck. In the occipital region the exciting cause is usually the irritation of head lice, and in all impetigos of the head and face the hair should be examined carefully for the pediculi and their ova.

The infection of the skin by the streptococcus rapidly leads to swelling and tenderness of the lymphatic glands which drain the area involved. The submental, submaxillary, and occipital glands are the most commonly affected, and suppuration may occur.

Erysipelas is a rare complication. Albuminuria may occur, and occasionally a scarlatiniform rash from toxæmia develops.

Intertrigo type. In the post-auricular sulcus and in the joint flexures, particularly the groins, impetigo takes a different form. The constant apposition, together with the warmth and moisture of the parts, causes premature rupture of the vesicles, and instead of the characteristic yellow crusts, red oozing surfaces are formed. Phlyctenules of the common type are often present at the margins of the raw areas and elsewhere, and they give a clue to the exact nature of the process. It must also be remembered that many intertrigos caused by chafing become impetiginised, and that pus infection is often an epiphenomenon in eczema and dermatitis due to irritants.

Bullous type. Sometimes a few blebs occur in association with the vesicles and crusts above described, but occasionally all or most of the lesions are of the bullous variety. Instead of rapidly drying up into crusts, the vesicles enlarge until blebs or blisters of considerable size are formed. They may be as large as a small walnut. The fluid contents are clear at first, but rapidly become opaque, and may get purulent. Occasionally I have observed the upper layers of the fluid in a bulla clear, while the dependent portion was purulent, a condition recalling hypopyon. Bullous impetigo may possibly be due to a special strain of streptococcus or to some peculiar local or general condition. The name " *Pemphigus contagiosus* " was given

Plate 16.

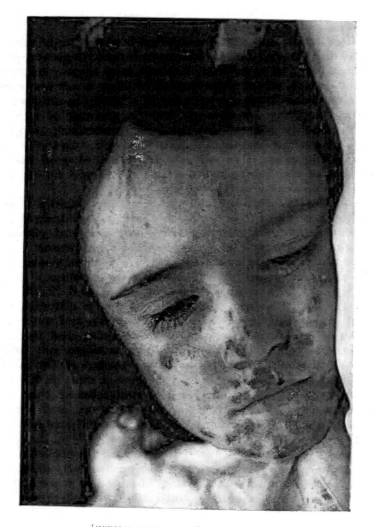

IMPETIGO CONTAGIOSA (STREPTOCOCCAL).

Phlyctenules and crusts of dried exudation scattered over the face. There
was also a phlyctenular whitlow on the right middle finger.

by Manson to epidemics of bullous impetigo seen in the tropics. Castellani believes them to be due to pyogenic staphylococci. Cantlie describes a virulent streptococcal infection occurring in hot seasons in the tropics, producing bullæ on the sole. The blebs rupture and are followed by desquamation. The disease may follow ringworm infection. There is intense itching.

Bullous impetigo of infants. "Pemphigus neonatorum." This form of impetigo requires special consideration. At one time classed as a variety of pemphigus it is now recognised as being caused by pus-cocci, and therefore finds its place among the impetigos. Early observers found staphylococci in the fluid of the lesions, but Sabouraud, Whitfield and others isolated streptococci by special methods, believing these organisms to be causal, and that the

FIG. 76.—Bullous impetigo. Pemphigus neonatorum.

staphylococci, which are found very early in the lesions, are a super-infection. The recent researches of Jadassohn and Hofmann suggest that this view must be reconsidered, and that some cases at any rate are primarily caused by staphylococci. Cole and Ruh in an epidemic in a maternity hospital found *staphylococcus aureus* in fluid from unbroken blebs in all cases examined, and in the pulmonary and hepatic veins in a fatal case. The clinical features certainly favour the streptococcal origin.

Clinical features. The eruption occurs in young infants usually before the umbilical stump has healed, and in many cases I have noticed that the umbilicus is in an unhealthy condition. It is possible that this, being the only breach of surface in the normal infant, is the site of infection.

The eruption consists of blebs or bullæ of all sizes from a small pea to a nut, and on the whole the large blebs predominate. The lesions are scattered widely over the trunk and less frequently upon the limbs, the palms and soles not being specially picked out by the eruption as in the congenital bullous syphilide. The blebs contain clear fluid which becomes opaque and eventually may be purulent. The surface left by the removal of the raised epidermis by friction or otherwise is raw, red or moist, and the lesions dry up with the separation of flakes from the margins.

The mother or the nurse may be suffering from impetigo of the common or bullous type, or from whitlow, and there may be common phlyctenular impetigo in other members of the family. Small epidemics sometimes occur in institutions or in the practice of a midwife or maternity nurse, if strict precautions are not taken against infection. The disease is dangerous, because the infection may become generalised. In the London Hospital clinic the mortality is about 30 per cent. In an autopsy upon one case I found the urachus distended with pus, and have several times seen suppuration in the course of the umbilical vessels. The organs generally show evidence of septic infection.

The bullous impetigo of infants has to be distinguished from the bullous congenital syphilide which appears occasionally at or within four or five days of birth. The spirochaetal eruption specially favours the palms and soles, and is usually accompanied by macular and other lesions of dull red colour on the face and elsewhere and by snuffles.

Some rare cases of generalised exfoliative dermatitis in infants first described by Ritter von Rittershain are believed by some authorities to be a severe form of infection by pyogenic cocci. Here, again, staphylococci are said to be the cause, but the disease has close relationships with the erythrodermias, with which it is considered (p. 400).

Circinate type. This variety of impetigo is rare except in the tropics. The lesions enlarge rapidly, but without much fluid exudation. The central parts heal, and thus rings are formed, which may cover large areas.

Ecthyma. In poorly-nourished and debilitated subjects, especially children, streptococcal infection may cause deeper lesions called "Ecthyma." Many cases of this type have occurred among the soldiers on active service, the pyogenic affection being secondary to scabies and pediculosis. The gluteal region and thighs were the parts most often involved. The eruption consists of vesicles which dry up to form crusts of a dirty brown colour, differing in this respect from the yellow scabs of impetigo. Around the crust a ring of small vesicles appears, and when the scab is removed a shallow, slightly cupped ulcer is found (Fig. 75A). There may be grave general symptoms, and in all cases the lesions are more difficult to heal than those of common impetigo, and leave permanent scars, and sometimes infiltrated nodules which may last a long time. Secondary warty growths occurred in numerous cases among soldiers in France (MacCormac). A similar affection without general symptoms, occurring chiefly in children in Ceylon and Southern India, is described as *Pyosis tropica* by Castellani. The vacciniform and varicelliform ecthymatous eruptions are dealt with elsewhere, being probably due to mixed infection (p. 186).

Chronic impetigo. Impetigo pityrodes. In some cases the phlyctenules of the common type are followed by dry scaly patches.

FIG. 77.—Chronic impetigo of the labial commissures.

Squamous areas are found about the upper lip and nose in children suffering from chronic nasal discharge, and about the ear in chronic otorrhœa. They are probably, as Adamson points out, streptococcal, but the organism has not yet been demonstrated in them. Sabouraud says that many of the dry scaly patches met with on the face and at the labial commissures in children are of coccal origin.

The diagnosis of impetigo. In most cases this is simple, but it must be remembered that many other conditions, especially itching eruptions, eczema, scabies, and prurigo, may become impetiginised. Impetigo is distinguished from eczema by the crusts appearing to be stuck on, by the scattered arrangement of the eruption, and the evidence of auto-inoculation. Scabies is characterised by the burrows, containing the acarus, and the affection of the interdigital clefts and inner side of the wrists, the penis and buttocks. Varicella may be mistaken for impetigo, but the glassy convex pocks coming out in crops, chiefly on the trunk, with pyrexia should enable one to make a diagnosis if the case is seen sufficiently early.

Bullous impetigo may be mistaken for pemphigus. True pemphigus is a grave disease and runs a chronic course, with constitutional symptoms, wasting, etc. In an early case advantage may be taken of the fact that the fluid in the fresh bullæ of pemphigus is sterile, and a bacteriological examination would be of great assistance.

Some of the chronic varieties suggest eczema, while the lesions in the flexures are often called intertrigo. The possibility of such conditions being due to coccal infection must be borne in mind and appropriate treatment applied.

Prognosis. The prognosis of impetigo is good, resolution under appropriate treatment taking place in four or five days to three weeks, unless there is a secondary staphylococcal infection of the follicles. Only in pemphigus neonatorum is there grave danger, and the mortality is about 30 per cent.

Treatment. The treatment of impetigo is remarkably successful even in the most extensive cases. All that is necessary is to remove the crusts completely and apply a mild antiseptic ointment. The removal of the crusts can be effected by the application of boric lint wrung out in hot water and covered with oil silk, or by boric starch poultices and by bathing. The best local applications are the dilute nitrate of mercury ointment or a weak ammoniated mercury ointment, 5 to 10 grains to the ounce. The unguentum metallorum is also a good formula.

> B. Plumbi acetatis, 10 grains,
> Zinci oxidi, 20 grains,
> Calomelanos, 10 grains,
> Ung. Hydrarg. Nitrat. dilut. to 1 ounce.

To prevent young children scratching the parts and removing the dressings it is a good plan to enclose the upper limbs in tubular splints made of thin card or stiff brown paper, bound top and bottom with lint to prevent chafing. The tubes should reach from just below the axillæ to just above the wrists. They prevent the elbow being bent, and consequently scratching is impossible.

In bullous impetigo the blebs should be opened with a sterile needle and the areas dressed with boric acid ointment.

In ecthyma the treatment for common impetigo is applicable, but it is necessary at the same time to treat the general condition by good feeding, tonics, and cod-liver oil. MacCormac found ecthyma among soldiers difficult to treat. Healing was slow, and new lesions appeared in the most disappointing manner. He recommends fomentation for three or four days followed by perchloride dressings. After disinfection a solution of nitrate of silver grs. 15, Spt. Aetheris nitrosi ʒj, is painted on. Vaccines are of little value.

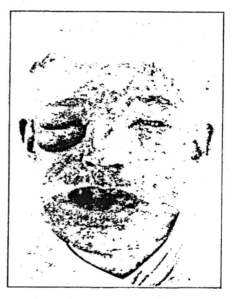

FIG. 78.—Chronic œdema from recurrent erysipelatous attacks. Streptococci isolated. Improvement under vaccine.

REFERENCES.—SABOURAUD. *Ann. de Derm. et de Syph.*, January, March, April, 1900. "Vacciniform Ecthyma of Infants." T. COLCOTT FOX. *British Journal of Dermatology*, June, 1907, XIX., p. 191. "Ecthyma Terebrans." JAMIESON and HUIE. *British Journal of Dermatology*, 1903, XV., p. 391. K. DOHI and S. H. DOHI. "A Clinical and Ætiological Study of Impetigo." *Archiv. f. Dermat. u. Syph.*, 1912, CXI., No. 2, p. 629. J. JADASSOHN. "Über Pyodermien." *Sammlungen Zwangloser Abhandlungen.* Marhold, Halle, 1, 2. COLE and RUH. *Journal American Med. Assoc.*, 1914, II., p. 1159. H. MACCORMAC. "Skin Diseases under War Conditions." *Trans. Royal Soc. Med.* (Dermat. Section), 1917, p. 121. Plates.

Recurrent Erysipelatoid Eruptions on the face leading to persistent œdematous swelling of the lips, eyelids, and other parts are not uncommon. They are believed to be of streptococcal origin, and are often associated with septic conditions of the nasal and oral mucosæ. The first attack is the most severe. A form of pseudo-elephantiasis may result (Figs. 78 and 170). Septic foci in the nose or mouth must be removed. Streptococcic vaccines have also been tried with advantage.

REFERENCE.—JAMES ADAM. *British Medical Journal*, October 2, 1909, p. 933.

Dermatitis gangrenosa infantum. Varicella gangrenosa.

This rather rare condition is characterised by an eruption of vesico-bullæ which rapidly necrose. It is peculiar to young infants and, curiously, is more common in girls than in boys. It occurs in marasmic children, or follows certain acute specific fevers, varicella, measles, and vaccination.

Pathology. The affection is doubtless microbic, and various organisms have been found by different observers. In all cases

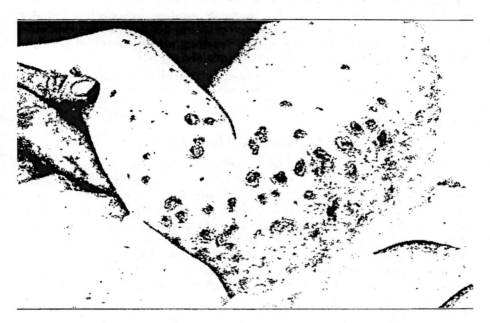

Fig. 79.—Dermatitis gangrenosa infantum.

there are pyogenic cocci, but the bacillus pyocyaneus has been found frequently in association with them. It is probable that there is always mixed infection.

Clinical features. The most frequent antecedent is chicken-pox, but instead of the vesicles drying up in the normal way they become inflamed and spread. They often become bullous, or may have an umbilicated appearance due to a central adherent black scab. Under the scab deep ulceration takes place, and around it there is a suppurative area. The enlargement and coalescence of adjoining lesions lead to the formation of ulcers with circinate margins. Deep scars are left. The eruption is scattered over the lower part of the body and thighs, and sometimes attacks the scalp and neck. In some cases it is widely disseminated. Abscesses frequently complicate the skin affection.

The general symptoms are high fever, grave exhaustion, wasting, diarrhœa, and convulsions.

About half the patients affected die with signs of septicæmia. In some cases miliary tuberculosis has been found post-mortem.

Treatment. Local treatment is of the highest importance. The child should have frequent baths containing boric acid, or boric acid fomentations frequently changed should be applied to the affected parts. Perchloride of mercury lotion 1-2,000 is also valuable. The general condition requires good feeding, and in hospital practice it is imperative to remove the child into the ward.

REFERENCES.—HUTCHINSON. "Clinical Lectures on Rare Diseases of the Skin," p. 235. H. RADCLIFFE CROCKER. *Med. Chir. Trans.*, 1887, p. 397.

Vacciniform Dermatitis.

This, again, is an affection peculiar to infants. It affects the buttocks, inner aspects of the thighs, and the genital regions. The lesions begin as vesicles, which rupture early and leave circular erosions or ulcers. The eruption is often mistaken for syphilis. The bacillus coli communis has been found, but Colcott Fox and Adamson believe the cause to be streptococci, which they isolated from unruptured vesicles. The condition should, if these observations are confirmed, be classed as a form of streptococcal impetigo. The local treatment for dermatitis gangrenosa is applicable here.

REFERENCE.—T. COLCOTT FOX. *British Journal of Dermatology*, 1907, XIX., p. 191.

Impetigo herpetiformis. Herpes pyæmicus.

A rare inflammatory disease, characterised by the formation of groups or rings of minute pustules. It occurs chiefly in the puerperium and is often fatal.

The patients are usually pregnant women, but very rarely a similar condition has been observed in men. The disease is undoubtedly a form of septicæmia or pyæmia. Its bacteriology has not yet been worked out.

Symptoms. There are grave general symptoms. The onset is attended with rigors and pyrexia, which are repeated with each successive crop of the eruption. The progress of the disease is attended with typhoid symptoms and albuminuria, the patient is delirious, the tongue dry and brown, and diarrhœa and vomiting hasten the fatal issue.

The eruption consists of nummular red spots, with some swelling upon which miliary pustules appear, and by the gradual increase of the areas of erythema and pustulation large tracts of the skin become involved. The centres heal up, and fresh pustules form at the periphery, so that a ringed and festooned arrangement is produced. Very often there are crusts in the centre of the rings. The eruption may gradually become universal, but the front of the trunk, the thighs, and the groins are the commonest sites. The mucous membranes may also be involved.

The disease is very rare, and in a large proportion of cases fatal.

REFERENCES.—Kaposi's Atlas, plates CXXVII., CXXVIII. SCHUBERG. *Archiv. f. Dermat. u. Syph.*, 1909, XCIV., p. 227. Case in a Man : GRAHAM CHAMBERS. *British Journal of Dermatology*, March, 1911, p. 65.

STAPHYLOCOCCAL INFECTIONS OF THE SKIN.

Staphylococci are cocci of rather variable size found in pus and growing easily on common media at the body temperature. Those met with in cutaneous disease are the *staphylococcus pyogenes aureus, albus,* and *citreus.* They liquefy gelatine easily and have considerable vitality.

The *staphylococcus epidermis albus,* which gives greyish cultures, often called the " morococcus " of Unna from its arrangement in mulberry-like masses, will be considered later in relation to " seborrhoic dermatitis " (p. 206).

Staphylococci are widely spread in the air. They are found in the mucous cavities and on the cutaneous surface. They infect the skin primarily or secondarily and have a special preference for the follicles.

The following conditions require consideration :—
(1) Follicular impetigo (Impetigo of Bockhart).
(2) Boils (Furunculi).
(3) Carbuncle.
(4) Sycosis menti.   Folliculitis of the beard region.
(5) Dermatitis papillaris capillitii.   Folliculitis of the scalp.
(6) Veld sore.
(7) Barkoo rot.

Staphylococcal infection may complicate impetigo contagiosa and is a marked feature of acne vulgaris.

Follicular Impetigo. (Impetigo of Bockhart.)

A staphylococcal infection of the skin characterised by suppurative lesions about the hair follicles.

Etiology. Follicular impetigo may occur at any age, but is commonest in children. Itching eruptions, causing scratching, such

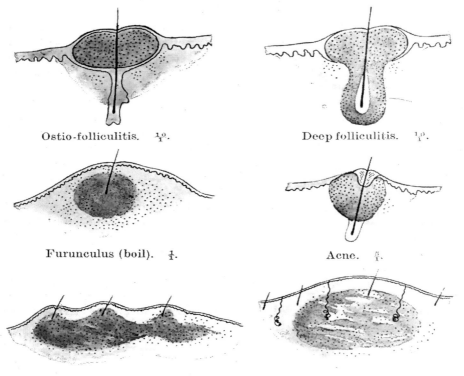

Ostio-folliculitis. $\frac{1}{1}$.

Deep folliculitis. $\frac{1}{1}$.

Furunculus (boil). $\frac{1}{1}$.

Acne. $\frac{5}{1}$.

Carbuncle. $\frac{1}{1}$.

Sweat-gland furuncle. $\frac{1}{1}$.

FIG. 80.—Diagram of types of staphylococcal follicular eruption (after Darier).

as scabies, local irritation, and dirt, are the commonest predisposing causes. The follicular type may also occur as a sequel to the phlyctenular (streptococcal) variety of impetigo. Impetigo of the follicular type has been rife among the troops on active service, and with secondary furunculosis has been a serious cause of invalidism.

Pathology. The staphylococcus pyogenes aureus is found in the lesions which are primarily small abscesses in the hair follicles. There is also perifollicular infiltration. The suppuration may be near the mouth of the follicle (ostiofolliculitis) or deep (Fig. 80).

Clinical features. The lesions are pustules varying in size from a pin's head to a small pea. Each pustule is surrounded by a small red halo, and a hair projects from its centre. The two points which distinguish this variety of impetigo from the phlyctenular type are the presence of suppuration from the beginning, and the central hair. The pus gradually dries up into crusts, which fall off, leaving a small scar at the mouth of the follicle.

The pustules are commonly multiple and may occur anywhere. They frequently follow traumatism, friction, the application of plasters, irritation by chemicals, and complicate irritable eruptions like scabies.

The course of this variety of impetigo is slower than that of the streptococcal form.

The **prognosis** is good, but the lesions may pass on to furuncles, and in infants to subcutaneous abscesses.

Treatment. In debilitated subjects iron is indicated. Purgatives are also beneficial at the onset. The local treatment consists in the application of fomentations of boric acid or of perchloride of mercury 1 in 4,000, or baths of the same, followed by white precipitate ointment. Sulphur lotions are also useful. In indolent cases a staphylococcus vaccine, preferably made from the patient's own organisms, may be required.

REFERENCES.—BOCKHART. *Monatschft. für Prakt. Dermatologie*, 1887, p. 450. R. SABOURAUD. *Annales de Derm. et de Syph.*, January, March, April, 1900.

Boil. Furunculus.

Boils are acute circumscribed follicular inflammations with necrosis and suppuration. They are often multiple.

Etiology. Follicular impetigo always precedes the boil. The conditions which predispose to multiple furuncles are the acute specific fevers, especially smallpox, septicæmia, diabetes mellitus, chronic renal disease, uræmia, and anæmia. Local irritation is the usual cause of a single boil, *e.g.*, the rubbing of the collar or cuff will irritate a follicular impetigo into a boil, and the furuncles on the buttocks of rowing men are determined by pressure and friction. Scratching in irritating eruptions like scabies may also determine the development of a furuncle.

Pathology. The *staphylococcus pyogenes aureus* is the cause of

Plate 17.

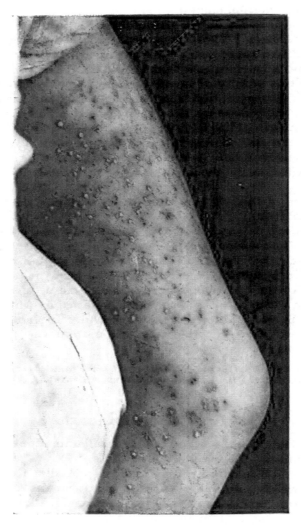

FOLLICULAR IMPETIGO OF THIGH (STAPHYLOCOCCAL).

The lesions are small abscesses centred by a hair and surrounded
by a zone of erythema.

the boil. It is found in the pus, sometimes also with the *staphylococcus albus* and *citreus*. Wright's observations have shown that in furunculosis there is a low resistance on the part of the patient to staphylococci, as shown by the opsonic index. The effect of the infection is to produce an acute inflammation with thrombosis of the vessels and necrosis. There is an extensive infiltration of round cells in and about the follicle (Fig. 80).

Clinical features. The boil starts as a painful red indurated spot, slightly raised above the level of the surrounding skin. The induration enlarges peripherally and the central part becomes raised to form a convex tumour. At first the colour is purplish red, with a halo of brighter redness, and the boil feels hard. Later, the centre softens and becomes of a yellow colour, the epidermis gives way, and by a single irregular opening (rarely more) pus is discharged. The necrosed tissue is extruded in fragments or as a " core," a whitish slough. On the rupture of the boil and the removal of the slough the inflammation at once begins to subside and the swelling and redness gradually disappear, though some induration may persist. The sloughed-out cavity heals up and a scar remains. The area may be discoloured for weeks or months after the lesion has quite healed.

Occasionally the process is arrested before suppuration occurs, and resolution takes place without actual necrosis. This condition is commonly called " blind boil."

Furuncles are exceedingly painful, especially those occurring in the external auditory meatus and the nostril, and there may be considerable constitutional disturbance until the pus is evacuated. The lymphatic glands are enlarged and tender, and they may suppurate. Lymphangitis of the lymphatics leading from the area of the boil is not uncommon.

Boils occur singly or in crops coming out for several weeks or months. The name " furunculosis " is applied to the latter condition. Small satellites often appear around a boil, usually as the result of improper treatment by dirty poultices, etc. Boils occur on any part of the body and limbs, but the neck, face, forearms, legs, and buttocks are the commonest sites. Small boils are also seen in the flexures, axillæ, gluteal clefts, and upper part of the thigh and adjacent part of the scrotum. Here the lesions are always small, and the infection is believed to begin in the large sweat glands in these regions (Fig. 80).

The **diagnosis** is easy.

Prognosis. Localised furunculosis or a single boil rapidly yields to treatment. Where there is tendency to recurrence much depends upon the possibility of removing the underlying cause. In many cases this can be done by vaccine treatment.

Treatment. General. Glycosuria and renal conditions require appropriate treatment. Purgatives are often desirable at the onset; iron, arsenic, and quinine are indicated in the debilitated, and especially in the furunculosis of convalescence.

Sulphide of calcium is recommended in doses of a quarter of a grain thrice daily, but I cannot say that I have seen it of obvious benefit. Yeast, on the other hand, raises the opsonic index to staphylococci and is well worth trying. Half a wineglassful of fresh brewers' yeast should be given night and morning. Twenty minim doses of dilute sulphuric acid in a wineglassful of water every four hours, as recommended by Reynolds, have proved of service in several cases under my care. Where there is troublesome furunculosis the best treatment is that by vaccines. If possible the vaccine should be made from the patient's own organisms, and of this a dose of 500 millions is injected every ten days. The dose may be increased, if necessary, up to 2000 millions. In many cases a polyvalent vaccine or stock preparation is quite sufficient. The vaccine is injected with strict antiseptic precautions into the patient's arm or back.

The local treatment of boils is important. Poultices should never be used, as they tend to produce fresh lesions around the original site of infection. A piece of Unna's carbolic mercury plaster cut a little larger than the boil, and with a hole in the centre, is applied, and over this is placed a pad of gauze. When pointing, the best treatment is incision or puncture with the cautery, followed by fomentations of boric lint wrung out in hot water. The hot antiseptic dressings promote healing. Some apply one or two drops of pure carbolic acid to the interior of the cavity. Another method is to apply cotton wool soaked in carbolic glycerine and covered with gutta-percha tissue. Bier's treatment is also useful. Abortive treatment may be tried if the boil is seen early. This consists in the injection of four or five minims of a one in twenty solution of carbolic acid into the base of the boil. Wassermann's Histopin, a staphylococcal extract, has been used in furunculosis with success. It is applied to and around the boil. The indurations left by boils may be treated with pastille doses of the X-rays every three weeks or by radium.

REFERENCES.—BOCKHART. *Monatschft. für Prakt. Dermatologie*, 1887, p. 450. T. C. GILCHRIST. "Bacteriology." *Johns Hopkins Hospital Reports*, Vol. XIV. A. E. WRIGHT. "Treatment by Staphylococcus Vaccines," *British Medical Journal*, 1904, p. 1075.

Nile Boils, a variety of tropical furunculosis, are seen in the Anglo-Egyptian Sudan. Chalmers and Marshall have shown that they are caused by a circular, non-motile coccus. Autogenous vaccine treatment (two doses of 500 millions) is curative.

REFERENCE.—CHALMERS and MARSHALL. *Journ. Trop. Med. and Hygiene*, 1915, p. 205.

Carbuncle.

A carbuncle is an acute phlegmonous inflammation of the skin and subcutaneous tissue leading to necrosis.

Etiology. The disease is rare before the fortieth year, and males are more commonly affected than females. Diabetes is frequently a predisposing cause, but other debilitating conditions may be complicated by carbuncle.

Pathology. Staphylococcal infection is the exciting cause. The inflammation begins, as in a boil, around the hair follicles (Fig. 80), and numerous foci of suppuration are found in the connective tissue about them. The affected areas undergo necrosis, and this process becomes very extensive by the confluence of the separate areas of infection. Ultimately large masses of slough form, and around them there is profuse suppuration. It appears probable that the arrangement of the connective tissue fibres in the region of the neck, running as they do vertically to the surface of the skin, and producing numerous columns of fat, leads to the evacuation of the pus by a number of small orifices. The induration about the carbuncle is due to massive cellular infiltration around the central gangrenous mass.

Clinical features. The carbuncle begins as a flat infiltration, usually on the nape of the neck. The area is purplish red and very tough. It gradually spreads and may eventually be as large as the palm of the hand. After increasing steadily for a week or more, numerous small points on the skin give way and spots of grey slough become visible, and a sanious pus exudes from the orifices. Later the skin over the middle of the carbuncle necroses and comes away, leaving an irregular crater-like ulcer, which slowly heals by granulation. A permanent scar remains. The carbuncle is exceedingly painful, and there is often grave prostration in the aged or debilitated. Pyrexia is not uncommon. Death may occur from septic absorption or from exhaustion.

Diagnosis. It is usually easy to diagnose a carbuncle from a boil. The carbuncle is single, its evolution is slower, it is larger and flatter, and there is brawny induration. The discharge of pus

s.   13

by cribriform openings instead of a single orifice is characteristic. There is also greater constitutional disturbance.

The **prognosis** is good, except in the elderly and debilitated and in the subjects of diabetes and chronic alcoholism. Carbuncles on the face and scalp are more dangerous than those on the back and neck, as there is some liability to septic thrombosis of the sinuses.

Treatment. General. A supporting diet is indicated, and in many cases stimulants are required. Any general predisposing condition, such as glycosuria, must be treated on the usual lines. Morphia may be required for the relief of pain.

Local. The possibility of the patient being able to take a general anæsthetic well modifies the line of treatment. Complete excision, if practicable, gives excellent results. After the removal, the cavity is packed with gauze and allowed to heal up. Another plan is to scrape out the slough and apply pure carbolic acid. The scraping must be carried out down to the deep fascia. The cautery may be necessary if there is much hæmorrhage. Skin grafts may be applied when the surface is clean.

Crucial incision with the injection of five to ten minims of carbolic acid in several parts is often practised. The lesion, after incision, is treated by boric acid or carbolic fomentations.

Vaccines may be tried, but have not met with so much success as in the treatment of boils.

If a carbuncle is seen early, the area should be painted with collodion or injected with carbolic acid. Fomentations are also useful, and the staphylococcus vaccine may be given.

Multiple Cutaneous and Subcutaneous Abscesses in Infants.

A staphylococcal infection characterised by the formation of multiple small abscesses in the subcutaneous tissue and deep parts of the skin.

Etiology. The patients are young infants, sometimes debilitated and suffering from impetigo of the common or of the bullous variety, or from impetiginised eruptions in the napkin area. In several cases under my observation the children have been in comparatively good health, but the disease may be associated with pneumonia and occasionally with tuberculosis. The pus contains staphylococci, often obtainable in pure culture. It has been suggested that infection may occur through the milk of mothers suffering from mammary inflammation, but the disease is not confined to nurslings. Adamson, pointing out the association with follicular impetigo and boils, believes that the infection of the skin is always primary, a Bockhart's impetigo, but I do not think this is always the case, for I have often seen the skin perfectly normal over the pea-like subcutaneous abscesses. I recognise the difficulty in believing that the infection is carried by the blood in cases where the general condition is good, but do not see any other explanation of the peculiarly widespread distribution of the lesions.

Clinical features. The lesions are numerous intradermic and hypodermic nodules about the size of a pea. They are elastic, and on incision a creamy pus is evacuated. The general condition is very variable, some of the infants being in a fairly healthy state without pyrexia, while others are gravely ill and have all the evidence of septicæmia.

The **prognosis,** in the absence of septicæmia, is generally good.

Treatment. Any cutaneous impetigo requires treatment in the usual way. The abscesses should be opened, and fomentations or mild antiseptic baths of boric acid hasten their healing. The internal administration of quinine without incising the abscesses has been recommended. I have given it a fair trial in several cases without success, and eventually have had to evacuate the pus.

Coccogenic Sycosis.

Sycosis is the name given to folliculitis of the beard and moustache regions. Coccogenic sycosis is caused by staphylococcal infection. Another form of pustular inflammation of the same regions is due to ringworm fungis (*vide* p. 162).

Etiology. The disease is fairly common in an out-patient department and is occasionally met with in private practice. It is usually contracted in the barber's shop. Sometimes a question may be raised as to the length of time which must elapse between infection and the appearance of the eruption, in order to trace the source of contagion. It is generally agreed that at least forty-eight hours elapse before the folliculitis is observed. Naturally, adult males are the sufferers, but a similar condition is observed very rarely on the eyebrows of women. Adamson draws attention to the fact that the follicular infection may be a sequel to a streptococcal impetigo which also occurs in the beard area.

Pathology. The essential feature is a suppurative inflammation of, and around, the hair follicles. The cause is the staphylococcus pyogenes aureus and albus. Temmadelli described a special

13—2

variety of organism which may cause the same type of inflammation. Each hair follicle is converted into an abscess; the papillæ may or may not be destroyed, according to the depth and intensity of the process. In the variety called "lupoid sycosis" the lesions are granulomatous, but there is no evidence of tuberculosis either in the structure or the presence of bacilli.

Clinical features. The primary lesions are papules about

Fig. 81.—Coccogenic sycosis.

the hairs. They rapidly become pustules in some cases, and in others enlarge to form nodules. The spots may be limited to a small area, but as a rule they spread rapidly until the whole of the beard region is involved. Each pustule has a hair at its centre, which at first is somewhat difficult to remove with the forceps, but when suppuration has occurred it is easy to bring away the hair, and its removal is followed by the exudation of pus. Scarring and permanent loss of the hair may be the result. Cheloid is a rare sequel. The process is essentially a chronic one, and frequently cases are seen which have lasted for several years, ten or more. In these very chronic cases there is a good deal of perifollicular infiltration.

Occasionally the abscesses are of some size from the coalescence of several suppurative areas. On such swellings a number of loose hairs stand up from the boggy fluctuating surface.

In several cases I have seen a chronic redness and scaliness with scattered small pustules lasting for years after the acute suppuration has cleared up.

Lupoid sycosis is a special variety in which the disease slowly spreads with a raised infiltrated margin. In the wake of this edge the follicles gradually undergo cicatricial atrophy. The disease is usually symmetrical. It is indistinguishable from common sycosis at its orign, and by some is believed to be always secondary to it. There is no reason to believe that it is a tuberculous process, as the name sycosis lupoides would imply. It is extremely refractory to treatment.

Diagnosis. It is important to bear in mind that some forms of ringworm of the beard region are also pustular. The lesions are circular or oval in shape, and localised, and these features should excite suspicion, which will be turned into certainty by an examination of the hairs or a scraping under the microscope.

Impetigo contagiosa differs from sycosis in not being confined to the hair follicles, and common phlyctenules are often present away from the beard region, but, as already mentioned, sycosis may follow a streptococcal impetigo. Eczema also is not confined to the beard area. The lesions are not specially follicular, but there may be some difficulty in diagnosis where there is secondary pus infection on an eczema of the chin. Syphilis sometimes simulates sycosis. This imitation most commonly occurs in the tertiary stage, but the removal of the crusts on the surface will disclose punched-out ulcers, and a complete examination of the patient will usually show other signs of syphilis. The tongue and throat must not be forgotten as throwing valuable light on an obscure case, and Wassermann's reaction should be examined.

Lupus vulgaris and lupus erythematosus might possibly be mistaken for lupoid sycosis. The history of the disease starting with the formation of pustules about the hairs would be a help in the diagnosis. I know one case of rodent ulcer beginning on the chin, a very unusual site, which was taken for years to be a lupoid sycosis. Here a biopsy would have prevented error.

Prognosis. Coccogenic sycosis is very chronic and difficult to cure. Recurrences after apparent removal are common. Lupoid sycosis may last for years.

Treatment. The rapid cure of coccogenic sycosis depends on whether the infected area can be thoroughly cleared of the hair.

This is best done by the X-rays. A full pastille dose is administered to the whole of the affected region. As a rule there is a rather marked exacerbation of the inflammation after the use of the rays, and the patient should be warned that this is likely to occur. At the end of a fortnight to three weeks the hair comes out, leaving the area bald. While waiting for the epilation I commonly advise frequent fomentation with boric acid lint. After the hair has fallen the Unguent. Hydrarg. Ammoniat. should be rubbed in twice daily until all sign of inflammation has gone. Even with this treatment relapses commonly occur.

If the X-rays are not available the hairs of the infected follicles

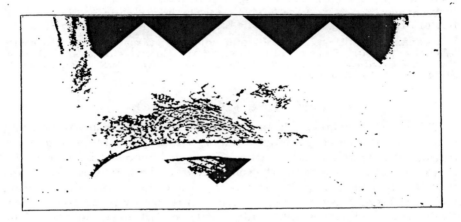

FIG. 82.—Sycosis nuchæ.

should be removed with epilation forceps, fomentations applied, and the white precipitate ointment rubbed in.

In obstinate cases I have had recourse to vaccine treatment with good results in some instances. A stock vaccine may be used, but it is best to have the vaccine prepared from the patient's own organism. The injections begin with a dose of 75 millions and may go on to 250 millions at intervals of ten days.

Stannoxyl may be tried in doses of four to eight tablets a day.

Sycosis nuchæ. Dermatitis papillaris capillitii. Acne cheloid.

This is a rare disease characterised by inflammation of the hair follicles of the nape and adjacent part of the scalp.

Pathology. The lesions are peri-follicular, with deep indurations. It is more nearly related to sycosis than to acne. *Staphylococcus pyogenes aureus* and *albus* are found.

Clinical features. A number of small closely-placed papules appear in the occipital region. They develop rapidly into vascular vegetations composed of granulation tissue. Crusts form and a fœtid secretion exudes. The process is very chronic, and after a duration of years the inflamed area undergoes a sclerotic change with irregular thickening. Between the cheloidal bands thus formed tufts of hair are usually present. I have seen two cases in this stage at the London Hospital, and each gave a history of prolonged suppuration. Castellani says the disease is common in native races.

Treatment. The X-rays offer by far the best means at our disposal, both in the inflammatory and the cheloidal stages.

REFERENCES.—UNNA. "Histopathology," translated by NORMAN WALKER, p. 490. BELOT and GOUIN. "Treatment by X-rays." *Archiv. d'electricité medicale.* January 25, 1911. H. G. ADAMSON. *Brit. Journ. Dermatology,* 1914, p. 69.

Veld Sore (Natal Sore).

This name is given to a form of pustular eruption closely resembling ecthyma. It was very common among the British troops and Boers during the South African war. It is believed to be caused by staphylococci, but restricted diet is held to be a factor. It begins with small itching papules, which rapidly become pustular forming a crusted lesion varying in size from a threepenny piece to a crown. Under the crust is a shallow ulcer with a festooned outline. The glands are enlarged and the lesions are painful and itching. There may be from one to twenty sores. The disease lasts from one to three months. The treatment required is that for Barkoo rot described below.

REFERENCE.—N. BISHOP HARMAN. *Journal of Pathology,* 1902.

Barkoo Rot.

A similar affection to veld sore occurring in dry weather in the back blocks of Australia. It has recently been observed among the troops operating in the Sinai desert. The absence of facilities for washing, tinned and salted foods and lack of fresh vegetables are important factors. The primary lesions are blebs containing watery pus, surrounded by an inflammatory areola. There may be a history of antecedent abrasions. The blebs reach the size of a sixpenny piece and generally rupture. The raw surface shows no tendency to heal and slowly spreads. The ulcer remains superficial unless secondarily affected by virulent cocci. After healing the affected areas are smooth and devoid of hair and sweat glands. The amount of scarring depends on the extent to which the corium is involved. The backs of the hands, forearms, feet and shins are affected. Auto-inoculation in the neighbourhood of the primary lesion is usual. The glands are not involved unless there is secondary infection. There is no constitutional disturbance.

C. J. Martin lays stress upon the infection of the hair follicles. The *Staphylococcus epidermidis albus* is the predominant organism, but some *S. citreus* and a few *S. aureus* are found. Martin insists on the importance of the removal of the infected hairs and also of the hairs round the lesions. The ulcers after thorough cleansing are dusted with calomel and covered with cotton wool. Extensive ulceration heals slowly.

REFERENCE.—C. J. MARTIN. *Medical Journal of Australia*, August 11, 1917, p. 118.

Granuloma pyogenicum. Botryomycosis hominis.

A fungating granuloma produced by pus-cocci.

Etiology. The term " botryomycosis " is used in veterinary surgery for a fungating granuloma met with in horses after castration. It occurs in the testicular cord and in the neighbourhood of the scrotum, and may become generalised. A similar condition is occasionally met with in man as a sequel to wounds, etc. It is, therefore, commonest on the uncovered parts.

Pathology. The lesions are inflammatory in character, granulomatous, and are little more than an exaggeration of the common excessive granulation tissue met with in the healing of wounds. The *staphylococcus pyogenes aureus* is obtained from the tissue, and there is no reason to believe that the granuloma is caused by other organisms, though amœbæ have been described by Letulle.

Clinical features. The tumours are of variable size, usually from a pea to a small cherry. They are of florid colour and usually pedunculated. They grow slowly and are probably always caused by suppurative processes.

Their importance lies in the possibility of mistaking them for malignant neoplasms. Removal is not followed by return *in situ*, and sections show the inflammatory character of the tumours.

REFERENCES.—" Botryomycose Humaine." BODIN. *Annales de Dermatologie*, 1902, III., p. 298. HARTZELL. *Journ. Cut. Diseases*, 1904, XXII., p. 520. LETULLE. *Journal de physiologie et pathologie*, 1908, X., p. 256. LENORMAND. *Annales de Dermatologie*, April, 1910, p. 161.

Diphtheria of the Skin.

The bacillus of Lœffler sometimes attacks pre-existing wounds or sores, and the characters of the lesions thus produced have been recognised for a long time. The ulcer or wound becomes covered with a characteristic white adherent membrane. The general symptoms may be severe and paralyses have sometimes followed. Cases in which a form of whitlow have developed are sometimes met with, but occasionally there is a generalised impetiginous and ecthymatous eruption. The latter cases are nearly always taken for a coccogenic infection as there is no diphtheritic membrane. The diagnosis has been made by cultivations from the lesions. In all the recorded cases both the *bacillus diphtheriæ* and staphylococci have been present. In other cases of a herpetic or bullous type the bacillus of Loeffler has also been found. In diphtheria of the skin antitoxin is as valuable as in the affection of the mucous membranes, and should be given without delay. .

REFERENCES to cases are given in an abstract in the *British Journal of Dermatology*, July, 1908, p. 239.

Anthrax (Malignant Pustule).

A specific disease with peculiar necrotic lesions due to the anthrax bacillus.

Etiology. Infection usually occurs from the hides, and occasionally from the bodies, of animals which have died from splenic fever. Workers in tanneries, wool-sorters, and butchers are consequently the most frequent victims. Carrying infected skins on the shoulders is the cause of the face and neck being so often the site of inoculation. The *bacillus anthracis* is found in the vesicles and later in the blood and organs.

Clinical features. The primary lesion appears, one to three days after infection, on an exposed part, usually the face, neck, or hand. It is a papule, and usually single. The papule soon becomes a vesicle or small bulla, containing blood at first, and later pus. The infected area rapidly becomes gangrenous and a black slough forms, around which a ring of tense vesicles develops. There are œdema and infiltration of the surrounding skin over a considerable area, and the patient complains of intense pain. Secondary lesions from auto-inoculation occur, but are very rare. The temperature rises to 104° to 105°; there are pains in the limbs, and vomiting. Prostration supervenes early, and the patient passes into a typhoid condition. In severe cases death occurs in two or three days, but occasionally mild cases are seen in which the constitutional symptoms are slight.

Diagnosis. The special features are the gangrenous spot with a ring of vesicles around it, and the infiltration and œdema beyond this.

The nature of the patient's employment will be of assistance in making a diagnosis, which is rendered absolute by the finding of the *bacillus anthracis* in the fluid from the vesicles.

Prognosis. The mortality used to be about 35 per cent., but it is now under 6 per cent.

Treatment. The lesions should be excised without delay, together with a wide margin of apparently healthy skin. General

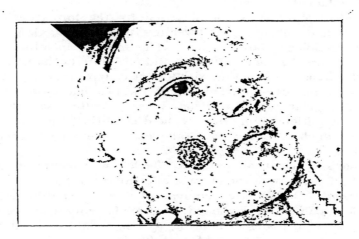

Fig. 83.—Anthrax.

tonic and stimulant treatment and good feeding are indicated. The anthrax serum of Sclavo in doses of 20 to 40 c.c. should be injected subcutaneously and the dose repeated in 24 hours if there is no abatement of the symptoms. Intravenous injection has been given in very grave cases. Legge reports that the mortality from anthrax at Bradford has been reduced from 35 to 5·4 per cent., partly owing to early treatment and largely to the use of Sclavo's serum.

REFERENCES.—DAVIES COLLEY. *Med. Chir. Trans.*, 1882, Vol. XLV. A. E. BARKER. *British Medical Journal*, June 5, 1895. Clinical lecture. Treatment by Sclavo's Serum. ROGER and BURVILL-HOLMES (15 cases). *Therap. Gazette*, June 15, 1908. FRANCESCO (11 cases). *Il Policlinico*, January 19, 1908. F. S. H. COUTTS. *Report Local Govt. Board*, 1917.

Equinia (Glanders. Farcy).

A contagious disease, rare in the human subject, due to the *bacillus mallei*, and characterised by cutaneous lesions and constitutional disturbance.

Etiology. The patients are men who come in contact with horses in the course of their work. The organism is the *bacillus mallei.*

Clinical features. After *local* inoculation of the skin with the microbe, a papule or pustule appears. It rapidly breaks down into an irregular ulcer with undermined edges. The ulcer spreads and the lymphatic vessels and glands in the neighbourhood become acutely inflamed.

Generalised equinia is characterised by the formation of small cutaneous and subcutaneous swellings which break down. These are the so-called "farcy buds." The mucous membrane of the respiratory tract becomes affected, and particularly the nasal cavity, in which extensive ulceration with foul discharge and crusts develops. Accompanying these cutaneous manifestations there is grave prostration with high fever and articular pains. Acute cases usually end fatally, the patient dying in a typhoid condition, but chronic cases occur in which recovery may take place after the lapse of some months.

Prognosis. Nearly all patients affected with acute equinia die. One-half of those with the chronic affection recover.

Treatment. Immediate removal of the inoculated lesions by the knife or curette offers the only chance of saving the patient in the acute type. Injections of mallein, $\frac{1}{20}$ c.c., should be tried. In the chronic cases some favourable results from injection have been reported. The general treatment is on the lines of pyæmia.

REFERENCE.—E. KLEIN. *British Medical Journal*, August 4, 1897, II., p. 385.

Verruga peruana.

Verruga peruana is an acute infectious disease occurring endemically in certain parts of Peru. In some valleys nearly every inhabitant is affected.

Pathology and etiology. The disease appears to be due to a special bacillus. Cole has been able to transmit the disease to apes.

The lesions are of the granulomatous type composed of mono-nuclear and polymorph leucocytes and connective tissue cells, and is very vascular.

Clinical features. After inoculation, there is a period of incubation, which varies from eight days to six weeks. The early symptoms are pyrexia, pains in the joints, and anæmia. The eruption appears from three weeks to six months after the onset of the illness. It first affects the face and the extremities, and then spreads to other parts, including the mucous membranes. The cutaneous lesions are red macules or vesicles, which itch. At a later date warty growths develop upon the sites of the macules. They may be small and numerous or form large discrete sessile or pedunculated tumours. As the disease subsides the growths become dry and horny. The mucous membranes and the larynx may be affected.

Septicæmia may supervene, with grave and even fatal results in two or three weeks.

Arsenic is of service, and the patient should, if possible, be removed from the infected district.

REFERENCES.—Abstract of paper by CHASTANG. *British Journal of Dermatology*, 1899, X., p. 59. H. N. COLE. *Archives of Internal Medicine*, December 15, 1912, p. 668.

CHAPTER IX.

MICROBIC AFFECTIONS (continued).

Pityriasis, Seborrhœa and the Acnes.

THE clinical features of this important group of skin diseases are distinctive, but divergent opinions are held as to the causes of the observed phenomena. Before discussing the histology and symptoms it will be of advantage to consider (1) the nomenclature ; (2) the micro-organisms believed to be concerned, and (3) the soil, *i.e.*, the peculiar characteristics of the skin of the subjects of these disorders.

(1) **Nomenclature.** This is particularly unfortunate, for in the first place the name " seborrhœa," which literally means flow of sebum, has been applied to (a) hypersecretion of sebum ; (b) the cause of this increased secretion ; (c) any kind of greasy exudation on the skin, whether from the sebaceous or from the sweat glands ; (d) dry scales upon the scalp, the so-called " seborrhœa sicca " ; and (e) a group of eruptions characterised by greasy scales. This terminology is especially inappropriate in the case of " seborrhœa sicca," a name given to the common dry scaling of the scalp, popularly known as " dandriff " or " scurf." There is no excess of sebaceous secretion in this condition, and the flakes are composed of epidermal scales containing micro-organisms, which are the probable cause. The name given by Willan, Pityriasis capitis, appears to be the most convenient, and it will be used here. Pityriasis, it may be mentioned, is commonly applied to some other scaling eruptions, pityriasis rosea, pityriasis rubra, pityriasis (tinea) versicolor, pityriasis rubra pilaris.

(2) **The microscopic flora** believed to be concerned in the production of these conditions are : (a) The *spores of Malassez,* or bottle bacillus of Unna, a parasite, probably more closely related to the ringworm fungi than to the bacteria, found in the epidermal scales of pityriasis capitis and in the other eruptions which have been grouped as " seborrhoides." Sabouraud points out the similarity of the epidermal affection it produces with pityriasis or tinea versicolor, which is caused by the microsporon furfur. The organism has not yet been cultivated.

(b) The *staphylococcus epidermidis albus*, a coccus growing on media in greyish white cultures. This organism, called by Unna the "morococcus" from its development in mulberry-like masses, is found in colonies in the greasy scales of pityriasis capitis and in the scaly eruptions with greasy scales upon the trunk and elsewhere. The organism is one of the common parasites present upon the skin, but under certain conditions of warmth and moisture, and probably an oily habitat, it becomes unduly prevalent and forms colonies.

(c) The *micro-bacillus of acne*. The *bacillus acnes* is a small rod-like Gram-positive organism, or group of organisms, growing preferably in anærobic media, found in the lesions of acne vulgaris, and in the oily plugs which can be readily expressed from the large sebaceous glands of the nose, etc., in oily seborrhœa.

(d) The *pyogenic staphylococci* are frequently found in acne and some of the seborrhoic eruptions.

(3) The **character of the skin** in patients liable to the affections under discussion is important. The colour is often dull, muddy or yellowish ; the surface is greasy ; and the sebaceous orifices are unduly patent. There is often hyperidrosis also, the sweat being not only excessive but oily, and luxuriant growth of hair is not uncommon at or about puberty. Later, hypertrichosis may be a great trouble to the female patients. The greasy condition of the skin tends to favour the growth of bacterial parasites.

(4) **Other etiological factors.** There is no doubt that inheritance and race are important ; and the evolution of the sexual function, attended with rapid development of the appendages of the skin, as indicated by growth of hair, etc., plays a prominent part in the etiology of the diseases here discussed. Excess of fatty, sugary and starchy foods is held by some to be a factor. Age has a marked influence, the common time for the appearance of pityriasis capitis being between six and ten years ; acne vulgaris is found between puberty and twenty-five ; a little later the common form of alopecia, which is secondary to pityriasis, develops, and in the forties acne rosacea is common. In the elderly we get the development of "seborrhoic warts" and keratomata. The distribution of the eruptions is also characteristic. Pityriasis affects the hairy parts, acne and oily seborrhœa favour the nose and naso-labial sulci and the temples, forehead and chin, and the back and chest. The "seborrhoides" particularly affect the sternal and interscapular regions and the flexures.

Pityriasis capitis.   "Seborrhœa sicca."   Dandriff. Scurf.

A chronic parasitic affection of the scalp characterised by the formation of easily detached scales and tending to atrophy of the hair.

Etiology.   Dandriff usually appears first in childhood, between the ages of six and ten.   It is exceedingly common, and if due to a parasite, as is believed, this organism must be widely spread, and there is, therefore, great difficulty in tracing contagion.   Many members of a family may be affected, and the tendency appears to be hereditary.   The use of brushes, etc., at the hairdresser's may be a prolific cause of the dissemination of dandriff.

Pathology.   In the *dry* scales of pityriasis large numbers of the spores of Malassez, or bottle bacillus of Unna, are found, and these are believed to be the cause of the affection.   The organism is confined to the superficial layers of the epidermis ; the scales themselves being composed of corneous cells, mostly without nuclei.   Sabouraud says that there is no alteration in the sebaceous glands.   In the *greasy* scales there is, in addition to the spores of Malassez, the *staphylococcus epidermidis albus*, growing in mulberry-like masses. The lesions consist of epidermal scales with spaces containing serum which has coagulated (Sabouraud).   The condition may become eczematised, when on removal of the scale or crust a moist oozing surface is found.   Sabouraud lays stress upon the exudation of serum (exoserosis) between the cells of the horny layer in pityriasis with greasy scales.   In the eczematous process a similar exoserosis takes place, but it is in the Malpighian layer.   It is, naturally, very difficult to say where the line is to be drawn between the two conditions.

Clinical features.   The affection is almost absolutely limited to the hairy scalp, and particularly attacks the vertex, upper parts of the parietal, temporal and the retro-auricular regions.   The affected areas are covered with greyish or earthy-coloured epidermic scales.   The squames are powdery, lamellar or branny, easily detached and constantly fall on the clothes.   At this stage the hair is unaffected.   The condition begins about the sixth year, and is exceedingly chonic, but occasionally disappears to return after a few months.   At puberty a change often occurs, the scales are thicker, and have a yellowish colour and look greasy.   They do not fall so easily, but the hair begins to come out, at first in small amount in the warm weather only, or after excessive perspiration, but later

the defluvium may occur all the year round.   The crown and the
temples are the parts most affected.   For a time there may be growth
of fresh hairs, but eventually they get thinner and atrophic, and,
finally, mere down, which ultimately gives place to a smooth shining
baldness (alopecia pityrodes).

In some patients the disease is of the dry scaly variety for years ;
in others the greasy character with early fall of hair is the important
feature.   Seborrhœa, using the term in the strict sense, is often

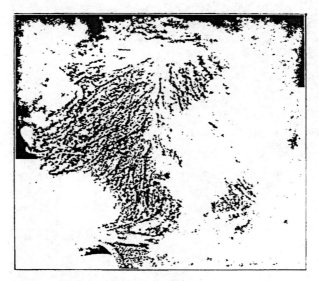

Fig. 84.—Pityriasis capitis, with secondary alopecia.

associated with pityriasis.   The skin becomes greasy, the sebaceous
glands are patent and acne vulgaris develops.

As already mentioned, there may be no active inflammation for
years, but the patient may complain of itching and heat from time
to time.   Then some alteration in the general health, worry or
anxiety, or perhaps the application of a stimulant lotion, causes a
change in the character of the disease.   The irritability of the scalp
increases, the surface becomes hot and red, and there is an excessive
production of epidermal scales of a flaky, greasy character.   The
inflammatory redness may not be limited exactly to the hairy scalp
but spread beyond it, forming a narrow band along the upper part
of the forehead and the temples.   This is sometimes called the
" corona seborrhoica," and is illustrated in Plate XVIII., where the

Plate 18.

"CORONA SEBORRHOICA."

The red area covered with greasy scales extends in a band below the
margin of the hairy scalp. The patent sebaceous follicles and greasy
character of the skin of the nose, etc., are shown. The patient has
since lost much of the hair on the temples.

greasy character of the skin is also shown. The affected area is usually dry, but slight irritation may cause considerable serous exudation, which on drying forms masses of crust. A similar condition may spread from the occipital region on to the nape of the neck and down the back, or in the retro-auricular sulcus.

This eczematisation of pityriasis led to the introduction of the term "seborrhoic eczema," which Unna applied widely to many forms of skin affection associated with pityriasis capitis. In the light of Sabouraud's researches it is more of the nature of an impetigo, being caused by cocci, and the association of staphylococcal infection is very common. One frequently meets with small pustules in the follicles, Bockhart's type of impetigo, on the nape and elsewhere in patients with greasy scales on the scalp ; boils may also occur.

In severe cases of pityriasis capitis the eyebrows may be affected. The areas are red, and covered with greasy yellowish scales, and they may become eczematised. I have several times seen blepharitis associated with this condition. The moustache region may suffer likewise, but if the beard area is affected the scales are generally of the dry powdery variety. Associated with the scalp affection there may be scaly patches on the face, but, according to Sabouraud, many of these are due to pyogenic cocci.

The "Seborrhoides" of the Glabrous Skin.

The glabrous skin of patients suffering from pityriasis of the scalp is very often the seat of eruptions of various types classed as "seborrhoides" or "seborrhoic dermatitis." There is considerable doubt whether they actually depend upon seborrhœa, using the term in the narrow sense. The skin is usually greasy, and there is often excessive perspiration of an oily character. There may be acne vulgaris and oily plugs in the dilated sebaceous glands, but these are not essential. Infrequent washing, the wearing of flannel constantly, the habit of sleeping in the vest worn by day, are often factors in the production of one form of the eruption (Flannel rash). The absence of facilities for bathing and changes of underclothing in the troops on active service have caused a wide prevalence of all forms of seborrhoic dermatitis. In many instances these have been associated with chronic impetigo. In practice the patient consults his medical attendant for the eruption on the body. He takes little heed of the pityriasis capitis ; he has had it for years, and beyond occasional irritation it has given no trouble.

Pathology. Sabouraud has demonstrated that there is an infiltration of serum in the superficial layers of the epidermis. There is a slight degree of thickening of the prickle layer, acanthosis. The greasy appearance is due to coagulation of serum. The scales contain numerous spores of Malassez, and colonies of *staphylococcus epidermidis albus*. The involvement of the sebaceous glands and their infection with the bacillus acnes is not essential, but often complicates the process. In the psoriasiform type besides the epidermal changes there are œdema and congestion of the papillæ, and some cellular infiltration of the true skin. In Sabouraud's opinion, the essential difference between this affection and true psoriasis is the early appearance in the latter of minute cellular infiltrations in the epidermis, an exocytosis, in contradistinction to exoserosis found in the seborrhoides and eczema.

Pityriasis circinata. Flannel Rash. Seborrhœa corporis (Duhring). Petaloid Type of Seborrhoic Eczema (Unna).

This has long been recognised as a clinical type of parasitic eruption affecting the trunk and spreading sometimes to the upper segments of the limbs. It is associated with pityriasis capitis. The lesions appear on the sternal and interscapular regions, and tend to keep to the middle line of the trunk, particularly involving the sweat furrow of the back. From these median areas the eruption may spread until large parts of the body and the upper arms and the thighs are affected. The primary spot is small, of a pink colour, and covered with a greasy scale. Each spot spreads to become a small disc, which usually clears up in the centre to form a ring. The rings, complete or broken, by their junction form the figured lesions to which Unna gave the appropriate name "petaloid." The margin of the ring is narrow, well-defined, red, and always covered by the greasy scale, while the centre often presents a pale dull yellow tint, which recalls tinea versicolor (Plate XIX.). Sometimes there is fine furfuraceous scaling in the middle of the rings. There is no infiltration. The patient may complain of itching, but this is not often severe.

Diagnosis. The condition is distinguished from pityriasis rosea by the tendency to form circinate figures, and the absence of the "herald" patch. In tinea versicolor the microsporon furfur is easily found under the microscope in the scales mounted in liquor potassæ. It should not give rise to difficulty, as there is no red margin

Plate 19

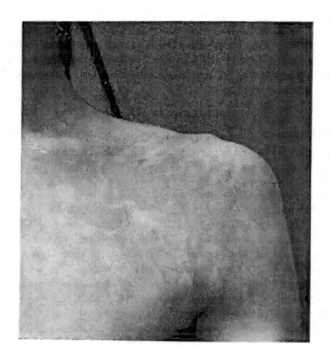

CIRCINATE SEBORRHOIDE.

Showing the petaloid arrangement of the lesions, which are scaly
at the margins. The trunk and upper parts of the arms and
thighs were affected.

to the patches.   Some forms of tinea of the scaly variety might show a similarity, but they are not likely to be limited to the middle line of the trunk, and if there should be any doubt the microscope at once dissipates it.

Psoriasiform Type of "Seborrhoide."

In this form the eruption is in the form of discs or of large plaques. The distribution is similar to that described above, viz., the middle

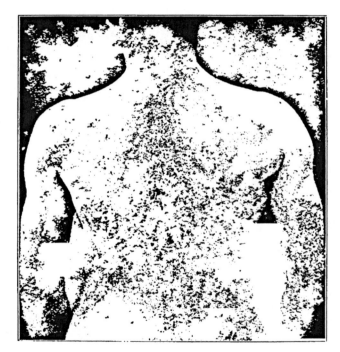

FIG. 85.—" Seborrhoide," showing distribution of eruption on the back.

line of the trunk (Figs. 85, 86). the sternal region, and submammary folds in women and obese men, the sweat furrow of the back, and there is often a large plaque in the hollow above the sacrum (Fig. 87). The axillæ and groins and the periumbilical area are also common sites.   The lesions are of varying size ; some coin-like. others, in the folds, elongated patches a couple of inches or so in length, apparently produced by the coalescence of neighbouring enlarging

14—2

discs. In the middle of the back and above the sacrum patches nearly as large as the palm may occur. The lesions are slightly raised above the surface, often a little infiltrated, of a red colour and covered with scales, usually characteristically greasy, but sometimes

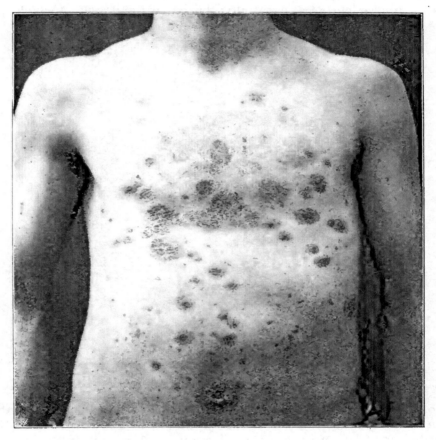

FIG. 86.—Scaly " seborrhoide," showing sternal submammary and umbilical distribution.

highly suggestive of psoriasis. According to Brocq, they show on scraping points of serous effusion which are not found in true psoriasis. It is, of course, quite possible that psoriasis may be altered by the " seborrhoic " condition. The skin of patients suffering from this psoriasis-like eruption shows the features which have already been noted, and the condition may be complicated by seborrhœa oleosa.

Sometimes this variety of "seborrhoide" when affecting the flexures becomes eczematised or infected with pus organisms.

Diagnosis. The practical point is to distinguish the seborrhoide from psoriasis. The distribution is an important feature. The lesions of psoriasis are more widely spread, they are not limited to the trunk, and nearly always there is some evidence of the disease on the extensor surfaces, especially the elbows and knees, which are

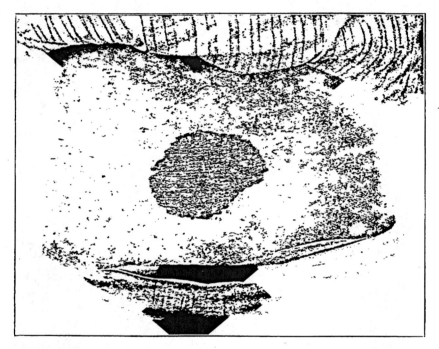

FIG. 87.—Psoriasiform seborrhoide. Large plaque in sacral region.

not affected in the psoriasiform seborrhoide. The presence of scales on the scalp should not mislead the student, for psoriasis attacks the scalp very frequently, but the affection is commonly in the form of nummular scaly patches. The scales of psoriasis are generally more abundant and silvery, and no points of serum escape upon their removal; there are simply minute hæmorrhages from the dilated capillary loops.

Prognosis. As a rule the "seborrhoides" yield rapidly to treatment, but pityriasis capitis is very prone to recur. Under service conditions, however, seborrhoic affections have been found by

MacCormac to have proved more resistant to treatment than any other cutaneous affection. A large number of the cases become impetiginised and relapses after apparent cure are common.

Treatment of pityriasis and the "seborrhoides." I have left the consideration of the treatment of these affections till the clinical features of the whole group have been described, for the trunk eruptions are so intimately connected with the scalp condition that one should not be treated without the other. From the point of view of prevention the treatment of the scalp is of greater importance. In dealing with this subject we can with advantage paraphrase Unna's dictum by stating that if the scalp disease were treated thoroughly in childhood we should have few "seborrhoic" eruptions in the adult.

Treatment of the scalp. Where there is a constant accumulation of scales shampooing at regular intervals is necessary. The following shampoo lotion is very useful : Soft soap and spirit equal parts, to which may be added thymol 10 grains to the ounce. The soap should be thoroughly washed out with fresh water. A quillaia shampoo may also be used, one to two teaspoonfuls of fluid extract of quillaia being added to half a basinful of warm water. The shampooing should be done every two or three weeks, but if the scalp is greasy the washing may be repeated more frequently. The regular use of lotions containing resorcin 15 to 20 grains to the ounce with 15 minims of glycerin, or spirit, is useful in mild cases. It is better not to use resorcin if the hair is very fair, as it may tend to darken it. Euresol, a monoacetate of resorcin, is of great service and is apparently free from this disadvantage. Instead of resorcin, salicylic acid may be used in the same strength or perchloride of mercury, 1 in 2,000, or the new colourless tar, anthrasol. In some cases an ointment suits the condition better, and the scalp, unless inflamed, will tolerate strong antiseptics such as salicylic acid 10 to 20 grains to the ounce, with or without sulphur, up to 30 grains to the ounce. Mercurials are sometimes advantageous, and the red or yellow oxide 5 grains to the ounce, with oil of cade or anthrasol ½ a drachm to the ounce, may be applied. If the patient has to go to work the ointment should be washed out in the morning and a little brillantine or almond oil applied.

In the eczematised condition it may be necessary to shave the head, beard or moustache to allow removal of the crusts by boric starch poultices, or boric acid fomentations, and when the surface is cleaned the remedies advocated above, but of half strength, should be used.

Internal treatment by alkalies is believed to be helpful.

Where the eruption spreads from the scalp to the face the calamine lotion or liniment is usually of service. Ichthyol 10 minims to the ounce may be added to the liniment.

For the seborrhoides of the trunk there is nothing so satisfactory as sulphur, which may be used in various strengths. A combination of sulphur and salicylic acid is particularly valuable. ℞ Sulphur præcipitata ½ a drachm, salicylic acid 10 grains to an ounce of petroleum ointment or in a paste with starch. Cinnabar is another useful remedy which may be combined with sulphur. ℞ Precipitated sulphur 15 grains. Cinnabar 15 grains. Vaselin to an ounce. If the eruption is of great extent the stronger preparations must be used with care, or part of the eruption should be treated at first to see how it bears the application. The addition of a little Liq. Carbonis detergens to the ointment is useful if there is much itching.

REFERENCES.—R. SABOURAUD. "Seborrhée, Acnés, Calvitie et Pityriases." Parts I. and II. of "Les Maladies du Cuir Chevelu," Paris, Masson, with copious plates and literature. UNNA'S article on Eczema in Mracek's "Handbuch der Haut Krankheiten," II., p. 168, should also be studied; a very full bibliography is appended. J. M. H. MACLEOD. Historical Review in *Practitioner*, May, 1904. W. ANDERSON. "Seborrhœa and its Results." *British Journal of Dermatology*, 1900, XII., p. 276. H. G. BROOKE. "Clinical Relations." *British Journal of Dermatology*, December, 1904, XVI., p. 205. BULKLEY. *Medical Record*, May 18, 1905.

Acne vulgaris.

A chronic parasitic inflammation of the sebaceous glands, occurring in young subjects, and characterised by the formation of comedones or black heads and suppuration. The eruption is found on the face and upper part of the trunk.

Etiology. The skin of the subjects of acne is oily, the sebaceous glands are unduly patent, the complexion is muddy, and there is usually pityriasis capitis. These conditions form a suitable soil for the development of the micro-organisms. Age is an important factor. acne beginning at puberty, and rarely lasting beyond the twenty-fifth year. The activity of the appendages of the skin at this age has already been mentioned, and this probably favours the bacillary invasion. Dyspepsia, constipation, and perhaps dietetic errors may play a part. Whitfield is of opinion that excess of starch, sugar or fat in the food increases the secretion apart from indigestion.

Pathology. The comedo is a worm-like mass composed of inspissated sebum, cells from the lining of the pilo-sebaceous follicle and a cocoon-like mass consisting of an enormous number of micro-bacilli, the bacillus of seborrhœa of Sabouraud or *bacillus acnes*. This organism, or, as Western has suggested, this group of organisms, is Gram-positive and grows by preference on anærobic media. Various investigators claim different characters culturally, and it is probable that there is not one form but several, and this would account for the difficulties attending treatment by inoculation. In the second stage the sebaceous glands are converted into pustules. There is infiltration of cells in and around the glands, and sometimes two or more adjoining lesions coalesce to form a deep-seated extensive abscess cavity. The abscesses may be superficial or deep, and usually run a very chronic course. From them are obtained the bacilli and also various forms of cocci which do not appear to be of the virulence of the pyogenic staphylococci. In some patients under

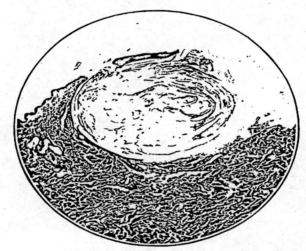

FIG. 88.—Acne vulgaris. Comedo. Microphotograph. 1 inch objective. Section kindly lent by Dr. Benians.

my care Western has been able to obtain from the suppurative lesions cultures of bacilli free from cocci. Gilchrist and Flemming report similar observations, showing that the bacillus under certain circumstances is pyogenic. H. C. Benians has devised a practical method of growing the acne bacillus from the comedo for making vaccines. The organism is grown in a tube of neutral broth, the surface of which is covered with about half an inch of sterile olive oil. The growth begins in three or four days and a vaccine can be prepared from it in eight to ten days.

Clinical features. The comedo is a small black or dark-brown point, slightly elevated above the surface. It varies in size from a pin's head to a millet seed, and is always situated at the mouth of a sebaceous follicle. By compression between the thumb nails a yellowish white greasy worm-like mass with a dark cap is extruded. These masses may be minute or a couple of lines in length. The cap is composed of keratinous material derived from the cells, and is not

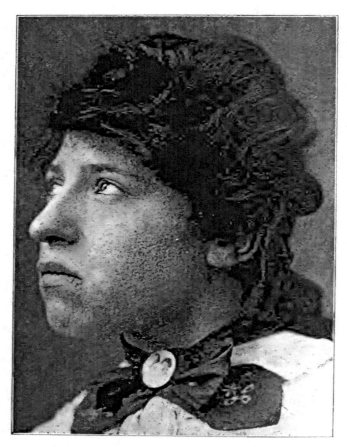

FIG. 89.—Scars left by acne vulgaris.

due to the deposition of dust. The comedones are found on the face, especially on the nose and nasolabial sulci, on the temples and cheeks, and often in the ears. The upper part of the chest and the back, sometimes nearly as low as the sacrum, are also affected in severe cases (Fig. 90).

In some patients the comedones are the special feature, in others the lesions pass on to a second stage, but comedones are always present. In this second stage the follicles are inflamed, the eruption consisting of papules of a red or purplish colour, slightly pointed, and after two or three days showing a minute yellow spot at the summit. The papules vary from a pin's head to a small pea in size. The yellow summit ruptures and a small quantity of thick

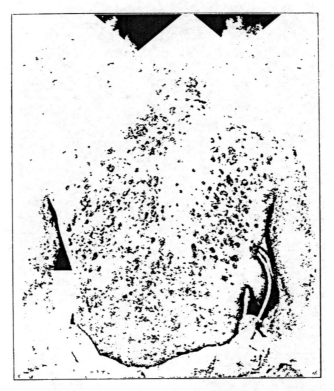

FIG. 90.—Severe acne of the back. Male, aged 17.

pus escapes, and the spot begins to dry up to form a brownish stain, with slight cicatrisation. In many instances the lesions undergo retrograde changes without the evacuation of pus. The face and the chest and back are the common sites of the eruption. There is little pain.

In some cases, however, the benign course described above is not followed. The abscesses increase to the size of a large pea or become irregular or elongated from the fusion of suppurative foci

Plate 20.

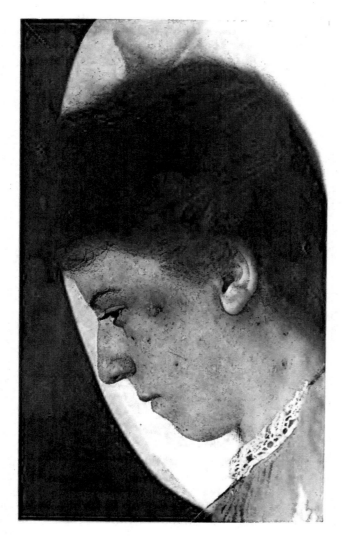

ACNE VULGARIS.

The skin is pale and greasy, the orifices of the sebaceous glands on the nose are patent; there are scattered comedones and a few suppurative foci.

in adjacent glands. The surface is purplish, the swelling indurated, and there is considerable pain. On evacuating such a lesion one is often surprised by the large quantity of thick inspissated pus which is removed. Permanent scars are left in this variety (Fig. 89).

The term " Acne punctata " is applied to a condition characterised by numerous comedones. The terms " Acne papulosa," " Acne pustulosa," and " Acne indurata " describe the other forms. The course of the eruption is essentially chronic, with periods of activity and remission, often depending to some extent upon the condition of the general health. The severe type illustrated (Fig. 90) is comparatively rare.

Diagnosis. The diagnosis of acne is usually easy. The presence of the comedones and the peculiar limitation to certain regions are characteristic. It must be remembered, however, that certain drug eruptions simulate acne very closely. Nearly every patient who takes bromides for a long time suffers from an acne-like eruption, and one form of iodide eruption is very like the pustular form of acne. The history would be of great assistance in the differential diagnosis, but the absence of characteristic comedones is of importance, and if necessary an analysis of the urine may be made. It is interesting to note that a third member of the halogen group of elements, chlorine, produces an acne-like eruption, often very severe, but closely simulating the common type. It occurs in chlorine workers. Tar and oil of cade ointments applied to the skin produce in some subjects a papulo-pustular eruption rather like acne, but the history would set at rest any doubt as to the cause.

Grouped comedones in infants are considered at p. 220.

Prognosis. A guarded prognosis should be given. Acne often runs a very chronic course, but tends to disappear spontaneously at the age of twenty-five.

Treatment. *General.* Exercise in the open air is important. The disfigurement, particularly in young girls, tends to their staying too much indoors. The diet requires supervision. Sweets, pastry, fatty and highly seasoned and salted foods, entrées, etc., should be avoided. Alcohol should be excluded, and excess of tea and coffee are bad. Plain simple food, with plenty of green vegetables, stewed or cooked fruit, and a sufficiency of fluid are advisable. The dental condition may require attention, and care should be given to thorough mastication. Any tendency to constipation should be met by salines. In many cases there is an anæmic tendency, and the old-fashioned mixture of sulphate of iron and magnesia should be given. In some cases in girls a mixture of iron and aloes is advantageous. Where there is debility, cod-liver oil and arsenic are indicated. As tending to increase the opsonic index fresh brewer's yeast, a tablespoonful twice a day, may be given, or one of the nuclein preparations, but the latter have not in my experience been so efficient as the yeast itself. In chronic cases the use of the vaccines has sometimes proved valuable. The vaccine should, if possible, be made from the patient's own organisms. The usual dose is seven and a half millions to nine millions of the acne bacillus every ten days with or without staphylococci.

The *local* treatment is very important. Where there are numerous comedones and little pustulation, the face should be washed with a 5 per cent. sulphur or sulphur and balsam of Peru soap, and bathed freely with hot water afterwards. The process is followed by brisk friction with a soft towel. This should be done nightly. Removal of the comedones is also advisable, but must be done with care. Where there is much pustulation the treatment must be less energetic. The bathing may be continued, and any deep-seated abscesses should be opened with a fine pointed knife and the pus evacuated. Some advise swabbing the cavities with carbolic, but, if properly emptied, they heal up satisfactorily. Lotions applied to the parts are often very useful. A good one is the following : Milk of sulphur, alcohol, water, equal parts, to which is added one-tenth part of gum mucilage, applied night and morning. In some cases high frequency electricity and radiotherapy are of great assistance, but in others there is little benefit.

REFERENCES.—R. SABOURAUD. "Seborrhœa, Acnés, Calvitie." Paris, Masson, 1902. T. C. GILCHRIST. *Johns Hopkins Hospital Reports*, IX., p. 409. FLEMMING. *Lancet*, 1909, 1, p. 1035. A. WHITFIELD. *Ibid.*, 1909, 1, p. 1207. G. T. WESTERN. "Vaccine Treatment." *British Journal of Dermatology*, XXII. E. H. MOLESWORTH. *British Medical Journal*, May 21, 1910, p. 1227. THIBIERGE. "Chlorine Acne." *Ann. de Dermat.*, July, 1900. H. C. BENIANS. *Lancet*, June 26, 1913, p. 1801.

Grouped Comedones in Infants.

A rather uncommon affection of young infants, and occasionally of school children, characterised by the formation of groups of black heads, which may sometimes pass on to suppuration.

Pathology. The cause is unknown, but the spores of Malassez are present in large numbers in the comedones. In several cases examined for me by Dr. G. T. Western no acne bacilli were found either in film preparations or in culture. Cultures grew staphylococcus albus only. Males are affected more frequently than females. There is often a history of local irritation, such as the application of tallow plasters, camphorated oil, or of chest protectors of dirty flannel.

Infection from caps is also a probable cause. When the condition occurs on the face contact with the mother's dirty shawl is apparently the cause.

Clinical features. The lesions are localised to a single area of variable size on the chest, and rarely on the forehead, scalp, or back.

FIG. 91.—Ulceration following grouped comedones.

The follicles are plugged with a horny mass with a black summit. There may be no evidence of inflammation, but sometimes there is an areola of redness round each comedone. In the case figured (Fig. 91) there was extensive inflammation with suppuration on the chest. The disease sometimes affects several members of a family.

Treatment. Thorough cleansing of the part and the avoidance of irritation are essential. Soft soap should be used when the comedones alone are present. If there be suppuration and ulceration, these are treated on the usual lines with boric acid fomentations, followed by boric acid ointment.

REFERENCE.—E. II. R. HARRIES. . " Grouped Comedones in Infants." *British Journal of Dermatology*, XXIII., p. 5.

Acne necrotica (Acne varioliformis. Acne frontalis).

A chronic parasitic affection of adults characterised by shotty papulo-pustules, commonly limited to the frontal area.

Etiology. The patients are usually sufferers from oily seborrhœa and pityriasis capitis. Sabouraud believes the cause to be the *staphylococcus aureus*.

Pathology. The lesions develop in the follicles and consist of

FIG. 92.—Acne frontalis. Male, aged 42.

papulo-pustules, with necrosis of the epidermis and of part of the true skin.

Clinical features. The eruption consists of small red swellings around the orifices of the follicles. They are soon surmounted by small pustules which dry to form yellowish crusts. On the fall of the scabs small depressed scars are left. The spots vary in size from a pin's head to a line in diameter. The shotty character of the pustules noticeable on palpation suggested the name " varioliform." The eruption comes out in crops, and particularly affects the forehead and temples, but it often extends on to the hairy scalp for a short distance. The auricles and the side of the nose may be affected, rarely the upper part of the trunk. Necrotic acne runs an extremely chronic course, and may last for years.

Treatment. The application of a sulphur soap, and rubbing in a sulphur or oil of cade ointment, cure the eruption in a few weeks. Engmann reports benefit from a staphylococcus vaccine.

Seborrhœa oleosa is dealt with under affections of the glands (p. 587), and **acne rosacea** with the toxic diseases (p. 384).

CHAPTER X

MICROBIC AFFECTIONS (continued).

Tuberculosis of the Skin.

Koch's bacillus is the cause directly or indirectly of a number of cutaneous affections. In some the organism is found in the affected areas in greater or less number; inoculation of portions of the morbid tissue produces tuberculosis in the guinea-pig, and a local reaction follows the injection of Koch's old tuberculin. The diseases in which these conditions obtain are classed as tuberculous diseases of the skin. But there are other affections in which the clinical history, the histological appearances, and the association of tuberculosis elsewhere strongly suggest a tuberculous origin, but the tubercle bacillus is very rarely found in the lesions, and positive results from inoculation are exceptional. To these conditions the name " tuberculides " has been given. It was supposed that they are due either to the circulation of toxines of tuberculous origin or to attenuated forms of Koch's bacillus. A more satisfactory explanation is that they are allergic phenomena (*vide* p. 249). The tuberculides are usually symmetrical in their distribution.

The tubercle bacillus may reach the skin (1) by the blood stream, as in miliary tuberculosis and some forms of lupus vulgaris ; (2) by auto-inoculation from open tuberculous lesions in the lung, bowel, or genito-urinary tract, as in acute tuberculous ulcer ; (3) by direct introduction of the microbe through breaches of the surface, as in tuberculosis verrucosa, and most likely in the majority of cases of lupus vulgaris ; (4) by extension from the mucous membranes, *e.g.*, from the nasal cavity in lupus vulgaris ; (5) by infection from broken-down tuberculous glands and sinuses leading to foci in the bones and joints, as in scrofulodermia and lupus vulgaris.

Clinical tests for tuberculosis. The injection of Koch's old tuberculin, von Pirquet's and Calmette's tests, and Moro's ointment may be used.

The *injection of Koch's old tuberculin* causes a general and also a local reaction. A general reaction indicates that the patient has some focus of tubercle, but the local reaction shows that the cutaneous lesion reacting is tuberculous. To observe the general reaction the temperature is taken two-hourly for twenty-four hours before the injection. The injection is made between the shoulders, preferably at about 7 p.m., and the rise of temperature should take place twenty-four hours later. If there is an elevation of 1° F. the reaction is positive. One-tenth milligram is given, and if there is no reaction one-third milligram is given at the end of three days. Should there again be no reaction the dose is increased to one milligram, and so on up to ten milligrams, the maximum for an adult being ten milligrams, for a child five. During the reaction the patient is kept at rest on a light diet. The local reaction is indicated by swelling and erythema of the cutaneous lesion.

Von Pirquet's test. The skin is scarified as in ordinary vaccination, and a 25 per cent. solution of old tuberculin (in a mixture composed of one part of 5 per cent. carbolic acid solution and two parts of normal saline) is applied. It is useful to scarify a corresponding area on some neighbouring part without applying the solution as a control. In a tuberculous subject at the site of inoculation a small red swelling appears, which the next day develops into a definite red papule. The lesion fades in a few days with slight desquamation. In some patients a wheal-like spot forms round the papule, and occasionally there are small vesicles. This reaction, of course, only indicates that the patient has some focus of tuberculosis at some part of the body.

Calmette's test. One drop of a freshly prepared 0·5 solution of old tuberculin is applied to the conjunctiva. The reaction appears in from three to six hours. The eye looks red and there is some degree of swelling of the lids. Congestion of the conjunctival surface increases, and the lachrymal caruncle becomes red and swollen. In some cases there is œdema, and there may be a fibrinous exudate and slight traces of pus. The test is exceedingly delicate, but must never be used where there is any suspicion of disease in either eye. Some unfortunate results leading to blindness have led to this test being rarely employed.

Moro's test. This is performed with an ointment containing 10 per cent. of Koch's old tuberculin. It is rubbed vigorously into an area of the chest or abdomen about three inches square. At the end of twenty-four to forty-eight hours an eruption of small red papules appears on the area treated. This is a useful and easily applied test.

As instances of the value of these tests I may mention that I have not failed to get positive reactions in a long series of cases of lupus vulgaris, scrofulodermia, warty tuberculosis, and tuberculides.

Cases suspected of being tuberculous, but proving by their healing rapidly under antiseptic fomentations to be septic, failed to react. A very fine example of the value of the cuti-test of von Pirquet and also of Moro's test occurred recently in my ward. A boy was admitted with an extensive ulceration of the neck extending from the mastoid process to the clavicle. The characters suggested scrofulodermia, but there was enlargement of the liver and spleen. Both von Pirquet's and Moro's tests gave negative results. Wassermann's test was made, and a positive result was obtained. The ulceration rapidly healed under mercurial inunction. I have several times applied the tests to cases of congenital syphilis for the purposes of control, and in young subjects have never obtained the tuberculin reaction.

Miliary Tuberculosis of the Skin.

Miliary tuberculosis of the skin is rare. It occurs as a part of general miliary tuberculosis. The patients are usually children, and there is often a history of a recent attack of measles or of some other acute specific fever. The lesions are acuminate red papules or papulo-vesicles, rarely minute pustules, varying in size from a pin's head to a hemp seed. The eruption comes out rapidly and is generally widely spread. The spots may disappear with the formation of small scales or crusts, but they occasionally break down into small ulcers. Microscopically the papules have a characteristic tuberculous structure, and Koch's bacilli are found in them in great numbers. The inoculation of guinea-pigs is followed by tuberculosis.

The prognosis is necessarily grave, and in most cases meningitis is the cause of death.

REFERENCE.—LEICHTENSTERN. *Münch. Med. Wochenschrift,* 1897, No. 1.

Acute Tuberculous Ulcer (Tuberculosis cutis orificialis).

The acute tuberculous ulcer is rare except in patients suffering from visceral tuberculosis. It has, however, been known to follow direct inoculation by virulent bacilli, *e.g.*, after ritual circumcision performed by a phthisical rabbi.

I have seen five cases in patients suffering from phthisis in whom the acute ulcer developed on the lower lip and buccal mucosa. Rarely the nares are affected. The infective agent is doubtless the sputa.

In tuberculosis of the bowel, and also in phthisis, tuberculous ulcer occurs about the anus, often in association with a fissure.

Mr. Hugh Lett recently sent me a boy of fifteen, with an acute ulceration of the glans penis, secondary to tuberculosis of the kidneys and bladder. I have seen one other case in which a similar ulceration occurred in genito-urinary tuberculosis.

Dr. Lewis Smith recently had a case in which an acute tuberculous ulcer developed in a tracheotomy wound.

Pathology. Tubercles containing giant cells and epithelioid cells are found in sections of the ulcer in great numbers, and Koch's bacilli are usually plentiful.

Clinical features. The lesions are small dull red swellings, which soon break down to form shallow ulcers with thin undermined edges. As a rule, they are circular or polycyclic from the fusion of neighbouring lesions, but an individual ulcer rarely exceeds half an inch in diameter. The base is somewhat irregular, and minute yellow granules are seen on its surface and at the margin. The ulcers are painless, except in parts which are liable to friction and movement, and then there is often great suffering. There is no tendency to spontaneous healing, but the lesions never become deep. The lymphatic glands are enlarged early.

Diagnosis. If the presence of visceral tuberculosis is known there is no difficulty in diagnosis, but care has to be taken to differentiate the lesions from soft sores, from Hunterian chancre, and from epithelioma. In any doubtful case the lesion should be scraped and the tubercle bacillus sought for, or a portion of the margin may be removed and stained for bacilli. In one case which came under my observation the ulcer on the glans penis was the first evidence that the patient had tuberculous disease of the urinary tract.

Treatment. If the patient suffers from visceral tuberculosis, no radical-treatment is usually advisable. The ulcers may be dressed with iodoform, or aristol or an ointment of peroxide of zinc (10 grains to the ounce), and to these preparations cocaine may be added if there be much pain. The application of the X-rays is also useful. In the absence of visceral disease the lesions should be excised.

Tuberculosis verrucosa (Anatomical Tubercle. Verruca necrogenica. Lupus verrucosus).

Warty tuberculosis is the result of the direct inoculation of the bacillus of Koch. It may occur in the subjects of phthisis from auto-inoculation, but is more commonly seen in medical men, nurses, and others who are in attendance upon patients suffering from

15—2

" open " tuberculous disease. I have seen several cases in which the hands have been infected by washing handkerchiefs used by phthisical patients. Warty tuberculosis is also met with in persons whose work brings them in contact with the bodies of those who have

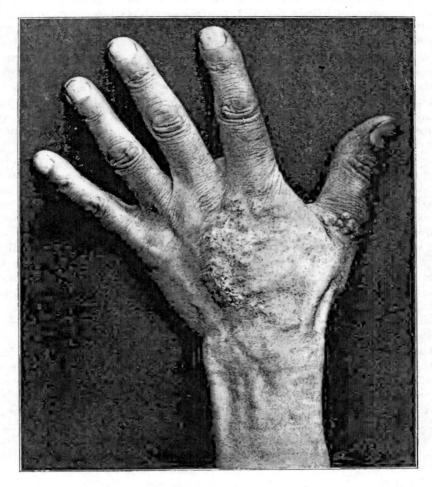

FIG. 93.—Tuberculosis verrucosa (chronic type).

died from tuberculosis, e.g., pathologists, post-mortem porters, etc. Veterinary surgeons, butchers, and others who handle the carcases of tuberculous animals are also liable.

Pathology. Tubercles with characteristic giant-cells, containing tubercle bacilli, are found in the lesions, and there are often miliary abscesses in the vascular layers of the skin. In some instances it is difficult to find the organism, but the inoculation of guinea-pigs generally gives a positive result.

Clinical features. The lesions occur usually on the fingers and backs of the hands, as these are the parts most likely to come in contact with the infecting organism. I have once seen the root of the nose affected. Two types may be recognised. In the first, a small red swelling develops at the site of inoculation, and upon it a small pustule appears. The swelling slowly enlarges to form a warty nodule with an infiltrated base, surrounded by a zone of erythema. The appearance suggests an infected wound, but the ordinary antiseptic applications have little or no effect. The pus removed from the small abscesses contains Koch's bacillus. The lymphatic glands enlarge early. In one such case, where the lesion was at the root of the nose, Mr. Russell Howard and I were for some time in doubt whether the sore was not syphilitic, as there was a hard bubo under the jaw. At that time examination for spirochætes was unknown. Wassermann's test was made several times, but was always negative. The bubo suppurated and tubercle bacilli were found in the pus.

In the second type of case an ovoid or lobulated warty swelling forms, cicatrises in the centre, and spreads at the edge, perhaps for several months or even years. The characters of the fully developed lesions are peculiar. There is a central depressed, often pigmented, cicatrix, around which is a ring of dark red warty nodules, covered usually with a crust resembling putty, and beyond this again is a zone of erythema, often of a purplish tint. The affection is generally attended with itching. The glands are involved early and the viscera are occasionally attacked. In a characteristic case under my care the primary infection took place in a butcher's shop, where the patient pricked the back of his left hand with a wire. The disease spread for three years, and when I first saw the case the whole of the back of the hand was affected, and the warty nodules were invading the fingers, an invasion I have several times noticed. The patient lost his arm from secondary infection of the elbow-joint from the epitrochlear gland.

Diagnosis. The tuberculous lesion is differentiated from the extragenital chancre by the finding of the spirochæte in the latter and of the tubercle bacillus in the former. Wassermann's test may be of value. Where it is impossible to carry out these examinations it may be necessary to wait for the appearance of secondary symptoms. Granulomata due to actinomyces and blastomyces are diagnosed by the finding of the respective organisms in the pus.

Treatment. In acute cases the diseased area should be excised or destroyed by the cautery. In chronic cases the warty masses may be removed by the curette and the parts then exposed to the X-rays, or a strong creosote and salicylic acid plaster (Leslie's) may be used to destroy the thickened areas. The Finsen light is of great service after the warty excrescences have been removed by the plaster.

Scrofulodermia.

Scrofulodermia is the name given to certain forms of tuberculous abscess and ulceration, usually associated with breaking down scrofulous glands or with caseous foci in the bones and joints.

Etiology. Children and young adults are most often affected with scrofulodermia, but occasionally the disease occurs in elderly subjects. The breaking down foci of tubercle in the glands, etc., lead to the formation of sinuses, and the skin is secondarily infected from them.

Pathology. Tubercles of the common type are found in the lesions, and Koch's bacilli may be demonstrated. A characteristic is the undermining of the skin by the softening process.

Clinical features. The neck, groins, and limbs are the common sites of scrofulodermia, but the face and trunk are sometimes attacked. I have seen several instances where the disease has developed over the buccinator muscle from breaking down of the buccal gland, which is sometimes present. This gland drains the buccal area inside the mouth and also a small part of the adjacent skin.

Scrofulodermia begins as a painless swelling in the subcutaneous tissue or the true skin. The epidermis over it becomes of a purplish red colour, and then the central part of the gummatous tumour softens. In rare cases there is spontaneous resolution, but usually the skin gives way and an ulcer with overhanging irregular bluish edges forms. The cavity is irregular, and its base is covered with pale flabby granulations. There may be pockets or fistulæ running in various directions, and several adjacent lesions may communicate by tracks under bridges of thin purplish skin. The discharge is sanious or serous or purulent, and tubercle bacilli may be found in it. The destruction may extend deeply into the tendon sheaths and bones when the extremities are affected. In some cases a chronic form of progressive ulceration extends from the cervical glands on to the face and neck. The scar left after healing is irregular and often presents fibrous knotty masses or bands and tags, and occasionally bridges.

It is usually adherent to the deeper structures, and the parts may remain pigmented for a long time. Conjunctivitis, keratitis, blepharitis, and nasal and aural discharges are sometimes found in association.

Diagnosis. Scrofulodermia is distinguished from common lupus by originating as a gummatous swelling associated with caseous glands and other local tuberculous disease, and especially by the absence of the apple-jelly-like nodules of lupus vulgaris. It is not, however,

FIG. 94.—Scrofulodermia. Secondary to tuberculous cervical glands.

uncommon to find the two conditions coexisting, and sometimes scrofulodermia is followed by true lupus.

The syphilitic gumma is distinguished by its more rapid development, by the absence of gland and bone disease, and in the ulcerating form by the punched-out character of the syphilitic ulcer. There are usually other evidences of syphilis present. The Wassermann test is often of great service.

Bazin's disease affects young women almost exclusively, and the lesions appear symmetrically on both legs, usually in the calves.

Actinomycosis, blastomycosis and sporotrichosis are differentiated by the presence of their respective organisms in the pus.

Mycosis fungoides usually occurs in adults, and there is generally a history of antecedent premycosic symptoms, *e.g.*, a scaly or eczematous eruption, urticaria or erythrodermia. Intense itching is a constant feature.

Prognosis. If the lesions can be removed or destroyed the prognosis is good. There is usually, however, evidence of general debility

FIG. 95.—Scrofulodermia. Secondary to tuberculous glands.

Treatment. If possible the original tuberculous disease should be treated surgically, when the removal of the infected glands and skin may be carried out at one operation, and an endeavour made to bring the parts together and obtain primary union ; or, if this is impossible, an epidermic graft may be applied either at once or when healthy granulation has been established. In many instances, where the skin affection is the chief feature, the overhanging edge may be removed and the area thus opened up treated by the X-rays, after thorough disinfection. Some excellent results are thus obtained. Curetting of the cavity with the subsequent use of the rays is also valuable. Iodoform, europhen, or aristol may be applied locally. In some cases I have seen good results from the injection of tuberculin.

In all cases the patient must have good food, and tonics such as cod-liver oil and iron are required. A prolonged residence by the seaside, especially on the east coast, is to be recommended.

Tuberculous lymphangitis is a variety of scrofulodermia.

It occurs chiefly on the limbs. The primary focus is generally a warty tuberculosis on the extremity, such as a toe or a finger. Following this there appear at intervals along the limb a series of gumma-like nodules, perhaps four or five, from the heel to the popliteal space, or along the forearm. These nodules are at first of a purplish or brownish tint, and break down into chronic indolent ulcers, discharging a sanious pus. The lesions heal up, leaving depressed pigmented scars. Besides the ulcers there is often solid œdema, *pseudo-elephantiasis* (Fig. 101), and sometimes the lymphatic trunks may be felt as an indurated band. The nodules are caused by emboli in the lymphatic vessels. Tubercle bacilli and sometimes pyogenic organisms associated with them have been found, and inoculation experiments are positive. The treatment is the same as that of scrofulodermia, but the solid œdema usually persists.

Tumour-like forms of tuberculosis of the skin. Fungating tumours, described variously as tuberculosis fungosa, tuberculosis vegetans and frambœsiformis, occasionally occur as the result of infection by Koch's bacillus. The lesions are red, irregular, soft tumours or nodulated plaques, and their surface may be ulcerated or covered with scabs. They are the result of direct inoculation or secondary to glandular, bony, or joint infection. The tumour, according to Pick, consists of a plate of infiltration in the cutis, the swelling above it being formed of granulation tissue, part of which has undergone caseous degeneration. The condition has to be distinguished from neoplasms of the sarcomatous type and from mycosis fungoides.

REFERENCE.—L. WICKHAM. *Annales de Dermatologie*, 1894, p. 321.

Chronic Tuberculous Ulcers.

Occasionally chronic ulcerations of a rounded or oval or irregular outline, and with a soft undermined edge, are met with in scrofulous subjects. There may be difficulty in determining whether the ulcers are syphilitic or tuberculous. The presence of an undermined edge, the chronicity of the lesions, and the absence of evidence of syphilis elsewhere will be a guide. In a doubtful case the tuberculin test should be made. The treatment consists in keeping the parts at rest, the application of antiseptic dressings, and attention to the general health. Small repeated doses of the X-rays appear to favour healing.

Lupus vulgaris.

Lupus vulgaris is a granuloma of tuberculous origin attacking the skin and adjacent mucous membranes ; it spreads by continuity and by the formation of fresh foci, and destroys the tissues involved, either by ulceration or by subepidermal cicatrisation.

Etiology. More than half the patients are attacked before the tenth and over 80 per cent. before the twentieth year. Exceptionally the disease may occur in advanced life. Females are more frequently the victims of lupus than males, the proportion in my clinic being 70 and 30 per cent. respectively. Although not confined to the poorer classes, lupus is much commoner in the children of the indigent and ill-fed than in those in better surroundings. Dirt, bad hygiene, and insufficient food have an important influence on the resisting power of the individual to infection, and it is in children living in these conditions that we find the most destructive types of the disease. An examination of the tuberculo-opsonic index of a large number of patients made by Dr. Wm. Bulloch showed that there is often a general predisposition, the index being subnormal in many instances. A history of tuberculosis in the family is found in an excessive proportion of the cases. In the patients seen at the London Hospital it is as high as 40 per cent. Lupus vulgaris is often associated with other tuberculous affections, particularly of the glands, bones, and joints, but phthisis is uncommon, though it may be a sequel to the cutaneous affection. It is exceedingly rare, however, to find that lupus occurs in more than one member of a family. Dr. D. E. Morley found twelve cases in the notes of the London Hospital clinic in thirteen years.

Climate appears to play an important part, and the disease is more common in northern latitudes than in Southern Europe and in tropical and sub-tropical regions.

The organism reaches the skin :—(1) By direct inoculation. Tattooing, piercing of the lobule of the ear for earrings, vaccination, morphia-syringe punctures, and, rarely, wounds have been followed by lupus. Scratching and picking the lesions of impetigo are probably also common causes. Infection of the inferior meatus of the nose may be caused by inhalation of infected dust, but more probably by direct inoculation from infected fingers. I have recently seen a case in which cold abscesses followed tuberculin injections for phthisis. These, in their turn, were followed by characteristic lupus vulgaris in three areas which had been the sites of inoculation. (2) By secondary infection of the skin from sinuses, etc., caused by the breaking down of tuberculous glands, and caseating foci in bones and joints. (3) By the softening of some distant focus and the escape of tubercle bacilli into the blood stream. This occurs most

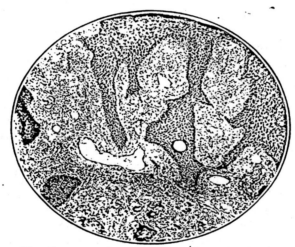

Fig. 96.—Lupus vulgaris. Microphotograph of section showing infiltration and giant cells. ⅔ in. obj.

commonly after certain acute specific fevers, especially measles (lupus post-exanthematicus).

Pathology. The lupus nodule is a granulation new-formation, consisting of masses of round nucleated cells in a delicate reticulum of connective tissue. Giant-cells may be seen and plasma-cells are common. Tubercle bacilli are present, but in very small numbers, and a large series of sections may have to be examined before one bacillus is detected. The centre of the lupus lesion tends to undergo fatty degeneration, but caseation does not occur. The process destroys the glands and the hair follicles, and finally all the normal structures of the skin are replaced by scar tissue. The epidermis may be unaffected, but in long-standing conditions it may undergo atrophy, or the horny layers may be greatly thickened. The injection of Koch's old tuberculin is followed by a local reaction in the affected tissues, and similar results may be obtained by rubbing a 10 per cent. tuberculin ointment into the part. The inoculation of guinea-pigs with lupus tissue gives positive results. Dr. Stanley Griffith has isolated both human and bovine types of Koch's bacillus

FIG. 97.—Widespread lupus of the trunk.

and modifications of both from my cases. Positive reactions are also obtained by von Pirquet's, Calmette's, and Moro's tests.

Clinical features. Lupus may attack any part of the integument, and may spread to the mucous membranes, or it may be primary in the mucous membranes, especially that of the nose, and invade the skin secondarily. In 78 per cent. of the cases seen at the London Hospital the face was affected first, the parts most commonly attacked being the nose, cheeks, and auricles. Next in frequency came the neck. The hairy scalp, forehead, and upper eyelids, were usually avoided. In only 8 per cent. of the cases were the trunk and

Plate 21.

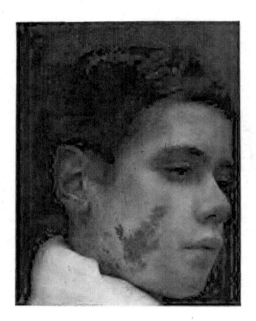

LUPUS VULGARIS.

Boy, aged twelve. The eruption was of eight years'
duration. The jelly-like nodules are well shown.
An area of scar is seen behind the main group.

extremities attacked, and the disease was exceedingly rare on the palms and soles, in the axillæ, and about the genitals and anus.

· The mucous membranes were affected in over 43 per cent. of the patients attending the London Hospital. In the Finsen Institute at Copenhagen, Christiansen found 80 per cent., but the type of lupus

FIG. 98.—Lupus vulgaris.

seen in Denmark is much more severe than that met with in this country. In a considerable proportion of the cases the mucous membranes are attacked primarily.

There are many clinical forms of lupus, but the primary lesion is nearly always a small " nodule " or spot slightly elevated above the surface. Its colour is pale yellow, or yellowish red, to dark red, with a translucency not unlike that of apple 'jelly (Plates XXI. and XXII.), but the translucency may be masked by scaling. The characters of the lupus nodule are best seen by examination in day-light under the pressure of a glass tongue depressor or diascope. The pressure removes the surrounding hyperæmia, and the non-vascular, apple-jelly-like spot stands out clearly. The primary focus is generally single, but multiple spots are not uncommon. I have seen as many as twenty-seven separate lesions scattered widely about the face, trunk and extremities. This variety is called lupus dissemi-natus, and commonly occurs after an acute specific fever. Lupus foci spread by peripheral growth, and adjacent areas often coalesce. In this way flat patches (lupus planus) or elevated plaques (lupus

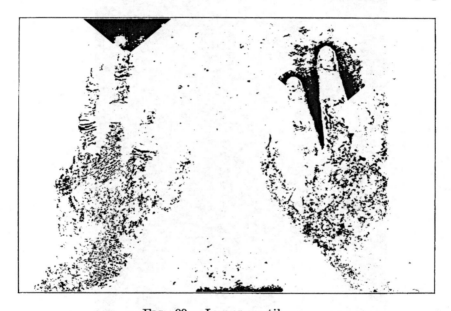

FIG. 99.—Lupus mutilans.

discoides) are formed. In other cases the disease extends by a nodular margin, while the centre undergoes spontaneous cicatrisation, and in this way ringed, gyrate, and festooned figures are formed. Sometimes, also, the disease creeps along the skin in one direction, leaving behind it a trail of scar.

There may be no breach of surface even in lesions which have lasted for many years, and this type of dry lupus has been named "lupus non-exedens." On the other hand, particularly in the more feeble and debilitated subjects, the nodules or patches break down to form ulcers—"lupus exedens or exulcerans." The dry forms of lupus may heal in part, very rarely entirely, without treatment. In

Plate 22.

LUPUS VULGARIS.

Extensive dry lupus, of over thirty years' duration. The colour
of the nodules and the scaling of the patch on the cheeks are
characteristic.

many instances there is an increase of the horny layers over the lupoid areas, causing scaly patches (resembling psoriasis) and warty nodules. In lupus exedens the lesions may be ulcerative from the onset, or they may begin as dry areas which subsequently break down. In many of the ulcerative cases the destruction is comparatively rapid, and about the nose, mouth, etc., may lead to grave deformity. The lesions may take a pustular, serpiginous or vegetative form. The lupus ulcer

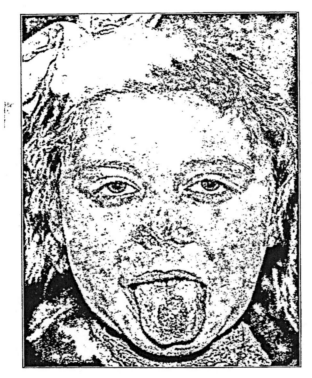

FIG. 100.—Lupus of nose, with ulceration of the tongue.

varies in depth and character in different subjects. Its edge may be raised and present characteristic jelly-like nodules, or it may be thickened and scaly or warty. The base is indolent and often covered with crusts, or with vegetations (lupus vegetans). Limited areas of ulcerative lupus may simulate impetigo or rupia. A pustular form affecting the hair follicles may resemble acne or sycosis. The bones and muscles are not implicated, but where the nose and ears are affected the cartilage is often destroyed, and great disfigurement results. Lupus vulgaris always leaves permanent scars. In rare instances the ulcerative process may be of phagedenic type (lupus

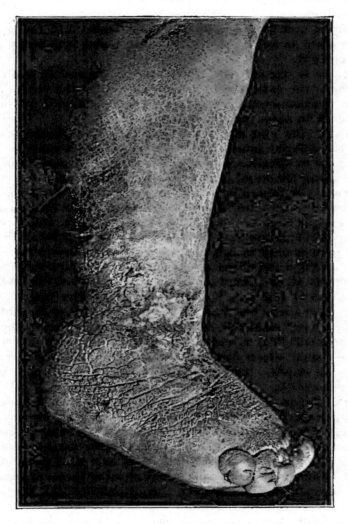

Fig. 101.—Tuberculous pseudo-elephantiasis. Female, æt. 44.

vorax), and when the extremities are attacked there may be destruction of the fingers, from coincident teno-synovitis, leading to grave deformity (lupus mutilans) (Fig. 99).

Lupus of the limbs may be associated with lymphangitis, leading to solid œdema, almost amounting to elephantiasis (Fig. 101). Thickening of the lips also occurs from coincident invasion of the skin and mucous surfaces and from recurrent attacks of erysipelatous inflammation.

The lupus scar is generally thin and white and fairly smooth, but it is often unsound, and may break down into fresh ulcers or become cheloid.

Variations in the activity of the process, depending upon varying conditions of the patient, and perhaps also upon the virulence of the organism, are common, while secondary infection with pus organisms always tends to more rapid destruction.

Lupus of the mucous membranes. The disease commonly attacks the inferior meatus of the nose, where it may be primary or secondary to affection of the skin. From the nose it may spread upwards along the nasal duct to the lachrymal sac, and even to the conjunctiva. Epiphora is a common symptom of early nasal lupus, and shows that the nasal duct is obstructed. The disease may also pass backwards from the nose to the naso-pharynx, and through the anterior palatine foramen to the front of the hard palate. Both hard and soft palates may be affected, and also the mucous membrane of the gums and lips and of the buccal cavity. The pharynx and larynx may be involved, and there is reason to believe that the disease may extend to the middle ear. The nose is by far the most frequently attacked, then come the lips and buccal mucosa and palate. The tongue is rarely affected (Fig. 100). The primary lesion on the mucous membrane is a slightly raised patch with a granular or uneven surfac, upon which small ulcers develop. In the nose the lesions are usually covered with crusts. The gums are swollen and red, and ulcerated loosening the teeth.

Course of lupus. The disease always runs a very chronic course, but the process is sometimes comparatively rapid when there is superadded pus-coccal infection. Cases lasting twenty and thirty years are not uncommon. Recurrences after apparent cure are frequent. The physique of the patient is, as a rule, poor, and there is a great tendency to the development of other forms of tuberculous disease. In many cases, however, the general health is not seriously affected.

The ulcerating forms of the disease lead to grave deformity—for instance, destruction of the nose, perforation of the cartilaginous septum, atresia of the nostrils, ectropion of the lower lids, contraction of the buccal orifice, and mutilation of the auricles and of the extremities.

Complications. *Erysipelas* is not uncommon, and sometimes has a beneficial and even curative effect on the lupus. *Visceral tuberculosis* is not frequent, but may lead to a fatal issue. Pulmonary complications are the most common, especially in connection with lupus of the naso-pharynx. Fifteen deaths occurred from phthisis and two from tuberculous meningitis in over a thousand

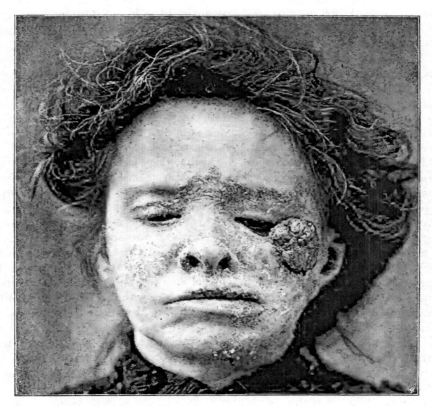

FIG. 102.—Epithelioma on lupus of 23 years' duration.

cases of lupus at the London Hospital. Bone and joint tuberculosis also occur.

Epithelioma (Fig. 102) develops upon cases of lupus of long duration. It was the cause of five deaths in a thousand cases at the London Hospital clinic. It rarely occurs unless the disease has been in progress for twenty years. Males are more liable than females, doubtless as the result of their being more exposed to irritation by climatic and other conditions.   Prolonged X-ray treatment of lupus vulgaris also tends to produce epithelioma.

Diagnosis.   Lupus has to be distinguished from other forms of cutaneous tuberculosis, from lupus erythematosus, and from syphilitic and other granulomata.

Scrofulodermia occurs in the same class of patient, and even in the same individual.   The lesions are primarily gummatous formations about caseating lymphatic glands, or tuberculous foci in the bones and joints.   There are no apple-jelly-like nodules, and the irregular ulcers have a thin undermined bluish edge.

The tuberculous ulcers which occur about the orifices of the body are only seen in advanced visceral tuberculosis.   They are acute in their development, and have thin undermined edges.   The conditions classed as tuberculosis verrucosa may be difficult to distinguish, but their warty character and appearance on the extremities, often with a history of infection, should make the diagnosis clear.   The early involvement of the lymphatic glands is a valuable point.

Lupus erythematosus should rarely give rise to trouble.   It is symmetrical nearly always, and affects the nose, cheeks, and auricles ; there are no apple-jelly nodules, and the disease usually starts at a later age.   The only difficulty lies in the superficial form of lupus of the face called Lupus tuberculeux erythemateux of Leloir, in which there are true nodules, but these are only recognisable upon biopsy.

Syphilis, especially the nodular and ulcerative tertiary forms, may lead to considerable difficulty, but the following points should be borne in mind.   Lupus takes years to cause the destruction which syphilis may cause in a few weeks to a few months.   The syphilitic gummata show no apple-jelly nodules, and the ulcers are round, or tending to be round, and punched out in character.   If the nose and palate are affected necrosis of bone points to syphilis.   Lupus does not destroy bone.   In doubtful cases one of the cellnial tests for tuberculosis may be applied, or Wassermann's test for syphilis may be used.

Lepra.   The nodules of leprosy are more raised than those of lupus ; they are of a dull earthy colour, and have no apple-jelly translucency.   Where there is any real doubt, a nodule should be excised.   In lepra, Hansen's bacilli are found in large numbers and recognition is quite easy.   The presence of anæsthetic patches and of a thickened ulnar nerve, of course, point to lepra.

In blastomycosis, actinomycosis and sporotrichosis the organisms of these diseases are easily demonstrable.

In lupoid sycosis the lesions are pustular from the onset, and even

16—2

in the most chronic cases pustules are seen about the hair follicles at the margin.

Treatment. The treatment of lupus vulgaris may be considered from three points of view: (1) Measures adapted to increase the resisting power of the patient to the invading organism ; (2) the destruction or removal of the bacilli ; and (3) the destruction or removal of the lesions produced by them with as little injury to the healthy tissues as possible.

The resistance of the patient is improved by good feeding, particularly the use of fat, milk, cream, cod-liver oil ; by attention to the general hygiene, a life in the open air being of great value ; and by the administration of tonics, such as iron and arsenic. Recently

FIG. 103.—Treatment of lupus vulgaris by the Finsen-Reyn lamp.

great use has been made of tuberculin in minute doses, controlled by the observation of the opsonic index as carried out by Wright. I regret that I cannot say that I have seen much benefit in true lupus from the " opsonic " treatment. In a few cases of lupus of the ulcerative variety distinct benefit has resulted, but in the ordinary dry type success from tuberculin injections is rare, and the results observed in my own clinic are supported by the experience of Reyn in the Finsen Institute at Copenhagen. Byrom Bramwell advocated the internal administration of thyroid gland, and its use has been attended with success in a certain number of cases, but the drug cannot be recommended for general use, as sometimes it has caused serious symptoms.

The *local treatment* of lupus has for its aim the removal or destruction of the tubercle bacillus and the products of its activity with as little destruction of the healthy tissue as possible. For this purpose chemical caustics, the cautery, erasion, scarification and excision, phototherapy and radiotherapy are all used. The chemical caustics, nitric acid, acid nitrate of mercury, caustic potash and chloride of zinc are not often employed, on account of their indiscriminate action and the unsightly scars they produce. For large areas on the limbs I have

FIG. 104.—Lupus vulgaris (dry variety), 25 years' duration.

used with advantage the strong creosote and salicylic acid (made by Leslies) with great advantage. The plaster is applied for forty-eight hours at a time, and after one or more applications the softer lupus nodules often slough out, leaving small pits, which heal up under an antiseptic dressing. This treatment is often advantageously combined with phototherapy and radiotherapy. I often use also an ointment composed of pyrogallic acid, salicylic acid, and ichthyol, of each forty grains to the ounce in vaselin. The caustic action of this preparation is used to thin down warty masses of lupus. Erasion still has many advocates, and the immediate results are often very satisfactory. The operation is performed under a general anæsthetic. The curette should be used boldly to clear away every part of the diseased area which will yield to its edge. After scraping, the area should be well swabbed over with phenol, in the hope of reaching any organisms which have not been removed by the curette, and to seal up the lymphatic spaces which have been torn open in the operation. Unless very thoroughly done, there appears to be some risk in the scraping leading to the infection of the surround'ng tissues, and I do not advocate it, except in some warty and fungating cases, as a preliminary to the application of the X-rays.

Scarification is sometimes useful. It consists in the mincing of the affected tissues by multiple linear incisions of the growth by a sharp scalpel or a special many-bladed knife. It is carried down to the fibrous tissue. This operation must be performed under an anæsthetic, and has been accused of tending to disseminate infection by setting free particles of infected tissue into the vessels.

Lang of Vienna has had some admirable results from excision of lupus areas, and this measure is strongly supported by many other surgeons. The operation is carried out under anæsthesia, and the incision should lie an eighth to a quarter of an inch outside the obviously affected area, and be carried down as deeply as possible. In facial lupus the removal should not go below the subcutaneous fat. If the wound is too large to be brought together by suture, grafts should be applied. Should the removal not be deep enough, the grafts may subsequently be infected, and any nodules which thus occur are extremely difficult to deal with. Excision cannot be recommended as a treatment for choice on the face unless the area is very small. On the limbs and elsewhere, where the resulting scar is of little moment, it is often the best method of treatment, as it has the great merit of rapidity.

Phototherapy by Finsen's method gives the best cosmetic results, and is the procedure to be advised if the lesions are on the face or exposed parts and of moderate size. It is very tedious and expensive, and requires an elaborate apparatus and skilled attention on the part of the nurses. It cannot be applied to an ulcerated area, and is not often practicable for the treatment of lesions of the mucous membranes. The procedure is the concentration of actinic light by means of rock-crystal lenses, fitted in a tube, on to the affected areas (Fig. 103). The light is produced by a powerful electric lamp, and the heat rays are absorbed by passing the beam through a column of distilled water. At the focus of the rays the skin is compressed by an apparatus consisting of two pieces of rock-crystal fixed in a metal ring. Through this compressor a current of cold water passes constantly. The compressor is held in position by an attendant, or, in some situations, fixed by a special holder, and the sitting lasts for at least one hour. Six hours after the application a blister forms, which is dressed with a soothing or antiseptic ointment, and healing takes place in from ten days to a fortnight. An area the size of a shilling can be treated at one sitting, and in an extensive case the treatment may have to be carried on for several months, and even years. The best results are obtained in cases of dry lupus which have

Fig. 105.—Lupus vulgaris. The same patient after Finsen treatment.

not been subjected to erasion or other measures which cause scarring. Relapses are not common, except in cases where there is disease also of the mucous membranes. In 1,039 cases treated by the Finsen method at the London Hospital, only 31 were uninfluenced by treatment, 730 cases were cured (99 being free from recurrence for ten years), 117 required occasional treatment, and 161 were improved but not cured. The Finsen-Reyn modification of Finsen's original apparatus is as satisfactory as the larger apparatus. It can be worked from the electric lighting mains served with a continuous current. Kromayer's mercury vapour lamp gives intense reactions with a ten minutes' application, but it is very fragile. The scars are not so smooth nor so supple as those produced by the Finsen apparatus. It is, however, of considerable service in extensive superficial lesions on the extremities. A tungsten arc lamp is also useful.

The application of the X-rays is of great value in the ulcerative forms of lupus, and in some of the mucous membrane lesions. The exposure is measured by the Sabouraud pastille. After the application, repeated at intervals of ten days, the ulcers dry up and the scar is usually sound. The rays, however, have less effect upon the dry forms of lupus, unless applied to such a degree that an inflammatory reaction occurs, and this is very liable to be followed by a pigmented atrophic telangiectatic scar. If pushed this treatment may result in epithelioma.

Radium may be used to destroy individual nodules. It causes a depressed scar, upon which telangiectases may appear.

I have found the method of treating intranasal lupus by nascent iodine devised by Pfannenstiel of great assistance. The patient is given 45 grains of sodium iodide in a mixture daily in divided doses, and the nasal cavity is packed with a gauze tampon, which is kept constantly moistened with a solution of peroxide of hydrogen. Free iodine is liberated in contact with the diseased tissue and rapidly promotes healing.

Recently my colleague, Dr. Western, has been successful in treating some intractable cases of mucous membrane lupus by intravenous injections of cyanide of gold and cantharidin (Spiess method).

REFERENCES.—" Multiple Lupus after Measles and other Fevers." H. G. ADAMSON. *British Journal of Dermatology*, 1904, p. 366, collected cases. " Lupus Secondary to Tuberculous Glands." H. EMLYN JONES. *Ibid.*, September, 1907, p. 305. " Lupus and Tuberculous Disease of the Ear, Nose, and Throat." H. F. TOD and G. T. WESTERN. *Practitioner*, May, 1908, p. 703. " Tuberculosis as a Cause of Death in Lupus." FORCHAMMER. *Archiv. f. Dermatologie*, XCII., p. 3. " The Finsen Treatment at the London Hospital," 1900—1913. J. H. SEQUEIRA. *Lancet*, June 14, 1913, p. 1655. " Observations on the Opsonic Treatment." A. REYN and KJER-PETERSEN. *Ibid.*, March 28, 1908, p. 919. The valuable series of papers in the Reports of the Finsen Institute are worth study. " Lupus and its Operative Treatment," by E. LANG, with results of 240 cases, Vienna, 1905. Pfannenstiel's Method. OVE STRANDBERG. *Berlin. Klin. Woch.*, January 23, 1911, p. 106, and J. H. SEQUEIRA. *British Journal of Dermatology*, XXIII., p. 327.

The Tuberculides.

The name " Tuberculides " was given by Darier to a group of cutaneous and subcutaneous affections whose characteristic features arc—(1) the patient is a tuberculous subject and reacts to tuberculin ; (2) the eruptions are generally bilaterally symmetrical ; (3) the histology of the lesions suggests tuberculosis ; (4) the tendency in the majority of cases is to spontaneous cure ; (5) the bacillus of Koch is almost invariably absent ; (6) inoculation of the guinea-pig is rarely successful.

To explain these phenomena it has been suggested that the lesions are a reaction of the tissues to a tuberculo-toxin derived from some antecedent glandular or other focus. Other observers hold that the eruptions are produced by the circulation of dead tubercle bacilli in the blood. The third hypothesis is that the tuberculides are caused by emboli of bacilli of low virulence. Rist and Rolland's researches, however, throw a new light on the tuberculides. They believe the cutaneous tuberculides to be a manifestation of allergy in subjects in whom there is a manifest or latent focus of tuberculosis. The tuberculides are therefore spontaneous examples of Koch's reaction. This reaction presents certain points of interest which are worthy of note in this place.

A primary inoculation of Koch's bacilli in a guinea-pig produces, after a latent interval of from two to twelve days, according to the dose of the organism and its virulence, a nodule which softens and ulcerates. The ulcer is rounded or irregular, its edges are raised and infiltrated, and it rests on a deep induration. It secretes a caseous pus or is covered with crusts. The primary lesion is a polynuclear abscess containing numerous tubercle bacilli. The nearest gland enlarges, and later there is bilateral glandular infection, and the ulcer retains its characters till the death of the animal in two or three months.

If, after an interval of a month or more, the animal is re-inoculated with Koch's bacilli, the lesion produced at the site of re-inoculation has quite different characters. There is oedema from the first day. In a few days a brown, indurated plaque forms, and in five or six days a slough begins to separate. The base of the sore left after the slough has come away is formed by the superficial muscular layer of the region. Cicatrisation goes on rapidly under a crust, and about a month after the re-inoculation a perfectly supple scar is left. Bacilli are extremely rare in sections of such lesions even twenty-four hours after re-inoculation. Everything points to a rapid destruction of the organisms introduced, and upon this depends the rapid healing of the lesions. Rist and Rolland suggest that the tuberculides are caused by endogenous re-inoculation, and clinically the lesions present many points of resemblance to the phenomenon of Koch, which is caused by exogenous re-inoculation.

The tuberculides are of several types, varying from pin-head-sized papules to large indurated tumours. They comprise—(1) lichen scrofulosus, chronic indolent papules causing no symptoms ; (2) indurated papular and nodular lesions, tending to undergo central necrosis and leaving scars. These conditions vary, and a large number of names, based upon their clinical characters, have been given to them, e.g., folliclis, acne scrofulosorum, acnitis, etc. ; (3) indurated tumours of the hypoderm, tending to necrosis and ulceration, leaving deep pigmented scars (erythema induratum of Bazin).

Recent observations suggest that some of the conditions which have been called erythema nodosum may be tuberculous. The subjects of the tuberculides commonly suffer from acroasphyxia and chilblains. The disseminated form of lupus erythematosus is sometimes regarded as a tuberculous exanthem, and would therefore be included in the " tuberculide " group. There appears to be some doubt as to the tuberculous origin of the chronic fixed form of lupus erythematosus, though a large proportion of the sufferers show signs of visceral or glandular tuberculosis. The consideration of these points is deferred to the chapter upon Lupus erythematosus (p. 387).

REFERENCES.—The tuberculides were the subject of discussion at the International Congress, Paris, 1900. In the transactions are valuable papers by Bœck, Colcott Fox, and many others. GOUGEROT and LAROCHE. " Experimental Reproduction of Cutaneous Tuberculides." *Archives de Médicine Expérimentale et d'Anatomie Pathologique*, September, 1908, No. 5, p. 581. E. RIST and J. ROLLAND. " Études sur la Réinfection tuberculeuse." (*Annales de Médicine*, tome II., No. 1, July 15, 1914.)

Lichen scrofulosus.

Lichen scrofulosus is the commonest tuberculide. Its relationship with tuberculosis has long been recognised.

Etiology. Most of the patients are children or adolescents, suffering from tuberculosis of the glands, bones, and joints, or of the skin, but rarely from phthisis. Injections of Koch's old tuberculin have occasionally been followed by the eruption, and the histology of lesions thus caused differs in no particular from those arising in connection with visceral or gland tuberculosis.

Pathology. The little papules consist of miliary tubercles of characteristic structure, containing epithelioid cells and giant cells. A local reaction is obtained in the majority of cases after the injection of tuberculin. The tubercle bacillus has very rarely been demonstrated in the lesions.

Clinical features. The eruption consists of rounded papules of a pale yellow or brownish tint, and occasionally almost the colour of the surrounding skin. They vary in size from a pin's head to a millet seed. There is sometimes a central depression to the papule, and a minute adherent scale may be attached to its summit. Rarely the lesion contains a minute bead of pus. The eruption is usually arranged in oval or crescentic patches composed of a number of discrete papules. There are no symptoms, and the affection is often unnoticed by the patient. The papules may last for months, and even years, and gradually clear up, usually without, but occasionally with, scarring. The eruption may occur. The trunk is most often affected.

Diagnosis. Lichen scrofulosus has to be distinguished from certain other papular eruptions. Lichen planus occurs on the forearms and fronts of the legs and on the thighs, occasionally on the trunk. The papules are of a peculiar lilac or violet tint, shiny and flat topped. Itching is usually pronounced, and there are white patches commonly in the mouth. There is no relation to scrofula. Acne is uncommon in children, and usually affects the face and upper part of the trunk. Comedones and secondary suppuration would be diagnostic of acne. Papular eczema is attended with itching, the onset is more acute, and vesication is common. The papular syphilide is of a brownish or hammy tint, the lesions are scaly at the margin, and there are other signs of syphilis. In pityriasus rubra pilaris the dorsal aspect of the fingers and the face are affected.

Prognosis. The prognosis of lichen scrofulosus is favourable, but its presence indicates that the patient is tuberculous.

Treatment. Cod-liver oil and general tonics, good feeding, and an open-air life are indicated. Arsenic internally is of service. Locally, inunction of cod-liver oil is advocated by many eminent authorities. Ointments of ichthyol, resorcin, and tar are also of value.

REFERENCE.—RÖNA. International Congress, Paris, 1900. LESELLIERS *Ann. de Derm. et de Syph.*, November, 1906, p. 897.

Papular and Nodular Tuberculides.

This group comprises a number of affections intermediate between lichen scrofulosus and the indurated tumour formations of Bazin's disease.

Colcott Fox collected twenty different names which have been given to eruptions of this type. The nomenclature depends upon probably accidental characters, such as the affection of the follicles of the skin, or the depth of the lesions and their tendency to necrotic changes. In all forms the eruption is symmetrical, and commonly associated with bad peripheral circulation, and has a tendency to affect the extremities.

Etiology. The patients are usually young, and the subjects of tuberculosis of the glands or lung, or of some other form of tuberculosis of the skin.

Pathology. Some of the lesions appear to be about the follicles, but in the majority of those recently examined the primary affection is a phlebitis, probably due to infected plugs. Infiltration of lymphocytes and fixed cells occurs about the small vessels of the

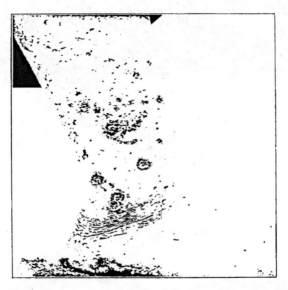

FIG. 106.—Necrosing tuberculide. Small type. Girl, æt. 11. The lesions were symmetrical.

dermis. Giant cells have been found, and in rare instances tubercle bacilli have been demonstrated.

Clinical features. Small necrotic type. "Folliclis." The lesions are flattened rounded papules in the deep part of the skin, giving the sensation of shot imbedded there. They vary in size from a pin's head to a lentil seed. The colour is dusky red, or purplish, and the papule is surrounded by an erythematous zone (Plate XXIII.). The subsequent course varies. In some instances the papules disappear spontaneously, leaving small pigmented stains. More commonly the summit is noticed to contain a little serous fluid, and finally a small pustule appears in the centre. This

Plate 93.

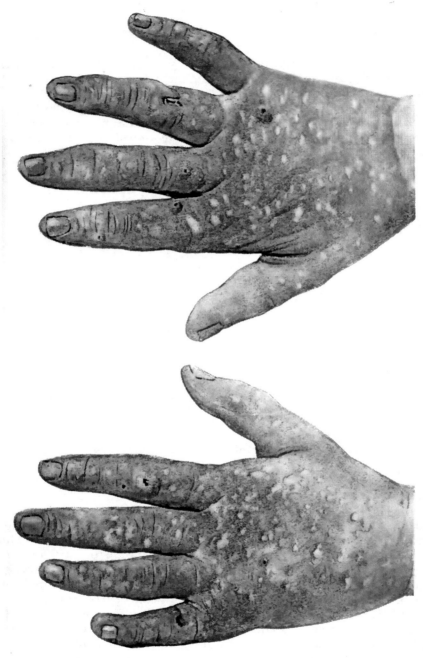

SMALL NODULAR TUBERCULIDE. Female, aged twenty-two. Active necrosing lesions, scars, &c. over phalanges.

dries up to form a small cone-shaped crust or scab, which on removal reveals a conical ulcer, which runs an indolent course. The coalescence of two or more neighbouring lesions may produce an irregular ulcer. The ulcers, on healing, leave depressed pigmented scars. The eruption is not painful, but there are tenderness, and, occasionally, itching. Crops of the spots may appear for several months or even years, but an individual lesion usually lasts for several weeks only. I have twice seen symmetrical painless effusion into the knee-joints in children suffering from this form of tuberculide. One of these patients when fifteen years of age came under treatment for erythema induratum (Bazin's disease).

The eruption appears in patients subject to acroasphyxia, and the hands and feet and the elbows and knees are the seats of election. The auricles are also frequently attacked, and the scarring may lead to atrophy. Occasionally the palms and soles are affected, but the face generally escapes. The outbreaks often occur during the spring and autumn.

Prognosis. This variety of tuberculide runs a chronic course, but the ultimate prognosis is good. Its presence must, however, be taken as evidence of tuberculosis.

Acne scrofulosorum. The patients are young subjects, usually suffering from tuberculosis of the glands.

The eruption consists of minute red papules the size of a millet seed. Each lesion has a small pustule at its apex from which a hair projects. The pus dries up to form a small scab or crust, and under this is a small ulcer. The ulcers leave pigmented scars, which may ultimately become pale. The seats of election are the upper and lower limbs, and the extensor surfaces are more affected than the flexor. The trunk and face are rarely involved.

Acne cachecticorum. This eruption occurs in the same type of patient. It appears on the face, back, chest, and lower limbs, and consists of papules and pustules varying in size from a pin's head to a lentil seed, of a livid purplish red colour, closely resembling a syphilide. In some cases there are hæmorrhagic lesions. The eruption may persist for several years, but clears up with the improvement in the general health of the patient. Small scars or pigmented spots are left.

Darier records the case of a patient who suffered from phthisis and scrofulous glands of the neck, axillæ and groins in whom there were lesions of the acne cachecticorum type on the trunk, folliclis on the limbs, and also tuberculous ulceration of the skin.

Acnitis (Barthélèmy). **Acne agminata** (Crocker). It is not yet agreed that this form of skin eruption is tuberculous, but there is good evidence that it is similar to the diseases described in this section. Varioliform acne, hydradenitis suppurativa, and acne telangiectodes are synonyms for this affection.

The eruption consists of rounded, brown papules imbedded in the skin. At first they are about the size of a millet seed, but they may reach the dimensions of a pea.

The forehead and temples are the seats of election, but the eyebrows and eyelids and the skin over the angle of the jaw may also be affected. In rare cases the trunk and limbs are attacked. There is no fever and no pain, but the patient may complain of itching. Soon after their appearance the papules become red, and soften ; small pustules form, and the scanty exudate dries up into crusts, which fall off, leaving small pigmented scars.

Differential diagnosis of the papular and nodular tuberculides. The predilection of the eruptions for the extremities is a point of importance. Variola is distinguished by the absence of fever, pains in the back, etc. In acne vulgaris the lesions are more acute ; there are black-heads, and the seats of election are the face and upper parts of the trunk. Lupus erythematosus involving the auricles might be mistaken, but it has no tendency to necrotic and ulcerative changes, and usually there are butterfly symmetrical patches across the middle of the face.

Treatment. Recognising that the subjects of these forms of eruption are tuberculous, attention must be directed to the improvement of the patient's general health. Cod-liver oil, iron and arsenic, combined with good food, plenty of milk, cream, and fat, and above all, where possible, residence by the sea, are of greater importance than the local treatment. Stimulant antiseptic ointments and lotions are the best local applications. The red oxide of mercury ointment is one of the most useful in my experience. If the lower extremities are affected, rest in the horizontal position must be enjoined. In some cases tuberculin, B.E. in 1—10,000 milligram doses, has proved of value.

REFERENCES.—" Tuberculides." T. COLCOTT FOX. *British Journal of Dermatology*, 1900, XII., p. 383. Discussion, International Congress, Paris, 1900. Tubercle bacilli found in lesions by MACLEOD and ORMSBY. *British Journal of Dermatology*, 1901, XIII., p. 367. PHILLIPSON. *Archiv. f. Derm. ü. Syph.*, February, 1901, p. 215. " Folliclis and Acnitis." BARTHÉLÈMY. *Annales de Derm.*, 1891, p. 532 ; 1893, p. 883 ; 1900, p. 856. " Acnitis." J. SCHAMBERG. *Journal of Cutaneous Diseases*, January, 1909. W. J. OLIVER. " Acne agminata." *British Journal of Dermatology*, XXVI,, p. 439 (Plate and Sections).

Tuberculides of the Hypoderm. Erythema induratum of Bazin.

Bazin's disease is a chronic malady affecting young girls almost exclusively. It is characterised by symmetrical node-like swellings of the legs and occasionally of the upper limbs. The lesions are chronic and tend to break down into indolent ulcers.

Etiology. Erythema induratum usually begins in adolescence, and is rare after twenty-five. The patients are nearly always young girls, and often those who have to stand at their occupations. It is therefore commonest in young shop assistants, domestic servants and the like. The patients are often overworked and underfed, and it is not uncommon to find evidence of tuberculosis in the glands, etc.

Pathology. It is believed that the affection starts in the hypoderm, and fluid removed from an unulcerated lesion resembles liquid fat. Giant cells and epithelioid cells have been demonstrated in the tissue. Granular necrosis of the cellular infiltration causes a softening of the tumour and destruction of the skin. Koch's bacillus has not been demonstrated in the tumours or in the fluid removed from them, but Colcott Fox and others have inoculated guinea-pigs with tuberculosis by injecting material derived from the lesions. Positive results are obtained with old tuberculin and with von Pirquet's and Calmette's and Moro's tests.

Western showed me a patient suffering from tuberculous disease of the ankle, for which he had been giving tuberculin (bacillary emulsion) in the usual way, and in whom lesions indistinguishable from Bazin's disease appeared in the leg. He has had a similar case, in which the cutaneous affection appeared after injection of the same tuberculin for scrofulous glands of the neck.

Erythematous nodules appear after the injection of tuberculin intradermically, but the swellings more closely resemble erythema nodosum, in some cases of which Marfan has been able to obtain positive reactions with von Pirquet's test. It therefore seems probable that some forms of erythema nodosum are related to Bazin's disease.

Clinical features. The lesions are red or purplish red, indurated, ill-defined plaques of various sizes, but usually about half to three-quarters of an inch in diameter. The seats of election are the lower part of the calf, and the outer aspect of the leg. As a rule there are several plaques on each leg. Occasionally similar indurations are seen on the upper extremities. The swellings appear subacutely, and vary in size from time to time. In many cases the nodes break down into rather deep ulcers with an irregular edge, a greyish or red base, surrounded by an area of infiltration. They run an indolent course, and when healed leave pigmented depressed scars which ultimately become white. The cicatrices simulate those of syphilitic gummata very closely, but they are nearly always symmetrically placed on both legs.

Diagnosis. Bazin's disease must be distinguished from several forms of hypodermic nodules and indurated plaques. The essential

FIG. 107.—Erythema induratum. Girl, æt. 16.

features are its occurrence in young girls, its predilection for the calves, its chronic course, and its symmetry. The syphilitic gumma usually occurs later in life ; it is generally asymmetrical, and there are other signs or a history of syphilis. Scrofulodermia occurs in relationship with breaking down tuberculous glands or caseating foci in the bones and joints. Lesions due to sporotrichia could only be differentiated by the finding of the organism. Varicose veins are associated with nodular infiltrations due to phlebitis, and the patient is usually older.

Treatment.   It is of the first importance that the patient should be kept in the horizontal position.   In the cases in which ulceration has not occurred this may be sufficient to effect a disappearance of the lesions, but they often recur when the patient resumes the vertical position, and especially if her occupation necessitates long standing.

FIG. 108.—Erythema induratum.   Ulcers and extensive scars.   Girl, æt. 18.

In the ulcerated cases rest is also imperative, and the ulcers usually heal up after a few weeks' confinement to bed, with the application of a stimulating ointment such as the Unguent. Hydrarg. Oxid. Rubr. Bier's congestion treatment is also of value, and small doses of the X-rays will help.   The patient requires good food and fresh air, and cod-liver oil and general tonics are often of service.   I have tried tuberculin, but am not impressed with the results, and in view of the cases of Western, in which similar lesions developed after the injection of the bacillary emulsion. I should not be inclined to push it.

REFERENCES.—WHITFIELD, A. *American Journal of Medical Sciences*, December, 1901, and *British Journal of Dermatology*, XVII., 1905, No. 7, p. 241, and XXI., 1909, p. 1. KRAUS. *Archiv. Derm.*, August, 1905, p. 85.

Hypodermic Sarcoids of Darier and Roussy.

Darier and Roussy have described a condition which appears to be related to Bazin's erythema induratum. The lesions are chronic indolent neoplasms in the hypoderm, but have no tendency to ulceration. They occur chiefly in females between the ages of thirty and forty. They vary in size from a pea to a nut, and often form nodular patches or cordons. They may occur anywhere, but are usually seen on the trunk in the costal regions. Giant cells and lymphocytes are found, and the lesions are surrounded by a fibrous envelope. The tuberculous nature of the disease has not been proved by inoculation, and Koch's bacilli have not been demonstrated.

REFERENCE.—DARIER and ROUSSY. *Archiv. de Med. Expérimentale et Anatomie Pathologique*, 1906, No. 1.

Multiple Benign Sarcoid of Boeck.

There are two forms of this rare affection, which, by its histological characters and its association with the papulo-necrotic tuberculides, appears to be related to tuberculosis.

In one form the lesions are hemispherical elevations of the skin varying in size from a millet seed to a pea. They are at first pink, then purplish, and finally brown. The surface of the papules is smooth, they are of soft consistence, but on examination with the diascope do not present the apple-jelly appearance of lupus nodules. The face is symmetrically affected, and papules appear also on the shoulders and extensor aspects of the limbs. Other parts are rarely involved. The eruption lasts for several years, and there is no ulceration. Eventually stains and atrophic scars are left.

Males are rarely affected. Most of the patients are females between fifteen and forty. The lymphatic glands may be enlarged, and there is often visceral tuberculosis. The lesions consist of masses of epithelioid cells, leucocytes, and occasionally giant cells.

In the nodular type the swellings may be as large as a small nut. They have a purplish tint, and occur as two, three, or a dozen discrete tumours on the forehead, chin, neck, shoulders, elbows, and knees.

The general health requires attention. Injections of tuberculin and of calomel are recommended. Arsenic in the hands of Bœck proved valuable.

REFERENCES.—BŒCK, C. *Archiv. für Dermatologie ii. Syph.*, 1905, LXXIII., pp. 71 and 301. KREIBICH and KRAUS. *Ibid.*, Vol. XCII., p. 173.

Leprosy.   Lepra.   Elephantiasis Arabum.

Leprosy is a chronic constitutional specific disease characterised by (1) the formation of granulomatous nodules in the skin and mucous membranes, or (2) peripheral neuritis with trophic disturbances, or (3) a combination of these.

Etiology.   Lepra is not now indigenous in this country, It occurs in Norway, Russia, and on the Mediterranean. It is endemic in India, China, and Japan, and in the West Indies, Central and South America, and the islands of the Pacific, in South Africa, and in Queensland. In the United States and Canada it occurs chiefly in the Scandinavians who have settled there.

The infective organism is the *bacillus lepræ* of Hansen. It is believed by Bayon and Kedrowski to exist in two stages : a nocardial or streptothrical form which is not acid-fast, and a bacillary and acid-fast stage. The latter closely resembles the tubercle bacillus. It has not been grown on artificial media, but successful inoculation of the monkey has been reported. It is believed that infection takes place commonly through the nasal mucous membrane, and occasionally through wounds, but there is little reliable evidence on this point. Hutchinson's attractive and brilliantly defended hypothesis that the infective element reaches the human subject by means of fish taken as food is not generally received, and there is no proof that Hansen's bacillus makes any variety of fish, fresh or in a state of decomposition, its habitat. It has recently been suggested that the bed-bug and perhaps other epiphytes may act as carriers of infection.

The period of incubation is unknown. It has been variously estimated at from a few weeks to several years. I have notes of a case in which the first symptoms were not noticed until the patient had been home from Burmah seven years, and another in which nine years elapsed between the probable time of infection and the appearance of symptoms.

Lepra is contagious in a low degree, and close and probably prolonged contact is apparently necessary. It is believed that cohabitation is a common cause of infection, although it is well known that a man may not give the disease to his wife even when they have been living together for many years. I know of one little group of three cases in one family. The mother, father, and one child out of three suffered from leprosy. There is no actual evidence of heredity, however, though probably a predisposition may be inherited. Some would prefer to consider lepra a household disease. It is curious that sometimes leprosy is introduced into a small community and persists there for generations, but segregation efficiently enforced tends gradually to stamp it out.

Pathology. The cutaneous and subcutaneous nodules are granulomatous infiltrations of the corium and of the hypoderm, and closely resemble the similar lesions of syphilis and tubercle. Hansen's bacillus is found in large numbers in the lesions in great contrast to the sparsity of the organisms in lupus and some other tuberculous conditions. The bacillus is found in the lymphatic glands and in the spleen and kidneys.

It is interesting to note that Wassermann's reaction is positive in many cases of leprosy, which may be taken as an indication that this reaction is due to chemical changes, and that the bacillus of Hansen produces an analogous change in the blood to that caused by the spirochæta. I have, however, seen three cases of the nervous type which gave a negative reaction.

In nerve leprosy there is an inflammation of the connective tissue of the nerves, and in this the bacillus is found. The nerves are irregularly thickened, and the fibrosis causes degenerative changes in the nerve fibres, leading to atrophy of muscles, trophic changes in the skin and deeper structures.

Clinical features. The three varieties of leprosy present such diverse features that they require separate consideration.

Nodular leprosy. (Lepra tuberculosa.) This variety is most co mon in temperate regions. In Norway more than half the cases are of this type, while in the tropics the proportion varies from 10 to 20 per cent.

Before any eruption appears there are prodromal symptoms, which may last from several weeks to a year or more. Attacks of intermittent fever, with chills and sweating, may suggest malaria. There are great prostration, malaise, pain in the bones, loss of appetite, diarrhœa, and epistaxis, with attacks of vertigo.

The eruption consists of smooth yellowish brown or reddish infiltrated spots, which vary a good deal from time to time, and may disappear temporarily. The next stage is the formation of nodules. At first they are small pinkish papules, which gradually enlarge, and by coalescence form infiltrated brown or yellowish brown plaques, with an irregular, rather nodular surface. At first the nodules are hyperæsthetic, but, later, sensation may be lost.

The eyebrows, nose, ears, and lips are the parts most frequently affected. The flexor aspects of the limbs, the chest, axillæ, and the scrotum and penis may also be involved. The palms and soles escape.

Enlargement of the nodules and the extension of the infiltration produce great deformity. The bosses on the eyebrows, cheeks, and nose give the patient a remarkable appearance, which has been called " leonine " (Fig. 109).

Fig. 109.—Nodular leprosy.

The nasal mucous membrane is studded with nodules, and this causes snuffling and a discharge containing crowds of the acid-fast bacilli. The buccal, pharyngeal, and laryngeal membranes are also affected, and a curious croaking voice is the result. The disease may even spread to the bronchi. The eyes are often severely affected in lepers. The eyelids, conjunctiva, cornea, and iris are attacked, and blindness may result. Dr. McLatchie and I had under observation a woman with leprous nodules as large as a pea on each cornea (Fig. 110). Similar lesions occur on the vaginal and uterine mucous membranes and on the penis. The testes undergo atrophy. Lepers of both sexes are usually sterile.

Course. Nodular leprosy runs a chronic course, with occasional exacerbations accompanied by febrile symptoms. The nodules tend to atrophy, leaving pigmented spots or scars, but in many instances they ulcerate, and large areas may be thus affected. The leprous ulcer is shallow, and crusted with dried discharge. It is remarkably

FIG. 110.—Nodular leprosy. Lepromata on the corneæ.

indolent, and rarely painful. The disease may last for many years, and although a fatal issue may be brought about by exhaustion, a large proportion of the patients die from intercurrent pulmonary, renal, or bowel disease.

Anæsthetic leprosy. (Nerve leprosy. Macular leprosy.) This variety is most common in the tropics, where it constitutes about two-thirds of the cases, while in Norway and other temperate regions it occurs in about one-third of the patients.

The prodromal period is usually longer, and there are no febrile attacks. The cutaneous affection is secondary to a peripheral neuritis. The commonest skin lesions are a number of erythematous

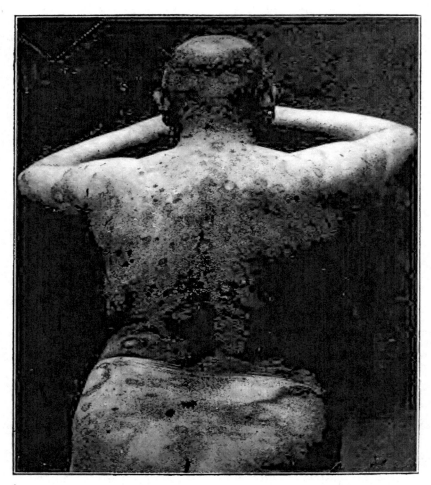

FIG. 111.—Maculo-anæsthetic leprosy.

patches of a reddish brown or bluish colour, and rounded in outline (Fig. 111). After a time the colour becomes duller, and ultimately a brownish pigmentation remains. In some instances the patches lose their colour from the centre, and finally become white. The affected skin tends to scaliness, and perspiration is diminished. The hair turns white or falls out; but, curiously, the scalp hair is usually unaffected. In old cases the areas of affected skin are pale and shining. By peripheral extension the patches may coalesce and form large areas with gyrate outlines (Fig. 111).

The primary nerve symptoms are paroxysmal pains, burning and itching. Later, the patches become anæsthetic; loss of sensation is however not limited to the areas of erythema and pigmentation, but extends over definite tracts supplied by the affected nerves. Paralysis and atrophy of the muscles supplied by the diseased nerves may ensue. The peroneal and ulnar nerves are those most commonly affected, and, as a result, there follow definite muscular atrophies in the hands, leading to the "leper claw" (Fig. 112) and to a corresponding deformity of the feet. Deep ulceration may occur in the

FIG. 112.—Nerve leprosy. The "leper claw."

sole, and a "plantar leprous ulcer" results. The enlarged thickened nerves are easily palpable, especially the ulnar, as it runs behind the internal condyle. In one of my cases the external cutaneous nerve of the forearm could be felt and seen, like a wire under the skin.

The bones of the fingers and toes undergo a rarefying osteitis, and atrophy without ulceration. The terminal phalanges may be lost by a process of gangrene, and leave ugly stumps, "lepra mutilans" (Fig. 113). It is characteristic that all this destruction is painless.

Occasionally the lesions of the skin in macular leprosy are bullous, and large blebs containing sterile clear fluid are formed. The blebs dry up, leaving a pigmented spot or superficial scar.

The mixed type. This is more common than the simple forms in some parts of the world. Usually the nodular lesions appear first, and at a later date the nerve affection develops and produces its characteristic phenomena.

Diagnosis. Advanced cases of the disease are usually diagnosed with ease. The early nodular manifestations have to be

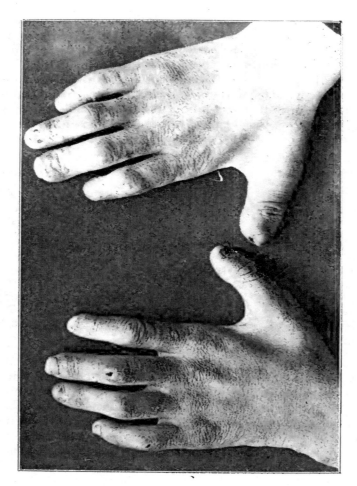

FIG. 1B.—Leprosy. Hands of a case of mixed nodular and anæsthetic varieties. Note the similarity with syringomyelia (Fig. 181). Case of Dr. Lewis Smith.

distinguished from nodular syphilis, from lupus vulgaris, and some of the rarer forms of granuloma caused by vegetable organisms. A definite diagnosis of lepra can be made by a biopsy and staining for bacilli.

Syphilitic nodules are redder than those of lepra; they are also usually smaller, and develop more rapidly. There are other symptoms to guide the practitioner, but it must be remembered that the Wassermann test may be positive in lepra as in syphilis. Lupus vulgaris is distinguished by the apple-jelly character of the nodules. It runs a very chronic course, and starts in childhood in the majority of cases. Lepra seen in this country is almost always in adults, and there is a history of residence abroad. The rarer granulomata due to vegetable parasites, blastomycosis, sporotrichosis, etc., tend to break down and suppurate, and the organisms can be recognised in the pus.

The macular form of lepra has to be distinguished from leucodermia, sclerodermia, from the premycosic stage of mycosis fungoides, and from syringomyelia. In leucodermia the white patches are simply areas of the skin devoid of pigment ; there is no atrophy. In sclerodermia there is in the late stages atrophy of the centres of the patches, but the margins have a peculiar pink or lilac tint, while the white areas are of an ivory colour. The areas of sclerodermia or mophœa tend to run along the limb and around the body. The ulnar nerve is not enlarged. In the premycosic stage of mycosis fungoides the eruption is either a generalised erythrodermia, or, if localised, it takes on the characters of eczema, or a scaly seborrhoide. The patient complains of intense itching. When the tumours develop, they are much larger than the nodules of lepra, they have a softish consistence, and tend to break down. In syringomyelia there is loss of sensibility to heat and cold, and no enlargement of the ulnar nerve. Cases of Morvan's disease, however, have given rise to considerable doubt, some authors maintaining that they are modified lepra, but this is disproved by the absence of Hansen's bacillus.

Prognosis. Lepra may be considered an incurable disease, but it undergoes many variations in its severity, and the removal of the patient to a temperate climate is usually of the highest benefit. As a rule, death occurs from intercurrent disease.

Treatment. The sufferer from leprosy requires good food, and as wholesome surroundings as are possible. Daily baths should be taken, and ulcerated surfaces demand the usual antiseptic applications. Chaulmoogra oil is undoubtedly of some value, and is well worth a prolonged trial. If the patient's digestive organs permit, the dose should be gradually increased from three minims of the oil up to a drachm or more thrice daily. The oil is given in capsule. An emulsion of chaulmoogra oil with camphorated oil and resorcin has been injected intramuscularly by Mercardo. Sir L. Rogers advocates the hypodermic injection of its active principle, gynocardate of soda (gr. ij. in 1 c.c. water), or the intravenous injection of $\frac{1}{10}$ grain gradually increased to $\frac{4}{5}$ grain once a week.

Anti-leprol, a refined constituent of chaulmoogra oil, is also used. Three to five c.c. are given by intramuscular injection or 15 minims to 2 drachms by the mouth. Gurgun oil has also been advocated. Many authors have strongly recommended mercurial treatment, and this should be carried out by intramuscular injection as in syphilis. Nastin, a fatty extract made from a streptothrix, which has been suggested as being peculiar to leprosy, mixed with benzoyl-chloride and dissolved in anhydrous olive oil, has been tried extensively. Beneficial results have attended the hypodermic injection of 10 c.c. once a week. I have seen it tried in several cases without appreciable improvement, but it has been attended with no untoward symptoms. Salvarsan and Neo-Salvarsan have also been given with doubtful results.

The nodules of lepra can be removed by the X-rays, but it is necessary to set up a distinct inflammatory reaction. The rays have no influence upon the course of the disease. Chaulmoogra oil rubbed in locally is believed to be advantageous.

In the nerve variety of leprosy strychnine has been recommended. Arsenic sometimes appears to be useful.

The question of the segregation and efficient treatment of the cases of leprosy which come into the British Islands from time to time has been under consideration, and an institution has been built for their accommodation.

REFERENCES.—For the recent literature the periodical *Lepra* should be consulted. *Transactions of the International Congress on Leprosy,* Bergen, 1909. "Résumé of Communications." *Journal des Maladies Cutan. et Syph.,* 1909, Fasc. VI., pp. 566—594. HANSEN. *Virchows Archiv.,* 1879, 88. HANSEN and LOOFT. "Leprosy in its Clinical and Pathological Aspects." Translation by Norman Walker, 1891. Wright, Bristol. UNNA, BAELZ, BUROW and WOLFF. "Lepra Studien," 1885. A. NEVE. "Ocular Leprosy." *British Medical Journal,* 1900, May 12. GRAHAM LITTLE. "Leprosy in Jamaica." *British Journal of Dermatology,* 1904, XVI., p. 441. H. BAYON. *South African Medical Record,* Cape Town, 1912. MINNET. *Journal of London School of Tropical Medicine,* 1912.

Rhinoscleroma.

A chronic microbic affection of the nose and upper lip, characterised by tumour formation of cartilaginous hardness, with involvement and closure of the nasal fossæ.

Etiology. Rhinoscleroma occurs endemically in Eastern Europe, especially in Austro-Hungary and Russia. It has also been observed in some tropical countries. It affects the poorer classes, beginning in youth or early adult life.

Pathology. The disease is caused by the bacillus of Frisch, which has some characters in common with Friedländer's pneumonia bacillus. The lesions are caused by a peculiar infiltration in the corium. There is dense small cell infiltration, but the special elements are large hyaline and colloid cells. In the large cells of the tumours and in the glands the bacillus is found. The sclerotic character is caused by dense fibrous connective tissue. The epidermis is little affected, but down-growths closely resembling cell-nests have been described.

Clinical features. The disease begins insidiously with the formation of painless pink or red nodules in the anterior nares, or on the surface of the nose or the adjacent part of the upper lip, sometimes in the buccal cavity and pharynx, and very rarely in the external auditory meatus. The lesions are well-defined, smooth infiltrations of the true skin or mucous membrane, of a peculiar cartilaginous or stony hardness. By their fusion plaques or masses form which may block up the anterior nares, or lead to stenosis of the naso-pharynx and even the larynx. The surface is smooth and tense, and tends to fissure or crack. The process is essentially chronic and may last for many years, death occurring usually from pulmonary complications. It is locally malignant, tending to recur after removal.

The **diagnosis** has to be made from syphilis, cheloid, and the malignant neoplasms.

Treatment. Surgical interference, except at the very earliest stage, is uniformly unsuccessful, and if the nares can be kept patent, there is little indication for treatment. Some improvement has been reported from the application of the X-rays.

REFERENCES.—V. FRISCH. *Wien. Med. Wochenschrift*, 1882, 32. NOYES. *Monatsheft. f. prkt. Dermatol.*, 1890, X., p. 341. WOLKOWITSCH. *Centralblatt f. Med. Wissenschaft*, 1886, 47. PAWLOWSKY. *International Congress of Berlin*, 1890. A case was described by SIR F. SEMON and DR. PAYNE. *Pathological Transactions*, XXXVI., 1885.

Keratodermia blenorrhagica.

A symmetrical horny eruption on the soles occurring in gonorrhœa. This very rare condition was first described by Vidal. A few instances have been recorded in France. The first case recognised in this country was reported by the author in 1910.

The patient was under the care of Dr. F. J. Smith, suffering from gonorrhœal arthritis and periarthritis of the right knee, right elbow, and right sterno-clavicular articulations. The left knee was also slightly affected. The man was in a very cachectic condition, anæmic and wasted. The urethral discharge had ceased after a few days' treatment with sandal-wood oil before the patient was admitted to hospital. The cutaneous condition was remarkable. Along the inner border of each foot was an irregular horny mass with a nodular surface. Smaller masses were present along the outer side of each sole, and the intervening areas were covered with yellowish brown parchment-like thickening of the epidermis. The nodules were of a dark brown or purple-brown colour, aptly likened by my clinical

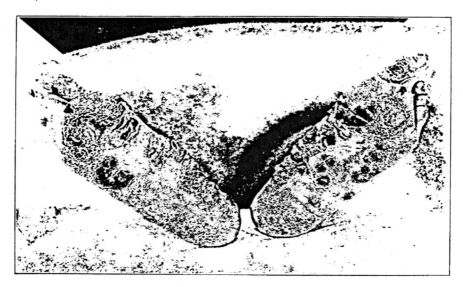

Fig. 114.—Keratodermia blenorrhagica.

assistant, Dr. Williams, to sloes embedded in the skin. The individual swellings measured 0·3 to 2 centimetres across. The masses as a whole closely resembled a mountain range on a relief map, a description which has been given by French authors. Although most developed on the soles, the excrescences crept towards the dorsum of the foot on both inner and outer aspects. The area affected was sharply defined by a narrow zone of hyperæmia. With the exception of small nodules at the base of the great toe, the digits were free. The lesions felt like horn, and no fluid could be withdrawn on puncture.

Dr. Turnbull found that the nodules were covered with a thick horny cap, and that the stratum granulosum and Malpighian layers were infiltrated with neutrophile leucocytes. There was also some œdema of the papillary layer with lymphocytic infiltration and plasma cells about the vessels.

Under treatment by gonococcus vaccine the arthritic lesions subsided and the carapace on the soles peeled off in large masses, leaving reddish brown stains, the whole duration of the keratodermia being about three months. This appears to be the usual course. Winkelried Williams, Graham Little, and others have since shown cases of this rare condition. In some instances the palms are also affected, but usually to a less extent than the soles. The disease is only met with in grave gonococcal infection with severe arthritic and general symptoms. Jacquet described a case in which three successive attacks of gonorrhœa were followed by keratodermia and articular disease.

REFERENCES.—VIDAL. *Annales de Dermatologie et de Syph.*, 1893, 3me serie, IV., p. 3. JACQUET. *Bulletin et Mem. Soc. Med. des Hôp. de Paris*, 1897, 3me serie, XIV., p. 93. J. H. SEQUEIRA. *Proc. Royal Society of Medicine, Dermatological Section*, 1910, p. 77.

Ulcus molle. Soft Chancre.

A highly contagious ulceration caused by infection with the strepto-bacillus of Ducrey.

Etiology. The infection almost always occurs in coitus by the inoculation of an erosion or herpetic sore with the pus from a soft chancre. Extragenital soft sores are extremely rare.

Pathology. The parasite is a short bacillus with rounded ends, sometimes occurring in pairs and often in chains, hence the name *strepto-bacillus*. It has been cultivated upon peptonised human skin and on blood-gelose. Monkeys and some other animals can be inoculated. The lesion is a destruction of the epidermis and part of the dermis, the surface of the ulcer being covered with pus containing the organism. Under the purulent layer lies a plasma-cell infiltration with inflammation of and around the vessels.

Clinical features. The soft chancre develops very rapidly. In two or three days after infection a small vesico-pustule appears, which soon develops into a small ulcer. The ulcer enlarges rapidly, but rarely exceeds a sixpenny piece in size. The edges are elevated and often fissured. The floor is covered with a greyish-yellow or greenish material, and exudes an abundant purulent secretion. The base of the ulcer is free from induration, and around it is a red slightly swollen areola. The soft chancre is rarely single. Auto-inoculation is exceedingly common, and multiple sores of all sizes are frequent. In the male the prepuce, glans, and frenum are the common sites.

In the female, the vestibule, the labia minora, clitoris and fourchette are most commonly affected. By auto-inoculation lesions often occur in the anal region, in the gluteal cleft, and on the pubic region and the inner sides of the thighs. The secondary chancres may be little larger than a lentil seed.

The lymphatic glands are swollen, painful and tender, and tend to suppurate early. The bubo is of large size, and on rupture forms an ulcer with fistulous tracks. Dr. Malcolm Simpson has called my attention to the fact that the gland swelling in ulcus molle may appear three to four weeks after the ulcer has healed and that it may then suppurate.

From mixed infection, phagedena and gangrene may occur, but they are rare.

Diagnosis. The multiplicity of the lesions, their early appearance after exposure to infection, the characters of the ulcers, and especially the absence of induration, are points which distinguish the soft sore from the Hunterian chancre. The early involvement of the glands, which are large, painful, and not shotty, is also a valuable diagnostic feature. In all cases the spirochæta pallida should be looked for. In my experience ulcus molle is much less common than syphilis, and a patient with supposed soft sore must be carefully watched for signs of the graver malady for at least a month and frequently examined for spirochætes. The inoculation of the patient with his own pus is sometimes practised. The inoculation is made in the deltoid region, and the characteristic sore appears in forty-eight hours.

Treatment. The best application is iodoform in powder. On account of its penetrative and distinctive odour it is sometimes replaced by europhen, airol, or iodol, but these substitutes are not so efficient. Silver nitrate solution (30 grains to the ounce) may also be used. Permanganate of potash in 1 per cent. solution is also valuable. The parts should be kept scrupulously clean, and frequent hot baths are of great service. Audry recommends the application of the thermocautery held a few millimetres away from the sore, the heat alone being sufficient to destroy the strepto-bacillus.

REFERENCE.—TOMASCZEWSKI. "Handbuch der Geschlechts-Krankheiten," II., p. 631, "Extra-genital Ulcus Molle." MERIAN. *Monatsheft. f. prakt Dermatol.*, November 15, 1911, p. 531.

Ulcus molle serpiginosum. A chronic spreading ulceration of the groins and adjacent parts which occasionally follows a soft sore in patients who have lived in the tropics. The process apparently begins with the breaking down of a suppurating gland secondary to ulcus molle. The ulcer gradually spreads until it may involve a large part of the thigh or of the abdominal wall. The edge of the ulcer is ragged and deeply undermined, the overhanging part being white, while outside the colour is first purplish and then red. The base is fleshy, uneven, and secretes freely. If improperly treated it may last for several years. Ducrey's bacillus is found in the lesions. Iodide of potassium up to 200 grains a day and local applications of camphphenol and iodoform are the best treatment (McDonagh). McDonagh suggests a relationship between· this condition and granuloma inguinale (p. 337), and this is supported by the fact that the intravenous injection of antimony has proved of great service (*vide* p. 338). The early cases described were nearly all of tropical origin, but a number of instances have been recently seen in soldiers who have been on service in Europe (Fig. 114A).

REFERENCE.—J. E. R. McDONAGH. *British Journal of Dermatology,* 1914, XXVI., p. 1, coloured plate and sections.

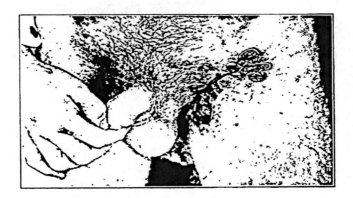

FIG. 114A.—Ulcus molle serpiginosum.

CHAPTER XI.

SYPHILIS.

Syphilis is a general infectious, contagious, and hereditary disease caused by the *Spirochæta pallida* (*Treponema pallidum*). The cutaneous manifestations only will receive special notice here.

Etiology. The *Spirochæta pallida*, discovered by Schaudinn in 1905, is a spirillar organism 6 to 14 μ long and 0·5 μ broad. It

Fig. 115.—Microphotograph of spirochætes, from a chancre. Preparation by Dr. McIntosh, London Hospital. Dark background illumination.

forms half-a-dozen or more spirals, and at either extremity there is a flagellum of extreme tenuity. Examined in hanging drop it preserves its motility for some hours. Noguchi has shown that the organism can be grown on agar and ascitic fluid in which are suspended small pieces of rabbit's tissue. The exact biological position of the spirochæta pallida is not yet determined. In 1908 Balfour demonstrated mobile granular bodies in the spirillar organisms. Noguchi showed (1911) round bodies attached to young spirochæta pallida as if they were sprouting from these spore-like bodies, and two years later demonstrated granules in pure cultures of the organism.   Meirowsky and Schereschewsky have shown what appear to be lateral and terminal bud-like bodies, and also fission of the spirochæta pallida, and on these grounds the organism would be classed as a vegetable parasite.   On the other hand McDonagh claims to have demonstrated intra-cellular stages of the organism with a sexual cycle.   E. H. Ross also described the development of the spirochæte from intra-cellular bodies.   The subject requires further investigation.

The spirochæta is found in large numbers in the primary sore, in the glands, mucous membrane lesions, recent papules and condy-

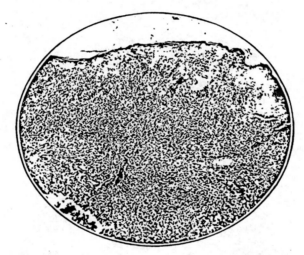

Fig. 116.—Primary chancre.   Microphotograph of section.

lomata.   It is less common in the macule.   In the stage of generalisation it may be detected in the blood, spleen, and adrenals. It is said that the organism may be demonstrated in the fluid raised by a blister applied to a dry lesion.   In tertiary lesions it is very rare, and apparently less active.

The spirochæta is abundant in the syphilitic fœtus and in the skin lesions and organs (liver, spleen, adrenals, and lungs) of the congenital syphilitic infant.

Monkeys can be inoculated, and the contagion can be conveyed, under special conditions, to rabbits, dogs, and sheep.

Immunity against inoculation may be inherited or acquired.   It is impossible to inoculate an individual (1) who is suffering from congenital syphilis (Profeta's law) ;   (2) who is already suffering from the acquired disease ; (3) a woman who has borne a syphilitic infant but has herself shown no signs of the disease (Colles' law). In the

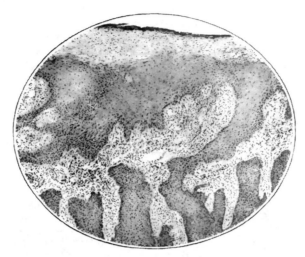

FIG. 117.—Papular syphilide, condyloma. Microphotograph of section.

FIG. 118.—Syphilitic gumma. Microphotograph of section.

last case the mother is suffering from latent syphilis, which may give a positive Wassermann reaction and show late gummatous lesions.

18—2

Pathology. The spirochæta is the cause of many types of lesion, but three conditions may be taken as representative of the pathological changes.

The primary sore consists of a cellular infiltration, with swelling of the connective tissue elements. The epidermis is the seat of a leucocytic and fibrinous infiltration. The vessels are inflamed, and the organism forms colonies in their walls, whence it passes by the vascular channels into the circulation, and by the lymphatics to the nearest gland.

The lenticular lesion may be taken as the type of the secondary manifestations. It consists of a cellular infiltration around the vessels. Occasionally giant cells are present. The epidermis may be unaffected, but in the scaly syphilides it is thickened, and in other forms œdematous and infiltrated, and it may undergo degeneration leading to superficial ulceration.

The gumma begins with venous thrombosis in the subcutaneous tissue. This is followed by excessive cell infiltration, which softens and liquefies. In all tertiary manifestations there is inflammation of the small vessels.

Vegetating syphilides are produced by hypertrophy and infiltration of the epidermis ; ulcerative lesions by necrosis and destruction of the epidermis and of the true skin. The hardness of the lesion varies with the amount of increase of the connective tissue elements.

Clinical Tests for Syphilis.

The demonstration of the spirochæta pallida.—The surface of the chancre may be scraped, but better results are obtained by driving a fine pipette into its substance. The serum thus obtained is placed on a slide with a few drops of normal saline solution and examined by the microscope ($\frac{1}{6}$ inch objective) by dark background illumination. The white spirochætes are seen in motion crossing the field. Or the serum may be mixed with a drop of distilled water and a drop of Chinese ink, or, as Harrison suggested, a solution of Collargol (Collargol 1, Aq. destillat. 19). A film is then made in the usual way by spreading the mixture with another slide, and the preparation is then allowed to dry. The examination is made with a twelfth oil-immersion lens. The white spirochætes are seen against the dark background of the Collargol solution. The organism is about twice as long as the diameter of a red corpuscle.

Similar preparations may be made from fluid obtained by puncturing the primary bubo, from moist papular and other lesions, and from the bullous congenital syphilide.

The Wassermann Reaction. By Dr. Paul Fildes.

The Wassermann reaction has now attained enormous importance in the diagnosis of syphilis. In many hospitals where facilities are available for its performance in large numbers it is becoming more and more the practice to confine the more expensive forms of treat ment to those patients only in whom the reaction is positive. The foundation for this method is based upon the extremely high incidence of the reaction in syphilis. Thus during the year 1912 an analysis of some 400 undoubted cases of active syphilis attending the London Hospital disclosed the following results :—

Primary syphilis	...	...	90 %	positive.
Secondary ,,	...	...	99 %	,,
Tertiary ,,	...	...	97 %	,,
Congenital ,,	...	...	100 %	,,

From such figures it is clear that the reaction is practically constant in undoubted cases of active syphilis, and therefore if such clinical diagnosis is insisted upon, in spite of a negative Wassermann reaction, it must be supported by extremely convincing evidence before it can be looked upon as probable.

On the other hand, although the test is admitted to be constant in syphilis, it is nevertheless necessary to show that it is invariably absent in non-syphilitic patients. A test which claims to be so absolute, and upon which so much must depend, must be absolutely specific.

Recently the suggestion has been advanced that the method is apt to give positive results in the absence of syphilis, and although such suggestions are purely speculative and have no foundation in some 10,000 cases, nevertheless it is impossible to disprove the allegation. If it were possible to select 1,000 persons known to be non-syphilitic, the constant occurrence of the negative reaction might readily be demonstrated, but when some 2 per cent. of all healthy persons have syphilis in all probability, and syphilis in an entirely latent and undiagnosable condition, the arrangement of such an investigation would be futile. In the *post-mortem* room of the London Hospital it was found that a certain high percentage of patients had syphilis, *but in very few had this condition been discovered before death.*

When the method here advocated was first introduced, 159 supposed non-syphilitic hospital patients were tested as controls and a small number of positive results were recorded. It was, however, possible on minute investigation to disclose in some cases proof of syphilis and in others a very strong probability.

Such considerations, taken with the fact that a positive result has never been brought forward in a patient in whom syphilis could be reasonably excluded, establishes the belief that the Wassermann reaction is specific for syphilis in the sense that it is never positive in the absence of syphilis or some allied disease.

It may be said that this belief is held by all observers in the leading laboratories of the world.

Technique. A detailed account of the principles and technique of the reaction would be out of place in this work.

As is well known, the "syphilitic antibody" in the patient's serum is permitted to interact upon the "antigen" representing the *Spirochæta pallida* and the "complement," with the result that the complement is fixed and prevented from causing hæmolysis of sensitised corpuscles subsequently added. A lack of hæmolysis will thus indicate a positive reaction and the presence of syphilis. If, however, hæmolysis supervenes it is clear that the complement added to the mixture has not been fixed by the antigen and serum, and thus the serum could not have emanated from a syphilitic individual.

For carrying out the test the following substances are required :—

1. *The serum to be tested.*—Although it is not to be expected that many practitioners will be able to carry out personally the rather complicated technique of the Wassermann reaction, it is within the power of all to take the necessary specimen of blood, which can be forwarded to a laboratory. As a general rule it will be found easier to remove the blood by a hypodermic syringe. A band should be placed round the upper arm, and, the bend of the elbow having been cleansed by ether or painted with iodine, the hypodermic needle should be passed longitudinally into the most prominent vein in front of the elbow, and at least two cubic centimetres of blood withdrawn. In some laboratories five cubic centimetres are demanded, and no doubt, when the arrangements are complete, the necessary capsules sent out from the laboratories will be accompanied by instructions as to the quantity required. Another method is to wind a rubber tube round the patient's thumb, making a puncture with a sterilised needle and drawing off the blood into a capsule of the type devised by Sir Almroth Wright. It is important to see that the ends of the capsule are carefully sealed by heat before posting to the laboratory. The serum is removed from the clot in the laboratory and "inactivated" by heat, since it is found that unheated normal serum will frequently give a positive reaction.

2. *The antigen.*—The antigen recommended is the heart-cholesterin mixture, which has been shown to furnish much better results than any other. The exact formula is a matter of great importance.

An alcoholic extract of human heart is first prepared, and this is mixed with a 1 per cent. solution of cholesterin in absolute alcohol in the proportion of 3 to 2. The mixture, if found to be satisfactory, is then diluted 1 in 15 with saline, and this dilution constitutes the antigen.

3. *The complement.*—This reagent is the fresh serum of a guinea-pig. Every sample must be standardised and found to be suitable. The serum is diluted 1 in 16 to 1 in 27 according to its capabilities, and is then ready for use.

4. *The corpuscle emulsion.*—The corpuscles used are those of the sheep. They are washed free from serum and suspended in saline solution in a strength of 5 per cent.

5. *The hæmolytic amboceptor.*—This substance is the serum of a rabbit which has been immunised against sheep's corpuscles. It is used in suitable quantities to "sensitise" the corpuscle emulsion.

The following table will indicate the mode of procedure. The various reagents are measured into test tubes in a rack in the following order and quantities and incubated at 37° C. as stated :—

TUBE No.

	1 2 Suspected Serum c.c.	3 4 Known Σ Serum c.c.	5 6 Known non-Σ Serum c.c.	7 8 Controls c.c.	
Serum . . .	0·1 0·1	0·1 0·1	0·1 0·1	— —	
Antigen 0·5 c.c.	1·0 —	1·0 —	1·0 —	1·0 —	Fixation Stage.
Complement 0·5 c.c.					
Saline 0·5 c.c. .	— 1·0	— 1·0	— 1·0	— 1·0	
Complement 0·5 c.c.					
	Incubate for 1 hour at 37° C.				
Sensitised Corpuscles	0·5 0·5	0·5 0·5	0·5 0·5	0·5 0·5	Stage of Hæmolysis.
	Incubate for 1 hour at 37° C.				

At the end of the period of hæmolysis it will be found that no hæmolysis has occurred in tube 3, while tubes 4, 5, 6, 7, and 8 are completely laked. Tube 2 will also be laked. In tube 1, however, the suspension of corpuscles may be laked or not according as the result is negative or positive or the serum derived from a non-syphilitic or syphilitic. It is desirable to confine the term " positive reaction " only to those sera which give complete inhibition of hæmolysis in tube 1.

The argument is often advanced against the validity of the Wassermann reaction that " paradoxical " results are sometimes obtained. That is to say, one and the same serum may be tested by different observers and found to be positive by some and negative by others. It is supposed by those unacquainted with the intricacy of the technique that such a result indicates a fundamental unreliability in the test. It must, however, be understood that the difference between a positive and negative reaction is not marked by any essential characteristic. It is merely one of degree, and since the standard of what constitutes a positive reaction differs among various observers, it is clear that in some cases the same serum will be evaluated differently. Such sera are usually of the slightly positive variety, and these may be reported positive or negative according as the result falls to one side or the other of the experimental error. (See "Report on the Diagnostic Value of the Wassermann Test," published by the Medical Research Committee.)

Noguchi's Luetin Reaction corresponds in syphilis to Von Pirquet's reaction in tuberculosis. Luetin is an extract prepared from cultures of the *Spirochæta pallida*. 0·1 c.c. is injected under the skin of the left arm and 0·1 c.c. of uninoculated culture medium as a control into the right arm. In syphilitic patients an anaphylactic action is set up which results in a local inflammation when the Luetin is inoculated. This reaction does not occur when the spirochætes are vigorous and abundant as in early untreated cases.

In a positive reaction the changes are :—At the site of inoculation after twenty-four hours there is an area of erythema varying in size from a pea to a threepenny piece, with a central papule of variable size. The papule is sometimes definitely elevated, firm and of a red colour. A couple of days later the lesion may increase in size and become darker and even suppurate. After several days it subsides leaving an indurated spot which gradually disappears, and may leave pigmentation. The Luetin reaction is more commonly obtained in tertiary and late heredo-syphilis than in the more acute stages. It is of far less practical value than the Wassermann reaction.

Acquired Syphilis. General Outline of the Course.

Infective contact is followed by a period of incubation, lasting as a rule from three to five weeks. In rare cases, this stage has been found as short as ten days and as long as three months. At the end of the period of incubation the **chancre,** or **primary sore,** develops at the site of infection. This lesion is the reaction of the tissues to the presence of the spirochæte. Within a week the nearest lymphatic gland is enlarged. A second period of latency lasting five or six weeks follows the appearance of the chancre, and then the **symptoms of generalisation,** the so-called "secondaries," appear. They are the reaction of the tissues generally to the organism brought to them by the blood stream. These manifestations consist chiefly of lesions of the skin and mucous membranes, and occasionally of the nervous system. The reaction of the tissues does not destroy all the spirochætes; some are left in the backwaters of the vascular system, where they may remain dormant. After a period of years, three or four to twenty or thirty, some of these organisms become free and, reacting on already sensitised structures, produce a violent reaction similar to that seen in the "tuberculides" (*vide* p. 248), and we have the **late syphilides,** usually gummata, in the skin, subcutaneous tissue, mucous membranes and viscera. These manifestations are frequently called "tertiary," but there is often no dividing line between the stages. From the practical point of view it is essential to distinguish the local (primary) stage and the stage of generalisation. It must, however, be recognised that in the late syphilides spirochætes are sparse, and that in this stage it is acknowledged that the patient may be considered as no longer in an infectious state. The nervous phenomena known as parasyphilis :—tabes, general paralysis of the insane, diseases of the great vessels, have been proved to be due to the spirochæta pallida in the central nervous and vascular systems, and they can no longer be considered a special stage of the disease.

The **chancre** appears at the site of infection. A breach of the surface appears to be necessary, the organism making its entry through a crack, fissure, a herpetic lesion, or a soft sore. Sexual intercourse, kissing, and medical examination are the commonest modes of infection. Contact with contaminated cups, towels, and the like are occasional causes.

The primary sore is usually single, but multiple chancres (two or three) are not uncommon. Before the general infection occurs, auto-inoculation may cause successive chancres.

The chancre is (1) a superficial erosion, moist and finely granular, and sometimes greyish; (2) an ulcer with a similar surface; or (3) an ill-defined red papule. It is rarely larger than a threepenny piece when it occurs on the genital organs. There is induration of the base, and when taken between the finger and thumb the lesion feels like a piece of cartilage. It may disappear in ten days to six weeks, but occasionally it lasts much longer. Very rarely, as

Sir Jonathan Hutchinson has pointed out, the induration may reappear *in situ*, after the lapse of two or three years (chancre redux).

Chancres vary very much in their appearance and size, especially the extra-genital, which are often much larger, and sometimes ulcerated. Chancres on the mucous surfaces are usually ulcerated when they come under observation.

Fig. 119.—Chancre on the chin.

Occasionally, a soft sore appearing three to five days after exposure to infection becomes indurated three to five weeks later. This is due to infection with the strepto-bacillus and the spirochæta simultaneously or within a few days. Other complications of the primary sore are herpes, which may precede, and indeed be the determining cause of, the infection, and phimosis. The gravest complication, fortunately rare, is phagedæna, which may lead to extensive destruction of the penis.

Position of the primary lesion. **Genital chancres** in the *male* occur on the side of the frenum, on the prepuce and glans, and in the sulcus behind the glands. In rare cases the meatus is the site, and urethral chancres have been observed. Occasionally the chancre develops on the body of the penis, or on the scrotum, or the skin over the pubes. Pawlow's statistics on the influence of circumcision on the incidence of genital chancres show that the operation affords some degree of protection.

In *women*, the labia, fourchette, clitoris, and the meatus urinarius are the common sites. Chancres on the cervix uteri are not very uncommon, but the vaginal wall is rarely affected. Spirochætes have been found in the cervical secretion without obvious lesions on the cervix or vaginal wall.

Extra-genital chancres may occur anywhere, but are commonest on the face and fingers. Of 50 consecutive cases of extra-genital chancre met with in my practice the sites were—lip, 29 (15 upper, 12 lower, 2 both lips); cheek, 3 ; nostril, 2 ; chin, 2 ; finger, 7 ; thumb, arm, shoulder, buttock, umbilicus, tongue, tonsil, 1 each. Kissing is a common cause of lip chancres, and Schamberg has reported six cases in girls who were infected in a kissing game. Infection of the scalp in a barber's shop has been reported by Dr. Walmisley, and Dr. Eardley Holland informs me he had a case in an infant whose scalp was infected at birth. In the buccal cavity, the tongue and the tonsil are most frequently involved. Finger chancres occur about the nails, and the infection is often the result of digital examination by medical men and midwives. Vaccinal chancres are now practically unknown. The nipple may be the site of a primary sore, and also the anus.

Extra-genital chancres on the mucous surfaces are usually ulcerative, and the surface of the ulcer is often covered with a greyish membrane resembling that of diphtheria.

I have no reliable figures as to the relative frequency of extra-genital chancres, but I should estimate it at less than five per cent. Of 141 adult males in my clinic, extra-genital infection was known to have occurred in 3·3 per cent. Of 136 adult females extra-genital infection was known to have occurred in 11 per cent. These figures are too high, as many women do not show signs of syphilis till the tertiary stage. Some Continental authors give the proportion as ten genital to one extra-genital chancre. In Russia it is said to be four to one.

Syphilis d'emblée, or, as Mr. Ernest Lane prefers to describe it, *cryptogenetic syphilis*, is the name given to spirochæte infection in which the primary manifestation is unnoticed or inconspicuous. In two cases occurring in medical men the infection was caused by needle-pricks at an operation. The initial lesions were so trivial that the sufferers, although trained observers, did not recognise them.

The **primary bubo** is usually a single large indurated gland, but occasionally there are small shotty glands as satellites. It appears about a week after the chancre, and persists long after it has disappeared. The syphilitic bubo does not suppurate.

Diagnosis of the primary chancre. The induration of the lesion and the hard bubo are usually sufficiently characteristic to make a diagnosis. The following conditions must be borne in mind, however—(1) traumatic ulcer, (2) herpes preputialis, (3) soft sore, (4) recurrent induration in the site of infection, (5) scabies, (6) erosive balanitis.

The first three conditions are distinguished by the absence of induration and of the indurated bubo. Soft sores are usually multiple, and appear a few days after exposure to infection, and the glands tend to suppurate. The recurrence of induration may take place two to five years after syphilitic infection, and may lead to a suspicion of re-infection. Scabies lesions are common on the penis, and mistakes are not uncommon if a general examination is omitted. Erosive balanitis is not indurated.

Extra-genital chancres are usually easily recognised when the condition is kept in mind. The finger sores may be mistaken for whitlow, but any such condition in a medical man or midwifery nurse should be carefully watched. I have seen one case in which a primary sore of the nipple was diagnosed as cancer.

If there be any doubt of the nature of a suspicious sore, a scraping of the surface should be made and examined by the Collargol method, or by dark background illumination for spirochætes.

Stage of generalisation. This begins from five to eight weeks after the appearance of the chancre.

General symptoms. There is often irregular fever, and I have once seen a pyrexia lasting for three weeks, the chart closely resembling that of enteric fever. The patient is anæmic, and an examination of the blood shows leucocytosis. The lymphatic glands all over the body are enlarged, hard and shotty. There may be enlargement of the spleen and albuminuria. The patient often complains of loss of strength and of wasting. Headache, and pains in the limbs, muscles and joints, and neuralgia are common. Loss of hair, iritis, and testicular inflammation may also occur. Pregnant women often abort. The cutaneous and mucous membrane eruptions are numerous and important.

General characters of the eruptions :—

(*a*) **Polymorphism.** The lesions are usually of several types. For instance, macules, papules, and scaly spots may coexist. But, although the type varies in different parts, or even in the same part, the size varies very little.

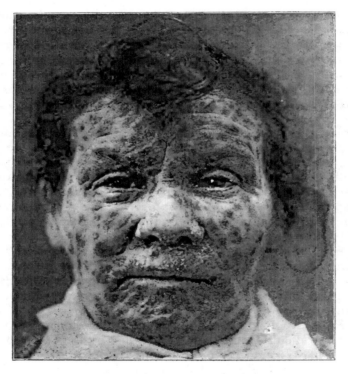

FIG. 120.—Lenticular syphilide.

(*b*) **Dissemination.** The early syphilitic rashes are widely spread and abundant.

(*c*) **Absence of itching.** As a general rule, the eruption is unattended with subjective symptoms. Its onset is insidious, and itching is rarely noticed. It must, however, be understood that this feature is not constant ; the presence of some pruritus is not evidence against syphilis.

(*d*) **Character of the individual lesions.** They are round, or tending to be round, and are often arranged in groups or rings. They have a reddish-yellow, hammy, or coppery colour. They disappear spontaneously, and often recur.

Special characters of the early eruptions. (*a*) The **macular syphilide** is the earliest manifestation, appearing about six weeks after the chancre, and lasting for three weeks to two months, occasionally recurring during the first year, and sometimes later. The

FIG. 121.—Moist papular syphilide (condylomata).

eruption consists of rose-coloured, round, or oval spots rarely larger than a threepenny piece. The margin of the macule is ill-defined ; there is no scaling and no itching. The roseola appears on the chest, flanks, back and abdomen, on the neck and limbs, and on the palms and soles. It is exceedingly rare on the face. The macules are occasionally circinate. The macular syphilide often escapes the notice of the patient, and it may be missed by the medical attendant if the examination is made in artificial light.

Plate 24.

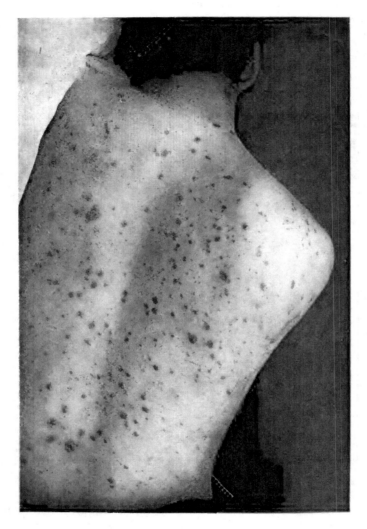

LENTICULAR SYPHILIDE.

The lesions are abundant, ham-coloured, and all about one size. Fine
scaling is seen at the margins of some of the spots.

(*b*) The **papular syphilides** take several forms. They usually appear on the sites of the macules, and both macules and papules may be present simultaneously, or they may arise independently of the rose spots. The eruption occurs in the first year, and lasts for a month to three months, sometimes longer.

The **lenticular syphilide** is the commonest form of papular eruption. The lesions are round, red or hammy-coloured spots, rarely coppery. The surface is shiny, and there is usually a narrow ring of fine scales

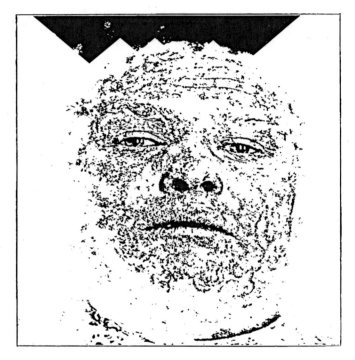

FIG. 122.—Circinate papular syphilide.

round the margin. On palpation the papules feel firm, and give the impression of infiltration. The lenticular syphilide is usually abundant on the trunk and limbs, the face, palms, and soles.

The **nummular syphilide** consists of flat, coin-like lesions about one-third of an inch to an inch in diameter. The plaques are of a dull red colour and of a round or oval shape. They may be dry, or moist, or covered with crusts. They occur on the neck and face, and in the flexures. The large moist flat papules in the neighbourhood of the anus and sometimes seen in the flexures are known as

condylomata (Fig. 121). The nummular eruption is commonly associated with the smaller papular syphilide.

Occasionally there is a **ringed or circinate papular** eruption. It forms rings, or parts of rings (Fig. 122), and occurs on the chin, neck, lips, and about the nostrils, and occasionally on the vulva. The papules are firm, small, and covered with fine scales. In the

FIG. 123.—Ringed syphilide. There were similar lesions at the bends of the elbows.

case illustrated (Fig. 123) there were concentric rings. The ringed eruption is particularly common in the negro.

(c) **Follicular syphilides.** In this type the eruption is localised to the hair follicles. The eruption appears from four to six months after the chancre, and often co-exists with the papular syphilides. It may last several weeks. The lesions are miliary, dull red spots, somewhat pointed, and often capped with a dry scale at the pilo-sebaccous orifice. They develop slowly, and are hard to the touch.

In some cases the apex of the follicle is capped by a small crust. Sometimes the follicular eruption is **pustular,** and the association of

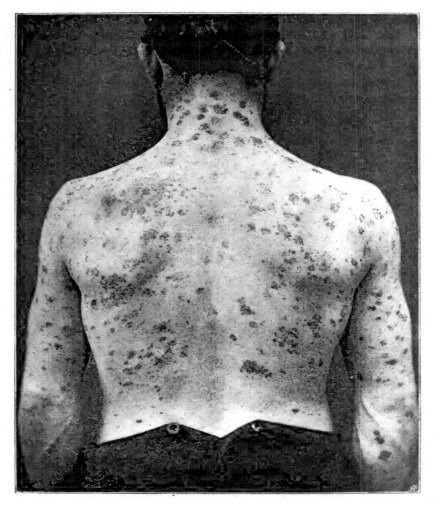

FIG. 124.—Papular and corymbose syphilide. The arrangement of the lesions should be examined with a lens.

pustules and papules is not uncommon (**papulo-pustular syphilide**). The individual lesions are dark red in colour and covered with a pus-crust. Various names have been given to modifications of the pustular follicular syphilides from their resemblance to other cuta-

s. 19

neous affections, *e.g.*, acniform, varicelliform, varioliform, vacciniform and herpetiform syphilides.

(*d*) The **corymbose syphilide** (Fig. 124) has special characters. It consists of a central brownish red infiltrated papule about one-fifth inch in diameter, and arranged round this are numerous papules the size of a pin's head, or a little larger. There may be several dozens of these small lesions forming a characteristic cluster around

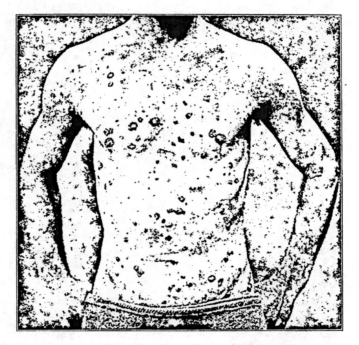

FIG. 125.—Ulcerative syphilide.

the central spot, which is sometimes covered by a scale or crust. The grouping is characteristic of syphilis, and the pigment stains which are left may last for several months and be of value in diagnosis.

(*e*) The **squamous syphilide** consists of rounded or ringed lesions of dull red colour covered with scales. The squames are less adherent than those of psoriasis, and the silvery character of the latter is absent. On their removal the papule is exposed, but there is no membrane of Bulkeley before the bleeding papillæ are reached, as in psoriasis. The squamous syphilide is also infiltrated, and this feature is valuable in the differential diagnosis. The eruption appears on the face, back,

Plate 25.

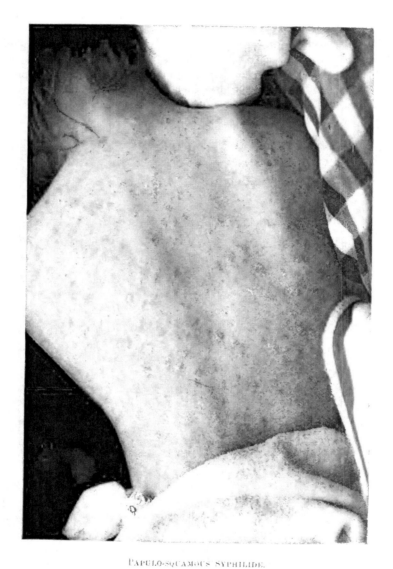

PAPULO-SQUAMOUS SYPHILIDE.

Abundant eruption; the lesions are all about one size. The colour and scaling
are characteristic.

and neck, in the bends of the elbows and behind the knees. The fronts of the knees and the points of the elbows escape.

(*f*) The **crusted and impetiginous** syphilides are moist flat papules of a yellowish brown colour, on which the exudation has dried to form crusts. On removing the crusts moist surfaces are exposed, but there is no ulceration as in rupia and ecthyma.

(*g*) The **vegetating (framboesiform) syphilide** is developed from the papule or pustule. It appears in the form of isolated plaques with fungating and papillomatous excrescences standing above the surface for perhaps a quarter of an inch (Fig. 126). It occurs on the

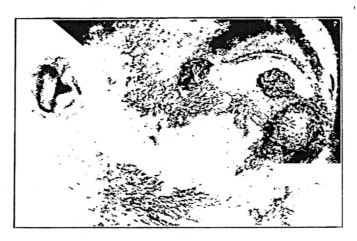

FIG. 126.—Framboesiform syphilide.

neck, face, and chest, and sometimes on the palms. Its evolution is slow, and its disappearance is followed by staining.

(*h*) **Ulcerative syphilides ; Rupia.** Ulcerative lesions are rare at this stage except in cachectic subjects. The more grave type occurs in those addicted to chronic alcoholism, and in malaria, scurvy, diabetes, chronic renal disease and grave anæmia. It is often associated with extensive ulceration of the mucous membranes. The patient wastes to a remarkable degree, and in some instances pulmonary and renal complications supervene, leading to a fatal issue (syphilis maligna). The eruption is irregularly disseminated, the ulcers being sometimes numerous and coalescing, and in other instances few and widely scattered (Fig. 125).

Each rupial lesion is a round or oval ulcer, with steep sides and purplish margin, and a soft base exuding a blood-stained pus, which dries to form a brown crust shaped like a limpet-shell. It leaves a deep characteristic scar. The rupial ulcer is rarely painful. The presence of the ulcer under the crusts is the diagnostic feature distinguishing this variety of syphilide from the massive crusts of psoriasis rupioides.

(*i*) **Keratodermia** of the **palms** and **soles** occasionally occurs. The early palmar syphilide is usually macular, affecting both palms, but occasionally the lesions are well-defined plaques or gyrate figures of a dull coppery-red colour covered by a thick horny layer. There is definite infiltration, and the margins of the scaly patches are surrounded by a zone of erythema. The later lesions are described at p. 303.

(*j*) **Pigmentary syphilides.** A large number of syphilitic eruptions leave stains which may last several weeks to several months, the pigment in these conditions being derived from the blood, but there is a remarkable pigmentary syphilide which is believed to be a true melanosis. There is some doubt as to whether it follows an eruption, or if it is always independent. It occurs almost exclusively in the first two years after infection, but may last an indefinite time. It consists of greyish or brownish staining of the neck, and is most abundant on the lateral aspects. The margin of the pigmented area is ill defined, but the surface is studded with white spots with a sharp outline, each spot varying in size from a split-pea to a shilling. The dappled appearance is very striking, and is characteristic of syphilis. This pigmentation occurs in women. It is exceedingly rare in men. The peculiar situation has led to the name of the " venereal collar " (Plate XXVI.).

(*k*) **Syphilitic alopecia.** In the first year after infection the hair tends to fall. In most cases there is a general thinning, but in other instances there are patches of baldness, depicted in Fig. 127. The areas differ from those of alopecia areata, resembling, when viewed from the side, glades in a forest, as certain authors have remarked. In alopecia areata the bald areas are of round or ovoid form and quite smooth. In pseudopelade, which is sometimes simulated, the bald patches are cicatricial. Cicatrisation is met with in the alopecia left by favus and pus infection.

(*l*) **Affections of the nails.** Onychia and perionychia occur in the stage of generalisation. In the former the nails are fissured, cracked and brittle (onychia sicca syphilitica) (Fig. 128). Sometimes the nail separates at the proximal end, and the matrix is inflamed and swollen. Ulceration and destruction of the nail may occur. In perionychia there may be scaly or inflammatory papules under the side of the nail or ulceration. The end of the finger is swollen and red, and the nail

Plate 26.

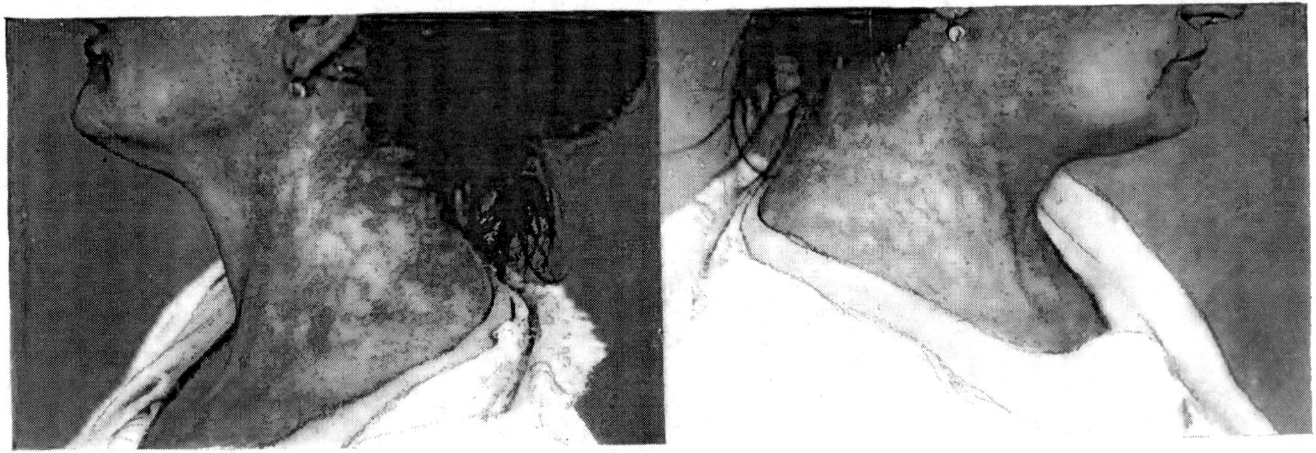

PIGMENTARY SYPHILIDE.

may be lost. The syphilitic affections of the nail are of slow evolution and attended with little pain, in great contrast to the whitlows caused by pyogenic infection.

Diagnosis of the early syphilides. It is unwise to make the diagnosis upon the character of the cutaneous manifestations alone, although it may be done with certainty in some cases. In the male there is often the history of the chancre, and the scar may be observed on the penis. In women, at any rate in general hospital and private practice, the primary lesion is rarely seen. Extragenital chancres

FIG. 127.—Syphilitic alopecia.

may be overlooked, and there is no doubt that many genital chancres even in the male escape notice. The history of the development of the symptoms must be carefully noted : the anæmic condition of the patient, his headaches, pains in the limbs, etc., will all be of value in diagnosis. The mucous membranes must be thoroughly examined, and often throw valuable light on the case. The glands above the bend of the elbow, in the neck and groins must be palpated, and a general shotty enlargement will be strong evidence in favour of syphilis. The eruption is polymorphous ; the individual lesions are round, or tending to be round, and except in the case of the roseola

they are usually infiltrated ; they are very much of one size, though
of different types ; their colour is dull red, hammy or coppery. They
rarely itch. The characters of the various types of lesion have been
sufficiently indicated in the preceding paragraphs. Their association
and order of development, first the rose rash, then the lenticular or
papular eruptions, are all important characteristics. It is a good
general rule when one meets with a cutaneous eruption which does
not conform to one of the common types to suspect syphilis and not to
diagnose some rare condition until syphilis has been excluded. As
Hutchinson long ago pointed out, syphilis is a great imitator, but
although the simulation of other diseases of the skin is very close,
there is usually some feature which leads one to doubt. For instance,
the scaly syphilide which affects the flexures may simulate psoriasis

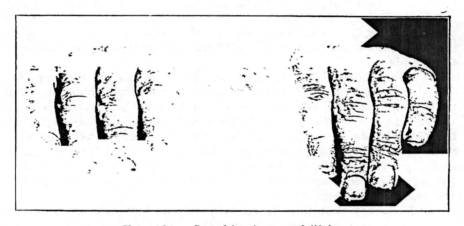

Fig. 128.—Onychia sicca syphilitica.

very closely, but one is struck at once by the fact that the lesions are
not in the common situation on the extensor surfaces. It is one's
duty to investigate the condition of the mucous membranes and the
glands, and to enquire into any antecedent rashes and their characters.
If there is the least doubt a specimen of the blood should be taken
and forwarded at once to the laboratory for the Wassermann test.
A positive reaction is obtained in nearly every case of secondary
syphilis. Again, one may be able, by scraping the surface of a
lesion, for instance, a nodule or rupial ulcer, to obtain fluid in which
the spirochæta can be demonstrated by dark background illumination, or by mixing with collargol and making a film preparation.
Failing these, there is, of course, the therapeutic test, the observa-

tion of the behaviour of the eruption under the influence of mercury or salvarsan.

In practice the commonest skin affections which are diagnosed as syphilis are :—(1) Pityriasis rosea. This is often mistaken for the roseola. The eruption appears on the trunk and adjacent parts of the extremities. The lesions are oval or lozenge shaped and also small round spots. They are pink in colour, and are covered with fine scales. There is itching, but there are no general symptoms, and the mucous membranes and glands are unaffected. The syphilitic macular eruption is pink, but it is never scaly. The scaly syphilides are infiltrated and of a dull red colour.

(2) Lichen planus is not infrequently diagnosed as a papular syphilide. The lichen spots are polygonal, flat topped and shiny. They have a peculiar lilac or violet tint. Itching is a prominent feature. The fronts of the forearms and the fronts of the legs and thighs are usually first affected. The mucous membrane lesions are white papules, or streaks or patches on the buccal mucosa, and sometimes on the tongue and palate. There is no general enlargement of the glands.

(3) The seborrhoides are also sometimes mistaken for syphilis. The eruption consists of rounded spots or circinate lesions covered with greasy scales. There is usually a remarkable distribution in the middle line of the trunk, back and front, and associated with the trunk affection there is pityriasis capitis. The red areas covered with greasy scales may encroach upon the forehead from the hairy scalp, producing the corona seborrhoica. There is no affection of the mucous membranes, and no general enlargement of the glands. Itching is often present.

(4) The scaly syphilides simulate psoriasis, but they are generally in the flexures and infiltrated, and the scales are not of the bright silvery type characteristic of psoriasis. There would also be other signs of syphilis present. The two diseases may, of course, be present simultaneously. The rupoid variety of psoriasis is simply a neglected condition, in which the scales have been allowed to accumulate. Their removal shows minute bleeding points, and not an ulcer as in rupia.

(5) Acne vulgaris is closely simulated by some of the follicular syphilides. The presence of comedones and early suppuration are important points in diagnosis. The difficulty arises in some bad cases of acne vulgaris of the back where there are numerous infiltrated spots with much scarring. As a rule there is a long history and many large comedones. Acne, of course, may coexist with syphilis.

(6) Certain drug eruptions sometimes give rise to difficulty. The

copaiba rash is one. It should not lead to error, as the eruption is of one type, resembling urticaria or measles (*vide* p. 342), and there is itching. The presence of gonorrhœa may lead to the suspicion of simultaneous syphilitic infection.

I have seen iodide eruptions diagnosed as syphilis, but the bullous character of the lesions, their tendency to affect the face and neck, etc. (Fig. 148), and the history of the patient taking a drug should be helpful points. The presence of iodide in the urine can be demonstrated.

Syphilis of the mucous membranes. Very few patients suffering from syphilis escape lesions of the mucous membranes. They may occur anywhere about the mouth, on the lips, tonsils, and pharynx, on the pillars of the fauces and on the gums about carious teeth, and in the nasal fossæ and larynx. The external genitals in both sexes may be affected, and also the anus. The eruptions are most severe in patients of dirty habits, and in the chronic alcoholic. In the mouth they are aggravated by smoking, by dental caries, pyorrhœa, etc.

Characters of the mucous membrane eruptions. Erythema. The simplest lesions are red spots, which may be observed on the lips and palate. *Mucous plaques* are circinate, slightly raised swellings with swollen epithelium of a whitish colour, but not ulcerated, closely resembling an area touched with the silver-stick. They are the commonest lesions, and occur on the palate and also about the vulva. In some instances the spots are covered with a diphtheroid membrane. *Erosions* are rounded, oval, or reniform superficial ulcers covered with a mucous secretion resembling the snail track. Such ulcers often occur symmetrically on the tonsils. Hutchinson called attention to red, dry, oval patches on the tongue. The disappearance of the papillæ gives these areas a peculiar peeled appearance. They are rather a late symptom. Another form is the *condyloma* or moist papule, which in dirty people may develop vegetations. These occur in the vulvar region, at the angle of the mouth and in the gluteal cleft, the genito-crural flexures, and on the tongue.

Deep ulceration of the mucous membranes is rare in the secondary stage.

Diagnosis of the mucous membrane lesions. The points already mentioned in considering the diagnosis of the secondary stage apply here. There are a few conditions to remember specially in considering the differential diagnosis. Aphthæ are rounded, yellow, painful superficial patches, occurring on the gums and buccal mucosa. The herpetic lesions of the mouth are also painful. Neither of these conditions would be associated with a cutaneous eruption or shotty glands. I have seen erythema multiforme with extensive erosions in the mouth diagnosed as syphilis, and treated unfortunately with mercury, which aggravated all the symptoms. The characters of the eruption of the extremities, the absence of general gland enlargements, and the common history of recurrences should obviate error. Lichen planus is another condition which may be mistaken. The buccal lesions are white spots, patches or streaks, and the cutaneous eruption is of a peculiar tint affecting the forearms and front of the legs. It has already been considered in the diagnosis of the cutaneous eruptions (p. 295).

Leukoplakia and exfoliative glossitis are unattended with cutaneous eruptions.

The genital mucous membrane lesions have to be distinguished from the soft sore and from herpes. The absence of general symptoms, and especially of the shotty glands, should prevent error. In all cases Wassermann's test should be used.

Late or Tertiary Syphilides.

The late manifestations of syphilis usually appear between the second and the tenth year after infection, but I have notes of several instances in which twenty years passed between the primary and the tertiary stages, and in one case thirty-five years. In quite 20 per cent. of the cases of undoubted tertiary syphilis there is no history or evidence of previous symptoms. In women it is exceptional to get direct evidence, but a history of miscarriages was obtained in 55 per cent. of the married women with tertiary syphilis attending the London Hospital clinic. In one case there had been eight miscarriages. Many women who have borne syphilitic infants, or who have had a series of miscarriages, present no cutaneous manifestation until the menopause is reached. In my own clinic the late manifestations are more common in the female than in the male in the proportion of 61 to 39 per cent. I think this must be due to the fact that in the male the earlier stages are more often recognised and treated; many women, as already mentioned, having syphilis without symptoms. One-third of the cases both in women and men occur in the third decade of life and one-fourth in the fourth decade. The limits of age in my cases were sixteen years and eighty-two.

The late eruptions are usually of a localised type, with considerable infiltration of the skin and subcutaneous tissues. They are commonly asymmetrical, tend to break down into ulcers, and leave scars or sclerotic conditions. Occasionally there is an **erythema** consisting of dark red or brownish red non-infiltrated patches free from scales. The lesions may be rounded or circinate. They occur on the trunk and the limbs and are rebellious to treatment. The tertiary erythema is distinguished from pityriasis rosea and from the seborrhoic eruptions by the absence of scales, and from drug eruptions by the colour and the absence of irritation.

The **nodular tertiary syphilide** consists of one nodule or a group

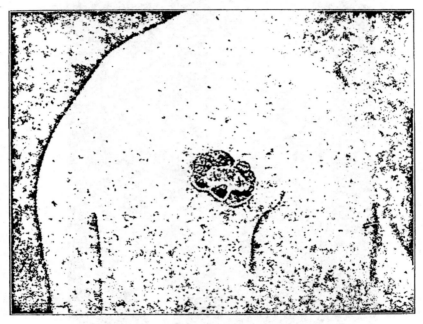

FIG. 129.—Gummatous syphilide.

of nodules of a reddish brown colour. The groups often form segments of circles. Such a group may be half an inch to three or four inches across. The individual nodules may be covered with scales or crusts, or they may break down into ulcers. On healing they leave some thickening of the tissues (sclerosis) or scars. The eruption often closely resembles lupus vulgaris, but it is distinguished from it by its rapid evolution—a matter of several weeks—and the absence of the apple-jelly nodules. The nose, forehead, and chin are the parts most commonly affected.

The **gummatous syphilide** begins at a circumscribed induration

Plate 27.

GEMMATOUS ULCERATION OF THE NOSE.

Duration three months.   Primary infection eight years before.

of the hypoderm or of the cutis. At first the surface is unaffected, and the gumma is more easily felt than seen. The swelling varies in size from a pea to a walnut. It gradually enlarges and the skin

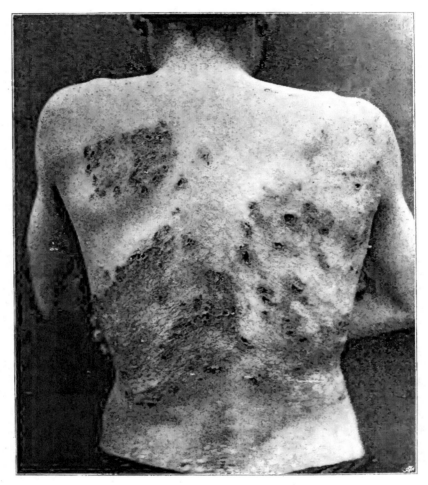

Fig. 130.—Gummatous syphilide, with extensive scarring.

becomes inflamed and reddened. The gumma then undergoes softening, the epidermis sooner or later gives way, and a punched-out ulcer is formed. In some instances, however, the gumma may clear up without undergoing this breaking down. The gummatous ulcer is characteristic ; the sides are steep, the base is covered with slough.

often of a wash-leather colour, and the discharge is sanious or purulent. Gummata are discrete or confined to regions, and are often grouped in a circinate fashion, a special feature being the polycyclic arrangement of circular or ovoid lesions (Fig. 129). In rare cases the ulcer formed by the breaking down of a group of gummata is of considerable size, as big as a five-shilling piece, with a festooned outline. The scars left by tertiary ulcers are generally thin, with

Fig. 131.—Gummatous syphilide.

irregular ridges, and their borders have the festooned outline of the ulceration (Fig. 130). By taking the scar between the finger and thumb and approximating the sides, the cicatrix wrinkles up like soft tissue paper. Hutchinson long ago described this as a characteristic feature. In some cases the gummatous ulcer is associated with considerable thickening of the subcutaneous tissue—sclerogumma.

Gummata may occur anywhere ; they are common on the face, nose and lips, about the mouth, on the scalp, trunk and extremities including the nails (Fig. 134). They are often associated with

Plate 28.

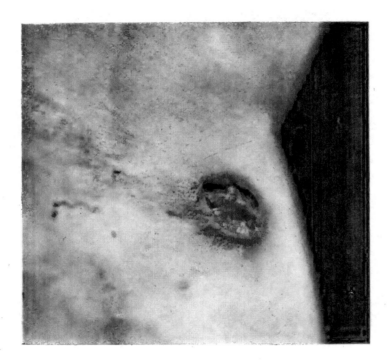

GUMMA OF BACK.

Showing characteristic punched-out ulcer.

similar lesions of the naso-pharynx, perforation of the palate, and leukoplakia and ulceration and gummata of the tongue.

Palmar syphilides. These deserve special attention. They may be early or late manifestations. The early eruptions are macular and occur in association with or independent of the lenticular form

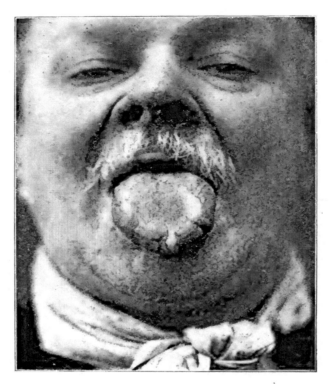

Fig. 132.—Leukoplakia, with fissures.

already described. The spots are dull red in colour, discrete, and vary in size from a pea to a bean. Both palms are affected.

The late palmar syphilide is always unilateral, and it occurs in two forms :—

(1) Nodular or gummatous, usually with a serpiginous outline, with or without ulceration.

(2) The more important squamous eruption, which may be circinate or diffuse, which affects the middle of the palm. The margin is usually sharply defined, the colour dull red, with adherent scale. There is no itching.

The differential diagnosis of these palmar eruptions is often difficult. The following points require attention :—

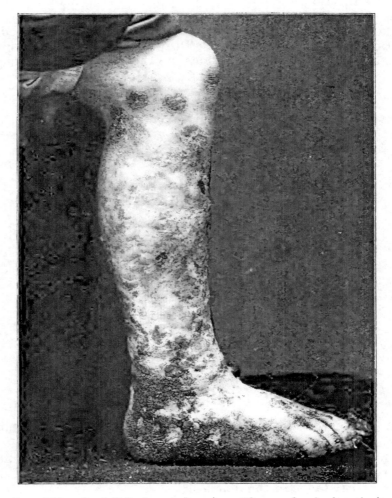

FIG. 133.—Syphilitic keratodermia, with pseudo-elephantiasis.

The early palmar syphilides are always bilateral, the later unilateral. They may be mistaken for—

(a) *Ringworm of the palm.* In this affection the margin is more inflammatory and very often vesicular, and fungus is demonstrable under the microscope.

(b) *Psoriasis.* This is usually bilateral. The scaling is often excessive (compare Fig. 186). Both palmar and dorsal surfaces may be involved. The nails may be pitted or show other signs of psoriatic affection, and psoriasis will be present elsewhere, *e.g.*, elbows, knees and scalp.

(c) *Chronic seborrhoic dermatitis.* The edge is well defined, the eruption itches and usually affects the palmar surfaces of the fingers, extending on to the palm. Lesions in other parts may be expected.

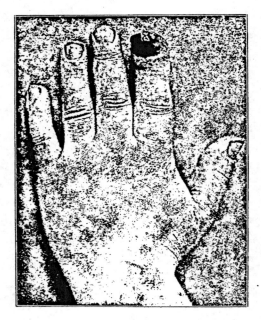

Fig. 134.—Tertiary onychia.

(d) *Arsenical keratosis* is bilateral, and the history that the patient has been taking the drug would be elicited.

A chronic scaly affection of the palm of one hand should always lead to a suspicion of syphilis, and the Wassermann reaction should prove of assistance in the diagnosis.

Among the rare tertiary manifestations, **keratodermia** of the sole must be mentioned. It is found, as a rule, on one foot only. The epidermis is enormously thickened, generally of a yellowish brown colour, and rough like shagreen leather. The hyperkeratosis extends all over the sole and encroaches on the sides of the foot. In some instances it is associated with **pseudo-elephantiasis** of the limbs (Fig. 133). The whole leg is swollen and does not pit deeply upon pressure. The condition is believed to be due to lymphatic obstruction, but it is rare to find palpable enlargement of the glands.

It is a noteworthy fact that enlargement of the lymphatic glands is exceptional in tertiary syphilis, and this point may be used in the differential diagnosis of gummatous from other forms of ulceration.

Diagnosis of the late or tertiary lesions. A thorough examination of the skin should be made, for there will often be found evidence of syphilis in the shape of scars of previous lesions. The tongue must also be inspected ; in 12 per cent. of my cases there was leukoplakia. Naturally, there was a greater proportion of tongue lesions in the males than in the females, on account of smoking, but the worst case seen in my clinic lately was in a woman, who had been a pipe smoker for many years. The pharynx should be inspected, and there are often indications of previous ulceration in the shape of scars or adhesions. In other cases an examination of the eyes will reveal irregularity of the pupil from old iritic adhesions, or choroiditis. In two patients attending my clinic tabes was associated with gummatous ulcers.

The rapidity of the destruction in the syphilitic disease is in great contrast to the slow evolution of the tuberculous affections, especially lupus vulgaris, which is the commonest disease in which mistakes are made. Necrosis of bone and deep ulceration of muscle do not occur in lupus. Epithelioma early infects the lymphatic glands, and if there is doubt a biopsy should at once be made. The rodent ulcer should not be mistaken for syphilis ; its very slow evolution and the rolled edge are sufficient to make the distinction. When gummatous infiltration affects particular regions there may be some difficulty. I have seen cases in which the lesions were confined to the beard region and the condition simulated sycosis. Where there is any doubt the Wassermann test should be made, if possible, and I have several times had to modify an opinion on the strength of the examination of the blood. If the practitioner is unable to get this test applied, or to do it himself, it is best to put the patient at once on anti-syphilitic treatment. In a couple of weeks many gummatous affections are so profoundly modified as to make the diagnosis certain.

Prognosis. Provided the patient's general health is not undermined by general disease, the tertiary syphilitic eruptions usually yield to treatment. Relapses are frequent, particularly in hospital practice, as it is difficult to keep the patients sufficiently long under treatment after the lesions have healed.

Congenital Syphilis.

The essential differences between the congenital and the acquired disease are the absence of the chancre and the mingling of the secondary and tertiary stages.

General symptoms. The infant at birth may be quite normal, and it may remain plump and well favoured for some weeks after the onset of the symptoms. In most instances, however, there is a peculiar facies which is characteristic. The skin is of a dull earthy

Fig. 135.—Congenital syphilis.

tint and shrunken, so that the face resembles that of a little wizened old man. As the disease advances the infant loses flesh rapidly.

It is not often possible to demonstrate general enlargement of the lymphatic glands, but sometimes shotty epitrochlear glands are palpable. In untreated cases visceral lesions may develop, particularly enlargement of the liver and spleen.

The earliest cutaneous manifestation is a **bullous eruption** on the palms and soles. The bullæ develop upon coppery or purplish spots, the epidermis being raised by clear or sanious fluid. The infant may be born with the eruption or with the remains of ruptured blisters, but, as a rule, the lesions do not appear until four or five days after birth. I have twice seen infants born alive with extensive

20

areas of ruptured bullæ nearly all over the trunk and extremities. One lived a few hours and the other two days. In both there was abundant evidence in the family history of the syphilitic nature of the eruption.

A constant **nasal discharge** of a serous or purulent character, tending to form yellowish or greenish crusts, is a common phenomenon. The rhinitis, commonly called " snuffles," prevents nasal breathing, and sucking is difficult.

Mucous patches occur about the commissures of the lips, where

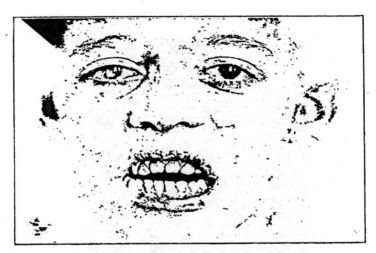

Fig. 136.—Congenital syphilis. Hutchinson's teeth, interstitial keratitis with deafness. Extensive ulceration of the leg.

radiating fissures form. Sometimes they ulcerate, and crusts develop upon them. The fissures may have an indurated base, and are attended with pain.

Between the third or fourth week and the third month, rarely later, a **polymorphous eruption** appears. It closely resembles the eruption of the secondary stage of the acquired disease, consisting of rounded erythematous spots of a dark red or pink colour on the buttocks and lower limbs, about the mouth, on the neck, and in the flexures. Some of these erythematous spots fade entirely, but others become scaly, and others again develop into papules. Circinate lesions due to marginate thickening occur, and in other instances the central parts become raised to form lenticular spots. Fine scaling is often present at the margin of the spots, but squamous patches are uncommon. Palmar and plantar bullæ may be present with the

Plate 29.

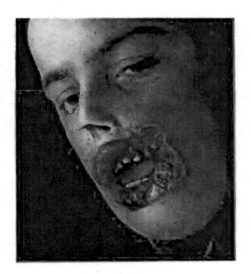

CONGENITAL SYPHILIS.

Rapidly destructive ulceration (some weeks only).
Scars of older ulceration of nose. Hutchinson's
teeth. Interstitial keratitis and choroiditis.

erythema and papules. An important feature of the congenital syphilides is the tendency of the eruption to affect the palmar and plantar surfaces.

In their later stages some of the lesions may become impetiginised and covered with crusts, or they may pass on to ulceration. These changes are most common in parts liable to irritation and maceration from contact with urine and fæces.

The **nails** may be affected, and ungual and periungual inflammation may lead to loss of the nails.

Condylomata are sometimes met with, even in children who have long passed the polymorphic eruption stage.

I have seen several instances of extensive **ulcerations of the tertiary type** occurring in children between the ages of seven and twelve. They are rapidly destructive, and attack chiefly the nose and oral region (Fig. 137). Gummatous swellings form, which rapidly break down, and, if not treated vigorously, cause grave deformity. In these cases the diagnosis of lupus vulgaris is commonly made. The process is so rapid that a great part of the nose may be destroyed in two or three weeks. The palate often suffers, and extensive necrosis of bone takes place, leading to a large opening between the nose and the mouth. The pharynx and tongue may also be affected.

True gummata of the skin and subcutaneous tissue are uncommon in congenital syphilis, but they may be met with after puberty. In these later manifestations Hutchinson's triad, the malformation of the incisor teeth, interstitial keratitis, and deafness, are stigmata which are of the highest value in diagnosis (Fig. 136). One child with gummatous ulceration of the nose cut characteristic teeth while under observation in my ward. The radiating scars about the lips and buttocks are sometimes valuable aids to diagnosis. Infantilism is another rare result of congenital syphilis, and deformities of the cranial bones and of the nose and tibiæ are not uncommon.

Diagnosis of congenital syphilides. It is useful to remember that an eruption on the hands and feet of a baby is usually either syphilis or scabies. The presence of burrows and the probable infection of the mother or other children will be points of importance in the diagnosis. The bullous syphilide has to be distinguished from the bullous impetigo of infants. The predilection for the palms and soles is an important feature. In doubtful cases the spirochæta may be sought for in the fluid, and the Wassermann test should be made. The polymorphous eruption, associated with the peculiar facies, snuffles, etc., is of a coppery or hammy colour; the lesions are not confined to the napkin region, and usually extend down the limbs

20—2

to the palms and soles. The differential diagnosis of the napkin eruptions is considered on p. 56. The history of a series of miscarriages in the mother is of value as an aid to diagnosis. The gummatous lesions have to be differentiated from tuberculous affections, particularly lupus vulgaris. If it is remembered that lupus is essentially a chronic disease, and that syphilis will cause as much destruction in a few weeks to a few months as lupus does in several

Fig. 137.—Congenital syphilis, gummatous type. Girl, æt. 11. There was a huge perforation of the palate. The spleen and liver were hypertrophied.

years, the mistake should not arise. I have under my care a little girl (Fig. 137) who had been treated at a dispensary as a case of tuberculous peritonitis for two years, and in whom a rapid ulceration developed on the nose. It was naturally thought to be lupus, and the child was sent to me for the Finsen treatment. There was already some necrosis of the palate when I saw the case, and the destruction of bone excluded lupus. The abdominal swelling was due to enlargement of the liver and spleen. The nasal ulceration healed in three weeks with mercurial inunction. Congenital syphilitics may give a positive Wassermann reaction for many years.

Prognosis of congenital syphilis. Where the infant is born with the bullous syphilide it rarely survives more than a few days, and the bullous eruption which appears about the fourth or fifth day is of grave omen. Infants thus affected rarely live. The common type in which the eruption appears about four weeks to two months after birth is usually amenable to mercurial treatment, and the majority of the infants do well. That the congenital disease is curable is shown by the fact that patients showing indubitable evidence of hereditary syphilis may acquire the disease in adult life. This fact must be borne in mind in the consideration of the very rare cases in which hereditary lues is said to have been transmitted to the second generation.

Treatment of Syphilis.

Syphilis is treated by mercury or salts of mercury, by certain arsenical compounds, and also by iodides. Antimony has also been used. Provided there are no contra-indications, I prefer to begin the treatment in the primary and secondary stages with an arsenical preparation and follow this by mercury.

TREATMENT BY MERCURY.

Mercury is the specific remedy which long experience has proved to be of curative value. After a few days' administration it is impossible to find the spirochæta in a chancre. Mercury also prevents the transmission of the disease to offspring, and may therefore be looked upon as prophylactic. Some years ago I saw in consultation a healthy woman, who had had two children, both developing a bullous eruption on the palms and soles a few days after birth. Both infants died within a couple of weeks of birth. The parents were exceedingly anxious to have healthy children. There was no history of any trouble in the wife, but not long before marriage the husband had had a mild attack of syphilis, which had only been treated for a few weeks, and was supposed to be cured. Both husband and wife were put upon courses of mercury, and have since had two healthy children without any stigmata of syphilis.

Mercury is administered (*a*) by the mouth, (*b*) by the rectum, (*c*) by inunction, (*d*) by intramuscular injection.

Before commencing the treatment it is of the utmost importance to be certain of the diagnosis. It is a serious matter to condemn a non-syphilitic patient to take so potent a drug as mercury for a period of years. We have now in the examination of the fluid from a chancre a method of demonstrating the organism, and in the later stages the Wassermann test, which should be used wherever there is a possibility of doubt.

Having determined that mercury is necessary, the patient should have carefully explained to him the necessity of carrying on the treatment for at least three years, and the grave risks there are in intermitting the cure simply because there are no symptoms. He should also thoroughly understand the risks of infecting others and the possibility of conveying the disease to offspring.

The next point of importance is an examination of the state of the mouth. If there are carious teeth the attention of the dentist is imperative, and lest he should be infected accidentally, it is well to take the precaution of letting him know the character of the case. During the treatment the hygiene of the mouth requires scrupulous care; the teeth should be cleaned after every meal with an antiseptic tooth powder. Carbolic acid or the potassium chlorate powders and pastes are the best. Smoking may be allowed in moderation, provided there is no soreness of the tongue or buccal cavity. Alcohol should be prohibited. There is nothing which tends to failure in the treatment of syphilis like the indulgence in alcohol in any form, and, as a rule, malignant forms of the disease occur only in the chronic alcoholic subject. The diet should be simple but sufficient ; it is generally wise to advise the avoidance of much fruit and vegetables, tending to cause looseness of the bowels, which will be aggravated by the mercury. If the patient can afford it, a sea voyage, or sojourn at the seaside, is beneficial. The question of continuing their employment is a serious one in many patients. Provided there are no breaches of the surface, there is little or no risk of conveying infection. The spirochæta has a very short life outside the body, so that the liability of indirect infection is small, but it must be remembered that cups, glasses, towels, etc., have been known to convey the contagion.

(a) *Oral administration* of mercury. This is the simplest method, but is less satisfactory than inunction or injection. Sir Jonathan Hutchinson's pill of one to two grains of Hydrarg. cum cret. with one grain of Pulv. ipecac. co. is usually well tolerated. It should be given three times a day after food, and can often be taken for two years on end without having to make any intermission. Some authors advise a primary course of six months, followed by an interval of a couple of months when the mercury is resumed. Two courses are given during the second and third years. Instead of the pill of mercury and chalk, grain doses of salicylate or tannate of mercury, or a third of a grain of the green iodide, may be used. In all cases it is wise to combine a little opium with the mercurial salt, either in the form of Dover's powder or of extract of opium. Mergal, which is a cholate of mercury with tannate of albumen, in three quarters of a grain doses, is also a satisfactory preparation. There is no advantage, but rather the reverse, in giving the solution of the perchloride of mercury, which I personally only prescribe in combination with iodides in the tertiary stages'. Arsenic may be combined with mercury in the form of Donovan's solution. Sometimes the administration of mercury by the mouth is attended with troublesome diarrhœa. This has two disadvantages—the patient is weakened, and the drug is hurried out of the system and is unable to act upon the parasite. In such cases inunction or injection should be used. McIntosh examined 160 cases treated by mercurial pills and found a positive Wassermann reaction after one year's treatment in 92 per cent., after two years' treatment in 54 per cent., and after three years' treatment in 30 per cent.

(b) *Rectal administration* of mercury has been tried by some Continental physicians, but it has no advantages over the oral method. Suppositories of cacao butter containing four parts in ten of grey oil (*vide infra*) are given,

(c) *Inunction.* This is one of the most rapid methods by which a patient can be brought under the influence of mercury. It has the disadvantage of being rather dirty, and the exact amount of the drug absorbed cannot be measured. For an adult, one drachm of Unguentum hydrarg. is rubbed in daily. The rubbing should take at least a quarter of an hour, so that the ointment is absorbed. The procedure is as follows. After a hot bath the ointment is well rubbed into a soft part of the skin, either by the patient, or preferably by an experienced rubber. The inner side of the thighs, the bends of the elbows, and the sides of the chest should be used in turn, care being taken to avoid parts that are hairy, as the mercury may set up a troublesome folliculitis.

For an infant suffering from congenital syphilis, the inunction of a quarter of a drachm of the ointment into the abdomen after the bath, followed by the application of a flannel binder, is most satisfactory.

The inunction treatment of the adult is carried out daily for five to six weeks, and two courses are given yearly for three years. The gums should be carefully watched during the treatment, and the rubbings must be suspended temporarily if there be much gingivitis. In my wards a glass rubber, consisting of a flat disc with a handle, is always employed if the inunction is performed by a nurse or male attendant.

(d) *Intramuscular injections*. The advantage of this method of introducing mercury is that the dosage is exact, and the treatment is completely under the observation of the practitioner. The site of injection is along a line drawn from the anterior superior spine of the ilium to the top of the gluteal cleft. In this situation there is no risk of injuring large vessels. The needle used should be two and a half to three inches long, and preferably made of irido-platinum. The syringe should be sterilisable entirely, and the site of injection should be carefully cleaned with ether or painted with iodine. The patient lying on his face, the injection is made deeply, alternately into each buttock along the line mentioned. After introducing the needle, it is wise to watch whether any blood comes away at the orifice, and if this should be the case the needle is withdrawn and reintroduced. The injection should be made very slowly, and on the removal of the needle finally the puncture should be closed with a small piece of gauze fastened with collodion. Some induration is left at the site of injection, but this clears up entirely. There is now a large choice of substances to be injected. They are of two classes : (1) insoluble; (2) soluble. As a rule, it is better to use the insoluble preparations, which are given once a week. The soluble preparations are generally given daily or several times weekly.

For ordinary use there is nothing better than the grey oil, consisting of metallic mercury ten parts, lanolin forty parts, vaselin (carbolised 2 per cent.) sixty parts. The preparation is slightly warmed before use, and ten minims are injected once a week. A more rapidly acting preparation is calomel three-quarters of a grain in seventeen minims of sterilised olive oil or vaselin. Injections are given once a week. The trouble is that the injection is attended with considerable pain. Another preparation which is less painful is the salicylate of mercury, one grain in ten minims of carbolised vaselin being the weekly dose.

The soluble preparations in use are the perchloride of mercury one-third grain, succinimate one-third grain, sozoiodolate one-third grain; and the benzoate and cyanides have also been used. Intravenous injections have been given, but they are attended with too great a risk of fat embolism to be advised.

The usual course of intramuscular injection for the insoluble salts is twelve weekly injections. There is then a period of rest. Two courses should be given each year for three years. If the soluble salts are used, about thirty injections are given in each course, at first daily and then twice or thrice a week.

If after the three years' treatment there should be any reminders, the iodides combined with mercury should be given as in the tertiary stage. Wassermann's test will prove the best guide as to when the mercurial treatment should cease. Harrison found that after one course of injections a positive Wassermann reaction was present in 83 per cent. of his cases, after two courses in 77 per cent., after three courses in 64 per cent., and after eight or more courses in 21 per cent. These observations show the importance of prolonged treatment.

The **tertiary lesions** of the skin demand the simultaneous use of iodide of potassium or sodium and mercury. As a rule, it is best to begin with a dose of ten grains of the iodide, and half a drachm to a drachm of the liquor hydrarg. perchlor. This may be combined with advantage with a bitter infusion, or with decoction of bark, or with extract of sarsaparilla. The treatment must be continued for some months after the lesions have cleared up. In grave tertiary disease of the skin mercurial inunction, with or without the internal administration of iodides, is often most valuable. The intramuscular injections may also be used, as in the secondary stage. Many sufferers from tertiary syphilis are in poor general health, and good feeding and change of air are advisable.

TREATMENT BY ARSENIC, SALVARSAN AND NEO-SALVARSAN.

It is well known that arsenic has a destructive influence upon the spirillar organisms, including the spirochæta pallida. The first serious competitor with mercury in the treatment of syphilis was atoxyl, but its use was attended with considerable risk; cases of optic atrophy, etc., occurring after its injection. Other arsenical preparations were tried, particularly the arylarsenates, but they again proved to be too toxic for general use. Ehrlich set to work to find a compound which, while sufficiently active to destroy the spirochæta, was not toxic in doses of the required strength. In conjunction with Hata he introduced "606," dioxy-diamido-arseno-benzol, with which a long series of experiments was made upon spirillar diseases in the lower animals, and finally he sent some of the new remedy to a number of clinicians for trial. Some was sent to Dr. Bulloch, and I placed at his disposal a number of cases of syphilis of all kinds, the injections being made by Drs. Fildes and McIntosh. The results obtained in these early cases were so satisfactory that when the new remedy in the form known as "salvarsan" was put on the market, I applied the treatment to all suitable cases.

The arsenical compounds in use are :

Salvarsan, 606, is dioxy-diamido-arseno-benzol-dihydrochloride ;—

$$\text{HClH}_2\text{N} \quad \underset{\text{OH}}{\bigcirc} \overset{\text{As} = \text{As}}{\quad} \underset{\text{OH}}{\bigcirc} \quad \text{NH}_2\text{HCl}$$

a canary-yellow powder sent out in sealed ampoules containing nitrogen. On exposure to air it easily oxidises and becomes highly toxic. Dissolved in water it gives an acid reaction, and for injection this must be exactly neutralised by caustic soda. It contains 34 per cent. of arsenic. The maximum dose to the human subject is 0·01 gramme per kilogramme of body weight. For an adult 0·6 gramme is the full dose.

Kharsivan, arseno-benzol (Billon), arseno-billon and diarsenol are chemically identical with salvarsan.

Neo-salvarsan, 914, is a condensation product of formaldehyde sulph-oxylate of soda with dioxy-diamido-arseno-benzol :—

$$\text{NaSO.O.CH}_2.\text{NH} \quad \underset{\text{OH}}{\bigcirc} \overset{\text{As} = \text{As}}{\quad} \underset{\text{OH}}{\bigcirc} \quad \text{NH}_2$$

Neo-salvarsan is a yellow powder easily soluble in water, the solution having a neutral reaction. On exposure to air it becomes highly poisonous, turning orange, then reddish, and finally dark brown. The full adult dose is 0·9 gramme, equivalent to 0·6 gramme of salvarsan.

Neo-kharsivan, novarseno-benzol (Billon), and novarseno-billon now take the place of neo-salvarsan.

Salvarsan-natrium, 1206, was Ehrlich's last contribution to the chemotherapy of syphilis. It is salvarsan neutralised by soda :—

$$\text{NH}_2 \quad \underset{\text{ONa}}{\bigcirc} \overset{\text{As} = \text{As}}{\quad} \underset{\text{ONa}}{\bigcirc} \quad \text{NH}_2$$

Salvarsan-natrium is a solid and is dissolved in water or 0·4 per cent. saline, forming an alkaline solution. Colonel Harrison found it a very convenient preparation, causing less reaction than those already mentioned. It is not at present available for general use.

Galyl, tetraoxy-diphosph-amino-diarseno-benzene, introduced by Mouneyrat, is a greenish grey powder put up in ampoules. It is easily soluble in water, and the solution has an alkaline reaction. The maximum dose for intravenous injection is 0·4 gramme.

Luargol is a combination of dioxy-diamino-benzene with antimony and silver. It was introduced by Danysz. The dose is 0·10 gramme to 0·15 gramme intravenously. Thrombosis at the site of injection is common, probably due to the alkalinity of the solution. This has been overcome by an improved preparation called disodoluargol, a dark brown powder. The solution, dark brown in colour, is more stable than neo-salvarsan. The dose is 0·3 gramme for intravenous injection.

In the administration of intravenous injections to children the best guide to the dose is the weight of the child. For each kilogramme of body weight the injection should be as follows :—

	Gramme.
Salvarsan, kharsivan, diarsenol . . .	0·01
Neo-salvarsan, neo-kharsivan, novarseno-billon	0·015
Galyl	0·006
Luargol	0·003

Selection of Cases. Treatment by these arsenical compounds is contra-indicated by renal disease of non-syphilitic origin, by " renal inadequacy," by grave heart disease and hepatic cirrhosis.

Preparation of the Patient. The urine being free from albumen, the patient is given an aperient pill on the night before the injection and a saline draught in the morning. It is best to avoid solid food for four hours before the injection.

The patient should be lying flat in bed with the arm chosen for the injection lying on a sterile towel. The bend of the elbow is well washed and then cleansed with ether or acetone or painted with iodine. Round the thick part of the arm a tourniquet or bandage is fastened, the compression being sufficient to render prominent the veins at the bend of the elbow.

If a small injection, say 10 to 15 c.c., is made it is injected with a syringe with a fine needle, care of course being taken that the whole of the syringe and the needle are thoroughly sterilised.

The novice should not attempt to use these highly concentrated solutions. If only a few drops of the strong solution, especially of galyl, are introduced into the connective tissue a severe reaction occurs. This may be followed by extensive sloughing. I have seen such cases take four months to heal.

When larger injections are made several forms of apparatus may be used. In one commonly employed the introduction of the solution is made by gravity (Fig. 138). Two sterile glass vessels are used, one containing normal saline (sterile) and the other the solution. From these vessels tubes supplied with taps pass downwards, to end in a single tube to which is attached the needle. The needle is introduced into the vein and a few c.c. of the saline are allowed to enter the vein ; this tap is now turned off and that connected with the neo-salvarsan solution is turned on. When all the solution required has entered the vein, the tap is turned off, and a small quantity of the normal saline is introduced, the object being to wash away any of the arsenical solution from the opening into the vein. The needle is then withdrawn and a pad and bandage applied.

I have been in the habit of using an ingenious apparatus devised by McIntosh and Fildes, by which the solution is introduced by air pressure (Fig. 139).

This apparatus consists of a flat-mouthed bottle with a rubber cork, through which pass (1) a glass tube reaching the bottom of the bottle, connected outside with a rubber tube attached to the needle ; in this rubber tube is a small window composed of glass tubing ; (2) a glass tube passing just through the cork and attached to a Higginson's syringe (the tube of the syringe is joined to the apparatus by a piece of glass tubing containing sterile cotton-wool); (3) a short tube provided with a clip.

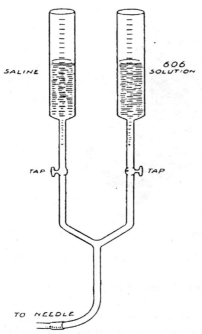

FIG. 138.—Diagram of gravity apparatus for intravenous injection.

The tourniquet being in position and the bottle filled with a sufficiency of the solution, the pump is blown up two or three times until the solution is seen to fill the needle. A clip is now placed on the rubber tube above the needle and the pressure in the bottle is relieved by opening the tube N. The needle is now inserted into the vein and the clip is removed for a minute. If the needle is in the vein, blood will appear at the little window L. The needle is then fastened in position with a strip of strapping. The tourniquet is now removed and the pressure in the bottle is raised by two or three pumps from the bulb. The solution will now flow into the vein steadily, the pressure being kept up by compressing the bulb occasionally. 40 c.c. will pass in in two or three minutes. As the last of the fluid is entering the tube the clip N is applied and the pressure in the bottle is relieved by removing the clip E. Blood will again appear at the little window, and this blood washes away any of the solution from the orifice of the vein. The needle is now withdrawn and a pad and bandage are applied. I prefer to keep the patient

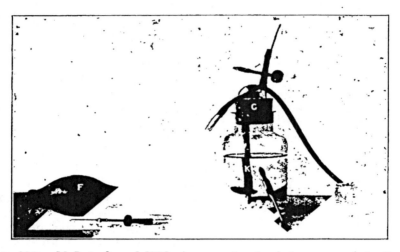

Fig. 139.—McIntosh and Fildes' apparatus for intravenous injection.

at rest until the next morning, when if there are no untoward symptoms he is allowed to go home.

Intramuscular injection of the arsenical compounds. The intramuscular method was the original procedure in treatment, but it had grave disadvantages. Persistent and severe pain was felt at the site of injection, and occasionally necrosis occurred, especially in adipose subjects. Encysted masses of salvarsan were found at the site of injection a year or more later. The intravenous method is painless and apparently more rapid in its action. Recently, however, Harrison and Miles have revived the older method, and report excellent results from the intramuscular injection of neosalvarsan.

The injection is carried out as follows:—0·6 gramme of neo-salvarsan is dissolved in 1 c.c. of 4 per cent. stovaine solution. This is then mixed with 1 c.c. creo-camph. (melting point 15° C.). The injection is given intramuscularly. In my experience the measure is not free from severe pain, but the results published by Harrison and Miles compare favourably with those obtained by intravenous injection.

Galyl, 0·35 to 0·4 gramme in glucose, is also given intramuscularly.

Rectal administration of salvarsan. Salvarsan may be used in the form of suppositories. Levaditi showed that a combination of liver extract added to arseno-benzol increases the lethal action in the blood. As pointed out by Sabouraud and Bagrov, rectal administration would secure the passage of the arseno-benzol through the liver. I have treated cases by this method with success. I had a child of nine suffering from acquired syphilis who was cured clinically by six suppositories containing 0·1 gramme of the original salvarsan.

The **management of the treatment** of a case of acquired syphilis should, in my opinion, depend upon the special features of the case. Although some authors lay down hard and fast rules which are intended to apply to all cases, I feel sure that the special circumstances of each require studying. It is generally recognised that the combination of arsenic with mercurial treatment gives the best and most lasting result. It is also agreed that our earliest anticipations of the cure of syphilis by one or two doses of an arsenical compound were too sanguine. Authors differ very much as to the quantity and frequency of doses of the arsenical compound. Colonel Harrison advocates a series of seven doses, beginning with 0·3 gramme of salvarsan and gradually increasing, the whole course being completed in fifty days, the minimum course prescribed at Rochester Row to average early cases of syphilis in the British Army at the present moment being as follows :—

Day of Treatment.	Doses of "606" injected intravenously (Gramme).
1	0·3
4	0·3
8	0·3
22	0·4
29	0·5
43	0·5
50	0·5
52 Wassermann test. If this is not completely negative, potassium iodide for two weeks, followed by—	

Day of Treatment.	Doses of "606" injected intravenously (Gramme).
69	0·3
76	0·4
83	0·5

The Wassermann reaction is taken thus early as the soldier has to return to duty.

Personally I prefer to give not more than four doses at weekly intervals, beginning with 0·6 gramme novarseno-billon or neo-kharsivan, or 0·3 gramme of galyl. The dose is increased 0·9 gramme of novarseno-billon and neo-kharsivan and 0·4 of galyl respectively after the first injection, the four doses being equivalent to 3·2 grammes of salvarsan. This course is followed by eight injections of one grain of mercury intramuscularly. The patient then waits *two months*, when the Wassermann test is made. In a large proportion of primary chancres and early secondaries the Wassermann reaction is found to be negative. Should it be positive a fresh series of injections is given. In secondary cases it will be wise to give a second series of three injections, even if the Wassermann reaction is negative. Should any of the untoward symptoms described develop, the dose should be diminished or the drug withheld, mercury alone being given.

I am strongly of opinion that every case should be under observation for at least two years, and that during that period occasional courses of mercury should be given even if the Wassermann reaction is negative. The mercury may be given by intramuscular injection, by inunction, or by the mouth.

In some cases, despite intravenous treatment, one is unable to obtain a permanently negative Wassermann reaction. I do not advise persisting in repeated intravenous injection of arsenical compounds over long periods in the hope of altering this condition, especially in tertiary cases. The dangers of arsenical poisoning, exfoliative dermatitis, etc., are too serious. In such cases I would rely upon the steady administration of mercury, as by Hutchinson's pills.

It is perhaps unnecessary to point out that the earlier a case is treated the better the results. In my own experience a patient who commenced salvarsan treatment five years ago, three days after a chancre was noticed—spirochætes being demonstrated by the dark background illumination—has never had a positive Wassermann reaction and no clinical symptoms of secondary infection. Such cases and a number of others in which a reinfection has occurred show that by early treatment the disease can be aborted. Gibbard and Harrison give an interesting table showing the advantages of early treatment, and I quote their statistics because they have had special opportunities of following their cases, opportunities impossible in civil practice :—

Period of Observation.	Stage of Disease.	Total Cases.	Clinical Relapses per cent.	Wassermann, Relapses without Clinical Signs.
12 months . . . {	Primary	70	4·2	7·1
	Secondary	130	7·6	26·1

The proportion of relapses, including both clinical and those only recognised by the blood test, was 11·3 when the treatment was begun in the primary stage, while it reached 33·7 when the treatment was postponed till the secondary stage. A comparison between the relapses under treatment by mercury alone and salvarsan plus mercury in the military hospitals is also most instructive. The following figures refer to relapses during the first year :—

—	Total Cases.	Clinical Relapses.			Total Relapses.	Percentage.
		Once.	Twice.	Three times or more.		
Mercury alone	378	151	115	49	315	83·0
Salvarsan and mercury .	152	6	...	...	6	3·9

To indicate the rapidity with which salvarsan acts I may mention two illustrative cases figured (Figs. 140 to 143).

To a young man with a chancre upon the lower lip and large primary bubo under the mandible an injection of " 606 " was given at 12 midnight, spirochætes being found in abundance in the serum of the chancre. Twelve hours later not one organism could be found (Figs. 140 and 141).

In secondary syphilis the eruption rapidly clears up; in the patient figured it had disappeared in eleven days. In tertiary syphilis the effects of the new remedy are even more remarkable. Gummatous ulcers heal up in a few days, and the absorption of swelling is very rapid, far exceeding anything which has been observed by treatment with mercury and potassium iodide.

In congenital syphilis cases have been treated directly and through the mother. Two cases of severe hereditary syphilis were admitted to my ward on the same day. One infant was injected with 0·02 gramme of " 606," while the mother of the other child, who was suckling her infant, received the full dose 0·6 gramme. It is interesting to note that the mother gave a negative Wassermann reaction

FIG. 140. 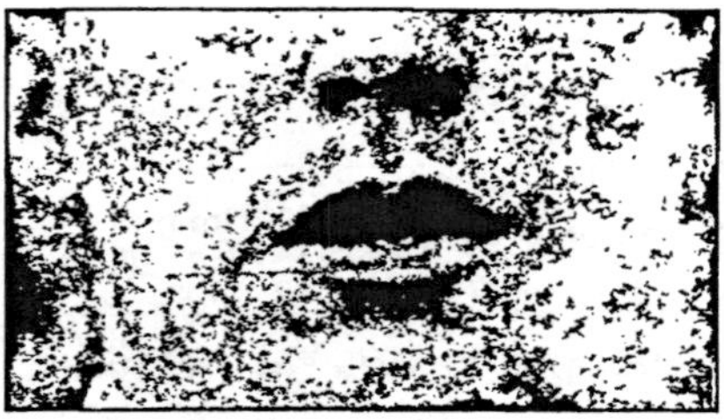   FIG. 141.

FIG. 140.—Chancre of lower lip. Numerous spirochætes found in fluid from scrapings. Twelve hours after injection of 0·6 gramme " 606 " no organism could be found.
FIG. 141.—The same patient eight days after injection.

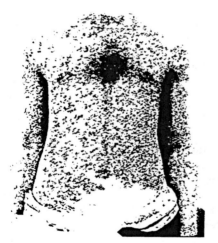
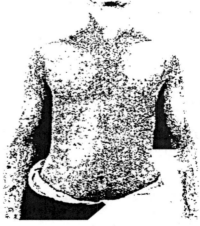

FIG. 142.   FIG. 143.

FIG. 142.—Copious secondary syphilide.
FIG. 143.—The same patient fourteen days after treatment with Ehrlich's " 606."

though there was a complete history of secondary syphilis three years before. In both infants the eruption cleared up remarkably rapidly, they put on weight, and lost all symptoms. It was thought that the child treated through the maternal milk improved less quickly than the other. Gummatous congenital syphilis does equally well, but prolonged treatment is required to produce a negative Wassermann reaction. Adults showing the stigmata of congenital syphilis, though free from any evidence of active disease for many years, often give a positive Wassermann reaction.

COMPLICATIONS AND DANGERS. The clinical phenomena which may attend or follow the intravenous injection of arsenical compounds are numerous and important.

(1) *Pyrexia* is a common symptom, especially after the first injection in florid secondary cases. The rise of temperature begins two or three hours after the injection and lasts for twenty-four hours. There may be mild rigors and headache. In my clinic the highest temperature was 106·2° F. A rise to 100° to 102° occurred in 14 per cent. of the cases. The more severe symptoms may be due to some fault in the technique of water distillation.

(2) *Vaso-motor disturbances.* The blood pressure is always lowered for two or three days after the injection.

Nitritoid crises are vaso-motor disturbances which may occur during or immediately after an injection. The face becomes congested, the pupils dilate, the pulse is rapid and may be dicrotic, the patient complains of constriction of the throat and precordial distress, sometimes accompanied by coughing. In some cases the face and tongue are swollen and there is severe dyspnœa with twitching of the limbs. In rare instances an acute *urticaria* follows. These phenomena closely resemble those seen after the administration of amyl nitrite, and they are also similar to the anaphylactic symptoms occasionally produced by serum injections. They are relieved by the intramuscular injection of 1·5 to 2 c.c. of adrenalin hydrochloride (1 in 1,000).

Syncope. Fainting during an injection is usually due to the taking of a heavy meal just before the injection, and is followed by vomiting. It may also be caused by fear.

A persistent slow pulse is sometimes seen after a course of injection.

(3) *Blood.* A moderate degree of leucocytosis and diminution in the number of erythrocytes occur.

(4) *Alimentary canal. Diarrhœa and sickness* are moderately common. They may be severe and attended with colic and cramps in the limbs. Sub-mucous hæmorrhages into the bowel wall have been found in fatal cases.

Jaundice is an occasional result. In one of my cases it persisted for twelve weeks. It has the usual characters of " catarrhal " jaundice. It is believed to be due to swelling at the orifice of the ductus communis. Acute yellow atrophy has been found in some fatal cases.

_ *Stomatitis* may occur during treatment by arsenic, but is less severe than that due to mercury.

(5) *Kidney.* *Albuminuria* following an injection is uncommon, but is to be regarded as a warning against increased dosage. Partial or complete *suppression of urine* has occurred in a few instances. In fatal cases hæmorrhages have been found into the kidneys, but the most constant features are cloudy degeneration of the glomeruli and convoluted tubules.

(6) *Skin.* *Urticaria* occurring with vaso-motor symptoms immediately after an injection has been already noticed. *Pruritus* is not uncommon. By some this is held to be a sign of intolerance and of caution as to dosage.

Erythema. An acute scarlatiniform or morbilliform rash occurs with high pyrexia (106° F.) soon after the first injection. In two cases under my care the eruption might easily have passed for that of scarlet fever. It was followed by desquamation. The patients were seriously ill for a week.

Exfoliative dermatitis is a more serious affection and occurs after repeated doses. I have known it to come on after five doses, but most cases I have seen have had at least eight doses. The eruption spreads all over the body, blebs or pustules developing, and their rupture causes crusting and scaling. The skin becomes a reddish brown tint and the epidermis exfoliates freely. There is intense itching. A noteworthy fact is the great swelling of the head. When the acute symptoms have died down the skin remains very pigmented, thin and atrophic. The loss of sleep caused by the irritation and general malaise affects the general health. In some cases there is high pyrexia with diarrhœa. The tongue is dry and brown, and the patient passes into a typhoid condition, which may end fatally with or without lung complications. In severe cases the eruption may be hæmorrhagic in parts. Dermatitis may persist for many months. The diet should be of the simplest character, and the patient should take plenty of fluid. A daily bran bath should be given ; boric starch poultices are used for the removal of crusts. If the eruption is merely erythematous, calamine lotion should be used, while ichthyol up to 10 per cent., either with calamine liniment or zinc paste, should be applied if there is pustulation. The patient complains of feeling cold, and every precaution should be taken against chill of the surface. Erythema may sometimes be aborted by venesection.

Herpes labialis and *zoster* are occasionally met with after an intravenous injection.

(7) *Nervous system.* Pain in the back associated with cramp may be met with immediately after an injection. Some patients also complain of pain in the teeth.

Abnormal sensations of *taste* are sometimes noted even during an injection. The taste or smell of ether is in my experience the commonest. A garlic odour has also been known.

Headache. Headache is commonly met with in association with rise of temperature, occurring soon after an injection, and this is usually relieved by ten-grain doses of aspirin, but a persistent headache associated with general asthenia occasionally occurs after a long course of injection. Insomnia is sometimes associated with these headaches.

The most severe *cerebral symptoms* are characterised by intense headache, epileptiform convulsions, and coma, often ending fatally. I have seen one such ; it occurred ⁀ ⁀ has usually been reported, in a late primary (early secondary) case. The cerebral symptoms began forty-eight hours after the second dose of salvarsan ; the temperature rose to 107°, and the patient's death occurred on the fifth day after the injection. These cases are extremely rare, and certainly fewer are on record than in the earlier days of treatment. Autopsies on these cases showed punctiform hæmorrhages with œdema of the brain. The capillaries are thrombosed, extravasation taking place from them.

Associated with these severe epileptiform seizures complete suppression of the urine may occur, and death from coma.

In rare instances a single epileptiform convulsion may occur and the patient recover. The treatment for these severe cerebral cases is venesection followed by infusions of saline. Lumbar puncture is also recommended, and intramuscular injection of adrenalin might also be tried.

Neuro-recurrences. In the early days of salvarsan treatment it was noticed that symptoms of the affection of the central nervous system supervened from six weeks to two months after injection, and that such occurrences were more frequent than under mercurial treatment. Auditory and facial paralyses are the most common, but the occulo-motor nerve may be affected. I have had one case of paraplegia, and hemiplegia has also been observed. It must be remembered that in generalised syphilis the meninges are affected early in most cases. It is believed that pains in the head and limbs and elsewhere are due to this cause. Moreover, as already mentioned, deafness is a common symptom in syphilis in the early generalised stages, and this is probably due to peri-neural inflammation. It has been established that neuro-recurrences are more frequent in cases that have been insufficiently treated by arsenic and mercury, and that they usually clear up rapidly with a further administration of the arsenical compound given intravenously.

(8) *General.* As a rule a patient having received an intravenous injection of the arsenical compound is remarkably benefited in his general condition; in fact, the remedy has a remarkable tonic influence, but occasionally after repeated injections one meets with loss of energy, loss of weight, and insomnia, which may last for some time.

(9) *Jarisch - Herxheimer reaction.* The administration of an arsenical compound, and, to a less extent, mercury, to a syphilitic patient is frequently followed by an exacerbation of the symptoms. The primary chancre may become swollen and surrounded with a red area the day after the first injection of salvarsan. The rash in the secondary stage also becomes more evident, and the Wassermann reaction may be intensified. Occasionally paralysis of a cranial nerve may come on a few hours after the injection, but a careful distinction must be made between these phenomena and the neuro-recurrences described above, which occur after the lapse of six or eight weeks. The severe cerebral symptoms mentioned above are not to be confounded with the Herxheimer reaction, as they commonly develop after the second day.

Phlebitis and *thrombosis* in the vein used for injection may be due to faulty technique and are dangerous from the risk of embolism.

The considerations enumerated show the importance of care in the selection of cases and of scrupulous asepsis in the administration of the remedy.

Local Treatment of Syphilis of the Skin.

The **local treatment of syphilis of the skin** is of minor importance, but it is often a valuable adjuvant to the other measures. The primary chancre may be dressed with dermatol, or with orthoform or iodoform. The powder is dusted over the surface and a dressing of lint worn. Ulcerated areas, whether of the secondary or tertiary stage, are dressed with lint soaked in black wash, or with the white precipitate ointment. In phagedæna of the penis I have obtained the best results from the use of an ointment of peroxide of zinc, 20 to 40 grains to the ounce. The prolonged bath is also of great efficiency in the treatment of this complication.

Treatment of congenital syphilis. Mercury is well borne by even the youngest infant. As a routine I prefer the method of inunction, and for this purpose a quarter of a drachm of unguent. hydrarg. is rubbed into the abdomen once daily, after bathing. A flannel binder is worn over the ointment, and the movements of the child promote absorption. The mother should be treated at the same time, if possible. The duration of mercurial treatment in the infant depends upon the severity and duration of the symptoms, and in future it will doubtless be controlled by the Wassermann reaction. Some authorities advise administration by the mouth in congenital syphilis. The usual form of mercury given is hydrarg. c. creta one-fourth to one-half grain with a little sugar of milk, thrice daily. Should there be diarrhœa, which is exceedingly uncommon, a quarter of a grain of Dover's powder may be added to the mercury and chalk.

The presence of snuffles sometimes prevents the child sucking, and in such cases feeding by the spoon must be employed.

Unless an infant is moribund, neo-salvarsan may be administered. The dose is 0·01 gramme per kilogramme of body weight. The injections may be made into the back. Treatment through the mother may also be tried (*vide* p. 321).

In congenital syphilis the rash usually disappears in from one to two weeks after the injection. Condylomata clear up in about the same time. Coryza and snuffles may take six weeks to three to six months to disappear. Lesions of the nails heal in about two months, but epiphysitis may disappear in a week to a fortnight. It may take eight or nine months to cause the absorption of hepatic and splenic enlargements. In the rare tertiary lesions of congenital syphilis mercury and iodides act with great rapidity, and equally good results follow the intravenous injection of neo-salvarsan.

Condylomata and other local lesions of congenital syphilis are treated by a calomel dusting powder.

PRECAUTIONS TO PREVENT INFECTION.

Medical men, midwives and nurses who are obliged to handle cases of syphilis should wear rubber gloves, especially if there be any abrasion or cut on the fingers. A parturient woman should never be digitally examined without inspection of the genitalia for condylomata. If rubber gloves are not available, washing with efficient antiseptic lotions is imperative. In the seventeen years during which I have had care of the dermatological cases arising in the nursing staff of the

London Hospital—and this includes a large number of midwifery nurses attending patients in their homes in the East End of London—I have seen only one case of syphilitic infection of the finger. A 1 in 2,000 perchloride solution is used to disinfect the hands immediately before and after all examinations of maternity cases.

Metchnikoff's ointment. Calomel 33 parts, lanolin 100 parts, vaselin 10 parts, applied within three hours of exposure to infection, destroys the spirochætes, and should be always available for those liable to infection. Disinfection of the external genitals by the application of this ointment after exposure to infection has proved of the greatest value. Failing the calomel ointment, the immediate use of a 1 in 1,000 permanganate of potash solution is advocated.

THE STATE AND SYPHILIS.

Since the last edition of this work appeared the policy recommended by the Royal Commission on Venereal Diseases has been adopted by the Local Government Board, and this body, in conjunction with the county councils, has introduced a scheme for the diagnosis and treatment of venereal diseases in areas comprising 83·9 per cent. of the population of England and Wales (January, 1918). There is no doubt that in the near future the scheme will be adopted in all parts of the British Isles. The policy adopted is to place within the reach of every one suffering from venereal disease, free of charge, the best modern methods of treatment. It is held that it is the duty of the State to give every opportunity for the early cure of venereal disease, because a patient suffering therefrom is a source of danger to the public health, and, moreover, sooner or later may become incapacitated by nervous or other affections. To attract every possible sufferer secrecy is enjoined, as there is no doubt many would fear to apply for the necessary assistance if there were a possibility of the nature of their illness becoming known.

(1) *Facilities for diagnosis.* Centres are established in connection with recognised laboratories for the gratuitous examination of discharges for spirochætes and of blood by the Wassermann test, and outfits for taking the required material are supplied by the health authorities.

(2) *Institution treatment.* This is provided free of charge to patients suffering from venereal disease under conditions of secrecy. The patient is known only by a number.

(3) *Private treatment.* Salvarsan or its substitutes are provided free of charge to practitioners who are qualified to use the newer methods of treatment. A list of medical men thus qualified is kept by the medical officer of health.

(4) *Facilities for instruction.* Facilities for instruction in the early diagnosis and methods of treatment are provided free of expense and clinical posts are offered to medical men in the venereal clinics. The expense of institutional treatment and of the free supply of salvarsan or its substitutes is borne partly by the Local Government Board and partly by the county and borough councils.

At present notification is not deemed practicable, and it is thought that it would be unwise to press for compulsory treatment, which is an end to be desired, until public opinion is more enlightened. A great deal of work has been done by the National Council for Combating Venereal Disease in educating the public as to the extreme importance of early diagnosis and treatment, and it is hoped that in time the more rigorous measure of compulsory treatment may be demanded by the public. The profession can, however, be of great assistance—

(1) *In the examination of contracts.* It is my practice, whenever possible, in the case of a married man presenting himself for treatment, to see the wife and to examine her and have a blood examination made. Likewise, if a married woman comes to the clinic and is found to be suffering from syphilis, every endeavour is made to induce the husband to come up for examination. Where there are children I have them brought up and they are examined. In one family the mother suffered from secondary syphilis acquired from her husband, her infant had congenital lues, while two other children in the house, one of them the mother's young sister, aged twelve, were suffering from primary lesions due to kissing. I have had families in which three generations were affected by kissing, etc.

(2) *In the treatment of women who have had reported miscarriages.* In my department we are working in collaboration with the obstetric department and with certain lying-in hospitals in this matter. Every woman who has had repeated miscarriages or still-births is examined by the Wassermann test, and if this is found positive she is urged to undergo treatment.

(3) *In the treatment of women infected during pregnancy.* Most satisfactory results have followed this measure. In many instances the children have been born at full term free from evidence of congenital lues.

(4) *In relation to the marriage of syphilitics.* Every patient must be warned as to the danger of marrying while in an infectious state. Wherever possible, treatment should be continued until the Wassermann reaction is negative. This specially applies to early syphilis. The Wassermann reaction should be watched for two years before permission to marry is given. In old tertiary cases a permanent

negative Wassermann reaction is unusual ; but such patients, if they marry, do not transmit the disease to offspring.

REFERENCES.—The literature of syphilis is enormous, and especially during recent years. On the clinical side the monographs of HUTCHINSON and FOURNIER are full of most valuable information. "La Syphilis," by C. LEVADITI and J. ROCHE, Masson, Paris, 1909, gives a full account of the history and recent work on the spirochæta and the pathology, with numerous plates. SCHAUDINN and HOFFMANN'S papers appeared in the *Arbeiten aus dem Kaiserlich Gesundheitsamt*, 1905, Vol. CXXII., fasc. ii., p. 527, and SCHAUDINN'S posthumous papers were published in the same periodical, 1907, Vol. XXVI., fasc. i., p. 11. LEVY-BING and LAFFORT give a good summary of experimental work in the *Annales des Maladies veneriennes*, May, 1909. The papers read at the International Medical Congress, London, 1913, should be studied. H. B. FANTHAM. "Spirochætes and their Granule Phase." *Brit. Med. Journal*, 1916, I., p. 409. MEIROW-SKY. *British Journal of Dermatology*, XXVI., p. 185, and his "Fortpflanzung von Bacterien, Spirillen ü. Spirochäten," Springer, 1914, deal with the development of the organism. Literature and plates. McDONAGH in *British Journal of Dermatology*, XXV., p. 1, describes the "life cycle" of spirochæte. NOGUCHI. *Journal Experimental Medicine*, 14, No. 2, 1911, on cultivation of spirochætes. BOAS'S valuable monograph on the Wassermann reaction, 2nd ed., 1914. McINTOSH and FILDES. "Syphilis from the Modern Standpoint." Arnold, 1911, and Brain, XXXVI., p. 193. L. W. HARRISON. "Critical Review of the Treatment of Syphilis." *Quarterly Journal of Medicine*, Vol. X., No. 40, p. 291. An excellent paper with copious references. "Diagnostic Value of the Wassermann Test." Report of Special Committee. H.M. Stationery Office, 1918.

CHAPTER XII.

EXOTIC SPIROCHÆTAL DISEASES AND LEISHMANIASIS.

Yaws (Frambœsia tropica). Parangi.

YAWS is a chronic infectious disease endemic in the tropics. It is characterised by nodular, vegetating and fungating lesions. It occurs commonly in the Orient, in Oceania, in Central Africa, and in Central and South America. In its course it resembles syphilis,

FIG. 144.—Yaws. From Dr. C. W. Daniels' "Tropical Medicine and Hygiene."

and for a long time many eminent authorities believed that the frambœsia tropica was a variety of syphilis. Recent researches have, however, shown that it is caused by a distinct, though morphologically similar, parasite.

Etiology. Yaws is caused by the *spirochæta pallidula* (treponema pertenue), discovered by Castellani in 1905. The organism is a spiral body with an undulating membrane closely resembling the spirochæta pallida. Neisser has shown that a patient suffering from yaws may contract syphilis, and monkeys inoculated with the spirochæta pallidula are not immune to infection by the organism of syphilis. Yaws is not a venereal disease, but is usually contracted in infancy through some breach of the surface, and Castellani believes that flies and other insects may introduce the parasite. It is highly contagious, and in the early stages autoinoculation is possible. When once fully developed it confers immunity upon the patient. It is not hereditary.

Pathology. The lesions show an increase in the horny layers of the epidermis, hyperkeratosis, and also parakeratosis. There

Fig. 145.—Yaws. From Dr. C. W. Daniels' "Tropical Medicine and Hygiene."

are numerous plasma cells, but no giant cells. The papillæ are much hypertrophied.

Clinical features. There is a period of incubation lasting from a fortnight to six months. In this stage there is slight fever, accompanied by headache, articular pains, and digestive disturbance. The primary lesion is a conical pinkish elevation, the centre of which necroses, becomes incrusted and indurated, and finally papillomatous. It occurs on the limbs or on the face. In some cases it is unnoticed or absent.   The eruption, which begins from one to three months after the primary lesion, is scaly, often circinate, and does not itch.   It is all of one type, and may affect the whole skin.   The plaques are from one-third of an inch to two inches across ;   they are covered with adherent brownish crusts, and sometimes there is a fœtid secretion.   Vegetations of a red or greyish colour form, and while the centre of the lesion tends to heal, bullæ develop around it. The areas affected are the skin about the orifices of the body, the lips, nostrils, genital regions, and the flexures.   The polycyclic character of the lesions suggests a hypertrophic fungating syphilide (Figs. 144, 145).   The Wassermann reaction is positive.

The eruption may last for some months and recur during several years.   The mucous membranes escape ; there are no visceral lesions, and alopecia is unknown.   The glands may or may not be generally affected.   Swelling of the joints and neuritis may occur.   Gummatous nodes are occasionally seen.

Treatment.   Mercury is often useful, but it is not so valuable as the iodides.   A mixture containing tartar emetic gr. 1, sodii salicylat. grs. 10, potass. iodid. grs. 60, sodii bicarb. grs. 15 in 1 oz. of water thrice daily is recommended by Castellani.   Salvarsan has proved remarkably successful, and sometimes one dose is sufficient to cure the disease.

REFERENCES.—" Yaws, its Nature and Treatment." N. RAT. 1891. Waterlow.   " Frambœsia Tropica."   A. CASTELLANI.   *Journal of Cutaneous Diseases*, April and May, 1908, Vol. XXVI., Nos. 4 and 5 (references). " Observations upon Treponema Pertenuis (Castellani) and the Experimental Production of the Disease in Monkeys."   ASHBURN and CRAIGS. *Philippine Journal of Science*, October, 1907, p. 441.   CASTELLANI and CHALMERS.   "Tropical Medicine," p. 1170.

Gangosa.

A slowly destructive ulcerative process involving the palate, nose, pharynx and skin.   The name " gangosa " signifies nasal voice. The disease is endemic in many tropical countries.

It is often mistaken for syphilis and leprosy, and is believed to be a sequel to yaws.   The disease attacks males and females equally.

Pathology.   The lesions consist of infiltrations of round cells, chiefly lymphocytes ;   giant cells are also found, and there is proliferation of the vessels and hæmorrhage into the affected tissues. The process ends in necrosis.

Clinical features.   The patient complains of sore throat, and a nodule may be seen in the pharynx or on the fauces or palate.   The nodule ulcerates, forming a brownish grey slough.   The process spreads and causes necrosis of bone, and ultimately the nose and mouth become one cavity. The skin may also be involved, and in advanced cases the whole of the middle of the face is eaten away. The dirty ulcerated surfaces have a foul odour. Ulcers may appear on any uncovered parts. The Wassermann reaction is positive.

There is often an osteitis as in syphilis.

The duration of the disease may be from a few months to ten or even thirty-five years, but it is rarely fatal.

The treatment consists in the local application of iodine, permanganate of potash, and the removal of the diseased areas by the cautery. Segregation of the sufferers from gangosa has been successful in Guam.

REFERENCE.—CASTELLANI and CHALMERS. "Tropical Diseases," p. 1275. Plates and literature.

Ulcus Tropicum. Aden Ulcer. Yemen Ulcer, etc.

A chronic sloughing ulcerative process, which may become phagedænic, occurring in many tropical and sub-tropical regions, and often denoted by the name of the country in which it occurs.

The disease is caused by the Spiroschaudinnia schaudinnii of Prowazek, a spirillar organism 10 to 20 μ in length.

The disease is not directly contagious, and it is possible that some carrier insect is the intermediary of infection.

Histology. The surface of the ulcer is covered by hyaline fibrin containing masses of the spirochætes and bacteria. The sides and base of the ulcer consist of granulation tissue. In the deeper parts there is an infiltration of lymphoid and plasma cells.

Clinical features. The ulcers occur usually on the lower third of the leg and on the dorsum of the foot, other uncovered parts being less commonly affected. The ulcer is usually single. The first stage of the lesion is a small, painful papulo-pustule with a dusky infiltrated areola. Suppuration occurs and sloughing follows. The fully-developed ulcer is perhaps a couple of inches or more in diameter, covered with a thick, dirty and very offensive secretion. The base is red or pale and covered with flabby granulations. The centre is often funnel-shaped. There is very little pain. In some cases there is a phagedænic process, and muscle, tendon, and bone may be exposed.

The course is chronic, and the ulcer usually lasts for months, showing no tendency to spontaneous recovery.

Treatment. The intravenous injection of salvarsan or neo-salvarsan gives excellent results. Calcium iodide is also·recommended. Locally the ulcer should be dressed with perchloride of mercury solution (1—1,000), peroxide of hydrogen, permanganate of potash solution, or an ointment of protargol 5 to 10 per cent.

REFERENCES. — PROWAZEK. *Arbeiten aus dem Kaiserlichen Gesundheitsamt*, XXVI., Heft 1. WOLBACK and TOD. *Journal of Medical Research*, 1912.

Ulcus interdigitale.

A tropical affection, in which the first symptom is itching between the toes. A fissure develops in a few days and extends to form an oval ulcer with sodden margin and dark red base. The ulcer·is very painful. Healing is rapid after disinfection with carbolic lotion and the application of a bismuth and boric acid ointment.

Oriental Sore. Dermal Leishmaniasis.

An endemic disease in certain parts of Asia and Africa, South America and Southern Europe, characterised by the formation of nodules, and ulcerating and vegetative lesions.

Many names are given to this affection, depending upon the district in which the disease is observed, *e.g.*, Aleppo or Delhi boil, Biskra button, etc. Nile boils as seen in the Anglo-Egyptian Sudan are caused by a non-mobile circular coccus (Chalmers and Marshall).

Etiology. The disease is caused by the Leishmania tropica and allied species. The infection is conveyed to the human subject through abrasions or small wounds and probably by insect carriers. Autoinoculation is common.

The lesions show atrophy of the epidermis, and extensive infiltration of the corium and papillæ by lymphoid, plasma and large round cells. These large round cells contain the parasite.

Clinical features. After an incubation period lasting from a few days to several weeks or longer one or more itching spots appear on uncovered parts of the skin. These lesions become indurated, and increase to the size of a bean. After three months the nodule ulcerates, and is covered with a dried crust. On the removal of the scab an ulcer about an inch in diameter is found. The edges of the ulcer are sharp, and the base is irregular and covered with reddish yellow granulations. The lesions run an indolent course and are slightly painful. The ulcer heals by granulation. There may be an intermittent fever before the development of the cutaneous lesions. Multiple sores from autoinoculation are not uncommon.

In some instances the mucous membranes of the nose and mouth are involved. Warty and non-ulcerative varieties of the disease occur in some countries.

The Leishman-Donovan bodies are found in blood expressed from the lesions. The prognosis is usually good, but occasionally phagedæna occurs and death may ensue from septicæmia. Scarring may cause considerable deformity.

Treatment. Dressing of the lesions with antiseptic lotions and ointments is recommended. X-ray treatment has proved unsatisfactory. Injections of atoxyl and of salvarsan have also been tried, but without benefit.

REFERENCES.—WRIGHT. *Journal of Medical Research*, 1903, p. 472. CASTELLANI and CHALMERS. "Tropical Medicine," p. 1548. Bibliography. Plates.

Espundia. Naso-oral Leishmaniasis.

A chronic ulcerating granuloma of the skin and mucous membranes of the mouth and nose caused by the Leishmania tropica.

The disease occurs in Peru and in other parts of South America. An Indian variety has also been described, and Europeans who have long resided in countries where the disease is endemic may be affected.

The parasite is believed to be introduced by an insect.

Clinical features. The disease begins with a chancre-like lesion on an exposed part of the mucous membrane. The primary lesion heals up in a few months and then ulcers appear in the nasal and oral cavities. The palate may be involved and also the nasal cartilages. The ulceration is attended with an offensive odour, and the destruction produces grave deformity. The disease runs a chronic course and may last for twenty to thirty years.

Excision of the primary lesion is recommended.

REFERENCES.—DE AMICIS. "Transactions of the International Congress," 1909. Buda-Pesth. Other references in CASTELLANI and CHALMERS' "Tropical Medicine," p. 1576.

Granuloma telangiectodes tropicum (von Bassowitz). Angio-Fibroma cutis circumscriptum contagiosum.

This affection, which appears to be closely allied to human botryomycosis, was described by von Bassowitz, who found it among the natives of Santa Victoria de Palma in Southern Brazil.

The infection is believed to take place through the mouth, the natives being in the habit of handing from one to another their pipes and also drinking vessels containing "mâte." The period of incubation is fifteen to twenty-five days.

The onset of the disease is quite acute, an eruption of bright red papules appearing on the face, neck, axilla or pubic region, and occasionally elsewhere. The papules rapidly develop into large, red, shining tumours, which are highly vascular and on slight injury give rise to severe and frequent hæmorrhages which may lead to grave anæmia. The tumours are painless and do not itch. There is no fever or interference with the general health. The glands are unaffected. The condition lasts about a year, and the prognosis is altogether favourable. von Bassowitz's account suggests a similarity to the appearance of the florid tumour about the mouth

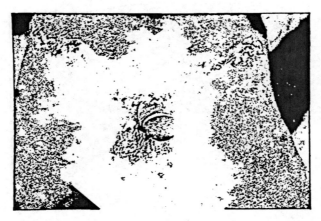

FIG. 145A.—Granuloma inguinale. (From Dr. C. W. Daniels' "Tropical Medicine and Hygiene.")

which was present in my case of granuloma inguinale tropicum (*vide infra*). The disease is distinguished from yaws by the absence of joint pains.

Microscopically the tumours consist of granulomatous tissue with dilated lymph spaces and vessels, developing from the vessels of the cutis.

Treatment. The tumours are removed after being injected with formaldehyde. Should they ulcerate they are treated with oxide of zinc and salicylic acid ointment. The X-rays would probably be useful, and intravenous injection of antimony should be tried.

REFERENCES.—BASSOWITZ. *Archiv. f. Schiffs. u. Tropische.* Hygiene, April, 1906. J. H. SEQUEIRA. *Trans. Roy. Soc. Medicine* (Dermatological Section), 1908, pp. 57 and 92, coloured plate.

Granuloma inguinale tropicum. Ulcerating granuloma of the pudenda.

A chronic ulcerative affection of the groin and neighbouring parts associated with papillary hypertrophy. In a case of my own there was a granulomatous swelling at the left angle of the mouth also.

The disease is most commonly met with in the West Indies, British Guiana and Brazil. It has also been observed in Fiji, India, West Africa, Australia and China. Imported cases are occasionally seen

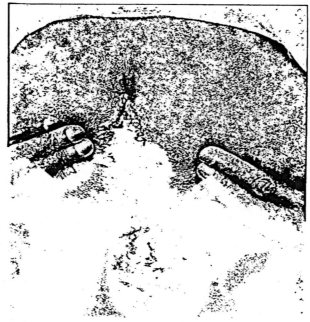

FIG. 146.—Granuloma inguinale. (From Dr. C. W. Daniel's "Tropical Medicine and Hygiene.")

in this country. McDonagh suggests a relationship between this affection and ulcus molle serpiginosum (*vide* p. 271).

My only patient was a negro born in Antigua, but who had spent the greater part of his life in Jamaica. He came to London as a ship's fireman in January, 1908. In April, 1907, he said that a swelling formed at the left angle of the mouth, and at the same time an infiltration developed in the right groin. Some months later an ulcer appeared on the dorsum of the penis. The tumour at the angle of the mouth at first sight suggested an epithelioma ; it extended in the form of a horse-shoe round the commissure of the lips, affecting both the skin and mucous surface. The growth was florid red and measured an inch and a quarter in its extreme width. It was soft to the touch and very vascular. On the surface there was some erosion which exuded a yellowish discharge. The glands were not palpable. In the left groin there was a line of infiltration running outwards from the pubic spine along Poupart's ligament nearly to the anterior superior spine of the ilium. It was of a pinkish colour and sclerosed in the greater part of its length, but in two or three places there was some superficial ulceration. The anal region and perineum are often involved (Fig. 146), and there are ulcers on the thickened skin of the penis. The whole of the lesions in my case cleared up with remarkable rapidity under repeated small doses of the X-rays.

The microscopical examination showed the growth to be a granuloma, but no organisms were recognised in the sections. The condition must be classed as an infective granuloma, probably of protozoal origin. It is distinguished from yaws by its peculiar localisation. The case mentioned above is the only one recorded in which the granuloma has been away from the pudendal and anal regions.

Intravenous injections of antimony (gr. 1 of antimonium tartaratum dissolved in 2 ounces of normal saline) repeated every third or fourth day have cured numerous cases. It may be necessary to give as many as twenty injections, and the dose may be gradually increased to $2\frac{1}{2}$ grs. (Aragao, Vianna).

REFERENCES.—CONYERS and DANIELS. *British Guiana Medical Annual*, 1896.   J. GALLOWAY.   *British Journal of Dermatology*, 1897, IX., p. 133. J. H. SEQUEIRA.   *Transactions of the Royal Society of Medicine* (Dermatological Section), 1908, pp. 57 and 92.   Coloured plate, p. 92.   H. RADCLIFFE CROCKER.   "Diseases of the Skin."   Plate, p. 1011.   G. C. LOW.   *British Medical Journal.*   1916, II., p. 387.

CHAPTER XIII.

ERUPTIONS CAUSED BY DRUGS, VACCINES, AND ANTITOXINES.

Drug Eruptions (Dermatitis medicamentosa).

A LARGE number of drugs administered internally may cause eruptions on the skin. In some cases there is idiosyncrasy, and the rash appears after the administration of small doses; in others there is defective elimination owing to renal and cardiac disease, but excess of dosage or, what is commoner, accumulation from prolonged administration may also be responsible.

In many instances the eruption is of an erythematous, urticarial, or petechial type, closely resembling the rashes of the exanthemata and those due to toxæmia; in others there are special characters, which may closely simulate some common dermatoses. The history of the case will usually be of assistance in making a diagnosis, but in the absence of knowledge that the patient has been taking drugs there may be great difficulty. In a few cases the examination of the urine for the presence of drugs will be helpful.

It will be convenient first to tabulate the common manifestations with a list of the drugs which cause them, and then to consider the more commonly used drugs and the various cutaneous eruptions which they may produce :

Erythematous eruptions may be produced by :—
Antipyrin, rash resembling measles and diffuse erythema.
Arsenic, occasionally.
Belladonna, scarlatiniform erythema.
Borax and boric acid.
Chloral, scarlatiniform rash with desquamation.
Copaiba and cubebs, eruption like measles.
Digitalis (rarely), scarlatiniform and measly eruption.
Iodoform, scarlatiniform.
Luminal.
Mercury (rarely), scarlatiniform erythema.
Midol, a derivative of Pyramidon, erythema.
Opium and morphia, rash resembling measles or scarlatina.
Pantopon.

Quinine, scarlatiniform erythema with desquamation sometimes attended with pyrexia.

Salicylates and salicylic acid, scarlatiniform.

Salvarsan and its allies, scarlatiniform erythema.

Sulphonal, macular and diffuse erythema.

Tar, erythema, sometimes morbiliform, with fever.

Veronal, itching erythema.

Urticarial eruptions.

Copaiba and cubebs.

Midol.

Quinine.

Salicylic acid and salicylates.

Santonin.

Tar and creosote.

Turpentine.

Valerian.

Erythema with Infiltration and œdema resembling erysipelas.

Aconite.

Bromide of potassium.

Iodide of potassium.

Vesicular and bullous eruptions.

Arsenic (rare).

Boric acid (rare).

Bromides.

Copaiba and cubebs (rare).

Iodides and iodoform.

Quinine.

Veronal.

Herpes zoster. Arsenic. Salvarsan.

Pustular eruptions.

Antimony.

Arsenic.

Bromides.

Iodides.

Sulphide of calcium.

Salicylic acid (rare).

Petechial eruption, Purpura.

Chloral, chloroform.

Copaiba.

Iodides.

Midol.

Cyanosis. Acetanilid.

Exfoliative dermatitis. Salvarsan, after repeated doses.
Pigmentation. Arsenic (brown), silver nitrate (slate colour).
Hyperkeratosis, Epidermic thickening.

Arsenic ; the hyperkeratosis may become malignant.

Borax, eruption like psoriasis (Gowers).

The eruptions may be caused by the direct action of the drugs circulating in the blood, or through toxic bodies developed in the alimentary canal or through changes produced directly or indirectly in the nervous system.

We will now consider shortly the commonly occurring eruptions in connection with the drugs in general use.

Antipyrin. The rash commonly resembles that of measles, but urticaria and diffuse erythema occur, and in rare instances vesicles and bullæ. General exfoliative dermatitis has been seen.

Arsenic in large doses, or if there is idiosyncrasy, may cause an urticarial or erythematous eruption and occasionally papules or vesicles. Salvarsan rashes and dermatitis are discussed on p. 323.

After prolonged administration a characteristic greyish-brown pigmentation of a dappled character appears on the trunk, together with hyperkeratosis of the palms and soles. In rare instances the warty lesions on the extremities may become epitheliomatous, as Hutchinson has pointed out. Herpes zoster is an occasional result of prolonged administration of arsenic, and I have once seen scattered blebs associated with herpes zoster and pigmentation.

Atophan may produce an œdematous swelling of the lips and eyelids accompanied by well-defined raised red plaques as large as a sixpence.

Belladonna produces a scarlatiniform eruption in certain subjects. The drug may be absorbed from a belladonna plaster.

Borax and **boric acid** may cause erythematous and vesicular eruptions. These sometimes occur when the patient is taking food to which boric acid has been added as a preservative. In the prolonged treatment of epilepsy by borax Gowers has seen scaly eruptions resembling psoriasis.

Bromides. Most patients who take bromides for a long time suffer from an *acneiform* eruption. The pustules occur on the face and upper part of the trunk and in hairy regions. In children, even those suckled by mothers taking bromides, a different type of eruption may develop. At first the rash resembles varicella, but the vesicles do not dry up. They run together, forming confluent patches which gradually increase in size and ultimately suppurate. The characteristic lesions thus formed are flat elevations covered with brownish crusts surrounded by a zone of erythema. Sometimes these plaques undergo papillary hypertrophy and form condylomatous tumours of soft consistence. The lower limbs and the lower part of the trunk are the parts most involved. Boils and carbuncles also occur, the former in the sites where acne is common and the latter on the face and limbs. Bullous lesions are met with occasionally, but the fluid in the blebs is small in amount, the cavity being largely occupied by papillomatous granulations. It is rather

Fig. 147.—Bromide eruption.

curious that the bromide lesions not infrequently develop upon the cicatrices of vaccination and other scar tissue. The presence of bromine in the urine may be detected chemically.

Chloral. The chloral eruption may be a transitory patchy erythema, resembling scarlatina ; the mucous membrane of the throat may be affected, and pyrexia sometimes occurs. The rash is usually very evanescent. On the other hand, there may be exudation and even hæmorrhage into the skin. Rarely papules, vesicles, and pustules are seen.

Copaiba and cubebs. In a severe case there are large dark red

Plate 80.

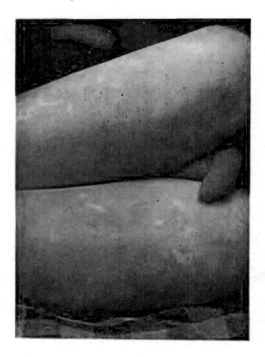

COPAIBA ERUPTION.

spots with purpuric lesions on the extremities, intense itching and burning. The seats of election are the fronts of the thighs, the lower thirds of the legs, the forearms and elbows, and sometimes the face and neck. The eruption is a confluent erythema. Plate XXX.,

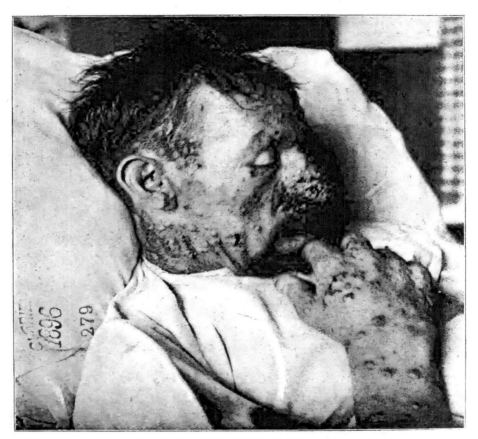

FIG. 148.—Iodide eruption in a patient suffering from cardiac disease.

and sometimes there are minute pustules upon it. Vesicular and bullous lesions may occur. The eruption may be mistaken for measles, scarlet fever, and for a macular syphilide. Febrile symptoms are not uncommon, and the throat is often congested. The odour of the urine may be characteristic; the contact nitric acid test shows a cloudy opacity at the line of junction of the acid and the urine, and sometimes a lilac or red tint is produced by floating the urine on nitric acid.

Formalin applied to dental cavities may, in susceptible subjects, produce an acute urticaria with œdema of the tongue and throat.

Iodides. The eruptions caused by iodides are most commonly seen in patients suffering from grave renal and cardiac disease, but occasionally there is a remarkable idiosyncrasy apart from conditions of defective elimination (Fig. 148).

The most characteristic eruption is bullous (hydroa). The bullæ are most often seen on the face and neck, and on parts exposed to pressure. The first symptom is a number of small vesicles or apparent vesicles, for they contain very little serous exudate. The lesions may ulcerate and form crusts. In other cases the eruption consists of distinct bullæ containing clear fluid, in which iodine can be demonstrated by chemical tests. The bullæ may be as large as a small nut, and the cavity is rapidly filled up by granulation tissue, producing lesions which resemble gummata, or mycosis fungoides, or even large molluscum contagiosum tumours. The danger of pushing the drug for the removal of these gummatous-like tumours is obvious. In cases where this has been done sloughing may occur with a fatal issue.

Purpura is another rare effect of iodism, and a fatal case was recorded by Mackenzie in a child after the administration of only $2\frac{1}{2}$ grains of the drug.

Acne-like lesions, nodules, and boils sometimes occur.

Iodine may be demonstrated in the urine.

Iodide of iron may cause characteristic iodide eruptions.

Iron. The administration of iron has been followed by the formation of acne-like pustules on the face, neck, and upper part of the trunk.

Luminal causes a widely-spread, intensely itching erythema with wheals.

Mercury. In rare cases the prolonged administration of mercury has been attended by the development of a scarlatiniform erythema, and even of pityriasis rubra. Herpetic lesions, impetigo, boils and ulcers have also been attributed to the drug.

Midol, a derivative of pyramidon, has been known to cause an itching erythema with urticarial wheals and purpura.

Opium and morphia. Opium and its alkaloids may cause an erythema resembling scarlatina or measles, or urticaria. The opium eruptions usually itch. Desquamation may follow.

Pantopon may produce an erythema.

Quinine. The commonest eruption due to quinine is a scarlatiniform erythema. It is sometimes attended with pyrexia and congestion of the fauces, and it may be exceedingly difficult to differentiate from the exanthem. Free desquamation follows. Occasionally urticarial, bullous and eczematous eruptions have been observed. Limited gangrene has followed the administration of quinine and urea hydrochloride.

Salicylic acid and the salicylates may produce erythematous eruptions of the scarlatiniform or urticarial types.

Silver. The slate-blue colour produced by the prolonged administration of silver had been seen rarely until the introduction of urethral injections of protargol, collargol, and allied substances. Several cases are on record in which the absorption probably took place through the damaged mucous surfaces. Local argyria may occur. Hexamine internally has diminished the discoloration.

Turpentine may cause a rash resembling that produced by copaiba and cubebs.

Veronal and allied drugs may cause an intensely itching erythema with vesication twelve to eighteen hours after taking the drug. Crusting and desquamation may follow.

REFERENCES.—PRINCE MORROW. *New Sydenham Society's Publications.* T. COLCOTT FOX and H. GIBBES. *British Medical Journal,* 1885, II., p. 971. S. MACKENZIE. *Path. Trans.,* 1884, XXXV., p. 400 (Iodides). H. G. BROOKE and LESLIE ROBERTS. *British Journal of Dermatology,* 1901, XIII., p. 122. "On the Effects of Arsenic on the Skin." PYE-SMITH, BEATTIE, and NUTT. "Arsenical Cancer." *Lancet,* 1913, II., pp. 214 and 282, with many references. ZEISLER. "Veronal Rashes." *Münchener Med. Wochenschr.,* 1912, p. 2169. HEIDINGSFELD. "Formalin Urticaria." *Journal Cutaneous Diseases,* April, 1916.

Vaccination Eruptions.

Ignorance and prejudice frequently attribute to vaccination a large number of cutaneous affections in childhood. It is, therefore, important that the practitioner should be familiar with the conditions which may be caused by the inoculation, and also with those which may reasonably be ascribed to it. It should be clearly understood that calf-lymph is made from animals which have been proved to be free from tuberculosis by the injection of tuberculin, and that the beasts are killed and their bodies examined before the lymph is sent out. Secondly, that the tubercle bacillus cannot live in glycerinated lymph. And lastly, that it is impossible for the calf to convey syphilis. In human lymph, as used in the old "arm to arm" vaccination, it was impossible to exclude these, though, thanks to the care of the operators, infection with either was extremely rare.

The use of calf-lymph and the performance of the operation with sterilised instruments and efficient disinfection of the sites of inoculation, followed by protection of the vaccinia lesions by antiseptic dressings, will further exclude infection by streptococci, staphylococci, and other organisms. In the absence of any of these precautions, and particularly of the want of care in the after-treatment, erysipelas, impetigo, furunculosis, etc., may still occur.

Eruptions caused by pure vaccine. The lesions caused by the inoculation of glycerinated calf-lymph may be papular, vesicular, or pustular. As a rule, there is an inflammatory areola around the developed vesicle. But sometimes, probably as the result of friction, scratching, or other injury, the redness and swelling are not limited to a small area round the vesicles, but spread until a large part of the arm, and perhaps the shoulder, are affected. The whole limb may become red, swollen, hot, tender, and painful, and there may be constitutional disturbance with pyrexia. Should an actual cellulitis supervene, mixed infection (*vide infra*) should be suspected. In a few cases, probably due to indididual idiosyncrasy, the local lesion may pass on to necrosis and ulceration.

Treatment consists in putting the limb at rest in a sling, and the application of soothing lotions of lead or calamine if there be simple erythema, and of boric acid ointment or boric fomentations if there be sloughing and ulceration.

Reinoculation. Autoinoculation is not uncommon. In some instances a few lesions develop in the neighbourhood of the vaccination. In others the eruption is widely spread. The infection is conveyed by scratching before the primary vesicles have healed, and consequently it may occur as late as the tenth day. In some of these cases the sites of autoinoculation have been areas of eczema, impetigo spots, and lesions of herpes, varicella, and the like. It is a wise precaution, therefore, not to vaccinate a person suffering from any skin affection.

Infections of this type may occur in the unvaccinated by contact with vaccination lesions. They occur sometimes on the face or hand of a parent inoculated from a vaccinated infant. In a woman seen by me at the London Hospital three spots appeared on the face nine days after her baby was vaccinated. They became confluent and formed an ulcer two inches and a half transversely and two inches in the vertical direction.

Generalised vaccinia. This name is given erroneously to cases of widespread vaccinia due to autoinoculation. There are, however, rare cases in which a pure generalised vaccinia occurs. It begins from four to nine days after inoculation. The lesions come out in crops, and pass through the stages of normal vaccination, papule, vesicle, and pustule. The affection may last for three weeks. Some cases are afebrile, and the fever, if present, varies with the extent of the eruption. In a recent smallpox epidemic I saw a woman of twenty-eight, in whom the resemblance to variola was so close that she was sent to the isolation hospital as a case of variola. I could not get any evidence of autoinoculation, and the eruption appeared too widespread to be due to that cause.

Concurrent varicella might lead to an erroneous diagnosis of generalised vaccinia.

No special treatment is indicated in these complications.

Toxic vaccination rashes. During the evolution of the vesicle, that is, from the fourth to the tenth day, transitory rashes are not uncommon. In my experience, which coincides with that of many others, these eruptions are commoner since calf-lymph has been used. They are of the same character as the rashes seen after the injection of diphtheria antitoxin and the coccal and other " vaccines." The following varieties occur :—

(1) Erythemata, generalised, punctate (like scarlatina), and roseolar.
(2) Erythema multiforme.
(3) Macular eruptions resembling measles.
(4) Urticaria.
(5) Papular eruptions.
(6) Vesicular and bullous eruptions, which are sometimes combined with (5).
(7) Hæmorrhagic rashes.

The erythematous, scarlatiniform and urticarial eruptions are the most common. The hæmorrhagic variety is very rare. Those resembling the exanthemata may lead to difficulties of diagnosis should there be an epidemic of scarlet fever or measles at the time. The papular and papulo-vesicular forms must be distinguished from lichen urticatus, which is common in infancy and which may co-exist.

Bullous dermatitis. It will be convenient here to mention that bullous eruptions have been seen in connection with vaccination. The eruptions have generally occurred after the vaccinia lesions have healed, but it is probable that they are toxic (Fig. 149).

Bowen described several cases in which there were erythematous and bullous lesions. Besides this polymorphism, the cases presented other features resembling dermatitis herpetiformis, viz., eosinophilia of the contents of the blebs and of the blood. Corlett and Stelwagon have described eruptions of bullæ, and in 1902 I showed, at the Dermatological Society of London, a man of thirty-nine with an extensive crop of bullous lesions which followed re-vaccination. I was informed that the first bleb appeared on one of the vaccination

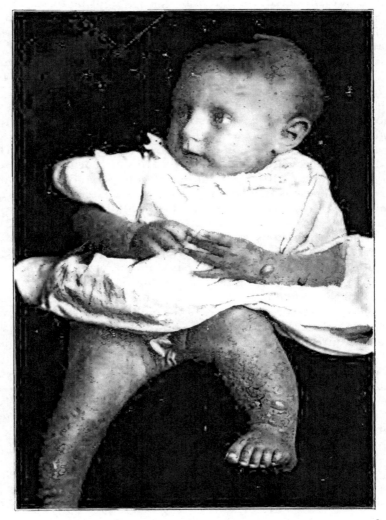

Fig. 149.—Vaccinal bullous erythema.

areas. The contents of the bullæ were sterile, and inoculation of animals gave a negative result.

The toxic eruptions of vaccination demand no special treatment.

Local infections. The operation of vaccination must be performed with scrupulous care. If properly prepared calf-lymph be used, and especially if the instruments be sterilised and the site of inoculation disinfected, foreign organisms cannot be introduced with the vaccine virus. Where these precautions have been omitted Fehleisen's streptococcus has been introduced, leading to erysipelas appearing on the second or third day, sometimes with fatal result. The streptococci and staphylococci may also cause impetigo and the like. Neither syphilis nor tuberculosis can be introduced if calf-lymph be used.

Infection of the vaccination lesions at a later date is less under the control of the doctor. He can apply a proper sterilised dressing and give instructions, but he cannot be sure that the dressing will be allowed to remain in position or be changed when required. He cannot, therefore, prevent infection of the sites of inoculation, especially when he is dealing with the children of careless and dirty parents.

The complications which may thus occur are : (1) Erysipelas ; (2) impetigo ; (3) furunculosis ; (4) cellulitis ; (5) ulceration ; (6) gangrene.

The coccal infections are the most common. Erysipelas may prove fatal if extensive. The eruption appears later than the third day, and is often easily traced to cases in the neighbourhood. Gangrene is fortunately rare, but if disseminated is fatal.

Tuberculosis, syphilis, and leprosy have to be considered. I myself have seen three cases of lupus vulgaris starting in early life in vaccination scars. The patients, however, had all been vaccinated before the introduction of calf-lymph, and it is possible that the tubercle bacillus had been introduced with vaccine virus. It is more probable that the introduction took place later.

Undoubted cases of syphilis have been recorded, but so far as I am aware these were all before the introduction of calf-lymph. It is, of course, possible that a recently vaccinated baby might be inoculated with spirochætes by contact with a syphilised person.

Leprosy has been noted, but in this country it does not need consideration.

The infections mentioned in this connection are treated on the lines indicated in the respective articles devoted to them. The important point is to prevent them, and this can be done with ease if the simple precautions mentioned above are taken.

Eruptions of doubtful connection. Only two conditions require serious consideration, viz., eczema and psoriasis.

It is exceedingly doubtful if vaccination ever causes eczema. Eczema is common in infancy, and occurs frequently independently of vaccination. We know, however, that some acute specific fevers, dentition, and other conditions which affect the general health predispose to it, and vaccination may act in like manner.

Psoriasis sometimes starts in a vaccination scar. But usually, according to Crocker, the patient is not an infant. We know that in predisposed persons slight injuries and wounds may be followed by psoriasis, and the vaccination wound is no exception. The complication is very rare.

REFERENCES.—"Debate on Vaccinal Eruptions." *Amer. Journ. Cut. and Gen. Urin. Dis.*, August, 1900. "Vaccination Rashes." M. MORRIS. *British Medical Journal*, November 29th, 1890. "Generalised Vaccinia." T. COLCOTT FOX. *Clinical Society Transactions*, XXVI., 1893, p. 108. HASLUND. *Archiv. f. Derm. u. Syph.*, 1899, XLVIII., pp. 205 and 371.

Cowpox Vaccinia.

Cases of direct infection of the human subject from the cow are comparatively uncommon, especially in large towns. In 1913, however, a cowman aged fifty-one attended my clinic suffering from cowpox. The left index and right little fingers were affected. Small inflamed spots appeared a few days after inoculation; they rapidly assumed the appearance of blebs with a flat surface somewhat umbilicated. On the tenth day the lesions were the size of a sixpence and threepenny piece respectively. They were covered with a black crust surrounded by a bluish indurated margin. The lesions were very painful and tender. There was some enlargement of the nearest lymphatic gland. On removal of the crust the ulceration healed up, leaving a foveated scar. The patient milked about a dozen cows twice a day, and frequently pricked his fingers with thorns in the hay, so that scratches may have been the sites of inoculation. The patient had been vaccinated in infancy and had not had smallpox. Cases have been described in which the face has been affected, and inoculation from one person to another by contact has been reported. The appearance and course of the affection is an exaggeration of the common phenomena of vaccination.

Serum Eruptions.

The injection of a serum derived from a horse or other animal into the human subject is frequently followed by an eruption and other toxic symptoms. These phenomena are independent of the antitoxic bodies present in the serum, for they may occur if pure serum is introduced. In practice these eruptions are seen after the use of diphtheria antitoxin, and the antistreptococcal, antitetanic, antityphoid, and other sera.

It is estimated that about 33 per cent. of the patients injected with diphtheria antitoxin develop an eruption. This is the proportion given by the committee of the Clinical Society of London, but in some hospitals the average is much higher and in others much lower. It is found that the serum of certain animals is more likely to produce these toxic effects than others.

After a period of incubation varying from a day to a month the temperature rises to 101° or 102° F., and occasionally as high as 104° or 105° F. The patient complains of headache and frequently of severe pains in the joints. There may be some articular effusion and muscular stiffness. In some cases there is evident prostration. A transitory albuminuria may occur and occasionally the cervical lymphatic glands are enlarged.

The eruption may appear as early as the first day or as late as a month after injection, but is most frequent between the seventh and the twelfth days. It consists most commonly of urticarial wheals or wheals mingled with erythematous patches. The next in order of frequency is a multiform erythema. In some cases the lesions are of a ringed character; in others they closely simulate scarlatina. In a few cases the rash resembles measles. Occasionally vesicles and bullæ and even hæmorrhages occur. A common characteristic is a combination of several types of eruption, particularly the urticaria and the polymorphic erythema.

The eruption varies greatly in its extent; in some cases the patches are few and far between, and in others the greater part of the surface is involved. No part of the body or limbs is exempt, but the extremities, the buttocks, and the trunk are most commonly affected. The rash lasts from forty-eight hours to five or six days, and relapses occasionally occur. Some desquamation is not uncommon.

Anaphylactic phenomena have been frequently noticed in serum reactions. If a patient has been injected with serum and is re-injected after an interval of at least three weeks, the second injection produces a very severe eruption within a few hours—" immediate reaction," or after a few days—" accelerated reaction." There may be rigors and high temperature, and even convulsions, vomiting and collapse, in the immediate cases. Sometimes there are asthmatic attacks and acute laryngitis. Goodall has seen an immediate reaction occur when 414 days separated the two injections and an accelerated reaction after over five years. Fatal cases have been reported.

Calcium salts are recommended if the reaction is severe, but the subcutaneous injection of 1 c.c. of pituitrin relieves the collapse and spasm of the bronchioles in a few minutes. The dose may be repeated. The injections are equally useful in serum rashes (Crofton). Irritation is relieved by evaporating lotions and joint pains by the local application of lead and opium.

REFERENCES.—" On the Supersensitisation of Persons by Horse-serum." *Journal of Hygiene*, 1907, VII., p. 607. " Report of the Committee on the Antitoxin of Diphtheria." *Clinical Society Transactions*, 1890, XXXI. "A study of the cause of sudden death following the injection of horse serum." Bulletin Hygiene Laboratory, United States Public Health Service, Washington, 1906, No. 29, etc.

CHAPTER XIV.

CUTANEOUS AFFECTIONS IN GENERAL AND VISCERAL DISEASES.

THERE are many general and visceral diseases in which cutaneous eruptions occur. As a general principle it may be stated that toxic conditions, whether autogenous or heterogeneous, may be accompanied by cutaneous lesions of the erythematous or petechial type, and it is probable that many of the rashes met with in association with visceral disease are due to toxic bodies developed as a result of the impairment of the functions of the organs involved.

In this chapter it is not proposed to do more than indicate the chief forms of cutaneous affection met with in the general and visceral affections, as many of them are dealt with in other parts of this work.

Acute specific fevers. The eruption may be :—

(1) A special feature of the disease, as in the exanthemata ;

(2) A minor feature, but yet of diagnostic importance, e.g., the rose spots of typhoid, the petechiæ and dusky mottling of typhus, and the petechiæ, mottling, rose spots, erythema, and herpes of cerebro-spinal meningitis ;

(3) An inconstant symptom, e.g., the erythema and petechiæ of diphtheria, the morbiliform and scarlatiniform erythemata of influenza, the herpes of pneumonia, the erythemata and purpura of acute rheumatism, and the erythemata of dengue, trypanaso-miasis, plague and cholera.

Septicæmia and pyæmia. Rashes of erythematous and petechial types occur in many cases of septicæmia and pyæmia, including infective endocarditis.

Diseases of the blood and ductless glands. *Pernicious anæmia* causes the skin to assume a peculiar lemon tint, and sometimes cutaneous hæmorrhages occur. I have had a case in which pernicious anæmia was associated with intense pigmentation of the whole skin, and complete loss of hair. The patient was cured by arsenic.

Scurvy, infantile scurvy and *hæmophilia* may be attended with purpura.

S.

Hæmochromatosis causes the skin to assume a slate-blue colour, or to become bronzed.

In *leukæmia,* itching, urticaria and sometimes eczematous lesions and general exfoliative dermatitis may occur. In rare cases leukæmic tumours develop in the skin.

In *Hodgkin's disease* pigmentation is common, and rarely cutaneous lymphoid tumours form.

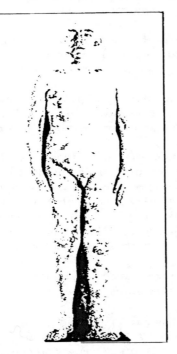

Fig. 150. — Hypopituitarism following injury to base of skull. Male æt. 20. Photograph kindly lent by Dr. Cecil Wall.

Hyperthyroidism, as in Graves' disease, is attended by anomalies of pigmentation. There may be melanodermia, or leucodermia, or both combined. Flushing, excessive sweating, and itching are common. Dystrophy of the nails is occasionally met with. Urticaria, œdema, and purpura may also occur. Hypertrichosis has been observed.

Hypothyroidism causes the dry, harsh, sometimes scaly skin of myxœdema. The hair tends to fall and there may be dystrophy of the nails. In the condition known as Lorain's infantilism, due to hypothyroidism, alopecia may be universal (*vide* p. 591).

Hyperpituitarism causes hyperplasia of the connective tissue of the cutis and hypertrichosis.

Hypopituitarism produces a smooth transparent skin free from moisture. The pubic and axillary hair is absent or ill-developed (Fig. 150).

Adrenal hypertrophy causes excessive growth of hair in the pubic regions, and in children this may be accompanied by precocious puberty.

In *Addison's disease* there is a remarkable excess of pigment in the areas normally pigmented and on the buccal mucosa.

In *thymic dwarfism* the hair is scanty and the skin dry and scaly. Pigmentation of the scalp has also been described.

Diseases of the alimentary canal. The absorption of toxic bodies from the alimentary tract is a common cause of urticaria. The toxines may be introduced from without or developed in the bowel by abnormal digestive processes or fermentations of bacterial origin. Besides urticaria it is probable that many of the conditions classed as erythema own this cause. Pigmentation is common in cases of chronic intestinal stasis.

The gum rash of infants (strophulus or lichen urticatus) is probably the result of alimentary canal toxæmia, but whether acting directly through the blood or through the nervous system is uncertain.

Acne rosacea is commonly associated with constipation and dyspepsia. Some forms of eczema are believed to depend upon disorders of the alimentary canal.

Oral sepsis must not be forgotten as a probable cause of erythema and purpura. One form of grave anæmia has been shown to be due to septic conditions of the buccal cavity, and cutaneous hæmorrhages are sometimes associated with it.

Hepatic disease is attended with xanthoma palpebrarum and xanthoma multiplex, and the presence of jaundice often induces intense itching of the skin. Acute yellow atrophy may be attended with cutaneous hæmorrhages.

Renal disease. The cutaneous affections of renal disease usually occur in the later stages when the patient may be assumed to be suffering from autointoxication. A peculiar erythema, erythema papulatum uræmicum, which sometimes takes a vesicular, bullous, or even hæmorrhagic form, is of grave import. In rare cases general exfoliation of the skin may supervene. It will be remembered that itching is sometimes the earliest symptom of renal disease.

The swelling and œdema of the legs cause erythema leve. and coccal infections, boils, etc., are common in chronic renal affections.

The albuminuria and nephritis which occur in certain cutaneous diseases are no doubt due to the conditions which cause the skin eruptions. Osler has pointed out the frequent co-existence of albuminuria and erythema in visceral disease, and Balean and I showed its presence in the acute type of lupus erythematosus.

In general exfoliative dermatitis and in pemphigus of the grave and foliaceous types the urine may be greatly diminished in quantity. and extreme hypoazoturia is not uncommon, but these conditions are parts of the general disease.

Diseases of metabolism. **Diabetes.** The skin is usually dry and pruritus is common. The hair and nails suffer. Erythema and urticaria may occur, and the local irritation of the sugar in the urine causes an eczematous dermatitis of the vulva and balanitis. Vesicular and bullous eruptions are rarely seen, but the skin of the glycosuric is particularly prone to coccal infection, causing boils and carbuncles.

Gangrene of the extremities is a serious complication and may follow a slight injury.

Xanthoma diabeticorum is a rare complication of glycosuria and may appear before sugar is found in the urine.

The bronzing of the skin described as of diabetic origin may occur in hæmochromatosis without glycosuria.

Gout. It is difficult to class any form of skin disease as definitely gouty. Eczema appears in gouty subjects on slight or even imperceptible irritation, but it is doubtful whether the presence of uric acid is of so much importance as the chronic intoxication from the alimentary canal.

Osteo-arthritis. Liveing and many French authors lay stress upon the association of osteo-arthritis with psoriasis occurring late in life, and my own experience tends to support their observations.

Dystrophies of the nails indistinguishable from ungual psoriasis occur in osteo-arthritis without any cutaneous psoriasis.

Pulmonary disease. Asthma may alternate with attacks of urticaria or may co-exist with it. Prurigo has been similarly associated. Eczema may disappear with the outbreak of acute pulmonary disease attended with fever, and other cutaneous eruptions clear up in pyrexial conditions. I have several times seen lupus vulgaris disappear with the onset of pulmonary tuberculosis.

Purpura may be a symptom of the late stages of tuberculosis of the lungs. The frequent occurrence of pityriasis versicolor in phthisis is accounted for by the excessive sweating.

Nervous diseases. Apart from the cutaneous affections which occur in relationship with organic disease of the nervous system, considered in another chapter (XVIII.), a number of cutaneous eruptions appear to be determined by acute nervous shock, violent emotion and anxiety. Among these may be mentioned fall of hair and changes in its colour, some eczemas, lichen planus, dermatitis, herpetiformis, the acute variety of lupus erythematosus, and pompholyx (dysidrosis). In hysteria eruptions are often produced artificially, but in rare cases it is believed that the skin affections develop spontaneously. Œdema and gangrene have been observed.

The vaso-motor diseases, of which erythromelalgia and Raynaud's disease may be taken as types, are considered at pp. 443 and 410.

Uterine disorders. Acne rosacea occurs in connection with the menopause, after the removal of the ovaries, and in some diseases of the female genital organs. Urticaria occurs in pregnancy, and in rare cases an extensive bullous eruption, hydroa gravidarum, develops. The rare disease known as impetigo herpetiformis appears only in the pregnant woman. Chloasma uterinum is a peculiar pigmentation of the face met with in pregnancy. Fall of hair is not uncommon in the later months of the puerperium or during lactation. Pruritus of the external genitals may be a symptom of disease of the internal apparatus.

Dermatitis symmetrica dysmenorrhoica occurs in women with dysmenorrhœa, and is believed to be due to toxic metabolism from ovarian derangement. The patients often suffer from cardiac and psychic disturbances. The eruption is symmetrical, and affects the limbs, face, and front of the trunk. The lesions are urticarial at the onset, and later vesico-bullous. They become crusted and leave stains. In models seen by the author the appearances suggested self-production, but this is said to have been excluded. (Matzenauer and Polland. *Archiv. f. Dermatologie*, October, 1912, p. 185.)

Withdrawal of the ovarian internal secretion in elderly women is characterised by hypertrichosis.

Sabouraud has confirmed the old observation that eunuchs do not suffer from the common masculine type of baldness.

REFERENCES.—A valuable contribution on this subject with extensive literature by S. E. DORE. *British Journal of Dermatology*, 1906, XVIII. "On Internal Secretions in Relation to Dermatology," by SIR MALCOLM MORRIS. *British Medical Journal*, May 17, 1913, p. 1027. "The Pituitary Body and its Disorders," by HARVEY CUSHING. "Alimentary Toxæmia." Debate. *Royal Society of Medicine Trans.*, VI., No. 5, Appendix.

CHAPTER XV.

TOXIC ERUPTIONS.

Erythema.

The term "erythema" is applied to certain cutaneous inflammations characterised by dilatation of the vessels with usually some degree of œdema or infiltration. The red colour of the lesions disappears on compression and returns when the pressure is removed. This point distinguishes the erythemata from purpura.

Erythema may be caused by mechanical irritation, by cold, heat, light, X-rays, and certain substances which act chemically on the skin. These conditions are considered elsewhere (Chapter IV.).

We have now to consider lesions of a similar character which are caused by the presence in the blood of toxic bodies.

Toxic erythemata may be due to :—

(1) The internal administration of certain drugs (p. 339).

(2) The introduction of calf-lymph in vaccination and of the various antitoxines and vaccines (p. 347).

(3) The acute specific fevers. Erythematous lesions are the essential features of the exanthems of scarlet fever, measles, rubella, etc. They are prodromal in variola, and an occasional feature in diphtheria, and in influenza.

(4) The poison of acute rheumatism. They occur in articular rheumatism, tonsillitis, etc.

(5) Septic conditions.

(6) The absorption of toxic bodies from the alimentary canal, in ptomaine poisoning, and pellagra (?).

(7) The development in the body of toxines produced by perverted digestive processes, by visceral disease, etc.

The rashes due to drugs, vaccination and antitoxines are dealt with in the preceding chapter. The exanthemata are discussed in the text-books on general medicine. In the present section the following varieties of toxic erythema will be considered :—

(1) Erythema multiforme.

(2) Erythema nodosum.

(3) Erythema scarlatiniforme.

(4) Pellagra.

s.

(5) Acrodynia.
(6) Urticaria.
(7) Urticaria pigmentosa.
(8) Angio-neurotic œdema.

Erythema multiforme. Erythema exudativum.

Erythema multiforme is a toxic inflammatory affection of the skin characterised by the formation of patches of redness of various forms and sizes. In some cases the exudation of serum raises the epidermis into vesicles and bullæ, and there may be hæmorrhagic lesions.

Etiology. Erythema multiforme is most common in childhood and adolescence. In thirty-two consecutive cases in my clinic twelve were males and twenty females. My youngest patient was four years of age and the oldest forty-five. The eruption is more prevalent in the spring and autumn. It may be due to (1) vaccination and the injection of diphtheria antitoxines and the " vaccines " ; (2) ptomaine poisoning ; (3) arthritic affections, including acute rheumatism ; (4) visceral disease, oral sepsis, gastro-intestinal, renal, pulmonary, and cerebral disease (Osler) ; (5) unknown causes. The fact that multiform erythema has sometimes appeared in small epidemics suggests the possibility of certain cases being due to some specific organism. In rare cases streptococci have been found in the blood. The existence of a specific variety of erythema multiforme is most probable, but the conditions mentioned produce lesions so remarkably similar that in the absence of specific characters we must leave the question open for further investigation.

The association of pain and swelling of the joints with the cutaneous eruption must not be taken as evidence of its rheumatic origin. Both arthritic pains and swelling occur after the injection of antitoxic sera and in many obviously toxic conditions. I think, however, that there is sufficient evidence in favour of acute rheumatism being one of the causes.

Pathology. The circulating poisons introduced from without or developed within the body may be considered as acting directly on the blood-vessels or indirectly through the nervous system. Those who prefer the second hypothesis look upon erythema multiforme as an angio-neurosis.

Microscopical examination of the lesions shows dilatation of the cutaneous vessels and cellular infiltration of the corium. In some instances there is serous exudation causing œdema and the elevation of the epidermis into vesicles and bullæ.

Plate 31.

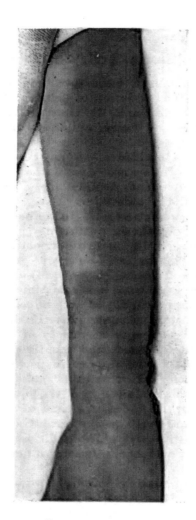

ERYTHEMA MULTIFORME.

Clinical features. General symptoms. The onset of the disease is attended with malaise, a slight degree of fever, and often with pain and swelling of one or more joints. Occasionally a persistent high temperature may be observed. I have seen one case in which the pyrexia lasted for more than three weeks, the chart closely resembling that of enteric fever. Itching is not common, but the patient often complains of a sensation of burning.

Local. The eruption comes out acutely in symmetrical patches, usually first on the backs of the hands and the dorsal aspect of the feet. The extensor surfaces of the extremities are favourite sites, the knuckles, wrists, elbows, knees and feet being often involved. Sometimes the face and neck are affected. The extent and characters of the eruption vary remarkably in different cases, but as a rule there is one predominant type in each. The colour and character of the lesions are well shown in the accompanying plate (XXXI.). The simplest lesions are *macules* of a purplish red tint, and on compression the colour entirely disappears. Various names are applied to indicate the different types of the disease, but it must be understood that they are simply descriptive appellations of the varieties of the polymorphous affection.

Erythema papulatum is a form in which the lesions are round, raised, blunt swellings smaller than a pea. Nodular areas larger than a pea also occur. I prefer to avoid calling the latter " erythema tuberculatum," to avoid confusion with affections due to the tubercle bacillus.

Larger patches in rings, with a central depression, are called *erythema circinatum.* In the centre of these rings there is often a vesicle which dries up, leaving a small scab or scale.

Erythema iris is an interesting form. It consists of concentric rings (Plate XXXII.) in which vesicles and small blebs appear. As the eruption spreads the central rings differ in colour from those at the periphery, and variations in tint from a rose pink to purple are seen. It has been aptly likened to a target. Recurrences are very common. Erythema iris has been observed in typhoid fever.

Erythema bullosum and *erythema vesiculosum* are terms used to denote the presence of swellings containing fluid associated with the erythematous lesions.

Erythema purpuricum is erythema multiforme associated with hæmorrhages into the skin. The association of purpuric with erythematous lesions is not remarkable when it is remembered that both conditions are due to circulating toxic bodies. One of my patients had hæmaturia at the same time.

Mucous membrane lesions. In bad cases there may be an outbreak of blisters on the buccal mucosa, tongue and pharynx, and also on the conjunctiva. I have met with several cases, and in one under the care of my colleague, Dr. Percy Kidd, the affection of the mouth was so severe that the patient was only able to take fluid nourishment with the greatest difficulty. In these cases the buccal cavity becomes very foul, and requires constant cleansing with antiseptics. Buccal lesions are common in erythema iris.

The disease lasts from one to three or four weeks, and tends to recur. Recurrences are most frequent in the iris variety.

Diagnosis. Urticaria is distinguished by the evanescent character and appearance of the wheals. The distribution is also different and there is much itching.

Measles may be suspected, but in erythema the catarrhal symptoms of the exanthem and Koplik's spots are absent. The eruption is also of one type.

Rubella is excluded by the absence of glandular swellings.

Erythema bullosum has to be distinguished from dermatitis herpetiformis, and the differential diagnosis may be difficult. In the latter condition there is much itching and a greater preponderance of vesicles and bullæ, usually arranged in some parts in herpetiform clusters. Eosinophilia is a common feature.

Lupus erythematosus occasionally simulates erythema multiforme very closely, when the face and the backs of the hands only are affected. Galloway and Macleod have called attention to the relationship of the two diseases, and I agree that both are due to circulating toxines. The chronic or fixed form of lupus erythematosus leaving scars should not present any difficulty in diagnosis.

The **prognosis** is favourable unless there is some underlying visceral trouble. The disease usually lasts from one to three or four weeks, but recurrences are common, especially in the iris cases, in which the eruption may return year after year.

Treatment. General. In febrile cases fluid diet should be enjoined, and rest is necessary. Bad cases require confinement to bed.

Medicinal. As the eruption in many cases depends upon gastrointestinal disorder, a nocturnal dose of calomel followed by a saline aperient in the morning should be administered. Salol, in five to ten grain doses thrice daily, and other intestinal antiseptics, such as benzo-naphthol, are often given, sometimes with benefit. Sodium salicylate, salicin, and aspirin are useful in the arthritic cases. I have seen benefit from the use of calcium lactate. Fifteen-grain doses are given thrice daily for two days, and repeated after an interval of three days. In cases where recurrence is the rule careful

Plate 32.

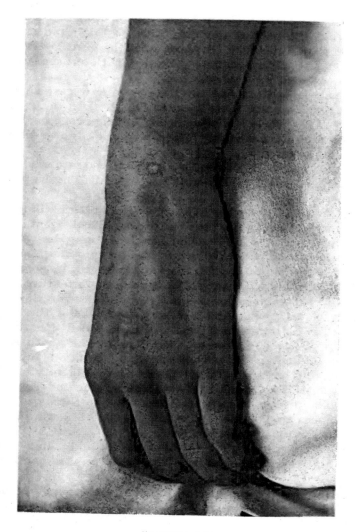

ERYTHEMA IRIS.

The patient (female, aged 28) had had eight attacks in two years. There were vesico-bullous lesions in the mouth.

investigation should be made to ascertain the underlying cause. In two cases I found the curdled milk treatment useful, and it is worth trying. Oral sepsis, if present, requires attention.

Local treatment. The application of tar and lead lotion or a calamine lotion is comforting to the patient, but has no curative influence.

REFERENCES.—W. OSLER. "Visceral Lesions of the Erythema Group." *British Journal of Dermatology*, 1900, XII., p. 227. J. GALLOWAY. "Ery- themata as Indicators of Disease." *British Medical Journal*, July 10th, 1903. ADAMSON. "Discussion on Erythema Multiforme." *British Journal of Dermatology*, 1912, XXIV., p. 429.

Erythema nodosum.

Erythema nodosum is considered by some to be a variety of erythema multiforme, with which it is sometimes associated. There are, however, special features which merit a separate consideration. The disease is characterised by the formation of painful node-like swellings on the limbs, particularly over the shins.

Etiology. Children and young adults are the most frequent sufferers, the commonest age of incidence being between ten and thirty. In my own cases females have been affected four times as often as males. Sir Stephen Mackenzie gave the proportion as five to one.

It has been suggested that this affection, like erythema multiforme, is a specific disease, and the term " nodal fever " has been applied to it. The fact that lesions of exactly the same type occur in associa- tion with the acute specific fevers, tuberculous meningitis, strepto- coccal infection, and with gastro-intestinal disturbance, ptomaine poisoning, and the administration of certain drugs, notably iodides, bromides, and antipyrin, shows that it is better to look upon it as an erythema which may be caused by various circulating toxines. Landouzy is of opinion that in the majority of cases erythema nodosum is a manifestation of septicæmia due to the bacillus tuber- culosis, and its occurrence after the intradermic injection of tuberculin favours this. The association of rheumatic fever (20 per cent. of my cases) is too frequent to be accidental, and the rheumatic poison must be considered as one of the causes. The remarks made above as to the association of joint pains with erythema multiforme of non- rheumatic origin apply here. The fact that erythema nodosum is accompanied by pain and swelling of the articulations is not proof of its rheumatic origin in any particular case, and in the absence of a specific test for rheumatism other signs of the general affection must be sought.

Pathology. The whole thickness of the skin and the subjacent connective tissue are involved. There are dilatation of the vessels, serous exudation and cellular infiltration. Small hæmorrhages are not uncommon. The change in colour of the subsiding eruption shows that there is escape of red blood cells from the vessels to a considerable extent, by diapedesis or by the actual rupture of small vessels.

Clinical features. General. The onset is acute, with malaise, fever, furred tongue, and pains in the joints. The local manifestations are round or oval, red, tense, shining swellings which appear over the front of the tibiæ. They vary in size from a nut to a small egg. Occasionally the forearms and rarely the body and face are affected. The nodal tumours are hard at first, but soften later, and look as if they would break down, but they never suppurate. The patient complains of pain, and the lesions are exceedingly tender.

Each node lasts from a week to ten days, but fresh crops appear during several weeks. Four or five to a dozen or more may be present at one time. During the period of devolution the pink colour passed through the various hues of a bruise, hence the old name " erythema contusiforme."

The **diagnosis** is usually easy. The condition might be mistaken for a bruise, but the absence of a history of trauma, the multiplicity of the lesions, the febrile symptoms and joint pains, could hardly lead to error. Abscess is usually single, and the presence of fluctuation is characteristic. Gummata are distinguished by their colour and the absence of acute tenderness. Moreover, the lesions of erythema nodosum do not break down.

Erythema induratum is usually painless, and not very tender. It is very chronic, and more frequently affects the calf than the shins. Ulceration is common. The patients are usually young females who have to stand a great deal at their work.

The **prognosis** is good. Recurrences are rare.

Treatment. General. Rest of the legs in the horizontal position is imperative. A low diet is advisable.

Medicinal. A laxative should be administered at the onset. Aspirin and the salicylates are useful for the relief of pain, but do not appear to have any specific influence on the disease.

Local. Lotio plumbi should be applied on lint.

REFERENCES.—S. MACKENZIE. *Clinical Society Transactions*, XIX., p. 215. L. LANDOUZY. *Gazette Medicale de Paris*, February 11th, 1914, p 37.

Erythema scarlatiniforme.

Erythema scarlatiniforme is characterised by a bright rash, closely resembling that of scarlet fever, due to various circulating poisons.

Etiology. A scarlatiniform erythema may follow the administration of quinine, salicylates, belladonna, mercury, and other drugs (see Drug Eruptions, p. 339). It occurs in certain specific fevers, as a prodromal symptom, *e.g.*, in variola, varicella, measles, enteric fever, and in diphtheria. It is also seen in ptomaine poisoning, and in septicæmia and pyæmia, and occasionally in rheumatism and malaria. It may follow the administration of an enema.

Clinical features. The onset is acute, and there may be pyrexia (100° to 103° F.) and malaise. The eruption may start on any part of the body, but it is rarely general. The face is sometimes affected, but not always. A close examination usually reveals a number of small bright red points, but in some cases the redness is diffuse. The rash may disappear in twenty-four hours, or it may last for five or six days. Desquamation begins early, about the third or fourth day, and may be in the form of branny scales or in large flakes.

There is a recurrent type in which the symptoms are more severe. Complete casts of the hands and feet may be shed and the nails and hair fall as in general exfoliative dermatitis. This form certainly suggests a relationship with the erythrodermias, a relationship to which Brocq has drawn special attention (see p. 400).

Diagnosis. The fact that eruptions of this type occur in such varied conditions is specially important in the diagnosis of scarlatina. The exanthem usually begins with vomiting and more severe general symptoms. The circum-oral pallor, strawberry tongue, and tonsillar inflammation in scarlet fever are not found in the erythema, but the fauces may be congested. A history of previous attacks is a useful point in favour of the scarlatiniform erythema. In any case of doubt it is wise to isolate the patient and treat the case as if it were scarlet fever.

The **prognosis** is good, unless the eruption is due to septic infection. The tendency to recurrence must be remembered.

Treatment. General. If there is fever the patient should be confined to bed.

Medicinal. A saline aperient should be given at the onset. Every endeavour should be made to ascertain the cause and remove it if possible.

Local. The eruption requires no special measures. Baths and the application of a simple ointment will help to remove the scales.

Megalerythema epidemicum (Erythema infectiosum).

An acute infectious disease, occurring in children between the ages of four and twelve, during the spring and early summer.

The incubation period varies from six to fourteen days. Usually the rash is the first sign of illness, but there may be slight prodromata, lassitude and sore throat. The rash begins on the cheeks as bright red confluent patches, which disappear on pressure. There is also some swelling. The erythema clears up in the centre, and the rash then consists of irregular red rings. The trunk is hardly ever affected, but the extensor surfaces of the limbs may be involved. The mucous membranes are unaffected, and there is no pyrexia. Epidemics are said to occur, and the eruption suggests a bacterial origin or a toxaemia.

An outbreak described by Fönss as erythema annulare in epidemic form appears to be of the same type.

REFERENCES.—RUHRAH's article in " Osler and McCrae's System of Medicine." A. L. FONSS. Abstract, *Brit. Journ. Derm.*, XXVII., p. 328.

Pellagra.

Pellagra is a general disease characterised by a cutaneous eruption, which in many respects resembles the erythemata, and nervous symptoms. Its cause is unknown, and it is provisionally placed in the group of toxic diseases, though evidence is accumulating in favour of its being due to an infecting organism.

Etiology. The disease is endemic in Southern Europe, particularly in Italy and Spain, and in Egypt and the Levant. It is probably widely spread, and recently attention has been drawn to cases in the British Isles and in the United States and South America. Systematic investigations have been undertaken to determine its exact cause.

The following hypotheses, among others, have been advanced :—

(1) The Zeist theory (Zea mais, maize). In maize, and perhaps other cereals, bodies are believed to be introduced into the blood, and these, under the influence of sunlight, become toxic (photo-dynamic theory of Rombitschek). Against this is the fact that jet-black negroes may suffer from pellagra.

Another hypothesis is that certain nitrogenous bodies which should be present in the maize are removed by processes of preparation, *e.g.*, steam-milling.

A third suggestion is that there is an individual susceptibility to maize or to some toxic body produced by maize alone or by the action of the bacillus coli on it.

A bad maize harvest is said to be followed by pellagra, the cereal being infected by fungi, bacteria or some foreign substance at present unrecognised.

(2) The parasitic theory. Tizzoni found a strepto-bacillus in maize and in the blood, cerebro-spinal fluid and organs of pellagrins,

FIG. 151.—Pellagra. (Photograph kindly lent by Dr. Box.)

but these observations have not been confirmed. Nematode worms, amœbæ and other parasites have also been found.

Sambon believes that pellagra is a protozoan infection spread by biting flies (Simuliidæ and allied species), and this opinion is supported by the Illinois Commission. The facts in favour of this hypothesis are that the disease occurs in rural districts, where there is moving water, that there is a seasonal incidence, and that many of the sufferers are field labourers. Both sexes are affected, though females suffer more than males. The disease may attack whole families, and no age is exempt. Sambon's hypothesis, however, does not account for the rapid spread of pellagra in Barbados in recent years. Simulium is not found in the island, but mosquitoes and sand-flies are numerous. Siler, who has investigated the conditions, is of opinion that the disease is an infection communicated from person to person.

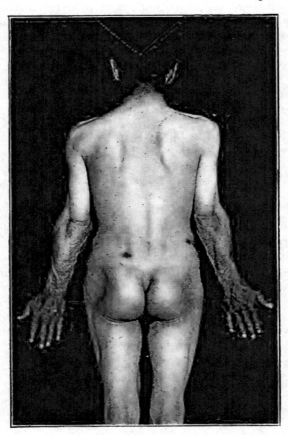

Fig. 152.—Pellagra.   Gastro-intestinal and nervous symptoms.   Melancholia.

It is now held that poverty and bad hygiene are only contributory causes.

Pathology. In the cutaneous lesions there is infiltration of the dermis, especially of the papillary layer, with œdema of the connective tissue. The rete Malpighii is infiltrated with cells. The stratum corneum shows parakeratosis. The red cells of the blood are diminished.

The chief changes in the nervous system are congestion of the posterior columns, with hæmorrhages, degeneration of the cells of the spinal ganglia, posterior cornua and Clarke's column. Degeneration of the nerve fibres in the posterior roots and columns and in the peripheral nerves also occurs. The cells of the brain cortex are swollen and disintegrated, and there is an increase in the neuroglia.

Clinical features. The incubation period is unknown, but is probably short. The eruption occurs on the face, neck and the backs of the hands, e.g., the parts exposed to light. The affected areas are bright red or livid and swollen, and there are sensations of burning and itching. The erythema has a distinct line of demarcation. The eruption disappears in the winter, but returns in the spring and lasts through the summer. In protracted cases the skin becomes thickened and pigmented and ultimately undergoes atrophy. There is often an associated nasal and facial " seborrhœa."

The lips, tongue and mouth are inflamed and covered with small vesicles and ulcers. The parotid glands are often swollen, and there is salivation. The bowels may be loose or constipated and abdominal pain is common.

There is progressive loss of strength, with attacks of vertigo and tremors. Melancholia, mental deterioration and insanity bring a number of patients into the asylums. Convulsions, tabetic symptoms, paralyses and optic neuritis and retinitis may occur.

Pellagra is a chronic affection and usually ends fatally in four or five years.

Prognosis. Slight cases recover, but the majority end fatally.

Treatment. Unfortunately very little can be done. Arsenic is advised, and good nourishing food and attention to the general hygiene are of the utmost importance.

REFERENCES.—"Pellagra in England." *British Medical Journal,* July 5th, 1913, p. 1, by C. R. Box, with coloured plate. "Histology of the Nervous System," by Dr. Mott, with plates. "Natural History of the Disease," by Dr. Sambon, in the same number. See also "The Study of Pellagra in England," by G. S. Blandy. *Lancet,* September 6th, 1913, p. 715, and case described by Dr. Cole in same number. Davenport and Muncey. *Eugenics Record Office Bulletin No. 16.* J. F. Siler. *Amer. Journ. Trop. Dis.,* October, 1915, p. 186.

Acrodynia.

This is a rare affection probably allied to pellagra. Some large epidemics have been recorded, chiefly early in the last century in France, Belgium, and elsewhere.

Symptoms. The eruption started on the hands and feet and spread to the limbs and trunk. It was erythematous, and followed by desquamation and pigmentation. Vomiting and diarrhœa suggested some poison taken as food. Cutaneous hyperæsthesia followed by anæsthesia, cramps and paresis were noted. The disease was rarely fatal.

Urticaria (Nettle-rash).

Urticaria is one of the commonest toxic affections of the skin. It is characterised by evanescent wheals and intense itching.

Etiology. Urticaria may occur at any age, but is more common in children than in adults. Females are more frequently affected than males. The disease is more often met with in the summer months, doubtless owing to the decomposition of food and the development of toxic bodies in it during the warm weather.

Urticaria may be caused by :—

(1) *Local irritation,* the sting of the nettle, bites of insects, jelly-fish, etc. In some susceptible persons high or low temperature may be an excitant. In others contact with flannel or with dyed under-clothing is sufficient to start an attack.

(2) *Toxic bodies introduced from without.*

(*a*) By the alimentary canal.

(i.) Some foods are toxic to certain individuals, *e.g.,* shell-fish, salted and tinned fish and meats, pork, pickles, mushrooms, oatmeal, strawberries, etc. ; (ii.) ptomaines arising from decomposing food ; (iii.) drugs ; copaiba, cubebs, quinine, salicylates, mercury, and many others ; (iv.) intestinal parasites, probably by toxic irritants produced in the bowel.

(*b*) By the blood-stream.

(i.) Vaccination ; (ii.) antitoxines and vaccines ; (iii.) puncture of hydatids.

(3) *Toxic bodies developed in the body.*

(i.) In gastro-intestinal disorders ; (ii.) in pregnancy and lactation ; (iii.) in visceral disease, glycosuria, jaundice, Bright's disease ; (iv.) after puncture of pleural effusion.

(4) In the premycosic and tumour stages of mycosis fungoides.

(5) Reflex (?). Urticaria is said to occur from emotional causes.

Pathology. Urticaria is generally considered an angio-neurosis, the poison being supposed to act through the nervous system. It is, however, more likely that there is a direct action of the circulating toxines upon the vessel walls. The lesion is a localised inflammatory œdema of the true skin with an enormous number of polynuclear leucocytes, increase in the number of lymphocytes and sometimes of the mast cells. At the centre the pressure of the effusion is great enough to cause anæmia, and this produces the white centre of the wheal. In pomphi developed artificially and excised for examination cellular infiltration is found to occur in a few minutes. After six hours eosinophiles were present (Gilchrist).

Clinical features. The onset of urticaria is acute, sometimes with

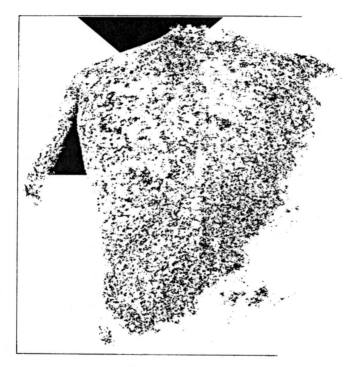

Fig. 153.—Urticaria.

a slight degree of fever (99·5° to 100° F.), but oftener without. The patient's attention is usually first attracted by the intense itching. There may be evidence of gastro-intestinal irritation, vomiting, diarrhœa, etc., but this is often absent.

The eruption consists of well-defined white or pink swellings of the skin, rarely more than an inch in diameter. The margin is often red, while the centre is pale. The lesion is exactly similar to the wheal produced by the stinging nettle. The scratching induced by the itching brings out fresh wheals, and mechanical irritation of any kind, such as rubbing, may excite them in the hypersensitive skin. A special characteristic of the urticarial wheal is its rapid development and its equally rapid and complete disappearance. It leaves neither scale nor stain. An individual wheal may last for a few hours to several days. Asymmetry is the rule, and there are remarkable variations in the extent of the eruption. In rare cases, nearly the whole of the cutaneous surface may be involved, and also the mucous membrane of the buccal cavity, pharynx, larynx, and probably the

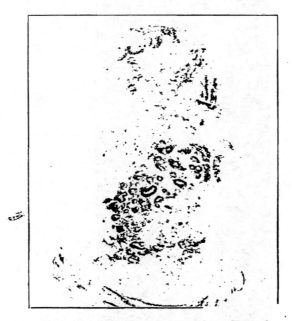

Fig. 154.—Bullous urticaria. Female child, æt. six months.

lining membrane of the hollow viscera, as indicated by asthmatic attacks and vomiting. In a unique case which I saw in consultation with Dr. Henry Head the urticarial attacks were associated with epileptiform seizures. The patient was a boy of sixteen, otherwise healthy.

Certain variations from the common type require mention. In *papular urticaria* the lesions are small, and the papular element persists after the disappearance of the wheal (*vide* Strophulus). In *U. gigans* the wheals are enormous, sometimes reaching the dimensions of an egg. *U. bullosa* is the name given to wheals in which the

Plate 83.

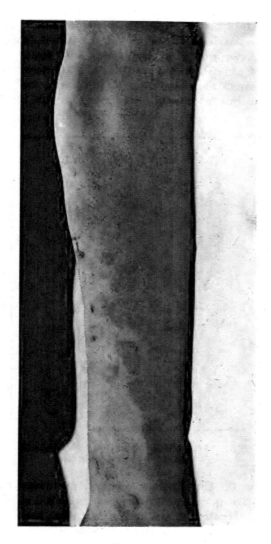

URTICARIA.

The flat wheals are distinctly raised and show the
characteristic white centre.

central part is raised by serous effusion into a blister. A bullous urticaria in an infant attending my clinic lasted for several months (Fig. 154). Hæmorrhage into the wheal is indicated by the term *urticaria hæmorrhagica*. The last variety may be associated with hæmorrhage from the kidney, stomach and bowel. *Factitious urticaria* is the name applied to wheal lesions produced by local irritation ; for instance, stroking the skin sharply with the finger nail or some sharp instrument causes an immediate development of linear pomphi in susceptible subjects (Fig. 155).

Urticaria tuberosa is a rare variety characterised by the rapid development of multiple asymmetrical subcutaneous or deep-seated swellings varying in size from a pea to an orange. The extremities, especially the fingers, hands, wrists, feet and knees, are most frequently affected. The fingers show fusiform swellings between the joints.

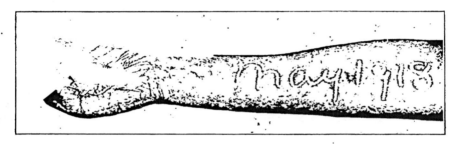

FIG. 155.—Urticaria factitia.

Aching, pain, stiffness and tingling or burning cause the patient sleepless nights, which are followed by languor and weakness. There is no fever, and the lesions, which usually develop at night, only last a few hours. They are distinguished from rheumatoid arthritis by the absence of articular changes, grating, etc. Recurrences are common.

The duration of urticaria varies a great deal. It is usually an acute affection lasting from a few hours to a few days or a week. But, in a few cases, it runs a chronic course, evanescent wheals appearing again and again, perhaps for months or years. In very rare instances, individual urticarial lesions last for some weeks to several months ; it is difficult to recognise these as urticarial lesions, but factitious pomphi may always be developed. It is most probable that such conditions own a different cause, similar wheal-like lesions being seen in leukæmia cutis and mycosis fungoides (*vide* also Prurigo nodularis, urticaria perstans verrucosa, p. 434).

Diagnosis. The diagnosis of nettle-rash is usually easy. Erythema multiforme is distinguished by the more persistent character of the lesions, their colour, distribution, and less irritation. I have known measles in an adult lead to difficulty. The urticarial eruption is more irritable, and there are no catarrhal symptoms, and the fever is less, or absent. Koplik's spots should be looked for. Rubella is attended by enlargement of the lymphatic glands in the neck.

Drug eruptions of urticarial type may lead to difficulty, but here the origin of the urticaria, and not its differential diagnosis, is at issue. Inquiry should be made as to the taking of drugs.

Prognosis. In its acute forms urticaria clears up in a few hours to a few days. The recurrent type is exceedingly difficult to cure, unless the underlying condition is recognised and removed.

Treatment. In acute cases a purgative should be given. A dose of calomel at night, followed by a saline aperient in the morning, is usually most efficient. If there is evidence of gastric disturbance, a simple emetic is also useful.

The local treatment consists in warm baths, with a teaspoonful of bicarbonate of soda to the gallon, or of potassa sulphurata half a drachm to the gallon. This should be followed by the application of a lotion of carbolic acid (1 in 50) or of the tar and lead lotion. Dusting the surface afterwards with a powder of zinc and starch is comforting. An ointment of beta-naphthol, half a drachm to a drachm to the ounce, or of salicylic acid, 2 per cent., relieves the irritation.

In chronic cases the underlying cause must be sought. Regulation of the bowels is necessary, and intestinal antiseptics, such as salol in ten-grain doses, beta-naphthol in five-grain doses, ichthyol in five-grain doses, thrice daily, are sometimes useful. In some cases, apparently dependent upon the absorption of bacterial toxines from the bowel, I have seen benefit from the sour milk treatment. Calcium lactate in fifteen-grain doses thrice daily for two days, followed by a period of intermission of three days, has also proved efficacious in certain cases.

To obtain a good night's rest, a full dose of antipyrin, or of quinine, given at bedtime, is often valuable. In young children a grain and a half to two grains of quinine, sugar-coated, can be given. The local treatment of chronic cases is similar to that of the acute variety.

It must be remembered that some of the recurrent cases depend upon the non-recognition that certain articles of food are toxic to the patient. An endeavour should be made to trace any relationship between the attacks and particular items in the dietary, with the object of eliminating the article which appears to be the exciting cause.

The treatment of urticaria tuberosa is on the lines described for the more common varieties.

REFERENCES.—"Blood-coagulability in Urticaria." E. PARAMORE. *British Journal of Dermatology*, July and August, 1906. "Experimental Urticaria." T. C. GILCHRIST. *British Medical Journal*, October 24, 1908, p. 1264. "Chronic Urticaria." KREIBICH. *Arch. f. Derm. u. Syph.*, 1899, XLVIII., p. 163. NIXON. "Urticaria Tuberosa." *Quart. Journ. Med.*, 1916, April, p. 245.

Angio-neurotic œdema. Giant urticaria. Quincke's œdema.

Etiology. Angio-neurotic œdema may begin in infancy, but is most common in early adult life. Both sexes are affected, females rather more frequently than males. The disease is less common in hospital than in private practice. Heredity occurs in a remarkable proportion of the cases. Of 141 persons in seven generations, 49 were affected and 12 died from suffocation caused by laryngeal œdema. Other predisposing causes are menstruation, hysteria, melancholia and Graves' disease. The exciting causes are cold, injury, diet, drugs, and nervous conditions, such as neurasthenia, worry, overwork, fright and insomnia. Digestive troubles are also known to cause an attack.

Clinical features. The majority of the attacks occur between 1 and 5 A.M. The eruption is characterised by circumscribed swellings which disappear spontaneously in a few hours to a few days. The swellings may be the same colour as the skin or of a waxy appearance, and cold to the touch or red and hot. In rare cases there are ecchymoses. The lesions are firm and elastic or hard. On the extremities they may be as large as a nut or an orange ; on the face and hands and external genitals the swellings may be enormous. The lesions are generally asymmetrical and may be widely separated. Itching and stiffness are experienced. The lips, palate, pharynx and larynx are often involved, and sometimes the trachea and intestines. The outbreaks occur at irregular intervals, and sometimes, like asthma, appear to depend upon certain localities. Hæmoglobinuria, albuminuria, tachycardia, and purpura, and also abdominal crises such as are seen in Henoch's purpura may occur. In 36 out of 170 cases collected by Bulloch death occurred from œdema glottidis.

The **diagnosis** of angio-neurotic œdema from lymphangitis of the face is not difficult, as the latter condition is more chronic and is attended with persistent swelling.

Treatment. Great care must be taken to find out whether any article of diet is an exciting cause. Quinine, arsenic, and strychnine are of service. The calcium salts may also be of benefit. Nitrites and nitroglycerine are also advocated. Adrenalin in four-minim doses injected at the onset was found by Codd to abort an attack. If given when the eruption was fully developed several hours elapsed before the rash disappeared. Suprarenal tablets given *per os* appear also to be of value. Tracheotomy or intubation may be necessary if the larynx is involved.

REFERENCES.—SIR WILLIAM OSLER. "System of Medicine," 1909, VI., p. 648, "On Heredity." W. BULLOCH. "Treasury of Human Inheritance," Part. III., 1909. (Family-trees). J. A. CODD. *Brit. Med. Journal*, 1917, I., p. 808.

Purpura.

Purpura, or hæmorrhage into the skin, is a symptom of many toxic conditions. Where the cause is known, the name " symptomatic purpura " is applied ; if the cause is unknown, the affection is classed as an " idiopathic purpura."

Hæmorrhage into the skin occurs :—

(1) As the result of traumatism.

(2) In the acute specific fevers, as a regular symptom in typhus and epidemic cerebro-spinal meningitis, and as evidence of malignancy in smallpox, scarlet fever, measles, diphtheria and yellow fever.

(3) In syphilis, malaria and tuberculosis as a rare symptom.

(4) In septic disorders, caused by streptococci, staphylococci, gonococcus, bacillus coli communis, and bacillus pyocyaneus, etc. It is thus a symptom of septicæmia, pyæmia and ulcerative endocarditis, and of cholera infantum, colitis, dysentery and pyogenic infections of the mouth, nose and middle ear.

(5) In auto-intoxications, as in over-exertion ; Bright's disease ; acute yellow atrophy and other diseases of the liver.

(6) In " blood diseases," pernicious anæmia, leucocythæmia, scurvy, infantile scurvy, and hæmophilia.

(7) In poisoning by tri-nitro-toluene (T.N.T.), death taking place in about a week. In these cases there is grave aplastic anæmia. (Information communicated by Dr. W. J. O'Donovan.)

(8) After the administration of certain drugs, iodides, bromides, chloral, quinine, salicylates, arsenic, etc.

(9) In chronic congestion due to varicose veins and to cardiac disease with failing compensation,

(10) As a special variety associated with rheumatism ; peliosis or purpura rheumatica.

(11) From unknown causes (probably toxic) in the forms of idiopathic purpura.

The idiopathic and rheumatic purpuras require special notice, as falling specially within the province of the dermatologist.

Pathology. The vessels of the superficial cutaneous plexus are dilated and filled with red corpuscles, and there are crowds of red cells in the tissues about them. There is no doubt about the rupture of the vessel walls, but how this comes about has not been ascertained. A reference to the above table shows that many of the conditions which cause purpura are microbic, and it is conceivable that embolism of a mass of organisms may cause such damage to the vessel walls as

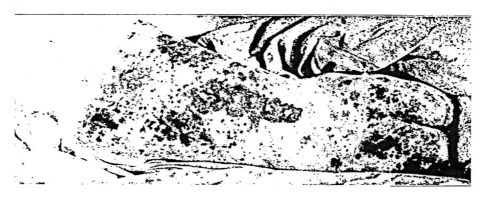

Fig. 156.—Purpura.   Extensive ecchymoses.

to lead to their rupture. Circulating toxines may be assumed to act similarly, first by damaging the walls, and secondly by causing dilatation of the vessels. In some of the conditions to be described hæmorrhages are found in the walls of the hollow and other viscera.

Clinical features. The lesions of purpura are (1) *petechiæ*, small red or purple well-defined areas, not raised above the level of the surrounding skin. The colour does not disappear on pressure. (2) *Ecchymoses*, large, flat, slightly raised red or purplish patches like bruises. (3) *Hæmorrhagic bullæ*, blisters containing blood. The lesions appear suddenly, and on fading pass through the colours of a bruise, purple, greenish and yellow. Several varieties of idiopathic purpura are recognised, but a comparison of their clinical features, and the difficulty in drawing hard and fast lines between them, suggest that they are merely differences in degree.

25—2

(1) **Purpura simplex.** In this form children are more frequently affected than adults. The eruption consists of petechiæ, varying in size from a pin's head to a sixpence, level with the surrounding skin. The lower extremities are usually affected, but the spots may also occur on the upper limbs. There is no fever, and beyond slight malaise there are no symptoms. The disease is probably toxic, the patient often being badly fed and living in unhygienic surroundings. Rest and good food lead to rapid recovery, but there may be relapses.

(2) **Purpura hæmorrhagica** (Werlhoff's disease) is a more severe affection, though it is often difficult to draw the line between this and the preceding variety. There may be an acute onset, with febrile symptoms and headache, but there are no articular pains. Sometimes the hæmorrhages into the skin precede the general symptoms. As a rule the eruption appears first on the legs ; but spots may come out on the upper extremities and on the trunk. The lesions are petechial at the onset, but generally there are some large ecchymoses—sometimes as large as the hand—and occasionally subcutaneous hæmorrhages, causing deep-seated swellings covered by unaltered skin. Bleeding from the lips, gums, mouth, nose, stomach, intestine or kidney occur. In the less severe cases it is common to find small hæmorrhages into the soft palate. In the grave cases the loss of blood from the vessels may cause a profound anæmia, but even then the mortality is not high.

(3) **Purpura rheumatica, Peliosis rheumatica** (Schönlein's disease). In this variety there are articular pains and swellings, in addition to the cutaneous lesions. The eruption is symmetrical, affecting the legs and feet and the arms and hands and occasionally the trunk. The petechiæ vary in size from a pea to a shilling. They are not flat, but raised like the lesions of erythema multiforme, which is often associated with the purpura. Urticarial wheals are also not uncommon. Recently I had a case in which the eruption was mainly purpuric on the lower extremities, while that on the upper limbs was erythematous, and at a later stage the upper part of the trunk was covered with urticarial wheals.

The general symptoms are pyrexia, malaise and joint pains. Occasionally there is vomiting. Evidence of valvular disease of the heart is sometimes present.

Peliosis rheumatica is peculiarly prone to recur, sometimes after the lapse of months, sometimes after several years.

(4) **Henoch's purpura.** This form occurs in children. The cutaneous lesions do not differ from those of the last group, viz., petechiæ with erythema and urticaria. There are occasionally

Plate 84

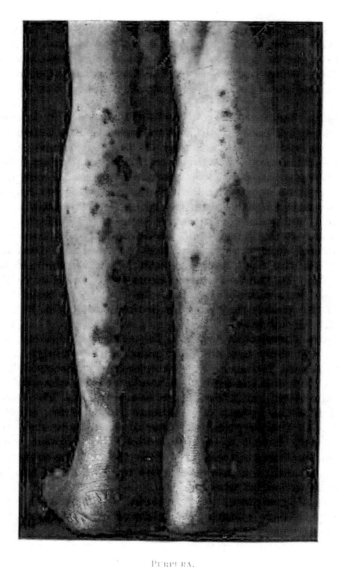

PURPURA.

The purple tint is well marked. The colour did not alter on pressure.

articular pains, but the distinguishing symptoms are gastro-intestinal. They comprise colicky pains and vomiting, and the passage of blood in the motions. The abdomen is tender, and there is usually pyrexia. The attacks of pain and sickness are recurrent and very suggestive of intussusception. They last for a few days. Albuminuria is common. Recovery is the rule, but relapses may occur.

It is believed that the abdominal symptoms are caused by hæmorrhage into the wall of the bowel and temporary paralysis of the section affected. Intussusception, which is simulated by the recurrent colic, and melæna, sometimes actually occurs from local paralysis of the gut.

(5) **Purpura fulminans.** In this fortunately rare type the hæmorrhages into the skin are extensive, but the mucous membranes are unaffected. The high pyrexia and death in a few hours suggest a microbic infection of peculiar virulence. Of sixty-five recorded cases eighteen followed scarlet fever.

Diagnosis. The lesions of purpura may be mistaken for those of erythema multiforme, but the colour does not disappear upon pressure. Occasionally, however, in peliosis and in Henoch's purpura there are both erythematous and hæmorrhagic lesions. Flea-bites are small punctate hæmorrhages, but they are surrounded by a zone of erythema at first, and do not come out in crops.

To say that a patient is suffering from " purpura " is merely to diagnose a symptom, and is of no more real value than the application of the name " epistaxis " to bleeding from the nose. The general condition must be carefully investigated with a view to determining the cause. In some instances it will be found that the dietary is at fault, and that the condition approaches scorbutus in character. In many cases, it must be admitted, it is impossible to determine the cause of the cutaneous hæmorrhages, and we are obliged to make the diagnosis of " idiopathic " purpura.

Prognosis. With the exception of the very rare cases of purpura fulminans, the prognosis is good. As indicated in the clinical history, peliosis rheumatica is very prone to recur, and it is not safe to give a promise of freedom from future attacks in this variety.

Treatment. The mild cases do not require any special treatment. If there is an extensive eruption, rest in bed should be enjoined. Any scorbutic tendency must be treated by giving plenty of vegetables in the diet, and lemon or lime juice and fruit, such as oranges.

An aperient at the onset is useful, and in mild cases nothing further is required. Some recommend arsenic internally. Turpentine is another remedy of proved efficacy. It should be given in doses of ten to fifteen minims in an emulsion, such as the following :—

℞ Ol. Terebinthinæ, ♏x.

Tr. Quillaiæ, ♏xx.

Aq. ad ℥j.

Septic conditions of the mouth and throat should be treated by antiseptic mouth-washes and gargles. Listerine, 10 per cent., is very useful. Intestinal disinfectants, such as salol or beta-naphthol, are also given where absorption from the bowel is suspected.

Calcium chloride, or the lactate in fifteen-grain doses, given thrice daily for two days, and repeated after an interval of three days, is given to increase the coagulability of the blood, and in some cases appears to be of great value. In purpura rheumatica many give salicylates and salicin or salipyrin, though the efficacy of the treatment cannot be said to be marked. In the chronic cases the patient should, if possible, be removed to the country and put under conditions of good hygiene.

Adrenalin chloride (1—1,000), in doses of two to three minims, has proved very serviceable in some grave cases.

Subcutaneous injections of horse serum (20 c.c.) at intervals of two to three days proved successful in a grave case of purpura hæmorrhagica under my care. In a severe case of the same type Emsheimer injected into the buttock 20 c.c. of whole fresh human blood obtained from a relative of the child with satisfactory results.

REFERENCES.—HENOCH. *Berl. Klin. Wochenschrift*, 1874. "On Henoch's Purpura." H. LETT. *Reports Soc. Diseases Children*, VIII., p. 307. S. BARLING. *Brit. Med. Journ.*, March 29, 1913, p. 659. "Purpura Fulminans." J. D. ROLLESTON. *Brit. Med. Journ.*, November 15, 1913. T. MCCRIRICK. *Brit. Journ. Children's Diseases*, IX., 1912, p. 154. EMSHEIMER. *Journ. Amer. Med. Assocn.*, 1916, I., p. 120.

Purpura annularis telangiectodes. This rare condition, first described by Majocchi, occurs most often in adolescence and early adult life. MacKee collected 38 cases in the literature—31 males, 7 females. It has three stages :—

(1) *Telangiectatic stage,* characterised by well-defined pink or red macules the size of a lentil. Under the glass they are seen to be composed of a network of dilated capillaries with numerous minute dark red puncta. The colour of the spots becomes paler on pressure, but the dark puncta are unaffected.

(2) *Hæmorrhagic pigmentary stage.* The lesions spread very slowly and may reach the size of a halfpenny. The central parts lose their red tint and become pigmented while the periphery is still bright red,

and contains many dark red puncta. The coalescence of these annular lesions produces various types of figure.

(3) *Atrophic stage.* After a period of quiescence the lesions lose their sharp outline, the edge becomes pale and of a brownish yellow colour, and finally the spots disappear, the pigment being lost after the lapse of months. Atrophy and alopecia of the affected areas may remain. The patient complains of pain and pruritus. The several stages may be present simultaneously in different areas.

The eruption is bilaterally symmetrical, and usually begins on the legs and dorsal aspects of the feet. The thighs, forearms, arms and trunk may be affected. The whole process is slow in evolution and may last from several months to a year. Histologically the essential feature is an obliterative endarteritis with cell-infiltration round the capillaries. In the hæmorrhagic stage areas of extreme dilatation and engorgement are present. The vessels chiefly affected are those in the deeper parts of the corium and in the hypoderm. In the atrophic stage the number of vessels is diminished and the cell-infiltration disappears, the papillæ are obliterated, and the glandular elements are atrophic.

The etiology is unknown.

REFERENCE.—G. M. MACKEE. *Journal Cutaneous Diseases*, XXXIII., pp.129, 186, 280 ; plates, sections, and review of literature.

Urticaria pigmentosa.

A rare affection characterised by the formation of macules or nodules which become urticarial upon slight irritation.

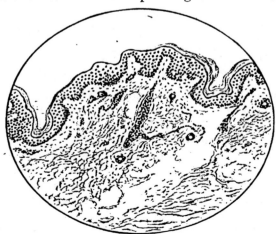

FIG. 157.—Urticaria pigmentosa (x. 75), showing infiltration of mast-cells along the vessels.

Etiology. The disease usually begins in early infancy, in more than 70 per cent. during the first year of life. Males are twice as frequently affected as females. There is no evidence of heredity, but occasionally two members of a family may be affected. The cause is unknown, and the eruption is compatible with perfect general health.

Pathology. The lesions are composed of infiltrations of mast-cells, especially about the vessels. These cells are present in some chronic inflammations, and are found in small number in the normal

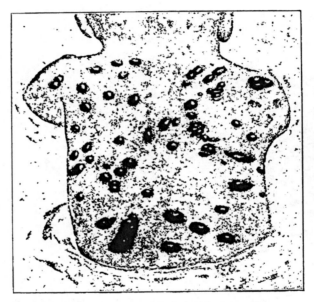

FIG. 158.—Urticaria pigmentosa. Nodular type. From a water-colour drawing lent by Dr. Graham Little.

skin, but in the lesions of urticaria pigmentosa they are a special feature, and more abundant than in any other condition. In fact this peculiarity may be taken as diagnostic of the disease. In the urticarial stage there is œdema of the whole skin, and the pigment of the lesions is chiefly in the deep layers of the epidermis.

Clinical features. The eruption begins with an urticaria, usually during the first year of life, though in rare cases it may not develop until after puberty. Recurrent attacks of urticaria, in which the lesions appear in the same sites, continue, and at last the characteristic macules are formed. These lesions are persistent, and are

Plate 35.

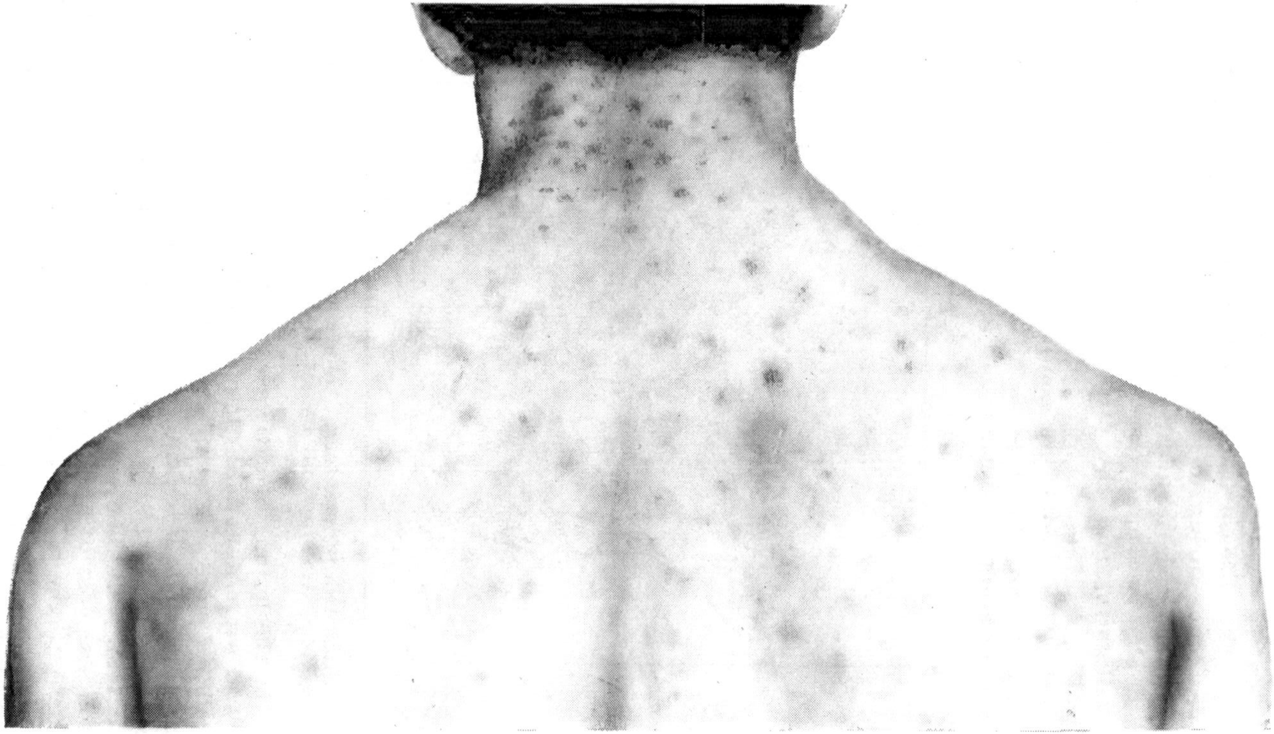

Urticaria Pigmentosa. Boy, aged nine. Showing widely spread pigment spots. They extended up to the scalp.

usually scattered thickly over the whole of the surface, or limited to certain areas.   In rare cases the macules are very few in number. There are two types of eruption, macules and nodules, and in some cases both forms are present.   The macular cases are by far the most common (Plate XXXV.).   The spots are pigmented patches the size of a split pea, of a buff to a brown colour, which on exposure to the air, or on slight friction, become turgid and wheal-like.   It is usually easy to provoke factitious urticaria by stroking the skin.   There is often itching, but this is not constant, and rarely severe. The neck and the trunk are more affected than the limbs and scalp, but no part of the body is exempt.   In the rare type, the lesions are nodules of a yellow colour (Fig. 158), closely resembling the tumours of congenital xanthoma, but differing from them in the presence of urticaria and of itching.   The pigmented spots and nodules persist for years, but often about puberty they begin to clear up, and ultimately disappear. It is interesting to note that the lymphatic glands may be generally enlarged, more than is accounted for by the scratching of the patient.

Prognosis.   Treatment is of little avail, and one can only hope for the disappearance of the eruption at puberty.

Treatment.   The itching may be relieved by the measures recommended for urticaria.   Dr. Radcliffe Crocker advocated small doses of arsenic internally, but there is rarely much benefit from any form of internal treatment. Any gastro-intestinal derangement should receive attention.

REFERENCE.—A collection of 154 cases by DR. GRAHAM LITTLE, with comments, contains most of the cases recorded to 1905.   See *Brit. Journ. Derm.*, 1905, XVII., p. 181, etc.   W. DUBREUILH, *Annales de Dermatologie*, August, 1912, III., p. 494.

Erysipeloïd (ROSENBACH).

Erysipeloïd is the name given to an eruption which resembles erysipelas, but which is caused by infection from animal matter undergoing decomposition.

Etiology.   Gilchrist, in 329 cases at Baltimore, traced all but six to bites of crabs, but elsewhere infection from decomposing fish and meat are recognised as causes.   The patients are usually those who deal in fish, butchers, etc.   Rosenbach described a cladothrix as the infective organism, but Gilchrist was unable to find it.

Clinical features.   The patient complains of heat and itching in the affected area.   There is no pyrexia, or sign of general illness. At the site of infection, usually the finger or hand, a purplish spot appears, and there is some swelling and tension of the skin.   The margin of the erythema is well defined ; the area slowly spreads, but much more slowly than in erysipelas. The affection lasts for from one to six weeks, and clears up without desquamation.

.**Treatment.** A 25 per cent. ointment of salicylic acid, or ichthyol 25 to 40 per cent., is applied to the affected area, and around it.

REFERENCES. —ROSENBACH. *Verhandlungen d. Deutsch. Gesellschaft f. Chirurgie,* April, 1907. ANDERSON and COLCOTT FOX. *British Journal of Dermatology,* 1899, XI., p. 121. T. C. GILCHRIST. *Journ. Ent. Diseases,* 1904.

Rosacea. Acne rosacea. Gutta rosea.

A chronic affection of the middle part of the face, forehead and chin, characterised by erythema, flushing, telangiectases, and the formation of pustules.

Etiology. Gutta rosea may begin about puberty, but it is most common in the fourth decade of life, and tends to disappear in advanced age. It is much more frequent in women than in men. It is often associated with the group of conditions classed as " seborrhoic," an oily condition of the skin, pityriasis capitis, etc., and acne vulgaris may precede it. The chief cause is undoubtedly derangement of the alimentary canal, many of the patients suffering from chronic dyspepsia, often due to chronic alcoholism, and from habitual constipation, and I have seen several cases in which the removal of a diseased appendix has been followed by remarkable improvement. In women, the menopause, oöphorectomy, and uterine and ovarian disease are frequently associated with rosacea, and it is usually worse just before the catamenia. Occasionally, the disease occurs in cardiac and chronic pulmonary disease, probably from the secondary congestion of the liver and other abdominal viscera. As local causes leading to exacerbation of the symptoms may be mentioned exposure to cold and changes of temperature.

Pathology. The vessels of the true skin are dilated, and there is inflammation of the sebaceous glands. The dilatation of the vessels often becomes permanent, leading to telangiectases, which are sometimes a prominent feature. The pustules which form in the sebaceous glands are not preceded by the formation of comedones.

In the condition known as rhinophyma, an occasional sequel of acne rosacea, there is hyperplasia of the connective tissue and of the sebaceous glands and vessels. Numerous mast-cells are found in the meshes of the connective tissue, and recurrent lymphangitis increases the swelling.

Clinical features. Acne rosacea begins by the formation of

Plate 36.

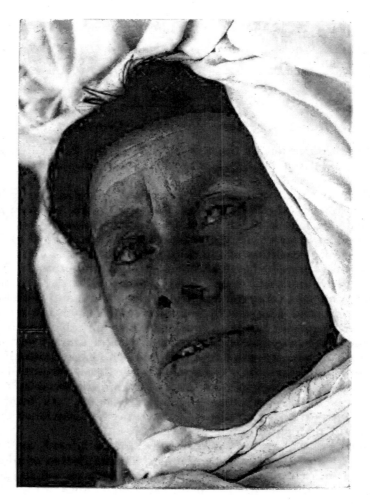

ACNE ROSACEA.

Female, aged 45. The plate shows the telangiectases and inflammatory papules on the flush area, forehead and chin.

diffuse or scattered red patches on the " flush area " of the cheeks, nose, and chin. Under the influence of changes of temperature the colour may become brighter or livid. After the taking of hot drinks, or sometimes after a meal, in many cases the midday meal, there is a tendency to flush, and the onset of the menstrual period often aggravates these symptoms. For a variable time these are the prominent features, but at length the vessels become permanently enlarged, notably in the naso-labial sulci and on the dorsum of the

Fig. 159.—Rhinophyma.

nose, on the cheeks, forehead, and chin. In the type called " couperose," by French authors, this condition persists. More commonly the sebaceous glands are obviously dilated, and are sometimes the seat of small red papules. Pustulation is a frequent complication. The pustules appear in small number from time to time, but are not preceded by comedones like acne vulgaris, and they rarely have the deep character of indurated acne. In some cases the pustulation is excessive, and there may be many abscesses scattered over the affected areas.

A variety characterised by small scattered papulo-pustules the size of a pin's head is described as a special affection by Brocq.

The lesions are usually most developed on the chin in women with uterine disorders.

Oily seborrhœa is a common symptom in all types. Nearly all patients suffering from acne rosacea suffer from coldness of the extremities.

In the hypertrophic form or *Rhinophyma* the nose is swollen,

Fig. 160.—Rhinophyma, after operation.

bulbous, and with soft nodular excrescences, covered by dilated vessels. The glandular structures are hypertrophic, and recurrent attacks of lymphangitis are common. This variety is most common in heavy drinkers. In the case illustrated the swelling was so great that the patient's vision was obstructed (Figs. 159, 160).

The disease is essentially chronic and may last for many years.

The diagnosis is usually remarkably easy, the symptom complex : —flushing, telangiectases, and papulo-pustules in the middle of the face and on the forehead and chin being characteristic. Lupus pernio might lead to difficulty, but it is a rare condition, in which the surface is chronically bluish, and is often associated with lividity of the extremities.

Treatment. The first point is to determine, if possible, the underlying cause and to treat the dyspeptic condition, constipation, etc. In many cases this at once relieves the symptoms. The diet should be extremely simple, alcohol must be avoided, and it is wise to limit the ingestion of hot fluids, particularly tea and coffee, but in so doing one must be sure that the patient takes a sufficiency of fluid, or there may be a tendency to constipation.

Ichthyol internally is often of great value in relieving the tendency to flushing. It should be given coated with keratin or in capsules in doses of two and a half to five grains thrice daily. Menthol half to two grains after meals is also of service in relieving this symptom. Large doses of citrate of potassium, a drachm thrice daily, and also quinine, are sometimes useful. Thyroid is recommended in rosacea occurring in women with hypo-thyroidism and in rhinophyma.

The local treatment is of importance. The application of a resorcin paste—Resorcin, 20 grains, zinc oxide and starch of each 22 grains, vaseline to one ounce—is often of service. Ichthyol ointment, 20 to 40 grains to the ounce, or a weak sulphur preparation, may be used. Where the flushing tendency is marked, the calamine lotion—Calamine two drachms, zinc oxide half a drachm, glycerine a drachm, and aq. calcis to four ounces—is useful to relieve the hyperæmia. The dilated veins are dealt with after the subsidence of the inflammatory symptoms. The best measure is electrolysis of the individual vessels, using a fine irido-platinum needle which is inserted into the vein, and a current of three milliampères is passed until the vein turns white. Measured doses of X-rays (about half the Sabouraud pastille dose) at intervals of fourteen days may be given when there are papulation and a moderate degree of hyperplasia. Radium also gives good results. In the hypertrophic cases the masses may be treated by multiple scarification, or, if of great size, pared away. The latter treatment was adopted, with good cosmetic results, in the case figured.

REFERENCE.—G. THIBIERGE. *La Pratique dermatologique*, 1900, Vol. I., p. 228.

Lupus erythematosus (Butterfly or Bat's Wing Lupus).

An inflammatory disease of probably toxic origin. The eruption is usually remarkably symmetrical, and tends to atrophy of the skin without ulceration. There are two types—(1) chronic and localised, and (2) disseminated.

Chronic Localised or Fixed Type.

Etiology. This is much the commoner. It occurs in both sexes, but is five times more frequent in the female than in the male. In over forty per cent. of the cases the disease begins in the third decade of life, in twenty-five per cent. between the ages of twenty and thirty. In about twenty per cent. between thirty and 'forty. It is rare in

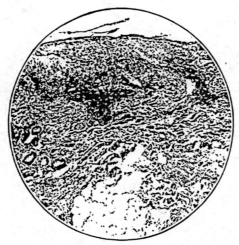

FIG. 161.—Lupus erythematosus. Microphotograph of section. ⅔.

young children, but has been seen as early as five. It is exceedingly rare for two members of one family to be attacked. Tuberculosis in the family is very common (one in three of my cases). Evidence of tuberculosis is present in at least one patient in five, usually in the form of strumous glands, or the scars of gland abscesses and bone and joint disease, but phthisis is rare. There is considerable diversity of opinion as to the exact relationship of this variety of lupus erythematosus to tuberculosis. Some hold that it is a tuberculous exanthem, and support is given to this view by the production of tuberculosis in guinea-pigs by the inoculation of material from patients. This has been done successfully by Gourgerot. On the other hand, it is exceedingly rare to get a positive reaction with tuberculin injected into the patient. Calmette's ophthalmic tuberculin test gave a positive reaction in fourteen out of twenty-one cases examined in my clinic. In none of these patients was there any clinical evidence of tuberculosis in the viscera or elsewhere. For the present it seems best to look upon lupus erythematosus of the fixed type as toxic, and that a tuberculous toxine may be one of the causes.

Local irritation may start an attack, the disease having been seen

FIG. 162.—Lupus erythematosus. Buccal mucosa and lips affected.

to begin at the site of a mosquito bite, and the area treated by a cantharides plaster.

Pathology. Lupus erythematosus is a peculiar form of inflammation of the skin beginning in the vascular layer about the sebaceous and sweat glands, and sometimes around the follicular orifices. There is hyperæmia of the corium and, later, cellular infiltration about the vessels. The infiltration consists of round cells, mast cells, and plasma cells, and occasionally giant cells have been observed. Finally, the infiltration undergoes cicatricial changes leading to destruction of the glandular elements of the skin, including the hair follicles. The tubercle bacillus has not been found in the tissue.

Clinical features. The lesions are erythematous and follicular. The former consist of flat red spots of various sizes with a dry and smooth or a scaly surface. There is sometimes some elevation above the level of the surrounding skin. In the follicular type there is hyperæmia at the margins of the patch, the centre of which is covered with an adherent scale, which finally may become of a greyish or yellowish colour. This scale is difficult to detach, and when removed a surface is exposed in which the dilated orifices of the glands are easily seen. On the under surface of the scale there are conical plugs which occupied the dilated gland orifices. In very rare instances the lesions may be nodular (Radcliffe-Crocker). The patch tends to extend at the margin and to heal in the centre, leaving a slightly depressed scar. The progress of the disease is always slow, and it may persist for years. Occasionally the inflammatory process clears up spontaneously, and if of the superficial type may leave very little cicatrix.

The seat of election is the face, usually the cheeks and the bridge of the nose, where the lesions form a butterfly patch. The eruption commonly starts as isolated symmetrical patches on the cheeks, but sometimes begins on the nose and spreads outwards from it. It frequently attacks the scalp, the patches at first being red and scaly, and ultimately areas of smooth scar, devoid of hair and surrounded by a narrow margin of redness covered with adherent scale. In rare instances the scalp is attacked first. The auricles are frequently affected, and the cicatricial contraction may lead to considerable deformity. The backs of the hands and the fingers are also commonly involved, the lesions closely resembling chilblains, but they do not clear up in the warm weather. Exceptionally, lesions of the common type occur on the trunk, the most frequent site being the shoulders and the limbs. In most cases the eruption is worse in the winter and spring, but this is not always the case.

The appearances vary somewhat in different types. In some there is excessive formation of scale, and massive crusts develop ; in others the scaling is confined to a narrow ring round the slowly-spreading scar. In the more superficial forms the scaling is very slight, and the resemblance to erythema is very close.

The mucous membranes are affected in 28 per cent. of the cases, the red margin of the lips being the most commonly attacked. Next in order of frequency come the buccal mucosa, the palate and

Plate 67.

LUPUS ERYTHEMATOSUS.

Duration seven years. The butterfly patches are characteristic. Their centres are atrophic and the margins scaly. Recently the disease has appeared on the trunk and extremities.

nasal cavity. Patches of lupus erythematosus of the lips often have the appearance of a dried layer of collodion, while on the buccal mucosa the lesions are symmetrical white patches, usually with a red margin. They sometimes leave whitish cicatrices (Fig. 162).

Disseminated Lupus erythematosus.

Etiology. All my patients have been young women, and with one exception between fourteen and thirty years of age. In two-

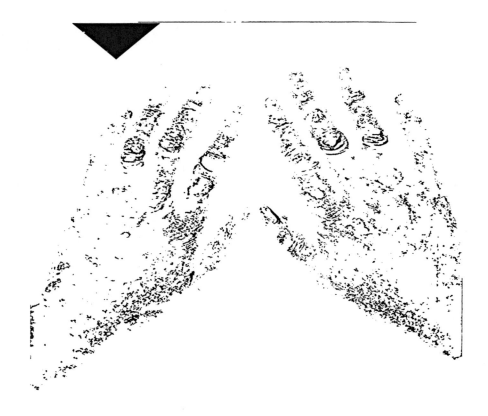

Fig. 163.—Lupus erythematosus of the hands.

thirds of the cases there was clinical evidence of tuberculosis— affection of the glands, scars of gland abscesses, or phthisis. It is usually held that lupus erythematosus of this type is a tuberculous exanthem, and there is some evidence in favour of this view, though

s.   26

cases are met with in which tuberculosis appears to be definitely excluded. There was a family history of tuberculosis in 80 per cent. of my patients. In many instances no exciting cause can be found,

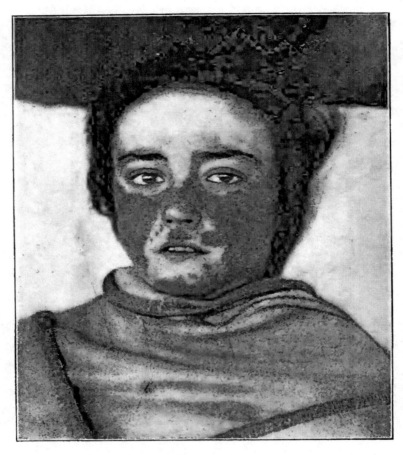

Fig. 164.—Acute Lupus erythematosus of exanthematic type. Fatal case under the care of the author.

but there are several instances on record in which the eruption started apparently as the result of mental or moral shock.

Clinical features. The acute affection occurs in young females already suffering from the disease of the chronic type, but occasionally it may run an acute course from the onset (Pernet). Recently I saw a patient of **Dr. Clive Rivière's** with a very acute outbreak. There were signs of bronchitis in the chest, and the young woman was

Plate 38.

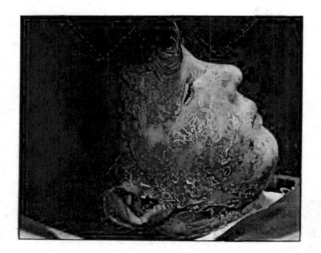

LUPUS ERYTHEMATOSUS.

Female, aged 27. Duration eight years. Widely spread eruption;
the limbs were affected. An epithelioma developed on the
right side of the face just outside the angle of the mouth.

.admitted to the Victoria Park Chest Hospital, and died there. At the autopsy, extensive tuberculosis of the lymphatic glands was found. There was a single fibrous focus in one lung. In another recent case there was no evidence of tuberculosis, the greatest care being taken at the post-mortem examination to investigate every possible site of the disease. In a third case there was glomerulo-tubular nephritis, which caused death, and a single fibrous nodule at the apex of one lung.

The eruption begins on the face as a number of pink or lilac coloured spots, which rapidly spread and become confluent, forming a butterfly patch across the middle of the face. The ears and scalp may be affected, and symmetrical spots appear on the trunk and extremities. As a rule, the scaling of the lesions is very slight, and at the onset the resemblance to erythema multiforme is very close. Hæmorrhagic areas occurred in a case of my own and in one under the care of Sir Stephen Mackenzie, and bullæ sometimes filled with blood may occur. The patient is gravely ill, and there may be high fever and prostration. In the later stages the fatal cases show the characters of acute septicæmia. Death occurs in about 8 per cent. of the cases, the fatal issue being determined by pneumonia, phthisis, nephritis and meningitis. In the acute stage, albuminuria is common. A subacute form occurs in which the eruption is of the disseminated type, but there are no grave constitutional symptoms, although the patient is usually in a weakly condition, easily tired and lethargic. Recurrences occur in this type, sometimes after long intervals.

Complications of lupus erythematosus. Epithelioma is the only serious complication of the chronic cases. It is very rare. I have seen two instances, and Dr. Pringle has reported a case in which there were multiple cancerous tumours on areas affected by lupus erythematosus. In one of my cases X-ray treatment appeared to be the exciting cause of the malignant growth.

Diagnosis. Lupus erythematosus is characterised by its symmetry and superficial character, by its marginal extension and the cicatricial destruction of the skin and its appendages. It, however, simulates very closely a number of conditions at its onset, and in some cases the progress has to be watched before a definite diagnosis can be made. The diseases resembling the early stage of lupus erythematosus are chronic eczema, psoriasis, acne, erythema, and chilblains.

From lupus vulgaris the diagnosis is generally easy. The eruption usually starts at a later age, it is symmetrical, and there are no apple-jelly nodules. Ulceration is also exceedingly rare. The only form of lupus which can lead to a mistake is the superficial type described

26—2

by Vidal, affecting the cheeks and nose, and in which the nodules are very small.

Prognosis. Very few skin affections are more difficult to treat than lupus erythematosus, and a favourable prognosis can never be given, even if the disease has only attacked a small area. The eruption tends to spread slowly for many years. In rare cases the lesions clear up spontaneously, and all that can be promised a patient is that eventually, perhaps after years, there may be gradual remission of the symptoms and scarring of the affected areas.

Treatment. Internal. Quinine is one of the best remedies. It should be given in doses of three to five grains, thrice daily. Salicin, in fifteen-grain doses, increased to twenty grains thrice daily, is sometimes of value in the early superficial type. Arsenic, iron and general tonics are often required, and ichthyol, in five-grain doses, thrice daily, is sometimes useful. The patient requires good food, plenty of fresh air, and, if possible, a residence in an equable climate. Tuberculin has been used on the supposition that the disease is of tuberculous origin, but a case of diffuse type reported by Ravogli, in which an injection was followed by acute fever and death in ten days, shows that this procedure may be attended with grave risk.

Locally, the treatment varies with the character of the eruption. In the erythematous and acute types, the application of soothing lotions, such as the lotion or liniment of calamine, are usually beneficial. If there be thick masses of scales, these can be removed by daily friction with a lotion composed of equal parts of soft soap and spirit. I have found the application of the creosote and salicylic acid plaster (Leslies) very useful in this type. Painting with tincture of iodine, combined with the internal treatment by quinine, as suggested by Hollander, I have used with satisfactory results in many cases. Painting for four days in succession with pure cyllin will also remove the thick scaly crusts.

I cannot say that I have ever seen benefit from the X-ray treatment, unless it has been pushed to the formation of a cicatrix with telangiectases, and in the acute variety I feel sure it is frequently harmful. The Finsen Light treatment is of value in a small proportion of the chronic cases, but undoubtedly may increase the area of the eruption in the more acute type. Sparking with high frequency apparatus and the ionic treatment with copper or zinc sulphate 2 per cent. have proved sometimes of temporary benefit. Radium may be applied with benefit to small areas.

Recently I have treated chronic patches with great temporary benefit by painting with carbon-dioxide snow dissolved in acetone, and also by the carbon-dioxide pencil.

It must be understood, however, that even the complete removal of any obvious lesions is often followed by recurrence, *in situ*, or elsewhere. It is for this reason that I do not advocate scarification and excision. The disease is, I believe, a toxæmia, and purely local measures are not likely to produce permanent benefit.

REFERENCES.—C. BOECK. "Die Exantheme der Tuberkulose." *Archiv. f. Dermatologie*, 1898, Bd. 42. H. GOUGEROT. "Tuberculoses cutanées atypiques non-folliculaires." *Revue de la Tuberculose*, BOUCHARD, 1898, pp. 444—446. J. H. SEQUEIRA and H. BALEAN. "A Clinical Study of Seventy-one Cases." *Brit. Journ. Dermatology*, 1902, XIV. The Transactions of the International Congress, Paris, 1900, contain valuable papers on the tuberculides, including lupus erythematosus. J. J. PRINGLE. "Carcinoma on Lupus Erythematosus." *Brit. Journ. Dermatology*, 1900, XII., p. 1, plate and references. H. RADCLIFFE CROCKER. "L. Erythematosus as an Imitator." *Amer. Jour. Cut. and Genito-Ur. Dis.*, 1894, XII., p. 1. RAVOGLI. *Journ. Cutaneous Dis.*, 1915, p. 206.

Lupus pernio. Chilblain Lupus.

This rare condition appears to be more closely related to Lupus erythematosus than to Lupus vulgaris.

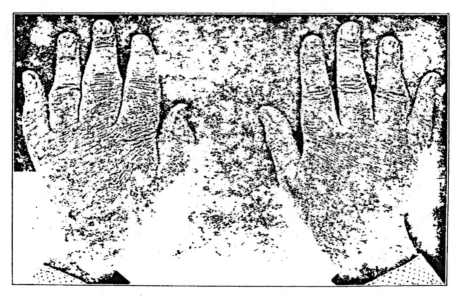

FIG. 165.—Lupus pernio.

The fingers and toes and the nose and ears are most commonly affected. The only characteristic case I have seen occurred in a married woman of thirty-six. The nose was enormously swollen, of a purplish-red tint and covered with dilated veins. The hands (figured here) were also cyanotic and so swollen that flexion of the fingers was very difficult. The surface felt doughy and pitted slightly on pressure. There was no scaling.

The condition was first noticed after a severe winter on the Continent, and had persisted for several years. There was slightly amelioration in the warm weather, but the affection has undergone no marked change while under my observation. I have seen another case in which the nose alone was slightly affected, and in this instance the erythema almost disappeared in the summer.

Treatment by X-rays, high frequency, and static electricity were tried in the severe case without material benefit.

GRANULOMA OF PROBABLY TOXIC ORIGIN.

Multiple Idiopathic Pigment so-called Sarcoma of Kaposi.

Histologically and clinically this condition should, in my opinion, be removed from the sarcomata. It appears to be a granuloma of peculiar type. The disease appears first on the hands and feet symmetrically, but it may spread to adjacent parts of the limbs and become generalised. In an early case recently under my observation the primary affection was a symmetrical purple congestion of the extremities on which small nodules of similar colour developed. There may, however, be small nodules from the onset. The small nodular tumours are always most numerous on the extremities. There is rarely much pain, and the lymphatic glands are not affected. The condition may remain stationary, or gradually undergo resolution. More rarely, the affection spreads and the lesions may ulcerate.

I have seen seven cases. A Galician Jew who was under Dr. Pringle and Sir Stephen Mackenzie, and who after having a leg amputated recovered. He died in the London Hospital under my care from heart disease secondary to emphysema. My second case, a London stonemason with severe gout, was for a long time under my observation. The hands and feet were affected, and the condition of one hand is shown in the figure. He improved gradually, and has not been seen for three years. A third case, shown at the Royal Society of Medicine, was also in a gouty patient, a German aged 80. Here the affection was also on the extremities, but more on one side than the other. Two cases recently in my ward were Polish Jews, aged 62 and 46 respectively.

The histology of the second case was investigated by Dr. Bulloch, who concluded that the lesions were inflammatory and not neoplastic. Spindle cells, round cells, and fibrous tissue with many dilated vessels were found. The pigment was, as Kaposi had described, entirely due to hæmorrhages. My cases had all the features which Sir J. Hutchinson described as "symmetrical purple congestion of the skin," and I have no doubt were of the same type. Dr. Turnbull, who has examined two of my cases histologically, found the earliest change to be a capillary hyperplasia. The pigmentation was due to multiple

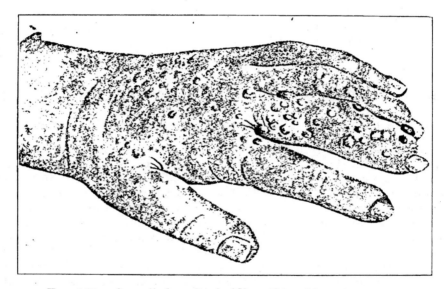

Fig. 166.—So-called multiple idiopathic pigment sarcoma.

hæmorrhages. The other changes were of an inflammatory nature. the infiltration consisting of fibroblasts and mononuclear cells. There was no evidence of sarcoma. The patients have nearly all been middle-aged or elderly men, but a very few cases have been described in women.

The cause of the disease is unknown. Two of the five cases I have seen suffered from severe gout, and Hutchinson gives this as the cause of his symmetrical purple congestion. Some of Kaposi's patients died with diffuse dark purplish patches widely spread on the skin and on the mucous membranes, the fatal issue being attended with extreme wasting, melæna, and hæmoptysis. Tumours similar to those on the skin were found post mortem in the viscera, but, as indicated above, a prolonged course and even recovery are not uncommon.

Treatment. Arsenic in large doses should be tried. Radio-therapy has proved useful in early cases.

REFERENCE.—J. H. SEQUEIRA. *Brit. Journ. Dermatology,* 1901, XIII., p. 201: coloured plate and literature.

CHAPTER XVI.

THE ERYTHRODERMIAS.

THIS group of diseases, probably of toxic origin, is characterised by persistent, extensive or universal inflammatory redness and scaling of the skin. Various names have been applied to members of the group, but the cases fall into four classes.

(1) Epidemic erythrodermias.

(2) Acute, subacute, and chronic primary erythrodermias.

(3) Secondary erythrodermias following eczema, psoriasis, etc.

(4) The erythrodermias of mycosis fungoides and leukæmia.

Etiology. Nothing is known upon this point. With the sole exception of the rare epidemic form, and possibly that described by Ritter v. Rittershain, there is no evidence of contagion. No specific organism has been found in the lesions. That the affections are toxic is generally admitted, but of the nature of the toxæmia we have no information. In some form, alcoholism appears to be a predisposing cause. The chronic form known as Pityrias rubra of Hebra usually ends with evidence of tuberculosis ; tubercles have been found in the skin lesions, and by some it is classed as a " tuberculide."

Pathology. There is congestion and cellular infiltration, especially in the papillary body, and the scaling is the result of parakeratosis. In the Hebra type, the papillæ in the late stages undergo atrophy, and the glandular elements are destroyed. Tubercles with giant cells and Koch's bacilli have been found by Jadassohn and others.

1. Epidemic Exfoliative Dermatitis.

In 1890, an epidemic of exfoliative dermatitis occurred in three London infirmaries, those of Paddington, St. Marylebone, and Lambeth. More than 19 per cent. of the inmates of the Paddington Infirmary were affected, the patients being usually elderly paupers. The eruption began as papular, erythematous or vesicular patches, which in one-half the cases spread until the whole surface was affected. The red areas desquamated freely, but in some cases the eruption throughout was of a moist eczematous character. The hair and nails were shed in the most severe cases, but there was little febrile disturbance. Wasting and prostration were noted in many of the patients, and death occurred in about 12 per cent. of those attacked. There seemed to be evidence pointing to the milk supply as the source of the infection, but this was not definitely proved.

A possibly similar condition was reported by Ritter v. Rittershain. During ten years, three hundred infants in the Foundling Asylum at Prague were attacked within the first five weeks of birth by an eruption of erythrodermic type. The affection usually started about the mouth, and spread all over the surface. The skin was of a purplish-red colour, and desquamated freely. Sometimes bullæ were present, and there is great probability that the condition was of the nature of a bullous impetigo. The malady was fatal in about a week. Though other observers on the Continent have met with this condition, it has not been seen in this country.

2. Primary Erythrodermias.

Erythrodermic xerodermia is a form of xerodermia in which the whole of the skin is red and dry. The affection is congenital, and the appearance is exactly similar to that met with in common xerodermia, except that the surface is red, and the flexures are as much affected as the rest of the skin (*vide* Xerodermia, p. 17).

Acute Erythrodermia. Recurrent Scarlatiniform Erythema.

Erythema scarlatiniforme has been described already (p. 365). Mention was there made of a form in which recurrences with excessive scaling are the prominent feature. The onset is acute, with a moderate degree of fever (100° to 101° F.), headache and shivering. After two or three days, the eruption appears in the form of red, itching patches in the flexures. These erythematous areas spread until the whole body and the limbs are involved, but the face usually escapes. In a few days the redness disappears, and is followed by extensive desquamation. In some parts the skin comes off in small branny flakes, and in others the scales are of large size, while the hands and feet peel in the form of sheets or casts. The subjacent skin is left smooth, but may continue to shed small flakes for some time after the primary desquamation. The nails are also slightly affected, the attack leaving a linear depression upon them. The hair does not fall. There is often associated congestion of the fauces, and of the conjunctivæ, and the tongue may peel. There is much freer and earlier desquamation than in scarlet fever, and a great tendency to relapse. The relapses occur at intervals of a few months or longer, but as time goes on, their intensity decreases. There is no evidence of the cause, but it is probably a toxæmia. In the

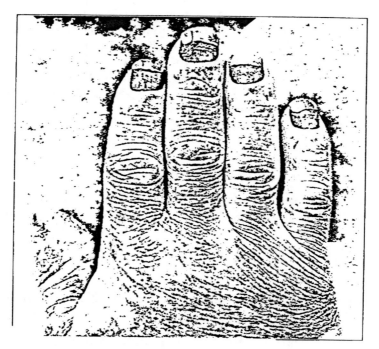

FIG. 167.—Exfoliative dermatitis. The photograph shows the affection of the nails.

differential diagnosis, care must be taken to eliminate drug eruptions. *e.g.*, the scarlatiniform rash of quinine, etc.

Subacute Form.   General Exfoliative Dermatitis of Erasmus Wilson.

The onset is very similar to that of the recurrent form or scarlatiniform erythema. There is moderate pyrexia as a rule, but sometimes the temperature is normal. The eruption may resemble erysipelas. or a simple erythema at the start, but it gradually extends. and may become universal. In the established cases there are three cardinal features, redness, desquamation, and a universal distribution.

(1) The skin is bright red, but may become pale on exposure to the air; compression with a piece of glass causes the red colour to disappear, but a pale yellowish tint remains. (2) The desquamation is copious. The flakes are large and abundantly formed and continuously shed, so that in the course of a few hours a dustpan full of flakes may be removed from the patient's bed. The scales are papery, or like the

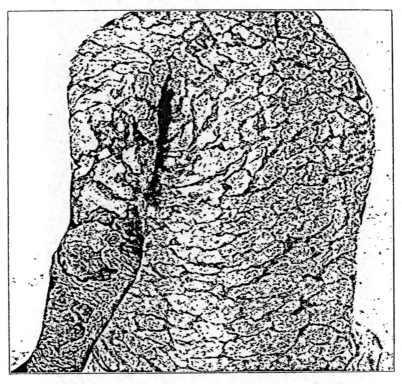

FIG. 168.—General exfoliative dermatitis. (From a drawing of a patient under the late Sir S. Mackenzie.)

flakes of pie-crust. (3) The affection is universal; in the majority of cases no part of the skin is unaffected. The hair, eyelashes and nails fall (Fig. 167), and the conjunctivæ are inflamed. The skin is tense, and sometimes appears to be thickened, while there may be œdema of dependent parts. The patient complains of cold, he loses flesh, and from time to time there are attacks of fever, the temperature reaching 102° to 103° F. The urine is sometimes albuminous, and there is usually grave diminution of the urea. In one of my

Plate 39.

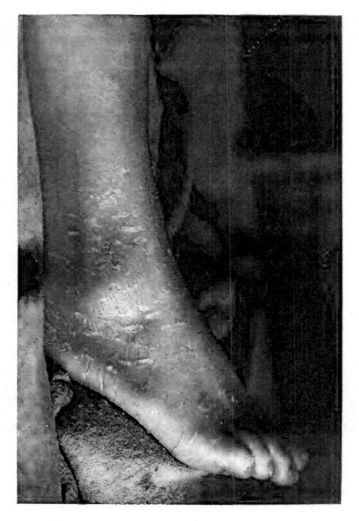

EXFOLIATIVE DERMATITIS.

The plate shows the characteristic redness and desquamation. The nails
and the hair were shed.

cases Dr. H. L. Tidy found marked diminution of urea, but excess of uric acid, the total nitrogenous output, however, being considerably below the amount of nitrogen taken in the food. Indicanuria is not uncommon.

Fright and severe mental strain have been followed by an acute outbreak. Exposure to cold and wet and alcoholism and mercurialism are believed to be exciting causes. Repeated intravenous injections of salvarsan may produce this form of dermatitis.

Death occurs in about 12 per cent. of the cases of this type. The disease usually runs a course of from three to twelve months, but occasionally lasts for years.

Chronic Type. Pityriasis rubra of Hebra-Jadassohn.

The eruption begins usually in the flexures, in the form of red scaly patches, without any infiltration. It gradually spreads, and at the end of some months, or perhaps not until the lapse of a year or more, it becomes universal. There is slowly progressive wasting and occasionally delirium in the febrile attacks. The skin gradually undergoes atrophy, and the movements of the body and limbs become difficult. The amount of itching varies, but the patient feels cold, and shivering is common. Pityriasis rubra runs a very chronic course, and after several years the patient succumbs to tuberculosis (Jadassohn). On this account, and from the finding of Koch's bacilli in the skin, this form of erythrodermia is sometimes included among the tuberculides.

Treatment of the primary erythrodermias. The patient must be kept in bed between blankets. The diet should be simple, and alcohol should be avoided.

I have usually followed Mackenzie in the local treatment. The patient is put into a pyjama suit made of lint, with a lint mask for the face. The suits are changed once a week. The lint is constantly soaked in the glycerol of lead lotion (glycerol of lead one ounce, glycerin one ounce, water to one pint). The lotion, just warmed, is applied to the lint suit from the outside, and the dressing is kept constantly moist with it. Care must be taken during the treatment to avoid chills, but a daily bath is a great comfort to the patient. The lead application soon relieves the irritation and burning, and tends to diminish the hyperæmia. When this occurs an ointment of glycerol of lead, or of equal parts of lanolin and vaselin, is applied. If the hyperæmia comes back on applying the ointment, a return is made at once to the lotion. Calamine liniment is another suitable application, and in the later stages Lassar's paste may be used. In some cases purified liquid paraffin is found to be a satisfactory application in the acute stage.

Medicinal treatment is of little avail. Quinine has sometimes proved of benefit, and in the chronic cases cod-liver oil and tonics are indicated.

3. Secondary Erythrodermias.

Strictly speaking, cases of generalised eczema, seborrhoic dermatitis, psoriasis, pemphigus foliaceus, and rarely lichen planus and pityriasis rubra pilaris come within the definition of erythrodermia, and in some instances closely simulate it. In universal eczema the eruption may be of the weeping or of the rubrum type, and there is often some grave disease of the kidneys. Seborrhoic dermatitis is very rarely general, but psoriasis may slowly involve the whole surface, but in parts it maintains its common characters. Pemphigus foliaceus in certain stages looks very like a general exfoliative dermatitis ; there is, of course, general exfoliation, but the scales are moist, and there is a history, if not actual evidence, of a bullous stage. The acute form of lichen planus soon shows the characteristic papules which make the diagnosis. Pityriasis rubra pilaris becomes universal exceedingly rarely. The **secondary erythrodermias** proper are sequels to any one of the diseases just mentioned. The characteristics of the eruption, whether eczema, seborrhoide, psoriasis, etc., change, and a dermatitis exfoliativa develops. I have seen such appear in cases of psoriasis as the result of treatment by chrysarobin and oil of cade ; and mercury has been known to cause it. Here the exfoliative dermatitis has the characters of the common type, but it generally runs a benign course. On the other hand, in some instances the erythrodermia is associated with rapid wasting, marasmus, partial suppression of urine, or grave hypoazoturia, and rapid death. In some cases excretion of urea by the skin has been noted. Erythrodermias of this type must be looked upon as infections or toxæmias developing upon the pre-existing cutaneous affection. In all probability they are of the same nature as the primary erythrodermias. The treatment is on the lines described above.

4. Erythrodermia in Mycosis fungoides and Leukæmia.

One of the eruptions occurring in the premycosic stage of mycosis fungoides is erythrodermia. Of three cases I have seen two were men and one a woman, in whom a number of red itching patches developed, and by extension covered the whole surface. In all there was a great deal of dry scaling, and the characteristic tumours developed in large numbers. The special features of this erythrodermia are the intense itching and the infiltration of the patches. In one of my cases there was general enlargement of the lymphatic glands.

A rare complication of leukæmia is an analogous erythrodermia with abundant scaling. The diagnosis is made by the examination of the blood and the enlargement of the spleen and glands. Radiotherapy affords relief.

REFERENCES.—BROCQ. "Etude critique et clinique." Paris, 1882. JADASSOHN. "Relationship of Pityriasis Rubra to the Tuberculides." *Archiv. f. Derm. u. Syphilis*, 1891, 1892. SIR S. MACKENZIE. *British Journal of Dermatology*, July, 1889, and "Allbutt's System," III. Discussion, *Brit. Journ. Derm.*, 1898, X., p. 437. "The Metabolism in Exfoliative Dermatitis." H. I. TIDY. *British Journal of Dermatology*, XXIII., p. 133.

CHAPTER XVII.

AFFECTIONS DEPENDENT UPON VASCULAR AND LYMPHATIC OBSTRUCTION, Etc.

IN this chapter I propose to review the affections contingent upon chronic obstruction of the blood and lymphatic vessels. Some of these have been dealt with elsewhere, and will be merely referred to in passing ; but the affections dependent upon varicose veins, and the forms of gangrene met with in cutaneous practice, and the varieties of elephantiasis demand special notice.

Affections due to Varicose Veins.

Varicose veins tend to produce a number of cutaneous affections, particularly if the subject is obliged to stand for long hours at his occupation. Primarily, varices cause a chronic congestion of the integument of the lower extremities, and consequent impairment of its nutrition. The lowered resisting power of the tissues renders them prone to bacterial invasion, particularly by the streptococci. Varicose veins may be the direct or indirect cause of (1) œdema, (2) pigmentation, (3) eczema, (4) ulcer, (5) phlebitis, (6) lymphangitis, (7) elephantiasis, (8) sclerosis.

The pigmentation is caused by the chronic congestion and the escape of red corpuscles into the tissues. The local predisposition to eczema has already been considered (p. 97). Phlebitis and lymphangitis are due to streptococcal infection, and if repeated tend to elephantiasis (p. 414). The sclerosis is the result of repeated attacks of inflammation of the derma and hypoderm.

Varicose ulcer. The so-called varicose ulcer may follow a bruise or slight traumatism. It may also be caused by (1) the rupture of a vein, (2) phlebitis, (3) eczema, (4) impetigo. In all these conditions a normal skin would be affected temporarily, and ulceration is uncommon, but where there are varicose veins the resisting power of the tissues is lowered and chronic microbic inflammations are often set up. One of the commonest is caused by streptococci, and a " streptococcal chancre," to use the name given by Sabouraud, forms. This inflammatory lesion is the usual precursor of the varicose ulcer.

Clinical features. The ulcer is commonly situated in the lower half of the leg and most frequently on the inner surface. It is ovoid or round, but by the fusion of neighbouring ulcers areas with a polycyclic outline may be involved. The varicose ulcer may be of large size, perhaps four or five inches in diameter, and it may extend round the greater part of the circumference of the leg. The edge is sometimes steep and sometimes undermined, and it may be indurated and adherent to the subjacent tissues. The base is red or purplish, and blood may ooze from it. In neglected cases the floor of the ulcer is often covered with greyish sloughs and fœtid sanious pus. If the parts are kept clean the exudation may be mainly serous. The ulcer is remarkably insensitive and callous, and, if the base is adherent to the bone, particularly intractable.

The lymphatic glands in the groins are enlarged.

The **diagnosis** of varicose ulcer may be attended with great difficulty. In practice it will be found that the ulcerating syphilides and gummatous ulcers give the most difficulty, but some of the chronic tuberculides and ecthyma may also require careful discrimination. The ulcerating tertiary syphilides are commonly multiple, and affect the extensor aspect of the limb. They are grouped in circles or parts of circles. The syphilitic gumma begins with a node-like swelling, which softens in the centre to form a punched-out ulcer with a wash-leather-like slough on the floor. In doubtful cases the Wassermann test should be applied if possible, or the effects of mercury and iodide of potassium should be tried. The tuberculous ulcers usually occur in younger subjects. In Bazin's disease they are bilaterally symmetrical, and affect the calf more than the inner side of the leg. In ecthyma the lesions are small and multiple, and the ulcer under the scab is comparatively superficial and has shelving margins. The concomitant symptoms—varicose veins, œdema, pigmentation and sclerosis—will be useful points in favour of varicose ulcer.

Prognosis. With rest in the horizontal position varicose ulcers tend to heal rapidly, but a return to the vertical position often leads to relapse. In patients of the labouring classes the limbs may be affected for years.

Treatment. The limb should be in the horizontal position with the foot slightly elevated. Mild antiseptic fomentations are of great value, but strong applications often irritate. The ulcer may be dusted with peroxide of zinc powder, or with aristol or europhen.

Stimulation of the callous surface with Lotio rubra (Zinc sulphate 2 grains, Tr. Lavandulæ Co. 12 minims, water to one ounce), or with a lotion of nitrate of silver 10 to 15 grains to the ounce, is often useful. In some of the chronic cases the application of the silver stick may be necessary.

Among other stimulating applications may be mentioned high frequency electricity and short exposures to the X-rays. Hot-air and light baths are said to be of service, and ionisation has also been recommended.

If the patient is unable to rest with the limb in the horizontal position the leg should be supported by " strapping " with Unna's gelatin bandage. The strapping is so arranged that the ulcer may be dressed with antiseptic and stimulating applications. After the healing of the ulcer the limb must be supported by an elastic bandage or stocking put on immediately upon rising in the morning. In bad cases surgical interference may be required to free the ulcer from its deep adhesions and permit of its contraction, or if of moderate size the ulcer may be excised and the area skin-grafted. In some instances amputation of the limb is necessary.

Cutaneous Gangrene.

Local necrosis of the skin may be due to—

(1) Severe traumatism.

(2) Physical causes :—intense heat, and cold (p. 62), prolonged exposure to the X-rays and radium (p. 78), powerful electric currents, high-frequency electricity.

(3) Chemicals :—strong acids, and alkalies, chloride of zinc, arsenic, carbolic acid, etc.

(4) In rare cases carbon-monoxide poisoning, chloral hydrate, iodides and arsenic may cause gangrenous eruptions.

(5) Virulent bacterial infection :—dermatitis gangrenosa infantum (p. 186), dermatitis vaccinformis (p. 186), noma, gas gangrene.

(6) Diabetes.

(7) Nervous diseases :—syringomyelia (p. 445), nerve leprosy (p. 262), and, in association with pressure, the bed-sore of myelitis, compression paraplegia, etc.

(8) Interference with or suppression of the blood supply :—

(a) Pressure on the vessels by neoplasms or exudations.

(b) Contraction of the muscular coat, in ergotism and Raynaud's disease.

(c) Diseases of the intima :—endarteritis obliterans, syphilitic ndarteritis, atheroma.

(d) Obstruction of the lumen by thrombus or embolus.

Some of these conditions are considered in other parts of this work, and others are more fittingly dealt with in the text-books on surgery.

Bed-sore.

The bed-sore is a form of gangrene of the skin and subcutaneous tissue caused by intermittent or continuous pressure in a patient suffering from acute or chronic disease.   It is particularly liable to occur in certain nervous affections, myelitis, compression paraplegia, hemiplegia, etc.

The areas commonly affected are the sacral and lower vertebral regions, the trochanters and malleoli, and the heels.   The parts first become congested and œdematous, and necrosis follows.   A greyish brown slough forms, and this covers an ulcer.   The ulcer may extend down to and expose or even involve the bone.   In some cases from secondary infection the gangrenous process is not limited to the parts exposed to pressure, but spreads widely beyond them.

Bed-sores are uncommon in patients who are carefully nursed. They can usually be prevented by frequently changing the position of the patient in bed, by the distribution of the pressure by water-beds and pillows, and by keeping the parts clean and dry.   The greatest difficulty occurs in nervous cases in which the excreta are passed into the bed.   In these, only the unremitting care of the nurse can prevent bed-sores.   Spirit lotion is used to harden the skin, and the parts are frequently dusted with powders of zinc oxide and starch or siliceous earth with boric acid.   If the surface is broken, the bed-sore may be dressed with Tr. Benzoin Co. or with boric acid ointment.   The ulcer itself should be surrounded with a circular water-pillow or a ring of thick plaster to prevent pressure.   If there be septic infection, boric acid or other antiseptic fomentations will be required.

Ergotism.

The prolonged use of ergot, or more commonly the use of rye infected with the *claviceps purpurea*, causes a local gangrene probably due to spasm of the arterioles.

The gangrenous process affects the toes and fingers, and occasionally the ears.   It is usually preceded by loss of sensation, or by tingling and pain.   There may also be spasms of the muscles. The necrosis is the result of stasis in the small vessels.   The treatment of the local conditions is on the same lines as that of peripheral gangrene.

Raynaud's Disease.

A vascular affection characterised by (1) local syncope, (2) local asphyxia, and (3) local gangrene. The extremities are usually affected and the phenomena are bilaterally symmetrical.

Etiology. Raynaud's disease occurs most frequently in adoles-

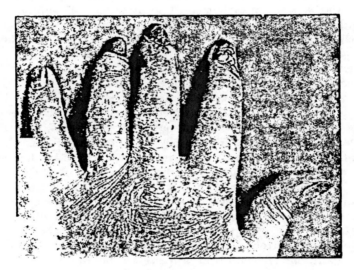

FIG. 169.—Terminal necrosis of phalanges.

cence and early adult life. Exposure to cold may determine an attack, but in some cases emotional disturbance and gastric disorder appear to be determining factors. The actual cause is unknown, but in some cases there is a syphilitic basis.

Pathology. The local syncope is believed to be caused by spasm of the peripheral arterioles. The asphyxial condition is due to stasis and dilatation upon the venous side. The gangrene is caused by complete or partial suppression of the blood supply.

Clinical features. (1) *Local syncope.* The condition is commonly known as " dead fingers." One or more fingers, or the distal part of the hand, becomes white and cold, and anæsthetic. The pallor may last for an hour or more, and then there is a gradual reaction, the parts become red and hot, and the patient experiences a sensation of burning.   In many cases there is a slight degree of asphyxia also, and different fingers may be affected with syncope or with asphyxia.

(2) *Local asphyxia.*   In its mildest form this is seen in the chilblain circulation.   The acro-asphyxia may follow the local syncope, or it may be independent of it.   The fingers and toes and the ears and occasionally the nose are affected.   In rare cases other parts of the limbs may be involved.

The fingers swell and become intensely congested ; they assume a livid colour, with perhaps bright patches of erythema upon the livid area.   The swelling of the digits impairs their mobility, and there are sensations of tension and actual pain.   In some cases the affected parts are anæsthetic.   The attacks of asphyxia return again and again over many years, and the recurrences are determined by exposure to cold or by emotional disturbance, and are sometimes associated with gastric disorder.

The general health is usually unaffected.

(3) *Local or symmetrical gangrene.*   The recurrent asphyxial attacks may leave small necrotic areas on the tips of the fingers or toes, or on the edges of the auricles.   In some cases there is considerable thickening of the distal parts of the digits.   In the more severe cases the terminal phalanges become insensible, black, and cold, and the skin necroses, forming blebs.   There is the usual line of demarcation of the gangrenous area, and a portion of the extremity sloughs.   The actual destruction is generally less than the severity of the phenomena would suggest, but parts of the fingers or of the nose or ears separate.   In some cases only one digit is affected.   In very rare instances the gangrenous process involves the limbs more extensively, and patches may occur on the trunk.   Some cases of multiple gangrene in children appear to be of the same nature. Spontaneous amputation of parts of the limbs has been observed.

It is interesting to note that some patients suffering from Raynaud's disease present symptoms showing that the affection is not purely local.   The most important of these is paroxysmal hæmoglobinuria occurring on exposure to cold.   Occasionally there are temporary loss of consciousness, giddiness, lethargy, headaches, transitory hemiplegia and peripheral neuritis.   Epistaxis may occur.

Treatment.   In the slighter cases no special treatment is necessary. In the more severe ones the patient should be kept in bed, and all exposure to cold must be avoided.   The affected parts should be wrapped in cotton-wool.   Massage may be found of value, but I have seen greater benefit from the constant current applied in the foot or hand bath.   Nitroglycerine and the nitrites have been found to be of temporary service.   The gangrenous conditions require the application of dry antiseptic dressings. The general health demands attention, and anti-syphilitic treatment should be given if required. The diet should contain plenty of fat.

Diabetic Gangrene.

Diabetic gangrene usually affects all the tissues of part or of the whole of an extremity, or of the genitalia. It may follow a slight injury, but often there is no history of traumatism. In some cases the gangrene is in the form of disseminated patches. This form originates as a spreading bullous eruption. The central lesions heal up while fresh blebs form at the margins of the affected area. In all probability this eruption is caused by streptococcal infection. The prognosis is not necessarily grave. In other cases the gangrenous process develops upon a pre-existing eczema or impetigo.

The treatment must be directed to the general condition. The parts must be protected by wrapping in cotton-wool, and strong antiseptic applications must be avoided. Surgical interference may be necessary.

Gangrene due to Obstruction of the Lumen of the Vessels.

This occurs in the aged (senile gangrene), from arteritis obliterans and syphilitic endarteritis. The cutaneous condition is only part of the disease.

Gas-gangrene.

In gas-gangrene the changes in the skin are first due to pressure, and secondly to infection. In some cases of gas-gangrene there is a general icteric tinge. In the early stages the local condition, *i.e.*, gas in the muscles, may show no sign beyond tension, and pallor due to stretching. When gangrene is definitely established the skin over the area is a dirty cream tint. Later, irregular purple areas with greyish skin around them develop. On the purple areas blebs form containing blood-stained fluid. In the final stage the skin has a dark yellowish green colour. The late changes are post-mortem changes due to bacterial action. A peculiar bronzing of the skin occurs with infected wounds of the trunk. It may be associated with crepitus in the subcutaneous tissue.

General symptoms and treatment. In *dry gangrene* there is interference with the arterial supply, but the return of blood and lymph is unchecked. The tissues become mummified, but there may be no septic infection. The areas are of a brown, purplish or yellow tint, slightly depressed below the surrounding skin. They are cold and hard to the touch and anæsthetic. The patient may complain of irritation, burning, tingling or of acute pain. In course of time a line of demarcation forms between the living and the necrosed tissue. The slough contracts and is eventually thrown off. Amputation is usually necessary, but where there is advanced disease of the vessels, or some grave constitutional cause, it is often better to avoid operation and allow the natural process of removal of the dead tissue to take place with as little interference as possible. The parts must be kept scrupulously clean and dry and dressed with antiseptics and wrapped in cotton-wool. The process of separation may take a long time and is often painful.

In *moist gangrene* the tissues generally are sodden because there is obstruction to the return of blood and lymph. Blebs form upon the dark purplish or greyish soft skin, and these blebs often contain blood. Such a condition is highly favourable to bacterial invasion, and upon this depends the rapidity and extent of the destruction. It may be necessary to amputate before there is a definite line of demarcation.

REFERENCES.—"Raynaud's Disease." "Allbutt and Rolleston's System of Medicine," VII., p. 120. "Arteritis Obliterans." PARKES WEBER. *Lancet*, 1908, I., p. 152. "Gas-gangrene : Colour Changes in Skin, etc." CUTHBERT WALLACE. *Brit. Med. Journ.*, 1917, I., 725, plates.

OBSTRUCTION OF LYMPHATICS.

Elephantiasis and Pachydermia.

Elephantiasis is a chronic hypertrophic affection of the skin and subcutaneous tissue caused by obstruction of the lymphatics and characterised by enormous enlargement of the affected parts and thickening of the integument. The term " pachydermia " is applied to thickening of the skin from chronic interstitial hyperplasia.

Etiology. In this country elephantiasis is caused by—

(1) Repeated attacks of erysipelas or cellulitis.

(2) Chronic ulcers.

(3) Chronic tuberculous or syphilitic inflammation.

(4) Obstruction of the lymphatic channels by pressure of neoplasms and cicatrices.

(5) Extensive removal of lymphatic glands.

(6) Rarely as a congenital anomaly.

In the tropics filariasis is the common cause, but elephantiasis is not a necessary consequence of filarial invasion, but appears to be due to repeated erysipelatous attacks predisposed to by the *filaria sanguinis hominis*.

Pathology. The tissue is hard and tough, and gelatinous in appearance on section, and plasma exudes from the cut surface. The derma may be from a half to one inch in thickness, and the subcutaneous tissue is twice or thrice its natural volume and intimately adherent to the subjacent tissues. The lymphatic channels and the veins stand widely open on the cut surface. The lymphatic glands are enlarged. Under the microscope the tissue is found to consist of round or spindle cells with masses of leucocytes and plasma cells in the meshes of the connective tissue. The walls of the vessels are thickened and infiltrated. The glands of the skin are atrophic. There is often increase in the fat of the hypoderm. The microscopic appearances show that the process is inflammatory and not simply a chronic œdema. In the pachydermatous skin the papillæ are elongated and there is hyperkeratosis.

Elephantiasis nostras.

(1) *From recurrent erysipelatous inflammation, etc.* In a considerable number of cases there is some evident breach of the surface which allows the entrance of the infecting organism, usually the streptococcus. There may be obvious lymphangitis with swelling, redness, pain, tenderness, and pyrexia, and enlargement of the lymphatic glands. In other cases there is erysipelas or cellulitis.

The inflammation passes off in a few days, but it is noticed that the parts are slightly swollen. From time to time, often at short intervals, fresh attacks of lymphangitis or of erysipelatous inflammation occur, and after each there is a further increase in the size of the part, ultimately resulting in chronic hypertrophy.

When the lower limb is affected the member may be nearly half as large again as the corresponding leg. The surface may be quite smooth and shining, or pigmented or purplish in colour. In some instances the surface is squamous, in others there are verrucose or papillomatous excrescences. In many instances there are soft compressible swellings which on puncture give exit to clear lymph or a milky fluid. Such swellings are lymph varices (lymphangiectases). Similar conditions follow ulcers of the legs, chronic eczema, etc. In some cases there are no inflammatory symptoms and no pyrexia, but a similar change is found in the tissue affected. There appears to be some general or local predisposition, for the erysipelatous attacks may have no obvious cause.

In adults the lower extremities are the common site. In young subjects the lips may be involved, and the swelling causes great disfigurement (Fig. 170). Recurrent attacks of erysipelas may lead to extensive swelling of the eyelids, the nose, the auricles, and other parts of the face (*vide* Fig. 78).

(2) *From disease or removal of the lymphatic glands.* Elephantiasis

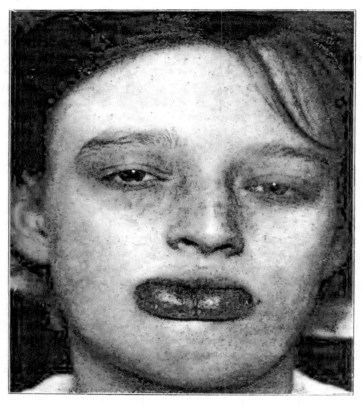

FIG. 170.—Elephantiasis of lip from recurrent streptococcal inflammation. Girl, æt. 15.

may follow extensive removal of the lymphatic glands, and also tuberculous disease, sclerosing syphilitic adenitis, and cancerous metastases.

The lower limbs and the external genitals are usually involved in the syphilitic forms, and both the upper and lower limbs may be affected in tuberculous gland disease. The upper limbs are involved in cancer of the breast. The affected parts become enormously swollen and painful. At first they pit on pressure, but ultimately they become indurated. In cancer en cuirasse the diffuse infiltration is often mainly due to lymphatic obstruction.

(3) *Secondary elephantiasis.* Pseudo - elephantiasis. Chronic swelling due to lymphatic obstruction occurs in certain tuberculous

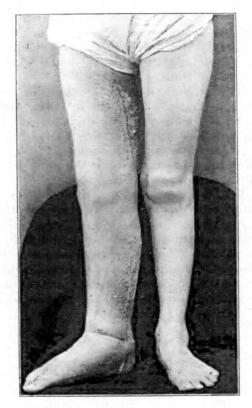

FIG. 171.—Congenital elephantiasis. Numerous vesicular lymph varices.

affections of the skin, *e.g.*, tuberculous lymphangitis (p. 233), lupus vulgaris (p. 240), and in tertiary syphilis (p. 303) and leprosy (p. 261).

In chronic ulcer of the leg it is usually associated with varicose veins.

(4) *Congenital elephantiasis.* In rare cases an elephantiasic condition is congenital. In the case figured here (Fig. 171), the patient, a girl of sixteen, had suffered from swelling of the leg and

thigh from birth. The limb was much enlarged, the surface white and glistening, and upon it there were numerous small translucent vesicles. Some of these ruptured spontaneously from time to time, giving exit to a milky fluid. The quantity lost was very large, and the girl was emaciated. On two occasions operations had been performed with the object of removing a tumour in the upper part of the thigh. I learned from one operator that the growth, which was evidently lymphangiomatous, extended into the abdominal cavity and could not be removed. I found that by removing fatty foods from the dietary the fluid became clear and translucent, but that the chylous character returned a few hours after the patient had taken a meal containing butter and milk.

Diagnosis. Where the elephantiasic condition follows disease or removal of the lymphatic glands there is no difficulty. In the inflammatory type the history of repeated attacks of erysipelatous inflammation or lymphangitis with the progressive enlargement of the affected areas are sufficiently characteristic.

Prognosis. If of long duration, and if the cause cannot be removed, there is no prospect of improvement.

Treatment. The acute attacks of inflammation are treated on general lines, the parts being kept at rest and the inflammation soothed by the application of lead lotions, ichthyol (40 per cent. in vaselin), or by fomentations. Quinine and salicin internally also appear to be of value. The general hygiene requires attention, and good food is essential. Compression of the swollen limb by properly-fitting bandages may be used with advantage where an extremity is affected. I have seen cases in which lymphangioplasty has been performed, but without obvious benefit.

Filarial Elephantiasis.

The most common sites are the legs, and also the penis and scrotum and the clitoris. The leg is enormously swollen, suggesting the leg of the elephant. The skin is greatly thickened, and adherent to the underlying structures. On palpation the limb feels like hide or wood, especially in the lower parts. The surface may be smooth and of the normal colour, or brownish or purplish in tint. In some cases it is covered with warty excrescences varying in size from a millet seed to a small nut. The warty growths may be closely aggregated and there may be numerous lymphangiectases which give exit to large quantities of lymph. The surface in cases of long duration undergoes maceration, and ulceration occurs, with the formation of sanious foul

discharge.   From time to time there are attacks of " filarial fever,"
attended with pyrexia and increase in the swelling of the limb.
These appear to be due to microbic invasion and are of the same
nature as the attacks seen in elephantiasis in temperate regions.

Filarial elephantiasis usually affects one leg, but occasionally
both lower extremities are involved.   The upper limbs are rarely

FIG. 173.—Filarial elephantiasis of Leg.   (From Dr. Daniels'
"Tropical Medicine and Hygiene.")

affected.   Next to the legs the external genitals are the parts most
frequently affected.   In the male the scrotum may be enormously
enlarged, often attaining the dimensions of the adult head.   The
swelling is pear-shaped, with the apex upwards, and the penis may
disappear in the swollen mass.   The surface of the scrotal tumour
may be smooth or warty.   In the female the vulva may be similarly
affected, the labia attaining an enormous size.

Filarial elephantiasis may be associated with chyluria, chylous ascites and hydrocele, lymph scrotum, etc.   It is, however, not the rule for patients with filariasis to suffer from elephantiasis, and sometimes it is impossible to find the filaria sanguinis hominis in the blood of patients with extreme elephantiasis.   There is still some doubt as to whether the parasite causes obstruction of the lymphatics or

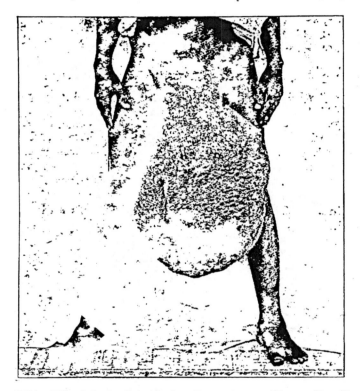

FIG. 173.—Filarial elephantiasis of scrotum. (From Dr. Daniels' "Tropical Medicine and Hygiene.")

predisposes to lymphatic inflammations of bacterial origin.   The phenomena of filarial fever point to the latter.   In extreme cases ligature of the femoral artery has been practised in elephantiasis of the leg.   Amputation of the enlarged scrotum may be necessary.   In early cases removal of the patient to a temperate climate has proved beneficial.   The injection of thiosinamin or fibrolysin, 2 to 4 c.c. daily, is recommended by Castellani.

REFERENCES.—C. DANIELS. *Journ. Trop. Med.*, XI., p. 280. G. C. LOW. *Ibid.*, March 5, 1911. SIR PATRICK MANSON'S article in "Allbutt and Rolleston's System," VI., p. 825.

Trophoedema (Meige).

A rare variety of pesudo-elephantiasis of probably nervous origin, characterised by chronic œdema which passes on to induration.

Clinical features. The lower limbs are the parts most frequently affected, but the upper extremities and the face are occasionally attacked. The onset may be attended with neuralgic pains, but there are no symptoms of inflammation. Sometimes there is exaggeration of the tendon-reflexes. The parts are swollen and œdematous, but the skin is smooth and retains its natural colour. There are, however, deep adhesions which prevent the integument being pinched up. In most cases the affected areas gradually become indurated and fibrous, in others the lesions are hard when first observed. The disease is unattended with any symptoms and remains stationary for years. · It only causes trouble by the impairment of movement. Spontaneous resolution may occur.

It is interesting to note that somewhat similar conditions have been observed in association with anterior polio-myelitis and lesions of the spinal cord.

Regular massage of the parts is advocated.

CHAPTER XVIII.

NEURODERMATOSES.

THE commonest form of neurodermatosis is itching, a peculiar subjective phenomenon which is caused by local irritation, by certain forms of cutaneous disease, and affections of the nervous system.

Itching is excited in every one by some forms of irritation, but the intensity of the subjective phenomena varies a great deal in different subjects. What would excite an uncontrollable desire to scratch in one person causes very little discomfort in another. Use dulls the sensibility, and explains the tolerance of animal parasites met with in the tramp, a tolerance which is inconceivable to a person of cleanly habits. On the other hand, some persons are morbidly sensitive, and suggestion, even the thought of one of the common parasites, is followed by a sensation of itching. In practice it is not uncommon to meet with an actual obsession, a parasito-phobia.

Contact with the hairs of the stinging-nettle, and of some forms of caterpillar, the peregrinations and bites of the flea, louse or bug, and the presence of the acarus scabiei in burrows in the skin all cause intense itching. In these cases the pruritus may be looked upon as physiological, scratching being the natural defence of the organism against intruders.

In many healthy persons exposure of the skin to the air, especially if the parts have been compressed by the corset, garters, etc., may cause pruritus.

Itching, again, is a frequent symptom of certain cutaneous diseases, and may precede or accompany obvious changes in the integument. It is most common in eczema, urticaria, lichen planus, dermatitis herpetiformis, mycosis fungoides and leukæmic eruptions and in some drug rashes.

The act of scratching itself may induce pruritus in the area scratched or in some distant part, and it may be difficult to determine how far the itching is primary or secondary.

Pruritus.

The name pruritus is given to certain neurodermatoses which appear to be independent of local irritation and of actual pathological changes in the skin. It may be local or general.

Etiology. Pruritus is most common between the ages of thirty and forty, but may occur at any age ; both sexes are equally affected. There is often a history of neuroses of other kinds in the family, and some races are more affected than others. Pruritus is very common in the United States, and among the Jews.

Predisposing causes. Some cases appear to depend upon seasonal variations, and upon climate. The subjects of pruritus are often worried, anxious, overworked or melancholic—the type of " neurotic " met with in our large cities. In other cases the predisposing cause is obesity, excess of nitrogenous food, or the abuse of alcohol, tea, coffee, or drugs, such as cocaine and morphia.

The circulation of toxic bodies in the blood may cause pruritus. It is a common feature in glycosuria, gout, jaundice, and some forms of uræmia, and in chronic dyspepsia and constipation. Pregnancy and uterine and ovarian disease are frequently accompanied by local or general pruritus, and the phenomenon may be toxic or reflex. Leukæmia and similar grave blood diseases are also often attended with intense pruritus. Itching is also met with in Graves' disease.

Itching is also an occasional symptom of organic disease of the nervous system, *e.g.,* tabes, general paralysis, hemiplegia and cerebral tumour.

Exciting causes. Nearly all forms of pruritus are made worse, and some are distinctly excited, by exposure of the skin to the air, by changes of temperature, and hot or cold baths. In some patients the ingestion of food, tea, coffee, or alcohol starts an attack. In others certain articles of diet, shell-fish, condiments, spices, even cheese, are the excitants. But in many of the most intractable cases no exciting cause can be traced, and the attack may waken the sufferer from an apparently sound sleep.

Symptoms. Pruritus is essentially subjective, and examination reveals nothing but the evidence of scratching. In a characteristic case of the severe type the patient is seized with an intense desire to scratch. He may make heroic endeavours to control this desire, but usually without success. Pressure, friction, or the application of heat or cold may be tried with little or no relief, and finally the sufferer gives way, and tears and mutilates the itching areas of skin with his nails. In a few cases an attempt is made to dig out the offending spots; I have seen this most marked in the pruritus of leukæmia, but it is not confined to this condition.

The excoriations produced by scratching are usually linear, but punctate lesions are not uncommon. Infection of the scratch lesions by pus cocci leads to impetigo and enlargement of the neighbouring lymphatic glands. In chronic cases an eczematous dermatitis is produced, or the parts may undergo a lichenification.

An attack of pruritus may last from a few minutes to several hours, and there is a tendency for the itching to return exactly in the same position after an interval.

Generalised pruritus. Where the itching is general, the first point in practice is to exclude the irritation of parasites, and careful examination should be made for scabies and pediculosis. Next, it is important to inquire as to constipation and dyspepsia, to examine the urine for albumen and sugar, and to inspect the patient in a good light to avoid overlooking jaundice. In the female, pregnancy and ovarian disease may be the cause of the pruritus, and these require careful inquiry and examination. The nervous system must not be forgotten, for itching is an occasional symptom of tabes, general paralysis, etc. Mycosis fungoides must be remembered as a cause of severe and persistent itching of the skin, which may long precede the evolution of the characteristic tumours. The possibility of the pruritus being due to leukæmia necessitates the examination of the blood.

Graves' disease and lymphadenoma may also be causes of general pruritus.

In certain cases, however, the cause eludes the most careful search, but only after a thorough examination is one justified in concluding that the pruritus is primary.

In true senile pruritus the skin is dry, inelastic and withered. There may be very little evidence of scratching, for the senile skin appears to be unusually resistant.

The prognosis depends upon whether the cause can be found and removed. In the true senile type treatment has little influence.

Treatment. The remarks made above emphasise the importance of treating the cause. The parasitic forms of pruritus are dealt with elsewhere. Glycosuria, renal disease, and other general affections are treated on the usual lines. If no definite cause can be found, the diet should receive careful attention. It should consist largely of milk and vegetables; meat should be taken in limited quantity, and alcohol in any form should be forbidden. Tea and coffee are also better avoided. The bowels should be regulated, and the condition of the teeth should be carefully examined, and, if necessary, the aid of the dentist should be invoked. In nervous subjects, rest, avoidance of worry, residence in the country or by the sea should be obtained if possible. In hospital practice a few weeks in the wards produce a remarkable improvement, which unfortunately often disappears on the patient's returning to the usual routine of life. Lumbar puncture has been advocated by some authors, but of its value I have no experience.

Internal medication. Bromides, valerian, phenacetin, antipyrin, and quinine may be given with advantage, especially at night. In overworked, nervous subjects iron, strychnine, and arsenic are often of value.

Local treatment. Bran, gelatine or oatmeal added to the bath, or weak alkaline baths, sometimes give relief. Tepid and warm douches applied to the affected parts daily for five minutes are also advocated. Static electric baths and high-frequency treatment may also be tried. In some cases short exposures to the X-rays every fourteen days relieve the itching remarkably. Tar and lead lotion ; carbolic acid, 2 to 5 per cent. ; salicylic acid, 2 to 10 per cent. ; chloral hydrate, 2 per cent. ; resorcin, 2 per cent. ; and menthol, 2 to 10 per cent., may all be tried, and it is often necessary to change the application from time to time. To protect the parts from air, plasters, pastes, and varnishes (see Formulæ) may be applied, but in the worst type of case the treatment taxes the ingenuity and the patience of the medical attendant, the remedies having to be changed frequently.

Local Forms of Pruritus.

Pruritus ani. Itching at the anus is the commonest form of local pruritus. The parts affected are the anal canal and a circum-scribed area about an inch wide around the orifice. The itching is often intense, and may lead to extreme nervous depression and melancholia. The peri-anal skin is often severely excoriated by scratching, and may be in an eczematous condition with radiating fissures. This eczematous eruption may extend forwards into the perineum and backwards into the gluteal cleft. In long-standing cases the skin becomes thickened, tough and parchment-like.

Etiology. Pruritus ani is more common in the male than in the female. It may occur at any age from local causes, but the peculiarly intractable neurotic form is most frequent in middle life and in old age. The local conditions which may cause itching must be carefully considered before any case is classed as being neurotic. They are :— (1) Thread-worms, which are the commonest cause of itching in this region in children, but it must be remembered that occasionally the oxyuris may persist to adult life ; (2) hæmorrhoids, fissures, polypi. A careful examination will often show that there are small superficial fissures or ulcers between the corrugations which are present in the skin of this region ; (3) chronic proctitis, with irritating discharges ; (4) chronic constipation, which may cause irritation by congestion and by the passage of hard scybalous masses ; (5) pelvic tumours also cause chronic congestion. In the female the presence of leucorrhœa may start a vulvar irritation, which spreads to the anal region.

The general conditions requiring attention are chronic constipation, hepatic cirrhosis, dietetic errors, alcoholism and the excessive use of coffee and tobacco, diabetes and renal disease.

The *prognosis* depends upon whether the local or general condition causing the pruritus can be removed. The intractable cases are those in which nothing but the evidence of scratching is found locally.

Treatment. The local conditions mentioned must be dealt with by appropriate measures. Glycosuria, renal disease, hepatic cirrhosis and the other general affections are treated on the usual lines. Alcohol, coffee and the excessive use of tobacco must be avoided, and the diet requires careful regulation. If necessary aperients must be administered to ensure a daily evacuation of the bowels, and it is important that the parts should be carefully cleansed after defæcation. This is best done with a pad of wet cotton-wool, and after careful drying a powder containing equal parts of zinc oxide and starch or talc should be applied. The addition of a little calomel (5 per cent.) to this powder is often of great service. If there is much thickening of the skin, benefit is derived by painting the part with pure carbolic acid, which causes exfoliation, and leaves a superficial denuded area, which heals up rapidly under Lassar's paste (Zinc oxid. 24 parts, Starch 24 parts, Acid salicylic 2 parts, Vaselin 50 parts). The patient should remain in bed until the parts are healed. If there is eczematisation or infection with pus-cocci, mild antiseptic ointments are most useful. An associated proctitis is treated by injections of warm boric acid lotion.

In the purely neurotic cases the patience of the sufferer and of his medical attendant is sorely tried, and the large number of remedies suggested is evidence of the intractable nature of the affection. It is frequently necessary to change the application to find out what suits the condition best. In some instances greasy applications appear to be irritant, in others they are the only form tolerated. In mild cases Lassar's paste or a zinc ointment with a little salicylic acid (2 per cent.) is useful. In others carbolic acid (1 in 20) in vaselin, menthol 2 to 10 per cent., weak tar or ichthyol ointments may be of service. The application of a sponge wrung out in hot water and applied to the part will sometimes give the patient sufficient relief to enable him to get off to sleep. It is sometimes necessary to have recourse to cocain and morphia, either in the form of ointment or as a suppository, but the risk in a neurotic subject of inducing a drug habit makes it imperative to give these remedies with great caution.

Great benefit is often obtained by the local use of the high-frequency electrode, but I have seen more general relief from the X-rays, a half-pastille dose being given every fourteen days. Care must, of

28—2

course, be taken to protect the scrotum in these applications. Radium on a flat applicator has also proved of service.

Hypnotics may be required at night, and bromides, valerian, phenacetin, and quinine may be tried. General tonic treatment and the avoidance of worry, with a change to the sea or a sea-trip, are of value in debilitated nervous subjects. Hypnotic suggestion has been tried with success in some cases.

Pruritus vulvæ is another common and most distressing form of local pruritus. It may be associated with a similar condition at the anus or be independent of it. Glycosuria is a common cause, and the irritation of thread-worms must not be forgotten. Local irritation by vaginal discharges must be looked for, and, failing evidence of this, the condition of the uterus, ovaries and tubes must be investigated. Pruritus vulvæ is a common phenomenon in pregnancy and is then apparently due to congestion. In some women there is pruritus at the catamenia, and it is not uncommon at the climacteric. The irritation may lead to masturbation, and it is believed this practice may cause the pruritus. Eczematisation of the parts may be induced by scratching, and local infection with pus organisms.

As in pruritus ani, some of the most intractable cases show no evidence of local disease, and a careful examination reveals nothing but the evidence of scratching. There is the same underlying neurotic condition, and the same mental depression and tendency to melancholia. The pruritus is rarely constant, but there are attacks of intolerable itching when warm in bed or on taking exercise.

The *prognosis* depends upon the recognition and appropriate treatment of the local causative conditions. Where none are found the outlook is very unsatisfactory.

The *treatment* is on the same lines as that of pruritus ani. In some mild cases soothing ointments and pastes containing zinc and a little salicylic acid are sufficient. In others the use of carbolic acid, menthol, chloretone and other analgesics may be of service. These remedies are applied on lint strips, which should be placed between the labia and extend on the cutaneous surface. The high-frequency treatment is sometimes useful, and great relief may often be obtained from applications of the X-rays (half the Sabouraud pastille dose every fourteen days). In a very intractable case, which had resisted all the usual remedies, including the X-rays and high frequency, I found that two applications of radium on a plate cured the pruritus.

The general treatment is that indicated in pruritus ani. Regular action of the bowels, a non-stimulating diet, the exclusion of alcohol and coffee, and in the neurotic cases general tonics are required.

In some cases excision of the itching area has been performed. The results are occasionally satisfactory, but I have seen several instances in which the pruritus has returned.

Pruritus of the external genitals in the male is not so common as in the female. It may be the result of glycosuria, and of urethral and prostatic affections, which require careful examination.

Pruritus sometimes occurs about the *nose* in association with intranasal conditions, naso-pharyngitis, etc. Dental caries and buccal sepsis may cause similar irritation about the *mouth*. The *scalp* is affected in association with pityriasis, etc.

Palmar and **plantar pruritus** are uncommon. They may occur in the auto-intoxications.

The treatment of the cause is indicated in all these local forms of pruritus. If no cause is evident the general lines indicated above should be followed.

REFERENCES. — "The Sensation of Itching." E. B. BRONSON. "Selected Monographs on Dermatology." *New Sydenham Society*, 1893. Also *British Journal of Dermatology*, VII., p. 291. (Discussion.) J. L. BUNCH. *Lancet*, 1910, I., 1251. "Pruritus due to Tobacco." BOTTSTEIN. *Monatsheft f. prakt. Dermatol.*, 1904, XXXIX., p. 577. "In Renal Disease." VEIEL. *Archiv. f. Dermat. in Syph.*, 1906, LXXX., p. 59. "Pruritus Ani." P. L. MUMMERY. *Practitioner*, 1907, p. 686. F. C. WALLIS. *Brit. Med. Journ.*, 1909, II., p. 452. "Pruritus Vulvæ." F. J. McCANN. *Polyclinic*, 1905, p. 130.

Prurigo.

The name " prurigo " is applied to a group of itching, papular eruptions. In the opinion of many authors, the pruritus is primary, and the papules are produced as a special reaction of the skin to scratching. By others the papules are looked upon as the essential feature, the itching being secondary. Prurigo, like other itching affections, is often complicated by pyogenic infection and with eczematous conditions produced by scratching.

Strophulus or gum rash is the commonest variety of prurigo. The more grave affection, called after Hebra, is uncommon in this country, and there are somewhat rare generalised and local conditions of milder type which require consideration in this place.

Strophulus (Gum Rash. Papular Urticaria. Lichen urticatus. Simple Prurigo).

Etiology. Strophulus is a disease of early infancy. It usually occurs about the period of dentition, and is so common that very few children do not suffer from it to a greater or less degree. Occasionally it may appear in older children. It is often associated with over-feeding and with improper feeding, and with gastro-intestinal troubles, constipation, diarrhœa, foul motions, etc. It is doubtful whether dental irritation is so important as the association of digestive disorders. By some strophulus is classed as a neurodermatosis, and it is considered as a form of prurigo. The actual cause is unknown, but there is great probability that it is a toxic affection.

Pathology. The papule of strophulus is a papillary œdema, with the infiltration of leucocytes and dilatation of vessels. The corpus mucosum is also œdematous, and under the stratum corneum there is a mass of imperfectly formed corneous cells, with a spongy condition of the cells of the epidermis resembling that seen in eczema.

Clinical features. The onset is acute, the child often being in good health, or perhaps a little out of sorts on account of the eruption of a tooth. The rash consists of papules and urticarial wheals. The wheal is evanescent, while the papule lasts for several days. Each papule is about the size of a pin's head, or a little larger, of a pale pink colour, or sometimes little different from the normal tint of the skin. The top of the papule often presents a tiny scale or yellowish point. In rare cases the lesion is vesicular. The papule is firm to the touch, and at the onset it is situated in the centre of a small wheal, which disappears in three or four hours. The papule itself lasts a week to a fortnight. Hence on examination the papules outnumber the wheals, but inspection at night will usually show fresh wheals. The top of the papule is often torn off by the scratching of the child, and a small blood crust is found at the apex. The lesions leave small brown stains.

The eruption occurs on the upper limbs and the trunk, and later on the lower limbs, preferring the extensor surfaces. In bad cases the face and neck may be affected, but the palms and soles nearly always escape. Crops of four or five to a dozen or more lesions appear, and continue to come out daily for weeks. All stages of the lesions are thus present in a marked case. The eruption, as a whole, may last for three or four weeks to as many months, and recurrences occur during the whole period of dentition in some children, and even after the eruption of the teeth has ceased. As a rule, however, strophulus clears up when the child is three years old, and, if it should persist, there is a probability that the condition is Hebra's prurigo (*vide infra*).

The itching is intense, the unfortunate child tearing itself constantly in the endeavour to find relief from the pruritus.

Diagnosis. Strophulus has to be distinguished from urticaria, which has no characteristic papule, and from scabies, which is characterised by burrows and specially affects the hands and feet, and from sudamina, where there will be excessive sweating. In older children the eruption may simulate papular erythema—which chiefly affects the backs of the hands and the elbows—and papular eczema, which is often associated with oozing areas, or there may be a history of weeping. The vesicular lesions may suggest varicella, but the long continuance of the eruption and the absence of the peculiar glassy vesicles of chicken-pox should prevent mistakes.

Prognosis. The eruption tends to recur during the period of dentition, and the attacks vary greatly in intensity, but usually clear up in three or four weeks to as many months.

Treatment. The condition of the alimentary canal and the diet require careful attention. The meals must be given at regular intervals, and the common practice among the poor of letting the infants have food more suited to older children and adults must be prohibited. Small doses of magnesia and rhubarb and fractional doses of calomel are usually given with great benefit. The child should be bathed in a weak alkaline solution, one drachm of sod. bicarb. to the gallon. The itching is usually relieved by the application of an ointment of naphthol, 2 per cent.

Hebra's Prurigo.

This form of prurigo is exceedingly chronic. It begins in infancy and persists to adult life. It is characterised by intense itching, a widespread papular eruption, and secondary changes in the skin produced by scratching.

Etiology. The cause is unknown. The disease has been seen associated with asthma.

Pathology. The prurigo papule has at the onset an urticarial character, viz., œdema of the true skin, with proliferation about the vessel walls. The horny layer of the epidermis is thickened and split to form vesicles, the papillæ and upper layers of the cutis are infiltrated with cells, while the arrectores pilorum are thickened and contracted, so that the hair follicles are in a state of erection. In the latter stages the vesicles in the stratum corneum become pustules. The ultimate condition of the skin is chronic thickening of the prickle and corneous layers, with obliteration of many of the fine furrows of the surface, flattening of the papillæ, and disappearance of the panniculus adiposus from compression. The whole integument is thus coarsened and toughened.

Clinical features. At the onset it is practically impossible to distinguish this affection from strophulus. It begins in the first year of life, and at the age of three is characterised by intense itching, the child constantly scratching, and producing innumerable excoriations of the punctate or linear type. Sometimes there are slight remissions in the severity of the symptoms, depending to some extent upon the seasons.

In a characteristic case the skin has an earthy colour, the surface resembles goose-flesh from the projection of the hair follicles, numbers of small pale or red papules are present, and, as a rule, large areas of excoriation, linear or punctate, with scabs or crusts. Localised or diffuse patches of eczematous dermatitis and of pus infection are produced by the constant scratching. In the advanced cases the whole integument feels thick and tough. The extensor surfaces of the limbs are the parts most affected ; the trunk is often involved, while the face is usually free. The lymphatic glands in the groins and axillæ are enlarged, and may suppurate (Fig. 174).

The children are irritable, nervous, and wasted, and insomnia from the itching is common. As a rule, the disease prevents the child from attending school, but at puberty, or, perhaps, as late as twenty-five, there is a tendency to spontaneous resolution, but in some cases the prurigo persists to adult life.

Different observers have described several types of the affection. In the type described by Hebra the intensity of the eruption is greatest on the lower limbs, while in the form to which Besnier's name is sometimes given the flexures of the knees and elbows, the face and neck are chiefly affected. Like the Hebra type, the disease usually begins in childhood, is intensely irritable, and produces a profound influence on the nervous system. The affected areas are diffusely lichenised, and attacks of weeping eczema with fissuring are common. It may persist to adult life.

Under the name *Prurigo Ferox*, Vidal described some fortunately rare cases, in which the lesions are larger and affect the face as well as the trunk and extremities. The itching is terrible.

Diagnosis. Hebra's prurigo has to be distinguished from other itching eruptions. It is impossible at the onset to detect any difference between this affection and strophulus, and some maintain that Hebra's prurigo is only a severe and persistent form of the common disease. The continuance of the prurigo beyond the age of three years should at once rai e the suspicion of the graver malady. Stress is laid upon the involvement of the lymphatic glands, which are rarely so much affected in other pruritic affections. I have, however, seen suppurating glands in the groin in a severe case of lichen planus. Scabies and other parasitic diseases are eliminated by the finding of the parasite. The early on-set of the affection excludes the pruriginous conditions associated with leukæmia and mycosis fungoides.

Prognosis. The disease is highly refractory to treatment.

Treatment. The patients as a rule require tonics. Cod-liver oil, iron and arsenic should be given, and good feeding is essential. Daily baths, preferably alkaline, and the use of soaps containing solutions of coal-tar or naph-thol are useful to allay the irritation, and I usually pre-scribe an ointment of naph-thol, 2 per cent., or liq. carbonis detergens, 20 minims and upwards to the ounce. Inunction of the surface with oil has been strongly recom-mended in the chronic cases, and I can endorse the efficacy of this measure.

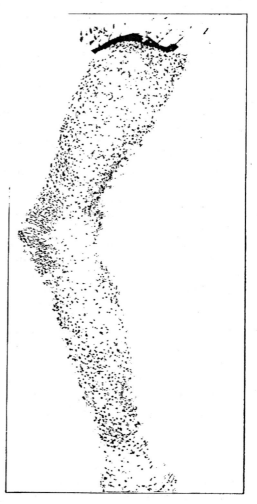

Fig. 174.—Hebra's prurigo in a boy, aged 13. The eruption had been pre-sent since infancy.

Common Prurigo.

Common prurigo is a less severe affection, and by many authors the difference is held to be one of degree only.

It may be *diffuse* or *localised*. In both forms there may be a history of heredity. The patients are often nervous, worried, and anxious. Errors in diet, alcoholism, etc., are alleged causes. The **diffuse form** may start in childhood, but is commonest between twenty and thirty, and is rare after fifty. The onset is acute, and one attack lasts for a few weeks. Recurrences are often seasonal. The itching is continuous, but always worse at night. Scratching may cause erythema and urticaria, but very soon the papular eruption becomes obvious. The papules are pale or red, of small size and ill-defined. The affected area may become deeply pigmented, while scratching causes eczematous dermatitis, excoriations, and impetigo. The disease may last for months or years, and is sometimes associated with asthma, hay fever, bronchitis, and uterine disorders.

Hutchinson's summer prurigo, which appears to be dependent upon exposure to sun, etc., and affects the face, the backs of the hands, and other exposed parts, has already been considered (*vide* p. 74).

The **circumscribed** varieties of **prurigo** are most common in women. The same etiological factors have been noticed. Of 35 cases, of which I have notes, 18 were males and 17 females, their ages varying from 13 to 82. Twenty-six of the 35 were between 30 and 60. The posterior part of the neck, the tops of the thighs, the genital region, and the gluteal cleft, the external surfaces of the legs, and the popliteal and axillary spaces are most often affected, but the disease may occur anywhere. In some cases constant friction is the cause, as of the inner side of the thigh in riding men, or of the elbows where occupation or habit induces leaning. Vidal described some of these cases under the name of **Lichen simplex chronicus.** The areas are usually oval, perhaps the size of the hand, of a violet-red colour, distinctly infiltrated, and with a peculiar quadrillated surface (Fig. 175). The margin is pigmented for about a quarter of an inch, and insdie it is an area on which the papules are closely set, of hemispherical shape, and often with excoriations caused by the scratching. In the centre there is a patch where the lichenisation reaches its maximum, the skin being deeply pigmented or devoid of pigment. The surface is often somewhat scaly, but in a flexure it becomes macerated by the warmth and moisture. The disease may last for several months to two years or more. Dr. Adamson recently showed a young woman at the Royal Society of Medicine, in whom the lesions had been present for eight years. Recurrences are frequent, and sometimes fresh plaques develop. The papular condition gradually disappears, leaving a brownish stain which may last for a long time, but cases are recorded in which leucodermia has been associated with localised prurigo. There is no general pruritus, and no urticaria factitia.

The **diagnosis** is sometimes attended with difficulty. The prurigos have to be distinguished from lichen planus, from the seborrhoides, from chronic eczema, and from some of the syphilides. The intense itching and the long duration are important features. The papules of lichen planus are flat and shining, their colour is peculiar, and Wickham's striæ and points are present, and there are often buccal lesions. The seborrhoides are associated with scaliness of the scalp, and their distribution is mainly in the middle line of the trunk and in the flexures. In chronic eczema there is usually a history of previous vesication, and in syphilis there are the general symptoms and absence of itching upon which the differential diagnosis is based.

FIG. 175.—Circumscribed prurigo. Lichen simplex chronicus. The inner side of the thigh of a woman, aged 52.

Treatment. The treatment of the chronic localised prurigos is often unsatisfactory. A simple plan is to cover the areas with an adhesive dressing of plaster, such as the leucoplast of Unna, but in chronic cases the X-rays in pastille doses at intervals of three weeks best relieve the itching and promote the absorption of the infiltration. The local application of the vacuum electrode is also recommended.

REFERENCES.—Discussion at the International Dermatological Congress, 1896. UNNA. "Histopathology" (translated by NORMAN WALKER), pp. 132 et seq. SIR MALCOLM MORRIS. "Prurigo, Pruriginous Eczema and Lichenification." *British Medical Journal*, 1912, I., p. 1469, and discussion, *British Journal of Dermatology*, 1912, p. 245. C. Rasch. "Besnier's Prurigo." Review, *British Journal of Dermatology*, XXVII., p. 104.

Prurigo nodularis. Urticaria perstans verrucosa. Under these and other names are described cases of an intensely pruritic dermatosis characterised by the formation of small, rounded nodules on the extremities. The eruption may remain unchanged or with slight remissions for years. The exact relationships of the condition are not clear. Schamberg has seen it in negroes.

References.—J. Zeisler. *Journ. Cut. Dis.*, 1912, p. 654. Hübner. *Archiv. f. Dermat.*, LXXXI., p. 1906.

Herpes simplex (Herpes labialis. Herpes genitalis).

An acute eruption of vesicles occurring on the lips, nostrils, or other parts of the face, on the genital organs, buttocks, nipples, and mucous membranes, but very rarely elsewhere.

Etiology. The cause is obscure. Herpes occurs at any age, but is commonest in adolescence and adult life. The disease is not contagious and not inoculable. A lymphocytic reaction has been found in the cerebro-spinal fluid in twenty-one out of twenty-six cases examined by Raveul and Darren. Herpes simplex is symptomatic in pneumonia, cerebro-spinal meningitis, and in influenza, "catarrh," etc. It occurs in association with dental caries, naso-pharyngeal catarrh, disease of the middle ear. and of the sinuses. Labial herpes sometimes recurs at the menstrual epoch. I have seen two cases in which recurrent patches appeared on the buttock at each menstrual epoch during several years. Traumatism may determine an outbreak, and dental operations are sometimes followed by labial herpes. In males. sexual excess, especially with different women, is a frequent cause. Recently I saw herpes appearing over the area of the mental nerve after the application of radium to a small tumour on the edge of the auricle on the same side. The herpetic outbreak followed each application of the radium. Fournier has pointed out that some syphilitic subjects suffer from recurrent labial herpes, which he suggests may be the result of the abuse of mercury.

Clinical features. There is often a premonitory sensation of heat or tension, which may last for some hours, and then a red spot appears, on which rounded vesicles rapidly develop. The vesicles are the size of a pin's head, and they vary in number from two or three to several dozens. Sometimes they are so closely packed that they become confluent. The contents are usually clear serum, but this soon becomes opaque, the vesicles dry up, and in the course of a week or ten days the yellowish-brown scale which is formed drops off, leaving a temporarily red spot. There is no scar. Sometimes the groups are multiple and irregularly placed. In a boy of six under my care both auricles and the upper and lower lips and the middle third of the tongue were involved. The nearest lymphatic glands are slightly swollen.

In very rare instances the serum is replaced by blood.

Herpes simplex occurs on the lips (*herpes labialis*). on the nostrils, or on any part of the face, and on the auricles (Fig. 176).

Herpes genitalis. In the male the eruption usually appears on

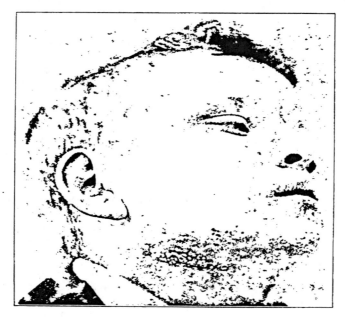

FIG. 176.—Herpes simplex.

the sulcus between the glans and the prepuce. On covered parts the vesicles early become erosions from friction and moisture. The lesions are very superficial. discrete and confluent, forming irregular figures. The eroded surfaces are red and slightly oozing, and occasionally covered with a diphtheria-like membrane. They are slightly painful, but there is no induration of the base, and if unirritated, they heal up in a week or ten days. If irritated. for instance with the silver-stick, they may ulcerate. the healing is delayed, and scarring may result.

In the female any part of the vulva may be affected. and in rare cases the vesicles appear on the vaginal wall and on the cervix uteri. Occasionally the symptoms are severe, there is slight fever and intense pain and œdema. From the vulva the eruption may spread to the pubic area and down the thighs. The ruptured vesicles are covered with a greyish-white membrane, and the exudation is fœtid. The glands in the groin are enlarged and tender, and the patient has to be confined to bed. These severe cases may last for two or three weeks. Genital herpes often follows illicit intercourse. The breaches of surface due to the herpetic lesions are doubtless a common source of syphilitic infection.

Rarer forms of recurrent herpes. Fig. 177 illustrates a case of recurrent *gluteal* herpes. This may occur at the menstrual periods,

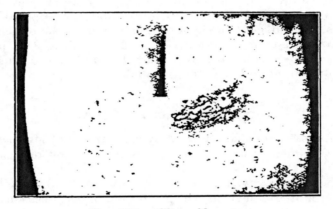

FIG. 177.—Gluteal herpes.

and I have seen a case in which there was a chronic prostatitis. Recurrent herpes of the edge of the *auricle* is occasionally seen. The cause is very difficult to locate. I have seen a recurrent herpes on the cheek in a child which ceased upon the removal of adenoids and hypertrophied tonsils. A medical friend suffered from recurrent herpes following irido-cychitis. In a boy of four I observed four attacks of herpes on the radial side of the left index finger in fifteen months. The first attack followed pneumonia. In another case already mentioned the application of radium to the ear was always followed by a herpes of the mental area on the same side. Such cases suggest a peripheral irritation which should be carefully investigated.

Herpes of the mucous membranes. Buccal herpes is very rare. The mucous membrane of the cheeks, palate and tongue may be involved. The vesicles are of short duration, but speedily become erosions. Similar affections of the pharynx and conjunctiva occur.

Diagnosis. As a rule herpes about the face offers no difficulty. Dr. Head insists on the essential difference of this form of herpes from herpes zoster. The diagnosis of the genital forms is often of the utmost importance. Herpetic lesions are often thought to be chancres, but the absence of induration should exclude syphilis, and the diagnosis can be made absolute by the finding of the spirochæte. Soft sores are more ulcerated, and the bubo which forms tends to suppurate.

Treatment. The essential point is to cover the lesions and protect them from irritation. This may be done by the application of powders of zinc oxide and starch or talc. Greasy and moist applications are best avoided, unless there is actual ulceration. Irritants should not be applied. Frequent bathing of the parts, especially in the genital cases, with boric acid lotion and the application of a powder usually suffice. In the severe vulvar cases the patient should be put to bed and fomentations applied to relieve the pain and swelling. If the condition is recurrent, the underlying cause should be carefully sought and, if found, treated.

Herpes zoster. Zona.

An acute infection characterised by an eruption of grouped vesicles upon an inflamed base, occupying a nerve area on one side of the body.

Etiology. Herpes zoster occurs at any age and in either sex. It is rather more frequent in the spring than in other seasons, and one commonly meets with pseudo-epidemics, several cases coming under observation about the same time, suggesting a climatic cause. Recently attention has been directed to the possible relationship of herpes and varicella. I have seen varicella develop in a child twelve days after the mother had an attack of herpes zoster, and many similar cases are on record. The actual origin is obscure, but the usual type may very probably be toxic or bacterial, for there are often general symptoms, the lymphatic glands are always enlarged, and there is an excess of polynuclear leucocytes in the blood. The actual changes in the posterior root ganglion cells are similar to those occurring in the anterior horn cells in anterior polio-myelitis. Head and Campbell found hæmorrhages or destructive inflammation leading to cicatricial changes in the ganglia. As Hutchinson long ago pointed out, the prolonged administration of arsenic may be followed by herpes zoster, and this drug has a peculiar effect upon ganglionic cells, as evidenced by the production of peripheral neuritis, affecting the motor side. In the active stage of herpes zoster, lymphocytosis of the cerebro-spinal fluid has been demonstrated, and Kernig's sign has been observed.

There are, however, two other conditions in which herpes zoster appears. It is symptomatic of certain affections of the spinal cord, viz., tabes, general paralysis of the insane, dementia, and meningomyelitis. Irritation of the nerve roots by traumatism, tuberculous infiltration. gummata and cancer may also cause herpes.

Fig. 178. —Herpes zoster.

Pathology. The actual lesions of herpes zoster are deep-seated vesicles, containing serous fluid, and in rare cases blood. The vesicles are unilocular, the base being formed of the papillary layer. The cavity is filled with swollen epithelial cells, which have lost their prickle processes. The papillæ are swollen and their vessels are dilated. Head and Campbell have shown that not only are the fine terminal twigs of the nerves in the lesions inflamed, but that the larger branches show degenerative changes ten days after the onset of the eruption.

Plate 40.

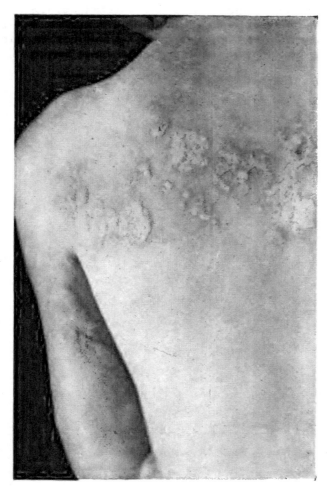

HERPES ZOSTER.

An early case, showing grouped vesicles on an inflamed base in band
form on the back and down the upper arm.   (Dorsal II. and III.)

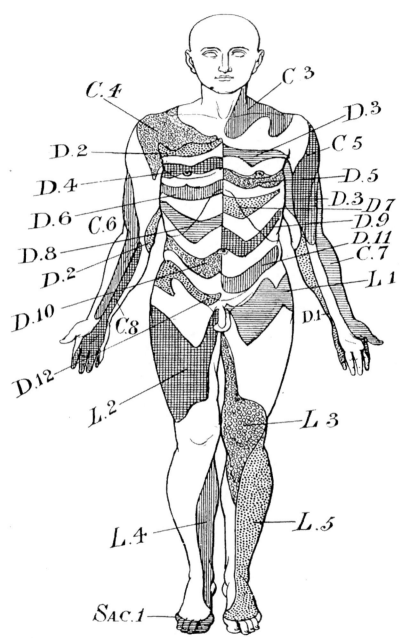

C.4 C.3 D.3 D.2 C.5 D.4 D.5 D.6 D.3 D.7 C.6 D.9 D.8 D.11 D.2 C.7 L.1 D.10 D.1 C.8 D.12 L.2 L.3 L.4 L.5 Sac.1

FIG. 179.—The areas of herpes zoster. (Reproduced by permission of Dr. H. Head.)

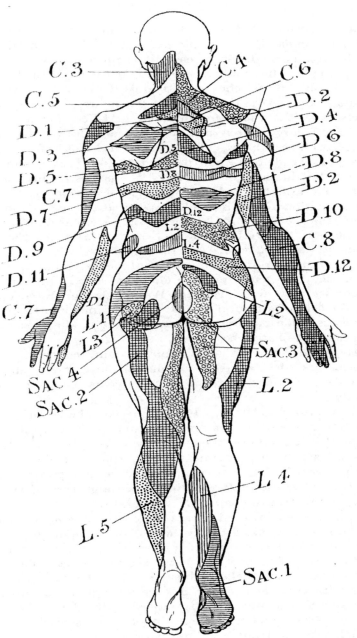

FIG. 180.—The areas of herpes zoster. (Reproduced by permission of Dr. H. Head.)

Clinical features. The eruption comes out acutely, sometimes without any premonitory symptoms, and is then noticed by the patient by accident. In other cases it is preceded by slight fever, malaise and pain, which may be severe. At the onset the lesions are oval or irregular red patches slightly raised above the level of the surrounding skin. After the lapse of a few hours vesicles appear and ultimately cover the whole of each patch. At first they are discrete, but as they enlarge, often run together and form irregular and confluent flat bullæ or blebs. The herpetic vesicle is at first about the size of a pin's head, tense and pearly in colour. The fluid is then quite clear, but in three or four days it becomes cloudy, and even purulent. Towards the end of a week the lesion begins to dry up, with the formation of a scab which drops off at the end of a fortnight. Sometimes the spots do not all come out at once, but appear in crops during the first two or three days. In rare instances the fluid is hæmorrhagic, and I have seen severe sloughing.

Herpetic vesicles rarely rupture spontaneously, but if they are ruptured, they present small circular erosions. In some cases permanent *scars* are left. Howard Warner demonstrated epithelial cysts in the scar of a frontal herpes, exactly similar to those seen in epidermolysis bullosa and pemphigus. " Glossy skin " has also been seen as a sequel to herpes zoster.

The *lymphatic glands* are always enlarged and tender.

Tenneson described aberrant vesicles in most cases, but, though I have looked carefully for them for some years, I have found them very rarely.

Pain is a variable feature. It may precede the eruption by two or three days, or longer. It may accompany the eruption, and in old people it often follows it and may be of a severe neuralgic type which is intractable to treatment. Sometimes burning sensations are complained of. The actual area may be anæsthetic, but more commonly it is hyperæsthetic, and in the neuralgic cases in the elderly exceedingly sensitive to changes of temperature.

In a recent case of frontal herpes under my care *hyperidrosis* was present for several weeks after the healing of the vesicles.

Paralysis, sometimes associated with wasting of muscles, has been reported in cases of herpes, *e.g.*, of the ocular muscles, in association with herpes of the ophthalmic division of the fifth nerve, and facial paralysis with cervical herpes. An interesting case of zoster with paralysis of the arm was recently published by Parkes Weber who gives a number of references to papers on the association of herpes with facial, cervical, trunk and limb paralyses.

Zoster fever is the name given to certain cases in which there is malaise, a temperature running up to 100° to 101° F. with furred tongue, anorexia, etc.

Areas affected (Figs. 179, 180). Intercostal herpes is the commonest. The cervical region is the next most frequently affected. The most troublesome cases are those in which the first division of the fifth cranial nerve is involved—herpes ophthalmicus. The frontal, nasal and palpebral regions are the seat of the eruption, and ocular complications are frequent. There may be conjunctivitis, keratitis punctata, and sometimes perforation of the cornea, and iritis, choroiditis and retinitis.

A special feature of herpes zoster is its unilateral distribution. Bilateral cases are very rarely met with, and some of these are of syphilitic origin. The disease occurs as a rule only once in a lifetime. I have seen a patient who had three attacks of herpes at three different levels, all on the right side. He had suffered from hemiplegia for many years. In another case the first attack was at the age of fifteen, and the second at the age of eighty. The patient had no obvious disease of the spinal cord.

Diagnosis. The presence of grouped vesicles upon an inflamed base, affecting one half of the trunk in band form, or along one limb, or involving the area supplied by one division of the fifth nerve, makes so characteristic a picture that mistakes are very rare.

Prognosis. The prognosis of herpes zoster is good, except in elderly patients. in whom the disappearance of the eruption may be followed by severe and persistent neuralgia. It is important to warn any patient in advanced life of the possibility of this complication, as popularly " shingles " is looked upon as a speedily cured and comparatively trivial malady. Again, where the lesions are in conspicuous parts, the medical man should inform the patient that there is a slight risk of permanent scarring. I have seen cheloid develop in such cicatrices.

Treatment. No moist applications should be used, and unless there is actual ulceration ointments are best avoided. I usually have the areas covered with cotton-wool, which is fastened to the skin at the margins by collodion. Powders of zinc oxide and starch may be applied. If there is ulceration and pustulation, they must be treated on general principles, with boric acid ointment spread on lint, or, if necessary, with boric acid fomentations. In the painful neuralgia of the elderly sufferers from herpes, aconite, gelsemium, aspirin, exalgine. and phenacetin may be tried, and sometimes give temporary relief. As far as possible endeavours should be made to relieve the pain without having recourse to opium or morphia. Cocaine may be used, provided it is kept under the control of the

Plate 41.

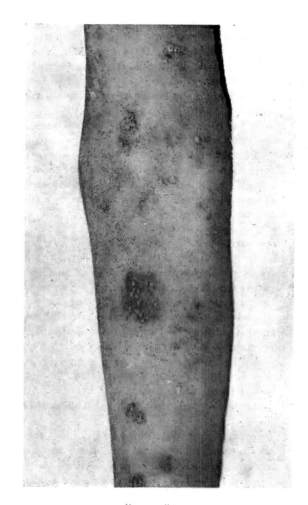

HERPES ZOSTER.

Grouped vesicles on inflamed base on the arm and forearm.
(Cervical VIII.)

physician. I have several times seen great benefit follow the use of the X-rays. Small repeated doses, with all precautions to prevent dermatitis, should be given. MacNab reports relief of pain in frontal herpes by ionisation with a solution of quinine.

REFERENCES.—v. BÄRENSPRUNG. "Charité Annales." 1861 - 1863. HEAD and CAMPBELL. "Pathology of Herpes Zoster and its Bearing on Sensory Localisation," 1900. Also DR. HEAD's admirable article in Allbutt and Rolleston's "System of Medicine." "Paralysis of Eye-Muscles." F. VOGEL. "Thesis. Leipsig," 1912. A. MACNAB. *Lancet*, March 22, 1913, p. 821. F. PARKES WEBER. *Brit. Journ. Dermatology*, XXVII., p. 408.

Dermatalgia and Erythromelalgia.

Dermatalgia. In a few rare cases there is a peculiar condition of the skin which has been called dermatalgia. The affection is a local one, and often located in the hairy parts. The only symptom is spontaneous pain, associated with hyperæsthesia. In some instances it appears to have a rheumatic origin.

Erythromelalgia is a related phenomenon, but the characteristic features are pain and patches of erythema. The pain is acute, and of a throbbing, burning, or darting nature, and it usually affects the lower limbs, particularly the feet; but occasionally the hands, and rarely the face, are involved. A dependent position and warm temperature aggravate the symptoms.

Erythromelalgia occurs in a number of nervous diseases, viz. : tabes, disseminated sclerosis, myelitis and syringomyelia, and in peripheral neuritis. Occasionally Raynaud's disease, or phenomena indistinguishable therefrom, co-exists. In some cases there is no obvious cause. Gangrene of a finger has occasionally occurred.

Dr. Parkes Weber has called attention to a curious type of spurious erythromelalgia, which occurs in young or middle-aged males. especially in Jews who have come from the eastern portions of Central Europe. The skin affection is characterised by redness or cyanosis, with intermittent attacks of pain in the sole. The affection is bilaterally symmetrical, and the colour does not fade on pressure. It depends upon a non-syphilitic arteritis obliterans. The cause is unknown.

The **treatment** of these conditions depends upon the cause ; blisters have been applied over the segment of the spinal cord, whence the affected parts are supplied, but other cases have been relieved by the administration of phenacetin and antipyrin. Aceto-salicylic acid might also be tried. The local application of menthol has also been recommended. The affection may be exceedingly chronic, but in some cases clears up spontaneously in a few weeks.

REFERENCES.—WEIR - MITCHELL. "Erythromelalgia." *Clinical Lectures on Nervous Diseases*, 1897, p. 179. R. CASSIRER. "Die Vasomotorischen Trophischen-Neurosen," 2nd ed., 1913. F. PARKES WEBER. *British Journal of Dermatology*, 1915, p. 196.

Atrophodermia neuritica. Glossy Skin.

Glossy skin is an uncommon affection, characterised by smooth, glossy patches on the extremities, following injury or disease of a nerve.

Etiology. Atrophodermia neuritica follows injuries to nerves in which there is incomplete solution of continuity, or neuritis following a wound. The present war has furnished many opportunities of observing this condition and the associated causalgia (thermalgia) caused by bullet wounds of nerves. It has also been observed in gouty neuritis, in anæsthetic leprosy, and after herpes zoster, and rarely in chronic diseases of the spinal cord.

Clinical features. The extremities are usually affected, commonly the fingers. The skin is dry, smooth, and glossy, and of a pink or red colour, or mottled. The appendages suffer also ; the parts are denuded of hair ; there is usually an absence of perspiration, though occasionally excessive sweating has been noticed, and the nails undergo peculiar and distinctive changes. The common condition is excessive curving of the nails both in the transverse and longitudinal directions, and whitlows are frequent. A specially important feature of this form of atrophy of the skin is intense pain, " causalgia " (thermalgia), described as burning, which precedes the changes in the skin and persists. Glossy skin tends to spontaneous cure, and the treatment consists in protecting the surfaces from cold and injury. The local application of cold water usually relieves the pain ; if this fails, very hot water should be tried.

REFERENCES.—WEIR-MITCHELL. "Gunshot Wounds and other Injuries of Nerves." J. S. B. STOPFORD. "Thermalgia (Causalgia)," *Lancet*, 1917, II., p. 195.

Acrodermatitis vesiculosa tropica. Under this name Castellani describes a rare tropical affection which he believes to be of nervous origin. The skin of both hands, and especially of the fingers, is glossy and tense and the fingers assume a tapering shape. Translucent millet-seed sized vesicles are deeply imbedded in the skin. Their contents are clear and amicrobic. They may disappear or rupture, leaving small superficial ulcers which heal up spontaneously. Intermittent pain is a constant feature. There is hyperæsthesia, but no pruritus. The affection may last for a few months to two or three years. Ichthyol internally and externally relieves the condition.

REFERENCE.—CASTELLANI and CHALMERS. "Tropical Medicine," p. 1621.

Morvan's Disease. Syringomyelia.

The cutaneous conditions occurring in this rare affection require notice in this place on account of their similarity to the lesions of nerve leprosy.

The disease begins sometimes in childhood, but usually between the ages of twenty and fifty, and it is commoner in the male than

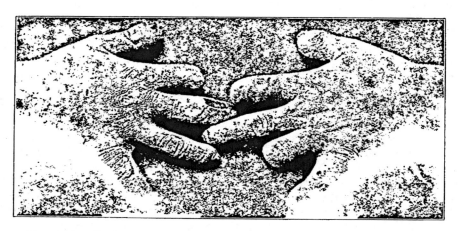

FIG. 181.—Syringomyelia, showing deformity of hands. (Case under Dr. Henry Head.)

in the female. The onset is insidious, with pain in the extremities, which is followed by analgesia, affecting first one side and then the other. In some cases the loss of sensation is an early, in others a late feature. The next, and perhaps the most characteristic, phenomenon is the development of whitlows, usually painless, but occasionally attended with great pain and tenderness when occurring in the early stages. The fingers are most commonly affected, but similar lesions appear on the toes. The inflammation about the terminal phalanges involves the bones, and necrosis occurs, the terminal segments of the digits falling off, leaving mutilated stumps. In the photograph, kindly lent me by Dr. Henry Head, the mutilations are well shown. The skiagram of the same case shows complete disappearance of the terminal phalanges in some fingers, and partial atrophy in other digits. Large bullæ, sometimes containing blood, may form upon the affected skin, and ulceration also occurs. As in other forms of trophic disturbance, the peculiar form of atrophy known as " glossy skin " develops in Morvan's disease.

The muscular weakness is followed by atrophy, and the contraction of the fingers leads to the formation of a claw-hand, " main en griffe."

Fig. 182.—Trophic ulcers in a case of anterior polio-myelitis.

There is retention of the sensation of touch, but loss of sensibility to heat and cold, and this feature is an important means of distinguishing Morvan's disease from nerve leprosy. It has, however, been shown that syringomyelia may develop in leprosy, and the thickening of the ulnar and other nerves must be looked upon as the most important diagnostic feature, in the absence of the recognition of the bacillus lepræ. In the mixed cases of lepra there is usually no difficulty in making a diagnosis. Morvan's disease lasts for many years ; there may be remission of the symptoms from time to time.

but the destructive process is slowly progressive, and treatment is of no avail.

REFERENCE.—Allbutt and Rolleston's "System," VII., p. 852.

Trophic Ulcer.

Trophic ulcers are occasionally met with in the limbs of children affected with anterior polio-myelitis. The muscles are wasted, the skin cold and purplish in tint, and one or more chronic indolent ulcers form, chiefly as a result of the impaired circulation. The illustration on p. 446 represents a characteristic case.

The treatment consists in keeping the limb warm by wrapping in cotton-wool and dressing the ulcers with antiseptic and stimulant ointment.

Perforating Ulcer.

A chronic ulceration of limited area, occurring usually on the sole of the feet, in the subjects of tabes dorsalis, diabetes, peripheral neuritis, leprosy and syringomyelia.

The seat of election is over the head of the metatarsal bone of the great toe or on the heel, *i.e.*, parts exposed to pressure. Both feet may be affected and the perforating ulcers may be multiple. Rarely similar ulcers occur on the fingers and on the dorsum of the foot.

A painful thickening of the skin appears first, and upon this a bleb may form, and ultimately a slough. Under the slough is a rounded ulcer with raised thickened edges. The necrosis may involve the tendons and even the bones, or open the joint. The ulcer is usually anæsthetic, but there may be tenderness on pressure.

Treatment. The affected part must be kept at rest. A salicylic acid plaster may be applied to soften the thickened skin, and the area is then fomented. Curetting of the surface followed by antiseptic dressing may also be tried. As a rule the ulcers heal, but in severe cases surgical interference becomes necessary.

CHAPTER XIX.

ERYTHEMATO-SQUAMOUS ERUPTIONS OF UNKNOWN ORIGIN.

THREE forms of eruption characterised by redness and scaling require consideration here. Pityriasis rosea, which in some of its characters resembles the circinate seborrhoide ; psoriasis, one of the commonest skin affections, with very definite characters ; and a group called parapsoriasis, approximating to psoriasis on the one hand. and the lichens on the other.

Pityriasis rosea.

Pityriasis rosea is characterised by an eruption of rose-coloured scaly spots of various sizes, chiefly confined to the trunk and the upper parts of the extremities.

Etiology. The cause is unknown. The eruption occurs most commonly in the young (my youngest case was a girl aged two years and four months, my oldest a man aged sixty-seven), and in females more than in males (40 females to 35 males in my private patients). It is more prevalent in the spring than at other seasons of the year. There is no evidence of contagion, but the history of a primary plaque, followed by a widely-spread crop of secondary lesions, suggests a microbic origin of the disease, a hypothesis which is supported by its definite course and absence of recurrence. Some authorities regard pityriasis rosea as an exanthem or a toxæmia. Others see a closer relationship with the tineas. Vidal in 1882 described an organism which he believed to be causative, the microsporon anamæon or dispar. Du Bois recently has demonstrated a cryptogamic organism with minute spores in the glandular orifices and follicles. The organism has not yet been cultivated or shown to be inoculable. The clinical characters are very similar to those of circinate seborrhoide, and, like it, the peculiar limitation of the eruption to the trunk and adjacent parts of the limbs rather suggests the vest as a source of contagion. The association of dilated stomach, described by Jacquet and Feulard. is believed by most dermatologists to be accidental.

Plate 42.

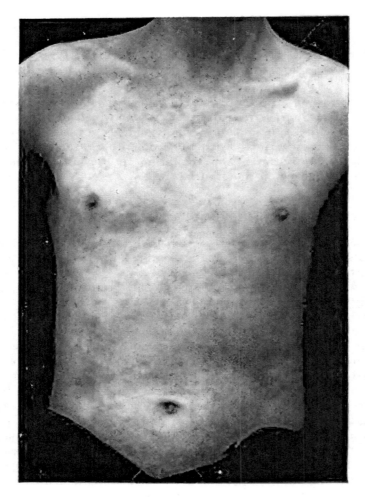

PITYRIASIS ROSEA.

The eruption was on the trunk and upper segments of the limbs. It
consisted of a primary or herald patch on the left flank, and medallions
and smaller spots covered with a fine scale.

Pathology. There is congestion of the papillary body, with œdema and infiltration of cells about the vessels. Sabouraud describes a spongiose condition of the epidermis with numerous histological vesicles containing mono-nuclear leucocytes. The scales are parakeratosic. The minute vesicles in the epidermis dry up without exudation. There is no mycelium, but Du Bois has found spores in the follicles and glandular orifices (*vide supra*).

Clinical features. There are two kinds of lesions, (1) irregularly rounded rose-coloured spots covered with a fine scale, and (2) medallions of oval form, pink in colour, scaly at the margin, and with a central yellowish area upon which there are marks resembling a watermark, due to fine ridges upon the epidermis. Some of the smaller lesions may have urticarial characters. The spots rarely exceed $\frac{1}{2}$ to $\frac{3}{4}$ inch in diameter.

The two forms of the eruption are in varying proportion in different cases. The disease affects the trunk and the upper segments of the limbs first—in fact, the area covered by the vest—but it may extend to the forearms. The face, hands, legs and feet are usually exempt.

The evolution of the disease is highly characteristic. There is an initial plaque or "herald spot," usually somewhere on the trunk, or on the neck or a limb. This patch is red and scaly, and may be mistaken for a spot of tinea circinata. The herald spot may itch slightly, but is often overlooked by the patient, especially if on the back. It is often obvious from its size and character when the generalised eruption has developed. The eruption of spots occurs from a few days to two or three weeks after the appearance of the primary or herald plaque. The outbreak consists of rounded spots and medallions, first on the trunk and then on the adjacent parts of the limbs. They may come out in successive crops, but the eruption is self-limited, and after lasting from about four to six weeks the spots fade, the scales fall off, and the skin resumes its normal appearance without scar or stain. It is exceedingly rare to meet with a second attack in the same subject. An instance was reported by Graham Little in 1915.

Slight pyrexia has been observed and also glandular swelling.

Pityriasis rosea gigantea (Darier). A very rare type in which the patches may cover an area of several square inches. The character of the eruption and the course are similar to the common type.

The **diagnosis** is important, and mistakes are not uncommon. Pityriasis is often diagnosed as syphilis, the eruption being taken for the macular syphilide. The essential points of difference are the colour, the variation in the size of the spots, and the scaliness. In syphilitic roseola the lesions are dull pink, all about one size, and free from scales. The scaly and lenticular syphilides are infiltrated and of a dull red colour. General enlargement of the glands and affection of the mucous membranes are absent in pityriasis.

Eczema is excluded by the oval medallion-like plaques and the primary patch and distribution of the eruption. Seborrhoic dermatitis affects often the same regions, but the scalp is usually scaly, and the trunk lesions are covered with greasy squames.

In psoriasis the spots are redder ; there is abundant silvery scaling, and fine bleeding points are found when the scales are removed by scraping. Erythema multiforme is distinguished by the purplish tint of the eruption, its predilection for the distal parts of the extremities, and the absence of scaling, and of the medallions.

Prognosis. Pityriasis rosea runs a self-limited course, and usually lasts from four to six weeks. Recurrences are exceedingly rare.

Treatment. Local treatment is sufficient to effect a cure. Mild antiseptic remedies are necessary. Weak tar ointments, ichthyol 2 per cent. in an ointment, and the boric acid ointment are the most useful. All strong or irritant preparations should be avoided.

REFERENCES.—SABOURAUD. "Pityriasis," p. 624. Masson : Paris, 1904. DU BOIS. *Annales de Dermatologie*, 1912, I., p. 32, plates. Discussion opened by GRAHAM LITTLE, Royal Soc. of Med. *Brit. Journ. Dermatology*, XXVI., p. 117. "Pityriasis Rosea Gigantea." PRINGLE, *Brit. Journ. Dermatology*, 1915, p. 307.

Psoriasis.

Psoriasis is a chronic inflammatory disease of the skin characterised by sharply-defined, red, rounded spots or patches, covered with silvery scales. It is one of the commonest cutaneous affections.

Etiology. We are in complete ignorance of the cause of psoriasis. Heredity is traceable in about one-third of the cases. The disease commonly begins in childhood or adolescence, and it is rare for the intitial attack to occur after the fourth decade. In some of the cases of late incidence there is osteo-arthritis, and I have several instances under observation in which this association is present, the small articulations of the extremities and also the large joints being affected. Gout and renal disease have also been suggested as possible causes, but in my opinion upon inadequate grounds. Schamberg and his colleagues found a positive Wassermann reaction in 18·7 per cent. of their cases, but there is no valid evidence that psoriasis is in any way associated with syphilis.

Many persons suffering from psoriasis are in good general health, but others are anæmic and debilitated. Nervous influences appear to determine an attack in some cases, and in women relapses are often associated with pregnancy and lactation. Sometimes an acute illness causes the disappearance of the eruption. Local irritation may determine a local outbreak as in other cutaneous conditions, *e.g.*, lichen planus.

Season has an influence, recurrences in many instances taking place in the spring and autumn.

There is one case, that of Destot, in which inoculation was followed by psoriasis, and in other instances the affection has appeared to spread by contagion, but no parasite has been isolated.

Pathology. The earliest histological change found in psoriasis is a number of small collections of round cells in the epidermis. This

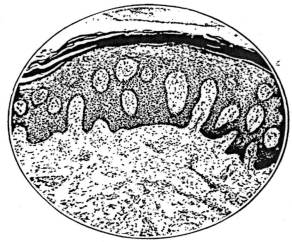

Fig. 183.—Psoriasis. Microphotograph of section

was described by Munro, and is accepted by Sabouraud, who distinguishes psoriasis by this particular feature, which he calls " exocytosis," from eczema and seborrhoic dermatitis, in which " exoserosis," or the exudation of serum, is the characteristic. The absence of bacterial infection is also an important feature.

The secondary changes are hyperplasia of the rete, with dilatation of the papillary loops and capillaries of the corium. The papillæ and the vascular layers are infiltrated with round cells. The scales are produced by a rapid but imperfect keratinisation, and their silvery appearance is due to the inclusion of small air bubbles between the epidermal cells.

Clinical features. The earliest lesions are red papules scarcely larger than a pin's head : they are sometimes covered with scales, but often these are not visible until the tops have been removed with the finger nail. The spots are always well defined and the skin around them has a normal aspect. They enlarge peripherally and various names have been applied to indicate the general size and shape of the lesions. To the smallest spots the name *psoriasis punctata* is given. When these have increased to form scaly plaques about the size of a pea the name *P. guttata* is applied. *Psoriasis nummularis* is the term used to describe plaques about the size of coins. By the

FIG. 184.—Psoriasis annularis.

coalescence of numerous enlarging patches large areas may be involved, and this condition is indicated by the name *psoriasis diffusa*. Sometimes an area tends to clear up in the centre, leaving a ringed scaly margin. This is called *psoriasis annularis* or *circinata* (Fig. 184). If the rings are not complete, polycyclic figures are produced, and the condition is called *psoriasis gyrata* or *figurata* (Fig. 185).

The type of lesion is always the same. The spots, patches, or rings are slightly raised above the level of the surrounding skin, silvery scales are present in abundance, and they can be scraped off

Plate 43.

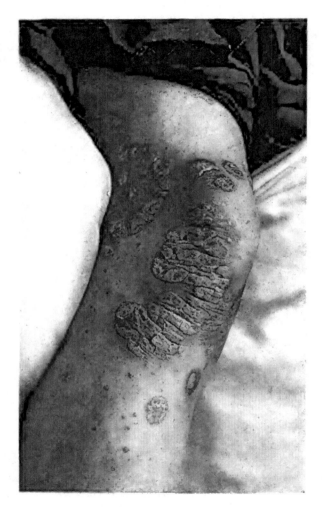

PSORIASIS.

Characteristic patches about the knee. The flat red plaques are covered with silvery scales. One of the upper spots has been denuded of scale to show the vascular surface under it.

with little difficulty, leaving a red area with a number of small bleeding points, due to the rupture of dilated capillary loops of the papillæ. Before the capillary hæmorrhages are seen, it is often possible to detect a fine membrane (Bulkeley). Unless irritated by scratching, psoriasis lesions are always dry. Occasionally in neglected cases the scales are very thick, and stand above the surface in yellowish or yellowish-brown masses, which in some instances

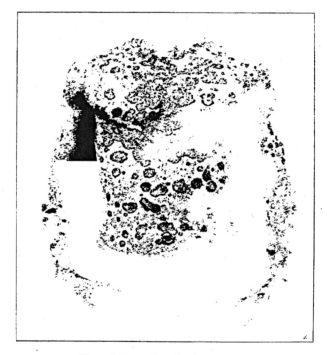

FIG. 185.—Psoriasis gyrata.

resemble the limpet-shell crusts of rupia. To this particular condition the name *psoriasis rupioides* has been given.

The eruption is commonest on the extensor surfaces of the limbs, particularly on the elbows and knees, and it may remain localised to these positions throughout an attack, or between exacerbations involving other parts. The next area favoured by psoriasis is the scalp, where the eruption takes the form of circumscribed scaly patches. In some instances the trunk is widely affected, but the face generally escapes. The palms and soles are occasionally involved.

Psoriasis attacks the nails. The earliest lesions are minute pits the size of a pin's point, or a little larger. In more severe cases the nails become thickened, opaque, yellowish in colour, and transversely ridged. In others there is an elevation of the distal part of the nail by a thickening of the bed.

Psoriasis tends to run a chronic course, but many untreated cases recover ; in nearly every instance, however, it recurs sooner or later. The lesions may for a long time be limited to the elbows and knees, and the recurrences may vary greatly in severity and extent. In young children the first attack is often confined to the trunk, but the

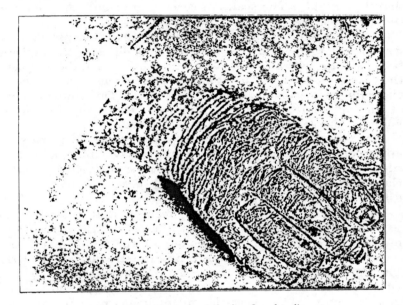

F ɪɢ. 186.—Psoriasis of the hand and nails.

characteristic elbow and knee patches soon appear and persist. In very rare instances the disease becomes generalised, and may pass into pityriasis rubra, or general exfoliative dermatitis.

In an elaborate research carried out under Schamberg's direction it was found that on a given diet a psoriatic patient eliminates less nitrogen in the urine, and that it takes a much less supply of energy in the form of food to keep the urinary nitrogen at a level than in the normal individual. These observers note a remarkable retention of nitrogen proportional to the extent and severity of the psoriasis. A similar observation was made by Tidy in some of my cases of exfoliative dermatitis. It seems likely that much nitrogen is lost in the scales which are shed.

Diagnosis. The diagnosis of psoriasis is usually easy. The sharp definition of the lesions, the silvery scales, and the healthy character of the surrounding skin, with the preference for the extensor surfaces, particularly the elbows and knees, produce a clinical picture which is characteristic. In ill-developed cases there may be some difficulty.

From squamous eczema psoriasis is distinguished by its more chronic course, its preference for the extensor surfaces, and its moderate itching. Patches of eczema are ill defined, while those of psoriasis are sharply limited. The scales of eczema are small and yellowish, and there is often a history of exudation.

The squamous syphilide may closely resemble psoriasis, but the general enlargement of the lymphatic glands and the mucous membrane lesions, with the absence of scales in parts of the eruption, make the diagnosis clear. The syphilide prefers the flexor aspects, and is exceedingly rare on the elbows and knees. On removal of the scales of the syphilide the base is dull red, and there are no bleeding points. The lesion is distinctly infiltrated.

Psoriasis is distinguished from " seborrhoic dermatitis " by the appearance of the scales, which are greasy and yellowish and not silvery. The base of the psoriasis plaque is vascular, while that of the seborrhoide is pale. The scaling of the " seborrhoic " scalp is diffuse and not in limited patches.

Lichen planus differs in so many respects that it is only the chronic patches below the knee and on the forearm which are likely to be mistaken for psoriasis. The colour of the lichen patch is lilac or violet, the scaling is fine and in minute streaks visible with a lens. The fronts of the legs and the fronts of the forearms are the common sites for chronic lichen patches, and there is generally a history of great itching. The buccal lesions of lichen may prove helpful in a doubtful case.

Psoriasis rupioides is distinguished from syphilitic rupia by the associated symptoms, the history, and especially by the presence of an ulcer on removing the rupial crust. In psoriasis rupioides the vascular points common to the disease alone are found.

The differential diagnosis of the palmar eruptions including psoriasis is considered at pp. 105 and 301.

Prognosis. Under appropriate treatment it is usually possible to get rid of the eruption, but in most cases, after an interval lasting several weeks, months, or even years, the disease recurs. It is important to remove all trace of the eruption, especially on the scalp, and to attack all recurrences as soon as they are noticed.

Treatment. In a disease which may persist with exacerbations for many years, and which is in itself benign, it is important to deter-

s.   30

mine how far it is necessary to remove the patient from his usual avocations. In acute cases it is certainly wise to advocate entire cessation of work, and to spend time in getting rid of the eruption. In the more chronic and limited cases it is usually impossible to convince the patient, especially if an old sufferer from the disease, that it is necessary to abstain from work.

Diet has received great attention in the treatment of psoriasis, and in practice one meets with patients who have benefited by a vegetarian diet, and others who have tried it without appreciable effect. The observations of Schamberg mentioned above suggest the advisability of limiting the intake of nitrogenous foods. Abstention from alcohol should be enjoined, and the amount of red meat taken should be limited. Highly-seasoned dishes and salted meats and fish, pastry and sweets, as being less easy of digestion, are better avoided.

Internal treatment. Any general condition such as gout, rheumatism, anæmia, and constipation will naturally receive attention, but the psoriasis is often unaffected. From the marked improvement which followed the treatment of pyorrhœa alveolaris in two adult patients suffering from chronic psoriasis I am inclined to look upon this condition as worthy of attention. Cook found vaccine treatment for pyorrhœa beneficial in some cases of psoriasis.

In acute cases arsenic should not be given. Salicin, as recommended by the late Dr. Radcliffe Crocker, has appeared to me to be of some benefit in the acute stage. The drug is given in fifteen to twenty grain doses thrice daily, either in cachet or tablet, or in a mixture with a little syrup of orange.

In the more chronic cases, and where the acute hyperæmia has passed, arsenic is of value. It is usually given in the form of Fowler's solution, beginning with three or four minims thrice daily after food, gradually increased according to the tolerance of the patient. When taken after food and well diluted it is rarely necessary to abandon it. If continued, however, over long periods, pigmentation of the trunk, occasionally herpes and keratosis of the palms and soles, may result. In rare instances peripheral neuritis may occur. Sir Jonathan Hutchinson has pointed out the danger of the development of malignant growths after prolonged administration of arsenic. I have recently tried intramuscular injection of Enesol—a compound of arsenic and mercury—as advised by Sabouraud. In some cases it appeared to be of great service. Thyroid gland has a marked effect on the eruption in some cases, but it is not a safe drug for regular and prolonged administration. Iodide of potassium in large doses is frequently used on the Continent, and sometimes with great benefit, but the depressing effect of the drug is against its lengthy use.

Small doses of antimonial wine, carbolic acid and turpentine have been advocated by different writers.

I have tried the autogenous serum treatment without obvious benefit. Twenty-five to thirty cubic centimetres of inactivated serum from the patient's own blood are injected at intervals.

Local treatment. The first measure is the removal of the scales. Hot baths containing a drachm of bicarbonate of soda or potash to each gallon are useful. The patient should remain in the bath for twenty minutes, and by friction with soap endeavour to get rid of as much of the scale as possible. In very thick troublesome patches, such as are often seen on the knees in neglected cases, soft soap and hot water, or equal parts of soft soap and spirit, should be used. It must not be forgotten that the scalp requires attention, and the soft soap and spirit lotion is most useful in getting rid of the scales.

After removal of the scales, the patches on the limbs and trunk are best treated with chrysarobin, if the patient can be under observation and in bed. I generally use Hutchinson's ointment :—

> ℞ Chrysarobin, five to forty grains ;
> Hydrarg. ammoniat., ten grains ;
> Liq. carbonis deterg., twenty minims ;
> Ung. petrolei to one ounce.

Sutton recommends the following formula :—

> ℞ Ol. rusci ten parts ;
> Acid salicylic, twenty parts ;
> Chrysarobin, twenty parts ;
> Lanolin anhydros, twenty-five parts ;
> Saponis mollis, twenty-five parts.

If the chrysarobin is used in the strength of 20 to 30 grains to the ounce, the ointment should only be used for four days in succession. The ointment must be well rubbed into the spots, and if a nurse is employed she must be careful to use a glass rubber. Chrysarobin has certain important disadvantages. It stains the skin temporarily, and the clothing and bed linen permanently. It is therefore impracticable to apply it in the form of an ointment to a patient going about his work. Again, if used over large areas, and in large doses, it usually causes an eruption of prune-juice colour, with great heat and irritation of the skin, and occasionally slight rise of temperature. The erythema cures the psoriasis, leaving the affected spots white, and around them is a zone of redness. Chrysarobin must not be used near the eyes, as conjunctivitis may be set up, nor on the scalp, as it stains the hair. If it should be required for areas of moderate size in a patient who has to be about, it may be used as a paint dissolved in traumaticin, ten grains or more of the chrysarobin to an ounce of traumaticin. This vehicle consists of gutta-percha dissolved in chloroform, and forms, when the chloroform evaporates, a layer on the parts treated.

The tars are very useful in psoriasis, but ordinary Unguentum picis is too dirty for common use. Anthrasol, a colourless tar, one drachm to an ounce of Ung. petrolei, is efficient. Oil of cade, also in an ointment one drachm to the ounce, may be used, but has a penetrating though not unpleasant odour. The white precipitate ointment with half a drachm of sulphur to the ounce is sometimes useful. Ichthyol and salicylic acid, as in the following formula, are one commonly used in my out-patient clinic. R. Ichthyol, forty grains; acid salicylic, ten grains; Ung. petrolei to one ounce.

Pyrogallic acid, or better, one of its derivatives, eugallol, acts very. like chrysarobin. It may be used in strengths varying from 10 to 30 grains to the ounce. It must be employed with care, and not over too large an area. It stains like chrysarobin. Eugallol may be applied as a paint with an equal proportion of acetone. After drying the areas are dusted with zinc powder.

As my experience has increased I am more impressed with the value of the X-rays in chronic cases. They are of especial service in small chronic patches and in palmar psoriasis. There is one point in their use in psoriasis which I have noticed two or three times, and that is that the subsequent administration of arsenic, even after several months, may excite an erythema in areas which have been submitted to the rays. The dose should be one-half the pastille dose, and an interval of at least a fortnight should intervene between the sittings. The sterilising effect of the rays should be remembered in applying them near the scrotum. High frequency applications have also proved beneficial.

The best treatment for psoriasis of the scalp in my experience is the rubbing in of an ointment of resorcin, a drachm to the ounce, after the scales have been removed by the soft soap and spirit lotion. Anthrasol may be used with the spirit lotion with advantage.

Residence at certain spas and bath treatment, especially sulphur baths, often benefit chronic cases, but the effect is uncertain. The waters of La Bourboule in France are advocated, as they contain arsenic. Injections of the Bourboule water are said to be more efficient than the administration by the mouth.

REFERENCES.—SABOURAUD. "Les Maladies Desquamatives," II., p. 539. Masson. 1904. NORMAN WALKER. Scott's Med. and Surg. Jour., April, 1908. SCHAMBERG, KOLMER, RINGER and RAIZISS. Journal Cut. Diseases, 1913, XXXI., p. 802. COOK. N. York Med. Journ., 1916, II., 255.

Parapsoriasis.

This name has been given by Brocq to a group of cases characterised by maculo-papular lesions covered with scales. In many of their features they resemble psoriasis, and in others lichen planus, but they are exceedingly resistant to treatment.

Three types are described : Guttate, lichenoid, and in plaques.

Guttate form. The following case under my own observation illustrates the essential features. The patient, a bank manager, thirty years of age, had suffered for four years from an eruption of rounded red spots varying in size from a threepenny piece to a shilling. Each spot was covered with a fine, somewhat adherent scale. The eruption was scattered all over the trunk and to a less extent upon the extremities. There was no scaliness of the scalp, and the mucous membranes were unaffected. There was no itching to speak of, and the patient simply wanted to get rid of the eruption on account of its appearance. He had been treated for four years for psoriasis, but one medical man had made the diagnosis of syphilis. Chrysarobin, tar, ichthyol, salicylic acid had all been tried in vain.

Lichenoid or **papular form.** The lesions are papules, somewhat more infiltrated than the guttate spots, and without much scaling. The spots are in groups on the trunk and extremities. They may be mistaken for lichen scrofulosus, lichen planus and for syphilides.

The **plaque-like form** consists of reddish-yellow or red patches, with little scaling, and without infiltration. They are usually of a rounded or oval form, and may take the form of bands. The surface of the plaque shows the normal lines of the skin somewhat accentuated, but scaling is uncommon. There is little itching. In a case seen with Dr. Hingston Fox, which I believe to be of this type, the question of mycosis fungoides had to be seriously considered, but the absence of irritation favoured the diagnosis of parapsoriasis. A biopsy was not obtained. The eruption formed curious wavy bands on the trunk. Seborrhoic dermatitis would be excluded by the absence of the greasy scale, and of pityriasis capitis, and syphilis by the duration of the eruption, and, if necessary, by the Wassermann test.

The guttate and papular type have been called by some authors parakeratosis variegata, and lichen psoriasis, while the eruption in the plaque form has been called erythrodermic pityriasis in disseminated plaques. Crocker and Pernet have applied the name xantho-erythrodermia perstans to it.

The *etiology* of parapsoriasis is unknown. It occurs in adults, and sometimes in the young. The pathological appearances have been studied by Civatte, J. C. White, Unna, and by Fox and Macleod.

The epidermis is œdematous, and there is slight leucocytic infiltration. The stratum lucidum and the stratum granulosum disappear. The corneous layer is thickened, and the cells are nucleated. The papillæ are œdematous and the vessels dilated. In old lesions the papillæ disappear, and there is much infiltration about the veins which may be obliterated. The whole process is that to which Unna has given the name of parakeratosis. Treatment is without any effect upon the eruption.

REFERENCES.—"Parakeratosis Variegata." UNNA. "Histopathology of the Skin" (trans. by NORMAN WALKER), p. 339. COLCOTT FOX and J. M. H. MACLEOD. *Brit. Journ. Derm.*, 1901, XIII., p. 319. "Xantho-erythrodermia Perstans." H. RADCLIFFE CROCKER. *Brit. Journ. Derm.*, 1905, XVII., p. 119.

Cheilitis exfoliativa.

A chronic, scaly, and crusted eruption occurring on the lips. It is difficult to place this disease, the cause of which is unknown. It occurs most commonly in young women, and is somewhat rare in men. It often lasts for several years.

Cracks develop in the lower lip, which bleed, and then dry and crust over. Later the upper lip becomes affected. The characteristic features are black or brownish scales or crusts consisting of dried blood. Under the crusts the skin is dry and shrivelled.

The mucous membrane may be involved.

The usual soothing applications have little or no effect upon the eruption. Applications of radium and X-rays should be tried.

CHAPTER XX.

PAPULAR ERUPTIONS OF UNKNOWN ORIGIN.

Lichen planus.

LICHEN PLANUS is characterised by an eruption of small inflammatory flat papules, polygonal in outline and of a dull red or lilac tint.

Etiology. The cause of lichen planus is unknown. The pathological appearances are compatible with a microbic origin, but of this there is no positive evidence. The subjects are usually nervous and irritable, and there is frequently a history of some shock, worry or anxiety with insomnia, antecedent to the eruption. These factors are so common as to suggest a " nervous " origin, but, on the other hand, cases are met with in which there is no obvious neurotic element. There has, however, been a notable increase in the number of cases seen in civil practice during the war, doubtless due to protracted mental strain. Local irritation may determine an outbreak, and scratching may increase the extent of the eruption, but there is no evidence that this is the sole cause, as has been suggested, for some of the patients have little pruritus. The disease is most common between the ages of thirty and sixty. Seventy-two per cent. of my cases were between these ages, and 36 per cent. in the fourth decade. Women, at any rate in England, suffer more frequently than men : females 60 per cent., males 40 per cent. among 200 private patients. Children are less commonly affected.

Pathology. The epidermis and the true skin are both involved. The stratum mucosum is hypertrophied, and in later lesions the horny layer is thickened. The stratum granulosum is increased, but the eleidine is irregularly thickened, and this causes the network of white striæ, which are pathognomonic of the eruption. At first the cells of the horny layer are not nucleated, but in older lesions the nuclei may be present. Giant cells of epidermic origin may be formed. Horny plugs are found at the mouths of some of the follicles. The papillæ are swollen, often into a spheroidal shape, and infiltrated with mono-nuclear cells. There is inter-cellular and intra-cellular œdema, and vesication may occur.   The lower margin of the infiltration is remarkably distinct in sections.

Similar conditions are found in the mucous membrane lesions.

Clinical features.   The elementary lesion is a smooth, flat-topped papule of polygonal outline, of a dull red to a violet or lilac colour, varying in size from a pin's head to a millet seed, or a little larger. The surface of the papule has a burnished appearance reflecting light, and this feature is a useful point in the differential diagnosis.   Some of the lesions have a slight depression in the centre indicating their origin around a duct or follicle.   Under a lens, and particularly if the surface has been moistened with oil and water, white opalescent

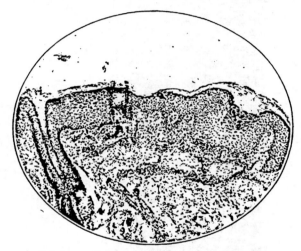

FIG. 187.—Lichen planus. Microphotograph of section ⅔.
Dr. W. J. Oliver.

points or striæ forming a fine network are visible.   The sign, first pointed out by Wickham, is pathognomonic.   Occasionally the papules are almost the colour of the normal skin.

The papules may be discrete, but usually by their aggregation form patches of rounded or irregular shape, covered with fine adherent scales, which are made more obvious by lightly scratching the surface with the finger nail.   Careful examination will show that even large patches are composed of aggregations of small papules, and even when the scaling is considerable, as in some of the thickened horny plaques below the knee, it is usual to find typical shining flat-topped papules at the margin of the scaly area, or in its vicinity. Patches of common lichen planus are never formed by the peripheral extension of a

Plate 44.

LICHEN PLANUS.

Eruption of lilac-coloured, flat-topped papules on
the front of the forearm. Close examination
shows the silvery striæ of Wickham.

papule, as in psoriasis, but in one rare form, to be described later, this method of extension may occur.

In most cases the burnished papules reflecting light and the peculiar lilac or violaceous tint of the lesions form a clinical picture which is highly characteristic (Plates XLIV. and XLV.).

On the disappearance of the spots pigmentation remains, and in well-marked cases a sepia-coloured stain may persist for months. This discoloration is independent of the administration of arsenic, though a prolonged course of the drug appears to increase it.

The eruption rarely appears on the face and scalp, but with these exceptions no part of the body is exempt. The commonest sites are the flexor surfaces of the wrists and forearms, the front of the legs, inner sides of the thighs, and the hips. The thenar eminences and the soles may also be involved. On the trunk the waist, particularly in women, owing to the pressure of the corset, is commonly affected, and the eruption sometimes occurs on the neck. The nails are rarely attacked. Fig. 188 shows the condition produced in an acute case under my care.

Lichen planus affects the mucous membranes in at least one-half of the cases, and the characteristic eruption in the buccal cavity is of great assistance in diagnosis. The affection of the mouth may precede the cutaneous manifestations, and indeed be independent of them. The inner aspect of the cheeks, opposite the teeth, is the favourite site of the eruption; less frequently the tongue and palate are involved; and I have occasionally seen the red margin of the lips studded with small white papules. The lesions are white porcelain-like patches of irregular shape, or a network of fine white striae, or white or yellowish discrete papules the size of a pin's head. Similar lesions occur on the labia and on the glans penis, but in the latter situation the papules may be the same colour as the mucous membrane. In rare cases the lesions may be confined to the buccal mucosa and the glans penis.

Itching is usually a predominant feature in lichen planus, but occasionally it is slight and intermittent. In some cases it is a terrible trial to the patient, preventing sleep and causing frantic scratching. It is usually worst at the beginning of the attack, but it may persist in chronic patches. The buccal lesions rarely trouble the patient. Diarrhœa occasionally occurs, and it has been suggested that this is due to an eruption of papules in the alimentary canal. The general symptoms depend upon the acuteness of the attack, and on the severity and duration of the itching.

Course. Lichen planus may run an acute or a chronic course. The chronic cases are by far the more common. The disease begins insidiously. and progresses slowly, the eruption gradually spreading for several months, and then remaining stationary, but commonly there are subacute exacerbations, in which fresh lesions appear, and new areas are attacked. Occasionally the disease persists for years. Resolution takes place slowly, the upper extremities clearing before the lower, but the spots affected may remain pigmented for months.

In the acute form large areas of the trunk and limbs are rapidly affected. In the severest type the skin may be diffusely red and

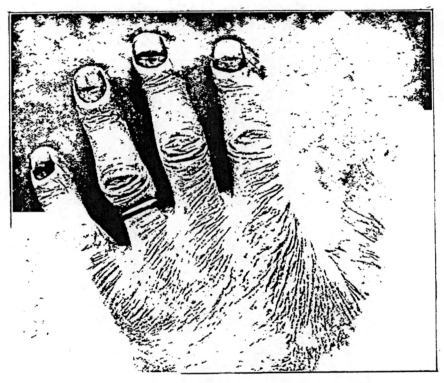

FIG. 188.—Affection of nails in severe lichen planus.

swollen, and small papules appear in large numbers on the affected areas. There is intense itching and fever and other systemic disturbance. The acute cases tend to clear up more rapidly than those of gradual onset, perhaps in a month or two, but sometimes they pass into the chronic type.

Variations. *Acuminate lesions* sometimes occur with the plane papules (L. plano-pilaris). They are elevations with a central

Plate 45.

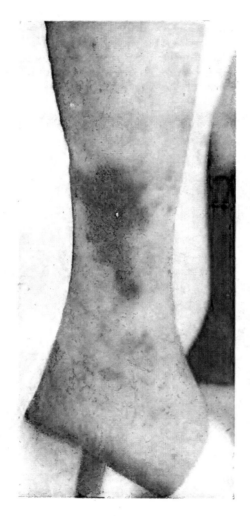

LICHEN PLANUS.

Patch of lilac tint on the lower part of the leg,
and a few scattered papules above and below.
The colour is quite characteristic.

follicular plug, and run together to form nutmeg-grater-like patches. The papules on the neck may have horny spines.

Vesicles and bullæ occasionally occur in association with the characteristic papules. As a rule they are transitory and of little importance.

Linear lesions. Associated with the discrete papules and patches, it is not unusual to see streaks formed of a line of closely-set papules. These commonly occur on the limbs in the line of a scratch.

Zoster-like lesions. In rare instances the eruption is limited to the area supplied by one or more cutaneous nerves on the trunk or extremities. There are several drawings of this variety in the collection given by the late Sir Stephen Mackenzie to the London Hospital Medical College.

Annular lesions. Instead of forming plaques, the papules may form rings varying from a quarter of an inch to three-quarters of an inch in diameter. The ringed lesions may be a prominent feature in the disease, but they are usually associated with the commoner discrete papules and patches. I have occasionally seen gyrate figures formed by broken rings.

Lichen planus atrophicus is a variety in which the papules in the centre of a patch become cicatricial, while fresh papules form at the periphery, until an area perhaps an inch or two in diameter is involved. The cicatricial area is pearly white, and sometimes minute horny plugs are seen at the mouths of the follicles.

Lichen planus obtusus. The lesions are disseminated, brownish, or violet-tinted swellings as large as a pea. They are not scaly, and the itching is slight. Kaposi described a rare variety as lichen planus obtusus moniliformis, in which the papules are large and arranged in chaplets.

Lichen planus verrucosus, or *Lichen hypertrophicus.* The lesions are warty elevations of the same colour as the common type, but they are covered with masses of horny adherent scales. They vary in size from a pea to a small coin. They may be discrete, or occur in groups. Itching is variable, and usually worse at night. The legs are the parts most commonly affected, but the thighs, elbows, and trunk may be involved. Some authors doubt this being a variety of lichen planus.

Diagnosis. Lichen planus is not uncommonly diagnosed as syphilis. The peculiar colour of the papules, and their burnished character, and the white striæ and points upon the surface of the lesions, are sufficiently distinctive to prevent this mistake. The lesions are of one type, and the spots and patches on the mucous membranes are quite different from those of secondary syphilis.

There is no general enlargement of the lymphatic glands, and, as a rule, there is intense itching.

The papules of strophulus are often rather flat and smooth, and may be mistaken for lichen planus. It must be remembered that lichen planus is uncommon in infancy, and the cases which have been called lichen planus infantum are really cases of strophulus.

Prurigo in the adult is circumscribed, the individual lesions are rounded, and not flat, and there are no white striæ.

Lichen scrofulosus occurs in strumous patients, and there is usually some obvious tuberculous disease. The papules are rounded and not flat, and they usually occur in groups on the trunk. They do not itch, and there are no mucous membrane lesions.

The rare conditions, parakeratosis of Mibelli, affecting the palms and soles could only cause difficulty if the lichen were limited to these regions. Parapsoriasis might offer difficulties also, but the lesions are not shining, and the striæ of Wickham are absent, and the mucous membranes are not affected.

Secondary lichenisation of patches of eczema, etc., should not cause difficulty if the history is known. In the rare cases of acute lichen planus one might suspect an erythrodermia at the onset, but the diagnosis would be cleared up by the appearance of the characteristic papules.

Prognosis. In the acute cases involving large areas, the course is generally more rapid than in the common type. The majority of cases, however, run a chronic course, and may persist for months, sometimes even for years. Recurrences after long intervals occasionally occur. I have notes of several cases in which four or five years have elapsed between the attacks.

Treatment. All forms of alcohol should be avoided, and also tea and coffee. Spiced and fermented foods should be excluded, and all preserved and tinned foods and fish; in fact, anything likely to disturb digestion.

In severe cases the patient is best at rest in bed, or at any rate away from business and worry.

Warm sedative baths are comforting, and relieve the irritation. Alkaline baths are also useful, a teaspoonful of sodii bicarb. being added to each gallon of water. The electric static bath and high-frequency treatment also afford relief. Chronic patches yield to weak doses of the X-rays.

In the early stages salicin in fifteen to twenty grain doses three times a day appears to lessen the inflammation and to diminish itching. Antipyrin is also useful given in full doses at night when the irritation is severe. Arsenic is a valuable remedy in the more chronic stages. It should be steadily pushed as far as the tolerance of the patient will allow. Mercury in the form of the biniodide is also of great service. Locally it is of the highest importance to relieve irritation, and for this purpose lotions, ointments, and pastes containing tar and carbolic acid are most useful. The following formulæ may be used :—

> ℞ Liquor plumbi, one drachm ;
> Liquor carbonis detergens, two drachms ;
> Water to six ounces.

Liquefied phenol ten to fifteen minims to the ounce, and menthol, ten to fifteen grains to the ounce, in lotion or ointment, or Unna's ointment :—

> ℞ Hydrarg. perchlor., two grains ;
> Glycerin, ten minims ;
> Phenol, twenty grains ;
> Ol. Olivæ, forty minims ;
> Ung. zinci to one ounce.

I have also found the lotion recommended by Sutton of service :—

> ℞ Menthol, one and a half drachms ;
> Thymol, two drachms ;
> Chloral hydrate, one drachm ;
> Chloroform, two ounces ;
> Eucalyptus oil, two ounces ;
> Oil of Gaultheria, four drachms :
> Alcohol to eight ounces.

REFERENCES.—"Lichen Planus : Its Varieties, Relations and Simulations." H. RADCLIFFE CROCKER. *British Journal of Dermatology*, 1900, XII., p. 421. Paper and discussion. On the "Association of Lichen Planus and Acuminate Papules" : see DR. ADAMSON's paper on "Lichen Pilaris." *British Journal of Dermatology*, 1905, XVII., p. 78. R. SABOURAUD. "Histology." *Annales de Dermatologie*, October, 1910, p. 491. SUTTON. *Journal American Association*, 1914, I., p. 175.

Lichen nitidus. Under this name Pinkus described a papular eruption characterised by numerous sharply-defined, flat-topped, shiny, pinhead-sized papules without any tendency to grouping or confluence and practically the same colour as the normal skin. It is commonest on the genitals, the abdomen, breast and about the anus. Arndt collected thirteen cases, all in males between the ages of twelve and forty-five. The lesions consist of epithelioid cells with giant-cells directly under the epidermis, and bounded laterally by a prolonged epithelial process. The cells are mono- and poly- nuclear leucocytes. There is no caseation, and no tubercle bacilli have been found. Arndt suggested that the condition is an infective granuloma, probably an atypical tuberculide.

REFERENCE.—PINKUS. *Archiv. f. Dermat. u. Syph.*, LXXXV., p. 11.

Lichen convex. Under this name Castellani describes a common disease in the natives of Ceylon, characterised by numerous smooth, convex pink or red follicular papules about $\frac{1}{12}$ to $\frac{1}{8}$ inch in diameter. The chest, back and shoulders are most affected. The eruption itches intensely and lasts for several months, and tends to recur. Antipruritic lotions are used.

Dermatitis nodosa tropica occurs on the face and trunk. The lesions are hemispherical, angry, red, hard non-scaly nodules as large as a pea. There is intense itching, but no urticaria. The lymphatic glands and the parotid are enlarged, and there is eosinophilia. The disease may last for six months to a year or more. The lesions leave no scar. Drugs have no influence on the condition. Antipruritic lotions are used to relieve the itching.

REFERENCE.—CASTELLANI and CHALMERS. "Tropical Medicine," p. 1895, plates.

Granuloma annulare.

An eruption occurring on the extremities and occasionally elsewhere, characterised by small papules arranged in rings, which after running an indolent course disappear spontaneously.

FIG. 189.—Granuloma annulare.

Etiology. The patients are usually children or young adults. The cause is unknown.

Pathology. The stratum corneum, the granular layer and rete are somewhat thickened. There is dense cell-infiltration in the pars reticularis and the hypoderm, the parts around the sweat ducts being especially involved. Focal accumulations of cells occur around the sweat coils and the hair follicles. No giant cells are found.

Clinical features. My first case was a male aged twenty-eight who had had the eruption for two years and a half. The patient was pale and thin, suffering from dyspepsia, and showing symptoms of cardiac disease. On the dorsum of each hand there was an irregular oval patch about the size of half-a-crown, its centre somewhat atrophic, and round the margin there were closely-set pale red papules free from scales measuring a twelfth to a sixth of an inch across. Similar and smaller ringed spots were present on the dorsum of both middle fingers. Still smaller and more recent rings were present on the back of the right middle finger. Six months later, wishing to show the patient at one of my classes, I wrote to him, and he attended the clinic, but the lesions had entirely disappeared. In another case, a female child aged eight, the disease had lasted several months. She had a ringed lesion as large as half-a-crown, made up of flat papules on the back of the right hand. Above it, close to the cleft between the first and second fingers, there was another ring as large as a shilling, and a third partly developed at the root of the middle finger, and one on the back of the index, and a fifth on the back of the right wrist. The condition is not very common, but the appearance of the eruption is characteristic, and the prognosis is good.

Treatment. In one case the application of a salicylic acid ointment was followed by the disappearance of the lesions, but if left alone they appear to clear up.

REFERENCES.—The earliest case appears to be that of COLCOTT FOX, *British Journal of Dermatology*, 1895, p. 91. DR. GALLOWAY published a case as lichen annularis. *British Journal of Dermatology*, 1899, p. 221. DR. RADCLIFFE CROCKER'S first case was reported. *British Journal of Dermatology*, 1902, p. 1. DR. GRAHAM LITTLE collected a large number of published and unpublished cases. *British Journal of Dermatology*, 1908, p. 213, etc.

Erythema elevatum diutinum.

Several cases have been recorded of an interesting and rare eruption of raised persistent nodules, beginning sometimes about the knees, and extending to the elbows and buttocks, and finally to the hands.

The lesions are convex, raised, well-defined, smooth, purplish-red and tender. They usually have a circular or oval outline, and are somewhat symmetrically arranged. Itching and tingling of the spots has been recorded. Dr. Radcliffe Crocker's case cleared up in about a year under arsenic. Dr. F. J. Smith's case was unchanged at the end of two years. Dr. Crocker's case was examined histologically, and the process was found to be chronic inflammation of the true skin about the sweat glands ; the corium being replaced in parts by a fibro-cellular structure. The nature and relationships of the condition are unknown.

REFERENCES. —" Erythema Elevatum Diutinum." RADCLIFFE CROCKER and CAMPBELL WILLIAMS. *British Journal of Dermatology*, Vol. VI., p. 1, plate. F. J. SMITH, *ibid.*, Vol. VI., p. 144. JUDSON BURY. *Illustrated Medical News*, May 18, 1889.

CHAPTER XXI.

FOLLICULAR KERATOSES AND ALLIED CONDITIONS.

THERE are several forms of keratosis which specially affect the follicles. Unfortunately they have been described and redescribed by many authors, with the result that the nomenclature is exasperatingly complicated (*vide* Dr. MacLeod's article, *British Journal of Dermatology*, XXI., p. 188). The commonest form is *keratosis suprafollicularis* or *keratosis pilaris*. These are names given to the rough, rasp-like surfaces so frequently met with in young subjects on the extensor surfaces of the limbs. *Lichen pilaris seu spinulosus* is a less common affection characterised by spiny projections from the mouths of the hair follicles. It occurs in young subjects and in adult women, and is sometimes associated with lichen planus. A follicular keratosis also occurs in association with kerion, and has been described as a secondary *lichenoid trichophytide* (*vide* p. 156). *Pityriasis rubra pilaris* is a rare disease in which there are horny plugs at the pilar orifices, and red, scaly patches on the face and scalp. *Keratosis follicularis*, or Darier's disease, is another rare affection characterised by hyperkeratosis of the follicles, with the formation of warty and vegetating tumours. The lesions are the seat of a special form of keratinisation, with the development of peculiar " bodies " formerly thought to be psorosperms, but now recognised as being degenerated epithelial cells. *Acanthosis*, or *keratosis nigricans*, is also considered in this chapter on account of its superficial resemblance to Darier's disease. It is characterised by warty pigmented and vegetating tumours chiefly developing in the flexures, in connection with cancer of the abdominal or pelvic viscera. *Porokeratosis* is another rare form of hyperkeratosis, affecting the extremities. The epidermis and the upper parts of the sweat glands are involved.

Keratosis pilaris. Keratosis supra-follicularis.

Keratosis pilaris is a common affection of childhood and adolescence characterised by the formation of rough, rasp-like patches on the skin. It is estimated that about one person in three is more or less affected. In some families the condition is constant. It is first noticed, as a rule, when a child is two or three years of age ; it tends to increase about puberty, and commonly disappears later in life. It is not infrequently associated with a degree of ichthyosis or xerodermia.

The pilo-sebaceous follicles are dilated and funnel-shaped and filled with horny plugs which project above the level of the skin to form acuminate papules. The lower portion of the follicles is atrophied and may contain an atrophied hair. The epidermis between the follicles shows hyperkeratosis as in mild degrees of ichthyosis (MacLeod). Unna and others believe the process to be inflammatory.

The parts most commonly affected are the extensor aspects of the arms and thighs, but the calves, forearms and knees, and the lower part of the trunk are sometimes involved. The flexures and parts where the skin is soft are unaffected. The skin is dry, and feels like a nutmeg-grater or rasp. The roughness is caused by numerous pointed papules formed by horny plugs in the mouths of the pilo-sebaceous ducts. The plugs are somewhat adherent, and a lanugo hair is attached to each. As a rule the colour of the lesions is normal, but in some instances the follicles and the adjacent skin are red. The little plugs can be picked out, leaving minute conical depressions. Even if untreated, the papules disappear, leaving minute punctate scars, the hair follicle and the sebaceous gland being atrophied.

MacLeod has reported three cases in one family associated with baldness of the eyebrows and scalp and absence of the eyelashes. There were no cicatrices as in the cases described by Taenzer (*vide infra*).

The **diagnosis** from lichen spinulosus is considered at p. 475.

Treatment. In mild cases, which are by far the most common, the patient rarely comes for treatment. Washing with soft soap and the application of greasy substances, olive oil and lanolin, glycerin, and weak salicylic acid preparations are useful. The general treatment is that of ichthyosis.

Keratosis pilaris rubra atrophicans faciei. Ulerythema ophryogenes of Taenzer. This is a rare disease, which has been studied by Taenzer, Unna and Brocq. It occurs more commonly in males than in females, and in young adults chiefly.

The parts affected are the outer-third of the eyelids and the lower part of the forehead, the scalp, and the cheek in front of the ear.

The lesions consist of prominent hair follicles on an area of diffuse redness. The hairs are destroyed, leaving small bald patches which are finely scarred. Brocq says that moniliform hairs are frequently found associated with this condition of the skin.

It is extremely difficult to treat, but the application of soft soap and of red plaster appear to improve the condition. Linear scarification carried out criss-cross is also advocated.

REFERENCES.—J. M. H. MacLeod. "Ichthyosis Follicularis associated with Baldness." *Brit. Journ. Dermatol.*, XXI., p. 171.

Lichen pilaris seu spinulosus.

Lichen pilaris is a rather uncommon disease characterised by the formation of fine filiform spines on the trunk and limbs. Two types may be recognised. The commoner is a disease of childhood, and

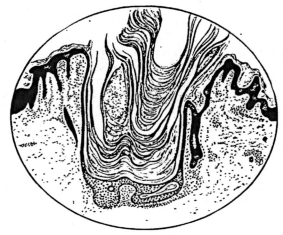

FIG. 190.—Lichen pilaris. (x 45.)

boys are affected more than girls. The rarer type is usually seen in middle-aged women, and is occasionally associated with folliculitis decalvans. What may possibly be a third type is seen in association with lichen planus—lichen plano-pilaris. The cause is unknown.

Pathology. There is some doubt as to whether the primary affection is inflammatory or not. Dr. Adamson agrees that the first spots may be slightly inflammatory on their first appearance, but his investigations of the histology lead him to believe that the essential part of the process is hyperkeratosis of the wall of the hair follicles. The section here illustrated is from an adult woman. It shows a plugging of the follicular orifice with a horny mass which projects above the surface. The plugs consist of concentric lamellæ around a hair. The lamellæ are made up of flattened epithelial cells. There is no perifollicular inflammation, and no micro-organisms are found in the plug, and the follicle below it is quite normal. It has been suggested that the eruption is toxic.

Clinical features. (1) *In children.* The lesions occur more or less symmetrically on the limbs, the neck, the buttocks, and sometimes on the face. They consist of groups of fine filiform spines arising from the pilo-sebaceous follicles. The follicles themselves are slightly raised to form papules the size of a pin's head. There are no symptoms and no active inflammation, the lesions being usually pale, but sometimes slightly redder than the normal skin.

The limbs are usually more affected than the trunk.

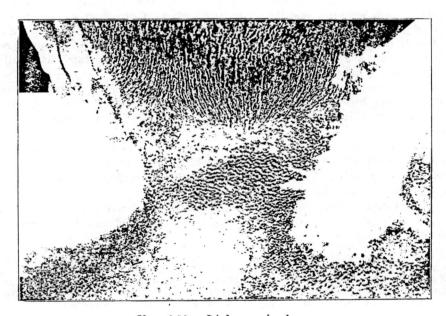

FIG. 191.—Lichen spinulosus.

(2) *In the adult.* The affection is much rarer. It seems to be peculiar to adult women. In a characteristic case recently under my care the eruption was most developed on the trunk, axillæ, groins and upper parts of the extremities. The larger lesions were brownish raised, rather blunt elevations situated in the hair follicles. The smaller were pointed papules. They were closely situated, and on passing the hand over the affected area the nutmeg-grater-like surface was easily recognisable. The spines could be picked out and a conical cavity was left. The affection was essentially chronic, but under treatment subsided after several months. At no time were

lichen planus papules observed. The hair was thin, but there were no bald areas. Graham Little, Dore and Wallace Beatty have described cases of this type associated with folliculitis decalvans. In Beatty's case the first symptom was a gradually developing alopecia, which became almost total. The follicular keratosis which was present on the scalp as well as on the trunk and extremities came on after some years' interval. Little's case was almost identical.

(3) In *lichen plano-pilaris* (Pringle) the spiny lesions are associated with characteristic lichen planus (*vide* p. 464).

Diagnosis. Lichen spinulosus is an affection of little importance ; but it has to be distinguished from several other diseases. Keratosis pilaris is a chronic condition of the extensor surfaces of the limbs consisting of small horny plugs covering a rolled-up lanugo hair. It is of common occurrence in persons who do not bathe frequently. Most cases are of congenital origin and are associated with mild degrees of ichthyosis.

Lichen scrofulosus may also be mistaken for lichen spinulosus. The lesions, however, are not spiny, but rounded, and occur in groups on the trunk in patients suffering from tuberculosis of the glands, etc.

Darier's disease is exceedingly rare. It is differentiated from the second group of lichen pilaris by its distribution, by its early onset and by its vegetative lesions, and the " corps ronds " found in the microscopical sections.

Treatment. The affected parts should be washed with soft soap, and an ointment containing ten grains of salicylic acid to the ounce applied.

REFERENCES.—H. G. ADAMSON. *British Journal of Dermatology*, 1905, XVII., pp. 24 and 77: plate illustrating histology. A critical analysis of the forms of cutaneous eruption with filiform spines. " Lichen Spinulosus with Folliculitis Décalvans." GRAHAM LITTLE. *Ibid.*, XXVII., p. 183. WALLACE BEATTY. *Ibid.*, XXVII., p. 331: plates and sections.

Pityriasis rubra pilaris (Devergie). Lichen ruber acuminatus (Kaposi).

A chronic affection characterised by an eruption of small, conical, or round papules about the hair follicles on the limbs and trunk, and by redness and scaling of the face.

Etiology. The disease is rare in this country. The patients I have seen have been between the ages of twelve and twenty-five years, but instances of earlier and later development are not uncommon. With one exception my patients were females, but on the

Continent males are in the majority. The cause of pityriasis rubra pilaris is unknown. Occasionally several members of a family are affected. It has been suggested that it is a tuberculide, and in a recent case I obtained a positive reaction with Moro's ointment and von Pirquet's test, but in two others the reaction was negative.

Pathology. The lesion is a hyperkeratosis of the follicular orifice around the hair. The stratum granulosum may be hypertrophic, while the corpus mucosum is thinned. The papillæ are congested and infiltrated with cells, and in the older papules the deep parts of the hair follicles are chronically inflamed.

Clinical features. Pityriasis rubra pilaris has very definite

FIG. 192.—Pityriasis rubra pilaris.   Microphotograph
of section $\frac{2}{3}$.

characters. The eruption consists of papules of a pale pink, red, brownish, or yellowish colour situated at the hair follicles. The individual lesions vary in size from a pin's head to a millet seed ; they are at first discrete, but in time become closely aggregated to form patches or plaques involving considerable areas. The papules are more closely set in the central part of the affected area than at the periphery.

The lesions are hard, and a surface covered with them feels like a very coarse rasp or nutmeg-grater. A close examination of a papule shows a central horny punctum which contains an atrophied hair often curled up.

The face is often the seat of a diffuse red scaly eruption, the

Plate 46.

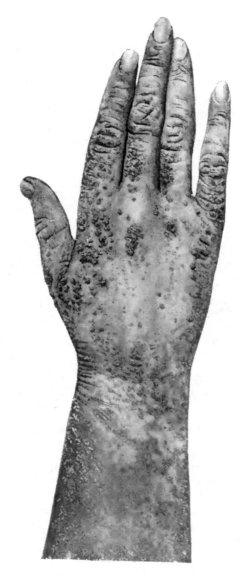

PITYRIASIS RUBRA PILARIS.

Showing the characteristic colour and distribution
of the papules on the fingers and wrist.

appearance sometimes suggesting that of a Red Indian. The scalp is covered with a copious branny scurf, while the palms and soles are dry and horny. On the elbows and knees the aggregation of the papules forms scaly plaques which simulate psoriasis.

On examination special attention should be given to the backs of

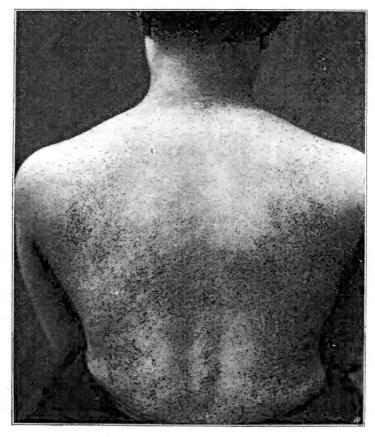

FIG. 193.—Pityriasis rubra pilaris.

the hands and the dorsal surfaces of the first phalanges of the fingers, where the lesions are in the form of minute horny plugs at the orifices of the hair follicles, or small groups of perifollicular papules with a scaly cap (Plate XLVI.). The elbows, knees, wrists and forearms are usually involved. On the trunk the eruption in some instances is more developed upon the upper part, the neck, shoulders and chest, while in others the waist and the lower abdomen are chiefly affected. In one of my cases the greater part of the trunk and limbs was involved (Fig. 193).

In rare instances the whole surface becomes scaly and red—a general exfoliative dermatitis (*vide* p. 404).

The nails are soft, and longitudinally striated like a cane.

There is a variable amount of itching, and the patient may complain of the skin feeling tense. The general health is unaffected. The disease runs a chronic course, with intermissions and relapses.

I have had under my care a child who at different times has suffered from psoriasis and pityriasis rubra pilaris. Dr. Adamson has also seen this association.

Diagnosis. The characteristic features of pityriasis rubra pilaris are the black conical plugs on the backs of the fingers and the rasp-like surfaces due to the closely-set hard papules. Exfoliative dermatitis (pityriasis rubra) is more hyperæmic, and scales are larger and more abundant. Papulation is absent. In psoriasis the lesions increase by peripheral extension, while in pityriasis rubra pilaris they are all about one size, and the face and scalp are the seat of diffuse red, scaling areas. Psoriasis rarely affects the face, and the spots are circumscribed. Ichthyosis, especially the form known as keratosis pilaris, might possibly lead to error, but the horny plugs are non-inflammatory, and develop in infancy and persist throughout life.

Prognosis. The general tendency of the disease is to spontaneous cure, but the duration is indefinite, and relapses are common.

Treatment. Thyroid extract in five-grain doses was strongly advocated by Radcliffe Crocker. Injections of pilocarpine to induce sweating are also recommended. Arsenic has also been used. Milian stated that injections of tuberculin proved satisfactory. The local treatment is on the same lines as that of psoriasis. Frequent baths containing sodium bicarbonate, with the free use of soap to remove the scales, are of great benefit. Eugallol, oil of cade, and resorcin in ointment form are used for their keratolytic effect. Mercurials may be added to the above remedies with advantage.

REFERENCES.—BESNIER. *Annales de Dermatologie*, 1889, Vol. X., p. 254. A. R. ROBINSON. *Journal Cut. and Genito.-Ur. Diseases*, Vol. VII., 1899, February and March. NEUMANN. *Archiv. f. Derm. u. Syphil.*, 1892, Vol. XXIV., p. 3. C. VIGNOLO-LUTATI. " Histopathology." *Archiv. f. Derm. u. Syph.*, April, 1906, p. 273.

Keratosis follicularis (Darier's Disease, Psorospermosis follicularis vegetans).

A chronic symmetrical disease characterised by follicular crusted papules with a peculiar form of keratinisation.

Etiology. The cause is unknown. The disease is rare, and according to Darier occurs rather more frequently in males than in

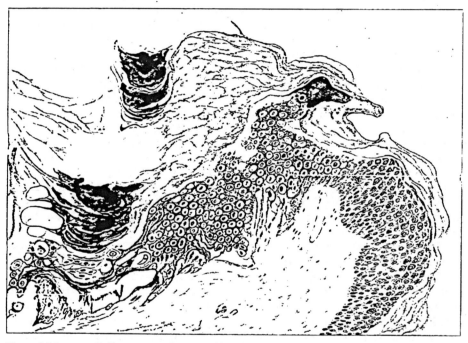

FIG. 194.—A. "Corps ronds" of Darier. B. Fissure in deeper layers of rete. C. Plug of stratified horn-cells and débris. Dr. Graham Little's case of Darier's disease.

females, though curiously the only cases I have seen have been females. Sometimes there are small family outbreaks which suggest contagion, but there is no proof. When Darier first described the disease in 1896 he called it "psorospermosis," because he believed that certain peculiar rounded bodies, to be described under pathology, were coccidia, or psorosperms, but he now recognises that these "bodies" are epidermal cells imperfectly keratinised.

Pathology. The top of the crust is formed by thickened horny epidermal cells, and these are mixed with curious grain-like cells which are horny and nucleated. In the corpus granulosum and in the mucous layer are found round bodies with a highly refracting membrane, and containing a nucleated protoplasm. These were supposed to be coccidia, but they are now known to be imperfectly developed elements of their respective layers. The papillæ are hypertrophied.

Clinical features. The primary lesion is a papule, varying in size from a pin's head to a pea, capped by a greyish-brown crust. On removing the horny crust a funnel-shaped cavity is exposed, from which a soft plug can be extracted. The cavity is a dilated sebaceous orifice. At the onset the skin is rough, and has a dirty appearance. As the disease progresses more and more follicular lesions appear and form wart-like masses. In parts which are moist, such as the groins

Fig. 195.—Darier's disease. Abdomen and thigh of woman, æt. 54
From water-colour drawing of Author's case.

and axillæ, they develop into vegetations of globular or crateriform form and give off an offensive odour.

The eruption is symmetrical and affects the face, especially the naso-labial furrows and the temples and the scalp, but it does not lead to baldness. It is also found over the sternum and between the scapulæ, in the flexures of the limbs, about the waist and the perigenital regions. Only in advanced cases is the extensor aspect of the limbs and the trunk involved. The hands and feet are sometimes affected, and there are often flat warts on the hand and minute points of hyperkeratosis on the palms and soles. In a case of mine the eruption appeared suddenly on the flexures of the elbows, and then slowly spread to the hands ; a little later the chest was involved, and then the abdomen and the thighs and legs. The patient complained of considerable irritation of the skin, especially in the warm weather. The skin of her face was coarse and dark, and there were scattered discrete papules of the same colour as the rest of the skin. The scalp was covered with masses of greasy scales, and the hair was coarse and scanty. On the chest and upper abdomen the papules were the size of pin's heads, and discrete, but on the abdomen some of the lesions were an eighth of an inch in diameter, and closely packed together. When admitted to my ward the colour of the skin in the groins and lower abdomen was so black as to suggest acanthosis nigricans, but after bathing the brown colour became apparent. On the labia majora and in the groins the lesions reached their maximum development, forming papillomatous tumours. The limbs were much less affected than the trunk, and the papules on them were always discrete and of small size. The nails were opaque and brittle. The mucous membranes were unaffected. The patient was forty-three years of age and had had the disease for many years. It usually starts between the ages of eight and sixteen, or later. There are no general symptoms, and the eruption remains stationary for an indefinite time.

The **diagnosis** is made by the curious appearance of the crusted papules and the funnel-shaped plugs seen when these are removed. In a doubtful case a microscopical examination should be made, when the appearance of the rounded bodies and the grain-like cells make the diagnosis clear.

Treatment. The disease is not easily influenced by treatment, but frequent bathing and the use of medicated soaps and ointments containing salicylic acid and resorcin improve the condition. Thyroid extract has been recommended.

REFERENCES. —DARIER. International Atlas of Rare Skin Diseases, 1893, Parts 8, 23, 24. SCHWENINGER. *Ibid.*, 25. J. H. ORMEROD and J. M. H. MACLEOD. *British Journal of Dermatology*, 1904, XVI., p. 321. Literature.

Acanthosis nigricans.

A very rare disease commonly associated with abdominal cancer, characterised by warty growths upon the skin and pigmentation.

Etiology. Three-fourths of the patients suffering from this peculiar condition are women, between the ages of 35 and 50. In the majority of the cases recorded there has been evidence of carcinoma of the alimentary tract or of the female genital organs. Sometimes the acanthosis has been the first sign of malignant disease. Professor Wild showed at Belfast, in July, 1909, a man in whom the supraclavicular glands were enlarged before the appearance of the cutaneous affection, the probable site of the primary growth being the cardiac end of the stomach.

Pathology. The probable cause is compression or irritation of the abdominal sympathetic centres, and sometimes growths have been found in the neighbourhood of the nerves adjacent to the adrenals. The cutaneous changes are hypertrophy of the horny and granular layers of the epidermis, and of the prickle-cell layer. The papillæ are elongated by the down growth of the interpapillary processes. The pigment is in the form of granules in the deep layers of the epidermis.

FIG. 196.—Acanthosis nigricans. (Block kindly lent by Prof. Wild, of Manchester.)

Clinical features. The skin generally is of a greyish-brown tint. The warty excrescences occur symmetrically, and affect the back of the neck and the perianal and genito-crural regions most commonly, but the axillæ, umbilical region, the bends of the elbows, the mammary region, and the hands and feet are involved to a greater or less extent. Warty growths also occur in the buccal cavity, but the mucosa is not pigmented. The pigmented skin varies in colour from a greyish-brown to a dark brown or even black tint ; it is somewhat thickened, and the surface is rugose from the exaggeration of the normal fissures. There is no scaling, but in the flexures, particularly the regions mentioned above, there are isolated warty excrescences or groups of warts varying in size from elevations just visible to the naked eye to lesions as large as a small pea. The skin of the hand is commonly warty and pigmented, the nails are brittle, and there is often considerable loss of hair. The warts are not painful, but there may be some itching. The onset is usually insidious, the patient first noticing the darkening of the skin in the axillæ or about the neck, or the development of one or more warts. In some instances itching has preceded any obvious change in the integument.

The **course** of acanthosis depends upon the activity of the malignant process, but the **prognosis** is always very grave.

The **diagnosis** of an advanced case is not difficult. The affection which most closely resembles acanthosis is Darier's disease, which usually begins early in life and affects males more than females. The pigmentation is not so marked in Darier's disease, the scalp is usually affected, and there are peculiar bodies in the lesions (pseudo-psorosperms). The pigmentation might suggest Addison's disease, but the presence of warty growths is sufficient to distinguish acanthosis nigricans.

Treatment. Unless the primary cause can be removed by operation nothing satisfactory can be done. Supra-renal extract has been suggested by Boeck. Thyroid extract is also recommended.

REFERENCES.—Plate in RADCLIFFE CROCKER'S Atlas, LIV. International Atlas of Rare Skin Diseases, X. and XI. MALCOLM MORRIS. *Med. Chir. Trans.*, 1894, LXXVII., p. 247: plates in colours. U. J. WILE. *Journ. Cutaneous Dis.*, 1912, XXX., p. 179.

Porokeratosis (Mibelli and Resphighi).

A chronic spreading hyperkeratosis affecting the extensor surfaces of the hands and feet, and rarely other parts, including the buccal mucosa.

Etiology. The cause is unknown. Males are more commonly

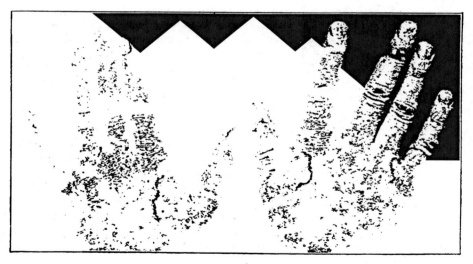

FIG. 197.—Porokeratosis of Mibelli. Photograph kindly lent by Sir James Galloway.

affected than females. The disease appears in childhood, and Gilchrist recorded eleven cases in four generations of one family.

Pathology. The horny layer of the epidermis and the upper part of the rete are affected. There is considerable increase of these layers (hyperkeratosis), and the sweat glands of the skin are involved in the process, hence the name Porokeratosis.

Clinical features. The eruption consists of a number of warty papules on the extremities, but occasionally the face and the genital organs are affected. The papule is conical with a crater-like depression, in which is a horny plug. The papules slowly increase to form irregular circinate spots or plaques of variable size and shape. The plaque may be only half an inch in diameter, or it may involve the whole of the affected limb. The early patches are circular, but the older ones have an irregular outline. The edge in the fully-developed plaque is well-defined, consisting of a row of papules which may be at the bottom of a furrow or groove. The centre of the area may be atrophic or scaly, but it is sometimes of normal appearance. The nail may be involved, an opaque area forming by extension from a finger lesion. The buccal mucosa and palate may be affected. The rim resembles a " fine silk thread." The disease begins in childhood, and progresses slowly for years.

Treatment. Patches of limited area have been successfully treated by electrolysis.

REFERENCES.—MIBELLI. *Monatsheft. f. Prakt. Dermatologie,* 1893, XVII., No. 9. RESPIGHI. *Ibid.,* 1894, XVIII., p. 70. T. C. GILCHRIST. *Bulletin Johns Hopkins Hosp.,* LXXIV. J. GALLOWAY. *Brit. Journ. Dermatology,* XIII., pp. 262, 300.

Keratoma plantare sulcatum is a hyperkeratosis of the soles and heels. The epidermis is greatly thickened and of a dark yellow colour, and split up by numerous deep fissures of straight, circular or ellipsoid forms. There is no sign of local inflammation, and the bases of the furrows when clear are white.

The disease occurs in the rainy seasons in Ceylon, India, and tropical Africa.

REFERENCE. — CASTELLANI and CHALMERS. "Tropical Medicine," p. 1599, plate.

Mossy foot is the name given to a peculiar vascular warty affection met with on the Amazons. The foot is covered with these vegetations, which are $\frac{1}{2}$ to $\frac{3}{4}$ inch thick. There is considerable pain. The leg may be affected by extension. The course is chronic, and Low has suggested that the disease is a type of warty tuberculosis.

REFERENCE.—THOMAS. *Trans. Soc. Tropical Medicine,* 1910.

CHAPTER XXII.

THE PEMPHIGUS GROUP.

The name " pemphigus," signifying blister, was formerly widely used and applied to any disease in which the formation of bullæ or blebs is an essential feature. The bullous impetigo of infants is still commonly called pemphigus neonatorum, and the outbreaks of bullous impetigo which sometimes occur in epidemics are called P. contagiosus. The congenital anomaly, already described as epidermolysis bullosa, is still sometimes referred to as Pemphigus traumaticus hereditarius. P. neuroticus is the name applied to bullous lesions appearing in certain nervous diseases and injuries, while P. hystericus is almost certainly due to self-inflicted injuries causing blisters. " Syphilitic pemphigus " is a term to be avoided, but is sometimes applied to bullous syphilides.

A bullous eruption may occur after the administration of certain drugs, notably the iodides. I have seen it follow vaccination, and Bowen described a series of ten such cases with six deaths. I have also reported a case in which a widely-spread bullous eruption was associated with gangrenous appendicitis in a young child. Anomalous conditions of this kind are difficult to explain, and the possibility of the eruption being due to toxic bodies developed at foci of infection has to be considered.

In this chapter I propose to describe a group of diseases with fairly well defined characters in which the formation of blisters is the predominant feature. It is impossible to classify them satisfactorily in the present state of our knowledge, for with the exception of one variety, which is probably of bacterial origin, we are in complete ignorance of their etiology. In a number of cases the relationships are so indefinite that many careful observers prefer to apply the name " bullous eruption," which has the advantage of being non-committal.

Acute Malignant Pemphigus.

A general infectious disease with a bullous eruption occurring in butchers and others who handle dead carcases.

Etiology. Bulloch found a diplococcus in the fluid from fresh blebs in two cases (Pernet's and Hadley's), and Demme has described a similar organism. It is supposed that the microbe is the cause of the disease.

Clinical features. The disease commonly follows a wound in the hand or elsewhere, and sometimes the bite of an animal. Its onset is marked by rigors, a temperature as high as 104°, sickness and diarrhœa, and there may be delirium.

The primary lesion may be a whitlow at the site of infection, but the characteristic bullæ appear at the end of twenty-four to forty-eight hours. The blisters are at first discrete and tense, and the contents are yellow serum or blood. They come out in large numbers, and may become confluent. Early rupture takes place in the flexures and where there is pressure, leading to the formation of raw surfaces which are covered by stinking, decaying epidermis. The mucous membranes of the mouth, tongue, conjunctiva, etc., are involved. The patient is in a prostrate condition, the urine contains albumen, and the symptoms suggest a grave infection, which ends fatally in 75 per cent. of the cases. Death occurs in from one to three weeks. In the minority of cases of recovery, convalescence begins in from three to four weeks.

Treatment. Every endeavour should be made to support the patient's strength, quinine should be administered, and the injection of artificial serum is advocated. The local treatment is similar to that described for pemphigus chronicus.

REFERENCES.—"Acute Pemphigus." G. PERNET and W. BULLOCH. *Brit. Journ. of Dermatology*, Vol. VIII., 1896, p. 157. Literature. "Bullous Dermatitis following Vaccination." BOWEN. *Journ. Cut. Diseases*, 1905, XXIII., p. 79. "Bullous Eruption associated with Gangrenous Appendicitis." J. H. SEQUEIRA. *Brit. Journ. Dermatology*, XXIII., p. 295.

Dermatitis herpetiformis (Duhring's Disease). Pemphigus pruriginosus. Dermites polymorphes douleureuses (Brocq).

A polymorphic eruption characterised by erythematous, vesicular and bullous lesions attended with intense itching, and with a great tendency to recurrence.

Etiology. Dermatitis herpetiformis is comparatively rare. It may occur at any age, but is more common between 20 and 40. Both sexes are equally affected. Exposure to cold, worry, exhaustion and shock are believed to be exciting causes, but of its exact nature nothing is known. No specific organism has been found in the lesions, and the disease is not inoculable or contagious. It has been suggested that it is due to a toxæmia, but of the nature of the toxine, and whether it is developed within the body or introduced from without, we are ignorant. From the remarkable excess of eosinophile cells found in the bullæ and in the blood, Leredde and Perrin brought forward the hypothesis that the primary cause of dermatitis herpetiormis is an affection of the bone marrow. Of this, again, there is no proof.

Pathology. The erythematous patches are congested and œdematous, and there is cellular infiltration of the papillæ. The cellular elements show a remarkable excess of eosinophiles. The bullæ are comparatively superficial, the roof being formed by the corneous

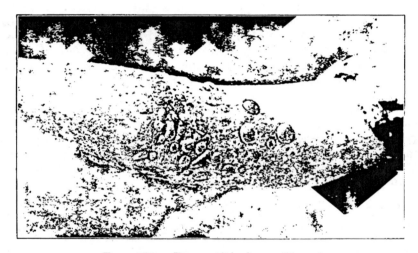

FIG. 198.—Dermatitis herpetiformis.

layer, or by the whole or part of the epidermis. The fluid in the blebs contains a large number of eosinophile cells, and the same cells are found in large numbers in the blood. There are no visceral lesions which are peculiar, and no changes in the nervous system.

Clinical features. There are four cardinal features of Duhring's disease—(1) the eruption is polymorphic, (2) it is attended with itching and sometimes with pain, (3) it is recurrent, and (4) the patient's health remains good.

The eruption consists of erythematous patches, usually well defined, of discoid shape, or with a gyrate outline from the coalescence of several neighbouring lesions. In rare cases there are papules. Vesicles appear on the patches, sometimes in groups like the vesicles of herpes, sometimes scattered irregularly over the surface of the plaque, or forming a marginal ring. The size of the vesicles varies much more than is usual in herpes, and bullæ as large as a pea or nut are common. In some cases there are blebs as large as a walnut or larger. Diversity in size of the bullous lesions is frequent. The vesicles and the blebs are not entirely confined to the erythematous patches, but may develop upon normal skin. The fluid in the bullæ and vesicles is clear at first, but it may become purulent, and in some rare cases, of apparently the same type, the fluid is puriform from the onset. Stained specimens of the fluid show a remarkable number of eosinophile cells, which may reach 20 to 90 per cent. of the cell elements present.

The disease presents many varieties, but these depend in the main upon the relative preponderance of the erythematous and vesicular lesions and upon the varying size of the bullæ.

The limbs are the parts most affected, and the forearms, perhaps, more than other parts, but no region of the skin is exempt. Buccal lesions are not rare. The eruption tends to come out in crops, but the duration of any one lesion is limited. The red areas become pale; the vesicles and bullæ rupture and dry up and leave moist or crusted spots. On the subsidence of the eruption pigmented stains are left, but scarring only occurs if the parts are severely scratched.

Subjective symptoms. The itching is intense. The Vienna school, refusing to separate the disease from true pemphigus, call it pemphigus pruriginosus. The pruritus may precede the eruption; it is always worse at night, and may be extremely distressing to the patient. Sometimes the affected areas are terribly excoriated by scratching. Complaints of burning sensations and of actual pain are also common.

General symptoms. The itching and pain may prevent sleep, and with the attacks there may be febrile phenomena, and sometimes diarrhœa, but there is no general wasting as in chronic pemphigus. In several cases I have examined the urine over long periods, but have failed to find the hypoazoturia which is described as occurring in this as in other members of the pemphigus group. A constant feature, and one of some importance in the diagnosis, is the excess of eosinophiles in the blood; a percentage of 10 or 15 is common, and recently I had a case in which it was as high as 30 per cent. Indicanuria may also occur.

Course. An attack may last for several weeks, or it may go on for a twelvemonth or more, and then the patient will probably have a period of freedom, which may, however, be of only a few weeks' duration or last several months. In some cases the eruption recurs throughout life, but the intervals between the attacks gradually

Plate 47.

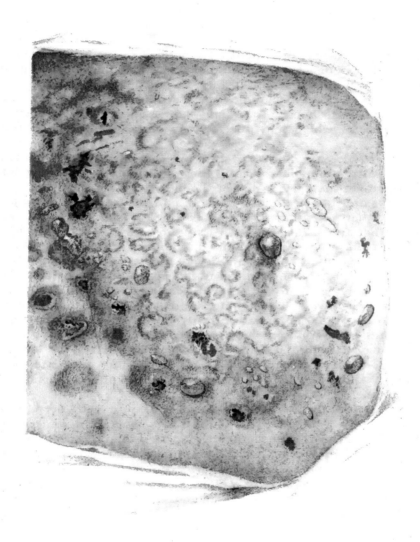

DERMATITIS HERPETIFORMIS.

Polymorphic eruption: erythema, vesicles and bullæ.

lengthen. A duration of ten or fifteen years is not uncommon. In rare instances Duhring's disease passes on to pemphigus foliaceus, and still more rarely vegetating lesions develop (*vide* Pemphigus vegetans). Dermatitis herpetiformis is one of the most distressing of skin diseases ; it unfits the patient for long periods from pursuing his avocations, but it is not dangerous to life, and death occurs from intercurrent disease.

Diagnosis. The intense itching and the maintenance of the general health serve to distinguish dermatitis herpetiformis from common pemphigus. The eosinophilia is also a useful guide. In urticaria with bullæ and in erythema bullosum the vesicular and bullous elements are not grouped, and are obviously an epiphenomenon. In erythema there is also less itching.

Prognosis. Under appropriate treatment most cases get well in a few weeks to several months, but there is in all a great tendency to recurrence. There are patients, however, who are rarely free from some degree of eruption for years.

Treatment. In the acute attacks the patients must be kept in bed. I have known cases of the milder form in which they have been able with some difficulty to pursue some occupation of a not very exacting character. A nutritious diet should be given, but milk should be the staple food in the acute stages. Alcohol should be forbidden. Arsenic in increasing doses, pushed to the limit of toleration, has a controlling influence upon the eruption, and salicin (15 to 30 grains thrice daily), as suggested by Dr. Radcliffe Crocker, has been used with advantage. Quinine has also its advocates, while antipyrin and phenacetin are used to relieve the itching. Darier has seen the injection of artificial serum in gradually increasing doses, up to a litre at a time, useful. A strict vegetarian diet with limitation of the quantity of fluid taken has been found to diminish the irritation. In some cases in which colitis was present autogenous vaccines are said to have been of service, but I have no personal experience of their use.

I have had no success with the injection of the patient's own blood serum.

Sulphur baths and ointments containing sulphur are generally very valuable. The B.P. sulphur ointment may be used. Where, however, the blister formation is very extensive, it is better to use dusting powders of zinc and starch or talc. The lotion of the glycerol of lead and calamine liniment are also useful for the treatment of large denuded surfaces. If the itching is very severe, liq. carbonis detergens, a drachm to four ounces, may be added to the lotions.

REFERENCES.—BROCQ. *Annales de Derm. et de Syph.*, 1888, IX., p. 1; X., p. 849. DUHRING. *Journ. Amer. Med. Assoc.*, 1884, August 30. *New Sydenham Society's Publication*, 1893. Monograph. J. M. H. MACLEOD. "Pemphigoid Eruptions." *Brit. Journ. Dermatology*, 1915, p. 201 : with report on discussion.

Hydroa gravidarum (Hydroa gestationis).

Hydroa gravidarum presents the same phenomena as dermatitis herpetiformis. It commonly occurs between the third and the sixth months of pregnancy, and often recurs with each successive pregnancy, and sometimes after delivery. As a rule the severity increases with each attack. Eosinophilia occurs in hydroa gravidarum as in Duhring's disease. It is believed to be caused by toxic bodies developed during gestation. It will be remembered that the urine of pregnant women has a high degree of toxicity, and rapidly causes death when injected into animals.

The treatment and general management are the same as in dermatitis herpetiformis. Recently great benefit is recorded as following the injection of 10 c.c. of inactivated serum made from the patient's own blood.

REFERENCE.—H. FRENCH. Goulstonian Lectures. *British Medical Journal*, May 2, 1908, p. 1029.

Hydroa puerorum (Unna) and **Hydroa aestivale** (Hydroa vacciniforme of Bazin, also called Hutchinson's recurring summer eruption) are sometimes classed as varieties of dermatitis herpetiformis. They have already been discussed among the diseases believed to be caused by the irritation of the sun. They begin in infancy or early childhood as red spots upon which appear round vesicles in groups. The uncovered parts are affected, and the disease tends to disappear about puberty (*vide* p. 75).

Hydroa vacciniforme leaves scars.

Pemphigus chronicus.

True pemphigus is a progressive disease characterised by the formation of blisters upon healthy skin. It is slowly progressive and often fatal.

Etiology. The patients are usually debilitated subjects over forty years of age. At the London Hospital an equal number of men and women are admitted to the wards, though Kaposi gave the proportion as three males to one female.

Pemphigus is not contagious, and no organism has yet been discovered which is specific to the disease. Worry, anxiety and the like are said to predispose to the affection. Parenchymatous changes in the spinal cord have been described, and it has been suggested that the disease is a toxæmia primarily acting on the nervous system and secondarily affecting the skin. Hendry has cultivated a short motile bacillus anærobically on human muscle which he believes to be the causative agent. Other organisms have been reported to be present, but the bacterial origin of the disease, though probable, has not yet been proved.

Pathology. The bullæ are formed as the result of the inflammation of the papillary layer, with exudation of fluid. Sections of a bulla show that its roof is formed in some cases by the horny layer and in others by the Malpighian layer. The derma is œdematous, but there are few migratory cells. There is no excess of eosinophiles as in dermatitis herpetiformis.

Clinical features. The eruption may first appear on the lips or in the mouth or on the front of the chest, and occasionally on other parts. The lesions are round or oval blisters about a fourth of an inch to an inch in diameter. They are usually tense, but may be flaccid. Their contents are clear serous fluid, which at the onset is always sterile. There is no excess of eosinophile cells in the fluid of the blebs as in dermatitis herpetiformis, pemphigus foliaceus, and pemphigus vegetans.

The bulla makes its appearance on healthy skin, but after the lapse of a few hours there is a red halo, and the lesion may suppurate. In blebs of even the second day both staphylococci and streptococci are commonly found. Whether the bullæ are allowed to rupture or not, they tend to dry up and form crusts which fall at the end of a week or ten days, leaving a brownish stain. The individual lesions do not increase in size, but numerous fresh blebs appear, sometimes in crops, though the development of crops is not nearly so marked a feature as in Duhring's disease. In advanced cases the abraded surfaces left by the bullæ do not heal well, and raw or scabbed areas with gyrate outlines are left. These are often surrounded by groups of fresh blebs. In this way large areas of the trunk and limbs may be affected, and in course of time the eruption may become general. Occasionally the bullæ contain blood, and in some instances the base may ulcerate, especially where there is friction or pressure. In the flexures, the neck, the axillæ, groins, and the anal and genital regions large raw areas sometimes covered with a diphtheroid membrane

are seen, and actual gangrene may occur.   In one case recently under
my care large intramuscular abscesses formed in each thigh.   Pure
cultures of streptococci were obtained from the pus.   *Nikolsky's sign.*
If the pulp of the finger be pressed on the skin the corneous layer of
the epidermis can be made to slide on the subjacent layer, and the

Fig. 199.—Pemphigus.   The photograph was taken early in the case,
which ultimately proved fatal.

pressure produces a bulla.   This sign is not peculiar to pemphigus,
but occurs sometimes in dermatitis herpetiformis and in epidermolysis
bullosa.

The mucous membranes are often affected in pemphigus.   As
already mentioned, the mouth may be the first part to be attacked,
but at all stages bullæ are common on the buccal mucosa, on the
palate, tongue, and pharynx.   Their early rupture leads to the

Plate 48.

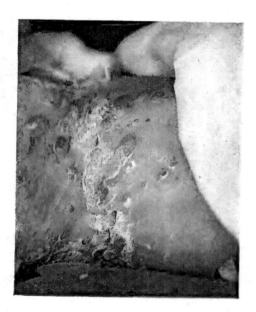

PEMPHIGUS.

Female, aged 52. The photograph shows bullæ
and ruptured bullæ on the flank.   The lower part is
somewhat obscured by zinc ointment.

formation of white patches which resemble the lesions of diphtheria, or ulcerative stomatitis. The lips are also affected. The mouth becomes very foul, and the taking of food may be extremely difficult and painful. The mucous membrane of the nose and the eyes and the vulva may be similarly involved. In one of my recent cases the ocular symptoms were curiously severe in proportion to the cutaneous eruption. The patient lost the sight of one eye, and there was "essential shrinking" of the conjunctiva. In rare cases an affection of the eyes of similar type occurs without any cutaneous lesions

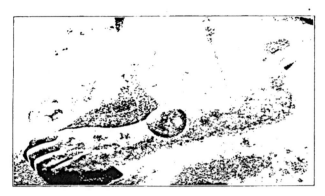

FIG. 200.—"Pemphigus solitarius." The bulla depicted was the sole lesion. The affection is probably of coccal origin.

whatever. It is, however, doubtful whether this condition is pemphigus.

Subjective symptoms. There may be no itching or burning, and the lesions are only painful when the surfaces are abraded from the rupture of the blisters. The buccal condition is extremely painful and causes much suffering.

General symptoms. The patient rapidly wastes, and there is loss of appetite and depression. The temperature is elevated at the onset and with the successive outbreaks. Ulceration and sloughing and the formation of abscesses tend to prolongation of the pyrexia. Vomiting and diarrhœa occur, and albuminuria and grave hypoazoturia are common symptoms. The patient frequently dies in from three to eighteen months, but the disease may pass on to pemphigus foliaceus (*vide* p. 495). Benign cases are seen, especially in children, but there is some doubt whether they are cases of true pemphigus. The curious cases in which a solitary large bulla develops, so-called "Pemphigus solitarius," are undoubtedly not, but their true nature is, unknown. In all probability they are due to coccogenic infection.

Diagnosis. The first point that the student must recognise is that all bullous eruptions are not pemphigus. The most common bleb eruption is caused by pus-cocci, a bullous impetigo, and sometimes this may be extensive enough to raise a suspicion of pemphigus. It usually clears up rapidly with mild antiseptic treatment. Dermatitis herpetiformis is differentiated by the polymorphism of the eruption and the intense itching, together with the tendency to the formation of herpetic groups and eosinophilia. Epidermolysis bullosa dates from early infancy, and bullous impetigo of the infant occurs during the first two weeks of life, and rarely later. So-called pemphigus in children is most likely a bullous impetigo due to streptococci. It must also be remembered that some drugs, and particularly iodides, cause bullous eruptions. No reliance can be placed upon bacteriological examination of the contents of the bullæ, unless the lesion is quite recent. All bullæ become secondarily infected with pyogenic cocci from the skin within a few hours, certainly by the second day. The bullous eruptions in certain nervous diseases may resemble pemphigus, but they are not likely to cause trouble in diagnosis, as the nervous phenomena are pre-eminent, and the skin affection is subsidiary. In hysterical girls and women bullous eruptions are met with from time to time, but there is grave doubt whether there is such a thing as pemphigus hystericus in the strict sense. Where such an eruption occurs the patient should be suspected of applying local irritants. For an account of such a case the reader is referred to p. 59.

Prognosis. True pemphigus is a grave disease, and in thirty patients admitted to the London Hospital with this diagnosis nineteen died in the wards, and this does not complete the tale of mortality, because some of the cases ran a very chronic course, and were transferred to the infirmary, or went home to die. It is exceedingly difficult at the onset of the disease to say whether it is going to develop into the grave type, and a very guarded prognosis should always be given. In this country the outlook appears to be slightly more favourable than that of cases seen in the Continental clinics.

Treatment. Arsenic in increasing doses is the usual remedy given, but in many cases has only a slight controlling influence. It appears to be more successful in the younger patients. Salicin in doses of fifteen to thirty grains thrice daily may also be tried. Quinine and general tonics are useful, and strychnine, advocated by Neisser, is sometimes of value. Leszczynski advocates intravenous infusions of quinine. Seven grains of quinine may be given dissolved in two pints of normal saline. Opium may be required to relieve pain and induce sleep.

The patient must be confined to bed, the parts being protected with dressings and powders. Zinc oxide and starch or talc, with addition of boric acid, form a useful powder. More generally it will be found. advisable to wrap up the affected areas in lint soaked in glycerol of lead lotion (glycerol of lead, one ounce ; glycerin, one ounce ; water, one pint). The calamine liniment is another soothing preparation (Calaminæ, thirty-five grains ; Ol. Olivæ and Aq. Calcis, of each half an ounce). The large abraded surfaces may be dressed with boric acid ointment spread upon lint. Prolonged immersion in warm baths kept at an even temperature (about 100° C.) is comforting, and tends to cleanse the surface, but the patient requires careful watching while submitted to this form of treatment.

The diet must be as supporting as the patient can take, but the foul condition of the mouth is often a great trouble, and requires constant attention. I usually have the buccal cavity swabbed out frequently with a peroxide of hydrogen and boric acid lotion, equal parts of peroxide of hydrogen (10 vols.) and lotio acidi borici being used.

REFERENCE.—LESZCZYNSKI. *Archiv. f. Dermat.*, 1912, CXIV., p. 29.

Pemphigus foliaceus.

This variety of pemphigus is characterised by the formation of flaccid bullæ, followed by a condition of general exfoliation of the skin. It may be primary, but is more frequently the sequel of common pemphigus, and rarely of dermatitis herpetiformis.

Etiology. Women are more often affected than men, and at the London Hospital the patients are always of Polish or Russian origin. The cause of the disease is unknown. It has been variously supposed to be of nervous, toxic, or hæmatic origin. When it supervenes upon common pemphigus, it suggests a superadded infection, and it is possible that it may be microbic.

Pathology. There is great dilatation of the vessels of the corium. The connective tissue is œdematous and swollen and shows hyaline and colloid degeneration. The glands are atrophic. The Malpighian layer shows an elongation of the interpapillary projections. The cells of the rete are swollen and lose their prickles. The exfoliation takes place below the stratum corneum or between the layers of the rete or between the rete and corium.

Clinical features. The characteristic lesions are flaccid bullæ, but on their rupture there is no tendency to the formation of healthy epidermis, but of lamellar scales which resemble leaves. They are usually moist, rarely dry, and cover red areas. The eruption may involve the entire surface of the body. The contents of the bullæ are turbid from the first, and speedily become purulent. The corium is left exposed and moist, and covered with a fœtid muco-pus. The epidermis splits into lamellæ, and there are fissures between the scales producing a peculiar tessellated appearance. Nikolsky's sign is present. There is little itching or burning as a rule, but in some cases they may be severe. The hair may fall, and the nails are atrophic and may be shed. The epithelium lining the buccal cavity and pharynx is destroyed, and the mouth is in a foul, painful condition.

The temperature is rarely raised above 100° F. The patient becomes extremely emaciated, and, on the whole, the disease runs a progressive course, but from time to time there may be intermissions in the severity of the symptoms, and parts of the skin may heal up, but in from two to three years, and sometimes much longer, pemphigus foliaceus ends fatally, by general asthenia, diarrhœa, or some intercurrent disease. In one of my cases uræmia closed the scene. In this connection it is of great interest to note that grave hypoazoturia is common. I have examined the urine carefully in several cases over long periods. In one the urea excreted was for many weeks under 1 per cent., and was once as low as 0·4 per cent. Dr. H. L. Tidy made a series of examinations of the total nitrogenous excretion, and found that the amount of nitrogen excreted by the kidneys was far below that taken in the food. We were led to believe that the residual nitrogen must be lost by the large areas of denuded skin.

Diagnosis. Pemphigus foliaceus has to be distinguished from the erythrodermias, in which there is general exfoliation, but these have no flaccid bulla formation. Generalised eczema is rarely if ever complete, and careful examination will show the absence of bullous formation.

Treatment is of no avail. The feeding of the patient may present difficulties, but it is remarkable how long strength is maintained. No internal medication affords any relief. Prolonged immersion in warm baths affords more comfort than any other measure. Failing these, the local applications mentioned under Chronic Pemphigus should be used.

REFERENCE.—R. CRANSTON LOW. *British Journal of Dermatology*, 1909, XXI., p. 101 : with literature to date.

Pemphigus vegetans.

This exceedingly rare disease is characterised by the formation of bullæ, at the base of which vegetations rapidly develop.

Etiology. Nothing is known upon this point. The disease is exceedingly rare, only one case having been seen at the London Hospital for many years. It occurs in adults, and is probably a true pemphigus with a superadded infection. The bacillus pyocyaneus has been found in the lesions and in the blood, and pyogenic cocci and diphtheroid organisms have been isolated.

Pathology. The early lesions do not differ in any respect from the bullæ of common pemphigus. In the vegetative period, excrescences from one-fourth to one-third of an inch high form. They consist of a very thick mucous layer, with numerous minute abscesses crowded with polymorph leucocytes and many eosinophile cells. There is no excess of eosinophiles in the blood. Pathological changes have been found in the central nervous system and in the viscera, but they are inconstant.

Clinical features. In one half of the cases the eruption begins in the mouth, nose or pharynx. The genitalia are also frequent sites of origin. In other cases the bullæ begin in the flexures, or about a nail. The onset is often insidious, and in some instances the first symptom is dysphagia from buccal or pharyngeal excoriations due to ruptured blebs. On the skin the bullæ are flaccid, and filled with sero-pus, which dries up to form crusts, and they may heal up in the centre and spread at the periphery. In five or six days the bottom of one or more bullæ ulcerates, and a swelling forms. This swelling rapidly becomes papillomatous and secretes a fœtid pus, under a brown crust. The lesions look very much like the mucous plaques seen in syphilis. By serpiginous extension and the confluence of the elements, large areas may be involved. Finally, the whole body may be covered with ulcerating vegetations, suppurating, fœtid and painful. The buccal cavity is the seat of a number of erosions covered with a diphtheroid membrane. There is often fever, and death ensues from marasmus in from two to six months. In rare cases in which the eruption runs a benign course the eruption is limited to the limbs and the trunk rather than the flexures. I have had one such case under my care ; the eruption closely resembled an iodide eruption, but this was absolutely excluded by the fact that the patient had for some time been under the care of Dr. Cursham Corner, who kindly gave me all information as to the prescriptions. There was also no iodine in the urine. This case ran a mild course without general symptoms, and was greatly relieved by simple bathing. In the mild cases there is a tendency to recurrence, and there appears to be the same relationship between them and the ordinary type as between true pemphigus and Duhring's disease. A case of Hallopean's " Pyodermite végétante " which is of this type was recently published by Douglas Heath.

Treatment. Hutchinson advocated the internal administration of opium in pemphigus vegetans. The foul condition of the surface requires fomentations of mild antiseptics such as boric acid, peroxide of hydrogen, or ointments of peroxide of zinc, ten to forty grains to the ounce. Continuous bathing, if it can be arranged, gives great relief.

REFERENCES.—NEUMANN. Congress, Paris, 1899. "Comptes Rendus," p. 81. H. RADCLIFFE CROCKER. *Transactions Royal Medico-Chirurgical Society*, LXII. Literature. WINFIELD. *Journal of Cutaneous Diseases*, 1907, XXV., p. 17. Literature. H. MacCORMAC. *British Journal of Dermatology*, XX., p. 277. DOUGLAS HEATH. *British Journal of Dermatology*, XXVII., p. 227.

Onyalai. An acute infectious disease of the tropics characterised by the formation of bullæ containing blood on the skin, soft palate and buccal mucosa. The bullæ vary in size from a split pea to lesions several inches in diameter. The temperature is raised, and the parotids are swollen and tender. It is believed that hæmorrhages occur in the internal organs. The mortality is 25 per cent.

REFERENCE.—MASSEY. *Journal of Tropical Medicine*, 1904, September 1, p. 269.

CHAPTER XXIII.

LEUCODERMIA, MELANODERMIA AND CHLOASMA.

THE congenital pigmentary anomalies, albinism and pigmented moles, have been discussed in Chapter III., and the effects of sunlight, heat, and X-rays in Chapter IV. We have noticed that various inflammatory conditions of the skin leave stains, and that some drugs, notably arsenic and silver, discolour the skin. Special attention was directed to the pigmentary syphilide (p. 292) and the changes which occur in leprosy (p. 263). The dyschromias associated with general and visceral disease, hæmochromatosis, ochronosis, jaundice, and pigmentation in Addison's and Graves' diseases, hyperpituitarism, chronic intestinal stasis, etc., have been considered in Chapter XIII. We have now to deal with the peculiar pigmentary affections known as Leucodermia and Chloasma. The cause of the former is unknown, and the latter occurs in pregnancy and in association with uterine and ovarian disease. In the chapter on Tumours of the Skin we shall consider the melanotic carcinomata which usually develop from pigmented moles.

Leucodermia. Vitiligo.

The name Leucodermia is given to affections of the skin characterised by the absence of pigment. This change in the skin may be primary or secondary, and it is to the primary form that the name Leucodermia or Vitiligo is given. It is always associated with increase in the pigment around the white spots.

Etiology. The affection is more common in adolescence and youth than in mature age. Females are more frequently affected than males, and the disease is commoner among the dark races than in fair people. The cause of leucodermia is unknown, but it has supervened upon shock, and has been observed in connection with Graves' disease and with tabes. I have now under my care a man who while employed on a lightship in the Channel during the first year of the war developed alopecia universalis with extensive vitiligo of the trunk and extremities. Occasionally leucodermia has occurred in connection with alopecia areata, lichen planus, prurigo, and sclerodermia. Cases are also recorded in which urticarial wheals could be easily produced (Dermographism).

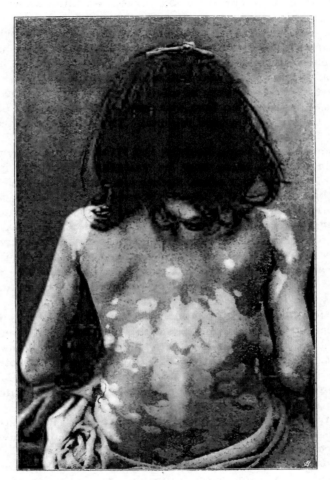

FIG. 201.—Leucodermia. Vitiligo.

Pathology. There is a complete absence of pigment in the leucodermic spots, and excess in the surrounding melanotic areas. A small round-celled infiltration is found round the vessels and glandular elements of the white spots. This is held to support the suggestion that the condition is of toxic origin.

Clinical features. The white spots are generally rounded at the onset, and the margin is well defined. The colour is milky, or like ivory. The spots are often limited, but they may extend over the greater part of the body. Schamberg pictures a negro who in seven years lost all the pigment of the skin except on small areas on the face and scrotum.

The increase of pigment is most marked around the white areas, and gradually shades away to the normal colour. The hair on the white patches is usually devoid of colour—leucotrichia. There are no symptoms, and the glandular functions are quite normal.

Any part of the body may be affected, but the commonest sites are the hands, forearms, the face and neck, and the lower part of the abdomen, thighs, and genital regions. The mucous surfaces are not involved.

Leucodermia may begin acutely, but its evolution is usually slow. From time to time there may be variations, and the increase of pigment in the summer often makes the white patches more conspicuous, but, as a rule, the progress is one of gradual extension, which by the coalescence of adjoining areas may involve large tracts.

The **diagnosis** is usually easy, but the discoloration may cause the affection to be mistaken for tinea versicolor, and for some of the conditions in which melanosis is a feature. The areas of pityriasis versicolor are of a *café-au-lait* tint and slightly scaly. The scales may be scraped off and the fungus demonstrated by examination under the microscope in a little liquor potassæ.

Syphilitic leucodermia is confined to the neck and occurs in women ; it has a peculiar dappled appearance (*vide* p. 292). Arsenical pigmentation is also dappled; but it affects the covered parts, the abdomen and chest. The pigmentation of Addison's disease, etc., is not associated with white areas, and the buccal mucosa is affected. Sclerodermia might give rise to difficulty, but is excluded by the toughness of the affected patches, which is completely absent in leucodermia. In the white patches of lepra there is anæsthesia, and the nerves are thickened. The atrophic patches of radiodermatitis are covered with telangiectases.

Prognosis. The disease is very little influenced by treatment.

Treatment. In a few cases improvement has followed the application of a lotion of perchloride of mercury 1-1,000. Some try to bleach the surrounding zone of pigmentation by peroxide of hydrogen, but I have never seen any appreciable effect. Heidingsfeldt has devised a tattooing apparatus with multiple needles to remedy the disfigurement. Tinting the white areas with weak walnut juice or permanganate of potash solution may be used where the spots are conspicuous. Castellani advocates the use of arsenic gr. $\frac{1}{50}$ in pill three times a day, or injection of atoxyl or soamin. Injections of adrenalin have also been recommended.

REFERENCES.—WILLMOTT EVANS. Erasmus Wilson Lectures. *Lancet,* February 16, 1907. Histology. PRINGLE and McDONAGH. Allbutt and Rolleston's System, IX., p. 561.

Chloasma uterinum.

A pigmentary discoloration of the face and rarely of other parts occurring in pregnancy and occasionally in uterine and ovarian disease.

Etiology. The affection is related in some way with the female genital organs, and has been variously ascribed to a toxæmia and to irritation of the sympathetic nerve centres in the abdomen.

Clinical features. Patches of a yellowish or brownish tint and of irregular outline appear on the forehead, temples, cheeks, and rarely on other parts of the face and trunk. The linea alba, the vulva, and the areolæ of the breasts are pigmented at the same time, especially in brunettes. Chloasma develops in pregnancy, and persists until menstruation returns, or even longer. It sometimes occurs in association with disease of the uterus and of the Fallopian tubes.

Treatment is unsatisfactory.

In rare cases a chloasma similar to that met with in pregnancy, etc., occurs in tuberculosis of the peritoneum, and in malignant disease of the abdominal organs.

Xanthoderma areatum. A yellowish or reddish-yellow pigmentation occurring in patches on the lower part of the legs. The onset is insidious, and the spots coalesce to form large irregularly outlined areas without infiltration. The affection occurs in the tropics, and runs a chronic course without symptoms. Its cause is unknown. The local application of resorcin and salicylic acid is recommended.

REFERENCE.—CASTELLANI and CHALMERS. "Tropical Medicine," p. 1614, plates.

Schamberg's Disease.

Described by Schamberg in 1901 as a "peculiar progressive pigmentary disease of the skin," this somewhat rare and probably often overlooked affection is characterised by groups of minute reddish-brown puncta which coalesce to form brown patches. All the recorded cases have been in males. I have had two instances under my observation. The lesions were on the legs between the knee and ankle. The red-brown spots, the size of a pin's head, were in groups, and here and there were brown macules about the size of a sixpence. The colour did not disappear on pressure, but there was some evidence of atrophy in the older lesions. There was no pain, tenderness or irritation.

The eruption persists for many years and slowly extends, and is apparently unaffected by treatment. The forearms may be similarly affected.

Histologically the lesions consist of dilatations by blood-vessels with localised cell exudation or proliferation. The pigment is not due to hæmorrhages, but to spindle-shaped collections of pigment-granules (Adamson).

The symmetry of the eruption and its histology differentiate it from angioma serpiginosum (p. 35).

REFERENCES.—SCHAMBERG. *British Journal of Dermatology*, XIII., p. 1. H. G. ADAMSON. *Ibid.*, XXVIII., p. 335.

Tattooing. The figures are produced by the introduction into the skin of Indian ink, indigo and vermilion. Infection of the tattoo marks with syphilis and tubercle is not very uncommon. Cheloid may also occur.

The dermatologist is sometimes consulted as to the possibility of the removal of tattoo marks. In some cases the pigmented area can be excised and a skin graft applied. Nieurowsky had some success by Finsen light treatment, but in two cases in which I tried it there was very little improvement.

CHAPTER XXIV.

ATROPHY AND SCLEROSIS OF THE SKIN.

Atrophodermia. Atrophy of the Skin.

ATROPHY of the skin is characterised by loss of substance of the whole thickness of the integument, or of some of its components.

Etiology. Atrophodermia may be primary or secondary.

Secondary atrophy may be caused by—

(1) Injury, traumatism, wounds, burns, scalds, the application of austics, X-rays, and radium.

(2) Xerodermia pigmentosa, and epidermolysis bullosa.

(3) Certain acute specific fevers, variola, vaccinia, varicella.

(4) Bacterial infections; acne vulgaris, and other suppurative lesions of the follicles; ulcers due to syphilis, tuberculosis, leprosy, etc.

(5) In favus of the scalp.

(6) Nervous disease: herpes zoster, glossy skin, syringomyelia, and nerve leprosy.

(7) Certain interstitial affections of the skin without actual ulceration : lupus vulgaris, lupus erythematosus, and lichen planus atrophicus.

(8) Hydroa vacciniforme, and occasionally pemphigus and dermatitis herpetiformis.

(9) Stretching of the skin as in lineæ atrophicæ.

(10) Senile degeneration.

The primary or idiopathic atrophies are of unknown origin. They may be diffuse or macular. Their special characteristics will be described in this chapter.

Pathology. In all cicatricial atrophies the essential changes are in the true skin, or at least in the papillary body. The epidermis may be thinned or thickened, and there is often irregularity, causing special characters of the surface. Under the epidermis lies a dense connective tissue, with a deficiency in the elastic fibres. The papillæ are usually absent, the vessels are diminished in number, and the usual arrangement of the plexuses is lost. In some cases, particularly in xerodermia pigmentosa and atrophic radiodermatitis, there are telangiectases. Many cicatricial atrophies are characterised by absence of pigment ; in others there is irregular or excessive pigmentation.   The hairs, sebaceous glands, and sweat glands are destroyed to a greater or less extent.   In some instances, especially in some forms of epidermolysis bullosa. pemphigus, and rarely herpes, there are solid epidermal cysts in the cicatrices.

.. The pathology of the primary atrophies is considered below.

Congenital atrophy. Developmental anomalies characterised by atrophy of the skin are rare.   They may be localised or widely spread, The pilo-sebaceous elements and the subcutaneous fat are absent.

Striæ atrophicæ.

Striæ atrophicæ are linear streaks of atrophy of the skin caused by stretching and occasionally by other conditions.   They are most commonly the result of pregnancy where they occur on the abdomen and upper parts of the thighs and buttocks and on the breasts. Obesity and occasionally swelling of the joints may cause them, but it must be noted that the striæ do not follow every kind of distension of the skin.   They are not seen over tumours or in ascites, nor after extensive hæmorrhages or dislocations, nor on herniæ.   Moreover, they occasionally appear after enteric and other fevers and in cachexia due to malignant disease.   Apparently there must be some predisposition on the part of the patient.   Though exceedingly common in women who have borne children, one occasionally meets with a patient who has had a large family in whom they do not develop.

The epidermis and the papillæ are wasted, and the connective tissue of the true skin is atrophic, but the special characteristic is the disappearance of the elastic tissue.

Striæ atrophicæ are streaks from the fraction of an inch to several inches in length with a wavy outline.   At first bluish or purplish in tint, they become pearly white, and occasionally pigmented.   To the touch they are soft and evidently atrophic.   The abdomen, flanks, buttocks, and upper parts of the thighs and the breasts are most often affected.   The striæ cannot be altered by any form of treatment.

REFERENCES.—UNNA.   "Histopathology," p.   997.   DUCKWORTH. *British Journal of Dermatology*, 1893, Vol. V.

Idiopathic Atrophies of the Skin.

Three conditions require consideration.   Strictly speaking, none of them is an idiopathic or primary atrophy, as each is the sequel of an inflammatory process of unknown origin.   The inflammatory

33.-2

process may escape notice, but it is usually evident in the histology of the lesions. To describe the remarkable laxity of the skin, the term "antedermia" is used in certain varieties, and writers often use the descriptive terms "erythematosa" and "erythromélic" to emphasise the inflammatory nature of these conditions.

Diffuse idiopathic atrophy. Atrophia cutis idiopathica progressiva. The cause is unknown. The patients are usually about forty years

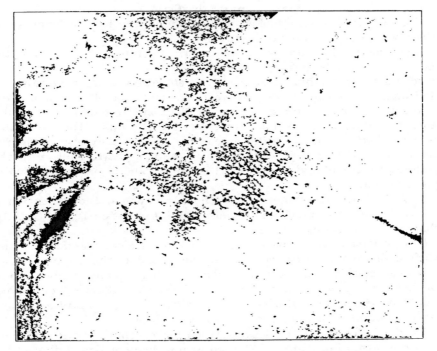

FIG. 202.—Idiopathic atrophy in a woman aged 28.

of age when the affection begins. Females are more frequently affected than males. The course is essentially chronic.

Pathology. The process is an inflammatory one. The epidermis is thin, and the papillæ are flattened. In the true skin the elastic fibres and the collagenous tissue are atrophied. There is an increase in the number of capillaries, and the vessels are dilated. An infiltration of mononuclear cells is found in the connective tissue about the vessels. The glands and hair follicles are atrophic and there is no subcutaneous fat.

Clinical features. The atrophy usually begins on both ankles and spreads slowly the whole length of the lower limbs, ending at the groins and buttocks.   In some cases the upper extremities are also involved, the process starting on the backs of the fingers or hands and extending to the shoulder.   The flexures and the palms and soles usually escape.   At the onset the affected areas are red or bluish and there may be some slight scaling of the surface.   By the coalescence of the extending circumscribed lesions diffuse areas are produced. In the later stages the skin is red or bluish or brownish in colour, atrophic and inelastic, and wrinkled and transparent.   The underlying veins and tendons are unusually distinct.

. The disease is distinguished from sclerodermia by the redness and the absence of the stage of induration.

Treatment.   Beyond the application of emollients to make the parts more supple nothing can be done.

Macular idiopathic atrophy.   Anetodermia erythematosa of Jadassohn.   In this variety there is an eruption of atrophic spots upon the trunk or limbs.   Usually they are rounded or irregular and do not exceed a shilling in size.   At the onset they resemble urticarial wheals or syphilitic macules.   At first they are a light red colour, but in the atrophic stage they assume a pearly white tint, the thinned areas feeling like holes in the skin.   The patients are usually young females.

Histologically the lesions are of the same type as those mentioned above, but in addition there are masses of fat in the cutis, due to fatty changes in the connective tissue.

The lesions have to be distinguished from cicatrices left by the various diseases and injuries already described in this chapter.

Acrodermatitis chronica atrophicans.   This name is given to a localised atrophy preceded by inflammatory infiltration occurring chiefly on the limbs.   Both sexes are equally affected, and the disease most commonly appears about the fortieth year.

In the early stage the lesions resemble erythema nodosum, but they are rather ill-defined.   The red or purplish colour is followed by a yellow tint.   The elbows, the inner aspects of the forearms, and the backs of the hands are the areas affected in the upper limb.   On the lower, the dorsal surfaces of the feet and the knees are the common sites.   Occasionally there is severe pain, but often there are no subjective symptoms.

REFERENCES.—UNNA.   *Neumann's Festschrift*, 1900, p. 910.   FINGER. *Wien. Med. Wochenschrift*, 1910, No. 2.   HERXHEIMER and HARTMANN. *Archiv. f. Dermatolog.*, Vol. XI., p. 57.   RONA.   *Reports of the German Dermatological Congress*, 1908, p. 462.

Senile Degeneration.

Senile atrophy of the skin (the Biotripsis of Cheatle) is characterised by a parchment-like thinning of the integument. The surface has a yellowish or reddish tint, and the natural elasticity is lost. If the skin is pinched up, it takes some time to return to its normal condition. The thinning of their covering exposes the outlines of the veins and the tendons. Parts exposed to the air are most severely affected. In some cases the surface is excessively dry and may suggest ichthyosis. Pigment spots are common and also telangiectases and small nævoid formations. Keratomata are not uncommon, and these may develop into epitheliomata (*vide* p. 524). In another type of senile atrophy the skin is not wasted, but thickened and wrinkled, soft to the touch and in folds, and of a pale yellow tint. The parts exposed, particularly the neck and the temples, are most affected.

Histologically the essential features are the degeneration of the elastic tissue in the common type, and in the rarer form a colloid change. The epidermis is thin and pigmented. The glandular elements are atrophic, while the vessels are dilated.

The senile skin is often the seat of pruritus, but it is curious that scratching affects it very little.

One condition already described in the group of congenital affections of the skin, xerodermia pigmentosa, may be looked upon as a precocious senility of the skin in its tendency to pigmentation, atrophy, wart formation, and epithelioma. In certain occupations in which patients are exposed to the vicissitudes of the weather, *e.g.*, seamen, coachmen, agricultural labourers, and the like, the exposed parts of the skin become very much like those observed in xerodermia and senile degeneration. I have now under my care a young agricultural labourer whose face is covered with freckles, atrophic spots, and telangiectases, and from whom I have removed a number of epitheliomatous tumours. The affection began in the third decade of life, and it is only in its late development that it differs from xerodermia pigmentosa. Unna described an analogous condition in seamen, followed by multiple epitheliomata. He called the cancerous stage " Seemann's Haut Carcinom." I have had examples under my own care.

REFERENCES.—" Epitheliomatosis of Solar Origin." DUBREUILH. *Annales de Derm. et de Syph.*, 1907, June, p. 387." Seaman's Skin Cancer." UNNA. " Histopathology," p. 719.

Leukoplakic vulvitis.

A chronic inflammatory condition of the vulva characterised by hyperæmia and cellular activity, followed by epithelial hypertrophy and sclerosis of the sub-epithelial tissue.

Pathology. Berkeley and Bonney describe a swelling of the epithelium and desquamation, with vascularity of the sub-epithelial tissue and lymphocytic infiltration. At a later stage plasma and connective tissue cells accumulate and lymph nodes form. In the final stage the epithelium becomes hypertrophied, the elastic fibres in the connective tissue disappear, and sclerosis is complete.

The cause of the affection is unknown. No evidence of syphilis can be obtained.

Clinical features. Four stages are described. In the first the parts are red, swollen, and look excoriated. In the second the labia minora decrease in size, and the area involved is of an opaque white colour, at first in patches, but ultimately diffuse. In the third stage there are cracks and ulcers, which may become carcinomatous. In the fourth stage the whole of the vulvar orifice is white, smooth and shiny, the labia minora and the clitoris being completely atrophied from contraction. The affection may spread beyond the vulva on to the inner sides of the thighs and into the perineum. The meatus urinarius and the vestibule escape the leukoplakic process. There is intense itching in the first two stages. In the third the fissures and cracks are painful, and in the last stage all symptoms disappear.

The disease has long been confounded with kraurosis vulvæ, but Berkeley and Bonney's researches show that they are distinct affections.

The **treatment** advised is the application of the X-rays to allay the irritation, but sometimes resinol ointment has afforded relief. If these fail a wide excision is recommended.

REFERENCE.—BERKELEY and BONNEY. *Trans. Royal Society of Medicine.* Obstet. Section, 1909, p. 29. Microphotographs of sections. The relationships to carcinoma are fully discussed.

Kraurosis vulvæ.

An atrophic condition of the vulva, with stenosis of the orifice.

Etiology. Kraurosis vulvæ occurs in sterile young women. after the menopause and after oophorectomy. It probably, therefore, is dependent upon deficiency of ovarian functions.

Pathology. The epithelium is thinner than normal and the papillæ atrophy. There is infiltration of plasma cells. lymphocytes.

and polymorpho-nuclear leucocytes under the flattened epithelium. The elastic tissue is present in the sub-epidermal layers.

Clinical features. The labia minora, the vestibule, the orifice of the uretha, and the vagina are affected. The lesions do not spread to the perineum and thighs. Two stages are described. In the first the muco-cutaneous surface is red and shiny and dotted over with bright red spots the size of a pin's head, or larger. There is usually a caruncle at the meatus urinarius. In the second stage the area becomes of a pale yellow colour with a glistening surface, which has been likened to the surface of a fatty liver. The muco-cutaneous junction is smooth, and all the ridges disappear ; the labia minora and clitoris atrophy and the mons veneris wastes.

The patient complains of soreness and pain. There is pain on micturition and dyspareunia. In the second stage these symptoms disappear. There is no tendency to malignant formation.

The **treatment** recommended is the removal of the affected areas and the enlargement of the vaginal orifice by operation.

REFERENCE.—BERKELEY and BONNEY. *Trans. Royal Society of Medicine.* Obstet. Section, 1909, p. 29. Microphotographs of sections.

Sclerodermia.

The name Sclerodermia is applied to a group of affections of unknown origin in which the skin and subcutaneous tissue become thick and tough, and ultimately atrophic.

One variety of sclerodermia, sclerema neonatorum, has been described already (p. 50). In it, it will be remembered, there is a remarkable induration of the integument, beginning a few hours to a few days after birth in the lower limbs, and gradually involving the whole or part of the surface. There are subnormal temperature, diarrhoea, etc., and the infant dies in the widely-spread cases from inability to take food. In the partial cases recovery may take place.

Etiology of sclerodermia. The cause of sclerema neonatorum is unknown, and we are equally ignorant of the cause of sclerodermia developing later in life. A survey of the literature shows that this cutaneous affection occurs in connection with such a variety of conditions that it is difficult to believe that many of the casual relationships which have been suggested can be accepted. Heller advanced the hypothesis that sclerodermia is due to a general or local lymphatic obstruction, and in support of this contention a case associated with obstruction of the thoracic duct was reported. Hoppe-Seyler, impressed with the occurrence of the disease in two children from the same place, suspected an infectious origin. No micro-organisms have been demonstrated in the cases examined, but it is worthy of note that the disease has been seen as a sequel to scarlatina, diphtheria, erysipelas, infectious tonsillitis, pneumonia, tuberculosis, influenza, malaria, measles, and other febrile illnesses.

The hypothesis most generally accepted is that sclerodermia is a tropho- or angiotropho- neurosis, caused by changes in the nervous system. The peculiar distribution seen in some cases of morphœic sclerodermia supports this contention. It is more difficult to accept this hypothesis in cases of diffuse sclerodermia, which may possibly have a different cause. Jacquet has described changes in the spinal cord, "myélite cavitaire," in sclerodermia, but Mott failed to find any evidence of disease. J. L. Steven found atrophy of the grey matter of the anterior horn of the cord on the same side as an area of localised sclerodermia.

Degeneration of the peripheral nerves and of the cord has been described by various authors, but there appear to be no recent observations. Brissaud maintained that the skin affection depended upon disease of the sympathetic, and its occasional association with anomalies of pigmentation may be held to be in support of the hypothesis, but there is no conclusive evidence.

Another hypothesis is that sclerodermia is the result of extensive endarteritis. In this connection it is interesting to note its occasional co-existence with Raynaud's disease.

This naturally opens up the question of there being a syphilitic basis in some cases of sclerodermia. Brocq and others have observed sclerodermia occurring in the course of syphilis. This must be very rare, as the Wassermann reaction was negative in every case I have had examined. More importance has been attached to the influence of internal secretions in the causation of sclerodermia. Thyroid atrophy is the commonest glandular defect, but Graves' disease, Addison's disease and acromegaly have all been seen in association with the cutaneous affection. In a woman under my care sclero-dermia of both legs developed after she had been taking thyroid extract for sixteen years for myxœdema.

Pathology. Peri- and end- arteritis with occlusion of the lumen of the vessels is believed to be the primary change, the alteration in the skin being secondary. The changes in the skin itself are a partial disappearance of the connective tissue with degeneration, but the elastic tissue is not destroyed as in a scar. The papillæ are flattened, and the horny layers of the epidermis are thickened. The glandular elements disappear. In some cases there is sclerosis of the subcu-taneous tissue and of the underlying muscles.

Clinical features. Sclerodermia in adults may be generalised or local. Of 22 cases under my care 18 were females and four males.

Generalised Sclerodermia.

This condition, sometimes called sclerema, is rare. In exceptional cases it may develop acutely. The patient first notices stiffness in the movements of the limbs and of the trunk, and his breathing becomes difficult. The malady progresses rapidly, and may be fatal in a few weeks to several months. The skin is thickened and indurated, and these changes spread widely.

The chronic form is less rare. It is preceded by wasting, pains in the joints and neuralgia, and from time to time there are febrile symptoms. Sometimes there are areas of local asphyxia (Raynaud's phenomena) or erythematous patches, with burning and itching. In other cases there is œdema or local swelling. This stage is followed by the peculiar induration and thickening of the skin, which may affect the whole integument, or large diffuse areas. On palpation the affected parts are found to be in a condition of solid œdema, they do not pit on pressure, and there is attachment to the deep structures. A remarkable immobility is thus produced. The expressionless face looks as if carved in marble, and speaking and taking food are exceedingly difficult. The stiffness of the neck and chest impede respiration, and sometimes swallowing is difficult. The proximal parts of the limbs are affected in greater or less degree, but the movements of the fingers are less impaired. The skin has a peculiar yellowish-brown tint, with greyish or pink spots. In the third stage a gradual atrophy supervenes, perhaps after a lapse of some months. The integument becomes fibrotic, the subcutaneous tissue is absorbed, the muscles themselves may become tough and fibrous. The skin is firmly attached both to them and to the bones. The unyielding envelope thus formed is the cause of the greatest distress to the patients. There is a constant sensation of cold, but the cutaneous sensibility is unaffected. Atrophy of the thyroid and also Graves' disease are occasionally present, but their relationship to the sclerodermia is not understood. Death usually occurs from some intercurrent disease, but also from the gradual loss of strength; but recovery may take place if the atrophic stage has not been reached.

Progressive Sclerodermia. Sclerodactyly.

This type differs in many respects from that just described. It begins at the periphery and slowly progresses. The onset is rather like that of Raynaud's disease, with darting neuralgic pains or a feeling of cold, associated with "dead" fingers (local syncope) or blueness of the extremities (acroasphyxia). Occasionally there is excessive sweating, and sometimes blebs form. As a rule, the affection begins on the fingers, but it may start on the auricles or on the nose.

The intensity of the symptoms varies greatly from time to time, but after the lapse of several months, or perhaps years, the fingers gradually waste, the skin atrophies and is attached to the bones. The digits cannot be extended or flexed, and the skin, which is firmly bound to the bones, is greyish or dull in tint. The process of mummification begins at the terminal phalanges, and gradually spreads up the fingers to the forearms. The gradual atrophy from the periphery

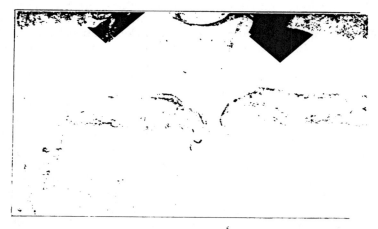

Fig. 203.—Sclerodactyly.

produces a tapering digit like an elongated radish. The subcutaneous tissue and the tendons are involved. Callous ulceration or necrosis with absorption of the bones leads to spontaneous amputation very similar to that observed in nerve leprosy. The nails are atrophic or claw-like. The process described as occurring in the fingers occurs to a less degree in the toes.

In a little girl at present under my care progressive sclerodactyly is associated with sclerodermia of the face. Her features are fixed like those of a mask or statue, the skin being a peculiar pale pink tint. The eyelids are closed with difficulty. As this rare condition advances the movements of mastication and deglutition are likely to become impaired. The tongue and the larynx may be involved. Sometimes the induration spreads to the trunk.

There remains one point to be mentioned, and that is pigmentation. This is always present, but it may not be confined to the sclerosed areas of skin.

Progressive sclerodermia always runs a very slow course, and death usually takes place from intercurrent disease. Sudden death without apparent cause is, however. not unknown.

FIG. 204.—Morphœa.

Diagnosis. At the onset it may be very difficult to determine whether the condition is Raynaud's disease or sclerodermia. Leprosy is distinguished by the anæsthesia and thickening of the nerves.

Syringomyelia is attended with peculiar alterations in the sensibility and by the absence of induration of the skin. The pigmentary changes of sclerodermia must be borne in mind in the differential diagnosis of melanodermia.

Localised Sclerodermia.
Morphœa.

This variety of sclerodermia differs from the previously described forms in being limited to plaques or bands. Here again the disease is much commoner in females than in males. The plaques appear, without any previous symptoms, as thickened, indurated, pink, or mauve coloured patches, which gradually extend. After a few weeks, or perhaps several months, the central part of the plaque becomes pale, and often assumes the colour of old ivory. As a rule the surface of the white area is smooth, but occasionally it may be nodular. The patches are oval or irregular, and the characteristic mauve zone about the pale central patch produces a very characteristic clinical picture. Occasionally there are minute telangiectases on the area, and rarely scaling. The plaque is tough, unpinchable, and attached to the deeper structures.

There is no hair on it, and sweating is absent. In most cases the plaques gradually extend to. a certain limit and then remain stationary. I had one case under my care in which there had been no extension for fifteen years. Some patients complain of itching or pricking, but this is usually in the early stages only. When the part is sclerosed, there is generally some degree of anæsthesia. The ultimate condition in most cases is a depressed atrophic area.

The band-like form of morphia is remarkable. It has similar characters to the plaque variety. There is the same zone of mauve or purplish erythema with a central pale area. The bands extend

Fig. 205.—Fronto-nasal morphœa.

the length of the limbs, or around the trunk, or around a digit. In one of my cases following an injury, a band extended from the level of the left great trochanter across the thigh along the line of the sartorius muscle to the inner side of the knee. The band here was about an inch and a half wide. Below the knee it widened out to take in the anterior and inner surfaces of the leg, ending on the foot just above the roots of the toes. Associated with this were patches of sclerosis and atrophy affecting the left half of the abdomen. The latter spots had the distribution of the anterior parts of cutaneous nerves, but the lateral and posterior parts were unaffected. The lesions of the trunk were on the same side as the band on the limb.

This case illustrated another feature of morphœa, the intractable character of the ulcerations produced by slight traumatism. A slight blow on the shin was followed by ulceration, which took many months to heal, and rapidly broke down on the patient leaving hospital. An interesting form is illustrated in Fig. 205. Here the sclerodermia affected the fronto-nasal area, causing a depressed scar-like lesion extending from the root of the nose on to the forehead to one side of the middle line. There was a groove in the frontal bone correspond-

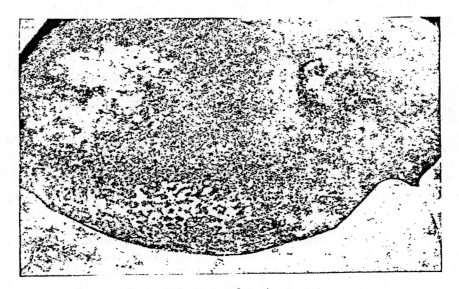

FIG. 206.—Sclerodermia guttata.

ing to the sclerosed area of skin. I have seen the band form of sclerodermia associated with anterior polio-myelitis.

The bands which occasionally form round the fingers or round the arm lead to œdema and swelling, and may even cause necrotic changes similar to those observed in ainhum.

The diagnosis of the band form of morphœa should not present much difficulty. There is nothing like the sclerosed tracts running along a limb. The local rounded patches are diagnosed by their toughness, by the impossibility of pinching them up from the deeper tissues, and the mauve margin to the pale areas. Cancer en cuirasse is usually described as being likely to be mistaken, but it is generally secondary to a mammary tumour, and only the rare apparently primary cases could be mistaken, and in them there are pain, involvement of the glands, and œdema of the arm.

Progressive hemiatrophy of the face, involving bone, muscle and skin, sometimes occurs in relation with morphœa.

Sclerodermia guttata.   White Spot Disease.

This somewhat rare condition has received much attention in recent literature.   The characteristic features are the development of a number of small pearly white indurated lesions.   In the characteristic case illustrated in Fig. 206 the groups of spots were on the right side of the abdomen and on the left leg.   Surrounding the groups of spots was a number of very fine telangiectases.   The patient was a woman aged fifty-five, and the history was that the eruption appeared as irritable papules which died away leaving white spots.   In one of my cases the band form of sclerodermia was associated with lesions of the guttate type.   Guttate sclerodermia must be differentiated from atrophic lichen planus, and here the history will be of service. Characteristic lichen papules will probably be present in some other part of the body, and there is usually severe irritation, especially in the early stages of lichen planus.

Treatment of sclerodermia.   In all cases the patient should be warmly clad, as relapses frequently follow chills and exposure. In view of the occasional association of Graves' disease and atrophy of the thyroid gland, thyroid treatment has been tried, but without much success.   Salicylates have also been recommended in the early stages.   Of the local treatments, the mercurial plaster, inunction and massage are generally advocated.   Of late, electric baths, galvanism, ionisation and electrolysis have been more used.   Electrolysis, using the negative pole, appears to give the best results in the localised form.   In the progressive and diffuse varieties little can be done beyond the avoidance of chills and attention to the intercurrent maladies as they arise.

REFERENCES.—H. RADCLIFFE CROCKER. Lectures.   *Lancet*, 1885, Vol. I., pp. 191, etc.   DINKLER.   "Sclerodermia."   Heidelberg.   1891. *Archives of Surgery*, Vols. V. and VI.   ZAMBINA.   "Histology and Literature."   *Archiv. Dermatol.*, 1901, p. 49.   J. H. SEQUEIRA.   "Sclerodermia associated with Thyroid Disease."   *Brit. Journ. Dermatology*, XXVIII., 1916, p. 31.   Literature.

Ainhum.

An endemic disease in certain tropical countries characterised by spontaneous amputation of the little toe.   It was first recognised on the West Coast of Africa, but is now known to be widely spread, occurring in Brazil, the West Indies, some of the Southern States of America, India, and the islands in the Indian and Pacific Oceans.

The disease affects young adults, and is commoner in males than in females. Heredity has also been recorded. It only attacks the dark races, but the cause is quite unknown. There is no association with leprosy.

The disease manifests itself by a furrow forming around the junction of the little toe with the foot. There is no inflammation, but the gradual constriction of the base leads to swelling and œdema of the toe. The toe is spontaneously amputated by a process of necrosis and ulceration at its base. The ulcerative stages are attended with great pain. The disease runs an essentially chronic course, often lasting several years. In rare cases other toes are attacked. Incision of the constricting band in the early stage is curative. Where the disease is advanced amputation of the toe is necessary.

REFERENCES.—EYLES. *Lancet.* September 25, 1886, p. 576. DA SILVA LIMA. *American Archives*, 1880, p. 367. MOREIRA. Abst., *British Journal of Dermatology*, 1900, p. 334. ARAGAO. *Dermatologie Tropicale*, Paris, 1910.

CHAPTER XXV.

TUMOURS OF THE SKIN.

THE tumours of the skin, like those of other organs, may be innocent or malignant. They may arise in the epithelial elements, including the invaginations which form the hair follicles, sebaceous and sweat glands ; from the connective tissue of the true skin ; from the smooth muscle of the arrectores pilorum ; from the blood and lymphatic vessels, and from the nerves. Some are of congenital origin, and these have already been considered.

Tumours of Epiblastic Origin.

To many of the innocent tumours of epithelial origin the term " papilloma " is applied. Strictly speaking, the name should only be given to conditions in which there is hypertrophy of the papillæ, but by common usage it is given to warty lesions of inflammatory and neoplastic origin.

The **callosity** and **corn** are hypertrophies of the horny layer of the epidermis, the result of local irritation (p. 57).

Verrucæ. Warts.

Warts are circumscribed elevations of the skin, due to hypertrophy of the epidermis and papillæ.

Verruca vulgaris. The common wart is usually seen on the fingers and hands. It varies in size from a pin's head to a pea. It is usually rounded or oval, and its surface may be rough or smooth. It is of a yellowish-brown or brownish-black colour, and may be single or multiple. Children and adolescents are most frequently affected (Fig. 207).

Verruca filiformis. The lesions are threadlike, often pointed excrescences, rarely more than an eighth of an inch long, of a pale pink colour, occurring on the face, frequently on the eyelids, nostrils, and on the neck.

Verruca digitata is a form of filiform wart in which there are numerous finger-like processes, arising from an area the size of a pea, or perhaps larger. The base is often constricted. These lesions occur also on the face, but more frequently on the scalp, often in " seborrhoic " conditions.

Verruca plana juvenilis. The juvenile warts are yellowish or pale brown flat lesions, varying in size from a millet seed to a small pea. They occur usually in large numbers upon the face, frequently on the forehead, in a line suggesting infection from the cap or hat, or about the mouth, probably from auto-infection from the hand, where there are often lesions of the common type (Fig. 208).

Verruca plantaris. Flat warty growths varying in size from

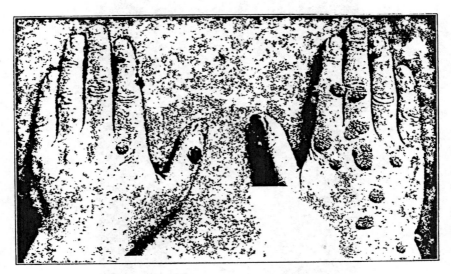

Fig. 207.—Verrucæ vulgares.

a pea to a threepenny piece occur not uncommonly on the sole. They are often multiple and most frequently form on the ball of the foot and the heel. The lesions are exceedingly tender, and the patient finds standing or walking very painful. The pain is usually worse in the early part of the day and becomes dulled later. In my experience they are more common in adolescence, but they may occur at any age (Fig. 209). The lesions are often taken for corns.

Etiology. It is almost certain that warts are caused by micro-organisms. There is no doubt that they are auto-inoculable and contagious.

Pathology. The common wart consists of an increase in the horny layers of the epidermis, and there is in addition a hyperplasia of the papillæ, in which there are dilated capillary loops. In the flat warts the essential change is in the prickle cell layer—acanthosis. In some of these the papillæ appear to be thinned and lengthened by the increase in the prickle layer, but there is no actual hypertrophy of the papillary body. In the digitate and filiform varieties the corneous

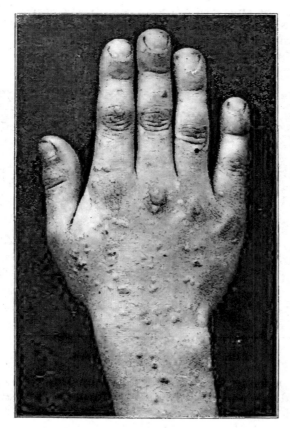

FIG. 208.—Verrucæ planæ.

layer is thin, the papillæ are very long and contain large capillarie (Fig. 210).

Treatment. Common warts may be removed by the local application of caustics, glacial acetic acid being the most convenient for ordinary cases. It should be painted on the wart with a camel-hair brush several times a day. Stronger caustics, such as nitric acid and caustic potash, require very careful application. Radium of strength

500,000 applied for an hour is often sufficient to remove warts, or the X-rays may be used, a pastille dose being given at intervals of fourteen days, the most striking success being seen in the case of plantar warts, where a single 1½ pastille dose applied exactly to the lesion may

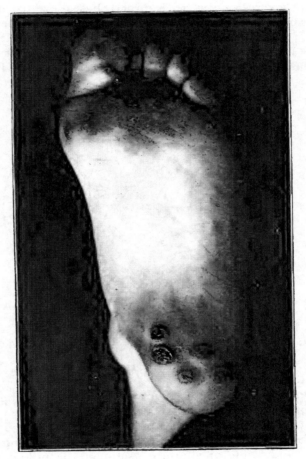

FIG. 209.—Verrucæ plantares. Female, æt. 14.

effect a cure. Sparking with the high frequency apparatus may also be used with success. The application of solid carbon dioxide is also valuable, and cataphoresis of magnesium sulphate is well spoken of.

In the multiple flat warts of young subjects the internal administration of lime water, to the amount of half a pint a day, is often followed by the disappearance of the warts. Dr. C. J. White recommends the proto-iodide of mercury in doses of $\frac{1}{4}$ grain three times a day. Small doses of magnesium sulphate are also advocated. The Kromayer lamp has proved of service in this type of wart.

Venereal warts. Verruca acuminata. The venereal warts are red or pink excrescences, with broad bases or distinct pedicles, occurring about the penis, vulva and anus, and sometimes about the mouth. They are usually soft, and grow very rapidly, producing tumours as large as a walnut. When they occur about the external genitals they are usually associated with an offensive purulent

FIG. 210.—Filiform wart. Microphotograph of section.

discharge. They are caused by irritating secretions, and are no doubt due to micro-organisms.

The lesions consist of hypertrophy of connective tissue and dilatation of blood-vessels and cellular infiltration.

The treatment consists in scrupulous cleanliness, the parts being bathed in astringent and antiseptic solutions. Dusting powders of starch, talc and oxide of zinc are useful in the milder cases. The larger excrescences require the application of carbolic acid, of the acid nitrate of mercury, or removal by the knife or cautery.

Verruca plana senilis. " Seborrhoic " wart. The senile wart is a circumscribed, rounded or oval flat elevation of the epidermis, varying in size from a pea to a finger-nail, and covered with an adherent horny or greasy scale, of a grey, brown or black colour. On the removal of the adherent covering an irregular or ridged surface is exposed. The lesions are usually multiple, and occur on the back and shoulders, on the chest, and about the waist, and occasionally on the forehead and temples (Fig. 211).

Both sexes are affected, and the lesions rarely appear before the age of forty.

Pathology. The lesions are not seborrhoic, but consist of a hyperplasia of the epidermis, with down-growths between the papillæ. The glandular elements are often atrophic, and there is no inflammatory exudation. These tumours differ from the senile keratoma, and have no tendency to epitheliomatous change.

They are often associated with vascular nævoid lesions on the trunk and with spots of pigmentation.

Treatment. Salicylic collodion, mercurial plasters, and even regular application of soft soap sometimes remove the lesions. The application of radium and treatment by electrolysis are most efficient.

Keratoma auriculare. I give this name to a rather rare affection which, in my experience, occurs in middle-aged men. The lesions consist of linear elevations about one line in height and about one sixth of an inch long, of a grey or greyish-brown colour and a rough surface, occurring on the edge of the auricle at the highest part. These warty excrescences are insignificant in appearance, but are extremely tender. The tenderness is so great that the patient may be unable to bear contact with the pillow on the affected side. If, as is often the case, the lesions are bilateral the discomfort seriously interferes with sleep. I have not been able to examine the lesions histologically, but in appearance they resemble warts. There is sometimes a history that they have followed prolonged exposure to cold. They differ from lupus erythematosus in being on the upper edge of the auricle and not associated with lesions on the face. They may be mistaken for gouty tophi, but they have not the white appearance of the gouty deposits. I have found the greatest relief from the application of radium and also from ionisation (copper sulphate 2 per cent.), but complete removal, except by operation, is difficult.

Keratosis senilis. Senile Keratoma.

Keratosis is seen most commonly on the face of elderly subjects. The condition is of great importance, as the lesions may develop into multiple epitheliomata.

The disease manifests itself first by the appearance of dry yellow or brownish spots, or by warty elevations resembling the senile wart, and sometimes as red telangiectatic spots with an irregular outline. The lesion becomes covered with a grey, or brown, or blackish layer with a rough surface.   This layer is very adherent, and sends conical processes into the skin, and its removal is usually attended with slight

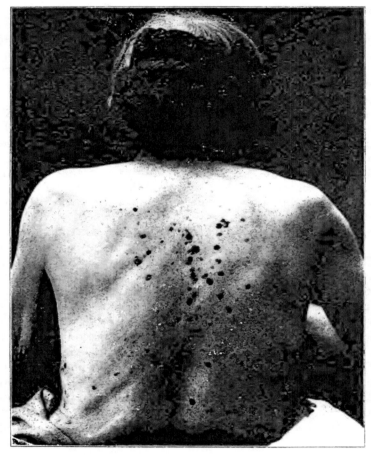

FIG. 211. —Verrucæ planæ seniles (Seborrhoic warts).   Female, æt. 70.

hæmorrhage.   Sometimes the central part of the spot shows some atrophic change.

The change to epithelioma may be unsuspected, but sometimes there is a rapid increase in the growth, and ulceration and infiltration of the derma and hypodermic tissue follow.

The patients are usually over sixty years of age, and the tumours form on the forehead, the temples, and other parts of the face, and sometimes on the backs of the hands, parts exposed to irritation. There is no tendency to spontaneous cure, and as age advances more and more lesions appear.

Pathology. The stratum corneum is hypertrophic, and sends down conical projections, the corpus mucosum is thinned, and the corium shows characteristic senile changes, notably an absence of elastic tissue which is transformed into elaccine, and there is colloidal degeneration of the connective tissue elements. The deeper parts of the epidermis are infiltrated with round cells, while plasma cells are found round the vessels.

Diagnosis. The senile keratoma has to be distinguished from the pigmented mole, which is congenital, from the lesions of syphilis, acne rosacea, and lupus erythematosus. The special distribution of the lesions and the age of the patient should suffice.

Treatment. The lesions may be removed by operation, or by the X-rays, or by radium. The carbon dioxide pencil also gives good results. In the early stages, resorcin and salicylic acid in the form of an ointment or paint are often sufficient. Trichloracetic acid applied on a glass rod after cleansing the surface of the wart with ether or benzine is also satisfactory. It is advisable to limit the action of the acid by applying vaselin around the lesion.

Tumours of the Appendages of the Skin.

New growths may develop from the sebaceous glands, from the hair follicles, and from the sweat glands.

The tumours of the *sebaceous glands* are (1) those characterised by typical or approximately typical hyperplasia of the sebaceous glands, including the symmetrical sebaceous adenoma of Pringle; (2) epithelioma of the sebaceous glands.

Tricho-epithelioma and epithelioma adenoides cysticum of Brooke are tumours arising from the *hair follicle*.

The tumours of the *sweat glands* are (1) hyperplasias; (2) simple or complex cystic tumours; (3) hidradénomes éruptifs of Jacquet and Darier, also called syringoma; (4) adenomata of the sweat glands of the labia; (5) epithelioma.

Growths of the sebaceous and sweat glands and from the hair follicles may be present in the same individual and in the same tumour. The malignant forms will be considered in the section on cutaneous cancer.

Sebaceous adenomata occur :—

(1) As a symmetrical affection of the face. The tumours are

numerous and occupy the naso-labial sulci, the root of the nose and the forehead. They begin in childhood, increase in number, and persist throughout life. The most characteristic type is that described by Pringle, where the lesions contain both vascular and glandular elements, and consequently have a red colour. This condition is congenital and may be considered as a symmetrical form of nævus. It has already been described at p. 43.

(2) Asymmetrical lesions of the same character occur in elderly subjects as pink, sometimes lobulated, tumours on the scalp, back, and face. They vary in size from a small pea to a nut. They are of

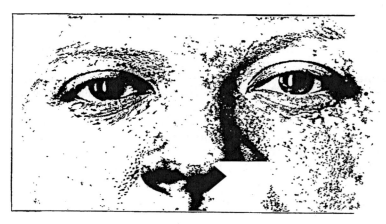

FIG. 212.—Tricho-epithelioma. Female, æt. 24.

little clinical importance, and the nature may not be recognised until sections are cut.

(3) Small sebaceous gland tumours sometimes occur on the inner aspect of the lips and cheeks. They form minute, usually multiple, creamy-white raised spots. The condition, which occurs after puberty, is called *Fordyce's disease*.

Tricho-epithelioma. A rare affection characterised by small papules in the skin about the eyes (Fig. 212), in the naso-labial grooves, and on the scalp, and less frequently on the chin and neck.

The tumours are the same colour as the skin or a little paler.

They vary in size from a pin's head to a lentil seed. They are most frequently seen in women of adult age, rarely in men. There may be a history of their development in the patient's family.

Histologically they consist of sharply defined lobulated downgrowths of epithelial cells, which are dilated at some places into cysts. Lanugo hairs are found in them, and they are believed to be derived from the hair follicles. The patients are usually girls or young women.

Epithelioma adenoides cysticum of Brooke. In this type the lesions are larger and more scattered over the face than in the preceding form. The tumours appear in childhood, and there is usually a history of heredity. The lesions consist of branching down-growths

FIG. 213.—Hidradénomes éruptifs. Tumours in intermammary and epigastric regions. Female, æt. 23.

of epithelial cells, in the centre of which there may be cystic formation around a lanugo hair. Milia are common in this type.

Hidradenoma Syringoma. Tumours of the sweat glands occur :—

(1) As single papillary or flat tumours, which may or may not have been noticed in childhood. In some of these tumours there are degenerate changes in the connective tissue of mucoid or hyaline character.

(2) An eruptive form, **Hidradénomes éruptifs,** characterised by the eruption of a large number of small tumours, varying in size from a pin's head to a split pea. Fig. 213 illustrates the distribution

in a girl of twenty-three. At the age of twenty a number of small growths were noticed on the chest and later on the back. They were confined to the intermammary triangle and epigastrium, the sides of the chest, and the scapular regions. The tumours were pale yellow, or nearly the colour of the skin, tense and hard to the touch. There were no subjective symptoms. Histologically the growths consisted of scattered epithelial tubes, with cystic dilatation. They are generally believed to arise from the sweat ducts. They are probably

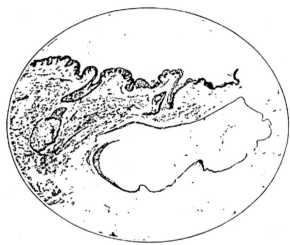

Fig. 214.—Hidradénome éruptif. Microphotograph of section.

derived from congenital anomalies, which become stimulated to growth for some unknown reason.

(3) Tumours of the sweat glands may be associated with vascular nævi.

(4) Small tumours of sweat gland origin are occasionally seen on the labia majora. They are to be distinguished from cysts of the glands of Bartholin.

Treatment. Benign tumours of the appendages of the skin may be excised, or, if small, treated by electrolysis or the cautery.

REFERENCES.—"Die Geschwülste der Hautdrüsen." RICKER and SCHWALB. Berlin, 1914. Full references and plates.

Cysts.

Cysts occur in the skin in the following varieties :—

. (1) [Sebaceous cysts varying in size from a millet seed to an egg, occurring in the true skin or subcutaneous tissue. They are of soft consistence, and fluctuation may be observed. The skin over them is normal, or perhaps a little thinned. There is no alteration of the colour, unless the lesions become infected with pus organisms. The contents are opaque and of a pasty consistence, and sometimes oily. Various names are given according to the character of the contents—steatomata, cholesteatoma, etc. The material contained in the cysts consists of epithelial cells and the products of their degeneration—fat, fatty acids, cholesterine, saponaceous bodies, and sometimes calcareous particles.

These are the common sebaceous cysts, which are dilated pilo-sebaceous organs. They are umbilicated, and their contents can be removed through the orifice by expression. Wens are multiple sebaceous and epidermal cysts which occur on the scalp and scrotum, usually in adults and in old age. They are deeper than the sebaceous cyst and have no orifice.

(2) **Dermoid cysts** are enclosures of embryonic elements, and occur, therefore, about the orbits, especially at the outer canthus, in the middle line of the nose, in the neck, and in the median line of the perineum and scrotum. They contain hairs and hair follicles, sebaceous glands, etc.

(3) **Milium** is the name given to the minute pinhead-sized tumours seen on the upper two-thirds of the face in adults. The lesions are of a pearly white colour, and do not increase in size. They are cyst-like bodies with a wall of flat epithelial cells and contain horny cells in concentric layers. They lie in the epidermis and are not connected with the sebaceous glands. Unna believes them to be derived from lanugo-hair follicles. The similar lesions occurring on the external genitals in adults are true retention sebaceous cysts. Milium in infants is also a retention cyst of the sebaceous glands.

(4) **Cicatricial epidermic cysts** are small, flat, circular, white or greyish-white lesions, the size of a pin's head to a millet seed, occurring in the site of bullous eruptions. They are most common in one form of epidermolysis bullosa (Fig. 10), but also occur in pemphigus, dermatitis herpetiformis, and in herpes zoster (Howard Warner). They also follow injury.

(5) **Kystes graisseux sudoripares** Under this name a very rare condition characterised by multiple cysts of the sweat glands has been described by Dubreuilh and Auché. The tumours are very numerous globular white cysts about the size of a pea, containing an oily material. In the cases described they were widely distributed, but were most numerous in the axillæ. Dr. Graham Little in 1915 showed a female patient, æt. 66, who had hundreds of itching cystic tumours of small size (the largest was $\frac{1}{4}$ inch in diameter) in the

axillæ, flexor aspects of the limbs, chest and abdomen. The skin was dry and in certain areas pigmented. Microscopically the lesions were cysts containing a mass of stratified epithelium continuous with the epidermis and closely resembling the cicatricial epidermal cyst.

REFERENCES.—DUBREUILH and AUCHÉ. *Transactions of International Congress of Dermatology*, London, 1898, p. 818. E. GRAHAM LITTLE. *Brit. Journ. Dermatology*, XXVII., p. 310.

Treatment of cystic tumours. If of large size, and the patient desires their removal, they should be excised. Wens may be injected with a few drops of ether at intervals, and when the resulting elimination of the tumour occurs, care should be taken to see that the cyst wall is removed. Milium is best treated by the curette or by electrolysis.

Hidrocystoma is a rare condition characterised by minute firm elevations of the skin with a pearly translucid appearance due to clear serous fluid. They vary in size from a pin's head to a pea, and occur in females, particularly on the face. The lesions tend to disappear in the winter and reappear in spring. It is believed that exposure to heat is an etiological factor.

The vesicles are formed by a dilatation of the ducts of the sweat glands (*vide* p. 586).

Molluscum contagiosum.

Small sessile, rarely pedunculated pearly white tumours, usually multiple, affecting the face, eyelids, genitals, and other parts.

Etiology. The affection is contagious, and I have seen a number of instances in which several members of one family have been affected. Fig. 217 shows it on the breast of a nursing mother and on the face of her infant. The disease is more common among the poor than in the well-to-do, and in females than males. In my clinic the proportion to all cases of skin disease is about 4 per 1,000, but this is higher than in other parts of London. I have seen seven cases in adults who have been in the habit of taking Turkish baths, and one in a hospital patient who had had hot-air baths for rheumatism. In one Turkish bath case in a lady there were over a hundred mollusca on the trunk. Whether the infection is conveyed to the skin by the massage after the bath, or whether the profuse sweating favours the infection, is a matter of doubt. The tumours are identical with the contagious epitheliomata of birds, and it has been shown that the causative agent in the latter will pass through a filter (Juliusberg).

Its nature is unknown. In successful inoculations of the human subject the period of incubation has been nine to ten weeks.

Pathology. The growths consist of lobules of a pear shape, with the apex upwards. They suggest a glandular origin, but it is now agreed that they do not arise in the sebaceous glands. The lobules consist of masses of ovoid cells of large size, derived from the prickle cell layer by a special transformation.

Clinical features. The lesions are hemispherical papules or flat, button-like discs, of a milky white, pearly or pink colour. There is a central depression in the centre of each, and on compression of the tumour between the thumb nails a semi-solid white mass can be extruded from the orifice. The tumours vary in size from a pin's

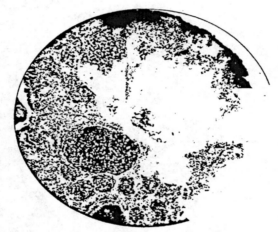

FIG. 215.—Molluscum contagiosum.

point to a large pea, or larger. There may be a few tumours of varying sizes, or there may be hundreds. In rare cases the mollusca become very large (molluscum giganteum), and some years ago Dr. Colcott Fox showed such a case in which there was a gradual transition from minute lesions to large growths as big as a small walnut.

The white pasty matter which can be expressed from the tumours consists of the large ovoid cells, which are easily identified under the microscope.

The face, eyelids, and neck and the genital organs are the parts most often affected. The tumours, however, may occur anywhere ; in the Turkish bath cases they are usually on the trunk. I have seen them about the nipple (Fig. 217).

If untreated, molluscum contagiosum lasts indefinitely, but there are no symptoms. The tumours increase in number by auto-inoculation. Sometimes, from infection with pyogenic organisms, they swell up and become red and inflamed, and suppurate.

Prognosis. The tumours, if left alone, last for a long time, but ultimately disappear (Hutchinson).

Treatment. The growth should be incised and the contents squeezed out. There is some hæmorrhage, but this is stopped at

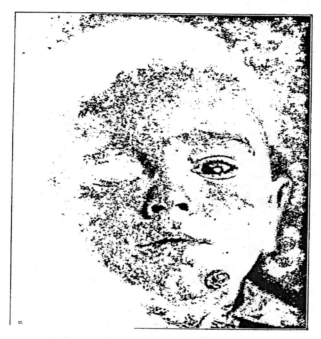

Fig. 216.—Molluscum contagiosum.

once by pressure. Some advocate swabbing out the cavity with tincture of iodine, or with a weak carbolic acid solution, or with nitrate of silver. Small tumours can be emptied by compression alone. Norman Walker finds the X-rays of value.

REFERENCES.—"On the Relations of Molluscum Contagiosum to the Bird Epithelioma," the paper of SHATTOCK, *Trans. Path. Society*, 1898, p. 394, may be consulted. GRAHAM LITTLE gives the proportions in different clinics in a paper in the *Brit. Journal of Dermatology*, June, 1910. P. JULIUSBERG. *Deutsch. Med. Woch.*, October 8, 1908.

CUTANEOUS CANCER.

Cancer of the skin may be primary or secondary. The primary carcinomata are malignant neoplasms developing from the epidermis and from the glandular and pilar organs derived therefrom. The secondary cancers invade the skin by extension from neighbouring mucous membranes, or from subcutaneous organs such as the mammary glands, and by metastasis from cancers of the viscera.

F IG. 217.—Molluscum contagiosum. Mother affected on the mamma. Child (æt. 2, but still suckled), tumours about eyelids and nose.

In the metastatic neoplasms the character of the tumour is essentially that of the primary growth, and the same holds good for the cancers invading the skin from the adjacent organs. Some primary carcinomata are squamous-celled tumours, but those derived from the basal layer of the epidermis and from the glandular elements of the skin have special characters. The malignancy of skin cancers varies greatly ; some have a high degree of malignancy and some are relatively benign. Again, some forms tend to early involvement of the neighbouring lymphatic glands and to metastatic development, while others are remarkable for their purely local malignancy.

It is of the highest importance for the medical practitioner to recognise the early stages of malignant tumours of the skin, for early radical treatment is more often attended with success in cutaneous malignant disease than in cancer of any other organ.

Etiology of cutaneous cancer. We are ignorant of the cause of skin cancer as of other forms of malignant disease. No parasite has been shown which has been able to stand the test of criticism, and the speculations of Cohnheim as to its development from embryonic cells or of heterotopic cells are interesting conjectures and nothing more.

The special features which stand out in a review of the causes of skin cancer are the age at which it appears, and the influence of local irritation and of certain precancerous conditions.

Age. Cutaneous cancer is very rare before forty. When it occurs in younger subjects there is usually a predisposing cause, *e.g.*, xerodermia pigmentosa or lupus.

Heredity apparently plays some part in this as in other cancers.

Sex. Males are more commonly affected than females.

Local irritation. The frequency with which the face is affected suggests that exposure, *i.e.*, irritation by wind and weather and by the rays of the sun, plays an important part. Unna recognised a special variety of cancer which he called seaman's skin cancer. I have shown that in lupus cancer males whose avocations necessitate exposure are more frequently affected than females. Frequently recurring traumatism may also start a malignant process. I have had under my care a man of twenty-eight with a rodent ulcer on the lower part of the face on an area which had been repeatedly struck by the recoil of a rifle.

Irritation by repeated small exposures to the X-rays or a severe acute radio-dermatitis produces a *precancerous state* which is liable to pass on to epithelioma. Workers in tar, chimney-sweeps, and men engaged in extracting paraffin from shale are liable to cancer of the skin. The history of the tar worker may be taken as an example. The earliest tar affection of the skin is a dermatitis ; this is followed by warts, some of which develop into papillomatous tumours, " tar molluscum " ; many of these fall off, but in men over forty there is a liability to their becoming malignant. Soot and paraffin act similarly. Tobacco is another irritant which, especially in association with leukoplakia, tends to cause cancer of the tongue and of the lower lip.

The prolonged administration of arsenic leads to hyperkeratosis, which, as Hutchinson first pointed out, may become epitheliomatous.

Other conditions predisposing to skin cancer are senile keratosis, a peculiar degeneration with a tendency to the development of warty growths, especially on the face. Multiple epitheliomata occur in this condition.

Xerodermia pigmentosa, which may be looked upon as a precocious senility of the skin, is the cause of epithelioma in the young, children six or seven years old developing characteristic epitheliomata, often multiple, on the affected skin of the face and hands.

Lupus vulgaris, lupus erythematosus, syphilitic and other scars, may be the seat of epithelioma.

Sebaceous cysts and wens may also undergo malignant change.

Bowen has called attention to a precancerous dermatosis occurring in late adult life characterised by chronic papular lesions covered with a horny crust. These spread to form nodular swellings which may become grouped or confluent. Under the crust is a red, oozing, slightly papillomatous surface. Cancerous degeneration has been observed by Bowen and Darier.

REFERENCE.—J. J. BOWEN. "Precancerous Dermatoses." *Journ. Cut. Dis.*, May, 1912; December, 1915.

Squamous-celled Carcinoma. Epithelioma Proper.

The lesions start in the epidermis and are characterised by the formation of cell-nests. Two distinct groups demand recognition.

FIG. 218.—Squamous epithelioma, showing numerous cell nests.

The first is primarily superficial and relatively benign, while the second is of deeper origin and highly malignant. It is important to

Plate 49.

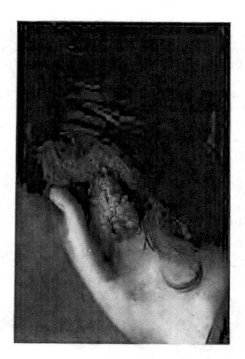

EPITHELIOMA.

An epithelioma behind the left ear; rapid involvement of glands. (Patient under Mr. Hunter Tod.)

recognise that the superficial forms may under certain circumstances infiltrate deeply, and they then assume the more malignant character of the second group.

Pathology. The tumour is composed of squamous epithelium with cell-nests. Large down-growths penetrate the true skin. The stroma is very little developed, but plasma cells are found in large

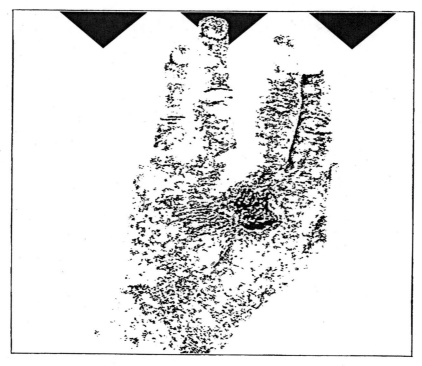

FIG. 219.—Squamous-celled carcinoma. Female, æt. 70. The axillary glands were involved.

numbers at the margin of the growth, and infiltrations along the lymphatic vessels are often present.

(1) **Superficial type.** This form is sometimes called papillary epithelioma. It occurs in three varieties.

(*a*) A warty excrescence which may develop upon normal skin or upon a senile keratoma. It occurs most frequently upon the face, or about the lips or neck, and occasionally on the back, and on the dorsal aspect of the hand (Fig. 219). For a long time it may have the appearance of a wart, and beyond a little bleeding which occurs when the top is removed by the towel or in washing it may cause the patient no uneasiness. Sooner or later the warty excrescence begins to increase in size and forms a disc-like tumour, with a superficial scab about the centre. The lesion bleeds easily and may ulcerate. Finally the infiltration may extend deeply and become highly malignant. The glands are usually involved late.

(*b*) Nodular non-warty lesions of a similar type are met with on the lips and on the mucous membrane of the mouth, and also on the glans penis and the vulva. The surface of the tumour is red,

Fig. 220.—Discoid or button-like epithelioma. Male, æt. 62. Tumour two years' duration.

shiny and smooth. After a comparatively long and slow course the lesion may become ulcerated and infiltrate deeply.

(*c*) *The malignant horn.* This rare form of tumour may begin on apparently normal skin or on a senile keratoma. The essential feature is an enormous development of horny cells. The lesion may be of large size, and in appearance sometimes closely resembles the ram's horn. The base is red and infiltrated. The face and scalp are the commonest sites, but the glans penis may be affected.

(2) **Deep type.** This form is sometimes called cancroid. It is highly malignant and penetrates deeply, and involves the glands early. It especially favours the muco-cutaneous junctions (Figs. 221, 222) and cavities, but also occurs on the scars of injuries, burns, syphilitic ulcers, and on lupus vulgaris, lupus erythematosus and in xerodermia pigmentosa. On the mucous surfaces it is frequently secondary to syphilitic and other forms of leukoplakia.

Developing upon normal skin, the primary lesion is a small nodule

FIG. 221.—Epithelioma, beginning at muco-cutaneous junction. Glands already involved (*vide* Fig. 222).

which is of a greyish colour and often covered with a small scale. Irritation by scratching and friction causes the nodule to increase in size and to extend deeply. The surface becomes red and inflamed, and ulcerates. Rapidly increasing in size, the nodule forms a tumour which projects above the skin and has an infiltrated base. The lesion is hard, and the edge becomes raised to form a rim, while the central parts are eroded, forming an irregular ulcer covered with a greyish exudate, and which bleeds easily. The tumour is painful and the glands are involved early.

Similar appearances occur when the tumour develops upon a scar (Fig. 223) or upon lupus (Fig. 97).

Squamous-celled epithelioma usually occurs late in life, but in xerodermia it may develop in early childhood, in lupus vulgaris and lupus erythematosus in adolescence and early adult life. Very occasionally epithelioma occurs independently of these conditions in childhood. *e.g.*, Battle and Maybury described a primary epithelioma

Fig. 222.—Epithelioma. The same patient four months later. A rapidly fatal type.

of the nipple in a girl of eleven, and lip cancer has been seen in a boy of fourteen.

Course. The tumour rapidly increases in depth, and sloughing perhaps of large masses of tissue takes place. The glandular growths also increase in size, and finally may fungate upon the surface. Involvement of the deep vessels may cause death by hæmorrhage, but more commonly the patient dies slowly by exhaustion. It is uncommon to find metastases in the viscera.

Baso-cellular and Glandular Tumours.   Rodent Ulcer.

We now have to consider the neoplasms which arise from the deep or basal layer of the epidermis and from the pilo-sebaceous glands.   To many of these conditions Continental writers apply the term " epithelioma," but in this country, from the clinical course, the name " **rodent ulcer** " is most commonly used.

Histologically, the tumours consist of ramifying, often pointed

Fig. 223.—Epithelioma, starting in a scar.   Eighteen months' duration
Recurrence after removal.   Rapidly fatal.

processes which invade the derma and subcutaneous tissue, or of lobules, composed of cells which have either the character of the basal cells of the epidermis, or of the cells lining the pilo-sebaceous ducts (Fig. 224).   Cells of true sebaceous gland type do not occur.   Some observers believe that the tumours may start in the sweat glands, but this must be exceedingly rare.   Sometimes the connection with the basal layer of the epidermis can be made out in sections, and in other cases the continuity with the pilo-sebaceous organs is demonstrable.   The amount of stroma varies, but is usually relatively large in amount.   It may be fibrous in the chronic types and embryonic in the more malignant forms.

Clinical appearances.   The disease usually starts in middle or advanced life, though I have once seen a case in which the lesions dated from the twelfth year and others in which the patients were thirteen and seventeen at the onset.   Senile keratosis is a common antecedent.   The seat of election is the face above a line drawn through just below the lobule of the ears and crossing the face below

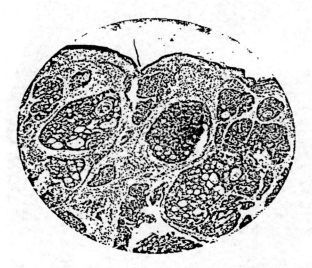

Fig. 224.—Rodent ulcer.   Basal-celled carcinoma.
Microphotograph ⅔.

the nose.   The inner and outer canthus, the side of the nose and particularly the alæ, and the auricles are the commonest sites (Fig. 225). Rarely the lesions may occur on the lip.   Basal-celled carcinomata of the trunk are rare.   I have seen them on the shoulder, under the scapular, in the mammary region, and on the back.   Gray showed a case in which a rodent ulcer started on a patch of psoriasis in the gluteal cleft.

The primary lesion is usually a firm nodule of a greyish or pearly tint, the size of a pin's head or a lentil, resembling a flat wart, or molluscum contagiosum, or an adenoma of a sebaceous or sweat gland.   The patient may complain of slight itching, and this fre-

Plate 50.

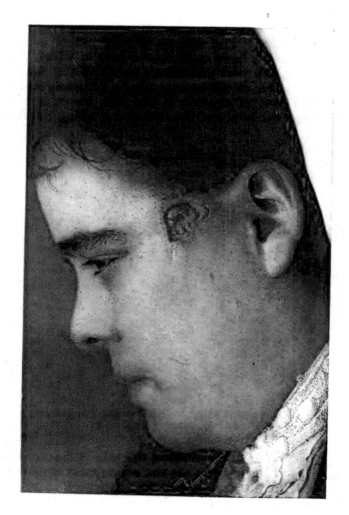

RODENT ULCER.

Of five years' duration. The smooth pink rim of the ulcer crossed by
fine vessels is well shown. The ulcer healed under radium, but a
relapse occurred, and the process has spread deeply.

quently causes the nodule to be picked, or scratched, perhaps with a little hæmorrhage. Not infrequently the lesion passes unnoticed until the top is cut off in shaving, or rubbed off with the towel. The nodule very slowly increases in size, and sooner or later the central part ulcerates, and a small scab forms. In the course of several years it may gradually spread peripherally, and occasionally takes on rapid growth. There is very rarely any large tumour, though exceptionally there may be deep infiltration with cystic formation. I have rarely

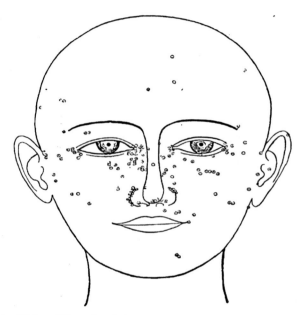

FIG. 225.—Site of origin in 200 cases of rodent ulcer.

seen cystic formation at the onset. There is in some cases a tendency to spontaneous cicatrisation in the central parts of the lesion while the periphery presents a ridge of spreading nodules.

(*a*) **Superficial cicatrising type.** This variety is seen most commonly on the temple and scalp, but also sometimes on the eyelids, nose, etc. The characteristic appearance is an irregular sclerotic scar surrounded by a rim of small greyish elevations with a smooth surface, often pearly, and crossed here and there by fine capillary vessels. This beaded margin is highly characteristic. The condition is essentially chronic, and may gradually spread for many years. Sometimes it takes on a more active course, and by deep ulceration involves the cartilages, the bones and muscles. The glands are scarcely ever affected. Recurrence after apparent cure is common.

(b) **Non-cicatrising type.** The initial growth and slow evolution resemble those of the cicatrising variety, but the lesion remains a chronic, indolent, slowly-spreading ulcer. It spreads superficially and also deeply, producing in the course of years grave deformity, especially when attacking the nose or the orbit.

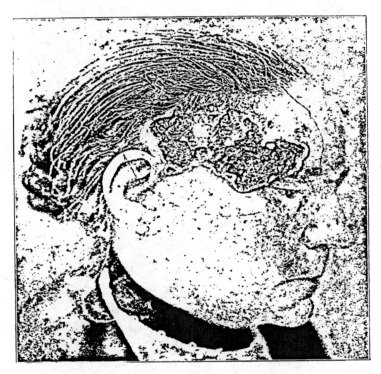

Fig. 226.—Rodent ulcer, of twelve years' duration. Superficial type. Parts spontaneously cicatrised.

(c) **Terebrant variety.** As a rule this form succeeds one of the varieties just described, but it may be highly malignant *ab initio*. The new formation and ulceration progress very rapidly in depth rather than on the surface, and produce huge excavations, with pruriform or foul sanious discharge (Fig. 228). The cavities are surrounded by induration which is moderately well defined. This form is very destructive and of great local malignancy. It is remarkable that the glands scarcely ever are affected, and very often the

FIG. 227.—Rodent ulcer, of seven years' duration, affecting inner canthus.
A common type, which usually invades the orbit.

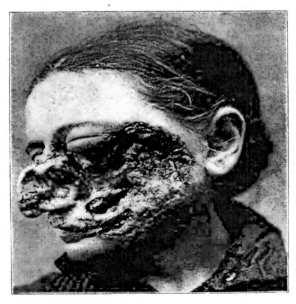

FIG. 228.—Rodent ulcer. Terebrant type. Duration sixteen years.
Glands unaffected.

general health is unimpaired.   Death is usually the result of
opening up of a deep vessel or of some complication or septic
infection.

Multiple rodent ulcers.   Occasionally rodent ulcers are multiple
(Figs. 229, 230).   Two or three characteristic tumours are not
uncommon.   In some of my cases there has been the condition known
as " tropical skin."   In the case illustrated in Fig. 230 the lesions

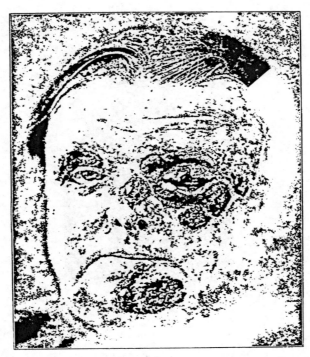

FIG. 229.—Multiple tumours, of rodent type, apparently following senile
     keratomata.   This patient lost the left eye, but all the tumours
     disappeared under the X-rays.

were all small.   Adamson has suggested a relationship of this type
with the multiple benign epitheliomata (*vide* p. 528).

The **cylindroma** is a rare variety of epithelioma, occurring especially
on the scalp.   It is generally considered to be a peculiar variety of
the baso-cellular epithelioma.   A number of explanations have been
given of the peculiar cylindrical appearance of the cellular growths
in the sections.   The stroma forms curious transparent cylinders
and oval masses which are found in between the epithelial cells proper.

Plate 51.

TURBAN TUMOUR (CYLINDROMA).

A rapidly growing fungating tumour on
the scalp. It diminished rapidly under
treatment by X-rays and was finally
excised. There was no recurrence.
The patient died some months after
from cerebral hæmorrhage.

Some authors class the lesions as endothelioma, others as varieties of sarcoma. They form extensive turban-like tumours on the scalp,

FIG. 230.—Multiple small pearly tumours on the face, tending to central ulceration. Microscopically they resembled rodent ulcer. The patient was 56 years of age, and had suffered for many years. The X-rays rapidly removed the growths.

rarely on the face ; ulceration is rare, and the course is relatively benign (Plate LI.).

Nævo-Carcinoma.

The name " Nævo-carcinoma " is applied to malignant tumours developing from nævi. Such tumours are usually melanotic, but occasionally non-pigmented growths occur.

Moles of any variety, whether pigmented or non-pigmented, hairy or not hairy, are liable to undergo malignant transformation in adult life, and especially in the aged. The pigmented spot may suddenly start growing, and form a large brown or black plaque, or a warty elevation may rapidly increase in size, become indurated, and eventually ulcerate. Sometimes new lesions appear in the immediate neighbourhood of the primary tumour. In the pigmented variety the glands are involved very early, and metastases, especially in the liver and lungs, are exceedingly common.

Pathology. The cells of the malignant nævi are globular or spindle-shaped, often pigmented and arranged in masses which are ill-defined. Sometimes there is a distinct alveolar arrangement. In a man aged thirty-two seen in my clinic in 1915 the growth began in the sweat glands on the back of the wrist. A very small part of

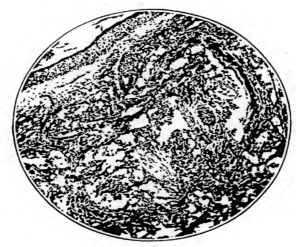

Fig. 231.—Melanotic carcinoma. Microphotograph of section. $\frac{2}{3}$.

the tumour was melanotic, the remainder resembling a basal-celled carcinoma. In some instances it is impossible to distinguish the cells from those of a sarcoma, and this resemblance is responsible for the difficulty at one time found in separating nævo-carcinomata from the sarcomata. Hence the term "melanotic sarcoma."

Secondary Carcinoma.

Secondary carcinoma of the skin occurs in connection with mammary cancer and in visceral cancer.

The lesions are hard, pink, purplish, or brownish tumours varying in size from a pin's head to a pea, or even a small nut. They may be isolated, or by coalescence form indurated irregular areas. The name " cancer en cuirasse " is given to tracts of infiltration thus formed by the aggregation of nodules, but is more often the result of lymphatic infection and subsequent solid œdema. The cancerous nodules may undergo atrophic changes, but more commonly they break down and form ulcers or fungate.

Pathologically the cells of these metastatic growths are similar to those of the primary tumour, e.g., if the primary growth is a columnar-celled carcinoma, the cells in the secondary deposit will be columnar (Fig. 232). The lesions appear to be produced by emboli

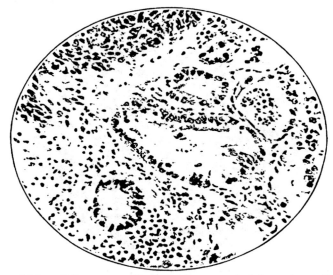

FIG. 232.—Columnar-celled carcinoma of skin. Secondary. Microphotograph of section. ⅙ obj.

of cancerous cells from the primary tumour. They are found in tracts along the vessels or lymphatic channels, or arranged in alveolar masses. They have no direct connection with the epidermis or the glandular elements of the skin.

Diagnosis of malignant growths of the skin. At the onset these affections have to be distinguished from warts and moles. In an elderly subject a growing mole or wart should always excite suspicion, and if there is the least doubt a biopsy should be made, or if the tumour is small it should be excised. The Hunterian chancre should not give rise to difficulty, but if necessary a scraping should be made and examined for the spirochæta. Tertiary syphilitic ulcerations may sometimes simulate a malignant ulceration.   Here the Wassermann reaction would be useful, or the effects of mercury and iodide of potassium may be tried for a couple of weeks.   A biopsy would of course be of value.   The superficial cicatrising type of rodent ulcer may cause trouble, as it may simulate lupus vulgaris or lupus erythematosus.   The presence of the beaded edge with capillaries running over its smooth surface is a help in diagnosis, but where there is doubt, a piece of the edge should be removed for microscopic examination.

Prognosis.   The prognosis in cases of epithelioma with glandular

Fig. 233.—Rodent ulcer, of nineteen years' duration, in a patient aged 32.

involvement is necessarily grave, but in the superficial forms of rodent uccer and the less malignant types of epithelioma, local measures, particularly radiotherapy and radium, may cure.   It is, however, impossible to promise that there will be no recurrence. Pigmentary nævo-carcinomata are of grave import unless treated radically at the earliest possible moment.

Treatment.   Malignant disease of the skin is treated (*a*) surgically, (*b*) by radiotherapy, (*c*) by radium.   These measures aim at the removal or destruction of the neoplasm and affected glands.   Failing this, purely palliative measures, *e.g.*, for the relief of pain, and prevention of septic infection, are required.

The surgical treatment consists in the complete removal of the growth and the glands by the knife. The possibility of complete removal is sometimes a difficult one, and the choice of measures must be left to the operator. In all cases it is important to make the incisions wide of the growth and to get below it. Any affected glands should be removed at the time of the operation or at a later date. The healed area after operation may be advantageously treated by a series of measured doses of X-rays through a screen of aluminium. Recently Mr. R. Warren removed for me a large epithelioma of the back of the right hand. The raw area was then treated by radium

FIG. 234.—The same patient cured by X-rays and
free from recurrence for six years.

and a large graft was applied. The graft took perfectly and the result has been most satisfactory.

The treatment of rodent ulcer by the X-rays is often very satisfactory (Figs. 233, 234). The superficial forms do best ; the ulcers clean and dry rapidly, and the healing is directly stimulated. cavities often filling up in a remarkable manner. Frequent small doses may be given, or preferably, massive doses through an aluminium screen. I now use as a rule exposures equivalent to two or three Sabouraud pastille doses (ten to fifteen H). Where the edge of the ulcer is thickened, the margin should be removed by the knife or curette prior to the application of the rays. This saves a great deal of time, and the cosmetic results are equally good. In some cases it may be found necessary to increase the dose, and if there is deep infiltration, I have found great benefit from a series of these massive doses. The filter cuts out the burning rays and prevents a chronic X-ray ulcer.

I have treated over 800 cases of rodent ulcer with radium, and if the lesion is of moderate size and free from attachment to bone or cartilage the results are excellent. I have patients who have been cured since 1902. The radium of strength one million units is applied for two

FIG. 235.—Crateriform ulcer.

hours on a suitable plate, covered with a varnish, and again covered with a single sheet of gutta-percha tissue. The applicator is fastened *in situ* with strapping or a bandage. Two or three such applications are often sufficient to cure a superficial lesion of moderate size (Figs. 235, 236). The reaction begins in about ten days, and at the end of three weeks a blackish slough falls off, leaving a smooth cicatrix. In some cases the application has to be repeated several times. Where there is deep infiltration, the radium, covered with a thin sheet of lead. is left in position for ten, twelve, or twenty-four hours.   The lead prevents any severe dermatitis, and sometimes the results are remarkably good.   In some cases the massive X-ray doses have given better results than these prolonged treatments by radium.   Diathermy is also of service.

The most troublesome cases are those in which the orbit is involved. The disease usually starts about the inner canthus and spreads to the

FIG. 236.—The same patient after treatment by radium.

bony margin of the orbit, and, as a rule, necessitates the complete clearance of the cavity.   Another type of case which leads to grave destruction begins at the angle of the nose, and rapidly involves the cartilage, and eventually the bone.   Here operative procedures may be combined with X-ray or radium treatment.   I have several times seen a deep recurrence, after apparent cure by radium and X-rays, in the malar and maxillary region.   The growth rapidly invades the bone. and may open the antrum and other accessory cavities of the nose.

Epithelioma of the lip should not be treated by X-rays or radium. Operation gives the best results, and the subsequent use of the X-rays sometimes appears to prevent recurrence. The slowly-growing epitheliomata of the crateriform and button type usually do well, with preliminary removal of the tumour and the subsequent application of the X-rays or radium. Occasionally one can get rid of such tumours in elderly people by radium alone.

Palliative measures. Where the ulceration or growth is very extensive, and the measures mentioned above are inapplicable, we are obliged to resort to opiates for the relief of pain, but sometimes great benefit is obtained by X-ray treatment. Care must be taken, however, not to give the applications frequently, or there may be stimulation of the growth, attended with increase in the painful symptoms. The constant cleansing of the ulcerations with antiseptic lotions such as peroxide of hydrogen (5 to 10 volumes), boric acid (saturated solution), lysol (a drachm to the pint), and the like are necessary to keep the parts from becoming foul.

REFERENCES. —"Rodent Ulcer." A. BOWLBY. *Path. Trans.*, 1894, XLV., p. 153. "Multiple Rodent Ulcer." ADAMSON. *Lancet*, October 17, 1908. "Epitheliomatosis of Solar Origin." DUBREUILH. *Annales de Derm. et de Syph.*, June, 1907, p. 387. "Seaman's Skin Cancer." UNNA. "Histopathology," English edition, p. 719. "Radium Therapy." "Treatment of Rodent Ulcer." J. H. SEQUEIRA. *British Medical Journal*, 1901. "Radiumtherapy." WICKHAM and DEGRAIS. English translation by S. E. DORE, 1910.

Paget's Disease. Malignant Papillitis.

Paget's disease is a chronic malignant affection of the nipple and areola occurring in women over forty years of age, characterised by infiltration, with an eczematous surface, followed by the formation of duct cancer in the mamma. In rare cases the same affection occurs in other parts, *e.g.*, the perineum, penis, vulva, pubic and umbilical regions.

Etiology and pathology. The cause of Paget's disease is unknown. Sampson Handley holds that the disease begins as a carcinoma in the smaller mammary ducts and permeates the lymphatics, blocking these vessels in the plexus under the nipple. He considers the changes in the skin to be due to this obstruction of lymphatics, *i.e.*, they are nutritional and not malignant. The dermis is thickened by solid lymphatic œdema. Secondary fibrosis leads to retraction of the nipple. Pathologically the stratum corneum is very slightly affected, and the granular layer is present. The prickle layer is thickened, and the interpapillary processes are lengthened. The deeper parts of this layer show rounded degenerate cells containing bright, oval, nucleated bodies, of which some are enveloped in a distinct capsule. The upper part of the corium shows dilatation of the vessels, and a dense infiltration consisting of plasma-cells. Proliferating epithelial cells are also found in small foci in this layer.

Symptoms. At the onset there is a small red area around the nipple, covered with a scab, or with a small quantity of sticky yellowish exudation. When fully developed, it forms a bright red erosion, with a finely granular glazed surface, sharply limited, and sometimes distinctly raised above the surrounding tissue. There is definite induration, and when taken between the finger and thumb the

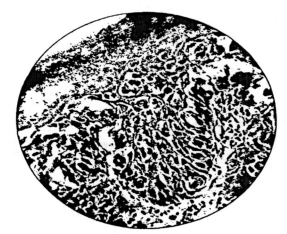

FIG. 237.—Paget's disease. Microphotograph of section.

lesion feels " like a penny felt through a cloth." There is no tendency to spontaneous healing, and the area affected slowly increases until a patch the size of the palm of the hand may be involved. The nipple may be retracted, but the lymphatic glands are not enlarged. The patient may complain of itching and burning.

Ultimately, after two or three, or rarely as many as twenty, years, the breast becomes infiltrated with duct cancer, the glands are involved, and death occurs from secondary deposits in the viscera or from cachexia.

The character of Paget's disease in other regions is similar.

Diagnosis. The red granular, glazed surface, seen on the removal of the crusts, and the induration with well-defined margins, together with the chronicity of the disease, distinguish it from chronic eczema.

Eczema of the nipple usually occurs in women who are suckling, and commonly both breasts are simultaneously affected.

The diagnosis is made certain by the examination of scrapings of

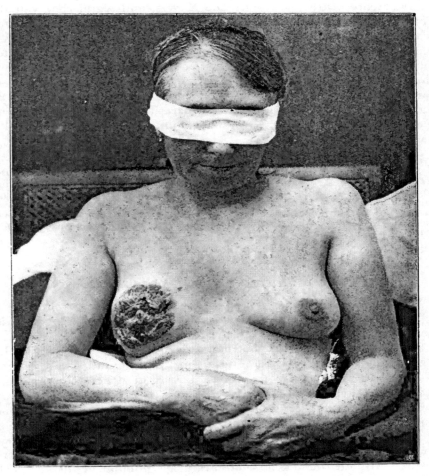

FIG. 238.—Paget's disease. of five years' duration. Patient, aged 61. The lesion cleared up under X-rays, but the mamma was involved early. Death eighteen months after.

the surface in liquor potassæ, showing the characteristic oval nucleated bodies in the cells or distinctly encapsuled.

Prognosis. Unless treated radically, Paget's disease tends to involve the breast, and to a fatal termination from dissemination of the malignant neoplasm.

Treatment. It is important to recognise that the process is malignant from the beginning, and the breast should be removed. together with the affected skin and glands, should any be involved. I have treated three cases with the X-rays, and regret that valuable time was lost by apparent cure. Two of these cases were entirely healed by radiotherapy, but in both of them the breast subsequently became infiltrated, and operative interference was required. Unfortunately both cases ended fatally. In the third case the disease was limited to the glans penis. The patient was a man aged 82. Temporary improvement followed the X-ray treatment, but later the glans penis had to be removed by operation, death occurring from uræmia. At the autopsy a rounded nodule of cancer was found in the bulbus urethræ.

REFERENCES.—PAGET. *St. Bartholomew's Hosp. Reports*, 1874, p. 87. H. T. BUTLIN. *Med. Chir. Trans.*, 1876, IX., p. 107. THIN. *British Medical Journal*, 1881, May 14 and 21. L. WICKHAM. Internat. Congress, Paris, 1889. *Comptes rendus.* J. HUTCHINSON, JNR. *Path. Soc. Trans.*, 1890, March 18. COLCOTT FOX and MACLEOD. "Paget's Disease of Umbilicus and other Rare Positions." *Brit. Journ. Derm.*, 1904, XVI., p. 41. W. SAMPSON HANDLEY. Hunterian Lecture. *Lancet*, 1917, I., p. 519.

TUMOURS OF MESOBLASTIC ORIGIN.

Xanthoma and Xanthelasma.

The name Xanthoma is applied to tumours of a yellowish or yellowish-pink colour. Xanthelasma is the name given to yellowish plaques on the upper and lower eyelids.

Etiology. One form of xanthoma occurs congenitally. Another is associated with glycosuria, and a third with jaundice and diseases of the liver. In a few instances nævi and other tumours may undergo a xanthomatous change.

Pathology. The lesions lie in the derma, where there is an accumulation of special fat-like material. The epidermis is normal. or it may be pigmented. The xanthomatous foci are rounded or in rows in the true skin, and they are separated by tracts of connective tissue. Around the vessels there are large globular or fusiform cells with rounded nuclei, containing granules or crystals. These granules are also found between the cellular elements. Chemically the material appears to be related to the fats, being soluble in ether and melting with heat. It can be fixed with osmic acid. Sudan III. stains it an orange-red colour. Pick has shown that the same substance is found in the blood and various organs of patients suffering from glycosuria and diseases of the liver. He considered the special material as a deposit of unknown origin. and independent of fat.

Pollitzer holds that xanthelasma palpebrarum is in no way related to the xanthoma tuberosum. It is in his opinion a peculiar degeneration of the muscles of the eyelid.

Clinical features. The lesions take three forms.

(1) **Xanthelasma palpebrarum.** Spots of an elongated shape, of a wash-leather or straw colour, with a well-defined margin, and very slightly raised above the surface. The affection is not uncommon in adults and in old people. It may be associated with

FIG. 239.—Xanthoma, of diabetic type. Male, æt. 24. The elbows and buttocks were affected.

cirrhosis and other affections of the liver, but the patients are often apparently quite well. It is, however, well known that a number of persons, particularly women, may have gall-stones without any symptoms. The regions affected are the inner ends of the upper and lower eyelids, close to the inner canthus. They are characteristic in appearance, painless and free from itching (Plate LII.). Xanthelasma may be associated with xanthoma tuberosum multiplex.

(2) **Xanthoma tuberosum multiplex.** The lesions are papules or nodules varying in size from a pin's head to a bean. Their colour varies : most have a yellow tint, with perhaps an areola of pink, others

Plate 52.

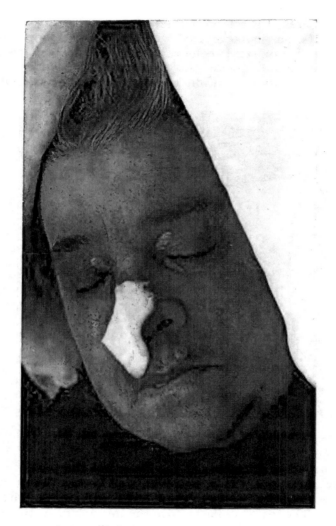

XANTHELASMA PALPEBRARUM.

The washleather-coloured plaques are on each lid at the inner ends.
The patient had also a rodent ulcer of the nose (partly treated and
covered with lint). There is also a nævoid tumour on the upper lip.

have an earthy colour, and others again are purplish, and the yellow colour can only be made out upon examination with the diascope. They vary in consistence, some being quite hard, while others are softish. The lesions develop slowly, coming out in crops and progressing in size, sometimes coalescing to form plaques. They are symmetrical, the favourite sites being the elbows, knees, shoulders, knuckles, buttocks and scalp. Extensor surfaces appear to be preferred. I have once seen a nodule on the prominence of the thyroid cartilage in a male who had an extensive outbreak on the hands and elsewhere.

Plaques also occur on the eyelids, and bands in the flexures and on the palmar and plantar regions.

In a remarkable case shown by Dr. Macleod there were irregular swellings of the wrist, elbow and knee-joints.

Children and adults may be affected, and both sexes are equally liable to the disease. In the adult a history of jaundice is common.

Xanthoma diabeticorum is held by many authors to be essentially different from the preceding form. The lesions are pinkish or orange-red papules, or nodules of small size. They come out acutely, affecting the extensor surfaces of the limbs, neck, loins, and buttocks. Sometimes they form rows, and in one of my cases the nodules resembled a string of yellow coral beads let into the skin about the knees. The nodules itch. The patients are middle-aged men, of stout, florid habit, and there is often a history of chronic alcoholism. Glycosuria is not always present, though it may appear after the eruption has cleared up. The papules and nodules may disappear in a few months, or occur intermittently.

I recently had a widely spread xanthomatous eruption in a boy of seven suffering from diabetes insipidus of non-syphilitic origin.

(3) **Xanthoma tumours** are seen occasionally ; they may be sessile, or pedunculated, and may reach the size of a small orange.

Prognosis. Except in xanthoma diabeticorum, the tumours tend to persist.

Treatment of xanthoma. The galvano-cautery at a dull red heat may be used to destroy the lesions. They also clear up usually under X-ray treatment. Where the case is of the diabetic type, the diet should be regulated, alcohol avoided, and the lesions usually disappear. Hepatic disease, if present, requires treatment on the usual lines.

REFERENCES. —" Xanthoma Diabeticorum." MORRIS. *British Medical Journal*, 1891, p. 1310. H. RADCLIFFE CROCKER. *Path. Trans.*, 1882, XXXII. J. M. H. MACLEOD. *Brit. Journal Dermatology*, XXV., p. 344, plates. POLLITZER. *Journ. Cut. Diseases*, December, 1910.

Fibromata and Neuro-fibromata.

Several conditions are included under the term Fibroma.

Fibroma simplex This name is applied to the common, soft, vascular, pedunculated tumours which occur on the face, neck and shoulders of elderly people. The lesions are rarely larger than a pea, and sometimes disappear, leaving hernia-like sacs.

Symmetrical ear-nodules, which are apparently fibromata, occur in the natives of tropical countries. The lesions are symmetrical nodules deeply placed in the lobules of the ears.

Recklinghausen's disease has already been mentioned in connection

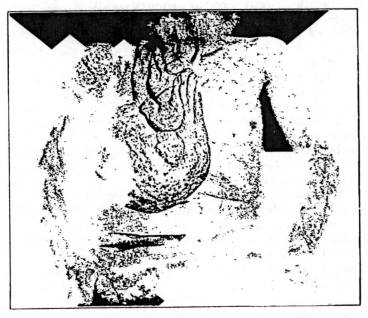

Fig. 240.—Dermatolysis. Pendulous fibroma. Male, 71.

with congenital tumours. The lesions are either multiple small tumours covered by normal skin, or pendulous growths, sometimes of large size. The two conditions may co-exist. The tumours vary in number from one or two up to several hundreds or more. The case figured at p. 46 is one of the most remarkable of this type. Pigmented patches occur in connection with this variety of fibroma, and the skin is usually coarse. There are also neuromata. Sloughing and ulceration may take place from pressure or friction. The pendulous tumours may attain large dimensions ; they occur at the occiput, neck and face, and also on the trunk and upper segments of the limbs (Fig. 240).

Dermatolysis is a variety of fibroma pendulum. Crocker described a remarkable case in which, after an accident attended with paraplegia, the buttocks and legs began to enlarge. Enormous pendulous folds of skin and subcutaneous tissue, " overlapping like flounces," hung from the lower part of the chest halfway down the thighs and down the leg below the knee. Small fibromata developed from time to time on the abdominal wall. There were no symptoms. " Elastic-skinned " men can draw the integument under the chin, over the face, and the like, and from examination of the skin of one such case it would appear that the primary condition is a myxomatous degeneration of the connective tissue.

The *cause* of all these conditions is unknown, but heredity plays some part. Congenital cases are not infrequent, and it is believed that in most there is some anomaly of development.

Von Recklinghausen showed that in some cases the tumours develop in connection with the lamellæ of the nerve sheaths. The connective tissue varies from tough fibrous tissue to masses of loose, imperfectly-formed fibres and gelatinous tissue. Unna describes mast-cells as occurring in large numbers.

Diagnosis. Fibromata have to be distinguished from moles, but these are usually pigmented. Sebaceous cysts contain pasty-white sebaceous matter which can be expressed. The rare cases of cysticercus of the skin may easily be mistaken for fibromata. Puncture and the finding of hooklets in the fluid would be the only certain method of diagnosis short of removal.

Prognosis. Fibromata give little trouble except from their position. They tend to increase in number and size.

Treatment. Excision may be practised if the position or size of the growths require it.

REFERENCES. —v. RECKLINGHAUSEN. *Ueber die Multiplen Fibrome der Haut.* Berlin, 1882. R. W. SMITH. *Syd. Soc. Reprints,* XI., "Atlas Illustrations of Pathology."

Neuromata.

These are exceedingly rare tumours arising from the neurilemma. They are chronic, painful, flat tumours imbedded in the skin, of small size, not exceeding a small pea or nut. Pain radiates from the growth when it is handled, and sometimes there are paroxysmal attacks. Removal of a portion of the nerve supplying the affected area has been found to relieve the symptoms.

I have recently had under my care a boy with multiple flat painless tumours on the palmar aspect of the wrist, thenar eminence, thumb and forefinger. One of the tumours was excised and found by Dr. Turnbull to be a plexiform neuroma (Fig. 241). As the tumours were painless, the lesions were probably congenital, and I considered the condition to be a localised form of Recklinghausen's disease.

REFERENCES.—DUHRING. "International Atlas of Rare Skin Diseases," Plate XXXV. R. W. SMITH. "Atlas Illustrations of Pathology." *Syd. Soc. Reprints*, XI.

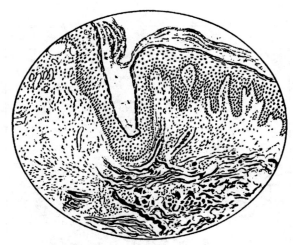

FIG. 241.—Neuroma. Nerve fibres: gold stain.

Cheloid.

Cheloid is a new growth of the corium occurring after injuries, and occasionally spontaneously.

Etiology. Cheloid occurs equally in both sexes and at all ages. It is commoner in certain races than in others, and negroes appear to be specially liable to it. There is undoubted predisposition, for some subjects develop cheloid after very slight irritation, such as the application of caustics, blistering, and contusions which would not even produce a cicatrix. I have seen it follow the bites of mosquitoes, acne vulgaris, vaccination, hypodermic injections, tattooing, perforation of the lobules of the ear for earrings, syphilitic ulcers, herpes zoster, etc. Burns and scalds, including burns from strong acids and alkalies, however, furnish the majority of cases. Spontaneous cases are very rare, and in many of them it is difficult to exclude slight traumatism.

Pathology. Cheloids are composed of masses of connective tissue bundles, running more or less parallel to the surface of the skin. The fibrous tissue develops around the blood-vessels, and the claw-like prolongations of the tumours are formed along the vascular channels. The papillæ are absent in the greater part of the growth, but not everywhere. There is no essential difference in the histology of the scar and the spontaneous cheloid.

Clinical features. The lesions may be single or multiple. The tumour is a well-defined, raised, ovoid or rounded plaque, or of

Fig. 242.—Cheloid, following a burn.

irregular shape. A characteristic feature, which is, however, not constant, is the claw-like prolongations, which spread from the central mass into the surrounding skin. The surface of a cheloid is smooth, often shining, and sometimes nodular. It may be white, or red, or purplish, the colour depending upon the presence of dilated vessels upon it. Where the muco-cutaneous junctions are affected, there may be grave deformity, and when situated at flexures the movements of the parts are impaired. Cheloids are often tender, and the patient may complain of pain, or of burning and itching. Sometimes the pain is intense, but in other cases there are no subjective symptoms. Scar cheloid may occur anywhere, and when following a burn or scald may be of considerable extent, as in the case figured (Fig. 242). It may spread beyond the actual scar area, but in the most extensive scars it is usual to find some areas of normal cicatrix, with the cheloid in patches. The most remarkable scar cheloid I have seen followed a burn of the face from sulphuric acid. The whole of the scar area was covered by an irregular quilted mass, with characteristic claw-like processes at the edges.

In the idiopathic form the lesion is usually single, and the trunk

FIG. 243.—The same case after treatment by X-rays.

is affected in one half the cases. This variety occurs more frequently in women than in men. The cheloid is of moderate size, with a well-defined margin. discoid, ovoid, or irregular in shape. with claw-like prolongations as in the scar variety. Tenderness and pain are also common.

After reaching a certain size, the cheloid remains stationary, or spreads slowly, or it may undergo spontaneous resolution. Malignant change is rare.

Diagnosis. Cheloid has to be distinguished from hypertrophic scar. The latter is limited to the original scar area. while the cheloid spreads beyond it. There is no importance in differentiating between a scar cheloid and the spontaneous variety.

Prognosis. Spontaneous resolution of cheloids sometimes occurs, and this is said to happen more frequently in young subjects. Usually the course is slowly progressive, and then stationary for a long period.

Treatment. Cheloids should not be excised. I have seen some immediately good results of operation, but unfortunately the cheloid usually recurs. In one such case treated by excision, the ultimate result was a linear cheloid with paired small nodules at the site of every suture. The most satisfactory treatment is by the X-rays or radium. A full pastille dose should be applied exactly to the diseased area at intervals of a fortnight. In every case I have thus treated there has been improvement, and in the majority the thickening has entirely cleared up. It is important to see that the patient understands that the thickening only can be removed, and that some scar, probably quite soft, will remain. The radium is applied on a button to the lesions for an hour at a time. Injection of thiosinamine and of fibrolysin may also be used, but in my experience they are not so satisfactory as the X-rays. Twenty minims of a 10 per cent. solution of thiosinamine are injected around the growth at intervals of a few days. Thyroid has been tried, but I have no experience of its use. Electrolysis is also advocated, but, of course, is painful, while the application of the X-rays is free from this drawback.

Lipoma.

Lipomata are dealt with in the surgical text-books. Sometimes they come under the observation of the dermatologist. They are usually multiple, subcutaneous tumours, varying in number, and from a pea to an orange in size, soft and lobulated, and with a peculiar pseudo-fluctuation. Lipomata occur anywhere. I recently showed at the Royal Society of Medicine an infant in whom there were symmetrical congenital lipomata attached to the plantar fascia.

Fatty growths may occur in fibromata, and angiomata and other tumours.

Lipomata should be treated surgically if necessary.

Colloid degeneration. Colloid milium. A rare affection occurring chiefly in men over forty-five who have been exposed to weather. The lesions are papules of transparent yellow or reddish-yellow colour on the nose, cheeks and upper lips. The mucous membranes, the conjunctiva, and lips may be involved. Pigmentation and atrophy of the exposed parts are common.   Colloid degeneration of the connective tissue of the cutis is found on microscopical examination. The lesions may be removed by the curette or electrolysis.

REFERENCE.—BOSELLINI.   *Annales de Dermatologie*, 1906, VII., p. 751.

Pseudo-xanthoma elasticum.   Elastorrhexis.   The tumours are of a yellowish tint arranged in groups or streaks, and are usually not larger than a lentil.   They occur on the abdomen, sides of the neck and in flexures.   In some cases there has been phthisis.   The growths cause no symptoms.   Microscopically giant cells are found associated with degeneration of the elastic tissue of the true skin.

REFERENCE.—BOSELLINI.   *Archiv. f. Dermatol.*, XCV., p. 3.

Myxoma.

Rarely tumours of myxomatous type occur on the genital organs and on the eyelids.   More often myxomatous degeneration takes place in fibromata, etc.

Myoma or Leiomyoma.

These remarkable tumours are composed of smooth muscle tissue, in the form of networks or bundles.   They arise from the arrectores pilorum, or from the muscular walls of the cutaneous

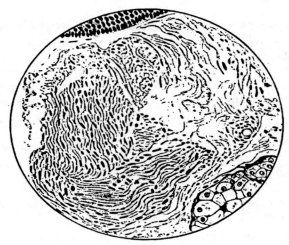

FIG. 244.—Leiomyoma.   Microscopic appearances.   (x 150.).

vessels. Myomata of the skin are rare, and are more common in women than men.

They form firm pinkish or brown tumours varying in size from a pea to a nut. They may be disseminated or in groups. They are tender on pressure, and the patient may complain of attacks of pain as the result of local irritation or of cold. Whitfield describes a case in which the lesions appear to have followed herpes. In a patient under my own care the tumours were remarkable for their unilateral distribution on the forehead and cheek.

REFERENCE.—WALLACE BEATTY. *British Journal of Dermatology*, 1907, XIX., p. 1 : photographs of patient, and sections and literature.

Calcareous Tumours.

These are of four kinds. (1) The most common are the small hard nodules the size of a small seed, occurring on the inner aspect of the tibiæ in old people. The condition is supposed to be due to calcification of fat lobules.

(2) In the second type the lesions are primarily inflammatory swellings, dermoids or neoplasms which have undergone calcareous degeneration. They may follow a cold abscess, phlebitis, etc.

(3) Calcification of tumours of supposed sebaceous gland origin occur in women and children. Sometimes the lesions are multiple and appear chiefly on the extremities. Their origin from the sebaceous glands is doubtful. In some cases the lesions appeared to be primarily of inflammatory origin, the chalky deposit lying in the connective tissue.

(4) **Subcutaneous calcareous granulomata** (**Calcinosis**). The subjects of this condition are usually young. After an injury a painless swelling occurs, often in the site of a subcutaneous bursa, such as that over the olecranon. The swelling is at first soft, and if opened a creamy fluid containing chalky matter escapes. Fresh lesions form from time to time, and the older ones become of stony hardness. Atrophy of muscles and immobility of the joints follow. The skin may be dry and pigmented in patches. Wasting and febrile symptoms, with albuminuria and hæmaturia and diarrhœa, may occur. The condition sometimes ends fatally.

The lesions resemble those of tuberculosis, but the central areas are filled by calcareous granules.

A microbic origin has been suggested. Treatment in the earlier lesions by operation is recommended.

REFERENCE.—JADASSOHN. *Archiv. f. Dermat. u. Syph.*, 1910. p. 317. PARKES WEBER. *Trans. Internat. Med. Congress*, 1913.

Telangiectases.

The word " telangiectasis " means a dilatation of the vessels farthest from the centre of the circulation, but, as generally used, the cutaneous nævi and angiomata are excluded. As Colcott Fox points out, it is often difficult to apply the term with strict accuracy, because some of the acquired dilatations appear to depend upon congenital anomalies of the vessels.

Etiology. Telangiectases may develop in early life, and are then probably of congenital origin. For convenience, the form called nævus araneus, which is often acquired, has already been described with the vascular nævi (p. 36).

Telangiectases are often associated with other cutaneous affections, usually of a congestive or inflammatory nature. The commonest causes are acne rosacea, adenoma sebaceum, lupus erythematosus, and some forms of sclerodermia. A similar condition occurs in the X-ray and radium cicatrices, and I have seen it after the reaction produced by the Kromayer mercury vapour lamp. Circulatory disturbance is another frequent cause. Telangiectases may occur in heart disease and in certain pulmonary affections, and in young subjects with a bad peripheral circulation (*vide* Angio-keratoma, p. 369), and in Graves' disease. Osler called attention to the frequent association of telangiectases and angiomata with hepatic disease, and Galloway described dilatations of the vessels in various abdominal diseases.

Besides these symptomatic telangiectases, there are several types which are primary or idiopathic. The following account of their important features is based upon the valuable article of Dr. Colcott Fox appended to an account of an interesting case under his own observation.

Clinical features of the primary telangiectases. (1) The dilatations of the capillaries may form *diffuse areas* of redness, or *networks*. A large part of the body, or certain regions only, may be affected. Cases are recorded as following vaginal hysterectomy, erysipelas, and chronic renal disease, and in an old syphilitic subject.

(2) The telangiectases may form *plaques*. The lesions may be macular dilatations of the vessels from a pin's head to a sixpence in size. Slight branny scaling may be present. Obesity and the menopause and mammary carcinoma have been associated conditions. In one case the telangiectases followed convulsions in a child, and in another were associated with urticaria at the menstrual periods. In one of the recorded cases the areas affected corresponded with those supplied by certain nerves, but were symmetrical.

(3) *Angiomata of the senile* (Dubreuilh). These occur on the trunk and upper parts of the limbs, in later middle life, and more commonly in men than in women. They are red points at first, but enlarge to the size of a millet seed or even a pea. The epidermis is unaffected. They bear no relation to malignant disease. In rare cases angiomata of this type occur on the face, and may attain a large size, and bleed freely if ruptured. In one case angiomata were found post mortem on the mucous membrane of the respiratory tract, the rectum and urethra, and in the liver.

(4) A *family affection* characterised by recurring epistaxis and multiple telangiectases of the skin and mucous membranes. Osler has specially drawn attention to this group, and the clinical features are thus summarised in a paper of Parkes Weber. The disease affects and is transmitted by both sexes. The hæmorrhage is in most cases only from the mucous membrane of the nose, and the epistaxis usually precedes the cutaneous manifestations by many years. The telangiectases first attract attention towards middle life, and the tendency to hæmorrhages and to the formation of angiomata increase with age. Grave anæmia may result. There is no tendency to hæmophilia, and no alteration in the coagulability of the blood. The telangiectases affect the face, lips, ears, and buccal and nasal cavity chiefly, but the trunk and extremities may be involved, and rectal hæmorrhages and menorrhagia have been recorded. Dr. Fox's own case was characterised by bilateral telangiectases on the trunk, with a marked history of epistaxis in childhood, and recent rectal hæmorrhage. There was no family affection. In a woman recently under my care the telangiectases began at the age of forty-one. Her brother and one sister and her paternal aunt suffered from epistaxis, which in two cases had necessitated plugging of the posterior nares.

Treatment, in the absence of known cause, must be purely symptomatic.

REFERENCE.—For literature see COLCOTT FOX's paper. *British Journal of Dermatology*, 1908, Vol. XX., p. 145.

Angio-keratoma.

A rare condition characterised by minute telangiectases with warty growths upon the extremities.

The patients are usually females, and all suffer from chilblains. Dr. Pringle recently showed four cases in one family, and similar instances of familial affection are on record. Some have suggested that the affection is a tuberculide, but of this there is no direct evidence.

Histologically the lesions consist of dilatations of the papillary blood-vessels. The stratum corneum is thickened, and there is inflammatory thickening of the papillary layer. The horny thickening is secondary to the vascular dilatation.

The disease begins in childhood or adolescence, in persons of poor physique. In most instances the telangiectases first appear as a sequel to chilblains.

The lesions are pin-head sized vascular growths in the backs of the fingers and toes (rarely on the ears). The vascular growths become warty, and by coalescence small horny, vascular patches may form. The larger tumours bleed easily.

The lesions can be removed by electrolysis. The general health usually requires attention.

REFERENCE.—J. J. PRINGLE. *Brit. Jour. Derm.*, 1891, p. 237, etc.

SARCOMATA OF THE SKIN.

Cutaneous sarcoma may be primary or secondary to tumours of the bones, viscera or glands. Kaposi's Multiple Idiopathic Sarcoma (so-called) is considered on p. 396.

Primary Sarcoma.

The growths may be composed of large or small round cells, or of spindle-cells, or of lymphoid cells. In some cases there is a great deposit of pigment derived from the blood. The cause of cutaneous sarcomata is unknown.

Generalised sarcomatosis. This rare affection may begin on any part of the body. The tumours vary from a couple of dozen to several hundreds. At first they are small, not exceeding a pea in size, but they may reach the size of a cherry, or form small flat plaques. The growths may start in the corium, or perhaps more commonly in the hypoderm. They are of a pale red or bluish-red colour, and in some cases the skin over them is covered with dilated capillaries. The clinical features and the rapidity with which the tumours are disseminated vary very much in different cases. Histologically, the more malignant tumours have been found to consist of round cells.

The affection may start early in life, and the prognosis is usually hopeless ; however, arsenic administered internally or by hypodermic injection has sometimes a remarkable influence. Kobner and Shattuck and others have reported cures. Coley's fluid might also be tried.

Boeck's Multiple Benign Sarcoid has alreay been discussed in connection with the cutaneous tuberculides (p. 258).

Secondary sarcoma of the skin is rare. I have had one case in which the primary disease was in the bones of the tarsus. The secondary tumours were in the scalp.

REFERENCES.—J. C. JOHNSTON. "Sarcoma and the Sarcoid Growths of the Skin." *Brit. Journ. Derm.*, 1901, XIII., p. 241. PERRIN. *Monatsheft f. Prakt. Derm.*, 1886, p. 331. FUNK. *Ibid.*, 1889, p. 91.

Mycosis fungoides. Granuloma fungoides.

It is difficult to place this remarkable disease. By some it is looked upon as an ally of the sarcomata and by others as connected with cutaneous leukæmia. It is best perhaps for the present to

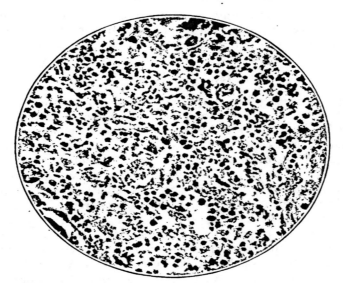

FIG. 245.—Mycosis fungoides. Microphotograph of section, ¼ obj.

consider it as a general disease characterised by a polymorphic eruption and tumours of peculiar type.

Etiology. The cause of mycosis fungoides is unknown. It is not hereditary and not contagious. It is more common in males than in females; in 74 cases collected by me there were 46 males and 28 females, and most of the patients were between thiry and fifty years of age, the extremes being fifteen and seventy-four. It has been suggested that it is due to a micro-parasite, and it would then have to be described as an infective granuloma. Rarely injury appears to be a cause.

Pathology. The tumours consist of round cells, lymphocytes from the blood or plasma cells. In early lesions there are compact

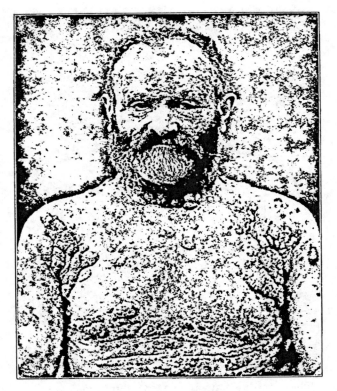

Fig. 246.—Mycosis fungoides.

masses of cells of various forms, some cuboidal, others rounded or irregular. contained in a fine stroma of connective tissue. A special small type of cell, the " daughter cell " or characteristic cell, is said to be peculiar to the disease. All the elements of the skin are rapidly destroyed by the growth, and the epidermis becomes distended or eroded with the increase of the tumour formation. In the premycosic erythrodermia there is a dense cellular infiltration of the papillary body. the cells being of lymphoid type in a fine connective tissue stroma. Similar cellular infiltration is found around the vessels. The epidermis is thickened and the horny layer desquamates.

Secondary deposits have been found in various organs, but metastases are rare.

Clinical features. The disease develops insidiously. In the majority of cases there is a premycosic stage, characterised by—

FIG. 247.—The same patient after treatment by X-rays. The tumours reappeared after several months.

(1) An intense pruritus ; (2) a polymorphic eruption ; or (3) erythrodermia. In rare cases the tumour formation is the first manifestation.

(1) *Onset with pruritus.* The itching is general and of very long duration, and unaccompanied by any obvious change in the skin. This condition may last for several months to several years.

(2) The *polymorphic eruption* may be transitory or persistent. There may be a primary patch, which precedes the generalised eruption. Various types of lesion occur. Sometimes they are

macular or in the form of plaques of a red or purplish colour, and occasionally blebs appear on them. They are of varying extent and their margins are ill-defined. In other cases the areas are like patches of dry eczema, slightly raised above the surface, ill-defined, and of purplish or yellowish tinge. The surface may be scaly, occasionally oozing, or covered with dry crusts. Infiltration may be present. In other cases, again, the lesions resemble a lichen. They vary in number and in extent, but are always attended by intense itching.

Sometimes the trunk is widely involved. The face may be affected, and if there is infiltration, an appearance which is leonine, like nodular lepra, may be produced.

Following these lesions, or coincident with them, there may be

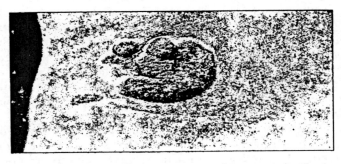

Fig. 248.—Mycosis fungoides. A group of tumours in the back of a man aged 56.

infiltrated plaques of a brick-red colour, with the surface of the skin finely mamillated like an orange, or there may be tumours.

(3) *Erythrodermia*. The initial lesions are red or violet-tinted plaques, chiefly in the flexures, but eventually the whole of the surface may be bright red. The skin is dry, and there may be fine desquamation. The hair may fall out all over the affected parts, but the nails are not affected. The itching is terrible. The skin later becomes œdematous, and the lymphatic glands everywhere become swollen. After a variable time, four to ten years, small nodules with characteristic structure may appear. Rarely death takes place without the development of the tumours.

The *tumours* appear rarely as the first symptom. Where this occurs the condition is described as mycosis fungoides à tumeurs d'emblée. Usually they develop as a sequel to the pruritus or to the polymorphic eruptions, or coincident with them. They may be in the form of infiltrated plaques of variable size, of a brick-red colour, with a mamillated surface, or rounded tumours. The mycosic tumour varies in size from a cherry to half an orange or more.   It may develop on one of the primary lesions or on previously healthy skin.   The tumours are soft, of a dull red colour, hemispherical or perhaps nodular on the surface.   They have often a narrow constriction at the base, and have been likened to a tomato on the skin. There may be semicircular or crescentic lesions.

They often ulcerate, destroying the epidermis, but extend peripherally.   Sometimes enormous tumours are seen, as big as a child's head, or large ulcers form, exuding a sanious discharge.   Gangrene is a rare sequel.

Curiously the tumours may disappear spontaneously, with or without scars and pigmentation.

Mycosis affects the trunk, the upper parts of the extremities, and the face.   The glands are always enlarged early.   Alopecia of the affected parts is usual.   There are no characteristic blood changes.

The disease may last for from two to twenty years, with spontaneous remissions, which simulate cure.   Intercurrent acute febrile illness sometimes causes disappearance of the tumours.   In the late stages the patient becomes asthenic, his digestive organs fail, and he dies in marasmus, or from complications.   One of my patients died from pulmonary embolism.

In the acute form described by Vidal and Brocq the tumours are localised to one region, appear in healthy skin, and the glands are not involved.   Brocq considers this form as closely related to the sarcomata.

Diagnosis.   The diagnosis in the premycosic stage is often exceedingly difficult.   " In all cases of ambiguous pruritic dermatoses which are prolonged and rebellious to treatment the possibility of the disease being the premycosic stage of mycosis fungoides should be borne in mind " (Besnier).   The chronicity of the disease and the characters of the plaques are suggestive. but the feature upon which reliance is to be placed are the persistence of a polymorphous eruption resembling eczema, lichen or psoriasis, with intense itching.   In a large number of cases, however, the nature of the disease can only be suspected until the development of the tumours.   A biopsy may be of value.   When the characteristic tumours appear the diagnosis is no longer in doubt.   Gaucher and others have reported successful complement-fixation tests in the pre-mycosic stage.

Prognosis.   Until the X-ray treatment was used for this affection the prognosis was hopeless.   In a number of cases the tumours and the erythrodermia have been entirely removed by radiotherapy, and patients have been free from recurrence for some years.   Our experience is, however, not yet sufficiently extensive to speak of cure. It must be remembered that spontaneous resolution sometimes occurs.

Treatment. The best results have been obtained by radio-therapy. In cases where the tumours were localised I have seen complete disappearance of the growths after six pastille doses administered at intervals of a week. In a case with erythrodermia and multiple tumours irradiation of the whole of the affected area with four pastille doses caused the entire disappearance of the eruption. This treatment naturally took a long time on account of the extent of the disease, but the patient remained quite free from recurrence at the end of a year. In another case the treatment has been continued for several months with large doses of X-rays, three pastille changes produced at one sitting, the rays being filtered through aluminium. The tumours slowly yielded, but recurred after some months.

Arsenic internally or administered by injection sometimes proves of value. Mercury has also been used with benefit. The ulcerating lesions are treated by the application of antiseptic lotions.

REFERENCES.—VIDAL. "Lymphadenie Cutanée." *Trans. International Congress*, 1881. PALTAUF. "On Lymphatic Skin Diseases." II. Internat. Dermat. Congress, Vienna, 1892. MAX WOLTERS. *Biblioth. Med.*, 1899. JAS. GALLOWAY and J. M. H. MACLEOD. *Brit. Journ. Dermat.*, 1900. Vol. XII., p. 153. J. H. STOWERS. Collected Cases. *Brit. Journ. Dermat.*, 1903, XV., p. 47. "Complement Fixation." GAUCHER, PARIS and GUGGENHEIM. *Bulletin et Mem. de la Société des Hôp.*, February 8, 1912, p. 150. A. JAMIESON. "Treatment by X-Rays." *Brit. Journ. Dermat.*, 1903, XV., p. 1. A. JAMIESON and HUIE. *Brit. Journ. Derm.*, 1904, XVI., p. 125. J. H. SEQUEIRA. *Brit. Journ. Dermat.*, XXVI., p. 213, and Discussion.

Lymphadenoma and Lymphosarcoma. Lymphadenoma of the skin has been described. The lesions closely resemble those of mycosis fungoides d'emblée (p. 574). They occur late in the disease.

Lymphosarcoma begins as a nodule in the true skin, usually about one of the orifices of the body. It gradually increases to form a flattened or lobulated tumour of large size. Eventually the tumour ulcerates. The glands are rapidly involved, and the tumours become generalised. The patients are usually young adults.

A form of prurigo also occurs in connection with lymphadenoma (*vide* p. 423).

Leukæmia cutis is very rare. In a case described by Rolleston and Wilfred Fox the eruption consisted of small blackish nodules in the skin of the abdominal wall. They rapidly reached the size of a raisin and spread all over the front of the trunk. The nodules were hard, shiny, and slightly tender. The infiltration consisted of myeloid cells in the corium.

REFERENCES.—"Lymphadenoma." ARNING and HENSEL. *Ikonographia Dermatologica*, 1909, IV., p. 127. "Leukæmia Cutis." ROLLESTON and FOX. *Brit. Journ. Dermat.*, XXI., p. 377.

CHAPTER XXVI.

DISEASES OF THE APPENDAGES.

Affections of the Sweat Glands.

THE sweat glands may be affected functionally or organically.

Functional affections. The excretion may be altered in quantity or in quality. The term Anidrosis is used for diminished excretion, Hyperidrosis for excessive secretion. Bromidrosis is the name given to offensive perspiration, and chromidrosis is used to designate alteration in colour.

Anidrosis. There does not appear to be any condition in which the excretion of sweat is completely suppressed, but it is diminished in quantity in certain general and local affections.

The general conditions causing anidrosis are diabetes, renal disease, myxœdema, and some cachexias due to malignant disease. Some degree of anidrosis is not uncommon in the aged from senile atrophy of the sweat glands.

Nervous affections sometimes cause local anidrosis, e.g., transverse myelitis, infantile paralysis, and anæsthetic leprosy.

Local conditions of the skin causing anidrosis are the congenital anomaly ichthyosis, and its less severe stage, xerodermia, senile degeneration of the skin. some forms of cutaneous atrophy, sclerodermia, and extensive psoriasis and eczema.

Where the anidrosis depends upon some cause like diabetes or myxœdema, the treatment is on the lines required by the general disease. Diaphoretics are of little use in the local forms, but benefit may be derived by treating such conditions as xerodermia, and the cutaneous eruptions like psoriasis, etc. Turkish baths may be of service and and pilocarpine may be used.

Hyperidrosis. There is a great deal of variation in the amount of sensible perspiration in different individuals without any alteration in the general health. Excessive sweating may be due to general or local causes.

General causes. Many toxic and bacterial diseases are attended with profuse perspiration. It is common in malaria, phthisis, septicæmia, typhoid fever, influenza, pneumonia, and in attacks of gout. It is a feature in defervescence in any febrile condition, and

occurs in the moribund from any cause. Rickets, obesity, exophthalmic goitre and allied conditions, chronic intoxications from
alcohol, lead and arsenic are also causes.

Nervous conditions cause hyperidrosis. Sufferers from neurasthenia, hemiplegia, tabes dorsalis, transverse myelitis, peripheral
neuritis, and affections of the sympathetic may all perspire excessively. Very rarely some gross organic disease of the brain, such as a
tumour, may cause local hyperidrosis. I have seen it also in the
area of herpes frontalis after the healing of the vesicles.

Local hyperidrosis occurs on the *scalp* in the bald and in many
sufferers from oily seborrhœa. In the latter condition the hat-lining,
pillows, etc., are constantly stained by the excretion, which appears
to be partly hyperidrosis and partly excess of oily matter from the
sebaceous glands.

The *face.* Unilateral sweating of the face is occasionally met
with. Some curious cases of heredity have been recorded. It may
be looked upon as an affection of the sympathetic. Mastication and
the ingestion of acids such as vinegar may excite it. I recently had
under my observation a man who carried about a supply of mustard
pickles, of which he partook to demonstrate the anomaly.

The *axillæ.* Sweating is often excited abundantly in the axillæ
of patients who strip for examination. This may be emotional or
due to exposure. Excess of sweat in the axillæ occurs in the gouty,
rheumatic, obese, and nervous subjects. In some cases it is particularly trying for the patient, especially women, as the clothing is
rapidly spoiled. In many instances there is fœtor (*vide* Bromidrosis).
Exertion and emotion increase the secretion.

The *groins* are affected in similar way to the axillæ, but the trouble
is rarely so severe.

The *extremities.* Hyperidrosis of the palms and soles is very
common. In many cases there is acro-asphyxia, the affected areas
being cold, clammy, and blue or dead white in colour. In others
there is evident hyperæmia. On the soles, owing to the retention of
sweat, the skin may become macerated, and vesicles and blisters
form, rendering walking painful and difficult. Secondary decomposition of the sweat with bromidrosis is common. Flat foot is often
associated with hyperidrosis, and the use of a proper valgus pad often
gives immediate relief.

Nose. **Granulosis rubra nasi** (of Jadassohn) is a rather rare
affection, occurring in children. The nose and occasionally the
upper lips and cheeks are involved. The affected areas are constantly
moist from the exudation of sweat, and there are a number of small
papules of a red colour about the size of a pin's head or little larger,

The surface of the nose generally is rather livid. Hallopeau points out that the affection may be hereditary.

Histologically, there is a cellular infiltration about the sweat glands. Mono-nuclears, plasma cells and giant cells are found and the sweat glands are dilated.

REFERENCES.—"Granulosis Rubra Nasi." JADASSOHN. *Archiv. of Derm. and Syph.*, 1901, LVIII., p. 145. Bibliography. MENEAU. *Journ. des Maladies Cut. et. Syph.*, 1909, XII., p. 894.

Treatment of hyperidrosis. Anæmia and other underlying conditions should be treated on the usual lines. Alcoholism is a common cause in adults and should be avoided. Atropine 1-100 grain subcutaneously injected, or given in pill, and belladonna may be tried, but require careful watching. Sulphur præcipitata in drachm doses twice a day, as suggested by Radcliffe Crocker, is very useful. It may be combined with Pulv. cret. aromat. if it tends to looseness of the bowels. Ichthyol may also be given.

Locally, great benefit is found from frequent bathing of the affected parts, followed by the application of ichthyol in ointment, 5 per cent., or lotions of permanganate of potash, 1 in 1,000, or a 3 per cent. solution of salicylic acid. Antiseptic soaps are also of service. Where the circulation is bad, electric baths, hot baths, and massage may be found beneficial. In sweating of the feet the parts should be bathed twice a day, the socks should be changed daily, and powders dusted over the parts and into the socks. Boric acid alone or in combination with salicylic acid, or resorcin 2 per. cent., may be used. For sweating of the armpits, hot sponging followed by a 1 per cent. solution of quinine in spirit or eau de Cologne is useful, or a dusting powder containing 3 per cent. of salicylic acid may be applied.

Recently advantage has been taken of the X-rays for the treatment of local hyperidrosis. A pastille dose is given at intervals of ten days. Four or five applications are usually necessary. I have seen it successful in some rebellious cases.

In granulosis rubra nasi similar astringent applications and also the X-ray treatment may be used, but the disease tends to spontaneous cure.

REFERENCE.—"Treatment by X-Rays." PIRRIE. *Lancet*. August 12, 1911, p. 433.

Bromidrosis. Fœtid sweating of the feet, axillæ, and groins. As a rule there is also hyperidrosis, the sweat undergoing decomposition, with secondary fermentative changes due to microbic infection.

Thin described a bacillus fœtidus which he believed to be the cause. This organism is probably a common parasite, and only becomes pathogenic under appropriate conditions.

Those who have to stand a great deal at their work, servants, and others, and particularly the flat-footed, are the most frequent sufferers from bromidrosis of the feet. Axillary bromidrosis is common, and a great annoyance to the patient. It is often dependent upon emotion.

Treatment. Boots and shoes soaked in the fœtid sweat should be got rid of. The feet should be washed twice daily, and an antiseptic such as potass. permanganat. 1-1,000, salicylic acid 3 per cent., or formalin ½ to 3 per cent. in alcohol and water applied. The socks should be changed every day, and in mild cases this daily change, with regular bathing and the application of boric acid powder, is sufficient. If the parts are excoriated, peroxide of hydrogen, xeroform or dermatol should be first applied. In bad cases the application of a 5 per cent. solution of chromic acid once weekly, as used in the German army, is attended with good results. There is sometimes great difficulty in getting rid of patches of thickened epidermis unless something of this kind is done. Another method of removing such horny patches is the application of diachylon plaster for twelve hours. After its removal the parts are treated with a dusting powder. The axillary cases are treated as for hyperidrosis, any underlying condition of the general health receiving attention. Castellani recommends the internal use of urotropine (grs. x. thrice daily).

Chromidrosis. Many of the recorded cases of coloured sweating are doubtless impostures, but there are a few authentic instances. The face, eyelids, cheeks, forehead, and (rarely) the hands and feet are affected. The sweat may be dark brown or black, the pigment probably being a derivative of indican, as the patients are always constipated. Blue sweating from pyocyanin, and green, yellow, and red varieties have been recorded. A pseudo-red sweat from growth of the bacillus prodigiosus in the moisture of the axillæ also occurs.

I have not met with a case of coloured sweating at the London Hospital, and the fact that it occurs nearly always in hysterical subjects should lead to careful investigation before the diagnosis is made. One girl of fifteen came to my clinic with a bright carmine-coloured deposit in the face. It was alleged to be a red sweat, but proved to be due to a dye. The colour was easily removed by washing with cold water. Attention to the general health and the use of aperients are necessary, and the local application of a mild antiseptic lotion may be required.

The sweat may also be coloured from the use of drugs, etc., pink by iodides, green from copper, blue from iron.

Phosphorescent sweat is rarely seen, but is said to occur after the use of phosphorus medicinally and from taking fish. Phosphorescent bacteria are the probable cause.

Hæmatidrosis. Bloody sweat has been described, but in most cases depends upon an error of observation or fraud. There are, however, genuine cases associated with grave toxæmia, purpura, and in neurotic subjects, in which blood has been seen to come from sweat glands. Dr. Still recently had a case in a girl of 12 at Great Ormond Street. Treatment must be directed to the general cause, if discovered.

Sudamina.

An eruption of small non-inflammatory superficial vesicles containing sweat.

Etiology. The eruption is common in the acute fevers, particularly acute rheumatism and enteric fever, in the crisis of pneumonia, and in the moribund, but it may occur independently.

Pathology. The vesicles lie in the stratum corneum, and the ducts of the sweat glands open into them.

Clinical features. The onset is sudden, the rash appearing on any part of the body or face, but it is most common on the chest and neck. The skin is of normal colour, and scattered over it are numbers of minute vesicles, usually discrete, but occasionally confluent, containing a clear fluid. There is usually no itching, and the vesicles dry up in a few days, leaving no stain. No treatment is necessary.

Miliaria rubra. Prickly Heat. Lichen tropicus.

An acute eruption of papules and minute vesicles at the orifices of the sweat glands, attended with itching.

Etiology. Miliaria rubra is a very common affection in the tropics among white people, the native races being unaffected. A similar affection occurs after severe exercise, after vapour baths, etc.

Pathology. The process is inflammatory, and in that respect differs from that of sudamina. There is a cystic dilatation of the ducts of the sudoriparous glands, with swelling of the horny cells at their orifices. Staphylococci are found in the lesions, chiefly the staphylococcus albus and citreus, and by some miliaria is looked upon as a form of impetigo; by others it is classed with eczema.

Clinical features The eruption develops acutely, with itching and burning. It is preceded and accompanied by sweating. The back and the trunk and the upper segments of the limbs are affected. The lesions are small acuminate papules and vesicles about the size of a pin's head, containing clear serum, and surrounded by a red areola. The proportion of papules and vesicles varies in different cases. The eruption lasts for a few days, the contents of the vesicles become opaque, and they finally dry up, leaving minute scabs· Owing to the itching and scratching and to pressure, the affected areas may become eczematised or impetiginised, especially in the flexures. In severe cases the buccal mucosa and fauces are acutely congested (Castellani). Miliaria has a great tendency to relapse, and the recurrences may be brought about by violent exercise, the taking of hot drinks, etc.

Treatment. The underclothing should, if possible, be of silk. Thick woollen materials should be avoided. Frequent changes are necessary, and care should be taken to avoid exertion and anything that may tend to free perspiration. The diet should be simple, very little fluid should be taken and no hot drinks ; alcohol should be avoided, and saline and diuretic mixtures given. Bathing the surface with eau de Cologne and water, or weak Condy's fluid, and powdering with starch and zinc, or some similar preparation, are comforting to the irritated surface. Lead and tar lotions may also be used, or the calamine liniment. Baths containing a small quantity of sodii bicarb., a drachm to the gallon, also afford relief.

Miliary Fever. Sweating Sickness.

Sweating sickness is an acute eruptive fever of which many epidemics are recorded. The onset is acute, with excessive sweating, often fœtid, headache, furred tongue, and general febrile symptoms. At the end of two or three days an eruption of papules upon erythematous areas develops. The papules become vesicular, and the clinical appearances are those of miliaria. The rash is widely spread, and similar lesions appear on the buccal mucosa. Desquamation follows. The most recent epidemic is described in the *Lancet* for October 1, 1887, p. 671.

Pompholyx, Cheiro-pompholyx, Dysidrosis.

An acute or subacute eruption of grouped vesicles or bullæ occurring on the hands and feet and associated with excessive sweating.

Etiology. The disease is more common in women than in men.

It often begins about puberty or early adult life.   It is generally said
that the patients are neurotic and overworked, but I have seen a
number of cases in persons in otherwise perfect health.   In a few
instances local irritation appears to be the exciting cause, for instance,
the use of antiseptics by medical men and nurses.   Spring and

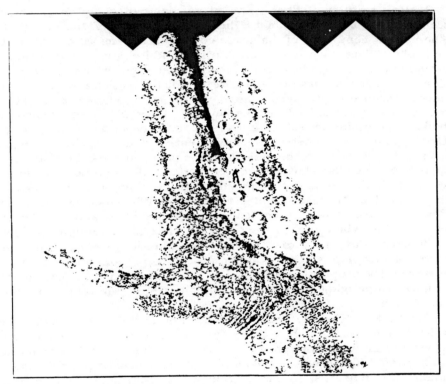

FIG. 249.—Pompholyx.   (Dysidrosis.)

summer are the seasons in which pompholyx occurs, and it often
returns year by year about the same time.

Pathology.   The lesions are rounded cavities in the corpus
mucosum, produced in a similar manner to the vesicles of eczema,
i.e., by spongiosis.   They do not arise from the sweat ducts, and
their contents are clear fluid, highly albuminous, and migratory cells.
The bacillus described by Unna, and believed by him to be the cause
of the eruption, has not been found by recent observers.   There is
some doubt whether pompholyx is a special disease or whether it is a

form of eczema with peculiar local characters. As already indicated, some local irritants in predisposed subjects produce a condition identical with pompholyx, and recent observations have shown that at a certain stage eczematoid ringworm of the extremities may produce a clinical picture which is identical with pompholyx with its peculiar tendency to recurrence at certain seasons.

Clinical features. There are often general symptoms which seem far out of proportion to the local character of the eruption. The patient complains of malaise, depression, and sensations of heat and cold. These symptoms, and burning and itching, and sometimes actual pain in the hands, usually precede the cutaneous manifestation. The lesions themselves are small, deeply-placed vesicles in groups or lines in the interdigital spaces, along the sides of the fingers and on the palms, rarely on the backs of the fingers. They have been likened to boiled sago grains embedded in the skin, and the simile is an apt one. On the palms there is often excessive sweating, but this is by no means constant. Very often the vesicles in the palms are so deep that they merely produce flat elevations of the surface which do not obviously contain fluid. In many cases the vesicles along the sides of the fingers and in the clefts and elsewhere tend to coalesce and form definite blebs. There is no tendency for the blebs and vesicles to rupture, but when pricked they exude a clear alkaline fluid. In ten to fourteen days they dry up and desquamation occurs. There is never a weeping surface. Relapses are very common. In rare instances the eruption may spread to the forearms and appear on the trunk. Impetiginisation of the lesions from scratching is not uncommon.

Diagnosis. The lesions in the interdigital clefts may be mistaken for scabies, but there are no burrows, and the eruption is usually limited. Care must be taken to eliminate the eczematoid ringworms which occur on the hands. Here the finding of the fungus makes the diagnosis. Whether the similar eruption occurring from local irritation should be classed as pompholyx or eczematous dermatitis is a matter of little diagnostic import.

Treatment. Any deviation from the general health must be attended to. Rest and change are often valuable adjuvants to local treatment, and iron, arsenic, and general tonics are often required. Arsenic is said to prevent relapses. Alcohol must be avoided, and tea and coffee should only be taken in moderation.

The most useful local applications are ointments of oxide of zinc, with a little salicylic acid, ten grains to the ounce, Lassar's paste, and the lotions of calamine and lead. It must be remembered that the lesions may easily be irritated and pass on to an eczematous condition by the use of irritant preparations. Pyogenic infection is best treated by boric acid baths or continuous fomentation.

Dysidrosis exfoliativa. In tropical countries excessive sweating on the palms is sometimes attended by the exfoliation of large flakes of epidermis. The condition is called dysidrosis exfoliativa. It differs from cheiro-pompholyx in the complete absence of vesication.

Hidrocystoma. Hidrocystoma is the name given to a cystic dilatation of the sweat glands and ducts occurring on the face in middle-aged women whose employment, such as laundry work, exposes them to heat and moisture.

Histologically the lesions are dilatations of the deeper parts of the sweat gland ducts, apparently produced by obstruction of their lumen in the upper part of the corium. The causation is obscure. Darier believes the condition is due to a congenital anomaly.

The lesions are discrete scattered vesicles upon the forehead and nose, eyelids and cheeks, and occasionally upon the lower parts of the face and upon the neck. The vesicles vary in size from a pin's head to a pea, and contain a clear slightly acid fluid, which gives them a clear or bluish tint. There is always profuse perspiration. The individual lesions dry up in a week or two, but the eruption persists during the hot weather and usually disappears entirely in the winter. In cases of unilateral sweating the condition has been observed in the affected side only.

Puncture of the vesicles with a sterile needle and the application of mild antiseptic lotions followed by an astringent powder are recommended.

REFERENCE.—LEBEL. *Annales de Dermatologie,* 1903, IV., p. 273.

Tumours of the sweat glands are considered at p. 528.

AFFECTIONS OF THE SEBACEOUS GLANDS.

A number of affections of the sebaceous glands have already been considered. The congenital tumours, sebaceous adenomata, are discussed on p. 43; the microbic affections, acne vulgaris, acne frontalis, and the conditions commonly called "seborrhoides" in Chapter IX. We have here only to deal with Asteatosis and Seborrhœa oleosa.

Asteatosis is a condition characterised by diminution of the sebaceous secretion. It does not appear to occur idiopathically, but is observed in ichthyosis, sclerodermia, and in psoriasis and prurigo. It is also met with on patches of nerve leprosy.

The application of certain soaps, spirit, etc., which remove the normal fatty secretion may also cause it.

The skin is harsh, dry, and frequently scaly; the epidermis may become thickened and fissured.

The treatment is to supply the absence of natural oil by the inunction of fatty substances, Ung. Aq. Rosæ, Lanolin, etc.

Seborrhœa oleosa.

A hypersecretion of sebum, but the name is also applied to excessive oily secretion from the sweat glands.

It is convenient to distinguish them.

(a) *Hypersecretion of sebum.* The characteristic features are the dilatation of the sebaceous gland orifices, with an accumulation of fatty material in the form of plugs which can be expressed. This material is composed of epidermal cells, of inspissated sebum, and of microbic parasites. One special organism, which is found in enormous numbers, is claimed by Sabouraud as the cause of the seborrhœa. It is the same parasite which occurs in the acne comedo. As already indicated, the oily habitat favours the growth of certain micro-organisms, but it is difficult to believe that this excess of a normal secretion is more than a suitable culture ground for the bacillus.

The sebaceous plugs are found in the middle of the face, especially on the nose and naso-labial sulci, but may be found in any part where the sebaceous glands are large.

(b) The greasy condition of the skin, which is a common feature in the subjects of the " seborrhoides," is characterised in its mildest form by a glistening oily surface, which stains tissue-paper. In some cases, on the other hand, there may be drops of oily fluid. This condition is usually accompanied by the dilatation of the sebaceous glands and the fatty plugs just described. There is still some doubt as to whether the secretion is simply sweat mixed with fatty matter from the sebaceous glands. It appears much more probable that it is really an excess of sweat secretion of oily character. The nose, the scalp, and the middle part of the trunk are chiefly affected.

These conditions are not seen before puberty; they are commonly associated with acne vulgaris and the " seborrhoides."

Treatment. Abstinence from fatty foods should be advised and any dyspeptic condition treated on the usual lines. The local treatment consists in the application of ethereal soaps, lotions containing ether or acetone, and sulphur. The expression of the oily plugs can be carried out by friction with a soft towel after washing.

DISEASES OF THE HAIR.

We have already discussed the affections of the hair follicles caused by pyogenic organisms, follicular impetigo (p. 189), boils (p. 190), sycosis (p. 195), folliculitis decalvans (p. 598).

In the chapter on Vegetable Parasites, ringworm of the scalp (p. 153), favus (p. 161), tinea barbæ (p. 162), piedra (p. 163), and trichomycosis axillaris (p. 163) were considered.

Keratoses of the hair follicles were described on p. 471, and neoplasms at p. 527.

We have now to consider certain special affections of the hair, and it is convenient to recall the fact that the growth of hair depends to a remarkable degree on certain internal secretions. Hypothyroidism and hypopituitarism are attended with decreased activity of the hair follicles.

Hypertrophy of the supra-renals is associated with excessive hair development even in young children.

The menopause is frequently followed by hypertrichosis, and a similar condition occurs after the removal of the ovaries.

Eunuchs do not suffer from the form of baldness so common in middle age (Sabouraud).

Canities.

Canities or greyness of the hair is usually acquired.

In the condition known as albinism the hair pigment is congenitally absent, and in some cases there is a local absence of hair pigment in a small area. The latter condition may occur through several generations.

Acquired canities is in most cases a senile change, but in many instances the hair becomes grey in early adult life and middle age. In some families there is a tendency to the early development of canities. Acute febrile illnesses and cachectic conditions may be followed by greyness, and there is no doubt that mental strain, worry, shock and the like play an important part in its development. Neuralgia and severe headaches are also sometimes followed by the appearance of white hair in the affected area. In characteristic cases of canities the blanching of the hair is first noticed on the temples, and later scattered hairs over the rest of the scalp, moustache and beard regions become white, producing a diffuse alteration in colour. Ultimately with exacerbations and retardations of the process the whole hair may become white.

Cases in which the hair has become grey or white in a few hours or a few days are very rare, but authentic instances are on record.

Patches of white hair are common in leucodermia (p. 499), and the new hair growing upon a patch of alopecia areata is usually non-pigmented at first, and, indeed, may never recover its normal colour (p. 593).

The whitening of the hair is due to absence of pigment or to the presence of air-bubbles in the cortex. The absence of pigment in the hair shaft may be dependent upon imperfect formation in the papilla or, as Ehrmann has suggested, to a defect in the transmission of the pigment to the hair-cells.

Cases in which the pigment has been restored after the development of canities are rare.

Treatment. The use of hair dyes is not to be recommended. Solutions of nitrate of silver (3 per cent.) are used to produce a black tint, and pyrogallic acid (2 per cent.) for a brown.

Several of the so-called harmless hair-dyes (Para-phenylene diamine, etc.) have been known to cause a severe dermatitis and even destruction of the hair. (*Vide* reference, pp. 95 and 597.)

Ringed hair. Leucotrichia annularis. This is a very rare condition characterised by alternate narrow rings of white and normal tint occurring in otherwise healthy hair. It is believed to be due to minute bubbles of air in the hairs. In some cases the condition has been congenital, and Dr. Galloway found it in two brothers. The cause is unknown.

Alopecia.

Alopecia may be congenital or acquired, local or general. The acquired forms may be cicatricial, and of nervous origin, but the cause of the common type is unknown.

Congenital alopecia is very rare, but sometimes runs in a family. I have had four cases of complete congenital absence of hair, two in brothers, and three cases in which the absence was partial and limited. The latter condition may be looked upon as a form of nævus. In one of the complete cases there was also a congenital dystrophy of the nails. (*Vide* Fig. 16.)

Cicatricial Alopecia.

Circumscribed patches of alopecia are caused by scars deep enough to destroy the hair follicles. The areas are bald, there are no downy hairs upon them, but here and there a solitary follicle may escape the atrophic process, and a hair of normal size and development remains.

Burns, scalds, the application of caustics, or the X-rays may leave bald scars. Favus leaves a peculiar irregular patchy baldness. Suppurative processes, impetigo, boils, dermatitis, papillaris capillitii (p. 198), and folliculitis decalvans (p. 598) are also causes. Similarly, syphilitic ulceration, lupus erythematosus, and lupus vulgaris destroy the hair follicles. The condition called "pseudo-pelade" is also an atrophic process. It will be considered later in this chapter.

An examination of the bald area will usually disclose the cicatricial character of the alopecia, and the history is often a useful guide.

Diffuse Alopecia. Alopecia pityrodes. "Seborrhoic Alopecia."

This is the commonest form of diffuse alopecia.

Etiology. It is a common sequel of pityriasis of the scalp, dandriff, the so-called "seborrhoea sicca." This condition often starts in childhood, but at puberty the dry scurfy condition gives place to a greasy scaliness, oily seborrhoea, and excessive sweating of the scalp.

Worry, anxiety, overwork, cachectic conditions, and probably dietetic irregularities favour its development. Want of attention to the scalp, heavy and ill-ventilated hats and caps are local causes. While much more common in the male than in the female, it is occasionally seen in greater or less degree in women.

Pathology. The fall of the hair depends directly upon the scalp condition, and this is believed to be ultimately of parasitic origin. The hair follicles undergo a gradual atrophy, very similar to the atrophy which is a senile change.

Clinical features. Premature baldness of this type begins at the vertex, and at the sides of the frontal region. It gradually, or sometimes rapidly, extends until the lateral bald areas on the forehead coalesce with the enlarging tonsure-like patch. Sometimes a small island of hair of normal length remains in the middle of the forehead, but ultimately the scalp becomes denuded, except in the occipital and temporal regions.

The "Hippocratic" scalp is shining, smooth, commonly pale, and the surface looks atrophic. From time to time scaliness may return, and there is often excessive perspiration.

There are many differences in the rapidity of the fall, and season has an influence in the early stages, the hair coming out more in the warm weather. Patients often ask how many hairs should be removed by the daily brushing in health. It may safely be said that if three dozen hairs are thus removed daily, there is a liability of premature baldness. At first the fallen hairs are replaced, but as time goes on the new hairs are of greater tenuity, and finally mere down appears, and this ultimately fails to develop, leaving the scalp smooth and shining.

Senile alopecia proper is not attended with the development of scales, but it is not uncommon to find cases in both sexes in which from want of attention brownish greasy scales form.

In the subjects of " seborrhoic dermatitis " the hair of the beard region, the eyebrows, and the hair of the trunk may be similarly affected. In women the affection of the scalp is rarely so severe as in men, but seasonal variations in the fall of the hair are common.

Prognosis. Provided the condition is treated early enough there is a possibility of retarding the development of premature baldness, but in advanced cases nothing can be done.

Treatment. The underlying " seborrhoic " condition requires the use of antiseptic lotions : resorcin, curesol (monoacetate of resorcin), sulphur and mercury being those most commonly used. (*Vide* Pityriasis, etc., p. 214.)

Any deviation from the general health must be attended to, and nerve strain, etc., must be avoided.

Alopecia of the Diffuse Type in General Diseases, etc.

Fall of hair, sometimes complete, occurs in the acute fevers, typhoid, erysipelas, pneumonia, etc., or it may be postponed to the convalescent stage. It has been particularly common after the recent influenza epidemic. I have seen a number of cases in which there has been a great loss of hair occurring with parturition. One patient under my observation lost her hair completely in three successive confinements, and after the third the alopecia was permanent. Grave mental shock has also been known to cause a rapidly-developing baldness.

In certain general skin affections the hair falls off; this is especially the case in general exfoliative dermatitis. Syphilitic alopecia is a special form. It occurs usually during the first year after infection ; the hair does not come out over large areas, but there are narrow bald patches, giving the appearance of glades in a forest.

Fall of hair is a common symptom of myxœdema. In the Lorain type of infantilism the alopecia may be universal. The response to thyroid treatment in this rare condition is well shown in a series of

photographs in the *Practitioner,* 1915, I., p. 26.   In many chronic
diseases attended with general cachexia loss of hair occurs.   In the
female it has been noticed after oophorectomy and ovarian disease.

Alopecia areata.

An affection of the hair characterised by one or more bald areas
without obvious change in the skin.   It usually affects the scalp.

Fig. 250. —Alopecia areata (common type).

Etiology. Three hypotheses have been advanced to explain
alopecia areata : (1) that it is caused by a parasite ; (2) that it is
of nervous origin ; and (3) that it is due to toxins.

In favour of the parasitic hypothesis it must be acknowledged
that now and again epidemics of alopecia occur in schools, etc.,
but these are of great rarity.   It will, however, be remembered
that there is a form of bald ringworm which may possibly account
for some of the recorded epidemics.   Innumerable experiments have
been made to inoculate the disease, but without success.   That there
are cases dependent upon nervous influence is certain, for occasionally

a particular area supplied by one nerve becomes bald ; but such cases are rare, and differ entirely from the characters of the majority. Jacquet believes in peripheral irritation as a cause of many cases, and

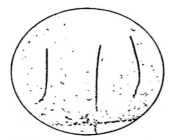

FIG. 251.—Hairs of alopecia areata magnified.

traces them to dental, ocular, or other forms of irritation. I had careful charts made of fifty consecutive cases, noting the dental condition and the position of the bald patches. The ocular state was also investigated. There was, I thought at first, some correspond-

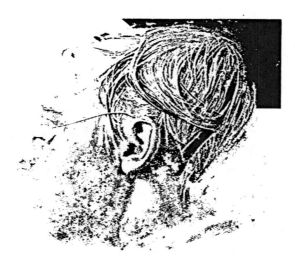

FIG. 252.—Leucotrichia following alopecia areata. The hair ultimately regained its normal colour.

ence, but an examination of fifty patients without alopecia resulted in an almost identical ratio of dental and other forms of irritation.

The toxic hypothesis is chiefly based upon the fact that baldness has been found to occur in animals after the injection of bacterial toxins and that acetate of thallium taken internally has produced rapid fall of the hair in the human subject. Hutchinson called attention to the fact that alopecia areata sometimes follows ringworm of the scalp, but as both diseases are common the sequence does not appear to be of etiological significance.

I have seen two instances in which alopecia areata followed partial thyroidectomy for Graves' disease. The possibility that an alteration or defect of internal secretion may be a cause must, therefore, be

Fig. 253.—Alopecia areata (ophiasic type).

considered. There is also no evidence that alopecia areata is produced by syphilis.

Histology. The follicles are atrophic, and there is often a small degree of cellular infiltration about the papillæ. In the late stages the papillæ are fibrotic. The sebaceous glands are atrophic.

Clinical features. *Common type.* The onset is insidious, the patient or a parent noticing that an area of the scalp has become bald. The patches are usually round or oval, often multiple, and they gradually spread, and sometimes, by extension and coalescence, may involve nearly the whole scalp. The areas are smooth, or, perhaps, covered with downy hair. Round the margins the hairs are frequently atrophic at their proximal ends, and of the usual diameter at the periphery, so that they resemble the note of exclamation (!). This appearance was once considered pathognomic of alopecia areata, but it is sometimes seen after the application of the X-rays. Occasionally the skin of the bald patch is thinned and easily wrinkled. In the stage of recovery the patches are covered with downy pale hairs, which subsequently become strong, but are often white for a time. In most cases, however, complete 'recovery of the strength and colour occurs (Fig. 252).

Any part of the scalp may be affected, and also the beard and moustache regions and the eyebrows. Occasionally the patches

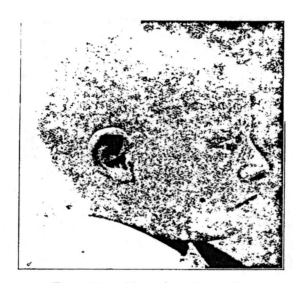

FIG. 254.—Alopecia universalis.

are remarkably symmetrical. In the *ophiasic* variety the bald [area runs round the margin of the hairy scalp (Fig. 253).

In some cases the areate patches fuse, and eventually the whole of the scalp becomes bald, **alopecia universalis.** The eyebrows and eyelashes are commonly affected also (Fig. 254).

Leuconychia may occur in connection with alopecia areata.

Nervous type. As already mentioned, alopecia areata sometimes affects a particular nerve area or areas. The most striking example I have seen was in a patient of Dr. Percy Kidd, suffering from anorexia nervosa. The scalp was void of hair over the area 'supplied by the first division of the fifth nerve on one side, and the area governed by the supratrochlear nerve on the other. On the one side the scalp was bald from the forehead to the lambdoid suture ; the lateral parts supplied by the second and third branches of the fifth and the area supplied by the occipitals being unaffected. On the other side there was a narrow band of baldness extending from the forehead as far as the coronal suture only. The patient made a complete recovery soon after the other nervous symptoms disappeared. I have also seen both occipital areas affected.

In this type the area supplied by the nerves is so exactly affected that one cannot be in doubt as to the relationship.

Diagnosis. Alopecia areata has to be distinguished from cicatricial alopecia, in which the presence of scar tissue is usually manifest. It has also to be diagnosed from some forms of ringworm. Here the examination of hairs from the margin of the patch for fungus will usually be sufficient. Pseudo-pelade will be considered in the next section.

Prognosis. In young subjects alopecia usually recovers after, perhaps, several months. In the ophiasic form the prospects are not so good. In older subjects the hair may never return.

Treatment. There does not appear to be any adequate reason for the removal of a child suffering from alopecia areata from school or from its playmates. As we are ignorant of the underlying cause, there are no indications for special general treatment. Any deviation from the general health will require attention. It is, perhaps, wise, in view of Jacquet's work, to remove any possible source of peripheral irritation, hence the teeth should be attended to and ocular strain relieved by appropriate glasses. The best results are attained by persistent local treatment with stimulant preparations. There are many methods in use. Friction and massage of the parts are advocated, but the application of lotions and paints containing rubefacients appear to be more valuable. An essential oil—*e.g.*, oil of nutmeg 1 part, olive oil 3 parts—daily rubbed in is a useful application. Cantharides in varying strengths is most valuable. I usually prescribe a daily painting with the following solution :— Emplastrum cantharidis liquid. 1 drachm, acetic acid 1 drachm, spirit 1 ounce. It is painted on lightly and allowed to dry. Should there be blistering the treatment is intermitted. Ammonia, turpentine, acetic acid are also used. (For formulæ, *vide* p. 622.) Recently high frequency applications and phototherapy have been advocated, and are sometimes attended with success, but I am not convinced that they are of greater value than other means of stimulating the circulation in the skin.

REFERENCES.—JACQUET. *Annales de Derm. et de Syph.*, August, September, 1900, and *Presse Medicale*, December 12, 1903. Debate, International Congress, 1900. BULKLEY and JANNEWAY. *Journ. Amer. Med. Assoc.*, July 25, 1908. (Observations on 1,129 cases of diseases of the hair.) ''Alopecia Areata treated by Light.'' KROMAYER. *Deutsch. Med. Woch.*, July 28, 1904. See also papers by SABOURAUD and discussion. *Transactions International Medical Congress :* Dermatological Section, London, 1913. ''Les Teintures Capillaires à la P. Phenylene Diamine,'' by E. ROSSEAU : Paris, 1914.

Alopecia cicatrisata. Pseudo-pelade of Brocq.

A chronic inflammatory disease of the hair follicles, terminating in cicatricial atrophy.

Etiology. The cause of the condition is unknown. Young

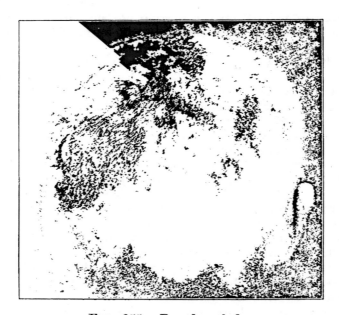

FIG. 255.—Pseudo-pelade.

subjects and adults are affected, and males suffer more commonly than females.

Pathology. The evolution and character of the lesions suggest a parasitic infection, but in spite of elaborate researches no fungus or bacterium has been discovered. The follicles are surrounded by dilated vessels and lymphocytic infiltration. The ultimate result is a cicatrix.

Clinical features. The onset is insidious,· the first lesions noticed being pale pink or rose spots round one or more hairs. There is also some slight scaling at the follicular orifice. The hairs fall and a minute scar remains. In well-marked cases the hairy scalp and occasionally the beard region are the seat of numerous irregular white or pale pink cicatricial bald patches. At first the bald areas are small, but by extension and the fusion of adjoining areas, form patches with a festooned outline or figures suggesting a group of islands on a map. The patches are devoid of hair, definitely cicatricial, and abruptly limited. There are no broken or deformed hairs.

Dystrophies of the nails occasionally occur in the subjects of pseudo-pelade.

Diagnosis. The condition differs entirely from common alopecia, but has close resemblance to the cicatricial alopecia following favus. There are, however, none of the yellow crusts containing the Achorion Schönleînii.

Patches of lupus erythematosus lead to cicatricial baldness, but their margins are red and scaly, and there are usually symmetrical lesions on the middle of the face and on the auricles.

Treatment. The treatment of pseudo-pelade is very unsatisfactory. Antiseptic lotions containing mercury, tar and sulphur are advised.

Folliculitis decalvans.

Under this name two conditions are described :

(1) The folliculitis decalvans of Quinquaud, a chronic affection of the hair follicles of the scalp causing extensive cicatricial alopecia. The clinical features are irregular bald patches rarely larger than a shilling with inflammation of the hair follicles at the margin. Pus-cocci have been found in the perifollicular inflammation, and Quinquaud described an organism which he believed to be peculiar to the condition. The hair is permanently lost.

The treatment recommended is the painting of the affected areas with tincture of iodine or with a solution of perchloride of mercury, one-sixth grain to the ounce. The X-rays would be worth trying.

(2) A chronic affection of the scalp causing cicatricial smooth, bald areas occurring in association with lichen pilaris (p. 473). The patients are women of middle age.

There is no evidence of inflammation, as in the Quinquaud type, but horny spines may be present in the follicles of the scalp. Apparently the destruction of the hair and cicatrisation is due to the same cause which produces excessive keratinisation with the formation of horny spines in the follicles of the glabrous skin. In this connection it is interesting to note that congenital keratosis follicularis may be associated with baldness.

REFERENCES.—QUINQUAUD. *Annales de Derm. et de Syph.*, 1889, 28, X., p. 99. "Folliculitis Decalvans and Lichen Spinulosus." GRAHAM LITTLE. *British Journal of Dermatology*, XXVII., p. 183. WALLACE BEATTY. *Ibid.*, XXVII., p. 331 : plates and sections. "Ichthyosis Follicularis associated with Baldness." J. M. H. MACLEOD. *Ibid.*, XXI., p. 171.

Hypertrichosis. Hirsuties.

Hypertrichosis may be congenital or acquired.

We have already discussed the congenital anomalies called hairy moles (p. 30) and the rare cases in which there is excessive development of lanugo hairs as a congenital peculiarity. This is a persistence of the fœtal hairs, which increase with age. The development is symmetrical, and parts are affected which normally are devoid of strong hairs. The whole of the face may be covered, producing the deformity which is sometimes on exhibition in shows, etc., dog-men, etc. The hair is always soft and woolly and fine. A case in which the face was extensively affected has already been mentioned (p. 42).

Hypertrichosis in adult life occurs in both sexes. In the male it is simply an exaggeration of the normal condition. It begins about puberty, or sometimes earlier. The regions ordinarily covered with hair are particularly affected, but the chest and back and the limbs may be covered with such a quantity of strong hair as to suggest an anthropoid ape. The hairy tufts in the lumbar region are usually associated with spina bifida (*vide* p. 42).

In women the hair development sometimes takes the masculine form. It occurs generally about the time of puberty, and also at the onset of the menopause. Usually the growth is excessive on the upper lip and upon the chin, and rarely an actual beard and moustache forms. In very rare instances the chest, mammary regions and limbs may be affected.

Heredity appears often to be the cause, and the affection is certainly more marked in certain races. Local irritation, such as the application of cosmetics, depilatories, and removal of growing hairs by forceps, etc., aggravates the growth. I have seen hirsuties follow mumps, the growth occurring on the lateral aspects of the cheeks. The connection with utero-ovarian disturbance is undoubted. seeing that the onset so often occurs about puberty and the menopause. Ewart has recently called attention to the frequency of hypertrichosis in insane women. In cases of precocious puberty, associated in some cases with neoplasms of the adrenals, I have seen excessive growth of hair in both sexes.

I have often noticed excessive growth of hair on parts treated by the Finsen light, and the frequent repetition of fomentations for ulcerations, etc., of the limbs produces it.

Treatment. Hypertrichosis in women is often a source of great mental worry, even inducing melancholia, and such cases frequently come to the dermatologist for treatment. The less conspicuous growths may be treated by peroxide of hydrogen, which bleaches the hair. Where the growth is marked and the hairs are strong, the best treatment is electrolysis. The negative pole is used, and to this is attached a very fine needle of irido-platinum. The needle is passed down to the base of the hair, and a current of three milliampères is passed until a few bubbles of gas appear at the mouth of the follicle. The hair is now loose, and can be removed with ease by the forceps. The passage of the current is attended with some pain, but usually about thirty hairs can be removed at one sitting. If the hairs are very numerous, the process is exceedingly tedious and trying both to the patient and to the operator.

For severe cases of hypertrichosis radiotherapy may be required. The application of the X-rays for this purpose demands great care. I give a full pastille dose through an aluminium screen, 0·25 millimetre in thickness. The hair falls out after an interval of fourteen days, and occasionally there is a transient erythema. The operation is repeated at the end of six weeks, and at longer intervals afterwards. Another method which I have found of service in bad cases is the administration of heavier doses, 4B through a 1·5 millimetre aluminium screen—three such doses being given in eight days. By either method some cases have given excellent results. There is some risk of a slight atrophy of the skin, but in grave hirsuties the patient whose life is thereby rendered miserable is willing to take the risk, which should be carefully explained to her.

Some women keep down the excessive growth by the use of pumice-stone. A depilatory containing barium sulphide ʒj, oxide of zinc ʒiij, starch ʒiij, made into a paste with water, is also applied for ten minutes, washed off, and the parts are then treated with a simple ointment or powder. This destroys the hair above the surface, but is little more than a chemical method of shaving.

Trichorrhexis nodosa.

An affection of the hairs of the scalp, beard, and pubic regions characterised by pale, fusiform, node-like swellings.

Etio'ogy. The affection is due to mechanical injury to hairs whose nutrition has been damaged. It is often associated with excessive dryness of the hair from the use of certain lotions and soaps. The same condition may be found in shaving-brushes and toothbrushes that have been in use for long periods.

Pathology. The lesions are produced by separation of the fibres of the hair. If the hair is broken across at one of the nodes, the broken ends are spread out into the form of a brush. An unbroken node appears like two brushes joined at their free ends.

Clinical features. The hairs present at intervals fusiform, white node-like swellings. The hair is exceedingly brittle at the nodes, and Adamson has shown that on laying the unaffected hairs from the same patient on a glass slide and striking them with the edge of a paper knife, typical nodes are easily produced. A normal hair, on the other hand, treated in the same manner is either broken straight across, or splits into two or three longitudinal bundles at the part struck. The nodes in trichorrhexis are more numerous at the distal ends of the hairs, and it is probable that brushing and combing are sufficient to produce the condition if the nutrition of the hair is impaired.

Treatment. Any underlying condition, such as pityriasis capitis, oily seborrhœa, etc., which may be recognised. requires treatment. The general health may also require attention. The local measures applicable are the cutting of the hair below the fractures and the use of greasy lotions, etc.

REFERENCES.—H. G. ADAMSON. *British Journal of Dermatology,* 1907, XIX., p. 99. LASSUEUR. *Annales de Derm. et de Syph.,* November, 1906, p. 211.

Trichoptilosis.

This name is given to longitudinal fracture of the hairs at their distal extremities. It occurs in cachectic conditions, but may also be due to excessive dryness of the hair.

The treatment is the same as for trichorrhexis nodosa.

Monilethrix.

This is a rare congenital and family affection characterised by an alternate narrowing and swelling of the hairs. The nodal portion is the normal thickness of the hair. The medulla is absent between the nodes and may be irregularly distributed. The hairs are dry, brittle and short, and the swollen parts are excessively pigmented. The scalp is scaly and dry.

It is suggested that the changes are due to alterations in the activity of the hair papillæ. The follicles are slightly prominent and finally cicatricial. The affected areas may be entirely denuded.

REFERENCES.—R. CRANSTON LOW. *Journ. Path. and Bact.*, 1910, XIV., p. 230. McKEE and ROSEN. *Journ. Cut. Diseases*, 1916, pp. 444, 506.

Leptothrix.

This name is given to a common condition of the hairs of the scrotum and axillæ, characterised by irregular lobulated concretions lying on the shafts.

Etiology. Warmth and moisture appear to be necessary for the development of leptothrix. Various organisms have been described in the lesions. In some cases it has been associated with red sweat due to the bacillus prodigiosus.

Clinical features. The affected hairs are brittle, and when removed show irregularly placed concretions attached to the shaft. In advanced cases the hair appears to be much thicker than normal, and on examination the thickening is found to consist of lobulated concretions the whole length of the shaft, the appearance suggesting the feathered end of an arrow. The fibres of the affected hairs may be split and the fractured ends may be clean-cut or brush-like.

Treatment. Shaving or close cutting of the hair and the application of antiseptic lotions, such as 1-1,000 corrosive sublimate, are recommended.

Trichotillomania is the name given to a neurosis of young women who pull out or break off the hair. It is often associated with other factitious dermatoses.

DISEASES OF THE NAILS.

The nail is a horny plate developed from the matrix, and also, according to Branca, from the whole bed, upon which it rests. The average rate of growth in health is about an eighth of an inch a month. Any condition, general or local, which interferes with the activity of the matrix causes changes in the growth of the nail. Should the activity of the matrix be temporarily diminished, a transverse furrow will appear upon the surface of the nail, and if the affection be prolonged, it may lead to extensive atrophy of the nail.

Levi and Rothschild state that the growth is improved by the administration of thyroid gland.

The nail-bed also plays a part in ungual affections, chiefly by raising the nail at its free border.

We have to consider both the general and the local conditions which may affect these appendages.

(1) **Congenital anomalies.** One nail, or perhaps several, may be congenitally absent, or there may be irregular formation, and rarely hypertrophy. Occasionally, tylosis raising the nail from its bed by the formation of a yellowish mass of epidermis has been observed. It is sometimes a family affection. (See report of family with photographs, by A. J. Wilson, *British Journal of Dermatology*, 1905, XVII., p. 13.)

(2) **Traumatic affections.** These are discussed in the text-books on surgery, and only require passing notice. The nail may be torn, there may be hæmorrhage under it, and inflammation of the matrix or bed, or of the periungual tissue as the result of injury.

Certain trades affect the nails. They may be worn down by friction with rough materials, or stained by various dyes. The latter conditions often throw light upon cutaneous eruptions produced by irritants, such as bichromates, anilin dyes, aurantia, etc. Chronic itching eruptions cause wearing away of the nails from constant scratching.

Grave dystrophy of the nails follows excessive exposure to the X-rays (*vide* p. 80).

(3) **Fungous affections** of the nails have been discussed elsewhere. (*Vide* Ringworm and Favus of the Nails, p. 145.)

(4) **Pyogenic affections.** In impetigo, whether due to staphylococci or streptococci, there is frequently inflammation of or about the nail. Such onychias may occur at any age, but they are most common in children and young subjects. The staphylococcal infection may be primary or secondary to traumatism. A small abscess forms under the corner of the nail, and the suppuration spreads along the nail bed, and in some cases detaches the nail. There is generally some perionychia, the periungual tissue being swollen, purplish-red and very tender, and suppuration is common.

Perionychia (whitlow) may also be caused by streptococci, or the matrix may become attacked by these organisms, causing a separation of the nail at the proximal end. The exposed matrix becomes gradually covered with an ill-developed nail which slowly grows forward. The resulting nail is deformed, but in time may be replaced by a healthy growth. I have seen a case of this kind in a nurse who had several nails affected while attending a case of impetiginised eczema. The treatment consists in the application of boric acid fomentations frequently changed, followed by dressing with the dilute nitrate of mercury ointment.

(5) Nail affections associated with cutaneous diseases.

(*a*) Eczema. In the acute forms the nails are thinned and atrophic, and in rare cases they may be shed. In the chronic cases the nails are cracked and fissured, the surface traversed by longitudinal or

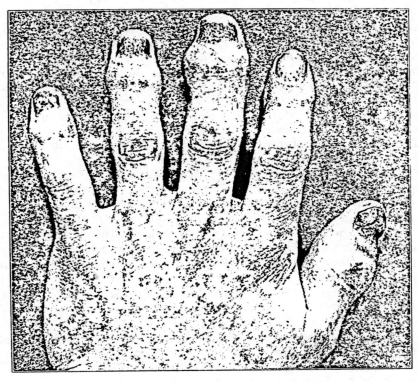

Fig. 256.—Psoriasis of nails in a patient suffering from osteo-arthritis.

transverse furrows, and sometimes there are small punctate depressions and erosions. The eczematous nails require protection with soothing dressings, the lines prescribed for eczema elsewhere being followed.

(*b*) Psoriasis. The commonest condition of the nails in psoriasis is pitting, the minute pit-like depressions being arranged in a transverse line if the affection is of short duration, but in chronic cases the whole nail may be covered with the indentations, so that it resembles the surface of a thimble. In other cases the free edge of the nail is detached and a thick mass of horny scales forms under it. These conditions may coexist. In very severe cases of psoriasis the nails are much deformed, presenting irregular ridges on a partly exposed nail bed (*vide* Fig. 186).

Psoriasis of the nails may be treated by the application of a 2 to 5 per cent. chrysarobin ointment, or by similar strengths of salicylic acid. Scraping of the surface before applying these is advisable. Ethereal lotions containing the same preparations have also been recommended.

(*c*) Lichen planus. In rare cases the nails are affected in severe lichen planus. The condition is illustrated in Fig. 188.

(*d*) Pityriasis rubra pilaris. In this disease the nail is thickened and reeded and of a yellowish colour, and there is some hyperkeratosis of the bed.

(*e*) In exfoliative dermatitis the nails may be completely or partially shed. This condition is illustrated in Fig. 167.

The bed of the nail may be left soft, or the nail may be detached in front or at the base.

Similar conditions are seen in pemphigus, pemphigus foliaceus, dermatitis herpetiformis, and in epidermolysis bullosa (Fig. 9).

(*f*) In Darier's disease the nails are brittle and striated.

(*g*) Alopecia is sometimes accompanied by atrophic changes in the nail, characterised by white striæ and fissuring and complete leuconychia (rare). These changes are more common in the universal alopecias. The association of dystrophic nails with congenital alopecia is illustrated in Fig. 16.

(*h*) In X-ray dermatitis the nails are gravely affected. They first become brittle and exfoliate, and ultimately atrophy. In advanced cases the end of the finger is rough, irregular, with narrow thickenings upon the site of the ungual plate. There is often onychia and perionychia, especially in the winter months. The affection is exceedingly painful and rebellious to treatment (*vide* p. 80).

(6) **Syphilis of the nails.** The primary chancre may appear about a nail. It is not uncommon in medical men and midwives at the angle of the nail. It may be a simple crack with some induration, or a chronic ulcer, or a large oval sore. An ungual chancre is painful, and a chronic painful ulcer about the nail in a person liable to infection should raise a suspicion and determine careful examination for spirochætes.

Onychia sicca syphilitica is a rare secondary condition characterised by a friable condition of the free border, leading to splitting and linear pitting. The whole nail may ultimately become opaque.

yellow, and like pith.   In another type the distal ends become thickened, and sometimes the whole nail may be shed.   The lesions are painless (*vide* Fig. 128).

Perionychia syphilitica.   In this condition a scaly or warty papule appears under the fold of the nail, and the areas swell up and become red and inflamed.   From pressure of the edge of the nail the lesion may ulcerate, but there is remarkably little pain.   The lesions are chronic and tend to recur.   They are treated by local applications of mercurials, black wash, etc., and the internal treatment on the usual lines.

(7) **Nail conditions in general diseases, etc.**   The acute specific

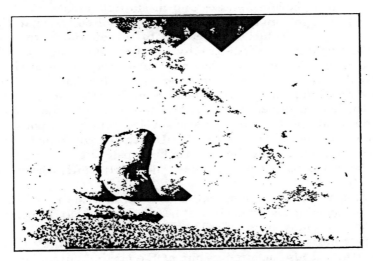

Fig. 257.—Onychogryphosis.   Male, 59.

fevers and any pyrexial conditions, such as pneumonia, tonsillitis, etc., may cause changes in the nails.   Grave injury, operation and shock may also affect them.   The local evidence is a transverse furrow on the nails due to a diminished activity of the matrix.   The furrows (Beau's lines) grow forwards at the rate of one-eighth of an inch a month, and may be a useful guide to the physician.   Chronic diseases may lead to atrophy of the nails, to fissuring and reeding, and to various deformities.   Reeding and splitting are said to occur specially in the gouty, but they are also simple senile changes.

(8) **Affections of the nails in nervous diseases.**   Injury to the nerves, neuritis, syringomyelia, Morvan's disease, tabes, hemiplegia, and nerve leprosy are accompanied by dystrophy of the nails.   The ungual appendages may simply fall or become brittle or atrophy, or

they may separate from the nail bed. Painless recurrent whitlows are characteristic of Morvan's disease. Sclerodermia, which is possibly a nervous disease, leads sometimes to gradual atrophy of the nails, which in sclerodactyly are merely small horny plugs.

(9) Unclassified conditions. Leuconychia. White spots commonly appear on the nails of children and young adults. They may be single or multiple, and are probably produced by slight injuries causing separation of the nail from its bed. The white spots are believed to be caused by minute bubbles of air under the nail plate.

Complete leuconychia, where the whole nail is white, is seen in some cases after severe illnesses and in alopecia areata.

The white spots may be concealed, if desired, by painting the nail with a weak solution of eosine to match the normal colour.

Onychogryphosis. Hypertrophy of the nail may be due to many causes. In onychogryphosis the increase in growth is in a forward direction, and the nail becomes twisted and bent laterally in an extraordinary way, sometimes resembling the ram's horn. The nail is thickened, ridged both in the transverse and the longitudinal directions, but the brownish-yellow surface retains its polish, and is usually more shining than normal. Under the thickened nail there is a mass of thickened epidermis of a brownish tint.

Onychogryphosis affects the toes, and particularly the great toes (Fig. 257).

Treatment consists in removal of the nail and the redundant part of the thickened mass under it. Where there is great hypertrophy a small, fine saw may be required.

Onychorrhexis. Extreme brittleness of the nails may be present from birth. It also occurs in some of the general cutaneous diseases already mentioned, viz., eczema and psoriasis, and occasionally in lichen planus. It may be necessary to protect the brittle nails by collodion.

Onychoschizia. Separation of the nails may be partial or complete, and occur at the free end or at the matrix. The various causes have been indicated.

Koilonychia. Spoon nails. This name is sometimes given to a variety of separation of the nail in which the free margin is raised above the central parts of the nail plate to form a spoon-like cavity. It may occur in certain general affections, typhoid fever, Raynaud's disease and some cutaneous affections, e.g., lichen planus.

REFERENCES.—HELLER. " Die Krankheiten der Nagel," 1900. HUTCHINSON. " Archives of Surgery," 1899, Vol. X., plates. PERNET. " Encyclopedia Medica," 1901, Vol. XIII. (Bibliography). RADCLIFFE CROCKER'S Atlas, Plate XC.

APPENDIX I.

———◆———

MINERAL WATERS.

MANY mineral waters are used in the treatment of cutaneous diseases. A number of them are supplied in bottles from the springs and are, therefore, available for home consumption ; but it must be remembered that patients often experience greater benefit by courses at the spas, the climatic conditions, change of environment, and the regular routine which is enforced being of equal or perhaps greater value than the actual taking of the waters.

The waters are here grouped according to their constituents, and the appropriate spas are indicated in connection with each group.

(1) **Alkaline Waters.** Useful in gouty conditions, chronic eczema, etc. Vichy, containing sodium bicarbonate. Dose, half a pint twice daily. Vals, similar to Vichy water. The same dose. Contrexéville. Dose, similar to Vichy water.

Suitable Spas. Bath, Buxton, Cheltenham, Leamington, Scarborough, Contrexéville, Royat (June to September), Vals, Vichy. Brides-Salines (June to September).

Droitwich has brine baths containing a saturated solution of sodium chloride ; the crystals can also be obtained for home use.

(2) **Arsenical Waters.** Suitable for psoriasis and chronic scrofulodermata.

La Bourboule, containing two grains of sodium arsenate to the gallon. Dose, half a pint.

Royat, an arsenical and ferruginous water. Dose, half a pint.

Levico, arsenical and ferruginous. Dose, a tablespoonful.

Roncegno. Dose, a tablespoonful.

Suitable Spas. La Bourboule (July and August), Royat (June to September), Roncegno, Levico.

(3) **Bromo-iodine Waters,** suitable in tertiary syphilis and scrofulous affections.

Woodhall water, containing $\frac{2}{3}$ grain iodine and seven grains of bromine to the gallon.

Suitable Spas. Woodhall, Roncegno, Salsomaggiore.

(4) **Ferruginous Waters.** These contain small quantities of iron salts in solution. They are of low therapeutic value, but are sometimes better borne than the usual iron tonics.

Spa water contains bicarbonate of iron, sodium, magnesium, and calcium. Dose, one-half to two pints per diem.

Flitwick water contains persulphate of iron.

Suitable Spas. Flitwick, Brighton, Cheltenham, Tunbridge **Wells,** Spa.

(5) **Sulphur Waters.** Suitable for chronic psoriasis and some eczemas in the gouty. Care in selecting cases is important.

Suitable spas. Harrogate, Llandrindod, Strathpeffer, **Moffat,** and Cheltenham. Aix-les-Bains (May to September) ; hot sulphur springs. Vernet-les-Bains (winter and spring). Schinznach (May to September).

APPENDIX II.

INTERNAL TREATMENT BY DRUGS.

THE special indications for the exhibition of drugs have been considered in the previous chapters. A short summary will, therefore, be all that is necessary in this place.

Analgesic and Antipruritic Remedies. — It is rarely necessary to give opium and morphia in cutaneous diseases. The exceptions are cases of malignant disease and a few obstinate cases of herpes zoster in the aged, and the graver forms of pemphigus. Relief of irritation and of painful sensations are often obtained by the administration of antipyrin (ten grains), antifebrin (five grains), phenacetin (five grains), acetyl-salicylic acid (ten grains), quinine (two to three grains). In the neuralgic pains of herpes, the tincture of gelsemium (five to fifteen minims) and butyl-chloral hydrate (five to twenty grains) may also be tried.

Aperients. In many acute conditions a mercurial purgative at night, followed by a saline draught in the morning, is highly beneficial. In all cases, constipation requires careful attention, and the regular use of saline aperients is often of value in chronic cases.

Antimony. Antimony has been found of great value in many of the acute forms of dermatitis, and is indicated in plethoric subjects suffering from acute inflammatory conditions. It is found serviceable in acute eczema, in some cases of psoriasis, lichen planus, etc. The wine of antimony in seven to ten minim doses is usually given in combination with salines.

Arsenic. The common form for the administration of this drug is Fowler's solution, but the Liq. Arsenici hydrochloridi may also be given. The dose of either is three to five minims gradually increased. If well diluted and taken directly after food, it can be administered in most cases over long periods. The addition of Tr. Lupuli (thirty minims) to each dose is said to be of advantage.

The Asiatic pill. Arsenious anhydride ($\frac{1}{12}$ grain), black pepper ($\frac{3}{4}$ grain), with gum acacia, is a favourite prescription on the Continent The dose is one to two pills daily.

Arsenic may be combined with iron, in the arsenate of iron. Dose $\frac{1}{16}$ to $\frac{1}{4}$ grain, or arsenious anhydride $\frac{1}{50}$ grain, ferrum redactum two grains, in a pill with a little syrup.

The indiscriminate use of arsenic in skin diseases is to be deplored. The drug is of great value in the erythemato-squamous eruptions of which psoriasis is the type, and in some of the chronic papular dermatoses, *e.g.*, lichen planus. It also appears to be of service in bullous eruptions, *e.g.*, pemphigus, hydroa, etc. It is also of use in chronic scaly eczema, but is undoubtedly harmful in acute inflammatory conditions.

Arsenic may be given subcutaneously and intravenously. The value of diamido-dioxy arsenobenzol (Ehrlich Hata's "606") and its derivatives has been considered at p. 313.

Hypnotics. It is often of the highest importance to obtain sleep in cases of acute skin disease. In some, the analgesic and antipruritic remedies mentioned above are of service. In others the bromides, cannabis indica, chloral, chloralamide, lupulin, sulphonal, trional, veronal and similar remedies may be used with greater advantage. Bromides should be given with caution, especially to children, in whom there is often a peculiar susceptibility.

Ichthyol. This remedy is frequently prescribed in cutaneous affections. It is of value in some forms of acne, particularly acne rosacea, attended with flushing. It is also recommended in lupus erythematosus. It certainly appears of use in cutaneous diseases at the menopause. The sulphur is excreted by the skin, and may have a local effect apart from the prevention of intestinal fermentation. Ichthyol is admitted in doses of two and a half to five or ten grains in pill or tablet covered with keratin, or in capsule. It should be given thrice daily after food.

Iodides. It is unnecessary to dilate upon the value of the iodides in tertiary syphilis, yaws, actinomycosis, and blastomycosis. They are also used in some clinics for the treatment of psoriasis. Potassium, sodium, or ammonium iodide may be given in doses from five to twenty or thirty grains in a bitter decoction or infusion, such as Decoct. Cinchonæ Co. or Ext. Sarsæ Liquid. a drachm, water to one ounce. The combination of mercury with the iodides is especially indicated in cutaneous gummata and the ulcers of the tertiary stage of syphilis. Donovan's solution of the iodides of arsenic and mercury in ten-minim doses is also of service.

Iron. Though it is difficult to particularise any skin affection as being directly dependent upon anæmia, we commonly meet with cutaneous eruptions in anæmic subjects, and the treatment of the general condition by iron assists the measures directed to the local affection. This is especially the case in acne vulgaris, and in some forms of eczema, etc., in the debilitated. One of the most valuable preparations is Startin's mixture—B Ferri. Sulph. two grains, Magnes. Sulph. a dram and a half, Acid. sulphuric dil. fifteen minims, Infus. Quassiæ to one ounce, thrice daily after meals. The citrates of iron and quinine and reduced iron are sometimes better borne than the sulphate. The syrup of the iodide is indicated in strumous subjects. It is given in half-drachm to drachm doses well diluted.

Mercury. The administration of mercury has been fully discussed in the chapter on Syphilis (p. 309). During the primary and secondary stages it has long been the practice to give mercury, but it is equally important in the tertiary manifestations in combination with iodides. The following formulæ are suitable :—Perchloride of mercury $\frac{1}{16}$ grain, Potass. iodid. five to fifteen grains, Spirit Ammon. Aromat. fifteen minims, Infusion of Calumba to one ounce. Liquor

Hydrarg. perchlor. half to one drachm, Potass. iodid. five to ten grains (or more), Extract. Sarsæ. Liquid. one drachm. Water to one ounce.

Donovan's solution, fifteen to thirty minims. Infus. Calimbæ or Decoct. Cinchonæ. Co. to one ounce.

The mercurials in combination with iodides are often of value in lichen planus as well as in syphilis.

Quinine. The influence of quinine in the alleviation of flushing was first pointed out by Dr. Payne. The drug is of value in some cases of acne rosacea, and in the acute varieties of lupus erythematosus. It is given in pill, tablet, or cachet, in doses of two to three grains and upwards. It may be combined with hydrobromic acid in a mixture. In pruritic affections, especially in infants, it is also of value, and may be given sugar-coated in doses of two grains to a young child.

Salicin and the Salicylates. The late Dr. Radcliffe Crocker used salicin in a number of acute eruptions. It sometimes appears to be beneficial in the early stages of lichen planus, psoriasis, and in lupus erythematosus. These drugs are often used in the treatment of erythemata believed to be of rheumatic origin. Salicin is better tolerated than the salicylates and is given in doses of fifteen to twenty or thirty grains thrice daily. It may be exhibited in cachet or in a mixture with a drachm of syrup of orange.

Salines are given in the early stages of inflammatory affections with or without antimony. The acetate of potassium, in fifteen-grain doses, or the Liq. Ammon. Acetatis, in drachm doses with the citrate and bicarbonate of potassium, are commonly used. Large doses of citrate of potassium, one drachm thrice daily, are sometimes useful in acne rosacea.

Tonics. The ferruginous and arsenical preparations are useful tonics, and particularly in debilitated and strumous subjects. Cod-liver oil may also be given with advantage.

APPENDIX III.

EXTERNAL APPLICATIONS TO THE SKIN.

In prescribing a local application it must be remembered that the normal epidermis is almost impermeable to watery solutions, but that fatty substances, ethereal and spirituous solutions, and gases penetrate to some extent. The normal excretion of sweat by the skin is an important factor in the regulation of the temperature of the surface, and measures which tend to its increase relieve heat and congestion, while applications which retain the perspiration tend to intensify congestion.

Baths, fomentations, and *lotions* are used to cleanse the surface, to remove scabs, crusts, etc., to soften the epidermis and render it more permeable. They also tend to relieve congestion.

Alcoholic and *ethereal solutions, acetone,* etc., are solvents of the fats and are used to remove greasy matter from the epidermis, and also as vehicles for the exhibition of drugs insoluble in water. They tend to irritate, and care must be used in selecting suitable cases for their use.

Powders are used to prevent chafing, to relieve congestion, and to dry moist surfaces. Starch, made from maize, wheat, potato or rice, is the basis of the " violet powders." It is often combined with zinc oxide and boric acid. Lycopodium is also a useful inert protective powder. It can be used in combination.

Talc, hydrated silicate of magnesium, also known as French chalk, if pure, is an excellent basis for powders to be applied to folds of the skin. Fuller's earth should only be used if well baked before use.

Diatomaceous earth (Infusorial earth, Kieselguhr) is nearly *pure* silica. If properly prepared it is an excellent basis.

Zinc oxide and zinc oleate are protective and soothing. Bismuth salts are mildly antiseptic. The subgallate and tannate are particularly serviceable.

Ointments are used to protect and soften the epidermis and to carry into it certain substances in combination. They are also useful for the removal of scales. By their retention of perspiration they tend to increase congestion and are thus heating.

The common bases for ointments are :—

Animal fats :—Lard (plain and benzoated), wool-fat (lanolin), hydrous wool-fat, beeswax, spermaceti, prepared suet. Wool fat is too hard for use alone, and it is usually used in combination with soft paraffin. Wool-fat, two drachms, soft paraffin, six drachms, make a suitable basis. The animal fats have the disadvantage of tending to rancidity.

Vegetable fats :—Cacao butter, almond oil, olive oil.

Hydrocarbons :—Hard paraffin, soft paraffin, liquid paraffin. The hydrocarbons do not become rancid and are therefore largely used.

Glycerina are solutions or suspensions of drugs in glycerine and are highly hygroscopic.

Pastes. The common bases of the pastes are with starch. Gelatine is also used. They are protective and permeable to perspiration.

Creams and many *liniments* are oleaginous preparations. Their bases are commonly olive, linseed, or almond oil combined with lime water.

Plasters and *mulls* containing a number of drugs are used in dermatological practice. They are convenient preparations for the prolonged application of caustic and other drugs.

Varnishes. Gum tragacanth five parts, glycerine two parts, distilled water 100 parts, is the formula for Pick's varnish. Various drugs may be added. Ichthyol forty parts, starch forty parts, albumen one part, water to 100 parts is the common formula of Unna's varnish.

Traumaticin. Chloroform nine drachms, gutta percha one drachm, produces after two or three weeks' digestion a thick solution to which such remedies as chrysarobin may be added. The chloroform evaporates and leaves a film containing the drug on the surface. Remedies applied in this form are useful if the patient is unable to leave off work.

FORMULÆ.

A. Soothing and Antiphlogistic Applications.

Baths.

1. Bran, 2 to 4 lbs. to bath of thirty gallons.
2. Starch, 1 lb.   ,,   ,,   ,,
3. Gelatine, 1 to 2 lbs. ,,   ,,   ,,
4. Size, 2 to 4 lbs.   ,,   ,,   ,,

Lotions.

5. Glycerine of the subacetate of lead one ounce, glycerine one ounce, water to one pint.
6. Liq. plumbi subacetat. one drachm, fresh milk two ounces, well shaken.
7. Calamine two drachms, zinc oxid. one drachm, glycerine two drachms, aq. calcis to four ounces.
8. Bismuth sub-nitrat. eight grains, zinc oxid. half a drachm, glycerine fifteen minims, hydrarg. perchlor. a quarter of a grain, rose water to one ounce.

Liniment.

9. Calamine thirty-five grains, lime water and olive oil of each half an ounce.

s.   40

Ointments.

10. Hydrous wool-fat six drachms, olive oil two drachms.
11. Hydrous wool-fat two drachms, soft paraffin six drachms.
12. Ung. aquæ rosæ.
13. Ung. zinci. oxid. benzoat.

Cream.

14. Zinc oxid. three drachms, hydrous wool-fat one drachm, lime water and ol. amygdalæ of each one ounce.

Plaster.

15. Zinc oxide 40 per cent., ichthyol 10 per cent. (Leslies.)

Pastes.

16. Zinci. oxid. two drachms, pulv. amyli. two drachms, soft paraffin half an ounce. (Lassar's.)

17. Zinc. oxid. one ounce, gelatine one ounce, glycerine two and a half ounces, water two and a half ounces. The gelatine is soaked in the water for twelve hours, and then dissolved by heat. The zinc oxide is rubbed up with the glycerine, and added to the gelatine. The preparation must be melted just before use, and applied with a brush. Cotton is often dabbed on while the paste is wet, to form a felt-like protective, which can be left on several days. (Unna's.)

B. Weak Antiseptic and Astringent Preparations.

Baths.

18. Liq. carbonis deterg. eight ounces to bath of thirty gallons.
19. Boric acid 4 lbs. to bath of thirty gallons.

Lotions.

20. Acid boric one drachm, water to four ounces.
21. Cupri. sulph. one grain, zinc sulphat. three grains, camphor water one ounce. (Impetigo.)
22. Alumen. four grains, plumbi acetat. twenty grains, water one ounce. (For weeping surfaces.)
23. Resorcin ten grains, glycerine ten minims, water one ounce.
24. Alcohol solution of thymol (1 per cent.) thirty minims, water to one ounce.
25. Tannic acid forty grains, acid. acetic. dilut. half an ounce, water to eight ounces. (Hyperidrosis and oily seborrhœa.)

Ointments.

26. Iodoform three to five grains, soft paraffin one ounce.
27. Europhen five grains, soft paraffin one ounce.
28. Calomel ten grains, ung. aq. rosæ one ounce.
29. Acid salicylic five to ten grains, soft paraffin one ounce.

30. Resorcin ten grains, soft paraffin one ounce.
31. Beta-naphthol ten grains, soft paraffin one ounce.
32. Ung. acid boric.
33. Calomel ten grains, lead acetate ten grains, zinc oxid. twenty grains, ung. hydrarg. nitrate dil. to one ounce. (Ung. Metallorum.)

Pastes.

34. Ichthyol twenty grains, zinc oxid. thirty-two grains, starch twenty-two grains, soft paraffin to one ounce.
35. Lassar's paste (No. 16) with salicylic acid ten grains, resorcin ten grains to the ounce.
36. Unna's paste (No. 17) with similar additions.

Powders.

37. Iodoform, airol bismuth oxyiodogallas, aristol thymol iodide, europhen, iodol, subgallate of bismuth (Dermatol), xeroform, peroxide of zinc, tannoform.

C. Stronger Antiseptics.

Baths.

38. Hydrarg. perchlor. one drachm, acid hydrochloric half an ounce to bath of thirty gallons.
39. Hydrarg. biniodid. one drachm, potassium iodide two drachms to bath of thirty gallons. (Syphilitic ulceration.)

Lotions.

40. Hydrarg. perchlor. one to two per 1,000.
41. Biniodide of mercury one, potassium iodide one, in 1,000.
42. Carbolic acid, one to 200 and upwards.
43. Liquor cresolis saponatus (Lysol) one drachm to a pint.
44. Cyllin. one in 150.

Colloids.

45. Collosol hydrargyrum 1 in 2,000. (Crookes.)
45A. Colloidal sulphur 1 in 1,000.

Solution.

46. Tincture of iodine.

Ointments.

47. Ung. hydrarg. ammoniat.
48. Ung. hydrarg. oxid. rubr.
49. Ung. hydrarg. oxid. flav.
50. Phenol one part, ung. sulphuris two parts. ung. hydrarg. nitrat. two parts. (Aldersmith's ointment for tinea capitis.)

Plaster.

51. Carbolic acid 16 per cent., mercury 45 per cent. (Made by Leslies.)

D. Antipruritic Applications.

Baths.

52. Starch, bran, gelatine. (*Vide supra*, Nos. 1—3.)
53. Sodii bicarb. one drachm to the gallon.

Lotions.

54. Aq. calcis.
55. Aq. lauro-cerasi.
56. Chloral hydrate ten grains, water one ounce.
57. Solution of chlorinated soda one drachm, water to one ounce.
58. Carbolic acid one in fifty to one in twenty.
59. Liq. carbonis deterg. half to one drachm, water one ounce.
60. Menthol one drachm, ol. olivæ one ounce.
61. Menthol a drachm and a half, thymol two drachms, chloral hydrate two drachms, chloroform two ounces, eucalyptus oil two ounces, oil of gaultheria four drachms, alcohol to eight ounces. (Lichen planus.)
62. Argent. nitrat. ten grains, spt. ætheris nitros. seven drachms, water one drachm.
63. Cocain hydrochloride 5 to 10 per cent.

Ointments.

64. Lard.
65. Ung. aq. rosæ.
66. Soft paraffin, white or yellow.
67. Lanolin two drachms, soft paraffin six drachms.
68. Naphthol ten to thirty grains, soft paraffin one ounce.
69. Menthol six grains, pulv. camphoræ six grains, chloral hydrate seven grains, vaselin to one ounce.
70. Menthol one drachm, soft paraffin one ounce.
71. Chloral hydrate twenty grains, soft paraffin one ounce.

Varnishes.

72. Pasta zinci et gelatini with ichthyol twenty grains.
73. Coal tar.

E. Keratolytic Applications for the Removal of Scales, Crusts, etc.

Baths.

74. Sodii bicarb. one drachm to the gallon.
75. Sodii biborat. half an ounce to one gallon.

Soaps.

76. Ichthyol, sulphur, balsam of Peru, coal tar, naphthol.

77. Soft soap half an ounce, rectified spirit half an ounce. (Pityriasis capitis, psoriasis.)

Lotions.

78. Alcohol, ether, acetone.

79. Sodii bicarb. half an ounce to one pint.

80. Sodii biborat. half an ounce to one pint.

81. Liq. carbonis deterg. one to two drachms, water one pint.

Fomentations.

82. Boric acid lint wrung out in hot water and covered with oil silk. (To remove impetigo and other crusts.)

Poultice.

83. Boric starch. A drachm of boric acid is made into a paste with half an ounce of starch and a little cold water. Boiling water is then poured on the paste and stirred to form a jelly. The jelly is spread in a layer three-quarters of an inch thick on lint, covered with muslin, and applied, when perfectly cold, to the part. (To remove impetigo and other crusts.)

Ointments.

84. Ung. paraffini.

85. Adeps benzoatus.

86. Ung. naphtholi 2 to 5 per cent.

In many cases where there is much crusting, as in long-standing lupus, the reducing agents are more serviceable.

F. Reducing Agents.

This group contains a number of valuable drugs ; the weaker are antiseptic, while the stronger produce exfoliation and irritation. They are specially useful in scaly eruptions, seborrhoides, dry eczema, psoriasis, parapsoriasis, and the lichens.

In the following list they are placed in order of activity :—

(a) Ichthyol and thiol.

(b) Pix liquida, oil of cade, ol. pini sylvestris, anthrasol.

(c) Lenigallol.

(d) Sulphur, aristol, resorcin, salicylic acid, mercurials.

(e) Pyrogallic acid, eugallol, chrysarobin.

Preparations.

Soaps.

87. Sapo mollis, oleum, cadinum, alcohol equal parts. Ol lavandulæ may be added.

88. Soft soap, spirit equal parts.

Lotions.

89. Sulphur præcip., alcohol. of each one ounce. (Acne.)
90. Liq. picis carbonis one part, spirit or water forty parts. (Painted on chronic eczema.)

Ointments.

91. Ichthyol forty grains, salicylic acid eight grains, soft paraffin one ounce.
92. Thiol one drachm, ung. paraffin one ounce.
93. Ung. picis.
94. Anthrasol one drachm, soft paraffin one ounce.
95. Oil of cade one drachm, soft paraffin one ounce.
96. Oleum rusci one drachm, soft paraffin one ounce.
97. Tar one drachm, camphor ten grains, lard one ounce.
98. Lenigallol twenty to forty grains, zinc oxid. one drachm, vaselin to one ounce.
99. Ung. sulphuris.
100. Resorcin ten to twenty grains, soft paraffin one ounce.
101. Salicylic acid up to one drachm to the ounce.
102. Pyrogallic acid forty grains, salicylic acid forty grains, ichthyol forty grains, soft paraffin one ounce. (To remove massive crusts in lupus.)
103. Perchloride of mercury two grains, glycerine ten minims, phenol twenty grains, ol. olivæ forty minims, zinc ointment to one ounce. (Lichen planus.)
104. Chrysarobin five to forty grains to the ounce.
105. Chrysarobin five to forty grains, liq. carbonis deterg. twenty minims, hydrarg. ammoniat. ten grains, ung. paraffini to one ounce. (Psoriasis.)

Plasters.

106. Salicylic acid, all strengths up to 50 per cent. (Made by Leslies.)
107. Creasote and salicylic acid, made by Leslies in two strengths, 33⅓ per cent. of each and 10 per cent. of each. The former is used with success in lupus vulgaris.
108. Pyrogallic acid 40 per cent. (Leslies.)

Varnishes.

109. Chrysarobin and other drugs mentioned above may be combined with traumaticin. (Gutta-percha one drachm, in chloroform nine drachms.)

G. Parasiticides (Animal).

Baths.

110. Soft soap.
111. Potassa sulphurata one drachm to the gallon. (Scabies.)

Solutions.

112. Slaked lime two ounces, sulphur four ounces, water one pint. Boiled together in an iron vessel and stirred with a wooden spoon. (Scabies.)

113. Balsam of Peru three parts, glycerine one part, painted all over the body. (Scabies.)

Ointments.

114. Ung. sulphuris. (Scabies.)

115. Sulphur half a drachm, ammoniated mercury five grains, sulphuret of mercury ten grains, olive oil two drachms, lard two drachms, creasote four minims. (Startin's ointment for scabies.)

116. Sulphur one ounce, potass. carb. half an ounce, lard six ounces. (Scabies.)

117. Naphthol fifteen parts, prepared chalk ten parts, soft soap fifty parts, lard one hundred parts. (Kaposi's ointment for scabies.)

118. Storax one drachm, methylated spirit one drachm, benzoated lard six drachms. (Scabies in young children.)

119. Ung. hydrarg. ammoniat. (Impetigo e pediculis and pediculi pubis.)

120. Ung. staphisagriæ. (Pediculi corporis.)

II. Parasiticides (Vegetable).

Solutions.

121. Sulphurous acid one part, water three parts. (Tinea versicolor.)

122. Sodium hyposulphite six drachms, water two ounces. (Tinea versicolor and tinea cruris.)

123. Hydrarg. perchlor. two grains, ol. terebinthinæ seven drachms, spirit one drachm. (Tinea.)

124. Tinctura iodi. (Tinea.)

Ointments.

125. Acid carbolic ten grains, dilute nitrate of mercury ointment one ounce. (Tinea circinata.)

126. Sodium chloride, soft paraffin, equal parts. (Tinea tonsurans.)

127. Phenol one part, ung. sulphuris two parts, ung. hydrarg. nitratis two parts. (Aldersmith's ointment for tinea tonsurans.)

128. Oleate of mercury up to 20 per cent. in soft paraffin. (Tinea.)

129. Oleate of copper one drachm, soft paraffin one ounce. (Tinea.)

130. Acid benzoic thirty grains, acid salicylic twenty-four grains, oleum lini, and wool-fat of each half an ounce. (Tinea cruris.)

Hair Lotions.

For Greasy Hair.

131. Acid tannic forty grains, resorcin three grains, spirit of lavender and spirit rosmarini, of each three ounces.

132. Tinct. cantharides forty minims, spirit of lavender and spirit of rosemary, of each three ounces.

133. Acid salicylic fifteen grains, spirit one ounce.

For Dry Hair.

134. Chloral hydrate three drachms, castor oil three drachms, distilled water eight ounces.

135. Resorcin ten grains, castor oil, half; drachm, Tr. quillaiæ fifteen minims, water to one ounce.

136. Oil of cade twenty minims, spiritus rectificat. thirty minims, liquid paraffin one ounce.

137. Hydrarg. perchlor. four grains, curesol two drachms, formic acid fifteen minims, castor oil one drachm, alcohol 70 per cent. to eight ounces. (C. J. White for alopecia seborrhoica.) If curesol cannot be obtained resorcin may be substituted.

Stimulating Lotions.

138. Liq. ammon. fort. one drachm, ol. amygdal. dulc. one ounce, spirit rosmarini four drachms, aq. mellis three drachms. (Wilson.)

139. Liq. ammoniæ half an ounce, ol. ricin half an ounce, spirit terebinth half an ounce, hydrarg. ammoniat. fifteen grains. (Tilbury Fox.)

140. Tr. cantharidis one ounce, acid acetic dil. one and a half ounce, glycerine one and a third drachm, spirit of rosemary one and a half ounce, aq. rosæ to eight ounces. (Tilbury Fox.)

141. Acetum cantharidis one ounce, glycerine six drachms, spirit rosmarini two ounces, aq. rosæ to eight ounces.

142. Emplastrum cantharidis liquid one drachm, acetic acid one drachm, spirit one ounce, to be painted on and allowed to dry. (Alopecia areata.)

143. Hydrarg. perchlor. two grains, spirit. vini. rect. one drachm, ol. terebinthinæ seven drachms. (Alopecia areata.)

144. Hydrarg. perchlor. half grain, acid acetic glacial three minims, resorcin five grains, chloral hydrate ten grains, spiritus vini. rectif. to one ounce. (Alopecia areata.)

145. Pilocarpin nitrat. thirty grains, quinine hydrochlor. forty grains, sulphur præcip. 150 grains, balsam of Peru six drachms, lard to three ounces. (Lassar, for baldness.)

INDEX.

s.   41

THE WHITEFRIARS PRESS, LTD., LONDON AND TONBRIDGE.

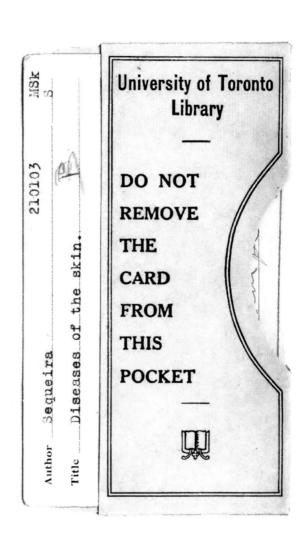

ImTheStory.com

Personalized Classic Books in many genre's

Unique gift for kids, partners, friends, colleagues

Customize:

- Character Names
- Upload your own front/back cover images (optional)
- Inscribe a personal message/dedication on the
  inside page (optional)

Customize many titles Including
- Alice in Wonderland
- Romeo and Juliet
- The Wizard of Oz
- A Christmas Carol
- Dracula
- Dr. Jekyll & Mr. Hyde
- And more...

Lightning Source UK Ltd.
Milton Keynes UK
UKOW04f1527161014

240129UK00013B/180/P